APPLIED CORPORATE FINANCE

A USER'S MANUAL

MAXIMIZE SHAREHOLDER WEALTH, NOT
VALUE OF FIRM
$$N_F = E_M + D_M$$

APPLIED CORPORATE FINANCE

A USER'S MANUAL

ASWATH DAMODARAN

STERN SCHOOL OF BUSINESS
NEW YORK UNIVERSITY

 JOHN WILEY & SONS, INC.
NEW YORK   CHICHESTER   WEINHEIM   BRISBANE   TORONTO   SINGAPORE

ACQUISITIONS EDITOR   Marissa Ryan
MARKETING MANAGER   Rebecca Hope
PRODUCTION EDITOR   Kelly Tavares
SENIOR DESIGNER   Ann Marie Renzi
ILLUSTRATION COORDINATOR   Anna Melhorn

COVER DESIGN: David Levy; COVER PHOTO: © 1992 Dale E. Boyer/Photo-Researchers, Inc.

This book was set in Times Roman by Carlisle Communications and printed and bound by Malloy Lithographing. The cover was printed by Lehigh Press.

This book is printed on acid-free paper. ∞

The paper in this book was manufactured by a mill whose forest management programs include sustained yield harvesting of its timberlands. Sustained yield harvesting principles ensure that the numbers of trees cut each year does not exceed the amount of new growth.

Library of Congress Cataloging in Publication Data:
Damodaran, Aswath
    Applied corporate finance: a user's manual/Aswath Damodaran
      p.   cm.
    Includes index.
    ISBN 0-471-23970-4 (alk. paper)
    1. Corporations—Finance.   I. Title
    HG4011.D26 1999

Printed in the United States of America

10 9 8 7 6 5 4 3 2

DEDICATION

To Michele, whose task is both more difficult
and more important than mine, and to
Ryan, Brendan and Kendra, who
contribute to making it so.

ABOUT THE AUTHOR

Aswath Damodaran received his MBA and Ph.D. from the University of California Los Angeles. His research interests include the examination of market efficiency, the fects of information and market structure characteristics, equity valuation, and issues real estate investing. He has published in the *Journal of Financial and Quantitative Analysis,* the *Journal of Finance* and the *Review of Financial Studies* and has written two widely used books on valuation—*Damodaran on Valuation* and *Investment Valuation* both published by John Wiley and Sons.

Dr. Damodaran was a visiting lecturer at the University of California, Berkeley, from 1984 to 1986, where he received the Earl Cheit Outstanding Teaching Award in 19—. He has been at New York University since 1986, where he received the Stern School Business Excellence in Teaching Award (awarded by the graduating class) in 1988, 1991 and 1992, and was the youngest winner of the university-wide Distinguished Teaching Award, in 1990. He was profiled in *Business Week* as one of the top twelve business school professors in the United States in 1994.

PREFACE

Let me begin this preface with a confession of a few of my own biases. First, I believe that theory, and the models that flow from it, should provide us with the tools to understand, analyze and solve problems. The test of a model or theory then should not be based upon its elegance, but upon its usefulness in problem solving. Second, in my view, the core principles of corporate finance are common sense ones, and have changed little over time. That should not be surprising. Corporate finance, as a discipline, is only a few decades old, while people have been running businesses for thousands of years. It would be exceedingly presumptuous of us to believe that they were in the dark until corporate finance theorists came along and told them what to do. To be fair, it is true that corporate financial theory has made advances in taking core principles and providing them with structure, but these advances have been primarily on the details. The story line in corporate finance has remained remarkably consistent over time.

Talking about story lines allows me to set the first theme of this book. This book tells a story, which essentially summarizes the corporate finance view of the world. It classifies all decisions made by any business into three groups—decisions on where to invest the resources or funds that the business has raised (the investment decision), decisions on where and how to raise funds to finance these investments (the financing decision) and decisions on how much and in what form to return funds back to the owners (the dividend decision). As I see it, the first principles of corporate finance can be summarized in Figure 1, which also lays out a site map for the book. Every section of this book relates to some part of this picture, and each chapter is introduced with it, with emphasis on that portion that will be analyzed in that chapter. (Note the chapter numbers below each section). Put another way, there are no sections of this book that are not traceable to this framework.

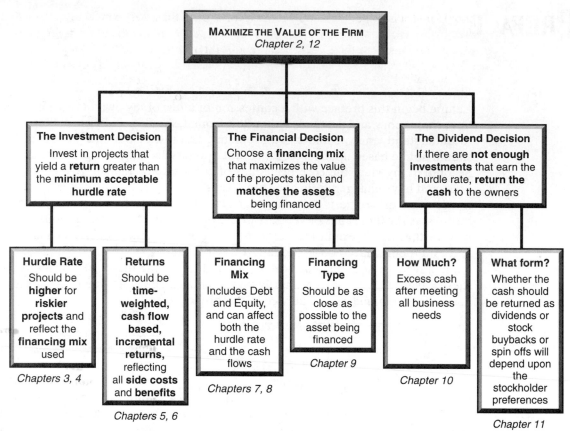

Figure 1   Corporate Finance: First Principles

As you look at the chapter outline for the book, you are probably wondering where the chapters on present value, option pricing and bond pricing are, as well as the chapters on short term financial management, working capital and international finance. The first set of chapters, which I would classify as "tools" chapters are now contained in the appendices; they are located there, not because they are unimportant, but because I want the focus to stay on the story line. It is important that we understand the concept of time value of money, but only in the context of measuring returns on investments better and valuing business. Option pricing theory is elegant and provides impressive insights, but only in the context of looking at options embedded in projects and in financing instruments like convertible bonds. The second set of chapters have been excluded for a very different reason. As I see it, the basic principles of whether and how much you should invest in inventory, or how generous your credit terms should be, are no different than the basic principles that would apply if you were building a plant, buying equipment, or opening a new store. Put another way, there is no logical basis for the differentiation between investments in the latter (which in most corporate finance books is covered in the capital budgeting chapters) and the former (which are considered in the working capital chapters). You should invest in either if and only if the returns from the investment exceed the hurdle rate from the investment; the fact that one is short term and the other is long term is irrelevant. The same thing can be said about international finance. Should the investment or financing principles be different just because a company is considering an investment in Thailand and the cash flows are in Thai Baht instead of in the United States and the cash flows are in dollars? I do not believe so, and separating the decisions, in my view, leaves readers with that impression. Finally, most corporate finance books that have chapters on small firm management and private firm management use them to illustrate the differences between these firms and the more conventional large publicly traded firms used in the other chapters. While such differences exist, the commonalities between different types of firms vastly outweigh the differences, providing a testimonial to the internal consistency of corporate finance. In summary, the second theme of this book is the emphasis on the *universality of corporate financial principles,* across different firms, in different markets and across different types of decisions.

Apply
Apply
Apply

Disney
Deutsche Bank
Aracruz Cellulose
Bookscape

The way this universality is brought to life is by using *four firms* throughout the book to *illustrate each concept;* they include a large, publicly traded U.S. corporation (Disney), a small, emerging market company (Aracruz Cellulose, a Brazilian paper and pulp company), a financial service firm (Deutsche Bank) and a small private business (Bookscape, an invented New York city book store). While the notion of using real companies to illustrate theory is neither novel nor revolutionary, there are, I believe, two key differences in the way they are used in this book. First, these companies are analyzed on every aspect of corporate finance introduced in this book, rather than used selectively in some chapters. Consequently, the reader can see the similarities and the differences in the way investment, financing and dividend principles are applied to four very different firms. Second, I do not consider this to be a book where applications are used to illustrate the theory. I think of it rather as a book where the theory is presented as a companion to the illustrations. In fact, reverting back to my earlier analogy of theory providing the tool box for understanding problems, this is a book where the problem solving takes center stage and the tools stay in the background.

Reading through the theory and the applications can be instructive and, hopefully, even interesting, but there is *no substitute for actually trying things out* to bring home both the strengths and weaknesses of corporate finance. There are several ways I have tried to make this book a tool for active learning. One is to introduce *concept questions* at regular intervals which invite responses from the reader. As an example, consider the following illustration from Chapter 7:

7.2   THE EFFECTS OF DIVERSIFICATION ON VENTURE CAPITALIST

You are comparing the required returns of two venture capitalists who are interested in investing in the same software firm. One venture capitalist has all of his capital invested in only software firms, whereas the other venture capitalist has invested her capital in small companies in a variety of businesses. Which of these two will have the higher required rate of return?

☑ The venture capitalist who is invested only in software companies   *higher risk .*

☐ The venture capitalist who is invested in a variety of businesses

☐ Cannot answer without more information

This question is designed to check on a concept introduced in an earlier chapter on risk and return on the difference between risk that can be eliminated by holding a diversified portfolio and risk that cannot, and then connecting it to the question of how a business seeking funds from a venture capitalist might be affected by this perception of risk. The answer to this question, in turn, will expose the reader to more questions about whether venture capital in the future will be provided by diversified funds, and what a specialized venture capitalist (who invests in one sector alone) might need to do in order to survive in such an environment. I hope that this will allow readers to see what, for me at least, is one of the most exciting aspects of corporate finance, which is its capacity to provide a framework which can be used to make sense of the events that occur around us every day and make reasonable forecasts about future directions. The second way in which I have tried to make this an active experience is by introducing *live case studies* at the end of each chapter. These case studies essentially take the concepts introduced in the chapter and provide a framework for applying these concepts to any company that the reader chooses. Guidelines on where to get the information to answer the questions is also provided.

While corporate finance provides us with a internally consistent and straight forward template for the analysis of any firm, information is clearly the lubricant that allows us to do the analysis. There are three steps in the information process—acquiring the information, filtering that which is useful from that which is not and keeping the information updated. Accepting the limitations of the printed page on all of these aspects, I have tried to put the power of online information and the Internet to use in several ways.

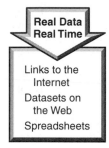

1. The live case studies that require the information are accompanied by *links to web sites* that carry this information.

2. The *data sets* that are difficult to get from the Internet or are specific to this book, such as the updated versions of the tables, are available on my web site and integrated into the book. As an example, the table that contains the dividend yields and payout ratios by industry sectors for the most recent quarter is referenced in Chapter 9 as follows:

There is a dataset on the web that summarizes dividend yields and payout ratios for U.S. companies, categorized by sector (**http:www.stern.nyu.edu/~adamodar/datasets/dividends.htm**).

3. The *spreadsheets* that are used to analyze the firms in the book are also available on my web site, and referenced in the book. For instance, the spreadsheet used to estimate the optimal debt ratio for Disney in Chapter 8 is referenced as follows:

This spreadsheet allows you to compute the optimal debt ratio firm value for any firm, using the same information used for Disney. It has updated interest coverage ratios and spreads built in. (**http:www.stern.nyu.edu/~adamodar/spreadsheets/capstr.xls**)

As a final point, I am delighted that technology has been put to good use in coming up with the supplements to this book. In particular, the accompanying software for this book, Corporate Finance 101, developed by Zoologic Inc., goes well beyond putting the ideas in this book into another format. This program presents the material in a way that emphasizes the key points that this book makes—the big picture, the internal connections, the universal principles and the application focus—while filling in for where the book has least depth, primarily in the understanding of the statistical and accounting tools that we draw on during the course of the analysis.

As I set to write this book, I had two objectives in mind. One was to write a book that not only reflects the way I teach corporate finance in a classroom, but, more importantly, conveys the fascination and enjoyment I get out of the subject matter. The second was to write a book for practitioners that students would find useful, rather than the other way around. I do not know whether I have fully accomplished either objective, but I do know I had an immense amount of fun trying. I hope you do too!

ACKNOWLEDGMENTS

I would like to acknowledge the hundreds of students who have patiently sat through my lectures, corrected my numerous errors and provided invaluable suggestions on ways to present this material better. Their enthusiasm and energy provided the fuel for this book.

I would also like to thank P. V. Viswanath, who knows this book as well as I do, having spent hours and hours going through it and pointing out ways to improve it. Any errors that remain, needless to say, are entirely mine.

Finally, I would like to thank Marissa Ryan at Wiley, who has backed this book enthusiastically from the time I initiated it, and Kelly Tavares, who has had the unenviable task of making sure it got done in time.

CONTENTS

CHAPTER 1

THE FOUNDATIONS

Every decision that a business makes has financial implications, and any decision which affects the finances of a business is a corporate finance decision. Defined broadly, everything that a business does fits under the rubric of corporate finance. It is, in fact, unfortunate that we even call it corporate finance, since it suggests to many observers a focus on how large corporations make financial decisions, and seems to exclude small and private businesses from its purview. A more appropriate title for this book might be *Business Finance,* since the basic principles remain the same, whether one looks at large publicly traded firms or small privately run businesses. All businesses have to invest their resources wisely, find a "good mix" of financing to make these investments, and return cash to the owners if there are not enough good investments.

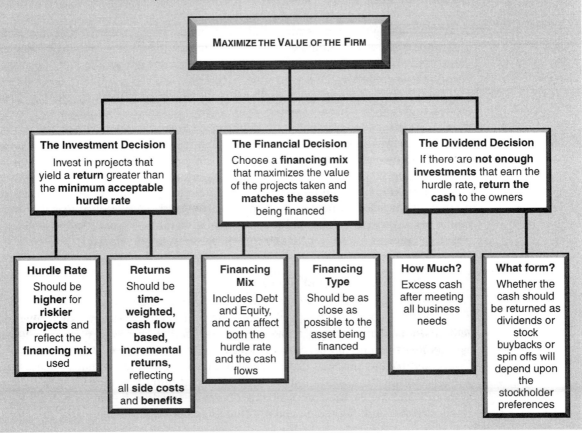

MAXIMIZE THE VALUE OF THE FIRM

The Investment Decision
Invest in projects that yield a **return** greater than the **minimum acceptable hurdle rate**

The Financial Decision
Choose a **financing mix** that maximizes the value of the projects taken and **matches the assets** being financed

The Dividend Decision
If there are **not enough investments** that earn the hurdle rate, **return the cash** to the owners

Hurdle Rate
Should be **higher** for **riskier projects** and reflect the **financing mix** used

Returns
Should be **time-weighted, cash flow based, incremental returns,** reflecting all **side costs** and **benefits**

Financing Mix
Includes Debt and Equity, and can affect both the hurdle rate and the cash flows

Financing Type
Should be as close as possible to the asset being financed

How Much?
Excess cash after meeting all business needs

What form?
Whether the cash should be returned as dividends or stock buybacks or spin offs will depend upon the stockholder preferences

1

FIRST PRINCIPLES

Every discipline has its first principles that govern and guide everything that gets done within that discipline. All of corporate finance is built on three principles, which we will call the Investment Principle, the Financing Principle, and the Dividend Principle.

- *The Investment Principle*   Invest in assets and projects that *yield a return greater* than the *minimum acceptable hurdle rate*. The hurdle rate should be *higher for riskier projects* and should reflect the *financing mix* used—owners' funds (equity) or borrowed money (debt). Returns on projects should be measured based on *cash flows* generated and the *timing* of these cash flows; they should also consider both *positive and negative side effects* of these projects.
- *The Financing Principle*   Choose a *financing mix* that maximizes the value of the investments made and *match the financing to the assets* being financed.
- *The Dividend Principle*   If there are not enough investments that earn the hurdle rate, *return the cash* to the owners of the business. In the case of a publicly traded firm, the *form of the return*—dividends and stock buybacks—will depend upon the *stockholders' characteristics*.

While making these investment and financing decisions, corporate finance is single-minded about the ultimate objective, which is assumed to be maximizing the value of the business. Any decision which increases value is a good one, while any decision that decreases value is a bad one.

These first principles provide the basis from which we will extract the numerous models and theories that comprise modern corporate finance, but they are also common-sense principles. It is incredible conceit on our part to assume that, until corporate finance was developed as a coherent discipline starting a few decades ago, people who owned businesses ran them randomly with no principles to govern their thinking. Good businesspeople through the ages have always recognized the importance of making more on their investments than they bear as a cost of raising the money for these investments. In fact, one of the ironies of recent years is that many managers at large and presumably sophisticated firms with access to the latest corporate finance technology have lost sight of these basic principles.

The Objective Function of the Firm

No discipline can develop cohesively over time without a unifying objective function. The growth of corporate financial theory can be traced to its choice of a single objective function and its development of models built around this function. *The objective in conventional corporate financial theory is to maximize firm value.* Consequently, any decision (investment, financial, or dividend) that increases firm value is considered a "good" one, whereas one that reduces firm value is considered a "poor" one. While the choice of this objective function has provided corporate finance with a unifying theme and internal consistency, it has come at a cost. To the degree that one buys into this objective function, much of what corporate financial theory suggests makes sense. To the degree that this objective function is flawed, however, it can be argued that the theory built on it is flawed as well. Many of the disagreements between corporate financial theorists and others (academics as well as practitioners) can be traced to fundamentally different views about the correct objective function for the firm. For instance, there are some who argue that firms should have multiple objectives where a variety of interests (stockholders, labor, customers) are met, while there are others who would have firms focus on what they view as simpler and more direct objectives, such as market share or profitability.

Given the significance of this objective function for both the development and the applicability of corporate financial theory, it is important that we examine it much more carefully and address some of the very real concerns and criticisms it has garnered: It assumes that what stockholders do in their own self-interest is also in the best interests of the firm; it requires the existence of efficient markets; and it is blind to the social costs associated with value maximization. In the next chapter, we will consider these and other issues and compare firm value maximization to alternative objective functions.

The Investment Principle

Firms have scarce resources that must be allocated among competing interests. The first and foremost function of corporate finance as a theory is to provide a framework for firms to make these decisions wisely. Accordingly, we define *investment decisions* to include not only those that create revenues and profits (such as introducing a new product line), but also those that save money (such as building a new and more efficient distribution system). Further, we argue that decisions about how much and what inventory to maintain and whether and how much credit to grant to customers, which are traditionally categorized as working capital decisions, are ultimately investment decisions, as well. At the other end of the spectrum, broad strategic decisions regarding which markets to enter and acquisitions of other companies can also be considered investment decisions.

Corporate finance attempts to measure the return on a proposed investment decision and compare it to a minimum acceptable hurdle rate in order to decide whether the project is acceptable. The hurdle rate has to be set higher for riskier projects and has to reflect the financing mix used, that is, the owner's funds (equity) or borrowed money (debt). In Chapter 3, we begin this process by defining risk and developing a procedure for measuring risk. In Chapter 4, we go about converting this risk measure into a hurdle rate both for entire businesses and individual projects.

Having established the hurdle rate, we turn our attention to measuring the returns on a project. In Chapter 5, we evaluate three alternative ways of measuring returns—conventional accounting earnings, cash flows, and time-weighted cash flows (where we consider both how large the cash flows are and when they are anticipated to come in). In Chapter 6, we consider some of the potential side-costs which might not be captured in any of these measures, including opportunity costs that may be created for existing investments by taking a new investment, and side-benefits, such as the options to enter new markets and to expand that may be embedded in new investments, and synergies, especially when the new investment is the acquisition of another firm.

Hurdle Rate: A hurdle rate is a minimum acceptable rate of return for investing resources in a project.

The Financing Principle

While we consider the existing financing mix and its implications for the minimum acceptable hurdle rate as part of the investment principle, we throw open the question of whether the existing mix is the right one in the financing principle section. While there might be regulatory and other real-world constraints on the type of financing mix that a business can use, there is ample room for flexibility within these constraints. We begin this section in Chapter 7 by looking at the range of choices which exist for both private businesses and publicly traded firms between owner's funds (equity) and borrowed money (debt). We then turn to the question of whether the existing mix of financing used by a business is the "optimal" one, given our objective function of maximizing firm value. While the tradeoff between the benefits and costs of borrowing are established in qualitative terms first, we look at two approaches to arriving at the optimal mix in Chapter 8. In the first approach, we examine the specific conditions under which the optimal financing mix is the one that minimizes the minimum acceptable hurdle rate. In the second approach, we look at the effects on value of changing the financing mix. Where the optimal financing mix is different from the existing one, we map out the best ways of getting from where we are (the current mix) to where we would like to be (the optimal) in Chapter 9, keeping in mind the investment opportunities that the firm has and the need for urgent responses because the firm is either a takeover target or under threat of bankruptcy.

Having outlined the optimal financing mix, we turn our attention to what type of financing a business should use (i.e., whether it should be long term or short term, whether the payments on the financing should be fixed or variable, and if variable, what it should be a function of). In Chapter 9, we state our basic proposition, which is that a firm will minimize its risk from financing and maximize its capacity to use borrowed funds if it can match up the cash flows on the debt to the cash flows on the assets being financed. We then add on additional considerations relating to taxes and external monitors (equity research analysts and ratings agencies) and arrive at fairly strong conclusions about the design of the financing.

The Dividend Principle

Most businesses would undoubtedly like to have limitless investment opportunities that yield returns exceeding their hurdle rates, but all businesses grow and mature. As a consequence, many of them reach a stage in their lives when the cash flow generated by existing investments is greater than the funds needed to take on "good" investments that yield surplus value (i.e., returns that exceed the hurdle rate). At that point, they have to figure out ways to return the excess cash to owners. In private businesses, this may just involve the owner withdrawing a portion of his or her funds from the business. In a publicly traded corporation, this will involve either paying dividends or the buying back of stock. In Chapters 10 and 11, we introduce the basic tradeoff that determines whether cash should be left in a business or taken out of it. For stockholders in publicly traded firms, we will note that this decision is fundamentally one of whether they trust the managers of the firms with their cash, and much of this trust is based upon how well these managers have invested funds in the past. We also consider the options available to a firm to return assets to its owners—dividends, stock buybacks and spinoffs—and investigate how to decide among these options.

CORPORATE FINANCIAL DECISIONS, FIRM VALUE, AND EQUITY VALUE

If the objective function in corporate finance is to maximize firm value, it follows that firm value must be linked to the three corporate finance decisions outlined above—investment, financing, and dividend decisions. The link between these decisions and firm value can be made by recognizing that *the value of a firm is the present value of its expected cash flows, discounted back at a rate that reflects both the riskiness of the projects of the firm and the financing mix used to finance them.* Investors form expectations about future cash flows based upon observed current cash flows and expected future growth, which, in turn, depend upon the quality of the firm's projects (its investment decisions) and the amount of its earnings it reinvests (the reinvestment rate). The financing decisions affect the value of a firm both through the discount rate and, potentially, through the expected cash flows.

This neat formulation of value is put to the test by the interactions among the investment, financing, and dividend decisions, and the conflicts of interest that arise between stockholders and bondholders on the one hand, and stockholders and managers on the other.

We introduce the basic models available to value a firm and its equity in Chapter 12, and relate them back to management decisions on investment, financial, and dividend policy. In the process, we examine the determinants of value and how firms can increase their value.

A REAL-WORLD FOCUS

The proliferation of news and information on corporations making decisions every day suggests that we do not need to use hypothetical businesses to illustrate the principles of corporate finance. We will use four businesses throughout this book to make our points about corporate financial policy:

1. **Disney Corporation**   Disney Corporation is a publicly traded firm with wide holdings in entertainment and media. While most people around the world recognize the Mickey Mouse logo and have heard about or visited Disney World or seen some or all of the Disney animated classics, it is a much more diversified corporation than most people realize. Disney's holdings include real estate (in the form of timeshares and rental properties in Florida and South Carolina), television (ABC and ESPN), publications, movie studios (Touchstone Pictures), and retailing (there are 610 Disney stores around the world). Disney will help illustrate the choices that large diversified corporations have to make as they are faced with

the conventional corporate financial decisions—Where do we invest? How do we finance these investments? How much do we return to our stockholders?

2. ***Bookscape Books***   This is a privately owned independent bookstore in New York City, one of the few left after the invasion of the bookstore chains such as Barnes and Noble and Borders Books. We will take Bookscape Books through the corporate financial decision-making process to illustrate some of the issues that come up when looking at private businesses with limited information available.

3. ***Aracruz Cellulose***   Aracruz Cellulose is a Brazilian firm which produces Eucalyptus pulp, and operates its own pulp mills, electrochemical plants, and port terminals. While it markets its products around the world for manufacturing high-grade paper, we will use it to illustrate some of the questions that have to be dealt with when analyzing a company in an environment where inflation is high and volatile, and where the economy itself is in transition.

4. ***Deutsche Bank***   Deutsche Bank is the leading commercial bank in Germany and is also a leading player in investment banking with its acquistion of Morgan Grenfell, the U.K. investment bank. We will use Deutsche Bank to illustrate some of the issues that come up when a financial service firm has to make investment, financing, and dividend decisions in a highly regulated environment.

A RESOURCE GUIDE

In order to make this book as interactive and current as possible, we will employ a variety of devices:

- This symbol precedes the illustrative examples using the four companies described above, where we will apply corporate finance principles to these firms.

- This symbol indicates the spreadsheet programs that can be used to do some of the analysis that will be presented in this book. (For instance, there are spreadsheets that calculate the optimal financing mix for a firm, as well as valuation spreadsheets.)

- This symbol designates updated data on some of the inputs that we need and use in our analysis that is available on the Web site for this book. Thus, when we estimate the risk parameters for firms, we will draw attention to the data set that is maintained on the Web site that reports average risk parameters by industry.

- This symbol turns up at regular intervals, where we stop and ask readers to answer questions relating to the topic at hand. These questions, which will generally be framed using real-world examples, will help emphasize the key points made in a chapter.

- This symbol stands for "In Practice," in which we look at issues that are likely to come up in practice and at ways of addressing these issues.

SOME FUNDAMENTAL PROPOSITIONS ABOUT CORPORATE FINANCE

There are several fundamental arguments we will make repeatedly throughout this book.

1. *Corporate finance has an internal consistency* that flows from its choice of maximizing firm value as the only objective function and its dependence upon a few bedrock principles: Risk has to be rewarded; cash flows matter more than accounting income measures; markets are not easily fooled; every decision a firm makes has an effect on its value.

2. *Corporate finance must be viewed as an integrated whole,* rather than as a collection of decisions. Investment decisions generally affect financing decisions, and vice versa; financing decisions generally affect dividend decisions, and vice versa. While there are circumstances under which these decisions may be independent of each other, this is seldom the case. Accordingly, it is unlikely that firms that deal with their problems on a piecemeal basis will ever resolve these problems. For instance, a firm that believes that it has a dividend problem and just cuts dividends may experience consequences for its financing and investment decisions.

3. *Corporate finance matters to everybody.* There is a corporate financial aspect to almost every decision made by a business; while not everyone will find a use for all the components of corporate finance, everyone will find a use for at least some *part* of it.

4. *Corporate finance is fun.* This may seem to be the tallest claim of all. After all, most people associate corporate finance with numbers and accounting statements and hard-headed analyses. While corporate finance is quantitative in its focus, there is a significant component of creative thinking involved in coming up with solutions to the financial problems businesses may encounter. It is no coincidence that financial markets remain the breeding grounds for innovation and change.

5. *The best way to learn corporate finance is by applying its models and theories.* While the body of theory that has been developed over the last few decades is impressive, the ultimate test of any theory is in applications. As we show in this book, much, if not all, of the theory can be applied to real companies and not just to abstract examples.

CONCLUSION

This chapter establishes the first principles that govern corporate finance. The investment principle, which specifies that businesses invest only in projects that yield a return that exceeds the hurdle rate; the financing principle, which suggests that the right financing mix for a firm is one that maximizes the value of the investments made; and the dividend principle, which requires that cash generated in excess of "good projects" needs be returned to the owners, are the core for what follows.

Chapter 2

The Objective

If you do not know where you are going, it does not matter how you get there.

Corporate finance's greatest strength and its greatest weakness is its single-minded focus on value maximization. By maintaining that focus, corporate finance preserves internal consistency and coherence, and develops powerful models and theory about the "right" way to make investment, financing, and dividend decisions. It can be argued, however, that all of these conclusions are conditional on the acceptance of value maximization as the only objective function.

In this chapter, we examine why we focus so strongly on value maximization, the assumptions needed for it to be the right objective function, the things that can go

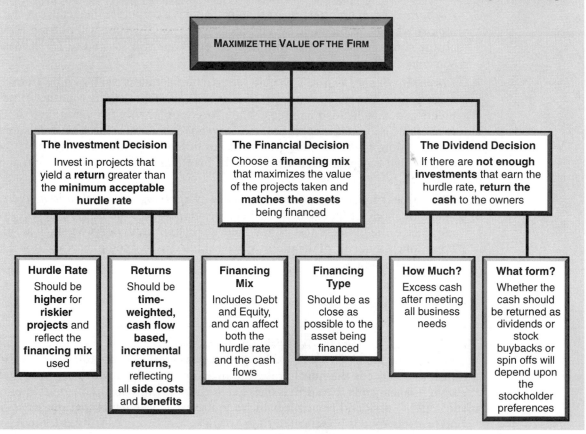

MAXIMIZE THE VALUE OF THE FIRM

The Investment Decision
Invest in projects that yield a **return** greater than the **minimum acceptable hurdle rate**

The Financial Decision
Choose a **financing mix** that maximizes the value of the projects taken and **matches the assets** being financed

The Dividend Decision
If there are **not enough investments** that earn the hurdle rate, **return the cash** to the owners

Hurdle Rate
Should be **higher** for **riskier projects** and reflect the **financing mix** used

Returns
Should be **time-weighted, cash flow based, incremental returns,** reflecting all **side costs** and **benefits**

Financing Mix
Includes Debt and Equity, and can affect both the hurdle rate and the cash flows

Financing Type
Should be as close as possible to the asset being financed

How Much?
Excess cash after meeting all business needs

What form?
Whether the cash should be returned as dividends or stock buybacks or spin offs will depend upon the stockholder preferences

8

wrong with firms that focus on value maximization, and at least partial fixes to some of these problems. We will argue strongly that, even though value maximization is a flawed objective function, it offers far more promise than alternative objective functions because it is self-correcting.

THE CLASSICAL OBJECTIVE FUNCTION

There is general agreement, at least among corporate finance theorists, that the objective of the firm is to maximize value or wealth. There is some disagreement on whether the objective is to maximize the wealth of stockholders or the wealth of the firm, which includes, besides stockholders, the other financial claim holders (debt holders, preferred stockholders, etc.). Furthermore, even among those who argue for stockholder wealth maximization, there is a debate about whether this translates into maximizing the stock price.

These objective functions vary in terms of the assumptions needed to justify them. The least restrictive of the three objectives, in terms of assumptions needed, is to maximize the firm value, and the most restrictive is to maximize the stock price.

Why Corporate Finance Focuses on Stock Price Maximization

There are three reasons for the focus on stock price maximization in traditional corporate finance. The first is that stock prices are the most observable of all measures that can be used to judge the performance of a publicly traded firm. Unlike earnings or sales, which are updated infrequently, stock prices are updated constantly to reflect new information coming out about the firm. Thus, managers receive instantaneous feedback on every action they take from investors in markets. A good illustration is the response of markets to a firm announcing that it plans to acquire another firm. While managers consistently paint a rosy picture of every acquisition that they plan, the stock price of the acquiring firm drops in a significant proportion of all acquisitions, suggesting that markets are much more skeptical about managerial claims.

The second is that stock prices, in a rational market, attempt to reflect the long-term effects of decisions made by the firm. Unlike accounting measures, such as revenues, or sales measures, such as market share, which look at the effects on current operations of decisions made by the firm, the value of a stock is a function of the long-term health and prospects of the firm. In a rational market, the stock price is an attempt on the part of investors to measure this value. Even if they err in their estimates, it can be argued that a noisy estimate of long-term value is better than a precise estimate of current earnings.

Finally, choosing stock price maximization as an objective function allows us to make categorical statements about the best way to pick projects and finance them.

2.1   WHAT DO YOU THINK THE OBJECTIVE FUNCTION OF THE FIRM SHOULD BE?

The following statement best describes where I stand in terms of the right objective function for decision making in a business:

☐   Maximize stock price or stockholder wealth, with no constraints.

☑   Maximize stock price or stockholder wealth, with constraints on being a good social citizen.

☐   Maximize profits or profitability.

- ☐ Maximize market share.
- ☐ Maximize revenues.
- ☐ Maximize social good.
- ☐ None of the above.

Organizational Structure and Classical Theory

In the modern corporation, stockholders hire managers to run the firm for them; these managers then borrow from banks and bondholders to finance the firm's operations. Stockholders then respond to information about the firm revealed to them by the managers, and firms have to operate and make decisions in the context of a larger society. By focusing on maximizing stockholder wealth, corporate finance exposes itself to several risks. First, the managers who are hired to operate the firm for stockholders may have their own interests which deviate from stockholder wealth maximization. Second, stockholders can be made wealthier by expropriating from lenders and other claim holders in the firm. Third, the information that stockholders respond to in financial markets may be misleading and noisy, and the response may be out of proportion to the information. Finally, firms which focus on maximizing wealth may create significant costs for society which are not reflected in the earnings of the firm.

These conflicts of interests are exacerbated further when we bring in two additional stakeholders in the firm. First, the employees of the firm may have little or no interest in stockholder wealth maximization and have a much larger stake in improving wages, benefits, and job security. In some cases, these interests may be in direct conflict with stockholder wealth maximization. Second, the customers of the business will probably prefer that the products and services they buy be priced lower to maximize their utility, but this again may conflict with what stockholders would prefer.

Potential Side Costs of Wealth Maximization

If the only objective in decision making is to maximize firm or stockholder wealth, there is a potential for substantial side-costs to society that may drown out the benefits from wealth maximization. To the extent that these costs are large relative to the wealth created by the firm, the objective function may have to be modified to allow for these costs. To be fair, however, this is a problem which is likely to persist even if an alternative objective function is used.

The objective of wealth maximization may also face obstacles when there is separation of ownership and management, as there is in most large public corporations. When managers act as agents for the owners (stockholders), there is the potential for a conflict of interest between stockholder and managerial interests, which in turn can lead to decision rules that do not maximize stockholder or firm wealth, but maximize managerial utility.

When the objective function is stated in terms of stockholder wealth, the conflicting interests of stockholders and bondholders have to be reconciled. Since stockholders usually control decision making and bondholders are not completely protected, one way of maximizing stockholder wealth is to take actions that expropriate wealth from the bondholders, even though such actions may reduce the wealth of the firm.

Finally, when the objective function is narrowed further to one of maximizing stock price, inefficiencies in the financial markets may lead to misallocation of resources and bad decisions. For instance, if stock prices do not reflect the long-term consequences of decisions, but respond, as some critics say, to short-term earnings effects, a decision that increases stockholder wealth may reduce the stock price. Conversely, a decision that reduces stockholder wealth, but creates earnings increases in the near term, may increase the stock price.

IN PRACTICE: WHAT IS THE OBJECTIVE FOR A PRIVATE FIRM OR A NON-PROFIT ORGANIZATION?

The objective of maximizing stock prices is a relevant objective only for firms which are publicly traded. How, then, can corporate finance principles be adapted for private firms? For firms which are not publicly traded, the objective in decision making is the maximization of firm value. The investment, financing and dividend principles we will develop in the chapters to come apply for both publicly traded firms, which focus on stock prices, and private businesses, that maximize firm value. Since firm value is not observable and has to be estimated, what private businesses will lack is the feedback, sometimes unwelcome, that publicly traded firms get when they make major decisions.

It is, however, much more difficult to adapt corporate finance principles to not-for-profit organizations, since their objective is often to deliver a service in the most efficient way possible, rather than to make profits. We will examine some of the factors that these organizations have to consider while making investment and financing decisions.

A Utopian World . . .

There is a scenario where it is reasonable to ask managers to concentrate on maximizing stock prices to the exclusion of all other considerations and not worry about side costs. For this scenario to unfold, the following assumptions must hold:

1. The managers of the firm put aside their own objectives and focus on maximizing stockholder wealth. This might occur either because they are terrified of the power stockholders have to replace them or because they own enough stock in the firm that maximizing stockholder wealth becomes their objective as well.

2. The lenders to the firm are fully protected from expropriation by stockholders. This might occur for one of two reasons. The first is that stockholders might be concerned enough about the reputation damage they will suffer if they expropriate wealth, and the consequences for future lending, that they will not take any actions that are intended purely to hurt the lenders to the firm. The second is that lenders might be able to protect themselves fully when they lend by writing in covenants proscribing the firm from taking any actions that expropriate wealth from the lenders.

3. The managers of the firm do not attempt to mislead or lie to financial markets about their future prospects, and there is sufficient information for markets to

The Classical Objective Function

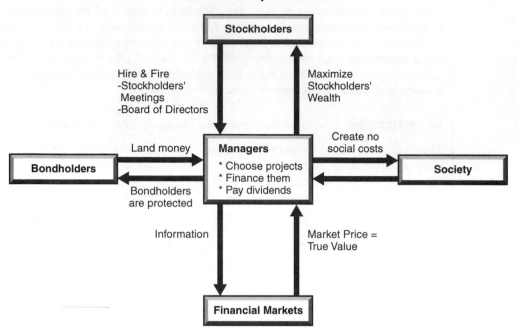

Figure 2.1   The Classical Objective Function

make judgments about the effects of the firm's actions on its long-term cash flows and value. Markets are assumed to be reasoned and rational in their assessments of these actions and the consequent effects on value.

4. There are no social costs. All costs created by the firm in its pursuit of stockholder wealth maximization can be traced and charged to the firm.

With these assumptions, there are no side-costs to stockholder wealth maximization and stock prices reflect stockholder wealth. Consequently, managers can concentrate on one objective—maximizing stock prices. Firm wealth maximization does not require the assumptions of market efficiency or bondholder protection, while stockholder wealth maximization as an objective adds on the assumption of bondholder protection. The assumptions needed for the classical objective function are summarized in pictorial form in Figure 2.1.

SO WHAT CAN GO WRONG?

Even a casual perusal of the assumptions we need for stock price maximization to be the only objective function suggests that there are potential shortcomings in each of the assumptions. Managers might not always make decisions which are in the best interests of stockholders, stockholders do sometimes take actions that transfer wealth from lenders, information about markets is noisy and sometimes misleading, and there are social costs that cannot be captured in the financial statements of the company. In the section that follows, we will consider some of the ways the four linkages—stockholders/managers, stockholders/lenders, stockholders/markets, and stockholders/society—might trigger a breakdown in the stock price maximization objective function.

Stockholders and Managers

Stockholders are assumed to have the power to discipline and replace managers who do not attempt to maximize their wealth. The two mechanisms that exist for this power to be exercised are the annual meeting, where stockholders can voice their displeasure with incumbent management and remove them if necessary, and the board of directors, whose fiduciary duty it is to ensure that managers serve the stockholders. While the legal justification is obvious, the practical power of these institutions to enforce stockholder control is debatable.

Consider first the annual meeting. Most stockholders do not go to the annual meetings, partly because they do not feel that they can make a difference and partly because it would not be economical for them to do so. They could exercise their power with proxies,[1] but in the absence of a proxy fight, incumbent management starts off with a clear advantage.[2] Many stockholders do not bother to fill out their proxies, and even among those who do, voting for incumbent management is often the default option. For larger stockholders, with significant holdings in a large number of securities, the easiest option when dissatisfied with incumbent management is to vote with their feet (i.e., sell their stock and move on). An activist posture on the part of these stockholders would go a long way toward making managers more responsive to their interests, and there are recent trends toward more activism, which will be documented later in this chapter.

The capacity of the board of directors to discipline management and keep them responsive to stockholders is also diluted by a number of factors.

Proxy Fight: In a proxy fight, an investor or a group of investors contests incumbent management by appealing to stockholders for their proxy votes.

1. Most individuals who serve as directors cannot spend much time on their fiduciary duties, partly because of other commitments and partly because many of them serve on the boards of several corporations. A study[3] by Korn-Ferry, an executive recruiter, in 1992, of directorial compensation and time spent by directors on their work, illustrates this very clearly. The average director spent 92

---

[1] A proxy enables stockholders to vote in absentia for boards of directors and for resolutions that will be coming to a vote at the meeting. It does not allow them to ask open-ended questions of management.

[2] This advantage is magnified if the corporate charter allows incumbent management to vote proxies that were never sent back to the firm. This is the equivalent of having an election where the incumbent gets the votes of anybody who does not show up to vote.

[3] Korn-Ferry surveys the boards of large corporations and provides insight into their composition. This study was quoted in a WSJ article on boards of directors.

hours each *year* on board meetings and preparation in 1992, down from 108 in 1988, and was paid[4] $32,352, up from $19,544 in 1988.

2. Even those directors who spend time trying to understand the internal workings of a firm are stymied by their lack of expertise on many issues, especially relating to accounting rules and tender offers, and rely instead on outside experts.

3. Though many directors are outsiders, they are not independent, insofar as the company's chief executive officer (CEO) has a major say in who serves on the board. Korn/Ferry's annual surveys of boards also found that 74% of the 426 companies that it surveyed relied on recommendations by the chairman to come up with new directors, while only 16% used a search firm.

4. The CEOs of other companies are the favored choice for directors, leading to a potential conflict of interest, where CEOs sit on each others' boards.

5. Most directors hold only small or token stakes in the equity of their corporations, making it difficult for them to empathize with the plight of shareholders, when stock prices go down. Institutional Shareholder Services, a consultant, found that 27 directors at 275 of the largest corporations in the United States owned *no* shares at all, and about 5% of all directors owned fewer than five shares.

The net effect of these factors is that the board of directors often fails at its assigned role, which is to protect the interests of stockholders. The CEO sets the agenda, chairs the meeting and controls the information, and the search for consensus generally overwhelms any attempts at confrontation. While there is an impetus toward reform, it has to be noted that these reforms were sparked not by board members, but by large institutional investors.

The failure of the board of directors to protect stockholders can be illustrated with numerous examples from the United States, but this should not blind us to a more troubling fact. Stockholders exercise more power over management in the United States than in any other financial market. If the annual meeting and the board of directors are, for the most part, ineffective in the United States at exercising control over management, they are even more powerless in Europe and Asia as institutions that protect stockholders. Students of the German and Japanese systems of corporate governance will argue that these systems have other ways of keeping errant management in line, but that is a claim that is difficult to back up with evidence.

■ ▲ A Case of a Captive Board: The Disney Example
▼ ●
The composition of the board of directors at Disney provides some insight into many of the problems associated with this institution. The following people were on the board in 1996:

---

[4]This understates the true benefits received by the average director in a firm, since it does not count benefits and perquisites—insurance and pension benefits being the largest component. Hewitt Associates, an executive search firm, reports that 67% of 100 firms they surveyed offer retirement plans for their directors.

Current Company Officials

- Michael D. Eisner, 54: chairman and chief executive.
- Roy E. Disney, 66: vice chairman, head of animation department.
- Sanford M. Litvack, 60: senior executive VP and chief of corporate operations.
- Richard A. Nunis, 64: chairman of Walt Disney Attractions.

Former Company Officials

- Raymond L. Watson, 70: Disney chairman in 1983 and 1984.
- E. Cardon Walker, 80: Disney chairman and chief executive, 1980–83. Received payments totaling $609,826 in fiscal 1996 with respect to films he invested in between 1963 and 1979 under a company incentive plan.
- Gary L. Wilson, 56: Disney chief financial officer, 1985–89.

Outsiders (?)

- Reveta F. Bowers, 48: head of school for the Center for Early Education, where Mr. Eisner's children attended class.
- Ignacio E. Lozano Jr., 69: chairman of Lozano Enterprises; publisher of *La Opinion* newspaper in Los Angeles.
- George J. Mitchell, 63: Washington, D.C. attorney; former U.S. senator. Disney paid Mr. Mitchell $50,000 for his consulting on international business matters in fiscal 1996. His Washington, D.C. law firm was paid an additional $122,764.
- Stanley P. Gold, 54: president and chief executive of Shamrock Holdings, Inc., which manages about $1 billion in investments for the Disney family.
- Thomas S. Murphy, 71: former chairman and chief executive of Capital Cities/ABC, Inc.
- The Rev. Leo J. O'Donovan, 62: president of Georgetown University, where one of Mr. Eisner's children attended college. Mr. Eisner sat on the Georgetown board and has contributed more than $1 million to the school.
- Irwin E. Russell, 70: Beverly Hills attorney whose clients include Mr. Eisner.
- Sidney Poitier, 69: Actor.
- Robert A. M. Stern, 57: New York architect who has designed numerous Disney projects. Mr. Stern received $168,278 for those services in fiscal 1996.

Without casting aspersions on any of these worthy individuals, it is worth noting the number of current and former Disney officials on the board, as well as the links of the outside directors to Mr. Eisner. In fact, it would take quite a stretch to expect some of them to be assertive in challenging Mr. Eisner.

In 1997, CalPERS: California Public Employees' Retirement System suggested a series of checks to see if a board was likely to be effective in acting as a counterweight to a powerful CEO. When they put the companies in the S&P 500 through these tests, Disney was the only company that failed all of the tests.

Fortune magazine, in its rankings of corporate boards in 1997, ranked Disney at the very bottom of its list of 500 companies.

When the Cat Is Idle, the Mice Will Play . . .

If the two institutions of corporate governance—annual meetings and the board of directors—fail to keep management responsive to stockholders, as argued in the previous section, we cannot expect managers to maximize stockholder wealth, especially when their interests conflict with those of stockholders. There are several examples where, arguably, managers put their interests above those of stockholders. The managers of some firms that were targeted by acquirers (raiders) for hostile takeovers in the 1980s were able to avoid being acquired by buying out the raider's existing stake, generally at a price much greater than the price paid by the raider. This process, called *greenmail,* has negative consequences for stock prices but it does protect the jobs of incumbent managers. Another widely used antitakeover device is a *golden parachute,* a provision in an employment contract that allows for the payment of a lump-sum or cash flows over a period if the manager covered by the contract loses his or her job in a takeover. While there are economists who have justified the payment of golden parachutes as a way of reducing the conflict between stockholders and managers, it is still unseemly that managers should need large side-payments to do that which they are hired to do—maximize stockholder wealth. Finally, firms sometimes create securities called *poison pills,* the rights or cash flows on which are triggered by hostile takeovers. The objective is to make it difficult and costly to acquire control. Greenmail, golden parachutes, and poison pills do not require stockholder approval and are usually adopted by compliant boards of directors.

 *We oppose hostile takeover!*

Greenmail: Greenmail refers to the purchase of a potential hostile acquirer's stake in a business at a premium over the price paid for that stake by the target company.

Golden Parachute: A golden parachute refers to a contractual clause in a management contract that allows the manager to be paid a specified sum of money in the event control of the firm changes, usually in the context of a hostile takeover.

Poison Pill: A poison pill is a security or a provision that is triggered by the hostile acquisition of the firm, resulting in a large cost to the acquirer.

Antitakeover amendments have the same objective as greenmail and poison pills (i.e., dissuading hostile takeovers), but differ on one very important count. They require the assent of stockholders to be instituted. There are several types of antitakeover amendments, all designed with the objective of reducing the likelihood of a hostile takeover. Among them are *super-majority requirements* (where the acquirer has to acquire more than a bare majority to acquire the firm), *fair-price amendments* (where the offer price has to exceed a price specified relative to earnings), and staggered elections to boards of directors (which prevent acquirers from getting control for several years). They do increase the bargaining power of managers and prevent two-tier takeovers.[5] For these rationales to be credible, however, managers should be viewed as acting in the best interests of stockholders, and that remains a stretch.

2.2 ANTI-TAKEOVER AMENDMENTS AND MANAGEMENT TRUST

If as a stockholder in a company, you were asked to vote on an amendment to the corporate charter which would restrict hostile takeovers of your company and give your management more power, in which of the following types of companies would you be most likely to vote yes to the amendment?

- ☑ Companies where the managers promise to use this power to extract a higher price for you from hostile bidders
- ☐ Companies which have done badly (in earnings and stock price performance) in the last few years *(maybe takeover is better ...)* *— maybe*
- ☑ Companies which have done well (in earnings and stock price performance) in the last few years *hostile takeover unlikely*
- ☑ I would never vote for such an amendment

There are many ways in which managers can make their stockholders worse off—by taking on bad projects, by taking on too much or too little debt, and by adopting defensive mechanisms against potentially value-increasing takeovers. The quickest and perhaps the most decisive way to impoverish stockholders is to overpay on a takeover, since the amounts paid on takeovers tend to dwarf those involved in the other decisions listed above. Of course, the managers of the firms doing the acquiring will argue that they never[6] overpay on takeovers, and that the high premiums paid in acquisitions can be justified using any number of reasons— there is synergy, there are strategic considerations, the target firm is undervalued and badly managed, and so on. The stockholders in acquiring firms do not seem to share the enthusiasm for mergers and acquisitions that their managers have, since the stock prices of bidding firms decline on the takeover announcements a significant proportion[7] of the time.

Synergy: Synergy is the additional value created by bringing together two entities and pooling their strengths. In the context of a merger, synergy is the difference between the value of the merged firm and the sum of the values of the firms operating independently.

---

[5]In a two-tier takeover, the acquirer offers a higher price for the first 51% who tender their shares and a lower price for those who tender afterwards.

[6]One explanation given for the phenomenon of overpaying on takeovers is given by Roll (1986), who posits that it is managerial hubris (pride) that drives the process.

[7]Jarrell, Brickley and Netter (1988) in an extensive study of returns to bidder firms note that excess returns on these firms' stocks around the announcement of takeovers declined from an average of 4.95% in the sixties to 2% in the seventies to −1% in the eighties. You, Caves, Smith, and Henry (1986) examined 133 mergers between 1976 and 1984 and found that the stock prices of bidding firms declined in 53% of the cases.

These illustrations are not meant to make the case that managers are venal and self-ish, which would be an unfair charge, but are manifestations of a much more fundamental problem; when there is conflict of interest between stockholders and managers, stockholder wealth maximization is likely to take second place to management interests.

 This data set has the breakdown of CEO compensation for many U.S. firms for the most recent year.

Stockholders and Bondholders

In a world where there are no conflicts of interest between stockholders and bond-holders, the latter might not have to worry about protecting themselves from expropriation. In the real world, however, there is a risk that bondholders who do not protect themselves may be taken advantage of in a variety of ways—by stockholders increasing leverage, paying more dividends, or undercutting the security on which the debt was based.

The Source of the Conflict

The source of the conflict of interest between stockholders and bondholders lies in the differences in the nature of the cash flow claims of the two groups. Bondholders generally have first claim on cash flows, but receive fixed amounts, assuming that the firm makes enough income to meet its debt obligations. Equity investors have a claim on the residual cash flows, but have the option of declaring bankruptcy if the firm has insufficient cash flows to meet its financial obligations. As a consequence, bondholders tend to view the risk in project choice and other decisions much more negatively than stockholders, since they do not get to participate on the upside if the projects succeed, and could bear a significant portion of the cost, if they fail. There are many issues on which stockholders and bondholders are likely to disagree.

Some Examples of the Conflict

Existing bondholders can be made worse off by increases in leverage, especially if these increases are large and affect the default risk of the firm, and these bondholders are unprotected. (The stockholders' wealth increases concurrently.) This effect is dramatically illustrated in the case of leveraged buyouts, where the debt ratio increases and the bond rating drops significantly. The prices of existing bonds fall to reflect the higher default risk.

Dividend policy is another issue on which a conflict of interest may arise between stockholders and bondholders. The effect of higher dividends on stock prices can be debated in theory, with differences of opinion on whether it should increase or decrease prices, but the empirical evidence is clear. Increases in dividends, on average, lead to higher stock prices, while decreases in dividends lead to lower stock prices. Bond prices, on the other hand, react negatively to dividend increases and positively to dividend cuts.

The Consequences of Stockholder-Bondholder Conflicts

Stockholders and bondholders have different objective functions and some decisions can transfer wealth from one group (usually bondholders) to the other (usually stockholders). An objective function that focuses on maximizing stockholder wealth may result in stockholders taking perverse actions that harm the overall firm but increase their wealth at the expense of bondholders.

It is possible that we are making too much of the expropriation possibility, for a couple of reasons. Bondholders are aware of the potential of stockholders to take actions that are inimical to their interests, and generally protect themselves, either by writing in covenants or restrictions on what stockholders can do, or by taking an equity interest in the firm. Furthermore, the need to return to the bond markets to raise further funds in the future will keep many firms honest, since the gains from any onetime wealth transfer are likely to be outweighed by the reputation loss associated with such actions. These issues will be considered in more detail in the next section.

Bond Covenants: Covenants are restrictions built into contractual agreements. The most common reference in corporate finance to covenants is in bond agreements, and they represent restrictions placed by lenders on investment, financing, and dividend decisions made by the firm.

The Firm and Financial Markets

There is an advantage to maintaining an objective function that focuses on stockholder or firm wealth, rather than stock prices or the market value of the firm, since it does not require any assumptions about the efficiency or otherwise of financial markets. The downside, however, is that stockholder or firm wealth is not easily measurable, making it difficult to establish clear standards for success and failure. It is true that there are valuation models, some of which we will examine in this book, that attempt to measure equity and firm value, but they are based on a large number of essentially subjective inputs on which people may disagree. Since an essential characteristic of a good objective function is that it comes with a clear and unambiguous measurement mechanism, the advantages of shifting to an objective function that focuses on market prices are obvious. The measure of success or failure is there for all to see. A successful manager raises the firm's stock price, and an unsuccessful one reduces it.

The trouble with market prices, of course, is that they are set by financial markets. To the extent that financial markets are efficient and use the information that is available to make measured and unbiased estimates of future cash flows and risk, market prices will reflect true value. In such markets, both the measurers and the measured will accept the market price as the appropriate mechanism for judging success and failure.

There are two potential barriers to this. The first is that information is the lubricant that enables markets to be efficient. To the extent that this information is hidden, delayed, or misleading, market prices will deviate from true value, even in an otherwise efficient market. The second problem is that there are many, both in academia and in practice, who argue that markets are not efficient, even when information is freely available. In both cases, decisions that maximize stock prices may not be consistent with long-term value maximization.

2.3   THE CREDIBILITY OF FIRMS IN CONVEYING INFORMATION

Do you think that the information revealed by companies about themselves is usually:

☐ Honest and truthful?

☑ Biased?

☐ Fraudulent?

1. The Information Problem

Market prices are based upon information, both public and private. In the world of classical theory, information is revealed promptly and truthfully to financial markets. In the real world, there are a couple of impediments to this process. The first is that information is sometimes suppressed or delayed by firms, especially when it contains bad news. While there is significant anecdotal evidence of this occurrence, the most direct evidence that firms do this comes from studies of earnings and dividend announcements made by firms. Penman (1987), in a study of earnings announcements, noted that those announcements which had the worst news tended to be delayed the longest, relative to the expected announcement date. In a similar vein, my study of earnings and dividend announcements by day of the week for firms on the New York Stock Exchange between 1982 and 1986 found that the announcements made on Friday, especially after the close of trading, contained more bad news than announcements made on any other day of the week. This suggests that managers try to time bad news announcements for when markets are least active or closed, because they fear that markets will overreact.

The second problem is a more serious one. Some firms, in their zeal to keep investors happy and raise market prices, release intentionally misleading information about the firm's current conditions and future prospects to financial markets. These misrepresentations can cause stock prices to deviate significantly from value. Consider the example of Bre-X, a Canadian gold mining company that claimed to have found one of the largest gold reserves in the world in Indonesia in the early 1990s. While the company was heavily touted by equity research analysts in the United States and Canada, the entire claim was fraudulent. When the fraud came to light in 1997, the stock price tumbled, and analysts professed to be shocked that they were misled by the firm.

The implications of such fraudulent behavior for corporate finance can be profound, since managers are often evaluated on the basis of stock price performance. Thus Bre-X managers with options or bonus plans tied to the stock price probably did very well before the fraud came to light.

Public and Private Information: Public information refers to any information that is available to the investing public, whereas private information is information that is restricted to only insiders or a few investors in the firm.

2.4   REPUTATION AND MARKET ACCESS

Which of the following types of firms is more likely to mislead markets?

☑ Companies which access markets infrequently to raise funds for operations—they raise funds internally.

☐ Companies which access markets frequently to raise funds for operations.

Explain.

2.5   ARE MARKETS SHORT TERM?

Focusing on market prices will lead companies toward short-term decisions at the expense of long-term value.

☑ I agree with this statement.

☐ I do not agree with this statement.

Explain.

2. The Market Problem

The fear that managers have of markets overreacting or not assimilating information well into prices may be justified. Even if information flowed freely and with no distortion to financial markets, there is no guarantee that what emerges as the market price will be an unbiased estimate of true value. In fact, there are many who would argue that the fault lies deeper, that investors are much too irrational and unreliable to come up with a good estimate of the true value. Some of the criticisms that have been mounted against financial markets are legitimate, some are overblown, and some are flat out wrong, but they all need to be seriously considered.

Financial markets do not always reasonably and rationally assess the effects of new information into prices. They can be volatile, reacting to no news at all in some cases; in any case, the volatility in market prices is usually much greater than the volatility in any of the underlying fundamentals. They sometimes overreact to information, as can be attested to by almost any firm that has had a significant negative earnings surprise. In some cases, they do look at the short-term effects of actions rather than their long-term implications. Finally, there are cases where insiders move markets.

IN PRACTICE: ARE MARKETS SHORT TERM?

There are many who believe that stock price maximization leads to a short-term focus for managers—see, for instance, Michael Porter's book on competitive strategy. The reasoning goes as follows: Stock prices are determined by traders, short-term investors, and analysts, all of whom hold the stock for short periods and spend their time trying to forecast next quarter's earnings. Managers who concentrate on creating long-term value, rather than short-term results, will be penalized by markets. Most of the empirical evidence that exists, however, suggests that markets are much more long-term than they are given credit for.

1. There are hundreds of firms, especially small and startup firms, which do not have any current earnings and cash flows, and do not expect to have any in the near future, but which are still able to raise substantial amounts of money on the basis of expectations of success in the future. If markets were in fact as short term as the critics suggest, these firms should be unable to raise funds in the first place.

2. If the evidence suggests anything, it is that markets do not value current earnings and cash flows enough and value future earnings and cash flows too much. Studies indicate that stocks with low price-earnings ratios (i.e., high

current earnings) have generally been underpriced relative to stocks with high price-earnings ratios.

3. The market response to research and development and investment expenditure is not uniformly negative, as the "short-term" critics would lead you to believe. Instead, the response is tempered, with stock prices, on average, rising on the announcement of R&D and capital expenditures.

The Bottom Line: To Believe in Markets, or Not . . .

The information that flows into financial markets is often delayed, incorrect, and misleading, and the prices that flow out are very noisy estimates of the true value. But this cannot take away from the central contribution of financial markets. They assimilate and aggregate a remarkable amount of information on current conditions and future prospects into one measure—the stock price. No competing measure comes close to providing as timely or as comprehensive a measure of a firm's standing.

The value of having market prices is best illustrated when working with a private firm as opposed to a public firm. While managers of the latter may resent the second-guessing of analysts and investors, there is a great deal of value to knowing how investors perceive the actions that the firm takes.

The Firm and Society

Most management decisions have social consequences, and the question of how best to deal with these consequences is not easily answered. An objective function of maximizing firm or stockholder wealth implicitly assumes that the social side-costs are either trivial enough that they can be ignored or that they can be priced and charged to the firm. In many cases, these assumptions may not be justifiable.

There are some cases where the social costs are considerable but cannot be traced to the firm. In these cases, the decision makers, though aware of the costs, may choose to ignore the costs and maximize firm wealth. The ethical and moral dilemmas of forcing a manager to choose between his or her survival (which may require stockholder wealth maximization) and the broader interests of society can be debated but there is no simple solution that can be offered in this book.

In the cases where substantial social costs exist, and firms are aware of these costs, ethicists might argue that wealth maximization has to be subjugated to the broader interests of society, but what about those cases where firms create substantial social costs without being aware of these costs? Johns Manville Corporation, for instance, in the fifties and sixties produced asbestos with the intention of making a profit, and was unaware of the potential of the product to cause cancer. Thirty years later, the lawsuits from those afflicted with asbestos-related cancers have driven it to bankruptcy.

To be fair, conflicts between the interests of the firm and the interests of society are not restricted to the objective function of maximizing stockholder wealth. They may be endemic to a system of private enterprise, and there may never be a solution to satisfy the purists who would like to see a complete congruence between the social and firm interests.

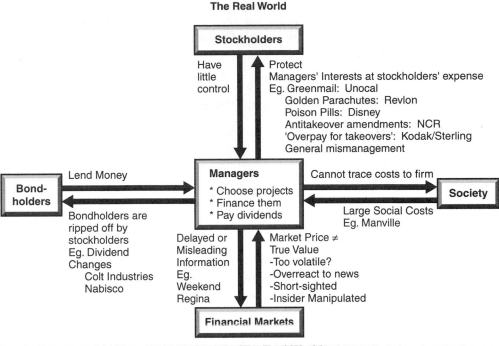

Figure 2.2   The Real World

2.6   CAN LAWS MAKE COMPANIES GOOD CITIZENS?

It has often been argued that social costs occur because governments do not have adequate laws on the books to punish companies that create social costs. The follow-up is that passing such laws will eliminate social costs.

☐   I agree with this statement.

☐   I do not agree with this statement.

Explain.

The Real World—A Pictorial Representation

We have spent the last few pages chronicling the problems in the real world with each of the linkages—managers and stockholders, stockholders and bondholders, firms and financial markets, and firms and society. Figure 2.2 summarizes the problems with each linkage in a pictorial representation.

So What Next?

There are obvious problems associated with each of the linkages underlying wealth maximization. Stockholders do not exercise control over managers, and managers consequently put their interests above those of stockholders. Bondholders who do not protect their interests often end up paying a price, when decisions made by firms transfer wealth to stockholders. Information is often erroneous and suppressed, and there are significant differences between price and market value. Finally, firms that maximize wealth may do so at the expense of society.

Given these problems, there are two alternative courses of action that we can follow. The first is to keep the objective function of maximizing stockholder wealth and minimizing its limitations. The second is to drop this objective function, and adopt an alternative.

MAXIMIZE STOCKHOLDER WEALTH, SUBJECT TO ...

There can be no complete solution to the problems discussed in the last section, but there are ways in which some of the problems can be alleviated. The objective is to reduce the conflicts of interest between stockholders, bondholders, and managers, and to reduce deviations between price and value.

Stockholders and Managers

There are clearly conflicts of interest between stockholders and managers, and the traditional mechanisms for stockholder control—annual meetings and boards of directors—often fail in their role of discipline management. This does not mean, however, that the chasm between the two groups is too wide to be bridged, either by closing the gap between their interests or by increasing stockholder power over managers.

Making Managers Think More Like Stockholders

As long as managers have interests which are distinct and different from the interests of the stockholders they serve, there is potential for conflict. One way to reduce this conflict is to provide managers with an equity stake in the firms they manage, by providing them with stock or warrants on the stock. If this is done, the benefits that accrue to management from higher stock prices may provide an inducement to maximize stock prices.

There is a downside to doing this, which is that while it reduces the conflict of interest between stockholders and managers, it may exacerbate the other conflicts of interest highlighted in the previous section. It may increase the potential for expropriation of wealth from bondholders and the probability that misleading information may be conveyed to financial markets.

Warrants: A warrant is a security issued by a company that provides the holder with the right to buy a share of stock in the company at a fixed price during the life of the warrant.

2.7   STOCKHOLDER INTERESTS, MANAGERIAL INTERESTS, AND MANAGEMENT BUYOUTS

In a management buyout, the managers of the firm buy out the existing stockholders and make the company a private firm. Is this a way of reducing the conflict of interest between stockholders and managers?

☑ Yes

☐ No

Explain.

Increasing Stockholder Power

There are many ways in which stockholder power over management can be increased. The first is to provide stockholders with better and more updated information, so that they can make better judgments on how well the management is doing. The second is to have a large stockholder become part of incumbent management, and have a direct role in decisions that the firm makes. Examples include Warren Buffett's role in the resuscitation of Salomon Brothers, and Larry Tisch's stint as CEO of CBS, Inc. In both cases, companies which were in serious trouble with declining stock prices were rescued by stockholders with large holdings, who reformulated policy to preserve and increase stockholder wealth.[8] The third is to have more "activist" institutional stockholders, who play a larger role in issues such as the composition of the board of directors, the question of whether to pass antitakeover amendments, and overall management policy. In recent years, institutional investors have used their considerable power to pressure managers into becoming more responsive to their needs. Among the most aggressive of these investors has been the California Public Employees Retirement System (CalPERS), one of the largest institutional investors in the country. The fourth change, pushed by these activist stockholders, is to make boards of directors more responsive to stockholders, by reducing the number of insiders on these boards and making them more independent of the CEO.

IN PRACTICE: Disney Stockholders Express Their Displeasure with Managers

In an earlier section, we pointed out the "inside" nature of the board of directors at Disney. While Disney is fond of pointing out that it has delivered superior returns to its stockholders, its stockholders are suspicious of the cozy relationship between their board and their CEO. In early 1997, after Disney had paid $38.8 million to former president Michael Ovitz to leave the firm, the board of directors extended the contract of the CEO, Michael Eisner, to run through the year 2006, and offered him a very generous package of options. At the annual meeting on February 25, 1997, 13% of Disney stockholders voted against the slate of directors up for reelection, and 8.2% voted against the pay package. While neither number may seem high, they represented the biggest "no" vote against a major U.S. corporation since Archer-Daniels-Midland Co.'s annual meeting in October 1995, when nearly 20% of the votes cast opposed the incumbent slate, according to the Investor Responsibility Research Center in Washington.

2.8 Inside Stockholders versus Outside Stockholders

There are companies like Microsoft where a large stockholder (Bill Gates) may be on the inside as the CEO of the concern. Is it possible that what is in Bill Gates' best interests as an inside stockholder may not be in the interests of a stockholder on the outside?

☑ Yes. Their interests may deviate.

☐ No. Their interests will not deviate.

If yes, provide an example of an action that may benefit the inside stockholder but not the outside stockholder.

---

[8] In the interests of the truth, it should be pointed out that neither was entirely successful in doing so.

The Threat of a Takeover

The perceived excesses of many takeovers in the eighties drew attention to the negative consequences of such actions. In movies and books, the raiders who were involved in these takeovers were portrayed as "barbarians," while the firms being taken over were viewed as hapless victims. While this may have been true in some cases, the reality was that in most cases companies that were taken over deserved to be taken over. A study by Bhide, for instance, found that target firms in hostile takeovers in 1985 and 1986 were generally much less profitable than their competitors and had provided sub-par returns to their stockholders, and that managers in these firms had significantly lower holdings in the company. In short, badly managed firms were much more likely to become targets of hostile takeover bids than well managed firms.

One implication of this finding is that takeovers operate as a disciplinary mechanism, keeping managers in check, by introducing a cost to bad management. Often, the very threat of a takeover is sufficient to make firms restructure their assets and become more responsive to stockholder concerns. It is not surprising, therefore, that legal attempts to regulate and restrict takeovers have had negative consequences for stock prices. One example was the antitakeover law devised by the Pennsylvania legislature to protect companies incorporated in the state against hostile takeovers, which was initiated in 1989 with much support from the state's chambers of commerce. Karpoff and Malatesta (1990) examined the consequences of this law for stock prices of Pennsylvania firms, and found that they dropped (after adjusting for market movements), on average, 1.58% on October 13, 1989, the first day a news story was carried on the law. Over the whole period, from the first news story to the introduction of the bill into the Pennsylvania legislature, these firms had a cumulative market-adjusted return of −6.90%.

The story of the Pennsylvania antitakeover law would not be complete without documenting the reactions to it from stockholders. Institutional investors in the firms that would have been covered by the law chose to fight it, expressed their displeasure to managers, and threatened to sell their stock in these firms. Their threats worked, because most firms chose to opt out of the law, an illustration of the power that stockholders can have if they choose to exercise it.

2.9   HOSTILE ACQUISITIONS: WHO DO THEY HURT?

Given the information presented in this chapter, which of the following groups is most likely to be protected by a law banning hostile takeovers?

☑ Stockholders of target companies
☑ Managers and employees of well-run target companies
☐ Managers and employees of badly-run target companies
☐ Society

The Consequences of Stockholder Power

As stockholders exercise their newfound power, managers are becoming more responsive to their interests. This helps alleviate, if not eliminate, the problems associated with the separation of ownership and management that we alluded to in the previous section.

IN PRACTICE: THE GERMAN/JAPANESE ALTERNATIVE TO STOCKHOLDER POWER

In the German and Japanese systems of corporate governance, firms own stakes in other firms, and often make decisions which are in the best interests of the industrial group they belong to, rather than in their own best interests. In this system, the argument goes, firms will keep an eye on each other, rather than ceding power to the stockholders. In addition to being undemocratic—the stockholders are, after all, the owners of the firm—it suggests a profound suspicion of how stockholders might use the power if they get it and is heavily skewed toward maintaining the power of incumbent managers.

While this approach may protect the system against the waste that is a byproduct of stockholder activism and inefficient markets, it has its own disadvantages. Industrial groups are inherently more conservative than investors in allocating resources, and thus are much less likely to finance high-risk and venture capital investments by upstarts who do not belong to the group. The other problem is that entire groups can be dragged down by individual firms that have run into trouble.

Deutsche Bank provides an illustration of this alternative mechanism for corporate governance. The largest single stockholder in Deutsche Bank is the German insurance company, Allianz, and Deutsche Bank is itself the single largest stockholder in the German auto maker, Daimler Benz. Through this elaborate system of cross-ownership, firms are supposed to keep an eye on each other. This system can fail on two counts. First, since all these firms have a vested interest in preserving the existing system, it is unlikely that any of them will have an incentive to challenge it. Second, none of these firms can be viewed as a pure equity investor in the other. For instance, Deutsche Bank is the lead commercial bank for Daimler Benz; consequently, it is both a leading stockholder and bondholder in the firm. It also does a substantial amount of investment banking business with Daimler Benz, and its equity research analysts have to pass judgments on whether Daimler Benz is fairly valued. Thus, it is not clear that what is in Duetsche Bank's best interests is in the best interests of other stockholders.

Stockholders and Bondholders

The conflict of interest between stockholders and bondholders can lead to actions that transfer wealth to the former from the latter—by taking risky projects, by paying more dividends, and by increasing leverage—without compensating bondholders for the loss of wealth associated with these actions. There are ways in which bondholders can obtain at least partial protection against some of these actions.

The Effect of Covenants

The most direct way for bondholders to protect themselves is to write in covenants in their bond agreements specifically prohibiting or restricting actions that may be wealth expropriating. Many bond agreements have covenants that do the following:

1. *Restrict the firm's investment policy:* Taking on riskier projects than anticipated can lead to a transfer of wealth from bondholders to stockholders. Some bond agreements put restrictions on where firms can invest and how much risk they can take on in their new investments, specifically to provide bondholders with the power to veto actions that are not in their best interests.

2. *Restrict dividend policy:* In general, increases in dividends increase stock prices while decreasing bond prices, because they transfer wealth from bondholders to stockholders. Many bond agreements restrict dividend policy, by tying dividend payments to earnings.

3. *Restrict additional leverage:* Some bond agreements require firms to get the consent of existing bondholders before issuing new secured debt. This is done to protect the interests of existing secured bondholders.

While covenants can be effective at protecting bondholders against some abuses, they do come with a price tag. In particular, firms may find themselves having to turn down profitable opportunities because of bondholder-imposed constraints and having to pay (directly or indirectly) for the legal and monitoring costs associated with the constraints.

Taking an Equity Stake
Since the primary reason for the conflict of interest between stockholders and bondholders lies in the nature of their claims, another way that bondholders can reduce the conflict of interest is by owning an equity stake in the firm. This can take the form of buying stock in the firm at the same time as bonds, or it can be accomplished by attaching warrants to the debt or making bonds convertible into stock. In either case, bondholders who feel that equity investors have enriched themselves at their expense can become stockholders and share in the spoils.

Firms and Financial Markets
The information that firms convey to financial markets is noisy and sometimes misleading. The market price that emerges from financial markets is often wrong, partly because of inefficiencies in markets and partly because of erroneous information. There are no easy or quick-fix solutions to these problems. In the long term, however, there are actions that will improve information quality and reduce deviations between price and value.

Improving the Quality of Information
While regulatory bodies like the Securities and Exchange Commission can require firms to reveal more information and penalize firms that provide misleading and fraudulent information, the quality of information cannot be improved with information disclosure laws alone. In particular, firms will always have a vested interest in when and what information they reveal to markets. To provide balance, therefore, an active market for information, where analysts who are *not* hired and fired by the firms they follow collect and disseminate information, has to exist. While analysts are just as likely to make mistakes as the firm, they have

greater incentive to unearth negative information about the firm and to disseminate that information to their clients.

Making Markets More Efficient

Just as better information cannot be legislated into existence, markets cannot be made more efficient by edict. In fact, there is widespread disagreement on what is required to make markets more efficient. At the minimum, these are necessary (though not sufficient) conditions for more efficient markets:

1. Trading should be both inexpensive and easy. The higher transactions costs are, and the more difficult it is to execute a trade, the more likely it is that markets will be inefficient.

2. At least some investors in this market should have access to information about the stocks being traded and the resources to trade on the information.

Restrictions imposed on trading, while well intentioned, often lead to market inefficiencies. For instance, restricting short sales may seem like good public policy, but it can create a scenario where negative information about stocks cannot be reflected adequately in prices.

Firms and Society

There will always be social costs associated with actions taken by firms operating in their own best interests. The basic conundrum is as follows. Social costs cannot be ignored in making decisions, but they are also too nebulous to be factored explicitly into analyses. One solution is for firms to maximize firm or stockholder value, subject to a "good citizen" constraint, where attempts are made to minimize or alleviate social costs, even though the firm may not be under any legal obligation to do so. The problem with this approach, of course, is that the definition of a "good citizen" is likely to vary from firm to firm and from manager to manager. There are companies, however, that have established reputations for being good corporate citizens, and have managed to use it to their benefit. Ultimately, the most effective way to make companies more socially responsible is to make it in their best interests economically to not create social costs. This can occur in two ways. First, firms that are construed as socially irresponsible could lose customers and profits. This was the galvanizing factor behind a number of specialty retailers in the United States disavowing the use of sweatshops and underage labor in other countries in making their products. Second, investors might avoid buying stock in these companies. As an example, many college and state pension plans in the United States have started reducing or eliminating their holdings of tobacco stocks to reflect their concerns about the health effects of the product.

There are clearly problems associated with wealth maximization, but some of these problems can be reduced by making some changes in how managers are hired and fired, and in how they are compensated, in bondholder agreements, and in financial markets. Figure 2.3 summarizes some of these changes.

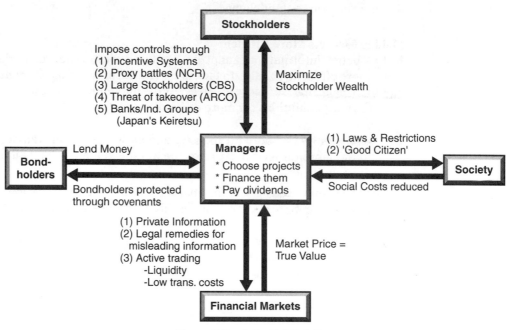

Figure 2.3   A Partial Solution

CHOOSING AN ALTERNATIVE OBJECTIVE FUNCTION

Given its limitations, the easy answer may be to cast aside wealth maximization as an objective function. The tough part is replacing it with another objective function. It is not that there are no alternatives, but that the alternatives come with their own sets of problems and it is not at all obvious that there is a benefit to switching, especially when the alternative objective is evaluated on the four criteria used to evaluate the wealth maximization objective. Is the objective function clear and unambiguous? Does it come with a measure that can be used to evaluate success and failure easily and promptly? Does it create side-costs that may exceed the overall benefits? Is it consistent with maximizing the firm's long-term health and value?

Most firms that choose not to maximize stockholder wealth choose an *intermediate objective* such as increasing market share, profits, or growth as an alternative. These intermediate objectives work well as long as the link to firm value remains strong, but can be very damaging when the link breaks down. Consider the objective of maximizing market share. Promoted by corporate strategists in the eighties, using Japanese companies as their examples of success, this strategy emerged as a double-edged sword. Companies that succeeded in increasing market share found that higher market share did not always lead to greater pricing power and profits in their markets.

There are firms, especially government-owned firms, which have objective functions which are *social welfare functions*. For instance, a firm that is directed to maximize the employment that it provides in the area in which it operates will make decisions accordingly, even though this may be fatal for its long-term health. A less extreme case would be a not-for-profit firm, say a hospital, whose mission might be to provide reasonable health care at an affordable cost. It is not clear what "reasonable" and "affordable" mean in this context, especially when scarce resources have to be allocated among competing uses.

A POSTSCRIPT—THE LIMITS OF CORPORATE FINANCE

Corporate finance has come in for more than its share of criticism in the last decade. There are many who argue that the failures of corporate America can be traced to its dependence on corporate finance. Some of the criticism is justified and based upon the limitations of a single-minded pursuit of stockholder wealth. Some of it, however, is based upon a misunderstanding of what corporate finance is about. Most of the criticism exaggerates the role corporate finance plays in significant decisions made by firms.

Economics was once branded the gospel of Mammon, because of its emphasis on money. The descendants of those critics have labeled corporate finance as unethical, because of its emphasis on the "bottom line" and market prices, even if this implies that workers lose their jobs and take cuts in pay. In cases like restructuring and liquidations, it is true that value maximization for stockholders may mean that other stakeholders, such as customers and employees, lose out. In most cases, however, decisions that increase market value also make customers and employees better off. Furthermore, if the firm is really in trouble, either because it is being undersold by competitors or because its products are technologically obsolete, the choice is not between liquidation and survival, but between a speedy resolution, which is what corporate financial theory would recommend, and a slow death, while the firm declines over time, and costs society considerably more in the process.

The conflict between wealth maximization for the firm and social welfare is the genesis for the attention paid to ethics in business schools. There will never be an objective function or decision rules that perfectly factor in societal concerns, simply because many of these concerns are difficult to quantify and are subjective. Thus corporate financial theory, in some sense, assumes that decision makers will not make decisions that create large social costs, even if their models suggest otherwise. This assumption that decision makers are, for the most part, ethical and will not create unreasonable costs for society or for other stakeholders, is unstated but underlies corporate financial theory. When it is violated, it exposes corporate financial theory to ethical and moral criticism, though this criticism may be better directed at the violators.

2.10 WHAT DO YOU THINK THE OBJECTIVE FUNCTION OF THE FIRM SHOULD BE?

Having heard the pros and cons of the different objective functions, the following statement best describes where I stand in terms of the right objective function for decision making in a business:

☐ Maximize stock price or stockholder wealth, with no constraints.

☑ Maximize stock price or stockholder wealth, with constraints on being a good social citizen.

☐ Maximize profits or profitability.
☐ Maximize market share.
☐ Maximize revenues.
☐ Maximize social good.
☐ None of the above.

CONCLUSION

Corporate financial theory is built around the objective function of maximizing either stockholder or firm wealth. This objective function has the potential to create significant side-costs, in the form of conflicts between stockholders and managers, stockholders and bondholders, and firms and society. These side-costs can be reduced by adopting strategies that reduce the likelihood of these conflicts—by increasing stockholder power over managers, by providing protection for bondholders, and by developing "good citizen" constraints. This may be the optimal strategy to adopt, since alternative objective functions come with their own set of baggage. Finally, much of the criticism of corporate finance can be traced to disagreements critics have with the value maximization objective function, though their prescriptions do not necessarily provide improvement.

PROBLEMS AND QUESTIONS

1. The objective of decision making in corporate finance is
   a. to maximize earnings.
   b. to maximize cash flows.
   c. to maximize the size of the firm.
   d. to maximize market share.
   e. to maximize firm value/stock prices.

2. For maximization of stock prices to be the sole objective in decision making, and to be socially desirable, the following assumption or assumptions must hold true.
   a. Managers act in the best interests of stockholders.
   b. There is no conflict of interest between stockholders and bondholders.
   c. Financial markets are efficient.
   d. There are no costs that are created by the firm that cannot be traced back and charged to the firm.
   e. All of the above.

3. There is a conflict of interest between stockholders and managers. In theory, stockholders are expected to exercise control over managers through the annual meeting or the board of directors. In practice, why might these disciplinary mechanisms not work?

4. Stockholders can transfer wealth from bondholders through a variety of actions. How would the following actions by stockholders transfer wealth from bondholders?
   a. An increase in dividends
   b. A leveraged buyout
   c. Acquiring a risky business

   How would bondholders protect themselves against these actions?

5. Financial market prices are much too volatile for financial markets to be efficient. Comment.

6. Maximizing stock prices does not make sense because investors focus on short-term results, and not on the long-term consequences. Comment.

7. There are some corporate strategists who have suggested that firms focus on maximizing market share rather than market prices. When might this strategy work, and when might it fail?

8. Antitakeover amendments can be in the best interest of stockholders. Under what conditions is this likely to be true?

LIVE CASE STUDY

I. CORPORATE GOVERNANCE ANALYSIS

Objective: This section is designed to analyze the separation between the different claimholders in the firm, and the consequences for the firm's objective function.

Key Questions

- Is this a company where there is a separation between management and ownership? If so, how responsive is management to stockholders?
- Is there a potential conflict between stockholders and lenders to the firm? If so, how is it managed?
- How does this firm interact with financial markets? How do markets get information on the firm?
- How does this firm view its social obligations and manage its image in society?

Framework for Analysis

1. The Chief Executive Officer
- Who is the CEO of the company? How long has he or she been CEO?
- If it is a "family-run" company, is the CEO part of the family? If not, what career path did the CEO take to get to the top? (Did he come from within the organization or from outside?)
- How much did the CEO make last year? What form did the compensation take? (Break down by salary, bonus, and option components.)
- How much stock and options in the company does the CEO own?

2. The Board of Directors
- Who is on the board of directors of the company? How long have they served as directors?
- How many of the directors are "inside" directors? (i.e., employees or managers of the company)?
- How many of the directors have other connections to the firm (as suppliers, clients, customers)?
- How many of the directors are CEOs of other companies?
- Do any of the directors have large stockholdings or represent those who do?

3. Bondholder Concerns
- Does the firm have any publicly traded debt?
- Are there bond covenants (that you can uncover) that have been imposed on the firm as part of the borrowing?

- Do any of the bonds issued by the firm come with special protections against stockholder expropriation?

4. Financial Market Concerns
- How many analysts follow the firm?
- How much trading volume is there on this stock?

5. Societal Constraints
- Does the firm have a particularly good or bad reputation as a corporate citizen?
- If it does, how has it earned this reputation?
- If the firm has been a recent target of social criticism, how has it responded?

Getting Information on Corporate Governance

To find out who the top managers in the firm are, as well as who sits on the board of directors, check out the company's annual report. You can get the annual reports of some companies on line at **www.reportgallery.com.** If that does not work, you can always try the home page for the company. Many companies have their annual reports online. To find out a little more about the people who serve on the board of directors, check out the web site called **people.edgar-online.com/people.** You can also get more information on recent filings with the SEC on insider trading and holdings from **www.freeedgar.com** as well as from the official SEC site which is **www.sec.gov/edgarhp.htm.** (For a description of the registration statement numbers and what's in them, look at the data set on my web site called **edgar.xls**).

To get some external perspective on how the board of directors of your company measures up in terms of keeping an eye on management, you might want to look at what one of our largest (and one of the earliest active investors) CALPERS has to say about the issue of corporate governance at **www.calpers.ca.gov/invest/corpgov/corpgov.htm.** They highlight 10 companies that they choose to focus on for severely underperforming their peer groups. You should also check *Business Week's* annual issue ranking the boards of directors of large U.S. companies. The most recent issue was on December 7, 1997 and can be obtained on line at **www.businessweek.com.**

To get a sense of how much and how your CEO is paid, you should check *Forbes,* which carry annual rankings on this matter. *Forbes* has an online site that ranks CEO compensation and provides the company's rankings in terms of performance—see **www.forbes.com/ceo.** If you dig a little deeper, this same site breaks down the CEO's compensation into its different components.

To get data on analyst coverage and views of this stock, try the site maintained by Zacks Investment Research. You can enter the symbol of a stock and get pretty detailed information on it at **www.zacks.com** in the Free Research Box. You can get the same information on the Morningstar site, under earnings estimates for your firm (**www.morningstar.net** - *quicktake reports*).

Finally, to get a sense of socially responsible investing, check out the web site for social investing at **socialinvest.org/sriguide/mfpc.htm.** One of the larger socially responsible funds, Calvert, has its site at **www.calvertgroup.com.** To get a labor perspective on firms, you can check the AFL-CIO labor site, with its distinct perspective on CEO pay and union labels (**www.aflcio.org**).

CHAPTER 3

THE BASICS OF RISK

Risk, in traditional terms, is viewed as a "negative." Webster's dictionary, for instance, defines risk as "exposing to danger or hazard." The Chinese symbols for risk, reproduced below, give a much better description of risk:

The first symbol is for "danger," while the second symbol is for "opportunity," making risk a mix of danger and opportunity. It illustrates very clearly the tradeoff that

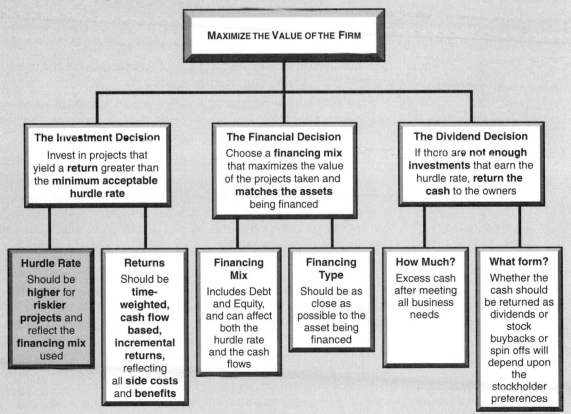

MAXIMIZE THE VALUE OF THE FIRM

The Investment Decision
Invest in projects that yield a **return** greater than the **minimum acceptable hurdle rate**

The Financial Decision
Choose a **financing mix** that maximizes the value of the projects taken and **matches the assets** being financed

The Dividend Decision
If there are **not enough investments** that earn the hurdle rate, **return the cash** to the owners

Hurdle Rate
Should be **higher** for **riskier projects** and reflect the **financing mix** used

Returns
Should be **time-weighted, cash flow based, incremental returns,** reflecting all **side costs** and **benefits**

Financing Mix
Includes Debt and Equity, and can affect both the hurdle rate and the cash flows

Financing Type
Should be as close as possible to the asset being financed

How Much?
Excess cash after meeting all business needs

What form?
Whether the cash should be returned as dividends or stock buybacks or spin offs will depend upon the stockholder preferences

every investor and business has to make—between the "higher rewards" that potentially come with the opportunity and the "higher risk" that has to be borne as a consequence of the danger. The key test in finance is to ensure that when an investor is exposed to risk, he or she is "appropriately" rewarded for taking this risk.

In this chapter, we will lay the foundations for analyzing risk in corporate finance and present alternative models for measuring risk and converting these risk measures into "acceptable" hurdle rates.

INGREDIENTS FOR A GOOD RISK AND RETURN MODEL

We will be presenting a number of different risk and return models in this chapter. In order to evaluate the relative strengths of these models, it is worth reviewing the characteristics of a good risk and return model.

1. It should come up with a measure of risk that applies to all assets and is not asset specific.
2. It should clearly delineate what types of risk are rewarded and what are not, and provide a rationale for the delineation.
3. It should come up with standardized risk measures; that is, an investor presented with a risk measure for an individual asset should be able to draw conclusions about whether the asset is above-average or below-average risk.
4. It should translate the measure of risk into a "rate of return" that the investor should demand as compensation for bearing the risk.
5. It should work well not only at explaining past returns, but also in predicting future expected returns.

GENERAL MODELS FOR RISK AND RETURN

To understand how risk is viewed in corporate finance, we will present the analysis in three steps. First, we will define risk in terms of the distribution of actual returns around an expected return. Second, we will differentiate between risk that is specific to an investment or a few investments and risk that affects a much wider cross-section of investments. We will argue that in a market where the marginal investor is well diversified, it is only the latter risk, called market risk, that will be rewarded. Third, we will look at alternative models for measuring this market risk and the expected returns that go with it.

I. Measuring Risk

Investors who buy assets have a return that they expect to make over the time horizon that they will hold the asset. The actual returns that they make over this holding period may be very different from the expected returns, and this is where the risk comes in. Consider an investor with a one-year time horizon buying a one-year Treasury bill (or any other default-free one-year bond) with a 5% expected return. At the end of the one-year holding period, the actual return that this investor would have on this investment will always be 5%, which is equal to the expected return. The return distribution for this investment is shown in Figure 3.1.

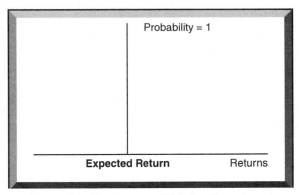

Figure 3.1   Returns on a Risk-free Investment

Variance in Returns: This is a measure of the squared difference between the actual returns and the expected returns on an investment.

This is a riskless investment, at least in nominal terms.

To provide a contrast, consider an investor who invests in Disney. This investor, having done her research, may conclude that she can make an expected return of 30% on Disney over her one-year holding period. The actual return over this period will almost certainly not be equal to 30%; it will be much greater or much lower. The distribution of returns on this investment is illustrated in Figure 3.2.

In addition to the expected return, an investor now has to consider the following. First, the spread of the actual returns around the expected return is captured by the *variance* or *standard deviation* of the distribution; the greater the deviation of the actual returns from expected returns, the greater the variance. Second, the bias toward positive or negative returns is captured by the *skewness* of the distribution. The distribution is said to be "positively" skewed, since there is a greater bias toward large positive returns than negative returns. Third, the shape of the tails of the distribution is measured by the *kurtosis* of the distribution; fatter tails lead to higher kurtosis. In investment terms, this captures the tendency of the price of this investment to "jump" in either direction.

In the special case, where distributions are symmetric and normal, investors do not have to worry about skewness and kurtosis, since there is no skewness and a normal distribution is defined to have a kurtosis of zero. In that case, it can be argued that investments can be measured on two dimensions—(1) the "expected return" on the investment comprises the reward, and (2) the "variance" in anticipated returns comprises the risk on the investment. Figure 3.3 illustrates the return distributions on two investments with symmetric returns. In this scenario, an investor faced with a choice between two investments with different standard deviations but the same expected returns will always pick the one with the lower standard deviation.

In the more general case, where distributions are neither symmetric nor normal, it is still conceivable, though unlikely, that investors still choose between investments on the basis of only the expected return and the variance, if they possess utility

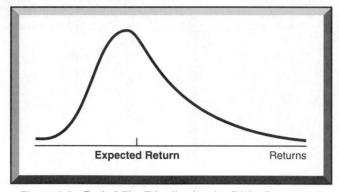

Figure 3.2 Probability Distribution for Risky Investment

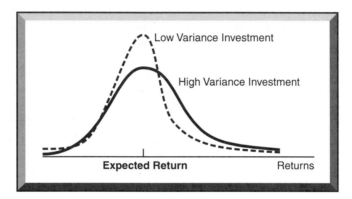

Figure 3.3 Return Distribution Comparisons

functions[1] that allow them to do so. It is far more likely, however, that they prefer positively skewed distributions to negatively skewed ones, and distributions with a lower likelihood of jumps (lower kurtosis) over those with a higher likelihood of jumps (higher kurtosis). In this world, investors will trade off the good (higher expected returns and more positive skewness) against the bad (higher variance and kurtosis) in making investments. Among the risk and return models that we will be examining, one, the capital asset pricing model (CAPM), explicitly requires that choices be made only in terms of expected returns and variances. While it does ignore the skewness and kurtosis, it is not clear how much of a factor these additional moments of the distribution are in determining expected returns.

---

[1]A utility function is a way of summarizing investor preferences into a generic term called "utility" on the basis of some choice variables. In this case, for instance, investor's utility or satisfaction is stated as a function of wealth. By doing so, we can effectively answer questions such as: Will an investor be twice as happy if he has twice as much wealth? Does each marginal increase in wealth lead to less additional utility than the prior marginal increase? In one specific form of this function, the quadratic utility function, the entire utility of an investor can be compressed into the expected wealth measure and the standard deviation in that wealth.

In closing, we should note that the return moments that we run into in practice are almost always estimated using past returns rather than future returns.
The assumption we are making when we use historical variances is that past
return distributions are good indicators of future return distributions. When this
assumption is violated, as is the case when the asset's characteristics have
changed significantly over time, the historical estimates may not be good measures of risk.

3.1   Do you Live in a Mean-Variance World?

Assume that you had to pick between two investments. They have the same expected return
of 15% and the same standard deviation of 25%; however, investment A offers a very small
possibility that you could quadruple your money, while investment B's highest possible payoff is a 60% return. Would you

☐ be indifferent between the two investments, since they have the same expected return
and standard deviation?

☐ prefer investment A, because of the possibility of a high payoff?

☐ prefer investment B, because it is safer?

Illustration **3.1**   Calculation of Standard Deviation Using Historical Returns: Disney

We collected the data on the returns we would have made on a monthly basis for
every month from January 1992 to December 1996 on an investment in Disney stock.
The monthly returns are graphed below:

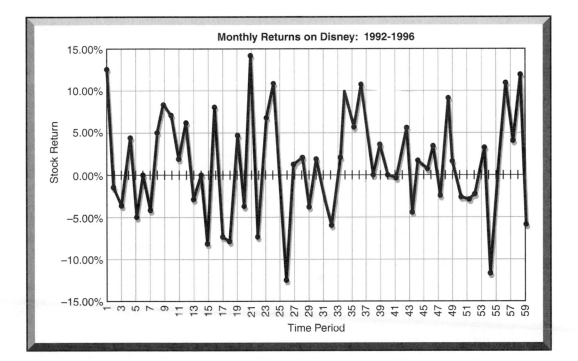

The standard deviation and the variance in these monthly returns were estimated to be:

Standard Deviation in Monthly Returns = 6.14%
Variance in Monthly Returns = 37.66%

These measures can be annualized[2] fairly simply as follows:

Annualized Standard Deviation = $6.14\% * \sqrt{12} = 21.26\%$
Annualized Variance = $37.66\% * 12 = 452\%$

This is a dataset on the Web that summarizes standard deviations of stocks in various sectors in the United States (**optvar.xls**).

3.2 UPSIDE AND DOWNSIDE RISK

You are looking at the historical standard deviations over the last five years on two investments. Both have standard deviations of 35% in returns during the period, but one had a return of −10% during the period, whereas the other had a return of +40% during the period. Would you view them as equally risky?

☐   Yes

☐   No

Why do we not differentiate between "upside risk" and "downside risk" in finance?

II. Rewarded and Unrewarded Risk

Risk, as we have defined it in the previous section, arises from the deviation of actual returns from expected returns. This deviation, however, can be caused by any number of reasons, and these reasons can be classified into two categories—those that are specific to the investment being considered (called firm-specific risks) and those that apply across all investments (market risks).

Diversification: This is the process of holding multiple investments in a portfolio, either across the same asset class (stocks) or across asset classes.

The Components of Risk

The risk that a firm faces when it makes a new investment comes from a number of sources, including the investment itself, competition, shifts in the industry, international considerations, and macroeconomic factors. Some of this risk, however, will be eliminated by the firm itself over the course of multiple investments and some by investors in the firm as they hold diversified portfolios.

The first source of risk is *project-specific risk*; an individual project may have higher or lower cash flows than expected, either because the analyst misestimated the cash flows for that project or because of factors specific to that project. When firms take on a large number of similar projects, it can be argued that much of this risk should be diversified away in the normal course of business. For instance, Disney,

---

[2]This procedure for annualization assumes that returns are uncorrelated across months, that is, that there is no relationship between the returns made in one month and the returns in the following month.

while considering making a new movie, exposes itself to estimation error—it may under- or overestimate the cost and time of making the movie, and may also err in its estimates of revenues from both theatrical release and the sale of merchandise. Since Disney releases several movies a year, it can be argued that some or much of this risk should be diversifiable across movies produced during the course of the year.

Project Risk: This is risk that affects only the project under consideration and may arise from factors specific to the project or estimation error.

The second source of risk is *competitive risk,* whereby the earnings and cash flows on a project are affected (positively or negatively) by the actions of competitors. While a good project analysis will factor the expected reactions of competitors into estimates of profit margins and growth, the actual actions taken by competitors may differ from these expectations. In most cases, this component of risk will affect more than one project, and is therefore more difficult to diversify away in the normal course of business by a firm. Disney, for instance, in its analysis of revenues from its Disney Store division may err in its assessments of the strengths and strategies of competitors like Warner Bros. Stores and Toys 'Я'Us. While Disney cannot diversify away much of its competitive risk, its stockholders can, if they have the capacity and willingness to hold stock in the competitors.[3]

Competitive Risk: This is the unanticipated effect on the cash flows in a project of competitor actions—these effects can be positive or negative.

The third source of risk is *industry-specific risk*—those factors that primarily impact the earnings and cash flows of a specific industry. There are three sources within this category. The first is *technology risk,* which reflects the effects of technologies that change or evolve in ways different from those expected when the project was originally analyzed. The second source is *legal risk,* which reflects the effect of changing laws and regulations. The third source is *commodity risk,* which reflects the effects of price changes in commodities and services that are used or produced disproportionately by a specific industry. Disney, for instance, in assessing the prospects of its broadcasting division (ABC), is likely to be exposed to all three risks: to technology risk, as the lines between television entertainment and the Internet are increasingly blurred by companies like Microsoft; to legal risk, as the laws governing network television change; and to commodity risk, as the costs of making new television programs change over time. A firm cannot diversify away its industry-specific risk without diversifying across industries, either with new projects or through acquisitions. Stockholders in the firm should be able to diversify away industry-specific risk by holding portfolios of stocks from different industries.

Industry-Specific Risk: These are unanticipated effects on project cash flows of industrywide shifts in technology, changes in laws or in the price of a commodity.

---

[3]Firms could conceivably diversify away competitive risk by acquiring their existing competitors. Doing so would expose them to attacks under the antitrust law, however, and would not eliminate the risk from as-yet unannounced competitors.

The fourth source of risk is *international risk*. A firm faces this type of risk when the currency in which the firm's earnings are measured and its stock is priced differs from the currency of its cash flows, as is the case when taking projects outside the domestic market. In such cases, the earnings and cash flows might be different than expected due to exchange rate movements or political risk. Disney, for instance, was clearly exposed to this risk with its 33% stake in EuroDisney, the theme park it developed outside Paris. Some of this risk may be diversified away by the firm in the normal course of business by taking on projects in different countries whose currencies may not all move in the same direction. Companies can also reduce their exposure to the exchange rate component of this risk by choosing a financing mix for projects that matches the cash flows on these projects, for instance, by borrowing money in Deutsche marks to take on projects in Germany. Investors who are restricted to domestic investments because of transactions costs or other constraints will also be exposed to currency and political risk if they hold stock in the company. An international investor who holds investments in multiple countries and currencies may be able to diversify away the international risk.

International Risk: This is the additional uncertainty created in cash flows of projects by unanticipated changes in exchange rates and by political risk in foreign markets.

The final source of risk is *market risk*—macroeconomic factors that affect essentially all companies and all projects, to varying degrees. For example, changes in interest rates will affect the value of projects already taken on and those yet to be taken on both directly, through the discount rates, and indirectly, through the cash flows. Other factors that affect all investments include the term structure (the difference between short- and long-term rates), the risk preferences of investors (as investors become more risk averse, more risky investments will lose value), inflation, and economic growth. While expected values of all these variables enter into project analysis, changes in these variables will affect the values of these investments. Firms cannot really diversify away this risk in the normal course of business, though they could conceivably do so by using interest rate or market derivatives. Investors also cannot diversify away this risk by creating portfolios of risky investments (such as stocks) since all risky investments bear some exposure to this risk.

Market Risk: Market risk refers to the unanticipated changes in project cash flows, created by changes in interest rates, inflation rates, and the economy, that affect all projects and all firms, though to differing degrees.

3.3   RISK IS IN THE EYES OF THE BEHOLDER

A privately owned firm will generally end up with a higher discount rate for a project than would an otherwise similar publicly traded firm.

☐   True

☐   False

Explain.

Why Diversification Reduces or Eliminates Firm-Specific Risk

Diversification reduces or, at the limit, eliminates firm-specific risk for two reasons. The first is that each investment in a diversified portfolio is a much smaller percentage of that portfolio. Thus, any action that increases or reduces the value of only that investment or a small group of investments will have only a small impact on the overall portfolio. The second is that the effects of firm-specific actions on the prices of individual assets in a portfolio can be either positive or negative for each asset for any period. Thus, in large portfolios, it can be reasonably argued that this risk will average out to be zero and thus not impact the overall value of the portfolio.

In contrast, the effects of marketwide movements are likely to be in the same direction for most or all investments in a portfolio, though some assets may be affected more than others. For instance, other things being equal, an increase in interest rates will lower the value of most assets in a portfolio. Being more diversified does not eliminate this risk, though holding assets in different classes may reduce the impact. Table 3.1 summarizes the different components of risk and the actions that can be taken by the firm and its investors to reduce or eliminate this risk.

Why Is the Marginal Investor Assumed to Be Diversified?

The argument that diversification reduces an investor's exposure to risk is not contested often, but risk and return models in finance go further. They argue that the marginal investor, who sets prices for investments, is well diversified; thus, the only risk that will be priced is the risk as perceived by that investor. The justification that can be offered is a simple one. The risk in an investment will always be perceived to be higher for an undiversified investor than for a diversified one, since the latter does not consider any firm-specific risks while the former does. If both investors have the same perceptions about future earnings and cash flows on an asset, the diversified investor will be willing to pay a higher price for that asset because of his or her risk perceptions. Consequently, the asset, over time, will end up being held by diversified investors.

While this argument is a powerful one for stocks and other assets, which are traded in small units and are liquid, it is less so for investments which are large and illiquid. Real estate in most countries is still held by investors who are undiversified and have the bulk of their wealth tied up in these investments. The benefits of diversification are strong enough, however, that securities such as real estate investment trusts and mortgage-backed bonds were created to allow investors to invest in real estate and stay diversified at the same time.

3.4   MANAGEMENT QUALITY AND RISK

A well-managed firm is less risky than a firm that is badly managed.

☐   True

☐   False

III. Measuring Market Risk

While most risk and return models in use in corporate finance agree on the first two steps of this process (i.e., that risk comes from the distribution of actual returns

Table 3.1 AN ANALYSIS OF RISK

Type of Risk	Examples	Firm Can Mitigate By	Investor Can Mitigate By	Private Firm	Effects on Analysis	
					Public Firm with Domestic Investors	Public Firm with International Investors
Project-specific	- Estimation mistakes - Errors specific to product or location	- Taking a large number of projects	- Holding more than one stock in their portfolios	- Should not matter if firm takes many projects - May matter if firm takes few projects	- Should not matter	- Should not matter
Competitive	- Unexpected response or new product/service from competitor	- Acquiring competitors	- Investing in the equity of competitors	- Will matter since owner is generally not well diversified	- Should not matter	- Should not matter
Industry	- Changes that affect all companies in an industry	- Diversifying into other businesses, through acquisitions/investments	- Holding a portfolio diversified across industries	- Will matter since owner is generally not well diversified	- Should not matter	- Should not matter
International	- Exchange-rate changes - Political changes	- Investing in multiple countries/currencies	- Holding a portfolio diversified across countries	- Will matter since owner is generally not well diversified	- Will matter since investors are not internationally diversified	- Should not matter
Market/Macro	- Interest rate changes - Inflation changes - Economic shocks			- Should matter	- Should matter	- Should matter

around the expected return and that risk should be measured from the perspective of a marginal investor who is well diversified), they part ways on how to measure the nondiverisifiable or market risk. In this section, we will provide a sense of how each of the four basic models—the capital asset pricing model (CAPM), the arbitrage pricing model (APM), the multifactor model, and the regression model—approaches the issue of measuring market risk..

A. The Capital Asset Pricing Model

The risk and return model which has been in use the longest and is still the standard in most corporate financial analyses is the capital asset pricing model.

1. Assumptions

While diversification has its attractions in terms of reducing the exposure of investors to firm-specific risk, most investors limit their diversification to holding a limited number of assets. Even large mutual funds are reluctant to hold more than a few hundred stocks, and many of them hold as few as 10 to 20 stocks. There are two reasons for this reluctance. The first is that the marginal benefits of diversification become smaller as the portfolio gets more diversified—the twenty-first asset added will generally provide a much smaller reduction in firm-specific risk than the fifth asset added, and may not cover the marginal costs of diversification, which include transactions and monitoring costs. The second is that many investors (and funds) believe that they can find undervalued assets and thus choose not to hold those assets that they believe to be correctly valued or overvalued.

The capital asset pricing model assumes that there are no transactions costs, that all assets are traded, and that investments are infinitely divisible (i.e., you can buy any fraction of a unit of the asset). It also assumes that there is no private information and that investors therefore cannot find under- or overvalued assets in the marketplace. By making these assumptions, it eliminates the factors that cause investors to stop diversifying. With these assumptions in place, the logical end limit of diversification is to hold all traded assets (stocks, bonds, and real assets included) in your portfolio, in proportion to their market value.[4] This portfolio of every traded asset in the marketplace is called the *market portfolio.*

2. Implications for Investors

If every investor in the market holds the identical market portfolio, how exactly do investors reflect their risk aversion in their investments? In the capital asset pricing model, investors adjust for their risk preferences in their allocation decision, where they decide how much to invest in a riskless asset and how much in the "market portfolio," which is a portfolio of all traded risky assets. Investors who are risk averse might choose to put much or even all of their wealth in the riskless asset. Investors who want to take more risk will invest the bulk or even all

---

[4]If investments are not held in proportion to their market value, investors are still losing some diversification benefits. Since there is no gain from overweighting some sectors and underweighting others in a marketplace where the odds are random of finding undervalued and overvalued assets, investors will not do so.

of their wealth in the market portfolio. Those investors who invest all their wealth in the market portfolio and are still desirous of taking on more risk, would do so by borrowing at the riskless rate and investing in the same market portfolio as everyone else.

These results are predicated on two additional assumptions. First, there exists a riskless asset, where expected returns are known with certainty. Second, investors can lend and borrow at this riskless rate to arrive at their optimal allocations. There are variations of the CAPM that allow these assumptions to be relaxed and still arrive at conclusions that are consistent with the model.

Riskless Asset: A riskless asset is one where the actual return is always equal to the expected return.

3.5 EFFICIENT RISK TAKING

In the capital asset pricing model, the most efficient way to take a lot of risk is to
- ☐ Buy a well-balanced portfolio of the riskiest stocks in the market.
- ☐ Buy risky stocks that are also undervalued.
- ☐ Borrow money and buy a well-diversified portfolio.

3. Measuring the Market Risk of an Individual Asset

The risk of any asset to an investor is the risk added on by that asset to the investor's overall portfolio. In the CAPM world, where all investors hold the market portfolio, the risk of an individual asset to an investor will be the risk that this asset adds on to the market portfolio. Intuitively, assets that move more with the market portfolio will tend to be riskier than assets that move less, since the movements that are unrelated to the market portfolio will be eliminated when an asset is added on to the portfolio. Statistically, this added risk is measured by the *covariance* of the asset with the market portfolio.

The covariance is a nonstandardized measure of market risk; knowing that the covariance of Disney with the market portfolio is 55% does not provide a clue as to whether Disney is riskier or safer than the average asset. We therefore standardize the risk measure by dividing the covariance of each asset with the market portfolio by the variance of the market portfolio. This yields the *beta of the asset:*

$$\text{Beta of an Asset i} = \frac{\text{Covariance of Asset i with Market Portfolio}}{\text{Variance of the Market Portfolio}}$$

Since the covariance of the market portfolio with itself is its variance, the beta of the market portfolio, and by extension, the average asset in it, is 1. Assets that are riskier than average (using this measure of risk) will have betas that exceed 1 and assets that are safer than average will have betas that are lower than 1. The riskless asset will have a beta of zero.

4. Getting Expected Returns

The fact that every investor holds some combination of the riskless asset and the market portfolio leads to the next conclusion, which is that the expected return on an asset is linearly related to the beta of the asset. In particular, the expected return on an asset can be written as a function of the risk-free rate and the beta of that asset.

> Expected Return on Asset i
> = Risk-Free Rate + Beta of Asset i * (Risk premium on market portfolio)
> = $R_f + \beta_i [E(R_m) - R_f]$

where,

> $E(R_i)$ = Expected return on asset i
> R_f = Risk-free rate
> $E(R_m)$ = Expected return on market portfolio
> β_i = Beta of investment i

Beta: The beta of any investment in the CAPM is a standardized measure of the risk that it adds to the market portfolio.

5. The CAPM in Practice

To use the capital asset pricing model, we need three inputs. While we will look at the estimation process in far more detail in the next chapter, each of these inputs is estimated as follows:

- The riskless asset is defined to be the return on an asset where the investor knows the expected return with certainty for the time horizon of the analysis. Consequently, the riskless rate used will vary depending upon whether the time period for the expected return is one year, five years, or ten years.

- The risk premium is the premium demanded by investors for investing in the market portfolio, which includes all risky assets in the market, instead of investing in a riskless asset. In practice, it is often estimated using historical data on the returns on risky assets (usually stocks) and the riskless return.

- The beta, which we defined to be the covariance of the asset divided by the variance of market portfolio, can be obtained directly by regressing past returns on the asset against past returns on the market portfolio, or some proxy thereof (usually a stock index). The slope of the regression is the beta.

In summary, in the capital asset pricing model all of the market risk is captured in one beta, measured relative to a market portfolio, which at least in theory should include all traded assets in the marketplace held in proportion to their market value.

3.6   WHAT DO NEGATIVE BETAS MEAN?

In the capital asset pricing model, there are assets that can have betas which are less than zero. When this occurs, which of the following statements describes your investment?

☐ This investment will make less than the riskless rate.

☐ This investment insures your "diversified portfolio" against some type of market risk.

☐ Holding this asset makes sense only if you are well diversified.

☐ All of the above.

B. The Arbitrage Pricing Model

The restricting assumptions in the capital asset pricing model and its dependence upon the market portfolio have long been viewed with skepticism by both academics and practitioners. In the late seventies, Ross (1976) suggested an alternative model for measuring risk called the arbitrage pricing model.

1. Assumptions

The arbitrage pricing model (APM) is built on the simple premise that investors take advantage of arbitrage opportunities. In other words, if two portfolios have the same exposure to risk but offer different expected returns, investors will buy the portfolio that has the higher expected returns and in the process adjust the expected returns to equilibrium.

Like the capital asset pricing model, the arbitrage pricing model begins by breaking risk down into firm-specific and market risk components. The first, firm specific, covers risk that affects primarily the firm. The second is the market risk that affects all investments, such as unanticipated changes in interest rates, inflation, or other macroeconomic variables. Incorporate this into the return model,

$$R = E(R) + m + \epsilon$$

where m is the marketwide component of unanticipated risk and ϵ is the firm-specific component. Note that this distinction is very similar to the distinction between firm-specific and market risk made in the capital asset pricing model.

2. The Sources of Marketwide Risk

While both the capital asset pricing model and the arbitrage pricing model make a distinction between firm-specific and marketwide risk, they part ways when it comes to measuring the market risk. The CAPM assumes that the market risk is captured in the market portfolio, whereas the arbitrage pricing model sticks with economic fundamentals, allowing for multiple sources of marketwide risk, such as unanticipated changes in gross national product, interest rates, and inflation, and measures the sensitivity of investments to these changes with factor betas. In general, the market component of unanticipated returns can be decomposed into economic factors:

$$R = E(R) + m + \epsilon$$
$$= E(R) + (\beta_1 F_1 + \beta_2 F_2 + \ldots + \beta_n F_n) + \epsilon$$

where

β_j = Sensitivity of investment to unanticipated changes in factor j (called factor beta)
F_j = Unanticipated changes in factor j

3. The Effects of Diversification

The benefits of diversification have been discussed extensively in our treatment of the capital asset pricing model. The primary point of that discussion was that diversification of investments into portfolios eliminates firm-specific risk. The arbitrage pricing model makes the same point and concludes that the return on a portfolio will not have a firm-specific component of unanticipated returns. The return on a portfolio can be written as the sum of two weighted averages—that of the anticipated returns in the portfolio and that of the factor betas:

$$R_p = (w_1R_1 + w_2R_2 + ... + w_nR_n) + (w_1\beta_{1,1} + w_2\beta_{1,2} + ... + w_n\beta_{1,n})\ F_1$$
$$+ (w_1\beta_{2,1} + w_2\beta_{2,2} + ... + w_n\beta_{2,n})\ F_2$$

where

w_j = Portfolio weight on asset j
R_j = Expected return on asset j
$\beta_{i,j}$ = Beta on factor i for asset j

4. Expected Returns and Betas

The fact that the beta of a portfolio is the weighted average of the betas of the assets in the portfolio, in conjunction with the absence of arbitrage, leads to the conclusion that expected returns should be linearly related to betas. To see why, assume that there is only one factor and that there are three portfolios. Portfolio A has a beta of 2.0 and an expected return of 20%; portfolio B has a beta of 1.0 and an expected return of 12%; and portfolio C has a beta of 1.5 and an expected return of 14%. Note that the investor can put half of his wealth in portfolio A and half in portfolio B and end up with a portfolio with a beta of 1.5 and an expected return of 16%. Consequently no investor will choose to hold portfolio C until the prices of assets in that portfolio drop and the expected return increases to 16%. By the same rationale, the expected returns on every portfolio should be a linear function of the beta, or there will be an opportunity for arbitrage. This argument can be extended to multiple factors, with the same results. Therefore, the expected return on an asset can be written as

$$E(R) = R_f + \beta_1\ [E(R_1) - R_f] + \beta_2\ [E(R_2) - R_f] ... + \beta_n\ [E(R_n) - R_f]$$

where

R_f = Expected return on a zero-beta portfolio
$E(R_j)$ = Expected return on a portfolio with a factor beta of 1 for factor j, and zero for all other factors

The terms in the brackets can be considered to be risk premiums for each of the factors in the model.

Note that the capital asset pricing model can be considered to be a special case of the arbitrage pricing model, where there is only one economic factor driving marketwide returns and the market portfolio is the factor:

$$E(R) = R_f + \beta_m\ (E(R_m) - R_f)$$

Arbitrage: An investment opportunity that requires zero investment, has no risk, and still yields a positive return is called an arbitrage opportunity.

5. The APM in Practice

The arbitrage pricing model requires estimates of each of the factor betas and factor risk premiums in addition to the riskless rate. In practice, these are usually estimated using historical data on returns on assets and a "factor analysis." Intuitively, a factor analysis examines the historical data looking for common patterns that affect broad groups of assets (rather than just one sector or a few assets). It provides two output measures:

1. It specifies the number of common factors that affected the historical data that it worked on.

2. It measures the beta of each investment relative to each of the common factors, and provides an estimate of the actual risk premium earned by each factor.

The factor analysis does not, however, identify the factors in economic terms.

In summary, in the arbitrage pricing model the market risk is measured relative to multiple unspecified macroeconomic factors, with the sensitivity of the investment relative to each factor being measured by a factor beta. The number of factors, the factor betas, and factor risk premiums can all be estimated using factor analysis.

C. Multifactor Models for Risk and Return

The arbitrage pricing model's failure to identify specifically the factors in the model may be a strength from a statistical standpoint, but it is a clear weakness from an intuitive standpoint. The solution seems simple: Replace the unidentified statistical factors with specific economic factors, and the resultant model should be intuitive while still retaining much of the strength of the arbitrage pricing model. That is precisely what multifactor models do.

Deriving a Multifactor Model

Multifactor models generally are not based on extensive economic rationale but are driven by the data instead. Once the number of factors has been identified in the arbitrage pricing model, the behavior of the factors over time can be extracted from the data. These factor time series can then be compared to the time series behavior of macroeconomic variables to see if any of the variables is correlated, over time, with the identified factors.

For instance, Chen, Roll, and Ross (1986) suggest that the following macroeconomic variables are highly correlated with the factors that come out of factor analysis: industrial production, changes in default premium, shifts in the term structure, unanticipated inflation, and changes in the real rate of return. These variables can then be correlated with returns to come up with a model of expected returns, with firm-specific betas calculated relative to each variable:

$$E(R) = R_f + \beta_{GNP}[E(R_{GNP}) - R_f] + \beta_I[E(R_I) - R_f] \ldots + \beta_\delta[E(R_\delta) - R_f]$$

where

β_{GNP} = Beta relative to changes in industrial production

$E(R_{GNP})$ = Expected return on a portfolio with a beta of 1 on the industrial production factor, and zero on all other factors

β_I = Beta relative to changes in inflation

$E(R_I)$ = Expected return on a portfolio with a beta of 1 on the inflation factor, and zero on all other factors

The costs of going from the arbitrage pricing model to a macroeconomic multifactor model can be traced directly to the errors that can be made in identifying the factors. The economic factors in the model can change over time, as will the risk premia associated with each one. For instance, oil price changes were a significant economic factor driving expected returns in the 1970s but are not as significant in other time periods. Using the wrong factor(s) or missing a significant factor in a multifactor model can lead to inferior estimates of cost of equity.

In summary, multifactor models, like the arbitrage pricing model, assume that market risk can be best captured using multiple macroeconomic factors and betas relative to each. Unlike the arbitrage pricing model, multifactor models do attempt to identify the macroeconomic factors that drive market risk.

Unanticipated Inflation: This is the difference between actual inflation and expected inflation.

D. Regression Models

All of the models described so far begin by thinking about market risk in broad intuitive terms and then developing economic models that might best explain this market risk. All of them, however, extract their parameters by looking at historical data. There is a final class of risk and return models that start with the returns and work backwards to a risk and return model by trying to explain differences in returns across long time periods using firm characteristics such as the size of the firm and its price multiples. These models are essentially regression models, and the firm characteristics that best explain differences in returns can be viewed as effective proxies for market risk.

Fama and French, in a highly influential study of the capital asset pricing model in the early 1990s, note that actual returns on firms over long time periods have been highly correlated with their price/book value ratios and their market capitalization. They suggest that these measures, and similar ones developed from the data, be used as proxies for risk and that the regression coefficients be used to estimate expected returns for investments. For instance, Fama and French report the following regression for monthly returns on stocks on the NYSE, using data from 1963 to 1990:

$$R_t = 1.77\% - 0.11 \ln (MV) + 0.35 \ln (BV/MV)$$

where

MV = Market value of equity (in millions)

BV/MV = Book value of equity/market value of equity

The values for market value of equity and book-price ratios for individual firms, when plugged into this regression, should yield expected monthly returns.

In summary, regression models measure market risk using firm characteristics as proxies for market risk. The firm characteristics are identified by looking at differences in returns across investments over very long time periods and correlating with identifiable characteristics of these investments.

Book-to-Market Ratio: This is the ratio of the book value of equity to the market value of equity.

A COMPARATIVE ANALYSIS OF RISK AND RETURN MODELS

All the risk and return models developed in this chapter have common ingredients. They all assume that only marketwide risk is rewarded, and they derive the expected return as a function of measures of this risk. The capital asset pricing model makes the most assumptions but arrives at the simplest model, with only one factor driving risk and requiring estimation. The arbitrage pricing model makes fewer assumptions but arrives at a more complicated model, at least in terms of the parameters that require estimation. The capital asset pricing model can be considered a specialized case of the arbitrage pricing model, where there is only one underlying factor and it is completely measured by the market index. In general, the CAPM has the advantage of being a simpler model to estimate and to use, but it will underperform the richer APM when the company is sensitive to economic factors not well represented in the market index. For instance, oil companies, which derive most of their risk from oil price movements, tend to have low CAPM betas. Using an arbitrage pricing model, where one of the factors may be capturing oil and other commodity price movements, will yield a better estimate of risk and higher cost of equity for these firms.[5]

The biggest intuitive block in using the arbitrage pricing model is its failure to identify specifically the factors driving expected returns. While this may preserve the flexibility of the model and reduce statistical problems in testing, it does make it difficult to understand what the APM beta coefficients for a firm mean and how they will change as the firm changes (or restructures).

Is beta a good proxy for risk, and is it correlated with expected returns? The answers to these questions have been debated widely in the last two decades. The first tests of the CAPM suggested that betas and returns were positively related, though other measures of risk (such as variance) continued to explain differences in actual returns. This discrepancy was attributed to limitations in the testing techniques. In 1977, Roll, in a seminal critique of the model's tests, suggested that since the market portfolio could never be observed, the CAPM could never be tested, and that all tests of the CAPM were therefore joint tests of both the model and the market portfolio used in the tests, i.e., all any test of the CAPM could show was that the model worked (or did not) given the proxy used for the market portfolio. It could therefore be argued that in any empirical test that claimed to reject the CAPM, the rejection could be of the proxy used for the market portfolio rather than of the model itself. Roll noted that there was no way to ever prove that the CAPM worked, and thus, no empirical basis for using the model.

---

[5]Weston and Copeland used both approaches to estimate the cost of equity for oil companies in 1989 and came up with 14.4% with the CAPM and 19.1% using the arbitrage pricing model.

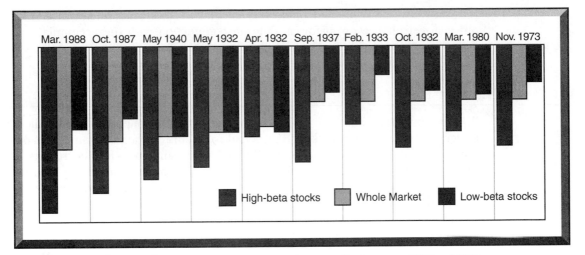

Mar. 1988   Oct. 1987   May 1940   May 1932   Apr. 1932   Sep. 1937   Feb. 1933   Oct. 1932   Mar. 1980   Nov. 1973

High-beta stocks   Whole Market   Low-beta stocks

Figure 3.4   Returns and betas: Ten worst months between 1926 and 1991.

In a damning indictment, Fama and French (1992) examined the relationship between betas and returns between 1963 and 1990 and concluded that there is no relationship between the two. These results have been contested on two fronts. First, Amihud, Christensen, and Mendelson, used the same data, performed different statistical tests, and showed that betas did, in fact, explain returns during the time period. Second, Chan and Lakonishok look at a much longer time series of returns from 1926 to 1991 and found that the positive relationship between betas and returns broke down only in the period after 1982. They attribute this breakdown to indexing, which they argue has led the larger, lower-beta stocks in the S & P 500 to outperform smaller, higher-beta stocks. They also find that betas are a useful guide to risk in extreme market conditions, with the riskiest firms (the 10% with highest betas) performing far worse than the market as a whole, in the ten worst months for the market between 1926 and 1991 (See Figure 3.4).

While the initial tests of the APM and the multifactor models suggested that they might provide more promise in terms of explaining differences in returns, a distinction has to be drawn between the use of these models to explain differences in past returns and their use to get expected returns for the future. The competitors to the CAPM clearly do a much better job at explaining past returns since they do not constrain themselves to one factor, as the CAPM does. This extension to multiple factors does become more of a problem when we try to project expected returns into the future, since the betas and premiums of each of these factors now have to be estimated. As the factor premiums and betas are themselves volatile, the estimation error may wipe out the benefits that could be gained by moving from the CAPM to more complex models. The regression models that were offered as an alternative are even more exposed to this problem, since the variables that work best as proxies for market risk in one period (such as size) may not be the ones that work in the next period.

Ultimately, the survival of the capital asset pricing model as the default model for risk in real-world application is testament both to its intuitive appeal and the failure of more complex models to deliver significant improvement in terms of expected returns. We would argue that a judicious use of the capital asset pricing model, without an overreliance on historical data, in conjunction with the accumulated evidence[6] presented by those who have developed the alternatives to the CAPM, is still the most effective way of dealing with risk in modern corporate finance.

MODELS OF DEFAULT RISK

When an investor lends to an individual or a firm, there is the possibility that the borrower may default on interest and principal payments on the borrowing. This possibility of default is called the "default risk." Generally speaking, borrowers with higher default risk should pay higher interest rates on their borrowing than those with lower default risk. This section examines the measurement of default risk, and the relationship of default risk to interest rates on borrowing.

In contrast to the general risk and return models described above, which focus on market risk, models of default risk examine the consequences of firm-specific default risk on expected returns. While the rationale for diversification can be used to explain why firm-specific risk will not be priced into expected returns, the same rationale does not apply for securities that have limited upside potential and much greater downside potential from firm-specific events. For instance, corporate bonds benefit only marginally from firm-specific events that increase the value of the firm and make it safer, while they bear the risk of any firm-specific events that lower the value of the firm and increase the probability of default. Consequently, the expected return on a corporate bond is likely to reflect the firm-specific default risk of the firm issuing the bond.

A General Model of Default Risk

The default risk of a firm is a broad function of two variables—the firm's capacity to generate cash flows from operations and its financial obligations—including interest and principal payments.[7] All else being equal,

- Firms that generate high cash flows relative to their financial obligations have lower default risk than do firms that generate low cash flows relative to obligations. Thus, firms with significant assets in place, which generate high cash flows, will have lower default risk than will firms that do not.

- The more stability there is in cash flows, the lower is the default risk in the firm. Firms that operate in predictable and stable businesses will have lower default risk than will otherwise similar firms that operate in cyclical and/or volatile businesses.

Most models of default risk use financial ratios to measure the cash flow coverage (i.e., the magnitude of cash flows relative to obligations) and control for industry effects, to capture the variability in cash flows.

---

[6]Barra, a leading beta estimation service, adjusts betas to reflect differences in fundamentals across firms (such as size and dividend yields). It is drawing on the regression studies that have found these to be good proxies for market risk.

[7]Financial obligation refers to any payment that the firm has legally obligated itself to make, such as interest and principal payments. It does not include discretionary cash flows, such as dividend payments or new capital expenditures, which can be deferred or delayed, without legal consequences, though there may be economic consequences.

Bond Ratings and Interest Rates

The most widely used measure of a firm's default risk is its bond rating, which is generally assigned by an independent ratings agency, using a mix of private and public information.

The Ratings Process

The process of rating a bond starts when the issuing company requests a rating from the ratings agency. The ratings agency then collects information from both publicly available sources, such as financial statements, and the company itself, and makes a decision on the rating. If it disagrees with the rating, the company is given the opportunity to present additional information. This process is presented schematically for one ratings agency, Standard and Poor's (S&P), in Figure 3.5.

Description of Bond Ratings

The two major agencies rating corporate bonds are Standard and Poor's (S&P) and Moody's. While the ratings assigned by the two agencies are fairly similar, there are some differences. Table 3.2 provides a description of the bond ratings assigned by the two agencies. In financial markets, bonds with ratings of BBB or higher (Standard and Poor's) are considered "investment grade."

Table 3.2   INDEX OF BOND RATINGS

Standard and Poor's		Moody's	
AAA	The highest debt rating assigned. The borrower's capacity to repay debt is extremely strong.	Aaa	Judged to be of the best quality with a small degree of risk.
AA	Capacity to repay is strong and differs from the highest quality only by a small amount.	Aa	High quality but rated lower than Aaa because margin of protection may not be as large or because there may be other elements of long-term risk.
A	Has strong capacity to repay; Borrower is susceptible to adverse effects of changes in circumstances and economic conditions.	A	Bonds possess favorable investment attributes but may be susceptible to risk in the future.
BBB	Has adequate capacity to repay, but adverse economic conditions or circumstances are more likely to lead to risk.	Baa	Neither highly protected nor poorly secured; adequate payment capacity.
BB,B, CCC, CC	Regarded as predominantly speculative, BB being the least speculative and CC the most.	Ba B	Judged to have some speculative risk. Generally lacking characteristics of a desirable investment; probability of payment small.
D	In default or with payments in arrears.	Caa	Poor standing and perhaps in default.
		Ca	Very speculative; often in default.
		C	Highly speculative; in default.

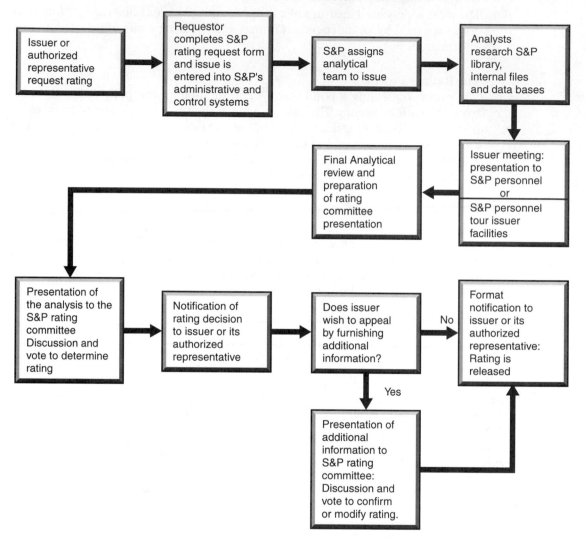

Figure 3.5 Standard and Poor's Ratings Process

Determinants of Bond Ratings

The bond ratings assigned by ratings agencies are primarily based upon publicly available information, though private information conveyed by the firm to the rating agency does play a role. The rating that is assigned to a company's bonds will depend in large part on financial ratios that measure the capacity of the company to meet debt payments and generate stable and predictable cash flows. While a multitude of financial ratios exist, Table 3.3 summarizes some of the key ratios that are used to measure default risk.

Ratio	Description
Table 3.3 FINANCIAL RATIOS USED TO MEASURE DEFAULT RISK	
Pretax Interest Coverage	= (Pretax Income from Continuing Operations + Interest Expense) / Gross Interest
EBITDA Interest Coverage	= EBITDA / Gross Interest Expense
Funds from Operations / Total Debt	= (Net Income from Continuing Operations + Depreciation) / Total Debt
Free Operating Cashflow / Total Debt	= (Funds from Operations − Capital Expenditures − Change in Working Capital / Total Debt
Pretax Return on Permanent Capital	= (Pretax Income from Continuing Operations + Interest Expense) / (Average of Beginning of the Year and End of the Year of Long- and Short-term debt, Minority Interest and Shareholders Equity)
Operating Income / Sales (%)	= (Sales − COGS (before depreciation) − Selling Expenses − Administrative Expenses − R&D Expenses) / Sales
Long-term Debt / Capital	= Long-term Debt / (Long-term Debt + Equity)
Total Debt / Capitalization	= Total Debt / (Total Debt + Equity)

There is a strong relationship between the bond rating a company receives and its performance on these financial ratios. Table 3.4 provides a summary of the median ratios from 1993 to 1995 for different S&P ratings classes for manufacturing firms. Note that the pretax interest coverage ratio and the EBITDA interest coverage ratio are stated in terms of times interest earned, whereas the rest of the ratios are stated in percentage terms.

 There is a dataset on the Web that summarizes key financial ratios by bond rating class for the United States in the most recent period for which the data is available.

Not surprisingly, firms that generate income and cash flows that are significantly higher than debt payments, that are profitable, and that have low debt ratios are more likely to be highly rated than are firms that do not have these characteristics. There will be individual firms whose ratings are not consistent with their financial ratios, however, because the ratings agency does bring subjective judgments into the final mix. Thus, a firm which performs poorly on financial ratios but is expected to improve its performance dramatically over the next period may receive a higher rating than that justified by its current financials. For most firms, however, the financial ratios should provide a reasonable basis for estimating the bond rating.

Bond Ratings and Interest Rates

The yield on a corporate bond should be a function of its default risk, which is measured by its rating. If the rating is a good measure of the default risk, higher-rated bonds should be priced to yield lower interest rates than would lower-rated bonds.

Table 3.4 FINANCIAL RATIOS BY BOND RATING: 1993–1995							
	AAA	**AA**	**A**	**BBB**	**BB**	**B**	**CCC**
Pretax Interest Coverage	13.50	9.67	5.76	3.94	2.14	1.51	0.96
EBITDA Interest Coverage	17.08	12.80	8.18	6.00	3.49	2.45	1.51
Funds from Operations / Total Debt (%)	98.2%	69.1%	45.5%	33.3%	17.7%	11.2%	6.7%
Free Operating Cashflow/Total Debt (%)	60.0%	26.8%	20.9%	7.2%	1.4%	1.2%	0.96%
Pretax Return on Permanent Capital (%)	29.3%	21.4%	19.1%	13.9%	12.0%	7.6%	5.2%
Operating Income/Sales (%)	22.6%	17.8%	15.7%	13.5%	13.5%	12.5%	12.2%
Long-term Debt/ Capital	13.3%	21.1%	31.6%	42.7%	55.6%	62.2%	69.5%
Total Debt/ Capitalization	25.9%	33.6%	39.7%	47.8%	59.4%	67.4%	61.1%

This "default spread" will vary by maturity of the bond and can also change from period to period, depending on economic conditions.

 There is a dataset on the Web that summarizes default spreads by bond rating class for the most recent period (**ratings.xls**).

IN PRACTICE: WHEN THERE ARE NO RATINGS AVAILABLE

An analyst looking at a firm has an information advantage when the firm is rated, since the rating provides an unbiased and public estimate of the default risk of the firm. Since bonds in a ratings class yield a default spread, the rating can also be used as a device to estimate the cost of debt for a firm, even when it has no bonds outstanding.

Some companies choose not to get rated. Many smaller firms and most private businesses fall into this category. While ratings agencies have sprung up in many emerging markets, there are a number of markets where companies are not rated on the basis of default risk. When there is no rating available to estimate the cost of debt, there are alternatives:

1. *Estimate a synthetic rating:* In markets like the United States, where thousands of firms are rated and financial information on these firms is widely available (see Table 3.4, for instance), the financial information that is available on a firm can be used to estimate a "rating" for the firm. For instance, assume that you

are looking at a private firm with a pretax interest coverage ratio of 6.15. Based upon the median ratios in Table 3.4, this firm should be expected to have a rating of A. This approach can be expanded to consider multiple ratios and to incorporate differences in market capitalization and earnings volatility.

2. *Recent Borrowing History:* Many firms which are not rated still borrow money from banks and other financial institutions. By looking at the most recent borrowings made by a firm, we can get a sense of the types of default spreads being charged the firm, and use these spreads to come up with a cost of debt.

Ultimately, it is important to keep in mind that ratings are a means to an end, with the end being the estimation of the cost of debt.

CONCLUSION

The notion that risk is a "negative" and needs to be rewarded is not contestable, though the precise model for estimating risk and reward is still a subject of debate. For equity investments, the models of risk and return that are widely used all measure risk in terms of nondiversifiable risk, though the capital asset pricing model measures it with just one "market" factor, whereas the arbitrage pricing and multi-factor models use several factors. For debt investments, where the holders have limited upside potential and significant downside risk, models of default risk are used to obtain estimates of appropriate returns.

While this chapter provides a background into the intuition behind and the assumptions underlying models of risk, the next chapter will look at the practical issues of how to estimate and use these models and how decisions made by firms affect their risk parameters.

QUESTIONS AND PROBLEMS

1. Suppose that we have three securities, A, B, and C, with the following parameters:

Parameter	A	B	C
Expected return	12%	10%	8%
Standard deviation	30%	40%	35%

Which security would you prefer and why?

2. The following historical returns data for the last 10 years have been gathered for stock X:

Year	Annual Return
1995	42.1%
1994	−10.9%
1993	20.4%
1992	12.5%
1991	10.3%
1990	45.8%
1989	−30.5%
1988	11.4%
1987	10.2%
1986	−2.2%

a. Estimate the average annual return and the standard deviation for the stock.

b. If the company pays no dividends for the last 10 years and the stock price was $25.6 at the end of 1985, what would be the stock price at the end of 1995?

c. What would be the annual compounding growth rate on the stock price over this 10-year period? Is it the same as the average annual return found in (a)?

3. You are interested in forming a portfolio based on two securities with the following characteristics:

Parameter	A	B
Expected return	12%	18%
Standard deviation	25%	40%
Correlation coefficient between A and B		0.8

    a. Calculate the expected return and the standard deviation for the equally weighted portfolio (equal amounts are invested in A and B).

    b. Would you choose to invest in this portfolio or invest in a single security (either A or B) and why?

4. There are two securities with the following parameters:

Parameter	A	B
Expected return	12%	15%
Standard deviation	25%	45%
Correlation coefficient between A and B		−1.0

    a. How can you construct a portfolio so that the portfolio will be risk-free?

    b. What will be the expected return of this particular risk-free portfolio?

    c. If you could get the same lending and borrowing interest rate of 8% from your local bank, how could you create a machine to reap arbitrage profits?

5. There are two securities with the following parameters:

Parameter	A	B
Expected return	15%	5%
Standard deviation	40%	0%

    a. What would be the correlation coefficient between A and B?

    b. If you constructed a portfolio with a standard deviation of 20%, what would be the weight in A and in B?

    c. What would be the expected return of this particular portfolio?

6. Three securities have the following parameters:

Parameter	A	B	C
Expected return	15%	20%	35%
Standard deviation	20%	40%	70%
Correlation coefficient between A and B		0.5	
Correlation coefficient between A and C		0.7	
Correlation coefficient between B and C		0.9	

If you invest 30% of the investment capital in A, 40% in B, and 30% in C, what will be the expected return and the standard deviation of this portfolio?

7. What would be the expected risk premium for a stock with a beta of 1.5, if the expected market risk premium were 10%?

8. What would be the expected return for a stock with a beta of 0.9 if the historical average return of stock market were 12.5% and the Treasury bills have an average yield of 5%?

9. Analysts have a consensus estimate of expected return on the stock market for the next year that is 2.5% higher than the historical average return. What would be the percentage increase in the expected return of this stock from the answer in Question 3.8?

10. A company's stock has an expected return of 15%, and the stock market has an expected return of 12%. What is the beta of the stock if the risk-free return is 5%?

11. The CAPM is often used to evaluate the performance of professional money management. Suppose that a mutual fund has a 10-year average annual return of 14%, whereas the beta is 1.4. The S&P 500 Index grew by 12% per year over the same period, and the average Treasury bill yield was 5%. The manager of this mutual fund would probably claim that it had beaten the market index by a margin of 2% per year. Do you really believe that the mutual fund outperforms the market if the CAPM is valid to represent the risk-return relationship?

12. The market's expected return is 12%, whereas the risk-free return is considered to be 5%. We construct a portfolio in the following fashion:

	A	B	C
Beta	1.2	0.9	1.8
Investment weight	0.4	0.3	0.3

What is the beta of this portfolio, and what is its expected return?

13. Investing only in an S&P 500 Index mutual fund that should have a beta of 1.0 and risk-free assets such as Treasury bills is probably the simplest asset allocation strategy. Assume that the expected return of the S&P 500 Index is 12%, while the expected return on the Treasury bills is 5%.
    a. If you want to get an expected return of 10% per year on your investment, what would be the weight on the S&P 500 Index and the weight on the Treasury bills?
    b. What would be the beta of this portfolio?

14. A typical diversified stock mutual fund invests in hundreds of stocks because it is not allowed to invest more than 5% of its total assets in any single security by law.
    a. What would you expect the beta of a mutual fund to be?
    b. What would you expect the average annual return before expenses to be for a typical mutual fund, if the S&P 500 Index had a historical average annual return of 12%?
    c. Would you be surprised to learn that about 80% of professional money managers underperform the S&P 500 Index after they deduct annual expenses of about 1% to 3% of total assets under management?

15. Assume that a four-factor APT holds, and you have estimated the parameters for a particular company as the following:

R_f	5%		
β_1	1.2	$E(R_1)$	6.5%
β_2	0.5	$E(R_2)$	4.3%
β_3	0.8	$E(R_3)$	8.0%
β_4	1.6	$E(R_4)$	7.5%

   a. What would be the expected return of this stock?
   b. If the actual parameters turn out to be
$$(R_1) = 7.2\%$$
$$(R_2) = 5.2\%$$
$$(R_3) = 6.3\%$$
$$(R_4) = 10\%$$

What will be the "surprise" on the stock's return?

16. You might want to apply Fama and French's estimated equation of $Rt = 1.77\% - 0.11 \, \ln(MV) + 0.35 \, \ln(BV/MV)$ in your portfolio decisions. You divide your securities into two groups based on the ratio BV/MV. The first group has an BV/MV of 0.3, while the other group has 1.2 as its BV/MV.

What is the expected difference on the average monthly return between these two groups of stocks?

17. Assume that the assumptions underlying the CAPM hold. Evaluate whether the following statements are true or false.
    A. A firm with high variance will have a higher beta than one with lower variance.
       True   False
    B. A portfolio is efficient if it has no unsystematic risk.
       True   False
    C. A firm which is highly correlated with the market will have a higher beta than one which is less correlated.
       True   False
    D. If the variance of the overall market goes up, the betas of all firms will go down.
       True   False
    E. A well-managed firm will have a lower beta than a badly managed firm.
       True   False
    F. The market portfolio is efficient and therefore contains only the best stocks in the market.
       True   False
    G. A risk-lover will hold the riskiest stocks in the market, where a risk-averse investor will hold the safest stocks.
       True   False

18. You are in a world where there are only two assets, gold and stocks. You are interested in investing your money in one, the other, or both assets. Consequently, you collect the following data on the returns on the two assets over the last six years:

	Gold	Stock Market
Average return	8%	20%
Standard deviation	25%	22%
Correlation		−.4

a. If you were constrained to pick just one, which one would you choose?

b. A friend argues that this is wrong. He says that you are ignoring the big payoffs that you can get on gold. How would you go about alleviating his concern?

c. How would a portfolio composed of equal proportions in gold and stocks do in terms of mean and variance?

d. You now learn that GPEC (a cartel of gold-producing countries) is going to vary the amount of gold it produces with stock prices in the United States. (They will produce less gold when stock markets are up and more when markets are down.) What effect will this have on your portfolios? Explain.

19. Assume that the average variance of return for an individual security is 50 and that the average covariance is 10. What is the expected variance of a portfolio of 5, 10, 20, 50, and 100 securities? How many securities need to be held before the risk of a portfolio is only 10% more than the minimum?

20. The CAPM has been attacked on several different dimensions. Summarize the criticism of the CAPM and evaluate whether it is justified.

21. You are comparing the arbitrage pricing model to the capital asset pricing model.

a. What are the similarities between the two models? What are the differences?

b. You are estimating the expected returns for a stock using both the CAPM and the arbitrage pricing model. Under what conditions would you get the same expected return? If the expected returns are different, how would you explain the difference?

LIVE CASE STUDY

II. STOCKHOLDER ANALYSIS

Objective: To find out who the average and marginal investors in the company are. This is relevant because risk and return models in finance assume that the marginal investor is well diversified.

Key Questions

- Who is the average investor in this stock? (Individual or pension fund, taxable or tax-exempt, small or large, domestic or foreign)
- Who is the marginal investor in this stock?

Framework for Analysis

1. Who Holds Stock in This Company?

- How many stockholders does the company have?
- What percent of the stock is held by institutional investors?
- Does the company have listings in foreign markets? (If you can, estimate the percent of the stock held by non-domestic investors.)

2. Insider Holdings

- Who are the insiders in this company? (Besides the managers and directors, anyone with more than 5% is treated as an insider.)
- What role do the insiders play in running the company?
- What percent of the stock is held by insiders in the company?
- What percent of the stock is held by employees overall? (Include the holdings by employee pension plans.)
- Have insiders been buying or selling stock in this company in the most recent year?

Getting Information on Stockholder Composition

To get information on the percent of stock held by insiders and institutions check out the Value Line page on this company; there is a box that lists out percent held by each. You can get more updated and detailed information at the SEC site (**www.sec.gov/edgarhp.htm**). The institutional ownership can also be obtained from the daily stocks web site, under **www.dailystocks.com**—*institutional ownership*. You can get an update on companies where there has been significant insider activity at **cda.com/investnet/periscope/periscope.html.** You can check my data set on typical insider and institutional holdings by sector for U.S. companies (**insider.xls**). You can get a sense of how this firm is classified (value versus growth, small versus large cap) by going into the Morningstar web site and entering the symbol for your firm (**www.morningstar.net**—*quicktake reports*). When you get the company's snap shot, click on *Investment Style.*

CHAPTER 4

RISK MEASUREMENT AND HURDLE RATES IN PRACTICE

In the previous chapter, we presented the argument that the expected return on an investment should be a function of the "market risk" embedded in that investment. In this chapter, we turn our attention to how best to estimate the parameters of market risk in each of the models described in the previous chapter—the capital asset pricing model, the arbitrage pricing model, and the multifactor model. We will present three alternative approaches for measuring the market risk in a project: the first is to use historical data on market prices for that asset or for the firm considering the asset to estimate the parameters, the second is to use the parameters estimated for other firms that are in the same business as the project being analyzed, and the third is to use accounting earnings or revenues to estimate the parameters.

In addition to estimating market risk, we will also discuss how best to estimate a "riskless" rate and a "risk premium" (in the CAPM) or "risk premiums" (in the

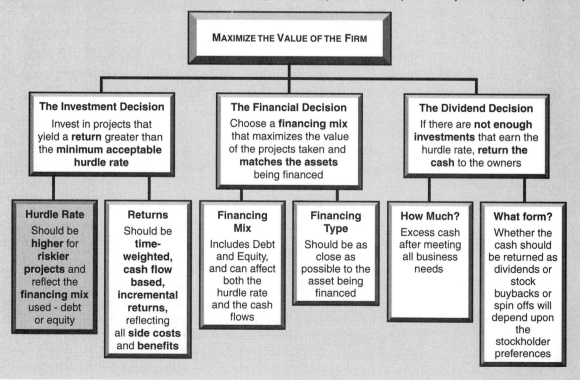

APM and multifactor models) to convert the risk measures into expected returns. We will present a similar argument for converting default risk into a cost of debt, and then bring the discussion to fruition by linking both the cost of equity and debt to a cost of capital, which will become the "minimum acceptable hurdle rate" for the project.

COST OF EQUITY

The *cost of equity* is the rate of return that investors require to make an equity investment in a firm. All of the risk and return models described in the previous chapter need a risk-free rate and a risk premium (in the CAPM) or premiums (in the APM and multifactor models). We will begin by discussing those common inputs before we turn our attention to the estimation of risk parameters.

I. Risk-free Rate

We defined a risk-free asset as one where the investor knows the expected returns with certainty. Consequently, for an investment to be risk-free (i.e., to have an actual return be equal to the expected return), two conditions have to be met:

- There has to be *no default risk,* which generally implies that the security has to be issued by the government.
- There can be *no uncertainty about reinvestment rates,* which implies that there are no intermediate cash flows.

Thus, the risk-free rate is the rate on a zero coupon government bond matching the time horizon of the cash flow being analyzed. Theoretically, this translates into using different risk-free rates for each cash flow on an investment—the one-year zero coupon rate for the cash flow in year one, the two-year zero coupon rate for the cash flow in year two and so on. Practically speaking, if there is substantial uncertainty about expected cash flows, the present value effect of using time-varying risk-free rates as opposed to using an average risk-free rate is generally so small that it is not worth the trouble. Using a *long-term government rate* (even on a coupon bond) as the risk-free rate on all of the cash flows in a long-term analysis will yield a close approximation of the true value. For short-term analysis, it is entirely appropriate to use a *short-term government security rate* as the risk-free rate.

IN PRACTICE: WHAT IF THERE IS NO DEFAULT-FREE RATE?

We have implicitly assumed in our discussion of risk-free rates that the government is a default-free entity and that it issues long-term bonds. There are a number of economies where one or both of these assumptions can be challenged. In some emerging market, where governments in the past have failed to meet their promised obligations, the government is not viewed as default free. There are many other markets where the government does not issue long-term bonds, and the best that one can obtain is a short-term government rate.

There are three solutions to this problem. One is to bypass it entirely by doing the analysis in a different currency (such as the U.S. dollar) where a risk-free rate is easy to obtain. The other is to find the rate at which the largest and safest corporations in that country can borrow long term in the local currency and reduce that rate by a small default premium (say 20 or 30 basis points) to arrive at a long-term risk-free rate. The third solution exists only if there are long-term forward contracts on the local currency. Since interest rate parity drives forward contract pricing, the long-term interest rate in the local currency can be obtained from the price of the forward contract and the long-term interest rate on the foreign currency.

In most analyses, there are other questions that need to be answered about the riskless rate. If working with a U.S. company, should the riskless rate always be a rate on a U.S. government security? Should the risk-free rate be nominal or real? The simplest way to answer these questions is to remember that the risk-free rate has to be defined in the same terms as the cash flows on the analysis. If the analysis is done in *nominal dollar terms,* the risk-free rate always has to be a *U.S. government security rate,* whether the firm doing the analysis is a U.S. firm or a non-U.S firm. This should be the case even if the country in which the company is located has its own U.S. dollar-denominated bonds,[1] which carry a default risk premium. The country default risk premium is best reflected in the risk premium component and not in the riskless rate. If the analysis is done in real terms, the risk-free rate has be a real risk-free rate.

IN PRACTICE: ESTIMATING AND USING REAL RISK-FREE RATES

Real risk-free rates do not include a premium for expected inflation and should be used if the cash flows are estimated using a similar premise. In practice, it is a good idea to steer away from nominal cash flows and discount rates when inflation hits double digits. One solution is to use a different currency which is more stable; in high-inflation economies, it is common to do investment analyses and valuations in U.S. dollars. The other is to use real cash flows and discount rates.

Obtaining real risk-free rates can be trivial if an inflation-protected government bond trades in the market. In the United States, for instance, the rate on inflation-linked bonds that were introduced in 1997 can be used as the real risk-free rate. Unfortunately, this option is generally unavailable in those high-inflation economies where the need to use real risk-free rates is the greatest. In those markets the real risk-free rate has to be estimated indirectly. We would propose that the real risk-free rate be set equal to the expected long-term real growth rate of that economy. While this rate may be about 3% for the U.S. economy, it is likely to be higher for other economies such as Brazil and China.

---

[1]To provide an illustration, Brazil has dollar-denominated long-term bonds called C-bonds which yield higher rates than the U.S. T-bond.

The correct risk-free rate to use in the capital asset pricing model

☐ is the short-term government security rate.

☐ is the long-term government security rate.

☐ can be either, depending upon whether the prediction is short term or long term.

II. Risk Premium

The risk premium(s) is clearly a significant input in all of the asset pricing models. In the following section, we will begin by examining the fundamental determinants of risk premiums and then look at practical approaches to estimating these premiums.

What Is the Risk Premium Supposed to Measure?

The risk premium in the capital asset pricing model measures the "extra return" that would be demanded by investors for shifting their money from a riskless investment to an average risk investment. It should be a function of two variables:

1. ***Risk Aversion of Investors*** As investors become more risk averse, they should demand a larger premium for shifting from the riskless asset. While some of this risk aversion may be inborn, some of it is also a function of economic prosperity (when the economy is doing well, investors tend to be much more willing to take risk) and recent experiences in the market (risk premiums tend to surge after large market drops).

2. ***Riskiness of the Average Risk Investment*** As the riskiness of the average risk investment increases, so should the premium. This will depend upon what firms are actually traded in the market, their economic fundamentals, and how good they are at managing risk. For instance, the premium should be lower in markets where only the largest and most stable firms trade.

Since each investor in a market is likely to have a different assessment of an acceptable premium, the premium will be a weighted average of these individual premiums, where the weights will be based upon the wealth the investor brings to the market. Put more directly, what Warren Buffett, with his substantial wealth, thinks about the premium will be weighted in far more than what you or I might think about it.

In the arbitrage pricing model and the multifactor models, the risk premiums used for individual factors are similar wealth-weighted averages of the premiums that individual investors would demand for each factor separately.

Assume that stocks are the only risky assets and that you are offered two investment options:

1. A riskless investment (say a government security), on which you can make 6.7%

2. A mutual fund of all stocks, on which the returns are uncertain

How much of an expected return would you demand to shift your money from the riskless asset to the mutual fund?

☐ Less than 6.7%

☐ Between 6.7–8.7%

☐   Between 8.7–10.7%

☐   Between 10.7–12.7%

☐   Between 12.7–14.7%

☐   More than 14.7%

Your answer to this question should provide you with a measure of your risk premium. (For instance, if your answer is 8.7%, your premium is 2%.)

Estimating Risk Premiums

There are three ways of estimating the risk premium in the capital asset pricing model—large investors can be surveyed about their expectations for the future, the actual premiums earned over a past period can be obtained from historical data, and the implied premium can be extracted from current market data. The premium can be generally estimated only from historical data in the arbitrage pricing model and the multifactor models.

1. Survey Premiums

Since the premium is a weighted average of the premiums demanded by individual investors, one approach to estimating this premium is to survey investors about their expectations for the future. It is clearly impractical to survey all investors; therefore, most surveys focus on portfolio managers who carry the most weight in the process. While a premium does emerge from these surveys, very few practitioners actually use these survey premiums. There are three reasons for this reticence:

1.   There are no constraints on reasonability; individual money managers could provide expected returns that are lower than the risk-free rate, for instance.

2.   They are extremely volatile; the survey premiums can change dramatically, largely as a function of recent market movements.

3.   They tend to be short term; even the longest surveys do not go beyond one year.

4.3   DO RISK PREMIUMS CHANGE?

In the previous question, you were asked how much of a premium you would demand for investing in a portfolio of stocks as opposed to a riskless asset. Assume that the market dropped by 20% last week, and you were asked the same question today. Would your premium

☐   be higher?

☐   be lower?

☐   be unchanged?

2. Historical Premiums

The most common approach to estimating the risk premium(s) used in financial asset pricing models is to base it on historical data. In the arbitrage pricing model and multifactor models, the raw data on which the premiums are based is historical data on asset prices over very long time periods. In the CAPM, the premium is usually defined as the difference between average returns on stocks and average returns on risk-free securities over an extended period of history.

In most cases, this approach is composed of the following steps. It begins by defining a time period for the estimation, which can range to as far back as 1926 for U.S.

data. It then requires the calculation of the average returns on a stock index and average returns on a riskless security over the period. Finally, it calculates the difference between the returns on stocks and the riskless return and uses it as a risk premium looking forward. In doing so, we implicitly assume that:

1. The risk aversion of investors has not changed in a systematic way across time. (The risk aversion may change from year to year, but it reverts back to historical averages.)
2. The average riskiness of the "risky" portfolio (stock index) has not changed in a systematic way across time.

In coming up with the average returns over past periods, a final measurement question arises: Should arithmetic or geometric averages be used to compute the risk premium? The arithmetic mean is the average of the annual returns for the period under consideration, whereas the geometric mean is the compounded annual return over the same period. The contrast between the two measures can be illustrated with a simple example containing two years of returns:

YEAR	PRICE	RETURN
0	50	
1	100	100%
2	60	−40%

The arithmetic average return over the two years is 30%, while the geometric average is only 9.54% ($1.2^{0.5} − 1 = 1.0954$). Those who use the arithmetic mean argue that it is much more consistent with the mean-variance framework of the CAPM and a better predictor of the premium in the next period. The geometric mean is justified on the grounds that it takes into account compounding and that it is a better predictor of the average premium in the long term. There can be dramatic differences in premiums based on the choices made at this stage, as illustrated in Table 4.1, which is based on historical data on stock and bond returns.

Geometric Mean: The geometric mean of a series is the average of the series, taking into account the effect of compounding on the data.

As you can see, the historical premiums can vary widely depending upon whether one goes back to 1926 or 1981, whether one uses T. bills or T. bonds as the risk-free

	Stocks—T. Bills		Stocks—T. Bonds	
Historical period	**Arith.**	**Geom.**	**Arith.**	**Geom.**
1926–1996	8.76%	6.95%	7.57%	5.91%
1962–1996	5.74%	4.63%	5.16%	4.46%
1981–1996	10.34%	9.72%	9.22%	8.02%

Table 4.1 HISTORICAL RISK PREMIUMS FOR THE U.S. MARKET

rate, and whether one uses arithmetic or geometric average premiums. While it is impossible to prove one premium right and the others wrong, we are biased toward:

1. ***Longer time periods*** (back to 1926), since stock returns are extraordinarily noisy[2] and shorter time periods can provide extreme premiums.

2. ***T. bond rates as riskless rates,*** since our time horizons in corporate financial analysis tend to be long term.

3. ***Geometric average premiums,*** since the arithmetic averages tend to overstate the premiums especially in markets like the United States, which have a survivorship bias,[3] leading to higher premiums. The geometric mean generally yields lower premium estimates than does the arithmetic mean.

These biases would lead us closer to the premium of 5.91% that is the geometric average premium for stocks over T. bonds from 1926 to 1996. In fact, we will use a premium of 5.50% in most of the examples involving U.S. companies in this book.

 There is a dataset on the Web that summarizes historical returns on stocks, T. bonds, and T. bills going back to 1926 (**histret.xls**).

While historical data on stock returns is most accessible in the United States, the premiums for other countries are updated in Ibbotson and Brinson (1991). Reliable historical data is not available for as long a time period as it is available for the United States, however, as seen in Table 4.2.

The premium earned by stocks over treasury bonds has typically been much lower in the European markets (not counting Britain) than in either the United States or Japan. We would argue that the changes in many of these markets and the economies underlying them have been so large that the historical premiums are useless. This point can be made even more emphatically when looking at the emerging markets. Thus, knowing the premium that an investor would have made in the Brazilian market from 1987 to 1996 would not be of much use for estimating the premium looking forward, given the substantial shifts in the Brazilian economy, especially since the Real Plan[4] in 1994.

If we cannot use historical premiums for other countries, how exactly can we get a premium to use in the CAPM? Returning to fundamentals, the risk premium should be a function of the volatility in the underlying economy and the political risk associated with that particular market. Other things remaining equal, we would expect markets which are riskier than the United States to have larger premiums than the United States, especially looking forward. While no direct measure of this risk

---

[2]Based upon the standard deviation in stock prices, it is estimated that one would need 150 years of reliable data before one could obtain a good estimate of the risk premium.

[3]When we look at markets like the United States that have survived for 70 years without significant breaks, we are looking at the exceptions. To provide a contrast, consider the other stock markets in which one could have invested in 1926; many of these markets did not survive, and an investor would have lost much of his or her wealth.

[4]The Real Plan reduced inflation from triple to double digits and, by doing so, changed the fundamental characteristics of the Brazilian economy.

Table 4.2 RISK PREMIUMS ACROSS THE WORLD: 1969–95					
	Equity			Bonds	Risk Premium
Country	Beginning	Ending	Annual Return	Annual Return	
Australia	100	898.36	8.47%	6.99%	1.48%
Canada	100	1020.7	8.98%	8.30%	0.68%
France	100	1894.26	11.51%	9.17%	2.34%
Germany	100	1800.74	11.30%	12.10%	−0.80%
Hong Kong	100	14993.06	20.39%	12.66%	7.73%
Italy	100	423.64	5.49%	7.84%	−2.35%
Japan	100	5169.43	15.73%	12.69%	3.04%
Mexico	100	2073.65	11.88%	10.71%	1.17%
Netherlands	100	4870.32	15.48%	10.83%	4.65%
Singapore	100	4875.91	15.48%	6.45%	9.03%
Spain	100	844.8	8.22%	7.91%	0.31%
Switzerland	100	3046.09	13.49%	10.11%	3.38%
UK	100	2361.53	12.42%	7.81%	4.61%
USA	100	1633.36	10.90%	7.90%	3.00%

Source: Ibbotson Associates

may exist, most countries are rated by ratings agencies based at least partially on these criteria. The advantages of these ratings are that they can be associated with default premiums that allow us to quantify the effect on the risk premium. For instance, the following table summarizes risk premiums for emerging markets in Asia, Latin America, and Eastern Europe:

COUNTRY	RATING	RISK PREMIUM
Argentina	BBB	5.5% + 1.75% = 7.25%
Brazil	BB	5.5% + 2% = 7.50%
Chile	AA	5.5% + 0.75% = 6.25%
China	BBB+	5.5% + 1.5% = 7.00%
Colombia	A+	5.5% + 1.25% = 6.75%
Czech Republic	A	5.5% + 1% = 6.50%
India	BB+	5.5% + 2.00% = 7.50%
Indonesia	BBB	5.5% + 1.75% = 7.25%
Korea	AA-	5.5% + 1.00% = 6.50%
Lithuania	BB+	5.5% + 2% = 7.50%
Malaysia	A+	5.5% + 1.25% = 6.75%
Mexico	BBB+	5.5% + 1.5% = 7.00%
Pakistan	B+	5.5% + 2.75% = 8.25%
Paraguay	BBB-	5.5% + 1.75% = 7.25%

COUNTRY	RATING	RISK PREMIUM
Peru	B	5.5% + 2.5% = 8.00%
Philippines	BB+	5.5% + 2.00% = 7.50%
Poland	AA	5.5% + 0.75% = 6.25%
Romania	BB-	5.5% + 2.5% = 8.00%
Russia	BB-	5.5% + 2.5% = 8.00%
Slovakia	BBB-	5.5% + 1.75% = 7.25%
Slovenia	A	5.5% + 1% = 6.50%
Taiwan	AA+	5.5% + 0.50% = 6.00%
Thailand	A	5.5% + 1% = 6.50%
Turkey	B+	5.5% + 2.75% = 8.25%
Uruguay	BBB	5.5% + 1.75% = 7.25%

The bond ratings are the local currency ratings for these countries, and the premiums are spreads earned over T-Bonds by corporate bonds in the United States with similar ratings. (We could have used country bonds for the default premiums, but they tend to be extremely volatile.)

There is a data set on the Web that contains the updated ratings for countries and the risk premiums associated with each (**ctryprem.xls**).

IN PRACTICE: ESTIMATING COUNTRY RISK PREMIUMS

The use of country bond ratings to estimate equity risk premiums for these countries may be disquieting to some. In defense, it should be noted that there is a high correlation between country bond premiums and country equity returns. Furthermore, many of the factors considered by the ratings agencies in analyzing country bond risk are also factors in evaluating country equity risk. If you do not want to use country bond ratings to arrive at risk premiums, you can use other measures that look at overall country risk. *The Economist,* for instance, assigns a numerical score to each country that it analyzes, ranging from 0 (least risky) to 100 (most risky). Then, a "risk spread" has to be assigned that corresponds to these ratings. An alternative approach exists when all of the country risk can be hedged away using market-traded instruments (options, futures and forwards). The annual percentage cost of hedging away the risk can be added on to the base country premium to arrive at the risk premium for a foreign market. For instance, assume that you are a U.S. investor, with a base premium of 5.5% for domestic investments, and that you can buy insurance against country-specific risk for 2% a year. The total premium used for this country will then be 7.5%.

3. Implied Equity Premiums
There is a third approach to estimating risk premiums that does not require surveys or historical data, but does assume that the market, overall, is correctly priced. Consider, for instance, a very simple valuation model for stocks:

$$\text{Value} = \frac{\text{Expected Dividends Next Period}}{(\text{Required Return on Equity} - \text{Expected Growth Rate})}$$

This is essentially the present value of dividends growing at a constant rate forever (see the time value appendix). Three of the four inputs in this model can be obtained externally—the current level of the market (value), the expected dividends next period, and the expected growth rate in earnings and dividends in the long term. The only "unknown" is then the required return on equity; when we solve for it, we get an implied expected return on stocks. Subtracting out the risk-free rate will yield an implied equity risk premium.

To illustrate, assume that the current level of the S&P 500 Index is 900, the expected dividend yield on the index is 2%, and the expected growth rate in earnings and dividends in the long term is 7%. Solving for the required return on equity yields the following:

$$900 = (.02*900) /(r - .07)$$

Solving for r,

$$r = (18 + 63)/900 = 9\%$$

If the current risk-free rate is 6%, this will yield a premium of 3%.

The advantage of this approach is that it is market-driven and current, and does not require any historical data. It is, however, bounded by whether the model used for the valuation is the right one and by the availability and reliability of the inputs to that model. For instance, in the above example, some might take issue with the use of dividends and the assumption of "constant" growth. Finally, it is based upon the assumption that the market is correctly priced.

The contrast between these premiums and the historical premiums is best illustrated by graphing out the implied premiums in the S&P 500 going back to 1960 in Figure 4.1.

In terms of mechanics, we used smoothed historical growth rates in earnings and dividends as our projected growth rates and a two-stage dividend discount model.

Note that this approach will not work for multifactor models since it will provide only an aggregate risk premium for all factors, and not the individual premiums for each factor separately.

4.4 IMPLIED AND HISTORICAL PREMIUMS

Assume that the implied premium in the market is 3%, and that you are using a historical premium of 7.5%. If you valued stocks using this historical premium, you are likely

☐   to find more undervalued stocks than overvalued ones.

☐   to find more overvalued stocks than undervalued ones.

☐   to find about as many undervalued as overvalued stocks.

 This data set on the Web shows the inputs used to calculate the premium in each year for the U.S. market (**implpr.xls**).

 This spreadsheet allows you to estimate the implied equity premium in a market (**implprem.xls**).

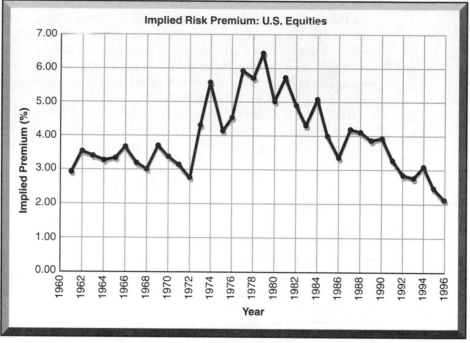

Figure 4.1   Implied Risk Premium: U.S. Equities.

III. Risk Parameters

The final set of inputs we need to put risk and return models into practice are the risk parameters for individual assets and projects. In the CAPM, the beta of the asset has to be estimated relative to the market portfolio. In the APM and multifactor model, the betas of the asset relative to each factor have to be measured. There are three approaches available for estimating these parameters: the first is to use historical data on market prices for individual assets, the second is to estimate the betas from fundamentals, and the third is to use accounting data. We will use all three approaches in this section.

A. Historical Market Betas

This is the conventional approach for estimating betas used by most services and analysts. For firms which have been publicly traded for a length of time, it is relatively straightforward to estimate returns that an investor would have made on their investments in intervals (such as a week or a month) over that period. These returns can then be related to a proxy for the market portfolio to get a beta in the capital asset pricing model, or to multiple macroeconomic factors to get betas in the multifactor models, or put through a factor analysis to yield betas for the arbitrage pricing model.

Standard Procedures for Estimating CAPM Parameters—Betas and Alphas
The standard procedure for estimating betas is to regress[5] stock returns (R_j) against market returns (R_m).

---

[5]The appendix provides a brief overview of ordinary least squares regressions.

$$R_j = a + b\,R_m$$

where

  a = Intercept from the regression
  b = Slope of the regression = Covariance $(R_j, R_m) / \sigma_m^2$

The *slope* of the regression corresponds to the beta of the stock and measures the riskiness of the stock. The *intercept* of the regression provides a simple measure of performance during the period of the regression, relative to the capital asset pricing model.

$$
\begin{aligned}
R_j \quad &= R_f + \beta\,(R_m - R_f) \\
&= R_f\,(1 - \beta) + \beta\,R_m \qquad \text{Capital Asset Pricing Model} \\[6pt]
R_j \quad &= a + b\,R_m \qquad\qquad\qquad \text{Regression Equation}
\end{aligned}
$$

Thus, a comparison of the intercept (a) to Rf $(1 - \beta)$ should provide a measure of the stock's performance, at least relative to the capital asset pricing model.[6]

If $a > R_f\,(1 - \beta)$ Stock did better than expected during regression period
If $a = R_f\,(1 - \beta)$ Stock did as well as expected during regression period
If $a < R_f\,(1 - \beta)$ Stock did worse than expected during regression period

The difference between a and $R_f\,(1 - \beta)$ is called *Jensen's alpha,* and provides a measure of whether the asset in question under- or outperformed the market, after adjusting for risk, during the period of the regression.

Jensen's Alpha: This is the difference between the actual returns on an asset and the return you would have expected it to make during a past period, given what the market did, and the asset's beta.

The next statistic that emerges from the regression is the *R-squared* (R^2) of the regression. While the statistical explanation of the R-squared is that it provides a measure of the goodness of fit of the regression, the financial rationale for the R-squared is that it provides an estimate of the proportion of the risk (variance) of a firm that can be attributed to market risk; the balance $(1 - R^2)$ can then be attributed to firm-specific risk.

The final statistic worth noting is the standard error of the beta estimate. The slope of the regression, is estimated with noise, and the standard error reveals just how noisy the estimate is. The standard error can also be used to arrive at confidence intervals for the "true" beta value from the slope estimate.

R-Squared: The R-squared measures the proportion of the variability of a dependent variable that is explained by an independent variable or variables.

ILLUSTRATION 4.1   Estimating CAPM Risk Parameters for Disney
In assessing risk parameters for Disney, the returns on the stock and the market index are computed as follows:

---

[6]The regression is sometimes calculated using returns in excess of the risk-free rate, for both the stock and the market. In that case, the intercept of the regression should be zero if the actual returns equal the expected returns from the CAPM, greater than zero if the stock does better than expected, and less than zero if it does worse than expected.

1. The returns to a stockholder in Disney are computed month by month from January 1992 to December 1996. These returns include both dividends and price appreciation and are defined as follows:

$$\text{Stock Return}_{\text{Disney}, j} = (\text{Price}_{\text{Disney}, j} - \text{Price}_{\text{Disney}, j-1} + \text{Dividends}_j) / \text{Price}_{\text{Disney}, j-1}$$

where

$$\text{Stock Return}_{\text{Disney}, j} = \text{Returns to a stockholder in Disney in month } j$$
$$\text{Price}_{\text{Disney}, j} = \text{Price of Disney stock at the end of month } j$$
$$\text{Dividends}_j = \text{Dividends on Disney stock in month } j$$

Dividends are added to the returns of the month in which the stock went ex-dividend.[7] If there was a stock split[8] during the month, the returns have to take into account the split factor, since stock prices will be affected. For instance, in a two-for-one stock split, the stock price will drop by roughly 50%, and if not factored in will result in very negative returns in that month. Splits can be accounted for as follows:

$$\text{Return}_{\text{Disney}, j} = (\text{Factor}_j * \text{Price}_{\text{Disney}, j} - \text{Price}_{\text{Disney}, j-1} + \text{Factor} * \text{Dividends}_j) / \text{Price}_{\text{Disney}, j-1}$$

where, to illustrate, the factor is set equal to 2 for a two-for-one split and to 1.5 for a three-for-two split.

2. The returns on the S&P 500 market index are computed for each month of the period, using the level of the index at the end of each month, and the monthly dividend yield on stocks in the index:

$$\text{Market Return}_{\text{S\&P}, j} = (\text{Index}_{\text{S\&P}, j} - \text{Index}_{\text{S\&P}, j-1}) / \text{Index}_{\text{S\&P}, j-1} + \text{Dividend Yield}_j$$

where Index_j is the level of the index at the end of month j and Dividend Yield_j is the dividend yield on the index in month j. While the S&P 500 and the NYSE composite are the most widely used indices for U.S. stocks, they are at best imperfect proxies for the market portfolio in the CAPM, which is supposed to include all traded assets.

Figure 4.2 graphs monthly returns on Disney against returns on the S&P 500 index from January 1992 to December 1996.

The regression statistics for Disney are as follows:[9]

a. *Slope of the regression = 1.40.* This is Disney's beta, based on returns from 1992 to 1996. Using a different time period for the regression or different return intervals (weekly or daily) for the same period can result in a different beta.

---

[7]The ex-dividend day is the day by which the stock has to be bought for an investor to be entitled to the dividends on the stock. It usually occurs a few weeks after the announcement date.

[8]A split changes the number of shares outstanding in a company without affecting any of its fundamentals. Thus, in a three-for-two split, there will be 50% more shares outstanding after the split. Since the overall value of equity has not changed, the stock price should drop by an equivalent amount $(1 - 100/150 = 33.33\%)$.

[9]The regression statistics are computed in the conventional way. The appendix explains the process in more detail.

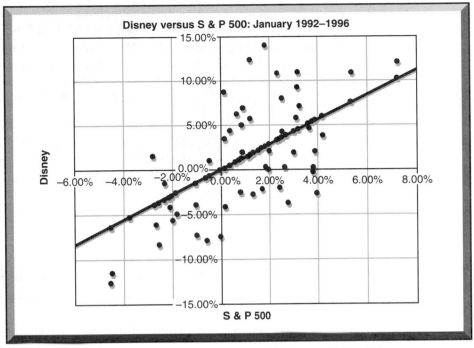

Figure 4.2   Disney versus S&P 500: January 1992–1996.

b. *Intercept of the regression = –0.01%.*   This is a measure of Disney's performance, when it is compared with $R_f(1 - \beta)$. The monthly risk-free rate (since the returns used in the regression are monthly returns) between 1992 and 1996 averaged 0.4%, resulting in the following estimate for the performance:

$$R_f(1 - \beta) = 0.4\%(1 - 1.40) = -0.16\%$$
$$\text{Intercept} - R_f(1 - \beta) = -0.01\% - (-0.16\%) = 0.15\%$$

This analysis suggests that Disney performed 0.15% better than expected, when expectations are based on the CAPM, on a monthly basis between January 1992 and December 1996. This results in an annualized excess return of approximately 1.81%.

$$\begin{aligned}\text{Annualized Excess Return} &= (1 + \text{Monthly Excess Return})^{12} - 1 \\ &= 1.0015^{12} - 1 = 1.0181 - 1 = 0.0181 \text{ or } 1.81\%\end{aligned}$$

By this measure of performance, Disney did slightly better than expected during the period of the regression. Note, however, that this does not imply that Disney would be a good investment looking forward. It also does not provide a breakdown of how much of this excess return can be attributed to industrywide effects, and how much is specific to the firm. To make that breakdown, the excess returns would have to be computed over the same period for other firms in the entertainment industry and compared with Disney's excess return. The difference would then be attributable to firm-specific actions. In this case, for instance, the average annualized excess return on other entertainment firms between 1992 and 1996 was 3.5%, suggesting that the firm-specific component of performance for Disney is actually −1.7%. (Firm-specific Jensen's alpha = 1.8% − 3.5%.)

c. ***R-squared of the regression − 32.41%.***   This statistic suggests that 32.41% of the risk (variance) in Disney comes from market sources (interest rate risk, inflation risk, etc.), and that the balance of 67.59% of the risk comes from firm-specific components. The latter risk should be diversifiable, and therefore unrewarded in the CAPM.

Disney's R-squared is slightly higher than the median R-squared of companies listed on the New York Stock Exchange, which was approximately 25% in 1997.

4.5 THE RELEVANCE OF R-SQUARED TO AN INVESTOR

Assume that, having done the regression analysis, both Disney and Amgen, a biotechnology company, have betas of 1.40. Disney, however, has an R-squared of 32%, while Amgen has an R-squared of only 15%. If you had to pick between these investments, which one would you choose?

☐ Disney, because its higher R-squared suggests that it is less risky.

☐ Amgen, because its lower R-squared suggests a greater potential for high returns.

☐ I would be indifferent, because they both have the same beta.

Would your answer be any different if you were running a well-diversified fund?

d. ***Standard Error of Beta Estimate = 0.27.***   This statistic implies that the true beta for Disney could range from 1.13 to 1.67 (subtracting or adding one standard error to beta estimate of 1.40) with 67% confidence and from 0.76 to 1.94 (subtracting or adding two standard errors to beta estimate of 1.40) with 95% confidence. While these ranges may seem large, they are not unusual for most U.S. companies. This suggests that we should consider regression estimates of betas with caution.

IN PRACTICE: USING ALPHAS

In practice, the intercept of the regression is often called the alpha and compared to zero. Thus, a positive intercept is viewed as a sign that the stock did better than expected and a negative intercept as a sign that the stock did worse than expected. In truth, this can be done only if the regression is run in terms of excess returns (i.e., returns over and above the risk-free rate in each month for both the stock and the market index).

If the return interval is short (days or weeks), the risk-free rate on a daily or weekly basis might be close enough to zero that the comparison can still be made to zero. Finally, if the beta is close to 1, the comparison will effectively be to zero again, since $R_f (1 − \text{Beta})$ will then also be close to zero.

Using a Service Beta

Most analysts who use betas obtain them from an estimation service: Merrill Lynch, Barra, Value Line, Standard and Poor's, Morningstar, and Bloomberg are some of the well-known services. All of these services begin with the regression beta described above and adjust them to reflect what they feel are necessary changes to make them better estimates for the future. While most of these services do not reveal the internal details of their estimation, Bloomberg is an honorable exception. The following is the beta calculation page from Bloomberg for Disney, using the same period as our regression (January 1992 to December 1996):

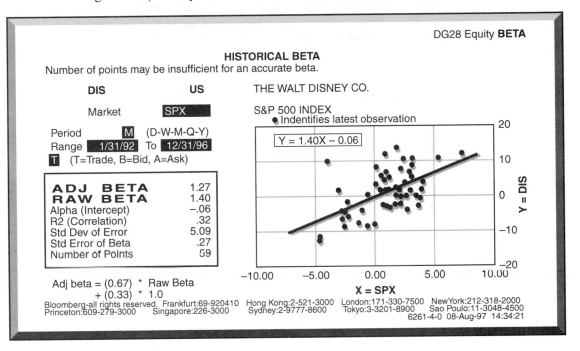

While the time period used is identical to the one used in our earlier regression, there arc subtle differences between this regression and the earlier one in Figure 4.2. First, Bloomberg uses price appreciation in the stock and the market index in estimating betas and ignores dividends. This does not make much of a difference for Disney, but it could make a difference for a company that either pays no dividends or pays significantly higher dividends than the market. Second, Bloomberg also computes what they call an adjusted beta, which is estimated as follows:

$$\text{Adjusted Beta} = \text{Raw Beta }(0.67) + 1\ (0.33)$$

These weights do not vary across stocks, and this process pushes all estimated betas toward 1. Most services employ similar procedures to adjust betas toward 1. In doing so, they are drawing on empirical evidence that suggests that the betas for most companies, over time, tend to move toward the average beta, which is 1. This may be explained by the fact that firms get more diversified in their product mix and client base as they get larger.

4.6   REGRESSION OF BETAS TOWARD 1

We have made the point that the betas of stocks tend to move toward 1 over time. Let us assume that you are looking at two companies—the first is Coca Cola, which has a history of staying focused on its beverage business and not expanding into other businesses, and the second is Pepsico, which has made repeated forays into other businesses (for instance, it bought restaurant chains in the 1980s). Assuming that both these companies currently have betas very different from 1 and that you expect these policies to continue, which of these companies should see its beta move more rapidly toward 1?

☐ Coca Cola, because of its focus on its core business.

☐ Pepsico, because it will get into other businesses over time.

☐ Both companies should see their betas move toward 1 at the same pace, because they will both become larger over time.

Estimation Issues

There are three decisions the analyst must make in setting up the regression described above. The first concerns the *length of the estimation period.* Most estimation services use five years of data, while Bloomberg uses two years of data. The trade-off is simple: A longer estimation period provides more data, but the firm itself might have changed in its risk characteristics over the time period. Disney, during the period of our analysis, acquired Capital Cities/ABC two years ago with substantial debt, changing its basic risk characteristics.

The second estimation issue relates to the *return interval.* Returns on stocks are available on an annual, monthly, weekly, daily, and even on an intra-day basis. Using daily or intra-day returns will increase the number of observations in the regression, but it exposes the estimation process to a significant bias in beta estimates related to nontrading.[10] For instance, the betas estimated for small firms, which are more likely to suffer from nontrading, are biased downward when daily returns are used. Using weekly or monthly returns can reduce the nontrading bias significantly.[11] In this case, using weekly returns for 2 years yields a beta estimate for Disney of only 0.98, while the monthly beta estimate is 1.40.

The third estimation issue relates to the choice of a *market index* to be used in the regression. The standard practice used by most beta estimation services is to estimate the betas of a company relative to the index of the market in which its stock trades. Thus, the betas of German stocks are estimated relative to the Frankfurt DAX, British stocks relative to the FTSE, Japanese stocks relative to the Nikkei, and U.S. stocks relative to the S&P 500. While this practice may yield an estimate that is a reasonable measure of risk for the parochial investor, it may not be the best approach for an international or cross-border investor, who would be better served with a beta estimated relative to an international index. For instance, Disney's beta between 1992 and 1996 estimated relative to the Morgan Stanley Capital Index, an index that is composed of equities from different global markets, yields a beta of 1.19.

---

[10]The nontrading bias arises because the return in nontrading periods is zero (even though the market may have moved up or down significantly in those periods). Using these nontrading period returns in the regression will reduce the correlation between stock returns and market returns and the beta of the stock.

[11]The bias can also be reduced using statistical techniques suggested by Dimson and Scholes-Williams.

IN PRACTICE: WHY BETA ESTIMATES VARY ACROSS SERVICES

It is not uncommon to find very different beta estimates reported for a firm by different services at the same point in time. There are several reasons for these differences:

1. The services might not be looking at the same historical time period. Value Line and S&P, for instance, use five-year estimates, while Bloomberg, in its default calculation, uses a two-year estimate.

2. The services also often use different return intervals to estimate betas. Bloomberg and Value Line use weekly returns to get their beta estimates while S&P uses monthly returns; there are services that even use daily returns.

3. The adjustments made to regression betas vary widely across the services. Bloomberg employs the simple adjustment toward 1 for all the betas that it estimates, whereas a service like Barra adjusts betas using a variety of fundamental information about the firm.

While these beta differences are troubling, note that the beta estimates delivered by each of these services come with a standard error, and it is very likely that all of the betas reported for a firm fall within the range of the standard errors from the regressions.

More Historical Beta Estimates
In this section, we will complete the beta estimation for the three other firms that we will be analyzing throughout this book—Bookscape Books, Aracruz Cellulose, and Deutsche Bank.

1. Estimating the Beta for Bookscape Books This approach to estimating betas, which uses historical data, works only for assets which have been traded and have market prices. Bookscape Books, being a private business, does not have a market price history. We will review, in the next section, an alternative approach to estimating betas for Bookscape.

Note that this constraint exists even for publicly traded firms which have been in existence only for a short period and for divisions of businesses which may want to estimate their costs of equity.

2. Estimating the Beta for Aracruz Cellulose An analyst estimating betas for U.S. companies has the luxury of working with different indices, and no individual stock dominates in most of the broader indices of the U.S. market (such as the S&P 500 and the NYSE composite). This is not the case when betas have to be estimated for non-U.S. companies. On the next page is the beta estimate for Aracruz Cellulose, the Brazilian paper and pulp manufacturing firm, using the default index in Bloomberg, which is the *Bovespa*, a trade-weighted index of stocks traded on the Sao Paulo exchange:

There are two problems with this regression. One is that data is available only for 36 months, reducing the power of the regression. The other is even more serious. The Bovespa is an index dominated by one stock, Telebras, which comprises almost half the index. Thus, the beta for Aracruz estimated relative to the Bovespa is really a beta for Aracruz versus Telebras. The equivalent in the Disney example would have been if Disney's beta had been estimated relative to AT&T instead of a market index.

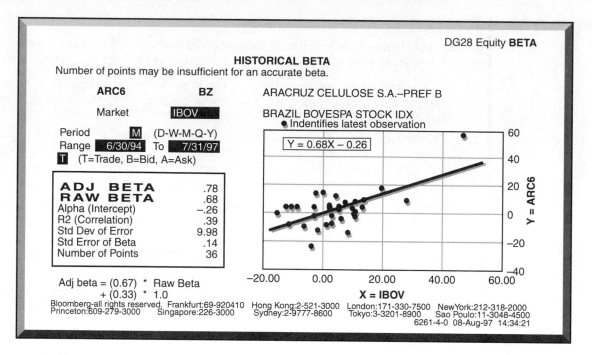

The follow-up then is that this beta is really not one that can be used in the CAPM. The alternatives, if one decides to stick with the regression approach, would include the following:

1. Replace the Bovespa with an equally weighted or a market-weighed index of Brazilian stocks.

2. Expand the index to include not only Brazilian stocks but stocks from other markets, such as an index of Latin American stocks or the Morgan Stanley Capital Index.

3. Estimate the beta for Aracruz Cellulose's ADR,[12] listed and traded on the NYSE, versus the S&P 500 or the NYSE Composite.

The betas from these regressions are summarized in the following table:

INDEX	BETA
Brazil I-Senn	0.69
S&P 500 (with ADR)	0.46
Morgan Stanley Capital Index (with ADR)	0.35

The Senn is a market-value weighted index of 50 large Brazilian companies.

We will argue that none of these betas are particularly reliable. We will instead estimate Aracruz's beta using fundamentals in the next section. It is worth noting, how-

---

[12]An ADR is a depository receipt that is traded in U.S. markets and denominated in U.S. dollars.

ever, that it is not any individual investor's portfolio profile that should drive the choice of the index, but the marginal investor's portfolio profile.

IN PRACTICE: WHICH INDEX SHOULD I USE TO ESTIMATE BETAS?

In most cases, analysts are faced with a mind-boggling array of choices among indices when it comes to estimating betas. Some analysts use only the local index, but others are willing to experiment. One common practice is to use the index that is most appropriate for the investor who is looking at the stock. Thus, if the analysis is being done for a U.S. investor, the S&P 500 index is used. This is generally not appropriate. By this rationale, an investor who owns only two stocks should use an index composed of only those stocks to estimate betas.

The right index to use in analysis should be determined by who the marginal investor in Aracruz is—a good indicator is to look at the largest holders of stock in the company and the markets where the trading volume is heaviest. If the marginal investor is, in fact, a Brazilian investor, it is reasonable to use a well-constructed Brazilian index. If the marginal investor is a global investor, a more relevant measure of risk may emerge by using the global index. Over time, you would expect global investors to displace local investors as the marginal investors, because they will perceive far less of the risk as market risk and thus pay a higher price for the same security. Thus, one of the ironies of our notion of risk is that Aracruz will be less risky to an overseas investor who has a global portfolio than to a Brazilian investor with all of his or her wealth in Brazilian assets.

3. Estimating the Beta for Deutsche Bank   The following is the estimate of a beta for Deutsche Bank from Bloomberg. Again, the initial estimate is obtained using the DAX, which is an index of large companies listed on the Frankfurt exchange.

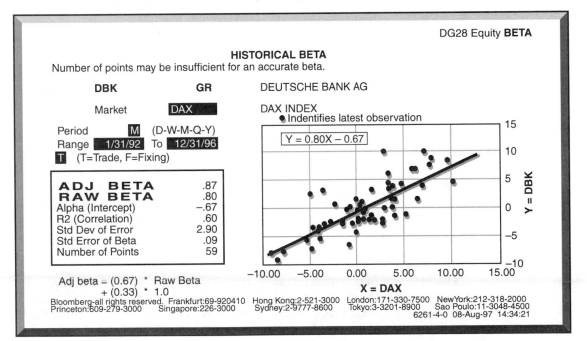

This regression also suffers from the fact that Deutsche Bank is a major component of the DAX. While the beta looks reasonable, we will develop approaches that can be used to check whether it is in fact so.

Standard Procedures for Estimating Risk Parameters in the
Arbitrage Pricing and Multifactor Models
Like the CAPM, the arbitrage pricing model defines risk to be nondiversifiable risk, but, unlike the CAPM, the APM allows for multiple economic factors in measuring this risk. While the process of estimation of risk parameters is different for the arbitrage pricing model, many of the issues raised relating to the determinants of risk in the CAPM continue to have relevance for the arbitrage pricing model.

The parameters of the arbitrage pricing model are estimated from a factor analysis on historical stock returns, which yields the number of common economic factors determining these returns, the risk premium for each factor, and the factor-specific betas for each firm.

Once the factor-specific betas are estimated for each firm, and the factor premiums are measured, the arbitrage pricing model can be used to estimate expected returns on a stock.

$$\text{Cost of Equity} = R_f + \sum_{j=1}^{j=k} \beta_j \, (E(R_j) - R_f)$$

where

R_f = Risk-free rate
β_j = Beta specific to factor j
$E(R_j) - R_f$ = Risk premium per unit of factor j risk
k = Number of factors

In a multifactor model, the betas are estimated relative to the specified factors, using historical data for each firm.

Factor Analysis: This is a statistical technique, where past data is analyzed with the intent of extracting common factors that might have affected the data.

B. Fundamental Betas

The beta for a firm may be estimated from a regression, but it is determined by fundamental decisions that the firm has made on what business to be in, how much operating leverage to use in the business, and the degree to which the firm uses financial leverage. In this section, we will examine an alternative way of estimating betas, where we are less reliant on historical betas and more cognizant of the intuitive underpinnings of betas.

Determinants of Betas
The beta of a firm is determined by three variables: (1) the type of business(es) the firm is in, (2) the degree of operating leverage in the firm, and (3) the firm's financial leverage. While much of the discussion in this section will be couched in terms of

CAPM betas, the same analysis can be applied to the betas estimated in the APM and the multifactor model as well.

1. Type of Business. Since betas measure the risk of a firm relative to a market index, the more sensitive a business is to market conditions, the higher is its beta. Thus, other things remaining equal, cyclical firms can be expected to have higher betas than noncyclical firms. For instance, companies involved in housing and automobiles, two sectors of the economy which are very sensitive to economic conditions, should have higher betas than companies which are in food processing and tobacco, which are relatively insensitive to business cycles.

Building on this point, we would also argue that the degree to which a product's purchase is discretionary will affect the beta of the firm manufacturing the product. Thus, the betas of food processing firms, such as General Foods and Kellogg's, should be lower than the betas of specialty retailers, since consumers can defer the purchase of the latter's products during bad economic times.

Cyclical Firm: A cyclical firm has revenues and operating income that tend to move strongly with the economy—up when the economy is doing well, and down during recessions.

4.7 BETAS AND BUSINESS RISK

Polo Ralph Lauren, the noted fashion designer, went public in 1997. Assume that you were asked to estimate its beta. Based upon what you know about the firm's products, would you expect the beta to be

☐ greater than one?

☐ about one?

☐ less than one?

Why?

IN PRACTICE: CORPORATE STRATEGY, MARKETING AND CORPORATE FINANCIAL RISK

It is true that firms have only limited control over how discretionary the product or service that they provide is to their customers. There are firms, however, that have used this limited control to maximum effect to make their products less discretionary to buyers, and by extension, lowered their business risk. One approach is to make the product or service a much more integral and necessary part of everyday life, thus making its purchase more of a requirement. (The push by online services, like America Online, for people to use e-mail and shopping services on the web is designed to make it less of a discretionary purchase.) A second approach is to effectively use advertising and marketing to build brand loyalty. The objective in good advertising, as I see it, is to make discretionary products or services seem like necessities to the target audience. Thus, corporate strategy, advertising and marketing acumen can, at the margin, alter the business risk and betas over time.

2. Degree of Operating Leverage. The degree of operating leverage is a function of the cost structure of a firm, and is usually defined in terms of the relationship between fixed costs and total costs. A firm that has high operating leverage (i.e., high fixed costs relative to total costs), will also have higher variability in earnings before interest and taxes (EBIT) than would a firm producing a similar product with low operating leverage. Other things remaining equal, the higher variance in operating income will lead to a higher beta for the firm with high operating leverage.

This has consequences for major strategic decisions that firms make on future direction. While there is much good that comes from updating plants and getting the latest technology, there might also be a hidden cost. By reducing the flexibility of the firm to respond to economic downturns, it may make the firm riskier.

While operating leverage affects betas, it is difficult to measure the operating leverage of a firm, at least from the outside, since fixed and variable costs are often aggregated in income statements. It is possible to get an approximate measure of the operating leverage of a firm by looking at changes in operating income as a function of changes in sales.

Degree of Operating Leverage = % Change in Operating Profit / % Change in Sales

For firms with high operating leverage, operating income should change more than proportionately, when sales change.

 ILLUSTRATION 4.2   Measuring Operating Leverage for Disney Corporation
In the following table, we estimate the degree of operating leverage for Disney from 1987 to 1996:

YEAR	NET SALES	% CHANGE IN SALES	EBIT	% CHANGE IN EBIT
1987	2877		756	
1988	3438	19.50%	848	12.17%
1989	4594	33.62%	1177	38.80%
1990	5844	27.21%	1368	16.23%
1991	6182	5.78%	1124	−17.84%
1992	7504	21.38%	1429	27.14%
1993	8529	13.66%	1232	−13.79%
1994	10055	17.89%	1933	56.90%
1995	12112	20.46%	2295	18.73%
1996	18739	54.71%	2540	10.68%
Average		**23.80%**		**16.56%**

The degree of operating leverage changes dramatically from year to year, because of year-to-year swings in operating income. Using the average changes in sales and operating income over the period, we can compute the operating leverage at Disney:

$$\text{Operating Leverage} = \% \text{ Change in EBIT} / \% \text{ Change in Sales}$$
$$= 16.56\% / 23.80 \% = 0.70$$

There are two important observations that can be made about Disney over the period, though. First, the operating leverage for Disney is lower than the operating leverage for other entertainment firms, which we computed to be 1.15. This would suggest that Disney has lower fixed costs than its competitors. Second, the acquisition of Capital Cities by Disney in 1996 may be skewing the operating leverage downward. For instance, looking at the operating leverage for 1987–1995:

$$\text{Operating Leverage}_{1987-96} = 17.29\%/19.94\% = 0.87$$

4.8 SOCIAL POLICY AND OPERATING LEVERAGE

Assume that you are comparing a European automobile manufacturing firm with a U.S. automobile firm. European firms are generally much more constrained in terms of laying off employees, if they get into financial trouble. What implications does this have for betas if they are estimated relative to a common index?

☐ The European firms will have much higher betas than the U.S. firms.

☐ The European firms will have similar betas to the U.S. firms.

☐ The European firms will have much lower betas than the U.S. firms.

IN PRACTICE: CHANGING OPERATING LEVERAGE

Can firms change their operating leverage? While some of a firm's cost structure is determined by the business it is in (an energy utility has to build expensive power plants, and airlines have to lease planes), firms in the United States have become increasingly inventive in lowering the fixed cost component in their total costs. Labor contracts which emphasize flexibility and allow the firm to make its labor costs more sensitive to its profitability, joint venture agreements, where the fixed costs are borne by someone else, and sub-contracting of manufacturing, which reduce the need for expensive plant and equipment, are only some of the manifestations of this phenomenon. While the arguments for such actions may be couched in terms of competitive advantage and flexibility, they do reduce the operating leverage of the firm and its exposure to "market" risk.

3. Degree of Financial Leverage. Other things remaining equal, an increase in financial leverage will increase the equity beta of a firm. Intuitively, the obligated payments on debt increase the variance in net income, with higher leverage increasing income during good times and decreasing income during economic downturns. If all of the firm's risks are borne by the stockholders (i.e., the beta of debt is zero),[13] and debt has a tax benefit to the firm, then,

$$\beta_L = \beta_u \left(1 + (1 - t)\,(D/E)\right)$$

---

[13]If debt has market risk (i.e., its beta is greater than zero), this formula can be modified to take it into account. If the beta of debt is β_D, the beta of equity can be written as:

$$\beta_L = \beta_u \left(1 + (1 - t)(D/E)\right) - \beta_D\,(D/E)$$

where

β_L = Levered beta for equity in the firm
β_u = Unlevered beta of the firm (i.e., the beta of the firm without any debt)
t = Corporate tax rate
D/E = Debt/equity ratio

The unlevered beta of a firm is determined by the types of the businesses in which it operates and its operating leverage. Thus, the equity beta of a company is determined both by the riskiness of the business it operates in, and by the amount of financial leverage risk it has taken on.

■▲ ILLUSTRATION 4.3   Effects of Leverage on Betas: Disney
▼● From the regression for the period from 1992 to 1996, Disney had a beta of 1.40. To estimate the effects of leverage on Disney, we began by estimating the average debt/equity ratio between 1992 and 1996, using market values for debt and equity.

Average Debt/Equity Ratio between 1992 and 1996 = 14%

Using a marginal corporate tax rate of 36%, we estimate the unlevered beta

Unlevered Beta = Current Beta / [(1 + (1 − tax rate) (Average Debt/Equity)]
= 1.40 / (1 + (1 − 0.36)) (0.14) = 1.2849

The levered beta at different levels of debt can then be estimated:

Levered Beta = Unlevered Beta * [1 + (1 − tax rate) (Debt/ Equity)]

For instance, if Disney were to increase its debt equity ratio to 10%, its equity beta would be

Levered Beta (@10% D/E) = 1.2849 *(1 + (1 − 0.36) (0.10)) = 1.37

If the debt equity ratio were raised to 25%, the equity beta would be

Levered Beta (@25% D/E) = 1.2849 *(1 + (1 − 0.36) (0.25)) = 1.49

Table 4.3 summarizes the beta estimates for different levels of financial leverage ranging from 0 to 90% debt.

As Disney's financial leverage increases, the beta increases concurrently.

This spreadsheet allows you to estimate the unlevered beta for a firm and compute the betas as a function of the leverage of the firm (**unlev.xls**).

More on Business Risk and Financial Leverage
Since financial leverage multiplies the underlying business risk, it stands to reason that firms which have high business risk should be reluctant to take on financial leverage. It also stands to reason that firms which operate in relatively stable businesses should be much more willing to take on financial leverage. Utilities, for instance, have historically had high debt ratios, but have not had high betas, mostly because their underlying businesses have been stable and fairly predictable.

Table 4.3   FINANCIAL LEVERAGE AND BETAS FOR DISNEY

Debt to Capital	Debt/Equity Ratio	Beta	Effect of Leverage
0.00%	0.00%	1.28	0.00
10.00%	11.11%	1.38	0.09
20.00%	25.00%	1.49	0.21
30.00%	42.86%	1.64	0.35
40.00%	66.67%	1.83	0.55
50.00%	100.00%	2.11	0.82
60.00%	150.00%	2.52	1.23
70.00%	233.33%	3.20	1.92
80.00%	400.00%	4.57	3.29
90.00%	900.00%	8.69	7.40

Breaking risk down into business and financial leverage components also provides some insight into why companies have high betas, since they can end up with high betas in one of two ways—they can operate in a risky business, or they can use high financial leverage in a relatively stable business.

IN PRACTICE: FINANCIAL LEVERAGE AND BETAS

The equity betas estimated for highly levered firms in practice tend to be much lower than the betas estimated from the levered beta equation developed in the preceding section. This difference can be attributed to one or more of the following factors:

1. The beta estimated from a regression of past returns on a stock against market returns will lag the true beta, when the leverage change is recent. This is because the returns are estimated over a long time period (2 to 5 years) and reflect the average leverage over the period rather than the most recent leverage. This can be fixed fairly easily by unlevering the beta using the average debt/equity ratio over the regression period, and then relevering it back using the current debt/equity ratio.

2. The equity betas estimated on the assumption that debt has no market risk will overstate the true betas because debt does bear market risk especially at higher debt ratios. This problem can be resolved by estimating a debt beta and calculating the equity beta using the expanded equation

$$\beta_L = \beta_u \left(1+(1 - t)(D/E)\right) - \beta_D(D/E)$$

3. The capital asset pricing models may not be the right model for risk, in which case the beta estimated may not reflect the true market risk exposure for a stock.

Bottom Up Betas

Breaking down betas into their business, operating leverage, and financial leverage components provides us with an alternative way of estimating betas, where we do not need past prices on an individual firm or asset to estimate its beta.

To develop this alternative approach, we need to introduce an additional feature that betas possess that proves invaluable. The beta of two assets put together is a weighted average of the individual asset betas, with the weights based upon market value. Consequently, the beta for a firm is a weighted average of the betas of all of the different businesses it is in. Thus, the bottom-up beta for a firm, asset, or project can be estimated as follows.

1. Identify the business or businesses that make up the firm, asset, or project.
2. Estimate the unlevered beta(s) for the business or businesses that the firm is involved in.
3. To calculate the unlevered beta for the firm, take a weighted average of the unlevered betas, using the market values of the different businesses that the firm is involved in. If the market value is not available, use a reasonable proxy such as operating income or revenues.
4. Calculate the leverage for the firm, using market values if available. If not, use the target leverage specified by the management of the firm or industry-typical debt ratios.
5. Estimate the levered beta for the firm (and each of its businesses) using the unlevered beta from step 3 and the leverage from step 4.

Clearly, this process rests on being able to identify the unlevered betas of individual businesses. Table 4.4 summarizes average betas, market debt ratios, and unlevered betas by industry in the United States as of March 1997.

 This data set on the Web has updated betas and unlevered betas by business sector in the United States (**Betas.xls**).

 Estimating Bottom-Up Betas for Disney, Bookscape, Aracruz, and Deutsche Bank The betas for the firms in our analysis can be estimated using the bottom-up approach and the average betas for the sectors in which each of the firms operate.

1. Bottom-Up Beta for Disney Disney has undergone a significant change in both its business mix and its financial leverage over the last five years. Not only did it acquire Capital Cities/ABC, giving it a major foothold in the television broadcasting business, but it borrowed almost $10 billion to finance this acquisition, leading to significant increase in its financial leverage. Since these events have occurred in the last two years, the regression beta does not reflect the effects of these changes. To estimate Disney's beta today, we broke their business into five major components:

1. **Creative Content,** which is the production and acquisition of motion pictures for distribution in theatrical, television, and home video markets as well as television programming for network and syndication markets.
2. **Retailing,** which includes the approximately 610 Disney stores, where Disney merchandise is sold.

Table 4.4   BETAS, D/E RATIOS AND UNLEVERED BETAS: BY SECTOR - MARCH 1997

Industry	Beta	D/E Ratio	Unlevered Beta
Advertising	.85	19.74%	.76
Aerospace/Defense	.93	18.68%	.83
Air Transport	1.20	93.17%	.75
Aluminum	.99	38.16%	.80
Apparel	.89	25.33%	.76
Auto & Truck	.96	133.99%	.52
Auto Parts (OEM)	1.02	37.22%	.82
Auto Parts (Replacement)	.80	37.88%	.65
Bank	.72	31.59%	.60
Bank (Canadian)	.77	27.62%	.66
Bank (Foreign)	.78	48.02%	.59
Bank (Midwest)	.73	29.26%	.62
Beverage (Alcoholic)	.71	24.46%	.62
Beverage (Soft Drink)	.88	12.13%	.82
Building Materials	.89	26.07%	.77
Cable TV	1.03	125.37%	.57
Canadian Energy	.75	43.80%	.58
Cement & Aggregates	.83	18.54%	.74
Chemical (Basic)	.89	23.85%	.78
Chemical (Diversified)	.85	25.76%	.73
Chemical (Specialty)	.89	16.83%	.80
Coal/Alternate Energy	.87	59.10%	.63
Computer & Peripherals	1.33	14.20%	1.22
Computer Software & Svcs	1.30	3.96%	1.27
Copper	.90	48.18%	.69
Diversified Co.	.82	23.77%	.71
Drug	1.28	8.48%	1.21
Drugstore	.84	18.46%	.75
Electric Util. (Central)	.70	91.49%	.44
Electric Utility (East)	.73	80.07%	.48
Electric Utility (West)	.73	90.90%	.46
Electrical Equipment	.98	9.39%	.92
Electronics	1.07	14.67%	.98
Entertainment	.88	43.35%	.69
Environmental	.89	37.92%	.72
Financial Services	1.00	76.02%	.68
Food Processing	.74	23.05%	.65
Food Wholesalers	.77	46.13%	.60
Foreign Electron/Entertn	.78	48.56%	.59
Foreign Telecom.	.94	26.35%	.80

Table 4.4 (CONTINUED)			
Industry	**Beta**	**D/E Ratio**	**Unlevered Beta**
Furn./Home Furnishings	.88	25.83%	.75
Gold/Silver Mining	.62	10.33%	.59
Grocery	.78	37.97%	.63
Healthcare Information	1.22	1.38%	1.21
Home Appliance	.90	61.05%	.65
Homebuilding	.87	104.04%	.52
Hotel/Gaming	1.07	33.14%	.89
Household Products	.97	13.90%	.89
Industrial Services	.86	26.79%	.73
Insurance (Diversified)	.82	17.16%	.74
Insurance (Life)	.86	15.86%	.78
Insurance (Prop/Casualty)	.80	8.62%	.76
Investment Co. (Domestic)	.55	39.67%	.44
Investment Co. (Foreign)	.64	8.70%	.61
Machinery	.85	30.25%	.71
Manuf. Housing/Rec Veh	1.04	11.75%	.96
Maritime	.86	103.19%	.52
Medical Services	1.06	23.61%	.92
Medical Supplies	1.11	8.92%	1.05
Metal Fabricating	.81	16.08%	.73
Metals & Mining (Div.)	.80	28.59%	.68
Natural Gas (Distrib.)	.58	57.47%	.42
Natural Gas (Diversified)	.82	47.99%	.62
Newspaper	.86	26.38%	.73
Office Equip & Supplies	1.04	34.10%	.85
Oilfield Services/Equip.	.86	11.43%	.80
Packaging & Container	.77	42.57%	.61
Paper & Forest Products	.84	61.73%	.60
Petroleum (Integrated)	.72	19.73%	.64
Petroleum (Producing)	.71	35.91%	.58
Precision Instrument	.97	11.07%	.91
Publishing	.89	25.08%	.77
R.E.I.T.	.69	109.42%	.40
Railroad	1.01	35.06%	.83
Recreation	.89	22.59%	.78
Restaurant	1.06	18.85%	.95
Retail (Special Lines)	1.07	19.13%	.95
Retail Building Supply	.98	12.33%	.90
Retail Store	1.00	47.93%	.77
Securities Brokerage	1.19	502.16%	.28

Industry	Beta	D/E Ratio	Unlevered Beta
	Table 4.4 (Continued)		
Semiconductor	1.45	4.41%	1.41
Semiconductor Cap Equip	1.43	3.95%	1.39
Shoe	1.01	10.93%	.94
Steel (General)	.83	27.09%	.70
Steel (Integrated)	.98	54.91%	.73
Telecom. Equipment	1.28	6.27%	1.23
Telecom. Services	1.08	34.12%	.89
Textile	.79	70.29%	.54
Thrift	.86	194.62%	.38
Tire & Rubber	1.03	18.61%	.92
Tobacco	.99	27.75%	.84
Toiletries/Cosmetics	1.00	7.50%	.95
Toys	.84	10.52%	.79
Trucking/Transp. Leasing	.77	71.16%	.53
Utility (Foreign)	1.00	37.16%	.81
Water Utility	.56	109.80%	.33

3. *Broadcasting,* which includes the ABC Television and Radio networks, and reflects the acquisition made in 1995. In addition, Disney has an extensive exposure in the cable market through the Disney channel, A & E, and ESPN (with the latter two acquired as part of the ABC deal).

4. *Theme Parks,* which include Disney World (in Orlando, Florida) and Disney Land (in Anaheim, California), as well as royalties from holdings in Tokyo Disneyland and Euro Disney. The hotels and villas at each of these theme parks are considered part of the theme parks, since they derive their revenue almost exclusively from visitors to these parks.

5. *Real Estate,* in the form of the Disney vacation club, which includes 175 units in Vero Beach, Florida, and 102 units in Hilton Head, South Carolina.

Each of these areas of business has very different risk characteristics, and we estimated the unlevered beta for each component by looking at comparable firms in each business. Table 4.5 summarizes the comparables used for each area and the unlevered betas we arrived at. The values for each of the divisions were estimated using the operating income[14] from each segment, and using a typical operating income multiple[15] for that type of business. The unlevered beta for Disney as a company in 1996 can be estimated by taking a value-weighted average of the betas of each of the different business areas. This is reported in the last column of Table 4.5 and is 1.0929.

---

[14]Note that Disney breaks its business down in its financial statements into three areas—creative content (which includes retailing), broadcasting, and theme parks (which includes real estate).
[15]The multiple we used was Value/EBIT, derived by looking at the average multiple for the sector. Alternatively, we could have just weighted on the basis of operating income.

Table 4.5   ESTIMATING UNLEVERED BETAS FOR DISNEY'S BUSINESS AREAS

Business	Estimated Value ($)	Comparable Firms	Unlevered Beta	Division Value Weight	Weight*Beta
Creative Content	$ 22,167	Motion picture and TV program producers	1.25	35.71%	0.4464
Retailing	$ 2,217	High end specialty retailers	1.5	3.57%	0.0536
Broadcasting	$ 18,842	TV broadcasting companies	0.9	30.36%	0.2732
Theme Parks	$ 16,625	Theme park and entertainment complexes	1.1	26.79%	0.2946
Real Estate	$ 2,217	REITs specializing in hotel and vacation properties	0.7	3.57%	0.0250
Firm	$ 62,068			100.00%	1.0929

The equity beta can then be estimated using the current financial leverage for Disney as a firm. Combining the market value of equity of $50.89 billion and the value of debt of $11.18 billion, we arrive at the current beta for Disney:

$$\text{Equity Beta for Disney} = 1.09\,(1+(1-.36)(11.18/50)) = 1.25$$

This contrasts with the beta of 1.40 that we obtained from the regression, and is, in our view, a much truer reflection of the risk in Disney.

2. Bottom-Up Beta for Bookscape Books   We could not estimate a regression beta for Bookscape Books, the private firm, since it did not have a history of past prices. We can, however, estimate the beta for Bookscape Books, using the bottom-up approach. We began by obtaining the betas and debt/equity ratios for other publicly traded booksellers in Table 4.6:

Table 4.6   BETAS AND LEVERAGE OF PUBLICLY TRADED BOOKSTORE FIRMS

Company Name	Beta	D/E Ratio	Market Cap $ (Mil)
Barnes & Noble	1.10	23.31%	$1,416
Books-A-Million	1.30	44.35%	$ 85
Borders Group	1.20	2.15%	$1,706
Crown Books	0.80	3.03%	$ 55
Average	1.10	18.21%	$ 816

Note that the debt/equity ratios are market value debt/equity ratios, and that these are much larger firms than Bookscape Books. The difference in the size of the firms, per se, should not affect the betas directly, but they might have an indirect effect, since smaller firms tend to have higher operating leverage. Assuming a marginal tax rate of 36%, the unlevered beta for book retailers can be calculated as follows:

$$\text{Unlevered Beta} = 1.10/(1+(1-.36)(.1821)) = 0.99$$

Since the debt/equity ratios used are market debt/equity ratios, and the only debt/equity ratio we can compute for Bookscape is a book value debt/equity ratio, we have assumed that Bookscape is *close to the industry average* in terms of leverage and used the average beta of 1.10 for Bookscape. We will return to examine whether this assumption is appropriate later in our discussion.

3. Bottom-Up Beta for Aracruz Cellulose   The bottom-up beta for Aracruz is difficult to estimate if we remain within its home market, which is Brazil, for two reasons. First, there are relatively few firms within the market that are in the same line of business as Aracruz (i.e., paper and pulp production). Second, the betas for all Brazilian firms are unreliable because the index used to estimate these betas, the Bovespa, is overweighted with Telebras.

There are three groups of comparable firms that we can use. One is to look across comparable firms in the business of manufacturing paper or paper products in Latin America and estimate their average beta and debt/equity ratio. The constraint which we will run into in doing this is that while the number of firms in our comparable group will be larger, the betas for these firms suffer from some of the same shortcomings as Brazilian firms (such as indices that are concentrated in a few companies). The second is to cast our net wider and look at companies in the United States that are in the paper products business. The advantage gained is not just in terms of the number of additional firms but also in terms of reliable betas. The final group that we examine is all paper and pulp firms listed around the world. While this group is the largest, some of the betas estimated relative to local indices are open to question. Since betas are measures of relative risk, we would argue that barring significant differences in regulation and monopoly power across markets, it is reasonable to compare betas across markets.

COMPARABLE FIRMS	AVERAGE BETA	D/E RATIO	UNLEVERED BETA
Latin American Paper & Pulp (5)	0.70	65.00%	0.49
U.S. Paper and Pulp (45)	0.85	35.00%	0.69
Global Paper & Pulp (187)	0.80	50.00%	0.61

The tax rates used were 35% for Latin companies, 36% for U.S. companies, and 40% for global companies, and the number of firms is provided in brackets. We will use an unlevered beta of 0.61, which is the beta based upon paper and pulp firms from around the world, as the beta for the paper and pulp business that Aracruz is involved in.

We can estimate the levered beta for Aracruz in two steps. First, we consider the assets that Aracruz has. In addition to being in the paper business, Aracruz had a cash balance of 800 million BR in 1995, which is roughly 20% of firm value. Since this is much larger than the typical cash balances of the companies on our comparable firm list, and the beta of cash is zero, the unlevered beta for Aracruz can be estimated as follows:

$$\text{Unlevered Beta for Aracruz} = (0.8)\,(0.61) + 0.2\,(0) = 0.488$$

Aracruz had gross debt outstanding of 1.6 billion BR in 1997 and a market value of equity of 2.4 billion BR leading to a debt/equity ratio of 66.67%. Allowing for a tax rate of 32%, the levered beta for Aracruz can then be estimated as follows:

$$\text{Levered Beta for Aracruz} = 0.49 \,(1 + (1 - .32) \,(.6667)) = 0.71$$

IN PRACTICE: GROSS DEBT OR NET DEBT

Many analysts prefer to subtract the cash from the gross debt to arrive at a net debt figure. While there is no conceptual problem with this approach, they should recognize that the unlevered beta that should be used for the firm should then be just the unlevered beta without the cash. Thus, for Aracruz, the unlevered beta, if net debt were our measure of debt, would be the unlevered beta of the paper business. The net debt ratio would be estimated as follows:

$$\text{Net Debt/Equity Ratio} = (\text{Gross Debt} - \text{Cash})/ \text{Market Value of Equity}$$
$$= (1.6 - 0.8)/2.4 = 33.33\%$$

The levered beta would then have been estimated using the net debt ratio:

$$\text{Levered Beta for Aracruz} = 0.61 \,(1 + (1 - .32) \,(0.3333)) = 0.75$$

The difference arises because netting out debt makes the assumption that the tax benefit from having debt is exactly offset by the tax effects of earning interest on cash. It is generally not a good idea to net debt if the debt is very risky (since netting is predicated on the assumption that debt and cash are both riskless) or if the interest rate earned on cash is substantially lower (or higher) than the interest rate paid on debt.

4. Bottom-Up Beta for Deutsche Bank   There are a few banks in Germany that can be viewed as competitors to Deutsche Bank, though none of them are as large as it is, or have as large a stake in investment banking. Here again, we will go across markets to estimate betas. Since the rules governing banking in the United States are different from the rules governing banks in much of Western Europe, we will look at the betas of Western European banks to estimate the beta for the commercial banking arm of Deutsche Bank. To estimate the beta of Morgan Grenfell, the investment banking arm, we use the betas of investment banking firms in the United States and the UK. The results are presented below:

COMPARABLE FIRMS	AVERAGE BETA
Commercial banks in Germany	0.90
U.K. and U.S. investment banks	1.30

Note that we do not adjust for differences in leverage, since regulatory constraints and the needs of the business keep the leverage of most commercial banks at high (and comparable) levels. The beta for Deutsche Bank as a firm can be estimated as a weighted average of these two betas. Using estimated market value weights of 90% for the commercial banking and 10% for the investment banking arms (based upon the income that Deutsche Bank made from each in the most recent year), we arrive at a beta for Deutsche Bank's equity:

$$\text{Deutsche Bank's Beta} = 0.9\,(0.9) + (.1)\,(1.30) = .94$$

This beta will change over time as the weights on each of these businesses changes.

Calculating Betas After a Major Restructuring

The bottom-up process of estimating betas provides a solution when firms go through a major restructuring, where they change both their financial mix and leverage. In these cases, the regression betas are misleading because they do not reflect fully the effects of these changes. Disney's beta, estimated from the bottom-up approach, is likely to provide a more precise estimate than the beta from a regression, given Disney's acquisition of Capital Cities and its increase in leverage. In fact, a firm's beta can be estimated even before the restructuring becomes effective using this approach. In the illustration that follows, for instance, we estimate Disney's beta just before and after its acquisition of Capital Cities/ABC, allowing for the changes in both the business mix and the leverage.

■ ▲
▼ ● ILLUSTRATION 4.4   Beta of a Firm After an Acquisition: Disney/Capital Cities

In 1995, Disney announced that it was acquiring Capital Cities, the owner of the ABC television and radio network, for approximately $120 per share, and that it would finance the acquisition partly through the issue of $10 billion in debt. At the time of the acquisition, Disney had a market value of equity of $31.1 billion, debt outstanding of $3.186 billion, and a beta of 1.15. Capital Cities, based upon the $120 offering price, had a market value of equity of $18.5 billion, debt outstanding of $615 million, and a beta of 0.95.

In order to evaluate the effects of the acquisition on Disney's beta, we do the analysis in two parts. First, we examine the effects of the merger on the business risk of the combined firm by estimating the unlevered betas of the two companies and calculating the combined firm's unlevered beta:

$$\text{Disney's Unlevered Beta} = 1.15/(1 + 0.64*0.10) = 1.08$$
$$\text{Capital Cities Unlevered Beta} = 0.95/(1 + 0.64*0.03) = 0.93$$

The unlevered beta for the combined firm can be calculated as the weighted average of the two unlevered betas, with the weights being based upon the market values of the two firms (market value of firm = value of equity + debt):

$$\text{Unlevered Beta for Combined Firm} = 1.08\,(34286/53401) + 0.93\,(19115/53401)$$
$$= 1.026$$

Then, we examine the effects of the financing of the merger on the betas, by calculating the debt/equity ratio for the combined firm after the acquisition, assuming that $10 billion is borrowed to finance the acquisition:

$$\begin{aligned}
\text{Debt} &= \text{Capital Cities Old Debt} + \text{Disney's Old Debt} + \text{New Debt} \\
&= \$615 + \$3,186 + \$10,000 = \$13,801 \text{ million} \\
\text{Equity} &= \text{Disney's Old Equity} + \text{New Equity used for Acquisition} \\
&= \$31,100 + \$8,500 = \$39,600 \text{ million}
\end{aligned}$$

where

$$\text{New Equity} = \text{Total Cost of Acquisition} - \text{New Debt Issued}$$
$$= \$18,500 - \$10,000 = \$8,500 \text{ million}$$

The debt/equity ratio can then be computed as follows:

$$\text{D/E Ratio} = 13,801/39600 = 34.85\%$$

This debt/equity ratio in conjunction with the new unlevered beta for the combined firm yields a new beta of:

$$\text{New Beta} = 1.026 (1 + 0.64 (.3485)) = 1.25$$

It is pure coincidence that this beta is equal to the beta that we estimated from the fundamentals.

C. Accounting Betas

A third approach is to estimate the market risk parameters from accounting earnings rather than from traded prices. Thus, changes in earnings at a division or a firm, on a quarterly or annual basis, can be regressed against changes in earnings for the market in the same periods, to arrive at an estimate of a "market beta" to use in the CAPM. While the approach has some intuitive appeal, it suffers from three potential pitfalls. First, accounting earnings tend to be smoothed out relative to the underlying value of the company, resulting in betas that are "biased down," especially for risky firms, or "biased up," for safer firms. In other words, betas are likely to be closer to 1 for all firms using accounting data. Second, accounting earnings can be influenced by nonoperating factors, such as changes in depreciation or inventory methods, and by allocations of corporate expenses at the divisional level. Finally, accounting earnings are measured, at most, once every quarter, and often only once every year, resulting in regressions with few observations and not much power.

■▲
▼● ILLUSTRATION 4.5　Estimating Accounting Betas—Bookscape Books

Bookscape Books, even though it is a private business, has been in existence since 1980 and has accounting earnings going back to that year. Table 4.7 summarizes accounting earnings changes at Bookscape and for the S&P 500 for each year since 1980. Regressing the changes in profits at Bookscape against changes in profits for the S&P 500 yields the following:

$$\text{Bookscape Earnings Change} = -.085 + 1.11 \text{ (S\&P 500 Earnings Change)}$$

Based upon this regression, the beta for Bookscape is 1.11. In calculating this beta, we used net income to arrive at an equity beta. Using operating earnings for both the firm and the S&P 500 should yield the equivalent of an unlevered beta.

Why We Do Not Estimate Accounting Betas for the Remaining Firms
Technically, there is no reason why we cannot estimate accounting betas for Disney, Aracruz Cellulose, and Deutsche Bank. In fact, for Disney, we could get net income numbers every quarter, which increases the data that we have in the regression. We could even estimate accounting betas by division, since the divisional income is reported. We do not attempt to estimate accounting betas for the following reasons:

1. To get a sufficient number of observations in our regression, we would need to go back in time *at least* 10 years. The changes that many large companies undergo over time makes this a hazardous exercise.

2. Publicly traded firms smooth out accounting earnings changes even more than private firms do. This will bias the beta estimates towards one.

Table 4.7	EARNINGS FOR BOOKSCAPE VERSUS S&P 500	
Year	**S&P 500**	**Bookscape**
1980	−2.10%	3.55%
1981	−6.70%	4.05%
1982	−45.50%	−14.33%
1983	37.00%	47.55%
1984	41.80%	65.00%
1985	−11.80%	5.05%
1986	7.00%	8.50%
1987	41.50%	37.00%
1988	41.80%	45.17%
1989	2.60%	3.50%
1990	−18.00%	−10.50%
1991	−47.40%	−32.00%
1992	64.50%	55.00%
1993	20.00%	31.00%
1994	25.30%	21.06%
1995	15.50%	11.55%
1996	24.00%	19.88%

 This data set on the Web has earnings changes, by year, for the S&P 500 going back to 1960.

IN PRACTICE: ESTIMATING SECTOR BETAS USING NON-MARKET DATA

The sector betas that we have talked about so far are estimated by averaging historical beta estimates across firms in each sector, and then unlevering the betas using the average debt/equity ratio for the sector. To the extent that this approach requires and uses market price data, it may not provide reliable estimates in markets where there is insufficient or very noisy information. An alternative approach is to estimate the total revenues in each sector in each period and run a regression of these revenues against the total gross national product of the economy over the same time periods. The slope of the regression will measure the sensitivity of each sector to overall economic movements. This "business risk beta" can then be used for any company in a sector, in conjunction with that company's operating leverage and financial leverage variables, to arrive at an estimate of a beta of the equity of the company.

Market, Fundamental, and Accounting Betas: Which One Do We Use?
For most publicly traded firms, the betas can be estimated using accounting data, market data, or from fundamentals. Since the betas will almost never be the same, the question then becomes one of choosing between these betas. We would almost never use accounting betas, for all of the reasons specified above. We are almost as reluctant to use historical market betas for individual firms because of the noisiness in beta estimates, the failures of the local indices (as in the Aracruz and the Deutsche Bank examples), and the inability of these regressions to reflect the effects of major changes in the business and financial risk at the firm (as in the Disney example). Fundamental betas, in our view, provide us with the best beta estimates because:

1. They allow us to consider changes in business and financial mix, even before they occur.
2. They use sector average betas, which tend to be less noisy than individual firm betas.
3. They allow us to come up with betas by area of business for a firm, which is useful both in the context of investment analysis and valuation.

In summary, we will use the fundamental estimates of equity betas of 1.25 for Disney, 1.10 for Bookscape, 0.71 for Aracruz, and 0.94 for Deutsche Bank.

IV. Estimating the Cost of Equity

Having estimated the risk-free rate, the risk premium(s), and the beta(s), we can now estimate the expected return from investing in equity at any firm. In the CAPM, this expected return can be written as:

$$\text{Expected Return} = \text{Risk-free Rate} + \text{Beta} * \text{Expected Risk Premium}$$

where the risk-free rate would be the rate on a long-term government bond, the beta would be either the historical, fundamental, or accounting betas described above, and the risk premium would be either the historical premium or an implied premium.

In the arbitrage pricing and multifactor model, the expected return would be written as follows:

$$\text{Expected Return} = \text{Risk-free Rate} + \sum_{j=1}^{j=n} \beta_j * \text{Risk Premium}_j$$

where the risk-free rate is the long-term government bond rate, β_j is the beta relative to factor j, estimated using historical data or fundamentals, and Risk Premium$_j$ is the risk premium relative to factor j, estimated using historical data.

The expected return on an equity investment in a firm, given its risk, has strong implications for both equity investors in the firm and the managers of the firm. For equity investors, it is the *rate that they need to make* to be compensated for the market (or nondiversifiable) risk that they have taken on investing in the firm. If after analyzing an investment, they conclude that they cannot make this return, they would not buy this investment; alternatively, if they decide they can make a higher return, they would make the investment.

For managers in the firm, the return that investors need to make to break even on their equity investments becomes the return that they have to try and deliver to keep these investors from becoming restive and rebellious. Thus, it becomes the rate that they have to beat in terms of returns on their equity investments in an individual project. In other words, this is the *cost of equity* to the firm.

ILLUSTRATION 4.6 Estimating the Cost of Equity for Disney, Bookscape, Aracruz, and Deutsche Bank

In the following analysis, we will estimate the cost of equity for Disney, Bookscape Books, Aracruz Cellulose, and Deutsche Bank using the CAPM. In doing so, we will use the fundamental betas since they best reflect the true riskiness of these firms. We will also estimate betas by division, within each of the two multibusiness firms, which are Disney and Deutsche Bank.

BUSINESS	UNLEVERED BETA	D/E RATIO	LEVERED BETA	RISK-FREE RATE	RISK PREMIUM	COST OF EQUITY
Creative Content	1.25	20.92%	1.42	7.00%	5.50%	14.80%
Retailing	1.50	20.92%	1.70	7.00%	5.50%	16.35%
Broadcasting	0.90	20.92%	1.02	7.00%	5.50%	12.61%
Theme Parks	1.10	20.92%	1.26	7.00%	5.50%	13.91%
Real Estate	0.70	50.00%	0.92	7.00%	5.50%	12.08%
Disney	**1.09**	**21.97%**	**1.25**	**7.00%**	**5.50%**	**13.85%**
Bookscape	**0.99**	**18%**	**1.10**	**7.00%**	**5.50%**	**13.05%**
Aracruz	**0.488**	**67%**	**0.71**	**5.00%**	**7.50%**	**10.33%**
Commercial Banks			0.90	7.50%	5.50%	12.45%
Investment Banks			1.30	7.50%	5.50%	14.65%
Deutsche Bank			**0.94**	**7.50%**	**5.50%**	**12.67%**

Note that each division of Disney has a different cost of equity, based upon differences in unlevered betas. We use Disney's overall debt/equity ratio to estimate the equity betas, by division, for all the divisions except real estate. This is done because none of these divisions carry their own debt. For the real estate division, which does carry its own debt (on the properties), we use a market value debt/equity ratio based upon comparable firms.

To estimate costs of equity, we use the rate on a long-term U.S. government bond for Disney and Bookscape (which yields a nominal dollar cost of equity), the rate on a long-term German Government bond for Deutsche Bank (which yields a nominal DM cost of equity), and the estimated real risk-free rate for Aracruz (which yield a real BR cost of equity).

IN PRACTICE: RISK, COST OF EQUITY AND PRIVATE FIRMS

Implicit in the use of beta as a measure of risk is the assumption that the marginal investor in equity is a well diversified investor. While this is a defensible assumption when analyzing publicly traded firms, it becomes much more difficult to sustain for private firms. The owner of a private firm generally has the bulk of his or her wealth invested in the business. Consequently, he or she cares about the total risk in the business rather than just the market risk. Thus, for a business like Bookscape, the beta that we have estimated of 1.10 (leading to a cost of equity of 13.05%) will understate the risk perceived by the owner of Bookscape. There are three solutions to this problem:

1. Assume that the business is run with the near-term objective of an initial public offering or sale to a large publicly traded firm. In such a case, it is reasonable to use the market beta and cost of equity that comes from it.

2. Add a premium to the cost of equity to reflect the higher risk created by the owner's inability to diversify. (This may help explain the high returns that some venture capitalists demand on their equity investments in fledgling businesses.)

3. Adjust the beta to reflect total risk rather than market risk. This adjustment is a relatively simple one, since the R-squared of the regression measures the proportion of the risk that is market risk.

$$\text{Total Beta} = \text{Market Beta} / \text{R-squared}$$

In the Bookscapes example, where the market beta is 1.10 and the average R-squared of the comparable publicly traded firms is 33%, this would lead to a total beta estimate of 3.30, resulting in a cost of equity of 25.05%.

FROM COST OF EQUITY TO COST OF CAPITAL

While equity is undoubtedly an important and indispensable ingredient of the financing mix for every business, it is but one ingredient. Most businesses finance some or most of their operations using debt or some hybrid of equity and debt. The costs of these sources of financing are generally very different from the cost of equity, and the minimum acceptable hurdle rate for a project will reflect their costs as well, in proportion to their use in the financing mix. Intuitively, the *cost of capital* is the weighted average of the costs of the different components of financing—including debt, equity, and hybrid securities—used by a firm to fund its financial requirements.

4.9 INTEREST RATES AND THE RELATIVE COSTS OF DEBT AND EQUITY

It is often argued that debt becomes a more attractive mode of financing than equity as interest rates go down and a less attractive mode when interest rates go up. Is this true?

☐ Yes

☐ No

Why or why not?

Calculating the Cost of Debt

The *cost of debt* measures the current cost to the firm of borrowing funds to finance projects. In general terms, it is determined by the following variables:

1. ***The current level of interest rates:***   As the level of interest rates increases, the cost of debt for firms will also increase.

2. ***The default risk of the company:***   As the default risk of a firm increases, the cost of borrowing money will also increase. One way of measuring default risk is to use the bond rating for the firm: Higher ratings lead to lower interest rates, and lower ratings lead to higher interest rates. If bond ratings are not available, as is the case in many markets outside the United States, the rates paid most recently by the firm on its borrowings may provide a measure of the default risk of the firm.

3. ***The tax advantage associated with debt:***   Since interest is tax deductible, the after-tax cost of debt is a function of the tax rate. The tax benefit that accrues from paying interest makes the after-tax cost of debt lower than the pretax cost. Furthermore, this benefit increases as the tax rate increases.

$$\text{After-tax Cost of Debt} = \text{Pretax Cost of Debt} (1 - \text{Tax Rate})$$

Default Risk This is the risk that a firm will fail to make obligated debt payments, such as interest expenses or principal payments.

4.10 COSTS OF DEBT AND EQUITY

Can the cost of equity ever be lower than the cost of debt for any firm at any stage in its life cycle?

☐ Yes

☐ No

ILLUSTRATION 4.7 **Estimating the Costs of Debt for Disney, Bookscape, Aracruz, and Deutsche Bank**

We will employ different approaches to estimate the cost of debt for the firms in our sample: For Disney and Deutsche Bank, we will use the current bond rating for the firm to arrive at a "market interest rate" at which each can borrow; for Bookscape, we will estimate a cost of debt based upon the rate at which it can borrow from a local bank; for Aracruz, we will use the interest coverage ratio to estimate a "synthetic rating" for the firm, which we will then employ to arrive at a real cost of debt.

For Disney, the current rating is AA, with an estimated spread of 50 basis points over the treasury bond rate, whereas Deutsche Bank's rating of AAA is estimated to yield a spread of 20 basis points over the German government bond rate. Bookscape is assumed to face a borrowing rate 1% above the Treasury bond rate, based upon rates charged by banks for firms of similar financial strength. For Aracruz, the rating is estimated based upon its interest coverage ratio at the beginning of 1996 to be AA, with a spread of 50 basis points over the real risk-free rate.

BUSINESS	APPROACH USED	INTEREST RATE	TAX RATE USED	AFTER-TAX COST OF DEBT
Creative Content	Bond Rating	7.50%	36%	4.80%
Retailing	Bond Rating	7.50%	36%	4.80%
Broadcasting	Bond Rating	7.50%	36%	4.80%
Theme Parks	Bond Rating	7.50%	36%	4.80%
Real Estate	Bond Rating	7.50%	36%	4.80%
Disney	**Bond Rating**	**7.50%**	**36%**	**4.80%**
Bookscape	**Recent Borrowing**	**8.00%**	**42%**	**4.64%**
Aracruz	**Synthetic Rating**	**5.50%**	**32%**	**3.74%**
Commercial Banks	Bond Rating	7.70%	45%	4.24%
Investment Banks	Bond Rating	7.70%	45%	4.24%
Deutsche Bank	**Bond Rating**	**7.70%**	**45%**	**4.24%**

Note that the after-tax cost of debt is significantly lower than the cost of equity for each and every one of the companies.

What the Cost of Debt Is Not

When firms borrow money, they do so often at fixed rates. When they issue bonds to investors, the rate that is fixed at the time of the issue is called the coupon rate. The cost of debt is not the coupon rate on bonds that the company has outstanding, nor is it the rate at which the company was able to borrow in the past. While these factors may help determine the interest cost the company will have to pay in the current year, they do not determine the after-tax cost of debt. Thus, a company that has debt on the books that it took on when interest rates were low cannot contend that it has a low cost of debt if the overall level of interest rates or its risk of default has increased in the meantime.

Calculating the Cost of Preferred Stock

Preferred stock shares some of the characteristics of debt (the preferred dividend is prespecified at the time of the issue and is paid out before common dividend) and some of the characteristics of equity (the payments of preferred dividend are not tax deductible). If preferred stock is viewed as perpetual, the cost of preferred stock can be written as follows:

$$k_{ps} = \text{Preferred Dividend per Share} / \text{Market Price per Preferred Share}$$

This approach assumes that the dividend is constant in dollar terms forever and that the preferred stock has no special features (convertibility, callability, etc.). If such special features exist, they will have to be valued separately to come up with a good estimate of the cost of preferred stock. In terms of risk, preferred stock is safer than common equity but riskier than debt. Consequently, it should, on a pretax basis, command a higher cost than debt and a lower cost than equity.

4.11   WHY DO COMPANIES ISSUE PREFERRED STOCK?

Which of the following are "good" reasons for a company issuing preferred stock?

☐   Preferred stock is cheaper than equity

☐   Preferred stock is treated as equity by the ratings agencies and regulators

☐   Preferred stock is cheaper than debt

☐   Other:

Explain.

ILLUSTRATION **4.8**   Calculating the Cost of Preferred Stock: General Motors Co.

In March 1995, General Motors had preferred stock that paid a dividend of $2.28 annually and traded at $26.38 per share. The cost of preferred stock can be estimated as follows:

$$\text{Cost of Preferred Stock} = \text{Preferred Dividend per Share} / \text{Preferred Stock Price}$$
$$= \$2.28 / \$26.38 = 8.64 \%$$

At the same time, GM's cost of equity, using the CAPM, was 13%, its pretax cost of debt was 8.25%, and its after-tax cost of debt was 5.28%. Not surprisingly, its preferred stock was less expensive than equity, but more expensive than debt.

Calculating the Cost of Other Hybrid Securities

In general terms, *hybrid securities* share some of the characteristics of debt and some of the characteristics of equity. A good example is a convertible bond, which can be viewed as a combination of a straight bond (debt) and a conversion option (equity). Instead of trying to calculate the cost of these hybrid securities directly, they can be broken down into their debt and equity components and treated separately.

Convertible Debt: This is debt that can be converted into stock at a specified rate, called the conversion ratio.

ILLUSTRATION **4.9**   Breaking Down a Convertible Bond into Debt and Equity Components: Unisys Corp.

At the end of 1992, Unisys had an 8.25% convertible bond, coming due in the year 2000, which was trading at $1400. It also had straight bonds, with the same maturity, trading in December 1992 at a yield of 8.4%. The convertible bond can then be broken down into straight bond and conversion option components:

$$\text{Straight Bond Component} = \text{Value of a straight 8.25\% coupon bond due in 2000}$$
$$\text{at a yield of 8.40\%. (8-year straight bond)}$$
$$= \$991.50$$
$$\text{Conversion Option} = \$1400 - \$991.50 = \$408.50$$

The straight bond component of $991.50 is treated as debt, while the conversion option of $408.50 is treated as equity.

4.12   INCREASES IN STOCK PRICES AND CONVERTIBLE BONDS

As stock prices go up, which of the following is likely to happen to the convertible bond (you can choose more than one)?

☐ The convertible bond will increase in value

☐ The straight bond component of the convertible bond will decrease in value

☐ The equity component of the convertible bond will increase as a percentage of the total value

☐ The straight bond component of the convertible bond will increase as a percentage of the total value

Explain.

Calculating the Weights of Debt and Equity Components

Market Value versus Book Value Weights

The weights assigned to equity and debt in calculating the weighted average cost of capital have to be based on market value, not book value. This rationale rests on the fact that the cost of capital measures the cost of issuing securities—stocks as well as bonds—to finance projects, and that these securities are issued at market value, not at book value.

There are three standard arguments against using market value, and none of them are convincing. First, it is argued that book value is more reliable than market value because it is not as volatile. While it is true that book value does not change as much as market value, this is more a reflection of weakness than strength, since the true value of the firm changes over time as both firm-specific and marketwide information is revealed. We would argue that market value, with its volatility, is a much better reflection of true value than is book value.[16] Second, it is suggested that using book value rather than market value is a more conservative approach to estimating debt ratios. This assumes that market value debt ratios are always lower than book value debt ratios, an assumption not based on fact. Furthermore, even if the market value debt ratios are lower than the book value ratios, the cost of capital calculated using book value ratios will be lower than the cost of capital calculated using market value ratios, leading to less conservative estimates, not more.[17] Third, it is claimed that lenders will not lend on the basis of market value, but this claim again seems to be based more upon perception than fact.[18]

---

[16]There are some who argue that stock prices are much more volatile than the underlying true value. Even if this argument is justified (and it has not conclusively been shown to be so), the difference between market value and true value is likely to be much smaller than the difference between book value and true value.

[17]To illustrate this point, assume that the market value debt ratio is 10%, while the book value debt ratio is 30%, for a firm with a cost of equity of 15% and an after-tax cost of debt of 5%. The cost of capital can be calculated as follows:

With market value debt ratios: 15% (.9) + 5% (.1) = 14%
With book value debt ratios: 15% (.7) + 5% (.3) = 12%

[18]Any homeowner who has taken a second mortgage on a house that has appreciated in value knows that lenders do lend on the basis of market value. It is true, however, that the greater the perceived volatility in the market value of an asset, the lower is the borrowing potential on that asset.

IN PRACTICE: ESTIMATING THE MARKET VALUES OF EQUITY AND DEBT

The market value of equity is generally the number of shares outstanding times the current stock price. If there is more than one class of shares outstanding, the market values of all of these securities should be aggregated and treated as equity. Finally, if there are other equity claims in the firm—warrants and conversion options in other securities—these should also be valued and added on to the value of the equity in the firm.

The market value of debt is usually more difficult to obtain directly since very few firms have all of their debt in the form of bonds outstanding trading in the market. Many of them have nontraded debt, such as bank debt, which is specified in book value terms but not market value terms. A simple way to convert book value debt into market value debt is to treat the entire debt on the books as one coupon bond, with a coupon set equal to the interest expenses on all of the debt and the maturity set equal to the face-value weighted average maturity of the debt, and to then value this coupon bond at the current cost of debt for the company. Thus, the market value of $1 billion in debt, with interest expenses of $60 million and a maturity of six years, when the current cost of debt is 7.5%, can be estimated as follows:

$$\text{Estimated Market Value of Debt} = 60 \left[\frac{(1 - \frac{1}{(1.075)^6})}{.075} \right] + \frac{1,000}{(1.075)^6} = \$930$$

■▲
▼●

ILLUSTRATION 4.10   **Difference Between Market Value and Book Value Debt Ratios: Disney, Bookscape, Aracruz, and Duetsche Bank**

In the following table we contrast the book values of debt and equity with the market values. For the firms other than Bookscape, the market value of equity is estimated using the current market price and the number of shares outstanding. For debt, we estimate the market value of debt using the book value of debt, the interest expense on the debt, the average maturity of the debt, and the pretax cost of debt for each firm. For Disney, the book value of debt is $12,342 million, the interest expense on the debt is $479 million, the average maturity of the debt is three years, and the pretax cost of debt is 7.50%. The estimated market value is as follows:

$$\text{Estimated MV of Disney Debt} = 479 \left[\frac{(1 - \frac{1}{(1.075)^3})}{.075} \right] + \frac{12,342}{(1.075)^3} = \$11,180$$

The market value of debt for Aracruz and Deutsche Bank is similarly estimated. While Bookscape has no debt on its books, it does have an operating lease commitment of $500,000 per year for the next ten years. This commitment can be converted into an equivalent debt amount by taking the present value of $500,000 at Bookscape's cost of debt which is 8%:

$$\text{Estimated MV of Bookscape Debt} = 500,000 \left[\frac{(1 - \frac{1}{(1.08)^{10}})}{.08} \right] = \$3.36 \text{ million}$$

The following table summarizes the book value and market value debt ratios of the four firms:

	BOOK VALUE			MARKET VALUE		
	Debt	**Equity**	**D/(D+E)**	**Debt**	**Equity**	**D/(D+E)**
Disney	$12,342	$16,086	43.41%	$11,180	$50,297	18.19%
Bookscape	$ −	$ 6	0.00%	$ 3.36	NA	NA
Aracruz	1581	2284	40.90%	1520	2001	43.17%
Deutsche Bank	110111	30295	78.42%	110111	62695	63.72%

For Disney and Deutsche Bank, where the market values of equity are well in excess of the book values, the market value debt ratio is much lower than the book value debt ratio. For Aracruz, the reverse is true, since the market value of equity is lower than the book value of equity. For Bookscape, absent a market value for equity, we will use the industry average debt ratio of 15.40%.

Estimating the Cost of Capital

In a general model, where a firm can raise its money from three sources (equity, debt, and preferred stock), the cost of capital is defined as the weighted average of each of these costs: the cost of equity (k_e) reflecting the riskiness of the equity investment in the firm, the after-tax cost of debt (k_d) reflecting the default risk of the firm and the tax advantages that the interest tax deduction confer on the firm, and the cost of preferred stock (k_{ps}) a function of its intermediate standing in terms of risk between debt and equity. The weights on each of these components should reflect their market value proportions, since these proportions best measure how the existing firm is being financed. Thus if E, D, and PS are the market values of equity, debt, and preferred stock respectively, the cost of capital can be written as follows:

$$\text{Cost of Capital} = k_e \left(E/ (D + E + PS) \right) + k_d \left(D/ (D + E + PS) \right) + k_{ps} \left(PS/ (D + E + PS) \right)$$

The Significance of the Cost of Capital

The cost of capital is a measure of the composite cost of raising money that a firm faces. When looking at the return on capital that a project makes, this is the minimum acceptable hurdle rate that the project has to beat. Note earlier that we suggested that the cost of equity can also be used as a hurdle rate. If it is, the return that we would be looking at in a project would be just the return on equity.

In estimating these costs of capital, we have in a sense conceded the status quo in terms of financing mix, since we have estimated the cost of capital at the existing mix. It is entirely possible that a firm, by changing its mix, could lower its cost of capital. The payoff from doing so would be immediate—they would not only have a lower hurdle rate for future projects, but all existing projects would earn a greater spread over the hurdle rate, making them more valuable. We will return to this question in Chapter 8.

ILLUSTRATION 4.11   Estimating Cost of Capital for Disney, Bookscape, Aracruz, and Deutsche Bank

Culminating the analysis in this chapter, we estimate the costs of capital for each of Disney's divisions, Bookscape, Aracruz Cellulose (in real terms), and for Deutsche Bank's divisions:

BUSINESS	E/(D+E)	COST OF EQUITY	D/(D+E)	AFTER-TAX COST OF DEBT	COST OF CAPITAL
Creative Content	82.70%	14.80%	17.30%	4.80%	13.07%
Retailing	82.70%	16.35%	17.30%	4.80%	14.36%
Broadcasting	82.70%	12.61%	17.30%	4.80%	11.26%
Theme Parks	82.70%	13.91%	17.30%	4.80%	12.32%
Real Estate	66.67%	12.08%	33.33%	4.80%	9.65%
Disney	**81.99%**	**13.85%**	**18.01%**	**4.80%**	**12.22%**
Bookscape	**84.60%**	**13.05%**	**15.40%**	**4.64%**	**11.75%**
Aracruz	**56.83%**	**10.33%**	**43.17%**	**3.74%**	**7.48%**
Commercial Banks	36.28%	12.45%	63.72%	4.24%	7.22%
Investment Banks	36.28%	14.65%	63.72%	4.24%	8.01%
Deutsche Bank	**36.28%**	**12.67%**	**63.72%**	**4.24%**	**7.30%**

These are the appropriate hurdle rates to use in analyzing projects in each of these companies, and within each company, in each division. Thus, a Disney movie project (which falls in the creative content category) would need to make a return on total investment of at least 13.07% to be value creating; alternatively, it would need to make a return on equity of at least 14.80%.

CONCLUSION

This chapter explains the process of estimating discount rates by relating them to the risk and return models described in the previous chapter:

- The cost of equity can be estimated using risk and return models—the capital asset pricing model (CAPM), where risk is measured relative to a single market factor; the arbitrage pricing model (APM), where the cost of equity is determined by the sensitivity to multiple unspecified economic factors; or a multiple factor model, where sensitivity to macroeconomic variables is used to measure risk.
  - In both the CAPM & APM, the key inputs are the risk-free rate, the risk premiums, and the beta (in the CAPM) or betas (in the APM). The last of these inputs is usually estimated using historical data on prices; in the case of private firms, they might have to be estimated using comparable publicly traded firms.
  - While the betas are estimated using historical data, they are determined by the fundamental decisions that a firm makes on its business mix, its operating and financial leverage.

- The cost of capital is a weighted average of the costs of the different components of financing, with the weights based on the market values of each component. The cost of debt is the market rate at which the firm can borrow, adjusted for any tax advantages of borrowing. The cost of preferred stock, on the other hand, is the preferred dividend.

- The cost of capital is the minimum acceptable hurdle rate that will be used to determine whether to invest in a project.

PROBLEMS AND QUESTIONS

1. You have been asked to assess the nominal risk free rate to use in the capital asset pricing model for a Chilean company. Which of the following rates would come closest to what you would use?
   a. Rate on short-term U.S. dollar denominated Chilean Government bonds.
   b. Rate on long-term U.S. dollar denominated Chilean Government bonds.
   c. Rate on short-term Peso-denominated Chilean Government bonds.
   d. Long-term Real Growth Rate in the Chilean Economy.
   e. Rate at which the largest and safest Chilean companies can borrow long term in Pesos.

2. The following multiple choice questions relate to the question of risk perspectives in assessing risk.
   A. If you owned a private business and you were trying to sell it, and you had two competing bidders for it—another private business person and a publicly traded company, which one would you generally expect to win the bidding war?
      a. The private business person.
      b. The publicly traded company.
      c. Not enough information.
   B. Given that individuals are less diversified than the investors in publicly traded companies, what would need to be true for the private business person to attach a higher value to the business?
      a. The capacity to generate higher cash flows than if the business were publicly traded.
      b. Localized information that is available only to specialized investors and

not to companies (which may increase cash flows and reduce risk).
      c. Tax advantages from being a private business.
      d. All or any of the above.
   C. Venture capitalists have traditionally been focused on sectors and have not been diversified. Given your answers to the first two questions, how would you explain this?
      a. They do not have the resources to diversify.
      b. They need information that is specific to the sector to value businesses, and this information is difficult and costly to acquire (they cannot be in more than one sector).
      c. They like taking risk.
      d. They need to be involved in the management of these companies, and they cannot spread themselves too thin.
      e. All of the above.
   D. Recently, mutual funds and banks have started funds to do venture capital investing. In what types of firms do you think these funds will have the most advantage over traditional venture capitalists?
      a. Firms which require a lot of resources.
      b. Firms where the returns are highest.
      c. Firms where information is easily available and understandable, and which have good management in place.
   E. Assume again that you run a private business. Would you maximize the value of the business to you as an investor or the best potential bidder (who might be a publicly traded company)?

a. Value to me as a private investor.
b. Value to the best potential bidder.
c. Depends upon whether and when I plan to sell; if I plan to sell soon, I will use the best potential bidder's price; if not, I will use my own value.

F. Real estate is one asset class where investors have traditionally been specialized and not diversified. Given our discussion so far, how would you explain this?
  a. Real estate investors are smarter than other investors.
  b. Real estate investors have bigger egos than other investors.
  c. Real estate investments require more localized knowledge for valuation, and more hands-on management on the part of investors.

G. Building on real estate, how would you explain the growth of real estate investment trusts?
  a. Investors want to diversify into real estate.
  b. Real estate is a good value.
  c. REITs have tax advantages.
  d. Real estate value is being driven less by localized information and more by general information.

3. You have run a regression of returns of Nike against the S&P 500 Index **using monthly returns** over the last 5 years, and arrived at the following regression:

$Return_{Nike} = 0.22\% + 1.20\ Return_{S\&P\ 500}$
$R\ squared = 15\%$ (0.38)

The standard error of the beta is in brackets below the beta.

a. Provide a confidence interval (range) for the beta, with 67% confidence.
b. If the treasury bond rate today is 6%, estimate the expected return for Nike.
c. Now assume that you are an investor interested in buying stock in Nike. The current stock price is $45 and you expect it to increase to $75 in five years. Assume that the stock does not pay dividends. Is this stock a good investment?

d. Now assume that Nike is considering a project in its existing business line (athletic shoes) that is expected to earn a return on equity of 14.5%. Should Nike take this project?
e. If the annualized riskfree rate during the last 5 years was 4.8%, evaluate whether Nike did better or worse than expected during that period, and measure the performance.
f. If you were an undiversified investor who buys stock in Nike, what percentage of the risk that you take on will not be rewarded?

4. You have been asked to estimate the beta for a large South Korean company, with large holdings in steel and financial services. A regression of stock returns against the local market index yields a beta of 1.10, but the firm is 15% of the index. You have collected the average betas for global companies in each of the sectors, as well as the average debt equity ratios in each sector:

Sector	Average Beta	Average D/E ratio
Steel	1.18	30%
Financial Services	1.14	70%

(The average tax rate for these firms is 40%) In the most recent period, the company you are analyzing earned 70% of its operating income from steel and 30% from financial services. The firm also had a debt/equity ratio of 150%, and a tax rate of 30%.
a. Estimate the beta for the company.
b. If the long-term government bond rate in nominal Won (the Korean currency) is 12%, Korea's rating is BBB (Corporate bonds with this rating earn a spread of 2% over the U.S. long bond rate), estimate the cost of equity for this company in nominal Won.
c. If the U.S. treasury bond rate is 6%, estimate the cost of equity for this company in U.S. dollars.

5. You have run a regression of returns of Devonex, a machine tool manufacturer, against the S&P 500 Index using monthly returns over the last 5 years and arrived at the following regression:

$$\text{Return}_{\text{Devonex}} = -0.20\% + 1.50 \ \text{Return}_{\text{S\&P 500}}$$

If the stock had a Jensen's alpha of +0.10% (on a monthly basis) over this period, estimate the monthly riskfree rate during the last 5 years.

6. You have been asked to analyze GenCorp, a corporation with food and tobacco subsidiaries. The tobacco subsidiary is estimated to be worth $15 billion and the food subsidiary is estimated to have a value of $10 billion. The firm has a debt to equity ratio of 1.00. You are provided with the following information on comparable firms:

Business	Average Beta	Average D/E Ratio
Food	0.92	25%
Tobacco	1.17	50%

All firms are assumed to have a tax rate of 40%. If the current long-term bond rate is 6%, estimate the current cost of equity of GenCorp.

7. Assume now that GenCorp divests itself of the food division for its estimated value of $10 billion.
   a. Estimate the beta for GenCorp if the cash is used to pay down debt.
   b. Estimate the beta for GenCorp if the cash is retained in the firm and invested in Government Securities.
   c. Estimate the beta for GenCorp if the cash if used to buy back stock.

8. You have run a regression on Multi-Brand Corporation, using monthly stock prices for the last 5 years and have estimated a beta of 0.90 for the company. The company had an average debt/equity ratio of 11.11% over these 5 years, but it has just borrowed $100 million and bought back $100 million worth of its stock. Prior to this transaction, it had $225 million in market value of equity and $25 million in debt outstanding. Estimate the beta that you would use for this company, looking forward. The company has a tax rate of 40%.

9. SunCoast, Inc. is a major appliance manufacturer and it is considering acquiring MF Capital, a corporation that provides financing for appliance buyers. At the time of the acquisition—

- SunCoast Inc. had debt outstanding of $100 million and 10 million shares trading at $50 per share. The beta for the stock is 1.2.
- MF Capital had debt outstanding of $100 million and 5 million shares trading at $10 per share. The beta for the stock is 0.9.

SunCoast plans to do a stock swap offering 1 million of its shares for all of MF Capital's outstanding stock. Estimate the beta for SunCoast Inc. after the acquisition. The company has a tax rate of 40%.

10. You have been asked to assess the implied risk premium on the Timbuktu Stock Exchange (TSE). The index is trading at 1050, and the dividend yield is 3%. The current long term bond rate is 6.5%, and the expected long term nominal growth rate in the economy is 6%. Estimate the implied risk premium for equities.

11. In December 1995, Boise Cascade's stock had a beta of 0.95. The Treasury bill rate at the time was 5.8%, and the Treasury bond rate was 6.4%.
    a. Estimate the expected return on the stock for a short-term investor in the company.
    b. Estimate the expected return on the stock for a long-term investor in the company.
    c. Estimate the cost of equity for the company.

12. Boise Cascade also had debt outstanding of $1.7 billion and a market value of equity of $1.5 billion; the corporate marginal tax rate was 36%.
    a. Assuming that the current beta of 0.95 for the stock is a reasonable one, estimate the unlevered beta for the company.
    b. How much of the risk in the company can be attributed to business risk and how much to financial leverage risk?

13. A biotechnology firm, Biogen Inc., had a beta of 1.70 in 1995. It had no debt outstanding at the end of that year.
    a. Estimate the cost of equity for Biogen, if the Treasury bond rate is 6.4%.
    b. What effect will an increase in long-term bond rates to 7.5% have on Biogen's cost of equity?
    c. How much of Biogen's beta can be attributed to business risk?

14. Genting Berhad is a Malaysian conglomerate, with holdings in plantations and tourist resorts.

The beta estimated for the firm, relative to the Malaysian stock exchange, is 1.15, and the long-term government borrowing rate in Malaysia is 11.5%.

a. Estimate the expected return on the stock.

b. If you were an international investor, what concerns, if any, would you have about using the beta estimated relative to the Malaysian Index? If you have concerns, how would you modify the beta?

15. You have just done a regression of monthly stock returns of HeavyTec Inc., a manufacturer of heavy machinery, on monthly market returns over the last five years and come up with the following regression:

$$R_{HeavyTech} = 0.5\% + 1.2\,R_M$$

The variance of the stock is 50%, and the variance of the market is 20%. The current Treasury bill rate is 3% (it was 5% one year ago). The stock is currently selling for $50, down $4 over the last year, and it has paid a dividend of $2 during the last year and expects to pay a dividend of $2.50 over the next year. The NYSE composite has gone down 8% over the last year, with a dividend yield of 3%. HeavyTech Inc. has a tax rate of 40%.

a. What is the expected return on HeavyTech over the next year?

b. What would you expect Heavy Tech's price to be one year from today?

c. What would you have expected HeavyTech's stock returns to be over the last year?

d. What were the actual returns on HeavyTech over the last year?

e. HeavyTech has $100 million in equity and $50 million in debt. It plans to issue $50 million in new equity and to retire $50 million in debt. Estimate the new beta.

16. Safecorp, which owns and operates grocery stores across the United States, currently has $50 million in debt and $100 million in equity outstanding. Its stock has a beta of 1.2. It is planning a leveraged buyout (LBO) whereby it will increase its debt/equity ratio to 8. If the tax rate is 40%, what will the beta of the equity in the firm be after the LBO?

17. Novell, which had a market value of equity of $2 billion and a beta of 1.50, announced that it was acquiring WordPerfect, which had a market value of equity of $1 billion, and a beta of 1.30. Neither firm had any debt in its financial structure at the time of the acquisition, and the corporate tax rate was 40%.

a. Estimate the beta for Novell after the acquisition, assuming that the entire acquisition was financed with equity.

b. Assume that Novell had to borrow the $1 billion to acquire WordPerfect. Estimate the beta after the acquisition.

18. You are analyzing the beta for Hewlett-Packard and have broken down the company into four broad business groups, with market values and betas for each group. (Corporate tax rate is 36%)

Business Group	Market Value of Equity	Beta
Mainframes	$2 billion	1.10
Personal Computers	2 billion	1.50
Software	1 billion	2.00
Printers	3 billion	1.00

a. Estimate the beta for Hewlett-Packard as a company. Is this beta going to be equal to the beta estimated by regressing past returns on HP stock against a market index. Why or why not?

b. If the Treasury bond rate is 7.5%, estimate the cost of equity for Hewlett-Packard. Estimate the cost of equity for each division. Which cost of equity would you use to value the printer division?

c. Assume that HP divests itself of the mainframe business and pays the cash out as a dividend. Estimate the beta for HP after the divestiture. (HP had $1 billion in debt outstanding.)

19. The accompanying table summarizes the percentage changes in operating income, percentage changes in revenue, and betas for four pharmaceutical firms.

Firm	% Change in Revenue	% Change in Operating Income	Beta
PharmaCorp	27	25	1.00
SynerCorp	25	32	1.15
BioMed	23	36	1.30
Safemed	21	40	1.40

   a. Calculate the degree of operating leverage for each of these firms.

   b. Use the operating leverage to explain why these firms have different betas.

20. A prominent beta estimation service reports the beta of Comcast Corporation, a major cable TV operator, to be 1.45. The service claims to use weekly returns on the stock over the prior five years and the NYSE composite as the market index to estimate betas. You replicate the regression using weekly returns over the same period and arrive at a beta estimate of 1.60. How would you reconcile the two estimates?

21. Battle Mountain is a mining company, that mines gold, silver and copper in mines in South America, Africa, and Australia. The beta for the stock is estimated to be 0.30. Given the volatility in commodity prices, how would you explain the low beta?

22. You have collected returns on AnaDone Corporation (AD Corp.), a large diversified manufacturing firm, and the NYSE index for five years:

Year	AD Corp.	NYSE
1981	10%	5%
1982	5%	15%
1983	−5%	8%
1984	20%	12%
1985	−5%	−5%

   a. Estimate the intercept (alpha) and slope (beta) of the regression.

   b. If you bought stock in AD Corp. today, how much would you expect to make as a return over the next year? [The six-month Treasury bill rate is 6%.]

   c. Looking back over the last five years, how would you evaluate AD's performance relative to the market? (The average risk-free rate during the period was 5%.)

   d. Assume now that you are an undiversified investor and that you have all of your money invested in AD Corporation. What would be a good measure of the risk that you are taking on? How much of this risk would you be able to eliminate if you *diversify?*

   e. AD is planning to sell off one of its divisions. The division under consideration has assets that comprise half of the book value of AD Corporation, and 20% of the market value. Its beta is twice the average beta for AD Corp. (before divestment). What will the beta of AD Corporation be after divesting this division?

23. You run a regression of monthly returns of Mapco Inc, an oil and gas producing firm, on the S&P 500 index and come up with the following output for the period 1991 to 1995:

Intercept of the regression = 0.06%
X-coefficient of the regression = 0.46
Standard error of X-coefficient = 0.20
R-squared = 5%

There are 20 million shares outstanding, and the current market price is $2. The firm has $20 million in debt outstanding. (The firm has a tax rate of 36%.)

   a. What would an investor in Mapco's stock require as a return, if the Treasury bond rate is 6%?

   b. What proportion of this firm's risk is diversifiable?

   c. Assume now that Mapco has three divisions of equal size (in market value terms). It plans to divest itself of one of the divisions for $20 million in cash and acquire another for $50 million (it will borrow $30 million to complete this acquisition). The division it is divesting is in a business line in which the average unlevered beta is 0.20, and the division it is acquiring is in a business line in which the average unlevered beta is 0.80. What will the beta of Mapco be after this acquisition?

24. You have just run a regression of monthly returns of American Airlines (AMR) against the S&P

500 over the last five years. You have misplaced some of the output and are trying to derive it from what you have.

a. You know the R-squared of the regression is 0.36 and that your stock has a variance of 67%. The market variance is 12%. What is the beta of AMR?

b. You also remember that AMR was not a very good investment during the period of the regression and that it did worse than expected (after adjusting for risk) by 0.39% a month for the five years of the regression. During this period, the average risk-free rate was 4.84%. What was the intercept on the regression?

c. You are comparing AMR Inc. to another firm that also has an R-squared of 0.36. Will the two firms have the same beta? If not, why not?

25. You have run a regression of *monthly* returns on Amgen, a large biotechnology firm, against *monthly* returns on the S&P 500 index, and come up with the following output:

$$R_{stock} = 3.28\% + 1.65 \, R_{Market} \quad R^2 = 0.20$$

The current one-year Treasury bill rate is 4.8%, and the current 30-year bond rate is 6.4%. The firm has 265 million shares outstanding, selling for $30 per share.

a. What is the expected return on this stock over the next year?

b. Would your expected return estimate change if the purpose was to get a discount rate to analyze a 30-year capital budgeting project?

c. An analyst has estimated, correctly, that the stock did 51.10% better than expected, annually, during the period of the regression. Can you estimate the annualized risk-free rate that she used for her estimate?

d. The firm has a debt/equity ratio of 3% and faces a tax rate of 40%. It is planning to issue $2 billion in new debt and to acquire a new business for that amount, with the same risk level as the firm's existing business. What will the beta be after the acquisition?

26. You have just run a regression of monthly returns on MAD Inc., a newspaper and magazine publisher, against returns on the S&P 500 and arrived at the following result:

$$R_{MAD} = 0.05\% + 1.20 \, R_{S\&P}$$

The regression has an R-squared of 22%. The current Treasury bill rate is 5.5%, and the current Treasury bond rate is 6.5%. The risk-free rate during the period of the regression was 6%. Answer the following questions relating to the regression.

a. Based on the intercept, you can conclude that the stock did
0.05% worse than expected on a monthly basis during the regression.
0.05% better than expected on a monthly basis during the period of the regression
1.25% better than expected on a monthly basis during the period of the regression.
1.25% worse than expected on a monthly basis during the period of the regression.
None of the above.

b. You now realize that MAD Inc. went through a major restructuring at the end of last month (which was the last month of your regression) and made the following changes:
- The firm sold off its magazine division, which had an unlevered beta of 0.6, for $20 million.
- It borrowed an additional $20 million and bought back stock worth $40 million.

After the sale of the division and the share repurchase, MAD Inc. had $40 million in debt and $120 million in equity outstanding.

If the firm's tax rate is 40%, reestimate the beta, after these changes.

27. Time Warner Inc., the entertainment conglomerate, has a beta of 1.61. Part of the reason for the high beta is the debt left over from the leveraged buyout of Time by Warner in 1989, which amounted to $10 billion in 1995. The market value of equity at Time Warner in 1995 was also $10 billion. The marginal tax rate was 40%.

a. Estimate the unlevered beta for Time Warner.

b. Estimate the effect of reducing the debt ratio by 10% each year for the next two years on the beta of the stock.

28. Chrysler, the automotive manufacturer, had a beta of 1.05 in 1995. It had $13 billion in debt outstanding in that year, and 355 million shares trading at $50 per share. The firm had a cash balance of $8 billion at the end of 1995. The marginal tax rate was 36%.

    a. Estimate the unlevered beta of the firm.

    b. Estimate the effect of paying out a special dividend of $5 billion on this unlevered beta.

    c. Estimate the beta for Chrysler after the special dividend.

29. You are trying to estimate the beta of a private firm that manufactures home appliances. You have managed to obtain betas for publicly traded firms that also manufacture home appliances.

Firm	Beta	Debt	MV of Equity
Black & Decker	1.40	$2,500	$3,000
Fedders Corp.	1.20	5	200
Maytag Corp.	1.20	540	2,250
National Presto	0.70	8	300
Whirlpool	1.50	2,900	4,000

The private firm has a debt equity ratio of 25% and faces a tax rate of 40%. The publicly traded firms all have marginal tax rates of 40% as well.

    a. Estimate the beta for the private firm.

    b. What concerns, if any, would you have about using betas of comparable firms?

30. As the result of stockholder pressure, RJR Nabisco is considering spinning off its food division. You have been asked to estimate the beta for the division, and decide to do so by obtaining the beta of comparable publicly traded firms. The average beta of comparable publicly traded firms is 0.95, and the average debt/equity ratio of these firms is 35%. The division is expected to have a debt equity of 25%. The marginal corporate tax rate is 36%.

    a. What is the beta for the division?

    b. Would it make any difference if you knew that RJR Nabisco had a much higher fixed cost structure than the comparable firms used here?

31. Southwestern Bell, a phone company, is considering expanding its operations into the media business. The beta for the company at the end of 1995 was 0.90, and the debt/equity ratio was 1. The media business is expected to be 30% of the overall firm value in 1999, and the average beta of comparable media firms is 1.20; the average debt/equity ratio for these firms is 50%. The marginal corporate tax rate is 35%.

    a. Estimate the beta for Southwestern Bell in 1999, assuming that it maintains its current debt/equity ratio.

    b. Estimate the beta for Southwestern Bell in 1999, assuming that it decides to finance its media operations with a debt/equity ratio of 50%.

32. The chief financial officer of Adobe Systems, a growing software manufacturing firm, has approached you for some advice regarding the beta of his company. He subscribes to a service that estimates Adobe System's beta each year, and he has noticed that the beta estimates have gone down every year since 1991—2.35 in 1991 to 1.40 in 1995. He would like the answers to the following questions:

    a. Is this decline in beta unusual for a growing firm?

    b. Why would the beta decline over time?

    c. Is the beta likely to keep decreasing over time?

33. You are analyzing Tiffany's, an upscale retailer, and find that the regression estimate of the firm's beta is 0.75; the standard error for the beta estimate is 0.50. You also note that the average unlevered beta of comparable specialty retailing firms is 1.15.

    a. If Tiffany's has a debt/equity ratio of 20%, estimate the beta for the company based on comparable firms. (The tax rate is 40%.)

    b. Estimate a range for the beta from the regression.

    c. How would you reconcile the two estimates? Which one would you use in your analysis?

34. In looking over the valuation of an Indonesian company, you notice that the valuation has been done in nominal U.S. dollars, and that the discount rate has been estimated using the dollar-denominated bonds issued by the Indonesian Government (which were trading at a yield of 9%, when the U.S. treasury bond rate was 6%) and a higher risk premium to reflect the additional risk of the Indonesian market (a premium of 8.5% was used instead of the U.S. premium of 5.5%).

a. Do you think that the discount rate has been estimated properly? If not, what would you do differently?

b. Given this process of estimating discount rates, what currency should the cash flows to the company be estimated in? Should there be expected inflation built in these cash flows?

35. In estimating risk premiums in the United States, we often use historical risk premiums - i.e., the excess return made investing in stocks as opposed to treasury bonds or bills. What are the implicit assumptions we are making about risk aversion of investors and the "average" risk investment, when we do this?

36. Now consider using the historical risk premium appoach to come up with risk premiums for the equity market in Thailand. What are some of the problems that you are likely to face in applying this approach?

37. When estimating real costs of equity, we have to use real riskfree rates. Answer the following questions relating to a real riskfree rate:

a. Why would real riskfree rates be different from nominal riskfree rates?

b. If your nominal riskfree rate was 7% and expected inflation was 3%, estimate the real riskfree rate.

c. Why might you want to do an analysis in real terms rather than nominal terms?

38. You have been asked to estimate the cost of equity for a private computer software company. You have collected data on publicly traded computer software firms, and arrived at an average beta of 1.40 for these firms; the average market debt-equity ratio at these firms is 15%. The average R-squared of these firms is 25%. The tax rate for all firms is assumed to be 40%.

a. Estimate the beta for the private computer firm, assuming that it has no debt.

b. How would your estimate change if the firm decided to move to the industry average debt/equity ratio?

c. Assuming that your firm had debt on its books, and a book value of equity, would you use this book debt/equity ratio to estimate the beta? Why or why not?

d. If the owner of this private business has all his wealth invested in the business, and has no plans to sell the firm or take it public, would your analysis be any different?

e. Would your answer change if the owner told you that he plans to take the firm public next year?

39. You have been asked to estimate the cost of capital for Allstate Insurance company and have been provided with the following information on the firm:

• The beta of the stock is 1.20, based upon a regression of Allstate stock returns against the S&P 500 Index.

• The share price is $ 93 and there are 430 million shares outstanding. The firm also has $ 2.5 billion in debt outstanding. (In book and market terms)

• The firm is rated AAA by the ratings agencies, and the default spread for AAA bonds is 0.20% over the treasury bond rate.

• The treasury bond rate is 6%.

a. Estimate the cost of equity for Allstate.

b. Estimate the cost of capital for Allstate.

c. Would your answer be any different if you were told that Allstate had no debt during the entire regression period (for the beta estimate above)?

40. You are trying to estimate the cost of debt for Food World, a privately owned grocery store. The store has no rating, but it does provide you with the following information:

• The debt on its books is three years old, and has a face value of $ 5 million and was originally borrowed at a rate of 10%.

• The store made earnings before interest and taxes of $ 3.5 million in the most recent year.

- The following table summarizes the relationship between interest coverage ratios, ratings and spreads over the long term bond rate for the most recent period.

Interest Coverage Ratio	Rating	Spread over T-Bond Rate
>12.5	AAA	0.20%
9.50 – 12.50	AA	0.50%
7.5 – 9.5	A+	0.80%
6.0 – 7.5	A	1.00%
4.5 – 6.0	A–	1.25%
3.5 – 4.5	BBB	1.50%
3.0 – 3.5	BB	2.00%
2.5 – 3.0	B+	2.50%
2.0 – 2.5	B	3.25%
1.5 – 2.0	B–	4.25%
1.25 – 1.5	CCC	5.00%
0.8 – 1.25	CC	6.00%
0.5 – 0.8	C	7.50%
<0.5	D	10.00%

- The firm faces a tax rate of 42% on its income.
- The treasury bond rate today is 6%. (It was 8% three years ago.)
  a. Use the ratings table to come up with a cost of debt for this firm.
  b. Why is this cost of debt different from the interest rate paid on the debt on the books.
  c. Under what conditions might you use the interest rate on the debt that is on the books as a cost of debt.

41. You have just done a regression of Sybase returns on the S&P 500 index, and arrived at a beta estimate of 1.10, with a standard error of 0.5. Looking at 25 comparable firms, however, you come up with an average beta of 1.50 and an average debt/equity ratio of 10%. Sybase has no debt outstanding.
  a. What beta estimate would you use for Sybase and why?
  b. If the treasury bond rate is 6%, what is your estimate of the cost of equity?
  c. An analyst who uses the CAPM to come up with a cost of equity for Sybase argues that the risk premium used in the model (which is multiplied by the beta) should be higher because Sybase is a risky firm. How would you respond?

42. In an analysis of Archer Daniels Midland, you notice that the beta estimate for the firm is 0.85, and that the firm has $ 3.4 billion in debt on its books. The interest expense on the debt in the most recent year was $ 225 million, and the average maturity of the debt is 4 years. The firm has 532 million shares outstanding at a market price of $ 22 per share; the shareholders equity on the books is $ 6.05 billion. The firm is rated AA, and AA rated bonds are trading at a spread of 0.70% over the long term treasury bond rate. The treasury bond rate today is 6%.
  a. Estimate the cost of capital, using book value debt and equity ratios.
  b. Estimate the cost of capital, using market value debt and equity ratios.
  c. Under what conditions will the first approach give you a higher cost of capital?

——————LIVE CASE STUDY

III. RISK AND RETURN

Objective: To develop a risk profile for your company, estimate its risk parameters and use these parameters to estimate costs of equity and capital for the firm.

Key
Questions

- What is the risk profile of your company? (How much overall risk is there in this firm? Where is this risk coming from (market, firm, industry or currency)? How is the risk profile changing?)

- What is the performance profile of an investment in this company? What return would you have earned investing in this company's stock? Would you have under or outperformed the market? How much of the performance can be attributed to management?

- How risky is this company's equity? Why? What is its cost of equity?

- How risky is this company's debt? What is its cost of debt?

- What is this company's current cost of capital?

Framework
for Analysis

1. Estimating Historical Risk Parameters (Top Down Betas)

Run a regression of returns on your firm's stock against returns on a market index, preferably using monthly data and 5 years of observations (or)

If you have access to Bloomberg, go into the beta calculation page and print out the page (after setting return intervals to monthly and using 5 years of data)

- What is the intercept of the regression? What does it tell you about the performance of this company's stock during the period of the regression?

- What is the slope of the regression?
  - What does it tell you about the risk of the stock?
  - How precise is this estimate of risk? (Provide a range for the estimate.)

- What portion of this firm's risk can be attributed to market factors? What portion to firm-specific factors? Why is this important?

- How much of the "risk" for this firm is due to business factors? How much of it is due to financial leverage?

2. Comparing to Sector Betas (Bottom Up Betas)
- Break down your firm by business components, and estimate a business beta for each component.
- Attach reasonable weights to each component and estimate an unlevered beta for the business.

- Using the current leverage of the company, estimate a levered beta for each component.

3. Choosing Between Betas

- Which of the betas that you have estimated for the firm (top down or bottom up) would you view as more reliable? Why?
- Using the beta that you have chosen, estimate the expected return on an equity investment in this company to
  - a short-term investor
  - a long-term investor
- As a manager in this firm, how would you use this expected return?

4. Estimating Default Risk and Cost of Debt

- If your company is rated,
  - What is the most recent rating for the firm?
  - What is the default spread and interest rate associated with this rating?
  - If your company has bonds outstanding, estimate the yield to maturity on a long-term bond? Why might this be different from the rate estimated in the last step?
  - What is the company's marginal tax rate?
- If your company is not rated,
  - Does it have any recent borrowings? If yes, what interest rate did the company pay on these borrowings?
  - Can you estimate a "synthetic" rating? If yes, what interest rate would correspond to this rating?

5. Estimating Cost of Capital

- Weights for Debt and Equity
  - What is the market value of equity?
  - Estimate a market value for debt. (To do this you might have to collect information on the average maturity of the debt, the interest expenses in the most recent period and the book value of the debt.)
  - What are the weights of debt and equity?
- *Cost of Capital*
- What is the cost of capital for the firm?

 Getting Information on Risk and Return

To get an extensive risk profile of your firm, visit the web site maintained by riskview.com (**www.riskview.com**). You can also get a 3-year monthly beta from the daily stocks web site (**www.dailystocks.com**—valuation, growth ratios).

You can get unlevered betas by industry in the data set on my web page (indbetas.xls). To get the breakdown of operating income and revenue by business sector, you might want to check the annual report (**www.reportgallery.com**) and the 10-K report (**www.sec.gov/edgarhp.htm**). The market value of equity and the inputs needed for estimating the market value of debt should be available in the same sources. (The maturity of the debt should be listed as a footnote to the balance sheet in the 10-K report.)

To find the rating for your company, you can check the handbook on ratings (available in most libraries) issued by Standard and Poor's. You can also e-mail a ratings request to Standard and Poor's at **ratings.standardpoor.com/ratings.** To get the spreads that go with the ratings, you can use the data set (**ratings.xls**) on my web page that lists the default spreads (over the long-term treasury bond rate) for each ratings class. If you want to estimate a synthetic rating, you should examine the table on my web site that lists ratings as a function of interest coverage ratios on my web site (**ratings.xls**)

If you have price and dividend data on your firm, on a monthly basis, for up to 5 years, you can use the excel spread sheet on my web site called **risk.xls** to run to regression and get the beta, alpha, and R-squared for your firm.

CHAPTER 5

MEASURING RETURN ON INVESTMENTS

In Chapter 4, we developed a process for estimating costs of equity, debt, and capital and presented an argument that the cost of capital is the minimum acceptable hurdle rate. We also argued that a project has to earn a return greater than this hurdle rate to create value to the owners of a business. In this chapter, we turn to the question of how best to measure the return on a project. In doing so, we will attempt to answer the following questions:

- What is a project? In particular, how general is the definition of an investment and what are the different types of investment decisions that firms have to make?

- In measuring the return on a project, should we look at the cash flows generated by the project or at the accounting earnings?

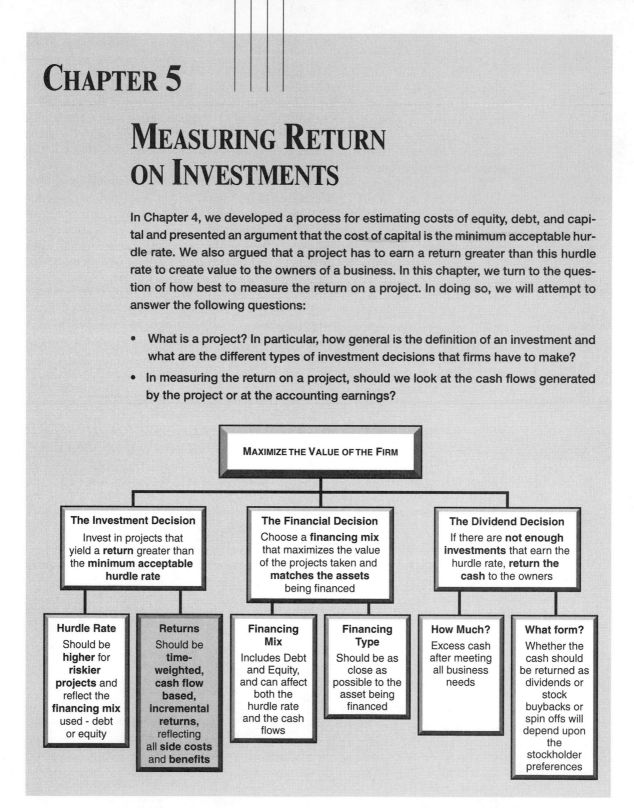

> - If the returns on a project are unevenly spread over time, how do we consider (or should we not consider) differences in returns across time?
>
> We will illustrate the basics of investment analysis using three hypothetical projects—an on-line book ordering service for Bookscape Books, a new theme park in Thailand for Disney, and a plant to manufacture linerboard for Aracruz Cellulose.

WHAT IS A PROJECT?

Investment analysis concerns which projects to accept and which to reject; accordingly, the question of what comprises a "project" is central to this and the following chapters. The conventional project analyzed in capital budgeting has three criteria: (1) a large up-front cost, (2) cash flows for a specific time period, and (3) a salvage value at the end, which captures the value of the assets of the project when the project ends. While such projects undoubtedly form a significant proportion of investment decisions, especially for manufacturing firms, it would be a mistake to assume that investment decision analysis stops there. If a project is defined more broadly to include any decision that results in using the scarce resources of a business, then everything from strategic decisions and acquisitions to decisions about which air conditioning system to use in a building would fall within its reach.

Salvage Value: This is the estimated liquidation value of the assets invested in the project at the end of the project's life.

Defined broadly then, any of the following decisions would qualify as projects:

1. Major strategic decisions to enter new areas of business (such as Disney's foray into real estate or Deutsche Bank's into investment banking) or new markets (such as Disney television's expansion into Latin America).
2. Acquisitions of other firms (such as Disney's acquisition of Capital Cities or Deutsche Bank's acquisition of Morgan Grenfell).
3. Decisions on new ventures within existing businesses or markets, such as the one made by Disney to expand its Orlando theme park to include an Animal Kingdom or the decision to produce a new animated children's movie.
4. Decisions that may change the way existing ventures and projects are run, such as decisions on programming schedules on the Disney channel or changing inventory policy at Bookscape.
5. Decisions on how best to deliver a service that is necessary for the business to run smoothly. A good example would be Deutsche Bank's decision on what type of financial information system to acquire to allow traders and investment bankers to do their jobs. While the information system itself might not deliver revenues and profits, it is an indispensable component for other revenue-generating projects.

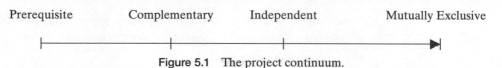

Figure 5.1   The project continuum.

Investment decisions can be categorized on a number of different dimensions. The first relates to how the project affects other projects the firm is considering and analyzing. While some projects are independent of other projects, and thus can be analyzed separately, other projects are mutually exclusive (i.e., taking one project will mean rejecting other projects). At the other extreme, some projects are prerequisites for other projects down the road. In general, projects can be categorized as falling somewhere on the continuum between prerequisites and mutually exclusive, as depicted in Figure 5.1.

Mutually Exclusive Projects: A group of projects is said to be mutually exclusive when acceptance of one of the projects implies that the rest have to be rejected.

The second dimension that can be used to classify decisions is the ability of the project to generate revenues or reduce costs. The decision rules that analyze revenue-generating projects attempt to evaluate whether the earnings or cash flows from the projects justify the investment needed to implement them. When it comes to cost-reduction projects, the decision rules examine whether the reduction in costs justifies the up-front investment needed for the projects.

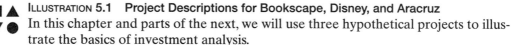

ILLUSTRATION 5.1   **Project Descriptions for Bookscape, Disney, and Aracruz**
In this chapter and parts of the next, we will use three hypothetical projects to illustrate the basics of investment analysis.

1. The first project we will look at is a proposal by Bookscape to add an on-line book ordering and information service. While the impetus for this proposal comes from the success of on-line book stores like Amazon, this on-line service will be more focused on helping customers research books and find the ones they need, rather than on price. Thus, if Bookscape decides to add this service, it will have to hire and train two well-qualified individuals to answer customer queries, in addition to investing in the computer equipment and phone lines that the service will require. This project analysis will help illustrate some of the issues that come up when private businesses look at investments and also when businesses take on projects that have a different risk profile from their existing business.

2. The second project we will analyze is a proposed theme park for Disney in Bangkok, Thailand. Bangkok Disneyworld, which will be patterned on Euro Disney in Paris and Disney World in Florida, will require a huge investment in infrastructure and take several years to complete. This project analysis will bring several issues to the forefront, including questions of how to deal with projects when the cash flows are in a foreign currency and what to do when projects have very long lives.

3. The third project we will consider is a plant in Brazil to manufacture linerboard for Aracruz Cellulose. Linerboard is a stiffened paper product that can be trans-

formed into cardboard boxes. This investment is a more conventional one, with an initial investment, a fixed lifetime, and a salvage value at the end. We will, however, do the analysis for this project from an equity standpoint to illustrate the generality of investment analysis. In addition, in light of concerns about inflation, we will do the analysis entirely in real terms.

MEASURING RETURNS: THE CHOICES

On all of the investment decisions described above, we have to choose between alternative approaches to measuring returns on the investment made. We will present our argument for return measurement in three steps. First, we will contrast accounting earnings and cash flows, and argue that cash flows are much better measures of true return on an investment. Second, we will note the differences between total cash flows and incremental cash flows and present the case for using incremental cash flows in measuring returns. Finally, we will argue that returns that occur earlier in a project life should be weighted more than returns that occur later in a project life, and that the return on an investment should be measured using time-weighted cashflows.

A. Accounting Earnings versus Cash Flows

The first and most basic choice we have to make when it comes to measuring returns is the one between the accounting measure of income on a project (measured in accounting statements, using accounting principles and standards) and the cash flow generated by a project (measured as the difference between the cash inflows in each period and the cash outflows).

Accountants have invested substantial time and resources in coming up with ways of measuring the income made by a project. In doing so, they subscribe to some generally accepted accounting principles (GAAP). Generally accepted accounting principles require the recognition of revenues when the service for which the firm is getting paid has been performed in full or substantially, and has received in return either cash or a receivable that is both observable and measurable. For expenses which are directly linked to the production of revenues (like labor and materials), expenses are recognized in the same period in which revenues are recognized. Any expenses which are not directly linked to the production of revenues are recognized in the period in which the firm consumes the services.

While the objective of distributing revenues and expenses fairly across time is a worthy one, the process of accrual accounting does create an accounting earnings number which can be very different from the cash flow generated by a project in any period. There are three significant factors that account for this difference.

1. Operating versus Capital Expenditure

Accountants draw a distinction between expenditures that yield benefits only in the immediate period or periods (such as labor and material for a manufacturing firm) and those that yield benefits over multiple periods (such as land, buildings, and long-lived plant). The former are called *operating expenses* and are subtracted from revenues in computing the accounting income, while the latter are *capital expenditures* and are not subtracted from revenues in the period that they are made. Instead, the expenditure is spread over multiple periods and deducted as an expense in each period—these expenses are called depreciation (if the asset is a tangible asset like a building) or amortization (if the asset is an intangible asset like a patent or a trademark).

While the capital expenditures made at the beginning of a project are often the largest and most prominent, many projects require capital expenditures during their lifetime. These capital expenditures will reduce the cash available in each of these periods.

5.1 WHAT ARE RESEARCH AND DEVELOPMENT EXPENSES?

Research and development expenses are generally considered to be operating expenses by accountants. Based upon our categorization of capital and operating expenses, would you consider research and development expenses to be

☐ operating expenses?

☐ capital expenses?

☐ either operating or capital expenses, depending upon the type of research being done?

Why?

2. Non-Cash Charges

The distinction that accountants draw between operating and capital expenses leads to a number of accounting expenses, such as depreciation and amortization, which are not cash expenses. These non-cash expenses, while depressing accounting income, do not reduce cash flows. In fact, they can have a significant positive impact on cash flows if they reduce the tax liability of the firm. Some non-cash charges reduce the taxable income and the taxes paid by a business. The most important of such charges is depreciation, which, while reducing taxable and net income, does not cause a cash outflow. Consequently, depreciation is added back to net income to arrive at the cash flows on a project.

For projects that generate large depreciation charges, a significant portion of the cash flows can be attributed to the tax benefits of depreciation, which can be written as follows:

$$\text{Tax Benefit of Depreciation} = \text{Depreciation} * \text{Marginal Tax Rate}$$

While depreciation is similar to other tax-deductible expenses in terms of the tax benefit it generates, its impact is more positive because it does not generate a con-current cash outflow.

Amortization is also a non-cash charge, but the tax effects of amortization can vary depending upon the nature of the amortization. Some amortizations, such as the amortization of the price paid for a patent or a trademark, are tax deductible and reduce both accounting income and taxes. Thus, they provide tax benefits similar to depreciation. Other amortizations, such as the amortization of the premium paid on an acquisition (called goodwill), reduces accounting income but not taxable income. This amortization does not provide a tax benefit.

While there are a number of different depreciation methods used by firms, they can be classified broadly into two groups. The first is *straight line depreciation,* whereby equal amounts of depreciation are claimed each period for the life of the project. The second group includes *accelerated depreciation methods* such as double-declining balance depreciation, which result in more depreciation early in the project life and less in the later years.

3. Accrual versus Cash Revenues and Expenses

The accrual system of accounting leads to revenues being recognized when the sale is made, rather than when the customer pays for the good or service. Consequently, accrual revenues may be very different from cash revenues for three reasons. First, some customers, who bought their goods and services in prior periods, may pay in this period; second, some customers who buy their goods and services in this period (and are therefore shown as part of revenues in this period) may defer payment until future periods. Finally, some customers who buy goods and services may never pay (bad debts). In some cases, customers may even pay in advance for products or services that will not be delivered until future periods.

A similar argument can be made on the expense side. Accrual expenses, relating to payments to third parties, will be different from cash expenses, because of payments made for materials and services acquired in prior periods and because some materials and services acquired in current periods will not be paid for until future periods. Accrual taxes will be different from cash taxes for exactly the same reasons.

When material is used to produce a product or deliver a service, there is an added consideration. Some of the material that is used may have been acquired in previous periods and was brought in as inventory into this period, and some of the material that is acquired in this period may be taken into the next period as inventory.

Accountants define net working capital as the difference between current assets (such as inventory and accounts receivable) and current liabilities (such as accounts payable and taxes payable). Differences between accrual earnings and cash earnings, in the absence of non-cash charges, can be captured by changes in the net working capital.

IN PRACTICE: THE PAYOFF TO MANAGING WORKING CAPITAL

Firms which are more efficient in managing their working capital will see a direct payoff in terms of cash flows. Efficiency in working capital management implies that the firm has reduced its net working capital needs without adversely affecting its expected growth in revenues and earnings. Broadly defined, there are four ways in which net working capital can be reduced:

1. While firms need to maintain an inventory to both produce goods and meet customer demand, minimizing this inventory while meeting these objectives can produce a lower net working capital. In fact, recent advances in technology which allow for just-in-time production have helped U.S. firms reduce their inventory needs significantly.

2. Firms which sell goods and services on credit can reduce their net working capital needs by inducing customers to pay their bills faster, and by improving their collection procedures.

3. Firms can also look for suppliers who offer more generous credit terms since accounts payable can be used to finance inventory and accounts receivable.

4. Firms which need cash for operational reasons can reduce their net working capital by keeping this cash balance to its minimum.

EQUITY LEVEL   Table 5.1   **ACCOUNTING EARNINGS VERSUS CASH FLOWS**

Accounting Earnings	Difference Is Due To	Cash Flow
Revenues	− Change in Inventory	Cash Revenues
− Operating Expenses	− Change in Accounts Receivable	− Cash Operating Expenses
− Depreciation & Amortization	+ Change in Accounts Payable	= Cash Operating Income
= Operating Income	+ Depreciation & Amortization	
Operating Income EBIT?	+ Change in Taxes Payable	Cash Operating Income
− Interest Expenses		− Interest Expenses
− Taxes		− Cash Taxes
= Net Income		= Cash Income
Net Income	− Change in Non-Cash Working Capital	Cash Income
	+ Depreciation & Amortization	− Capital Expenditures
	− Capital Expenditures	− Principal Repayment
	− Principal Repayments	+ New Debt Issues
	+ New Debt Issues	= FCFE

[where AR is accounts receivable, INV is inventory, AP is accounts payable, TP is taxes payable, and the subscripts refer to beginning balances (Beg) and ending balances (End)]

In Summary

The three factors outlined above can cause accounting earnings to deviate significantly from the cash flows. When doing investment analysis, we can estimate the returns purely from the perspective of just the equity investors (in which case the hurdle rate will be the cost of equity) or estimate returns to the entire capital base of the firm (in which case the hurdle rate is the cost of capital). In Table 5.1 we summarize the differences between accounting income and cash flows.

In fact, if we define net non-cash working capital as the difference between the sum of Accounts Receivable and Inventory on the one hand, and the sum of Accounts Payable and Taxes Payable on the other; the cash flow equation can be summarized as follows:

$$\text{Cash Flow to Equity (FCFE)} = \text{Net Income} + \text{Depreciation \& Amortization} -$$
$$\text{Change in Non-Cash Working Capital} - \text{Capital Expenditures} - \text{Principal}$$
$$\text{Repayments} + \text{New Debt Issues}$$

If the objective is to estimate the cash flows to all claimholders in the firm (and not just the equity investors), this analysis is done prior to interest expenses and principal repayments, as shown in Table 5.2. Using the notation for change in non-cash working capital, the cash flow to the firm can be estimated as follows:

$$\text{Cash Flow to Firm (FCFF)} = \text{EBIT}(1 - t) + \text{Depreciation \& Amortization} -$$
$$\text{Change in Non-Cash Working Capital} - \text{Capital Expenditures}$$

Table 5.2   OPERATING EARNINGS VERSUS CASH FLOW TO THE FIRM

Accounting Earnings	Difference Is Due To	Cash Flow
Revenues − Operating Expenses − Depreciation & Amortization = Operating Income	− [Change in Inventory + Change in Accounts Receivable − Change in Accounts Payable + Depreciation & Amortization	Cash Revenues − Cash Operating Expenses = Cash Operating Income
Operating Income *EBIT* − Taxes = After-tax Operating Income	Change in Taxes Payable	Cash Operating Income − Cash Taxes = After-tax Cash Operating Income
After-tax Operating Income *EBIT (1−t)*	+ Change in Non-Cash Working Capital + Depreciation & Amortization − Capital Expenditures	Cash Income − Capital Expenditures = FCFF

5.2 EARNINGS AND CASH FLOWS

If the earnings for a firm are positive, the cash flows will also be positive.

☐ True

☐ False

Why or why not?

IN PRACTICE: MANAGING EARNINGS

Companies, which have seen the effect on their stock prices of not meeting analyst expectations on earnings, have learned over the last decade to manage their earnings. Accounting standards, strict as they are for U.S. companies, still allow some leeway for firms to move earnings across periods by delaying revenues or expenses, or choosing a different accounting method. Companies like Microsoft not only work at holding down expectations on the part of analysts following them, but also use their growth and flexibility to move earnings across time to beat expectations. In January 1997, Microsoft reported earnings per share of 57 cents for the quarter, beating - consensus estimates of 51 cents per quarter, the 41st quarter out of 42 that Microsoft had beaten expectations.

The phenomenon of managing earnings has profound implications for a number of actions that firms may take, from how they sell their products and services, to what kinds of projects they take or firms they acquire and how they account for such investments. While Microsoft has not been guilty of accounting manipulation and has worked strictly within the rules of the game, other companies which have tried to replicate its success have had to resort to far more questionable methods to report earnings that beat expectations.

---

[1]The convention in capital budgeting and valuation is to estimate the taxes as if there were no interest expenses; the operating income is multiplied by the tax rate to arrive at taxes. The tax benefit from interest is reflected in the hurdle rate, through the after-tax cost of debt. If the cash flow is increased by the tax benefit from interest expenses, there will be a double counting of the same benefit.

The Case for Cash Flows

When earnings and cash flows are different, as they are for many projects, we must examine which one provides a more reliable measure of performance. We would argue that accounting earnings, especially at the equity level (net income), can be manipulated at least for individual periods, through the use of creative accounting techniques and strategic allocations. In a book entitled *Accounting for Growth,* which won national headlines in the United Kingdom and cost the author his job, Terry Smith, an analyst at UBS Phillips & Drew, examined 12 legal accounting techniques commonly used to mislead investors about the profitability of individual firms. To show how creative accounting techniques can increase reported profits, Smith highlighted such companies as Maxwell Communications and Polly Peck, both of which eventually succumbed to bankruptcy.

The second reason for using cash flow is a much more direct one. No business that we know off accepts earnings as payment for goods and services delivered; all of them require cash. Thus, a project with positive earnings and negative cash flows will drain cash from the business undertaking it. Conversely, a project with negative earnings and positive cash flows might make the accounting bottom line look worse, but will generate cash for the business undertaking it.

 ILLUSTRATION 5.2   Operating Earnings versus Cash Flows to Firm: Disney Corporation

The following table compares the operating income at Disney in 1996 with the cash flow to the firm, using the framework devised above:

ACCOUNTING EARNINGS		DIFFERENCE IS DUE TO		CASH FLOW	
Revenues	$18,739	− Change in Inventory	− 127	Cash Revenues:	$17,189
Operating Expenses	− $12,046	− Change in Accounts Receivable	− 1,550	− Cash Expenses:	$8,060
− Depreciation & Amortization	− $ 1,134	+ Change in Accounts Payable	+ 4,113	= Cash Oper. Income	$9,129
		+ Depreciation & Amortization	+ 1,134		
= Operating Income	= $ 5,559				
Operating Income	= $ 5,559	Changes in Taxes Payable	− 0	Cash Operating Income	$9,129
− Taxes	− $ 2,001			− Cash Taxes	$2,001
= EBIT (1−t)	= $ 3,558			= Cash OI after taxes	$7,128
EBIT (1−t)	= $ 3,558	−Change in Non-Cash WC	− (−2,436)	Cash Income	$7,128
		−Depreciation & Amortization	+ 1,134	−Capital Expenditures	$1,745
		−Capital Expenditures	− 1,745	−FCFF	$5,383

This cash flow to the firm can also be obtained using the change in non-cash working capital:

Cash Flow to Firm = EBIT(1 − t) + Depreciation & Amortization − Change in Non-Cash Working Capital − Capital Expenditures = $5,559 mil (1 − .36) + $1,134 mil − (−$2,436) − $1,745 mil = $5,383 million

The cash flow to the firm is significantly higher than the after-tax operating income because the working capital decreased (became more negative) by $2,436 million, which creates a cash inflow of an equivalent amount.

This cannot be sustained in the long term but they did come together in 1996 to create a surge in cash flows. This cash flow calculation does not reflect the acquisition of Capital Cities during the course of the year. If that investment of $18,500 million is added on to the capital expenditures, the cash flow to the firm changes dramatically:

$$\text{Cash Flow to Firm} = \text{EBIT}(1-t) + \text{Depreciation \& Amortization} - \text{Change in}$$
$$\text{Non-Cash Working Capital} - \text{Capital Expenditures} = \$\,3,024 \text{ mil}$$
$$+ \$3,944 \text{ mil} - (-\$2,436) - \$20,245 \text{ mil} = -\$12,084 \text{ million}$$

This negative cash flow is much more reflective of the true cash position at Disney, and the shortfall was covered by borrowing to acquire Capital Cities.

There is a dataset on the Web that summarizes, by sector, the differences between after-tax operating income and cash flows to the firm (**indoi.xls**).

B. Total versus Incremental Cash Flows

The objective in good investment analysis is to take investments that make the entire firm or business more valuable. Consequently, we will argue that the cash flows we should look at in investment analysis should be the cash flows that the projects add on to the business (i.e., incremental) and should be after taxes. The total and the incremental cash flows on a project may be different for many reasons, and we will examine some of them below.

1. Sunk Costs

There are some expenses related to a project that might be incurred before the project analysis is done. One example would be expenses associated with a test market done to assess the potential market for a product prior to conducting a full-blown investment analysis. Such expenses are called *sunk costs*. Since they will not be recovered if the project is rejected, sunk costs are not incremental and therefore should not be considered as part of the investment analysis. This contrasts with their treatment in accounting statements, which do not distinguish between expenses that have already been incurred and expenses that are still to be incurred.

One category of expenses that consistently falls into the sunk cost column in project analysis is research and development, which occurs well before a product is even considered for introduction. Firms that spend large amounts on research and development, such as Merck and Intel, have struggled to come to terms with the fact that the analysis of these expenses generally occurs after the fact, when little can be done about them.

---

[2]The convention in capital budgeting and valuation is to estimate the taxes as if there were no interest expenses; the operating income is multiplied by the tax rate to arrive at taxes. The tax benefit from interest is reflected in the hurdle rate, through the after-tax cost of debt. If the cash flow is increased by the tax benefit from interest expenses, there will be a double counting of the same benefit.

IN PRACTICE: WHO WILL PAY THE SUNK COSTS?

While sunk costs should not be treated as part of investment analysis, a firm does need to cover its sunk costs over time or it will cease to exist. Consider, for example, a firm like McDonald's, which expends considerable resources in test marketing products before introducing them. Assume, on the ill-fated McLean Deluxe (the low-fat hamburger introduced in 1990), that the test market expenses amounted to $30 million and that the net present value of the project, analyzed after the test market, amounted to $20 million. The project should be taken. If this is the pattern for every project McDonald's takes on, however, it will collapse under the weight of its test marketing expenses. To be successful, the *cumulated* net present value of its successful projects will have to exceed the *cumulated* test marketing expenses on both its successful and unsuccessful products.

2. Allocated Costs

An accounting device created to ensure that every part of a business bears its fair share of costs is *allocation,* whereby costs that are not directly traceable to revenues generated by individual products or divisions are allocated across these units, based upon revenues, profits, or assets. While the purposes of such allocations may be rational, their effects on investment analyses has to be viewed in terms of whether they create "incremental" cash flows. An allocated cost that will exist with or without the project being analyzed does not belong in the investment analysis.

Any increase in administrative or staff costs that can be traced to the project is an incremental cost and belongs in the analysis. One way to estimate the incremental component of these costs is to break them down on the basis of whether they are fixed or variable, and, if they are variable, what they are a function of. Thus, a portion of administrative costs may be related to revenue, and the revenue projections of a new project can be used to estimate the administrative costs to be assigned to it.

ILLUSTRATION 5.3 Dealing with Allocated Costs

Case 1: Assume that you are analyzing a project for a retail firm with general and administrative (G&A) costs currently of $600,000 a year. The firm currently has five stores, and the new project will create a sixth division. The G&A costs are allocated evenly across the stores; with five stores, the allocation to each store will be $120,000. The firm is considering opening a new store; with six stores, the allocation of G&A expenses to each store will be $100,000.

In this case, assigning a cost of $100,000 for general and administrative costs to the new store in the investment analysis would be a mistake, since it is not an incremental cost—the total G&A cost will be $600,000 whether or not the project is taken.

Case 2: In the analysis above, assume that all the facts remain unchanged except for one. The total general and administrative costs are expected to increase from $600,000 to $660,000 as a consequence of the new store. Each store is still allocated an equal amount; the new store will be allocated one-sixth of the total costs, or $110,000.

In this case, the allocated cost of $110,000 should not be considered in the investment analysis for the new store. The *incremental* cost of $60,000 [$660,000 − $600,000], however, should be considered as part of the analysis.

IN PRACTICE: WHO WILL PAY FOR HEADQUARTERS?

As in the case of sunk costs, the right thing to do in project analysis (i.e., considering only direct incremental costs) may not add up to create a firm that is financially healthy. Thus, if a company like Disney does not require individual movies that it analyzes to cover the allocated costs of general administrative expenses of the movie division, it is difficult to see how these costs will be covered at the level of the firm. Assuming that these general administrative costs serve a purpose, which otherwise would have to be borne by each movie, and that there is a positive relationship between the magnitude of these costs and the number of movies produced, it seems reasonable to argue that the firm should estimate a fixed charge for these costs that every new movie has to cover, even though this cost may not occur immediately or as a direct consequence of the new movie.

3. Product Cannibalization

Product cannibalization refers to the phenomenon whereby a new product introduced by a firm competes with and reduces sales of the firm's existing products. On one level, it can be argued that this is a negative incremental effect of the new product, and the lost cash flows or profits from the existing products should be treated as costs in analyzing whether or not to introduce the product. Doing so introduces the possibility that the new product will be rejected, however. If this happens, and a competitor now exploits the opening to introduce a product that fills the niche that the new product would have filled and consequently erodes the sales of the firm's existing products, the worst of all scenarios is created—the firm loses sales to a competitor rather than to itself.

Thus, the decision whether or not to build in the lost sales created by product cannibalization will depend on the potential for a competitor to introduce a close substitute to the new product being considered. Two extreme possibilities exist: The first is that close substitutes will be offered almost instantaneously by competitors; the second is that substitutes cannot be offered.

1. If the business in which the firm operates is extremely competitive and there are no barriers to entry, it can be assumed that product cannibalization will occur anyway, and the costs associated with it have no place in an incremental cash flow analysis. For example, in considering whether to introduce a new brand of cereal, a company like Kellogg's can reasonably ignore the expected product cannibalization that will occur because of the competitive nature of the cereal business and the ease with which Post or General Foods could introduce a close substitute. Similarly, it would not make sense for Compaq to consider the product cannibalization that will occur as a consequence of introducing a Pentium notebook PC since it can be reasonably assumed that a competitor, say IBM or Dell, would create the lost sales anyway with their versions of the same product if Compaq does not introduce the product.

2. If a competitor cannot introduce a substitute, because of legal restrictions such as patents, for example, the cash flows lost as a consequence of product cannibalization belong in the investment analysis, at least for the period of the patent

protection. For example, Glaxo, which owns the rights to Zantac, the top-selling ulcer drug, should consider the potential lost sales from introducing a new and maybe even better ulcer drug in deciding whether and when to introduce it to the market.

In most cases, there will be some barriers to entry, ensuring that a competitor will either introduce an imperfect substitute, leading to much smaller erosion in existing product sales, or that a competitor will not introduce a substitute for some period of time, leading to a much later erosion in existing product sales. In this case, an intermediate solution, whereby *some* of the product cannibalization costs are considered, may be appropriate. Note that brand name loyalty is one potential barrier to entry. Firms with stronger brand name loyalty should therefore factor into their investment analysis more of the cost of lost sales from existing products as a consequence of a new product introduction.

Product Cannibalization: These are sales generated by one product that come at the expense of other products manufactured by the same firm.

5.3   PRODUCT CANNIBALIZATION AT DISNEY

In coming up with revenues on its proposed theme parks in Thailand, Disney estimates that 15% of the revenues at these parks will be generated from people who would have gone to Disneyland in California, if these parks did not exist. When analyzing the project in Thailand, would you

☐ use the total revenues expected at the park?

☐ use only 85% of the revenues, since 15% of the revenues would have come to Disney anyway?

☐ use a compromise estimate that lies between the first two numbers?

Explain.

The Argument for Incremental Cash Flows

When analyzing investments it is easy to get tunnel vision and focus on the project or investment at hand, and to act as if the objective of the exercise is to maximize the value of the individual investment. There is also the tendency, with perfect hindsight, to require projects to cover all costs that they have generated for the firm, even if such costs will not be recovered by rejecting the project. The objective in investment analysis is to maximize the value of the business or firm taking the investment. Consequently, it is the cash flows that an investment will add on in the future to the business (i.e, the incremental cash flows) that we should focus on.

ILLUSTRATION 5.4   Estimating Cash Flows for an On-line Book Ordering Service: Bookscape

As described in Illustration 5.1, Bookscape is considering an on-line book ordering and information service that will be staffed by two full-time employees. The following estimates relate to the costs of starting the service and the subsequent revenues from it:

1. The initial investment needed to start the service, including the installation of additional phone lines and computer equipment, will be $1 million. These investments are expected to have a life of four years, at which point they will have no salvage value. The investments will be depreciated straight line over the four-year life.

2. The revenues in the first year are expected to be $1.5 million, growing 20% in year 2, and 10% in the year following, and 5% in year 4.

3. The salaries and other benefits for the employees are estimated to be $150,000 in year 1, and to grow 20% a year for the following three years.

4. The cost of the books is assumed to be 60% of the revenues in each of the four years.

5. The working capital, which includes the inventory of books needed for the service and the accounts receivable (associated with selling books on credit), is expected to amount to 10% of the revenues. At the end of year 4, the entire working capital is assumed to be salvaged.

6. The tax rate on income is expected to be 42%.

The following table summarizes the operating earnings from the on-line investment each year for the four-year life of the project.

	1	2	3	4
Revenues	$1,500,000	$1,800,000	$1,980,000	$2,079,000
Operating Expenses				
Labor	$150,000	$165,000	$181,500	$199,650
Materials	$900,000	$1,080,000	$1,188,000	$1,247,400
Depreciation	$250,000	$250,000	$250,000	$250,000
Other Expenses *WC*	$150,000	$180,000	$198,000	$207,900
Operating Income	$50,000	$125,000	$162,500	$174,050
Taxes	$21,000	$52,500	$68,250	$73,101
After-Tax Operating Income	$29,000	$72,500	$94,250	$100,949

To get from operating income to cash flows, we add back the depreciation charges and subtract out the working capital requirements (which are the changes in working capital from year to year):

YEAR	1	2	3	4
After-tax Operating Income	$29,000	$72,500	$94,250	$100,949
+ Depreciation	$250,000	$250,000	$250,000	$250,000
− Δ WC	$30,000	$18,000	$9,900	
After-Tax Cash Flow (ATCF)	$249,000	$304,500	$334,350	$350,94

(WC: Working Capital)

why not 150,000

Note that there is an initial investment in working capital which is 10% of the first year's revenues, invested at the beginning of the year. Each subsequent year has a change in working capital that represents 10% of the revenue change from that year to the next. Bringing the initial investment in computer equipment and phone lines into the analysis as well as the salvage of working capital provides us with a more complete picture of the cash flows on this project:

YEAR	0 (NOW)	1	2	3	4
Investment in Equipment	−$1,000,000				
After-tax Operating Income.		$29,000	$72,500	$94,250	$100,949
+ Depreciation		$250,000	$250,000	$250,000	$250,000
− Δ WC	$150,000	$30,000	$18,000	$9,900	−$207,900
Net ATCF	−$1,150,000	$249,000	$304,500	$334,350	$558,849

5.4 THE EFFECTS OF WORKING CAPITAL

In the analysis above, we assumed that Bookscape would have to maintain additional inventory for its on-line book service. If, instead, we assumed that Bookscape could use its existing inventory (i.e., from its regular bookstore), the cash flows on this project

☐ would increase.

☐ would decrease.

☐ would remain unchanged.

Explain.

IN PRACTICE: ESTIMATING CASH FLOWS FOR A PRIVATE FIRM

While the definition of cash flows is the same for both private and public firms, there are some special concerns associated with cash flow estimation for the former. The first is the tendency of private businesses to *understate profits for tax purposes.* While publicly traded firms also do this, they have to weigh the effects on stock prices and perceptions of reporting smaller profits. It is, therefore, particularly important to estimate cash flows on projects rather than earnings. The second is the *failure on the part of many private business owners to distinguish between a management salary and a return on investment,* since both are taxed at the individual tax rate. Private business owners who do not charge adequately for their time can overstate the returns on projects. There are two solutions to this problem. The first is to compute an opportunity cost for the owner's time, based upon the compensation he or she would have earned *at the next best alternative occupation.* Thus, an investment banker who quits his job to run his own business can charge a cost equivalent to what he would have made at his investment banking job. The limitation of this approach is that it charges this opportunity cost for all activities in which the owner engages, and does not distinguish between activities that can be done by others at much lower cost, and more important activities. The second solution is more flexible; it involves assigning a cost to each activity in which the owner is involved, based upon how much it would cost to hire a *third party to provide the service.* Thus, if the owner spends three hours a week on accounting tasks, the cost of hiring an accounting agency to provide the same service will be the assigned cost. The final issue is that many private business owners *do not and often cannot maintain a rigid barrier between personal and business expenses.* Thus, some of the expenses that show up for the business might be really personal expenses, and some of the employees on the payroll might be close relatives of the owner. From the perspective of project cash flows, it is critical that these expenses be stripped out from the project cash flows.

Illustration 5.5   Estimating Cash Flows to Firm for a Disney Theme Park

The theme parks to be built near Bangkok, modeled on Euro Disney in Paris, will include a "Magic Kingdom" to be constructed beginning immediately and becoming operational at the beginning of the second year, and a second theme park modeled on Epcot Center at Orlando to be constructed in the second and third year and becoming operational at the beginning of the fifth year. The following is the set of assumptions that underlie the investment analysis:

1. The cash flows will be estimated in nominal Thai Baht. The expected inflation rate in Thailand is 15%, while the expected inflation rate in the United States is 3%.

2. The cost of constructing Magic Kingdom will be 109.078 billion Baht, with 70 billion Baht being spent right now and 39.078 billion Baht to be spent one year from now. Disney has already spent 17.5 billion Baht researching the proposal and getting the necessary licenses for the park; none of this investment can be recovered if the park is not built.

3. The cost of constructing Epcot II will be 67.987 billion Baht, with 43.63 billion Baht to be spent at the end of the second year and 24.357 billion Baht at the end of the third year.

4. The revenues at the two parks and the resort properties at the parks are assumed to be the following, based upon projected attendance figures until the tenth year and an expected inflation rate of 15% in Thailand. Starting in year 10, the revenues are expected to grow at the inflation rate:

Year	Magic Kingdom	Second Theme Park	Resort Properties	Total Revenues
1	0 Bt	0 Bt	0 Bt	0 Bt
2	43,630 Bt	0 Bt	8,726 Bt	52,356 Bt
3	68,199 Bt	0 Bt	12,178 Bt	80,377 Bt
4	92,461 Bt	0 Bt	16,317 Bt	108,778 Bt
5	121,451 Bt	30,363 Bt	22,772 Bt	174,586 Bt
6	149,161 Bt	37,290 Bt	46,613 Bt	233,064 Bt
7	183,193 Bt	45,798 Bt	57,248 Bt	286,238 Bt
8	224,989 Bt	56,247 Bt	70,309 Bt	351,545 Bt
9	276,321 Bt	69,080 Bt	86,350 Bt	431,752 Bt
Terminal Year	317,769 Bt	79,442 Bt	99,303 Bt	496,515 Bt

5. The operating expenses are assumed to be 60% of the revenues at the parks and 75% of revenues at the resort properties.

6. The depreciation schedule and capital maintenance expenses on the properties for the next 10 years:

YEAR	DEPRECIATION	CAPITAL MAINTENANCE EXPENDITURES
1	0 Bt	0 Bt
2	16,361 Bt	6,545 Bt
3	18,389 Bt	10,047 Bt
4	20,088 Bt	13,597 Bt
5	19,356 Bt	21,823 Bt
6	20,467 Bt	23,306 Bt
7	23,090 Bt	22,899 Bt
8	25,764 Bt	26,366 Bt
9	28,816 Bt	32,381 Bt
Terminal Year	33,138 Bt	33,138 Bt

After year 10, both depreciation and capital expenditures are assumed to grow at the same rate as inflation.

7. Disney will also allocate the following portion of its general and administrative expenses to the theme parks. It is worth noting that a recent analysis of these expenses found that only one-third of these expenses are variable (and a function of total revenue) and that two-thirds are fixed. After year 10, these expenses are also assumed to grow at the inflation rate.

YEAR	ALLOCATED G & A COSTS	CHANGE IN WORKING CAPITAL
1	–	–
2	8,726 Bt	2,618 Bt
3	10,717 Bt	1,096 Bt
4	13,162 Bt	952 Bt
5	16,165 Bt	2,657 Bt
6	19,853 Bt	1,907 Bt
7	24,383 Bt	1,301 Bt
8	29,946 Bt	1,598 Bt
9	36,778 Bt	1,963 Bt
Terminal Year	42,295 Bt	723 Bt

8. Disney will have to maintain net working capital (primarily consisting of inventory at the theme parks and the resort properties, netted against accounts payable) of 5% of revenues initially, with additional investments in working capital being made at the end of each year. The changes in working capital are included in the table above.

9. The income from the investment will be taxed at a marginal tax rate of 36%.

The projected operating earnings at the theme parks, starting in the first year of operation (which is the second year), are summarized in Table 5.3. These operating earnings can be contrasted with the after-tax cash flows in Table 5.4, with the projected capital expenditures shown as part of the cash flows. In estimating these cash flows, we did the following:

- Added back the depreciation and amortization each year, since it is a non-cash charge.
- Subtracted out the maintenance capital expenditures in addition to the primary capital expenditures since these are cash outflows.
- Added back the portion of the allocated general and administrative costs that are fixed and therefore not an incremental effect of the project; this amounts to two-thirds of the allocated cost in each year from Table 5.3. (We added back the after-tax cost to the after-tax earnings)
- Subtracted out the working capital requirements each year, which represent the change in working capital from the prior year. In this case, we have assumed that the working capital investments are made at the end of each year. The initial investment of 2.6 billion Baht in year 2 is 5% of the second year's revenues. In each year after that, the change in working capital is shown in the table above.

The investment of 109.078 billion Baht in Bangkok Magic Kingdom is shown at time 0 (as 70 billion Baht) and in year 1 (as 39.078 billion Baht). The investment of 17.5 billion Baht that will not be recovered because it has already been spent is not considered in the cash flows because it is a sunk cost.

5.5 DIFFERENT DEPRECIATION METHODS FOR TAX PURPOSES AND FOR REPORTING

The depreciation that we used for the project above is assumed to be the same for both tax and reporting purposes. Assume now that Disney uses more accelerated depreciation methods for tax purposes and straight line depreciation for reporting purposes. In estimating cash flows, we should use

☐ the depreciation numbers from the tax books.

☐ the depreciation numbers from the reporting books.

☐ neither.

Explain.

This spreadsheet allows you to estimate the cash flows to the firm on a project (**capbudg.xls**).

Table 5.3 **OPERATING EARNINGS AT DISNEY THEME PARKS IN BANGKOK**

	2	3	4	5	6	7	8	9	10
Revenues									
Magic Kingdom	43,630 Bt	68,199 Bt	92,461 Bt	121,451 Bt	149,161 Bt	183,193 Bt	224,989 Bt	276,321 Bt	317,769 Bt
Second Theme Park	0 Bt	0 Bt	0 Bt	30,363 Bt	37,290 Bt	45,798 Bt	56,247 Bt	69,080 Bt	79,442 Bt
Resort & Properties	8,726 Bt	12,178 Bt	16,317 Bt	22,772 Bt	46,613 Bt	57,248 Bt	70,309 Bt	86,350 Bt	99,303 Bt
Total	*52,356 Bt*	*80,377 Bt*	*108,778 Bt*	*174,586 Bt*	*233,064 Bt*	*286,238 Bt*	*351,545 Bt*	*431,752 Bt*	*496,515 Bt*
Operating Expenses									
Magic Kingdom	26,178 Bt	40,919 Bt	55,477 Bt	72,871 Bt	89,496 Bt	109,916 Bt	134,993 Bt	165,793 Bt	190,662 Bt
Second Theme Park	0 Bt	0 Bt	0 Bt	18,218 Bt	22,374 Bt	27,479 Bt	33,748 Bt	41,448 Bt	47,665 Bt
Resort & Property	6,545 Bt	9,134 Bt	12,238 Bt	17,079 Bt	34,960 Bt	42,936 Bt	52,732 Bt	64,763 Bt	74,477 Bt
Total	*32,723 Bt*	*50,053 Bt*	*67,714 Bt*	*108,167 Bt*	*146,830 Bt*	*180,330 Bt*	*221,473 Bt*	*272,004 Bt*	*312,804 Bt*
Other Expenses									
Depreciation & Amortization	16,361 Bt	18,389 Bt	20,088 Bt	19,356 Bt	20,467 Bt	23,090 Bt	25,764 Bt	28,816 Bt	33,138 Bt
Allocated G&A Costs	8,726 Bt	10,717 Bt	13,162 Bt	16,165 Bt	19,853 Bt	24,383 Bt	29,946 Bt	36,778 Bt	42,295 Bt
Operating Income	($5,454 Bt)	1,218 Bt	7,814 Bt	30,897 Bt	45,913 Bt	58,436 Bt	74,362 Bt	94,154 Bt	108,277 Bt
Taxes	($1,963 Bt)	438 Bt	2,813 Bt	11,123 Bt	16,529 Bt	21,037 Bt	26,770 Bt	33,895 Bt	38,980 Bt
Operating Income after Taxes	($3,490 Bt)	779 Bt	5,001 Bt	19,774 Bt	29,384 Bt	37,399 Bt	47,592 Bt	60,259 Bt	69,297 Bt

Table 5.4   OPERATING CASH FLOWS AT DISNEY THEME PARKS IN BANGKOK

Year	0	1	2	3	4	5	6	7	8	9	10
Operating Income After Taxes			(3,490 Bt)	779 Bt	5,001 Bt	19,774 Bt	29,384 Bt	37,399 Bt	47,592 Bt	60,259 Bt	69,297 Bt
+ Deprec'n & Amortization			16,361 Bt	18,389 Bt	20,088 Bt	19,356 Bt	20,467 Bt	23,090 Bt	25,764 Bt	28,816 Bt	33,138 Bt
- Capital Expenditures	70,000 Bt	39,078 Bt	50,175 Bt	34,404 Bt	13,597 Bt	21,823 Bt	23,306 Bt	22,899 Bt	26,366 Bt	32,381 Bt	33,138 Bt
- Change in Working Capital			2,618 Bt	196 Bt	952 Bt	2,657 Bt	1,907 Bt	1,301 Bt	1,598 Bt	1,963 Bt	723 Bt
+ Fixed Allocated Expense			3,723 Bt	4,573 Bt	5,616 Bt	6,897 Bt	8,471 Bt	10,403 Bt	12,777 Bt	15,692 Bt	18,046 Bt
Cashflow to Firm	(70,000 Bt)	(39,078 Bt)	(36,199 Bt)	(11,759 Bt)	16,155 Bt	21,548 Bt	33,109 Bt	46,692 Bt	58,169 Bt	70,423 Bt	86,620 Bt

IN PRACTICE: ADJUSTING CASH FLOWS FOR CONSTRAINTS ON FOREIGN PROJECTS

The normal assumption in estimating project cash flows is that the after-tax cash flow can be withdrawn by the firm and used elsewhere, presumably where returns are higher. While this is generally justified in regular projects, it may not hold in countries that *restrict cash withdrawals* from projects; the parent company might be forced either to leave the cash idle in the foreign currency or to invest it back into that country. This may not be an onerous assumption when there are numerous projects with excess returns available in that country. It may end up costing the company, however, if it is forced to keep the proceeds in sub-standard projects until it can remit the cash. In such cases, only that portion of the cash that can be remitted each period should be considered in the capital budgeting analysis. Since the remaining cash earns below-market returns, this will make the project much less attractive.

The second factor to consider in estimating cash flows is *taxes.* The parent firm may find itself facing different tax obligations in the foreign country and domestically, depending upon how much of the cash it chooses to transfer from the subsidiary to itself and how it does so. For instance, a U.S. firm that has a subsidiary in France will pay French taxes on the income the subsidiary makes. It may also have to pay domestic taxes if it remits the cash in the form of a dividend from the subsidiary to the parent. Depending upon the tax rates in the two locales, and the laws on offsetting taxes paid in a foreign locale, the after-tax cash flows will vary as a function of the remittance policy of the firm.

ILLUSTRATION 5.6   **Estimating Cash Flows to Equity for a New Plant: Aracruz**

Aracruz Cellulose is considering a plan to build a state-of-the-art plant to manufacture linerboard. The plant is expected to have a capacity of 750,000 tons and will have the following characteristics:

1.   It will require an initial investment of 250 million BR. At the end of the fifth year, an additional investment of 50 million BR will be needed to update the plant.

2.   Aracruz plans to borrow 100 million BR, at a real interest rate of 5.5%, using a 10-year term loan (where the loan will be paid off in equal annual increments).

3.   The plant will have a life of 10 years. During that period, the plant (and the additional investment in year 5) will be depreciated using double-declining balance depreciation, with a life of 10 years. At the end of the tenth year, the plant is expected to be salvaged at book value.

4.   The plant will be partly in commission in a couple of months, but will have a capacity of only 650,000 tons in the first year, 700,000 tons in the second year, before getting to its full capacity of 750,000 tons in the third year.

5.   The capacity utilization rate will be 90% for the first three years and rise to 95% after that.

6.   The price per ton of linerboard is currently $400, and is expected to keep pace with inflation for the life of the plant.

7. The variable cost of production, primarily labor and material, is expected to be 55% of total revenues; there is a fixed cost of 50 million BR, which will grow at the inflation rate.

8. The networking capital requirements are estimated to be 15% of total revenues, and the investments have to be made at the beginning of each year. At the end of the tenth year, it is anticipated that the entire working capital will be salvaged.

9. The selling and distribution expenses related to this plant are shown in Table 5.5.

Table 5.5 summarizes the net income from plant investment to Aracruz each year for the next 10 years. The interest payments on the debt are estimated in the following table:

YEAR	TOTAL PAYMENT	INTEREST EXPENSES	PRINCIPAL REPAYMENTS
1	13,267 BR	5,500 BR	7,767 BR
2	13,267 BR	5,073 BR	8,194 BR
3	13,267 BR	4,622 BR	8,645 BR
4	13,267 BR	4,147 BR	9,120 BR
5	13,267 BR	3,645 BR	9,622 BR
6	13,267 BR	3,116 BR	10,151 BR
7	13,267 BR	2,558 BR	10,709 BR
8	13,267 BR	1,969 BR	11,298 BR
9	13,267 BR	1,347 BR	11,920 BR
10	13,267 BR	692 BR	12,575 BR

Note that while the total payment remains unchanged, the breakdown into interest and principal payments changes from year to year.

In Table 5.6 we estimate the cash flows to equity from the plant to Aracruz. To arrive at these cash flows, we do the following:

- Add back depreciation and amortization, since they are non-cash charges.
- Subtract the capital expenditures, both initially and in year 5, since these are cash outflows.
- Subtract the changes in working capital; since investments in working capital are made at the beginning of each period, the initial investment in working capital of 35.1 million BR is made at time 0 and is 15% of revenues in year 1. The changes in working capital in the years that follow are 15% of the changes in revenue in those years. At the end of year 10, the entire investment in working capital is recovered as salvage.
- Subtract the principal payments that are made to the bank in each period, since these are cash outflows to the nonequity claimholders in the firm.
- Add the salvage value of the plant in year 10 to the total cash flows, since this is a cash inflow to equity investors.

Table 5.5 ESTIMATED NET INCOME FROM PAPER PLANT INVESTMENT: ARACRUZ CELLULOSE

	1	2	3	4	5	6	7	8	9	10
Revenues										
Capacity (in '000s)	650	700	750	750	750	750	750	750	750	750
Utilization Rate	0.90	0.90	0.90	0.95	0.95	0.95	0.95	0.95	0.95	0.95
Production Rate	585	630	675	713	713	713	713	713	713	713
Price per ton	400	400	400	400	400	400	400	400	400	400
Revenues (*in 000s*)	*234,000*	*252,000*	*270,000*	*285,000*	*285,000*	*285,000*	*285,000*	*285,000*	*285,000*	*285,000*
Operating Expenses										
Cash Expenses	178,700 BR	188,600 BR	198,500 BR	206,750 BR	206,750 BR	206,750 BR	206,750 BR	206,750 BR	206,750 BR	206,750 BR
Depreciation	50,000 BR	40,000 BR	32,000 BR	25,600 BR	20,480 BR	26,384 BR	21,107 BR	16,886 BR	13,509 BR	10,807 BR
Selling Expenses	1,696 BR	7,488 BR	12,640 BR	16,848 BR	18,486 BR	16,597 BR	18,286 BR	19,637 BR	20,717 BR	21,582 BR
Operating Income after Taxes	*3,604 BR*	*15,912 BR*	*26,860 BR*	*35,802 BR*	*39,284 BR*	*35,269 BR*	*38,857 BR*	*41,728 BR*	*44,024 BR*	*45,861 BR*
−Interest Expenses	5,500 BR	5,073 BR	4,622 BR	4,147 BR	3,645 BR	3,116 BR	2,558 BR	1,969 BR	1,347 BR	692 BR
Taxable Income	*(1,896 BR)*	*10,839 BR*	*22,238 BR*	*31,655 BR*	*35,638 BR*	*32,153 BR*	*36,299 BR*	*39,759 BR*	*42,677 BR*	*45,170 BR*
−Taxes	*(607 BR)*	*3,469 BR*	*7,116 BR*	*10,130 BR*	*11,404 BR*	*10,289 BR*	*11,616 BR*	*12,723 BR*	*13,657 BR*	*14,454 BR*
Net Income	*(1,289 BR)*	*7,371 BR*	*15,122 BR*	*21,526 BR*	*24,234 BR*	*21,864 BR*	*24,684 BR*	*27,036 BR*	*29,020 BR*	*30,715 BR*

Selling expenses are expenses related to distribution and sales of production from this plant.

Table 5.6 CASH FLOWS TO EQUITY FROM PAPER PLANT: ARACRUZ CELLULOSE

	0	1	2	3	4	5	6	7	8	9	10
Investment in Plant	−250,000 BR										
Net of Debt	+100,000 BR										
Equity Investment	−150,000 BR										
Net Income		(1,289 BR)	7,371 BR	15,122 BR	21,526 BR	24,234 BR	21,864 BR	24,684 BR	27,036 BR	29,020 BR	30,715 BR
+ Deprec'n & Amort.		50,000 BR	40,000 BR	32,000 BR	25,600 BR	20,480 BR	26,384 BR	21,107 BR	16,886 BR	13,509 BR	10,807 BR
− Capital Expenditures		0 BR	0 BR	0 BR	0 BR	50,000 BR	0 BR	0 BR	0 BR	0 BR	0 BR
− Δ Working Capital	35,100 BR	2,700 BR	2,700 BR	2,250 BR	0 BR	0 BR	0 BR	0 BR	0 BR	0 BR	(42,750BR)
− Principal Repayments		7,767 BR	8,194 BR	8,645 BR	9,120 BR	9,622 BR	10,151 BR	10,709 BR	11,298 BR	11,920 BR	12,575 BR
+ Salvage Value: Plant											43,228 BR
Cashflow to Equity	(185,100BR)	38,244 BR	36,477 BR	36,227 BR	38,006 BR	(14,907BR)	38,097 BR	35,082 BR	32,624 BR	30,609 BR	114,925 BR

*Note that Δ working capital is subtracted from earnings to arrive at cash flows. Thus, the negative amount in year 10 is the salvage value (and it increases the cash flow in that year).

The cash flows to equity measure the cash flows that equity investors at Aracruz can expect to receive from investing in the plant.

5.6   THE EFFECTS OF DEBT FINANCING ON CASHFLOWS TO EQUITY

In the analysis above, we assumed an additional capital expenditure of 50 million BR in year 5, financed entirely with funds from equity; the cash flow to equity in year 5 (from Table 5.6) is − 14.907 million BR. If, instead, we assumed the 50 million BR had come from new borrowing, the cash flow to equity in year 5

☐   would increase by 50 million BR.

☐   would decrease by 50 million BR.

☐   would remain unchanged.

Explain.

This spreadsheet allows you to estimate the cash flows to equity on a project (**capbug.xls**).

C. Time-Weighted versus Nominal Cash Flows

Very few projects with long lifetimes generate earnings or cash flows evenly over their life. In sectors with huge investments in infrastructure, such as telecommunications, the earnings and cash flows might be negative for an extended period (say ten to twenty years) before they turn positive. In other sectors, the earnings may occur earlier in time. Whatever the reason for the unevenness of cash flows, a basic question that has to be addressed when measuring returns is whether they should reflect the timing of the earnings or cash flows. We will argue that they should, with earlier earnings and cash flows being weighted more than earnings and cash flows later in the project life.

Why Cash Flows Across Time Are Not Comparable

There are three reasons why cash flows across time are not comparable, and a cash flow in the future is worth less than a similar cash flow today:

1.   Individuals *prefer present consumption to future consumption*. People would have to be offered more in the future to give up present consumption—this is called the *real rate of return*. The greater the real rate of return, the greater will be the difference in value between a cash flow today and an equal cash flow in the future.

2.   When there is *monetary inflation,* the value of currency decreases over time. The greater the inflation, the greater the difference in value between a cash flow today and a cash flow in the future.

3.   Any *uncertainty (risk)* associated with the cash flow in the future reduces the value of the cash flow. The greater the uncertainty associated with the cash flow, the greater will be the difference between receiving the cash flow today and receiving an equal amount in the future.

The process by which future cash flows are adjusted to reflect these factors is called *discounting,* and the magnitude of these factors is reflected in the *discount rate*. Thus the present value of a cash flow(CF_t) at a point in time t in the future, when the discount rate is r, can be written as follows:

$$\text{Present Value of Cash Flow} = \frac{CF_t}{(1+r)^t} = CF_t\left(\frac{1}{(1+r)^t}\right)$$

Note that the second term in the brackets $\left(\frac{1}{(1+r)^t}\right)$ is called the discount factor and effectively weights the cash flow by when it occurs. The differences in weights across time will depend entirely upon the level of the discount rate. Consequently, when discount rates are high, which could be due to high real rates, high inflation, and/or high uncertainty, returns that occur further in the future will be weighted less. Appendix 1 includes a more complete discussion of the mechanics of present value.

The Case for Time-Weighted Returns
If we accept the arguments that cash flows measure returns more accurately than earnings, and that the incremental cash flows more precisely estimate returns than total cash flows, we should logically follow up by using discounted cash flows (i.e., time-weighted returns) rather than nominal cash flows, for two reasons:

1. Nominal cash flows at different points in time are not comparable and cannot be aggregated to arrive at returns. Discounted cash flows, on the other hand, convert all cash flows on a project to today's terms and allow us to compute returns more consistently.

2. If the objective in investment analysis is to maximize the value of the business taking the investments, we should be weighting cash flows that occur early more than cash flow that occur later, because investors in the business will also do so.

5.7 TIME HORIZONS AND TIME WEIGHTING
Calculation of present values for cash flows leads to a greater weighting for cash flows that occur sooner and a lower weighting for cash flows that occur later. Does it necessarily follow that using present value (as opposed to nominal value) makes managers more likely to take short-term projects over long-term projects?

☐ Yes

☐ No

Why or why not?

D. Investment Decision Rules
1. Accounting Income-Based Decision Rules
Many of the oldest and most established investment decision rules have been drawn from the accounting statements and, in particular, from accounting measures of income. Some of these rules are based on income to equity investors (i.e., net income) while others are based on pre-debt operating income.

Return on Capital
The expected *return on capital* on a project is a function of both the total investment required on the project and its capacity to generate operating income. Defined generally,

$$\text{Return on Capital (Pretax)} = \frac{\text{Earnings Before Interest and Taxes}}{\text{Average Book Value of Total Investment in Project}}$$

$$\text{Return on Capital (After-Tax)} = \frac{\text{Earnings Before Interest and Taxes } (1 - \text{Tax Rate})}{\text{Average Book Value of Total Investment in Project}}$$

To illustrate, consider a one-year project with an initial investment of $1 million and earnings before interest and taxes of $300,000. Assume that the project has a salvage value at the end of the year of $800,000, and that the tax rate is 40%. In terms of a timeline, the project has the following parameters:

Earnings Before Interest & Taxes = $ 300,000

Book Value = $ 1,000,000   Salvage Value = $ 800,000

Average Book Value of Assets = $(1,000,000+800,000)/2 = $ 900,000

The pretax and after-tax returns on capital can be estimated as follows:

$$\text{Return on Capital (Pretax)} = \frac{\$\,300,000}{\$\,900,000} = 33.33\%$$

$$\text{Return on Capital (After-Tax)} = \frac{\$\,300,000\,(1 - 0.40)}{\$\,900,000} = 20\%$$

While this calculation is rather straightforward for a one-year project, it becomes more involved for multiyear projects, where both the operating income and the book value (BV) of the investment change over time. In these cases, the return on capital can either be estimated each year and then averaged over time, or the average operating income over the life of the project can be used in conjunction with the average investment during the period to estimate the average return on capital.

Consider, for instance, a four-year project requiring an initial investment of $1,500, which will have the following operating income over time:

EBIT		$ 300	$ 400	$ 500	$ 600
EBIT $(1 - t)$		$ 180	$ 240	$ 300	$ 360
BV of Assets	$ 1500	$ 1300	$ 1100	$ 900	$ 700
Return on Capital		21.43%	33.33%	50.00%	75.00%

The book value of the assets decreases over time, as the assets are depreciated down to a salvage value of $700. The return on capital (ROC) can be estimated each year and then averaged over time as depicted in Table 5.7.

The average (based on arithmetic averages) pre-tax return on capital over the four years is 44.94%, while the after-tax return on capital is 26.96%. The geometric averages are 43.58% for the pre-tax return on capital and 26.40% for the after-tax return on capital. The return on capital can also be estimated from the average operating income and the average book value of assets over time:

Average EBIT = $ 450
Average After-Tax EBIT = $ 270

Year	1	2	3	4
	Table 5.7 **EBIT ON FOUR-YEAR PROJECT**			
EBIT	$ 300	$ 400	$ 500	$ 600
Average BV of Assets	$ 1400	$1200	$ 1000	$ 800
Pre-tax ROC	21.43%	33.33%	50.00%	75.00%
After-Tax ROC	12.86%	20.00%	30.00%	45.00%

Average Book Value of Investment = ($1500 + $ 700)/2 = $ 1100
Return on Capital = $450 / $1100 = 40.91%
After-Tax Return on Capital = $270 / $1100 = 24.54%

The differences between the two approaches will widen as more accelerated depreciation methods are used, with the first approach providing higher estimates of return on capital.

 Accelerated Depreciation: This is a depreciation method that yields higher depreciation in the early years, and less in the later years.

The after-tax return on capital on a project has to be compared to a hurdle rate that is defined consistently. Most firms use the cost of capital as the hurdle rate, since the return on capital is a return to the firm rather than to equity investors.

DECISION RULE FOR RETURN ON CAPITAL FOR INDEPENDENT PROJECTS

If the after-tax return on capital > Cost of Capital ⇒ Accept the project
If the after-tax return on capital < Cost of Capital ⇒ Reject the project

When choosing between mutually exclusive projects of equivalent risk, the project with the higher return on capital will be viewed as the better project.

ILLUSTRATION 5.7   Hurdle Rates for Projects: Bookscape, Disney and Aracruz
We spent the previous chapter estimating the costs of equity and capital for Disney, Aracruz Cellulose, and Bookscape. We will draw on that analysis to estimate the hurdle rates for the projects being analyzed in this section:

1. For the Bookscape On-line Book Ordering Service, we will not use the costs of equity and capital that we estimated for Bookscape Books as a firm, since that was based upon traditional bookstores. Instead, we will use the average beta of 2.0 of companies that derive all or the bulk of their revenues from on-line commerce as the beta for Bookscape's equity:

Cost of Equity = 7% + 2 (5.5%) = 18%

Using the debt ratio of 15.40% that we used for Bookscape as a firm, the cost of debt of 8%, and a tax rate of 42%, we can estimate the cost of capital:

Cost of Capital = 18% (.846) + 8% (1 − .42) (.154) = 15.94%

2. For Disney, we estimated the cost of capital by division, and the cost of capital for the theme park division was 12.32%. This assumes, however, that the analysis is done in U.S. dollar terms. Since we estimated the earnings in Thai Baht, we will estimate the cost of capital in Baht terms:

$$\text{Cost of Capital (in Baht)} = \text{Cost of Capital in \$} * \frac{1 + \text{Expected Inflation}_{\text{Baht}}}{1 + \text{Expected Inflation}_{\$}}$$

$$= 12.32\% * \frac{1.15}{1.03} = 25.41\%$$

3. For Aracruz, we will use the real cost of equity of 10.33% that we estimated in the previous chapter, since our cash flows are to equity and in real terms.

In summary, the hurdle rates we use are determined by the way we estimate our cash flows—the currency we use, the risk associated with the cash flows, whether they are to equity investors or to the firm, and whether they are real or nominal.

IN PRACTICE: SHOULD THERE BE A RISK PREMIUM FOR FOREIGN PROJECTS?

Some financial managers argue that taking a project in another country allows the company to diversify across economies and thus reduce risk, suggesting that the discount rate (in domestic unit terms) should be lower for foreign projects. There are others who argue for the use of a higher discount rate to reflect the additional risks associated with taking on projects in other countries. In particular, they note that foreign projects expose firms to exchange rate and political risk. The assumption underlying both arguments is that investors in the company cannot accomplish the diversification themselves.

The question of whether or not discount rates should be different for foreign projects cannot be answered without looking at the stockholders in the firm and the availability of instruments to hedge risk. If stockholders are well diversified internationally and/or firms can hedge risk at low cost, it can be argued that exchange rate and political risk should not affect discount rates.

If we decide that a risk premium should be attached to discount rates to reflect the political or other risk that cannot easily be diversified away, the magnitude of the premium has to be estimated. The most reliable approach is to use the country bond ratings assigned by ratings agencies as a way of estimating their political risk. Since ratings are linked to default spreads, these spreads can be used as a proxy for the risk premium for investing in real projects in a country.

In the investment analysis of Disney's theme park in Thailand, we have chosen to use the same dollar cost of capital for this theme park as we would have for a domestic theme park. Implicitly, we are assuming that Disney's stockholders are diversified enough to take care of exchange rate and political risk on their own. If we had not made this assumption, we would have estimated a risk premium of 1% for Thailand based upon its A rating in July 1997. This spread can be added on to the company's dollar cost of capital of 12.32% for U.S. theme parks to reflect the additional risk associated with investing in Thailand, resulting in a dollar cost of capital of 13.32%.

Table 5.8	**RETURN ON CAPITAL ON BOOKSCAPES ON-LINE**				
	0	**1**	**2**	**3**	**4**
After-Tax Operating Income (See Illustration 5.4)		$29,000	$72,500	$94,250	$100,949
Beginning Book Value	$1,000,000	$1,000,000	$750,000	$500,000	$250,000
−Depreciation		$250,000	$250,000	$250,000	$250,000
Ending Book Value	$1,000,000	$750,000	$500,000	$250,000	$ 0
Average Book Value		$875,000	$625,000	$375,000	$125,000
Return on Capital		3.31%	11.60%	25.13%	80.76%

ILLUSTRATION 5.8   Estimating and Using Return on Capital in Decision Making: Disney and Bookscape

In Illustrations 5.4 and 5.5, we estimated the operating income from two projects—an investment by Bookscape in an on-line book ordering service and an investment in a theme park in Bangkok by Disney. We will estimate the return on capital on each of these investments using the estimates of operating income. Table 5.8 summarizes the estimates of operating income and the book value of capital at Bookscape.

The average after-tax (AT) return on capital anticipated on the project was 30.20%. Since this exceeds the cost of capital of 15.94% that we estimated earlier for this project in Illustration 5.7, the return on capital approach would suggest that this is a good project.

In Table 5.9, we estimate operating income, book value of capital, and return on capital for Disney's theme park investment in Thailand. The operating income estimates are from Table 5.3.

The average after-tax return on capital is 16.72%. Here, the return on capital is lower than the cost of capital that we estimated in Baht terms to be 25.41%. It is worth noting, however, that this project is assumed to last beyond year 10, and that the return on capital after year 10 is well in excess of 25.41%.

Biases, Limitations, and Caveats

While the return on capital is a simple and intuitive measure of the profitability of a project, its adherence to accounting measures of income and investment expose it to some serious problems:

- The measure works better for projects that fit the conventional pattern (i.e., have a large up-front investment and generate income over time). For projects that do not require a significant initial investment, the return on capital has less meaning. For instance, a retail firm that leases store space for a new store will not have a significant initial investment, and may have a very high return on capital as a consequence.

- The focus on operating income rather than cash flows exposes this measure to potential problems when the operating income either lags or is very different from the cash flows generated by the project. Furthermore, changing depreciation methods and inventory costing may lead to changes in operating income and the return on capital, even though the underlying cash flows might be unaffected.

Table 5.9   RETURN ON CAPITAL FOR DISNEY THEME PARK INVESTMENT

Year	AT Operating Income	Beg. Book Value	Depreciation	Capital Expenditure	Ending Book Value	Average BV	ROC
0			0 Bt	87,500 Bt	87,500 Bt		
1	0 Bt	87,500 Bt	0 Bt	39,078 Bt	126,578 Bt	107,039 Bt	
2	($3,490 Bt)	126,578 Bt	16,361 Bt	50,175 Bt	160,391 Bt	143,484 Bt	−2.43%
3	779 Bt	160,391 Bt	18,389 Bt	34,404 Bt	176,406 Bt	168,399 Bt	0.46%
4	5,001 Bt	176,406 Bt	20,088 Bt	13,597 Bt	169,915 Bt	173,161 Bt	2.89%
5	19,774 Bt	169,915 Bt	19,356 Bt	21,823 Bt	172,382 Bt	171,149 Bt	11.55%
6	29,384 Bt	172,382 Bt	20,467 Bt	23,306 Bt	175,221 Bt	173,801 Bt	16.91%
7	37,399 Bt	175,221 Bt	23,090 Bt	22,899 Bt	175,030 Bt	175,126 Bt	21.36%
8	47,592 Bt	175,030 Bt	25,764 Bt	26,366 Bt	175,632 Bt	175,331 Bt	27.14%
9	60,259 Bt	175,632 Bt	28,816 Bt	32,381 Bt	179,198 Bt	177,415 Bt	33.96%
10	69,297 Bt	179,198 Bt	33,138 Bt	33,138 Bt	179,198 Bt	179,198 Bt	38.67%
Average							16.72%

- The book value of the assets may not be a very good measure of the investment in the project, especially over time. Since depreciation reduces the book value of investments, the return on capital will generally increase over time, as it did in the example above.

- Finally, the average return on capital does not differentiate between profits made in the early years of a project and profits made in later years. Thus $100 in operating income in year 1 is counted the same as $100 in operating income in year 4.

Note that all of the limitations of the return on capital measure are visible in Illustration 5.8 in the Disney theme park analysis. First, the Disney example does not differentiate between money already spent and money still to be spent; rather, the sunk cost of 17.5 billion Baht is shown in the initial investment of 87.50 billion Baht. Second, as the book value of the assets stagnates (depreciation is largely offset by capital expenditure) the operating income rises, leading to an increase in the return on capital. Third, the average return on capital is taken over 10 years, even though this project's life is much longer, resulting in an underestimation of the true returns on the project.

Return on Equity

The return on equity looks at the return to equity investors, using the accounting net income as a measure of this return. Again, defined generally:

$$\text{Return on Equity} = \frac{\text{Net Income}}{\text{Average Book Value of Equity Investment in Project}}$$

To illustrate, consider a four-year project with an initial equity investment of $800, and the following estimates of net income in each of the four years:

Net Income	$140	$170	$210	$250

BV of Equity	$800	$700	$600	$500	$400

Return on Equity	18.67%	26.15%	38.18%	55.56%

Like the return on capital, the return on equity tends to increase over the life of the project, as the book value of equity in the project is depreciated.

Just as the appropriate comparison for the return on capital is the cost of capital, the appropriate comparison for the return on equity is the *cost of equity,* which is the rate of return equity investors demand.

DECISION RULE FOR ROE MEASURE FOR INDEPENDENT PROJECTS

If the Return on Equity > Cost of Equity	⇒	Accept the project
If the Return on Equity < Cost of Equity	⇒	Reject the project

The cost of equity should reflect the riskiness of the project being considered and the financial leverage taken on by the firm. When choosing between mutually exclusive projects of similar risk, the project with the higher return on equity will be viewed as the better project.

■▲
▼●
ILLUSTRATION 5.9   Estimating Return on Equity: Aracruz Cellulose
Consider again the analysis of the paper plant for Aracruz Cellulose that we started in Illustration 5.6. The following table summarizes the book value of equity and the estimated net income (from Table 5.5) for each of the next ten years in thousands of BR.

YEAR	NET INCOME	BEG. BV: ASSETS	DEPRECIATION	CAPITAL EXP.	ENDING BV: ASSETS	DEBT	BV: EQUITY	AVERAGE BV: EQUITY	ROE
0		0	0	250,000	250,000	100,000	150,000		
1	(1,289)	250,000	50,000	0	200,000	92,233	107,767	128,883	−1.00%
2	7,371	200,000	40,000	0	160,000	84,039	75,961	91,864	8.02%
3	15,122	160,000	32,000	0	128,000	75,395	52,605	64,283	23.52%
4	21,526	128,000	25,600	0	102,400	66,275	36,125	44,365	48.52%
5	24,234	102,400	20,480	50,000	131,920	56,653	75,267	55,696	43.51%
6	21,864	131,920	26,384	0	105,536	46,502	59,034	67,151	32.56%
7	24,684	105,536	21,107	0	84,429	35,793	48,636	53,835	45.85%
8	27,036	84,429	16,886	0	67,543	24,495	43,048	45,842	58.98%
9	29,020	67,543	13,509	0	54,034	12,575	41,459	42,254	68.68%
10	30,715	54,034	10,807	0	43,228	0	43,228	42,343	72.54%

The increase in the return on equity over time occurs because the net income rises while the book value of equity decreases.

The average real return on equity of 40.12% on the paper plant project is compared to the cost of equity for this plant, which is 10.33%, suggesting that this is a good investment.

Biases, Limitations, and Caveats

The return on equity measure suffers from many of the same biases and limitations that plague the return on capital measure. First, it is much too dependent on accounting measures of income and investment, and accordingly, is susceptible to changes in accounting methods. Second, it tends to increase over time, as the book value is depreciated, and to provide unrealistically high values when the project does not require a significant initial investment. Finally, like the average return on capital, this measure does not differentiate between net income in the early years and net income in later years.

Returns on Capital and Equity for Entire Firms

Our discussion of returns on equity and capital have so far revolved around individual projects. It is possible, however, to calculate the return on equity or capital for an entire firm, based upon its current earnings and book value. This return, on a firmwide basis, can be used as an approximate measure of the returns that the firm is making on its existing investments or assets, as long as the following assumptions hold:

1. The income used (operating or net) is income derived from existing projects and is not skewed by expenditures designed to provide future growth (such as R&D expenses) or onetime gains or losses.

2. More importantly, the book value of the assets used should measure the actual investment that the firm has in these assets.

3. The depreciation and other non-cash charges that usually depress income are used to make capital expenditures that maintain the existing asset's income earning potential.

If these assumptions hold, the return on capital becomes a reasonable proxy for what the firm is making on its existing investments or projects, and the return on equity becomes a proxy for what the equity investors are making on these investments.

With this reasoning, a firm which earns a return on capital that exceeds its cost of capital can be viewed as having, on average, good projects on its books. Conversely, a firm which earns a return on capital that is less than the cost of capital can be viewed as having, on average, bad projects on its books.

From the equity standpoint, a firm which earns a return on equity that exceeds its cost of equity can be viewed as earning "surplus returns" for its stockholders, while a firm that does not accomplish this is taking on projects that destroy stockholder value.

 ILLUSTRATION 5.10   Evaluating Current Investments: Disney, Aracruz, Bookscape, and Deutsche Bank

In the following table, we have summarized the current returns on capital and costs of capital for Disney, Aracruz, Bookscape, and Deutsche Bank.

COMPANY	EBIT	EBIT (1 − t)	BV: DEBT	BV: EQUITY	ROC	COST OF CAPITAL	ROC-WACC
Disney	5,559	3,558	7,663	11,368	18.69%	12.22%	6.47%
Bookscape	2,500,000	1,450,000	3,180,000	5,500,000	16.71%	11.75%	4.96%
Aracruz	15	10	1,369	2,115	0.29%	7.48%	-7.19%
Deutsche Bank	13,369	7,353	103,824	29,444	5.52%	7.30%	-1.78%

(We adjusted Disney's EBIT to reflect amortization in 1996.)

The average book value of debt and equity for 1995 and 1996 is used for each of these firms to compute capital, and the operating income for 1996 is used to compute the return on capital. For Deutsche Bank, we used only the long-term debt and computed the earnings before long-term interest expenses. For all of the other firms, we used total debt and earnings before any interest expenses. For Bookscape, we used the earnings before lease expenses, since we are treating the present value of lease expenses as debt. The marginal tax rates used in Chapter 4 are used here as well. While this analysis suggests that only Disney and Bookscape are earning excess returns, the following factors should be considered:

1. The book value of capital is affected fairly dramatically by accounting decisions. In particular, Disney's capital invested increased by almost $10 billion from 1995 to 1996 as a result of the acquisition of Capital Cities and Disney's decision to use purchase accounting.

2. We have not made any adjustments to the earnings before interest and taxes. To the extent that each of these companies has operating expenses designed to create future growth rather than support current operations the returns on capital are understated.

3. For Aracruz, we are assuming that since the book values are adjusted for inflation, the return on capital is a real return on capital and can be compared to the real cost of capital. The 1996 EBIT for Aracruz was well below 1995 EBIT (which was $271 million).

The analysis can also be done in purely equity terms. The returns on equity and costs of equity are summarized for Disney, Aracruz, Bookscape, and Deutsche Bank in the following table:

COMPANY	NET INCOME	BV: EQUITY	ROE	COST OF EQUITY	ROE-COST OF EQUITY
Disney	2,836.4	11,368	24.95%	13.85%	11.10%
Bookscape	1,160,000	5,500,000	21.09%	13.05%	8.04%
Aracruz	47	2,114.65	2.22%	10.33%	-8.11%
Deutsche Bank	2,134	29,444	7.25%	12.67%	-5.42%

The conclusions are similar, with Disney and Bookscape earning excess returns. Note that the equity differentials tend to be larger than the differentials on capital.

 There is a dataset on the Web that summarizes, by sector, returns on equity and capital as well as costs of equity and capital (**eva.xls**).

IN PRACTICE: ECONOMIC VALUE ADDED (EVA)

Economic value added is a value enhancement concept that has caught the attention of both firms interested in increasing their value and portfolio managers looking for good investments. EVA is a measure of dollar surplus value created by a firm or project and is measured by doing the following:

$$\text{Economic Value Added (EVA)} = (\text{Return on Capital} \times \text{Cost of Capital})$$
$$(\text{Capital Invested})$$

where the return on capital is measured using "adjusted" operating income, where the adjustments[3] eliminate items that are unrelated to existing investments, and where the capital investment is based upon the book value of capital but is designed to measure the capital invested in existing assets. Firms which have positive EVA are firms which are creating surplus value, and firms with negative EVA are destroying value.

While EVA is usually calculated using total capital, it can be easily modified to be an equity measure:

$$\text{Equity EVA} = (\text{Return on Equity} \times \text{Cost of Equity})$$
$$(\text{Equity Invested in Project or Firm})$$

Again, a firm which earns a positive equity EVA is creating value for its stockholders, while a firm with a negative equity EVA is destroying value for its stockholders. The measures of excess returns that we computed in the tables in Illustration 5.10 can be easily modified to become measures of EVA:

COMPANY	ROE	COST OF EQUITY	BV: EQUITY	EQUITY EVA	ROC	WACC	BV: CAPITAL	EVA
Disney	24.95%	13.85%	11,368	1,262	18.69%	12.22%	19,031	1,232
Bookscape	21.09%	13.05%	5,500,000	442,250	16.71%	11.75%	8,680,000	430,100
Aracruz	2.22%	10.33%	2,115	−171	0.29%	7.48%	3,483	−250
Deutsche Bank	7.25%	12.67%	29,444	−1,597	5.52%	7.30%	133,268	−2,376

Note that EVA converts the percentage excess returns in these tables to dollar excess returns, but it is affected by the same issues of earnings and book value measurement.

---

[3]Stern Stewart, which is the primary proponent of the EVA approach, claims to make as many as 168 adjustments to operating income to arrive at the true return on capital.

5.8 STOCK BUYBACKS, RETURN ON CAPITAL, AND EVA

When companies buy back stock, they are allowed to reduce the book value of their equity by the market value of the stocks bought back. When the market value of equity is well in excess of book value of equity, buying back stock will generally

☐ increase the return on capital but not affect the EVA.

☐ increase the return on capital and increase the EVA.

☐ not affect the return on capital but increase the EVA.

☐ None of the above.

Explain.

There is a dataset on the Web that summarizes, by sector, the economic value added and the equity economic value added in each (**eva.xls**).

2. Cash Flow Based Decision Rules

Payback

The payback on a project is a measure of how quickly the cash flows generated by the project cover the initial investment. Consider a project that has the following cash flows:

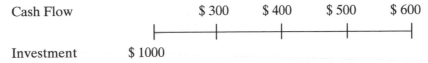

| Cash Flow | $ 300 | $ 400 | $ 500 | $ 600 |

Investment $ 1000

The payback on this project is between two and three years and can be approximated, based upon the cash flows, to be 2.6 years.[4]

As with the other measures, the payback can be estimated either for all investors in the project or just for the equity investors. To estimate the payback for the entire firm, the free cash flows to the firm are cumulated until they cover the total initial investment. To estimate payback just for the equity investors, the free cash flows to equity are cumulated until they cover the initial equity investment in the project.

Payback: The payback for a project is the length of time it will take for nominal cash flows from the project to cover the initial investment.

ILLUSTRATION 5.11   Estimating Payback for the Bookscape On-line Service
The following example estimates the payback from the viewpoint of the firm, using the Bookscape On-line Service cash flows estimated in Illustration 5.3.

YEAR	FCFF (FREE CASHFLOW TO FIRM)	CUMULATED FCFF
0	($1,150,000)	($1,150,000)
1	$249,000	$(901,000)
2	$304,500	$(596,500)
3	$334,350	$(262,150)
4	$558,849	$296,699

---

[4]This assumes that cash flows occur uniformly over time.

The initial investment of $1.15 million is made back by the fourth year, leading to a payback of approximately 3.5 years.

Using Payback in Decision Making

While it is uncommon for firms to make investment decisions based solely on the payback, surveys suggest that some businesses do in fact use payback as their primary decision mechanism. In those situations where payback is used as the primary criterion for accepting or rejecting projects, a "maximum" acceptable payback period is typically set. Projects that pay back their initial investment sooner than this maximum are accepted, while projects that do not are rejected.

Firms are much more likely to employ payback as a secondary investment decision rule and use it either as a constraint in decision making (e.g., accept projects that earn a return on capital of at least 15%, as long as the payback is less than 10 years) or to choose between projects that score equally well on the primary decision rule (e.g., when two mutually exclusive projects have similar returns on equity, choose the one with the lower payback).

Biases, Limitations, and Caveats

The payback rule is a simple and intuitively appealing decision rule, but it does not use a significant proportion of the information that is available on a project.

- By restricting itself to answering the question "When will this project make its initial investment?" it ignores what happens after the initial investment is recouped. This is a significant shortcoming when deciding between mutually exclusive projects. To provide a sense of the absurdities this can lead to, assume that you are picking between two mutually exclusive projects with the cash flows shown in Figure 5.2.

  On the basis of the payback alone, project B is preferable to project A, since it has a shorter payback period. Most decision makers would pick project A as the better project, however, because of the high cash flows that result after the initial investment is paid back.

- The payback rule is designed to cover the conventional project that involves a large up-front investment followed by positive operating cash flows. It breaks down, however, when the investment is spread over time or when there is no initial investment.

- The payback rule uses nominal cash flows and counts cash flows in the early years the same as cash flows in the later years. Since money has time value, however, recouping the nominal initial investment does not make the business whole again, since that amount could have been invested elsewhere and earned a significant return.

3. Discounted Cash Flow Measures

Investment decision rules based on discounted cash flows not only replace accounting income with cash flows, but explicitly factor in the time value of money. The two most widely used discounted cash flows rules are *net present value* and the *internal rate of return*.

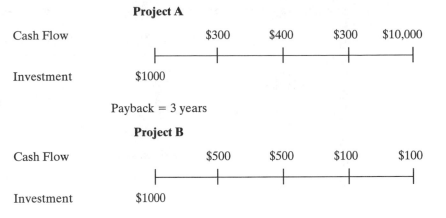

Project A

Cash Flow $300 $400 $300 $10,000

Investment $1000

Payback = 3 years

Project B

Cash Flow $500 $500 $100 $100

Investment $1000

Payback = 2 years

Figure 5.2   Using payback for mutually exclusive projects.

Net Present Value (NPV)

The *net present value* of a project is the cumulation of the present values of each of the cash flows—positive as well as negative—that occur over the life of the project. The general formulation of the NPV rule is as follows

$$\text{NPV of Project} = \sum_{t=1}^{t=N} \frac{CF_t}{(1 + r)^t} - \text{Initial Investment}$$

where

CF_t = Cash flow in period t
r   = Discount rate
N   = Life of the project

The net present value of a project with a discount rate of 12% can be written as shown in Figure 5.3.

Net Present Value (NPV): The net present value of a project is the sum of the present values of the expected cash flows on the project, net of the initial investment.

The net present value of a project can be computed from one of two standpoints:

1. It can be calculated from the perspective of all investors in the project by discounting *free cash flows to the firm* at the *cost of capital,* and netting out the *total initial investment* in the project.

2. It can also be calculated from the perspective of equity investors in the project by discounting *free cash flows to equity* at the *cost of equity,* and netting out the *initial equity investment* in the project. The cost of equity should reflect the riskiness of the project.

The key is to remain consistent in matching up discount rates and cash flows. Once the net present value is computed, the decision rule is simple since the hurdle rate is already factored in the present value.

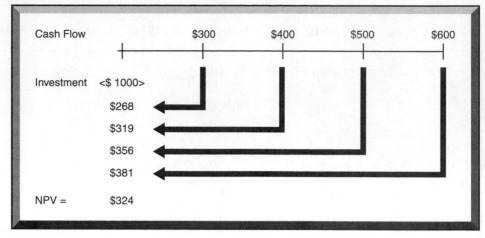

Figure 5.3 NPV of a project.

DECISION RULE FOR NPV FOR INDEPENDENT PROJECTS

If the NPV > 0   ⇒   Accept the project

If the NPV < 0   ⇒   Reject the project

Note that a net present value that is greater than zero implies that the project makes a return greater than the hurdle rate. The following examples illustrate the two approaches.

 This spreadsheet allows you to estimate the NPV from cash flows to the firm on a project (**capbudg.xls**).

5.9 THE SIGNIFICANCE OF A POSITIVE NET PRESENT VALUE

Assume that you have analyzed a $100 million project, using a cost of capital of 15%, and come up with a net present value of $1 million. The manager who has to decide on the project argues that this is too small of a NPV for a project of this size and that this indicates a "poor" project. Is this true?

☐ Yes. The NPV is only 1% of the initial investment.

☐ No. A positive NPV indicates a good project.

Explain your answer.

 ILLUSTRATION 5.12   NPV from the Firm's Standpoint: Bookscape On-line

Table 5.10 calculates the present value of the cash flows to Bookscape, as a firm from the proposed on-line book ordering service, using the cost of capital of 15.94% as the discount rate on the cash flows. (The cash flows are estimated in Illustration 5.4 and the cost of capital is estimated in Illustration 5.7)

This project has a net present value of −$184,939, suggesting that it is a project that should not be accepted, based on the projected cash flow and the cost of capital of 15.94%.

	Table 5.10 FCFF ON BOOKSCAPE ON-LINE	
Year	**FCFF**	**PV of FCFF (at 15.94%)**
0	($1,150,000)	($1,150,000)
1	$249,000	$214,762
2	$304,500	$226,517
3	$334,350	$214,522
4	$558,849	$309,259
NPV		$(184,939)

■▲
▼● ILLUSTRATION 5.13   **NPV from the Firm's Standpoint: Disney's Theme Park in Bangkok**
In estimating the cash flows to discount for Disney's theme park in Thailand, the first point to note when computing the net present value of the proposed theme park in Thailand is the fact that it has a life far longer than the ten years shown in Table 5.4. To bring in the cash flows that occur after year 9, when cash flows start growing at the same rate as inflation forever, we draw on a present value formula for a growing perpetuity (see Appendix 1):

$$\text{Present Value of Cash Flows after Year 9} = FCFF_{10} / (WACC - g)$$
$$= 86,620 \text{ Bt} / (.2541 - .15)$$
$$= 832,421 \text{ Bt}$$

where the free cash flow to the firm in year 10 is 86,620 Bt, the cost of capital is 25.41% and the expected inflation rate is 15%. This present value is called the *terminal value* and occurs at the end of year 9.

The net present value of the proposed theme parks in Thailand is estimated using the incremental cash flows in nominal Thai Baht, from Table 5.4, and Disney's cost of capital, in Baht terms, of 25.41%.

YEAR	FCFF	TERMINAL VALUE	TOTAL FCFF	PV OF FCFF
0	($70,000 Bt)		($70,000 Bt)	(70,000 Bt)
1	($39,078 Bt)		($39,078 Bt)	(31,161 Bt)
2	($36,199 Bt)		($36,199 Bt)	(23,017 Bt)
3	($11,759 Bt)		($11,759 Bt)	(5,962 Bt)
4	16,155 Bt		16,155 Bt	6,532 Bt
5	21,548 Bt		21,548 Bt	6,947 Bt
6	33,109 Bt		33,109 Bt	8,512 Bt
7	46,692 Bt		46,692 Bt	9,572 Bt
8	58,169 Bt		58,169 Bt	9,509 Bt
9	70,423 Bt	832,421 Bt	902,843 Bt	117,694 Bt
NPV				28,626 Bt

The net present value of this project suggests that it is a good project which will earn surplus value for Disney.

PV in year 9   Isn't this already PV   in year 9 !

IN PRACTICE: THE CURRENCY EFFECT: COMPUTING NPV

One of the debates that analysts often engage in when doing investment analysis is whether the analysis should be done in one currency or another. Intuitively, an analysis of whether a project is a good or bad one should not depend upon what currency the analysis is done in. In the Disney theme park analysis, for instance, the net present value was computed in Thai Baht to be 28,626 Bt. The entire analysis could have been done in dollar terms. To do this, the cash flows would have to be converted into dollars and the discount rate would then have been a dollar discount rate. It would have required the following steps:

Step 1: Estimate the Expected Exchange Rate for Each Period of the Analysis.

While forward rates might be available for some currencies for a few periods, there are very few cases where forward rates will be available for the entire project life. To estimate the expected exchange rate, we will draw on purchasing power parity that argues that changes in exchange rates between two countries will reflect differences in inflation in those countries. In the Disney example, since we assume the inflation rate to be 15% in Thailand and 3% in the United States and the current exchange rate is 35 Bt per dollar, the projected exchange rate in one year will be:

Expected Exchange Rate in Year 1 = 35 Bt * (1.15/1.03) = 39.08 Bt

Similar analysis will yield exchange rates for each of the next 10 years.

Step 2: Convert the Expected Cash Flows from Baht to Dollars in Future Periods Using These Exchange Rates.

Step 3: Discount the Expected Cash Flows at a Dollar Discount Rate.

In the case of Disney, this would mean using the dollar cost of capital of 12.32%, estimated in the previous chapter as the cost of capital for theme parks.

The following table summarizes exchange rates, cash flows, and the present value for the proposed Disney theme parks, with the analysis done entirely in dollars.

YEAR	CF/(IN Bt)	Bt/$	FCFF	TOTAL FCFF	PV AT 12.32%
0	−700000	35.00	$ (2,000)	$ (2,000)	$ (2,000)
1	−39078	39.08	$ (1,000)	$ (1,000)	$ (890)
2	−36199	43.63	$ (830)	$ (830)	$ (658)
3	−11759	48.71	$ (241)	$ (241)	$ (170)
4	16155	54.39	$ 297	$ 297	$ 187
5	21548	60.73	$ 355	$ 355	$ 198
6	33109	67.80	$ 488	$ 488	$ 243
7	46692	75.70	$ 617	$ 617	$ 273
8	51869	84.52	$ 688	$ 688	$ 272
9	902843	94.37	$ 9,568	$ 9,568	$ 3,363
NPV					$ 818

Note that the net present value of $818 million is exactly equal to the net present value computed earlier in Baht of 28,626 Bt, converted at the current exchange rate of 35 Bt per dollar.

5.10 CURRENCY CHOICES AND NPV

A company in a high-inflation economy has asked for your advice regarding which currency to use for investment analysis. The company believes that using the local currency to estimate the NPV will yield too low a value, because domestic interest rates are very high—this, in turn, would push up the discount rate. Is this true?

☐ Yes. A higher discount rate will lead to lower NPV.

☐ No.

Explain your answer.

ILLUSTRATION 5.14 NPV from the Equity Investors' Standpoint: Paper Plant for Aracruz

The net present value is computed from the equity investors' standpoint for the proposed linerboard plant for Aracruz, using real cash flows to equity, estimated in Table 5.6, and a real cost of equity of 10.33%. (See Table 5.11.)

The net present value of 32.28 million BR suggests that this is a good project for Aracruz to take on.

5.11 EQUITY, DEBT, AND NET PRESENT VALUE

In the project described above, assume that Aracruz had used all equity to finance the project, instead of its mix of debt and equity. Which of the following is likely to occur to the NPV?

☐ The NPV will go up, because the cash flows to equity will be much higher; there will be no interest and principal payments to make each year.

☐ The NPV will go down, because the initial investment in the project will be much higher.

☐ The NPV will remain unchanged, because the financing mix should not affect the NPV.

☑ The NPV might go up or down, depending upon: . . . k_e vs k_D

Explain your answer.

Table 5.11 FCFE ON LINERBOARD PLANT

Year	FCFE	PV of FCFE
0	(185,100 BR)	(185,100 BR)
1	38,244 BR	34,663 BR
2	36,477 BR	29,966 BR
3	36,227 BR	26,974 BR
4	38,006 BR	25,649 BR
5	(14,907 BR)	(9,119 BR)
6	38,097 BR	21,122 BR
7	35,082 BR	17,629 BR
8	32,624 BR	14,859 BR
9	30,609 BR	12,636 BR
10	114,925 BR	43,001 BR
NPV		32,280 BR

IN PRACTICE: REAL AND NOMINAL NET PRESENT VALUE CALCULATIONS

In the project analyses in this chapter, we have used nominal cash flows and discount rates for the Disney and Bookscape investments, and real cash flows and discount rates for the Aracruz analysis. If done consistently, each analysis should yield the same net present value. For instance, the Disney theme park analysis could have been done entirely in real Baht, and discounted back at the real cost of capital. The real cost of capital can be estimated from the nominal cost of capital of 25.41% and the inflation rate of 15%:

$$\text{Real Cost of Capital} = 1.2541/1.15 - 1 = 1.0905 \text{ or } 9.05\%$$

The real cash flows can be obtained by deflating the nominal cash flows at the inflation rate of 15%. Thus, the real cash flow in year 2 can be estimated from the nominal cash flow in year 2:

$$\text{Real Cash Flow in Year 2} = 36{,}199 \text{ Bt}/1.15^2 = 27{,}371 \text{ Bt}$$

YEAR	NOMINAL CF (Bt)	REAL CASHFLOW	PV AT REAL COST OF CAPITAL
0	(70,000 Bt)	(70,000 Bt)	(70,000 Bt)
1	(39,078 Bt)	(33,981 Bt)	(31,161 Bt)
2	(36,199 Bt)	(27,371 Bt)	(23,017 Bt)
3	(11,759 Bt)	(7,731 Bt)	(5,962 Bt)
4	16,155 Bt	9,237 Bt	6,532 Bt
5	21,548 Bt	10,713 Bt	6,947 Bt
6	33,109 Bt	14,314 Bt	8,512 Bt
7	46,692 Bt	17,553 Bt	9,572 Bt
8	58,169 Bt	19,015 Bt	9,509 Bt
9	902,843 Bt	256,644 Bt	117,694 Bt
			28,626 Bt

The net present value is identical to the one computed using nominal cash flows in Illustration 5.13.

The choice between nominal and real cash flows therefore boils down to one of convenience. When inflation rates are low, it is better to do the analysis in nominal terms since taxes are based upon nominal income. When inflation rates are high and volatile, it is easier to do the analysis in real terms.

Properties of the NPV Rule

The net present value has several important properties that make it an attractive decision rule.

1. Net Present Values Are Additive

The net present values of individual projects can be aggregated to arrive at a cumulative net present value for a business or a division. No other investment decision rule has this property. The property itself has a number of implications.

- The value of a firm can be written in terms of the net present values of the projects it has already taken on as well as the net present values of prospective future projects:

Value of a Firm = Σ Present Value of Projects in Place + Σ NPV of expected future projects

The first term in this equation captures the value of *assets in place,* while the second term measures the value of *expected future growth.* Note that the present value of projects in place is based on anticipated future cash flows on these projects.

- When a firm terminates an existing project that has a negative present value based on anticipated future cash flows, the value of the firm will increase by that amount. Similarly, when a firm takes on a new project, with a negative net present value, the value of the firm will decrease by that amount.

- When a firm divests itself of an existing asset, the price received for that asset will affect the value of the firm. If the price received exceeds the present value of the anticipated cash flows on that asset to the firm, the value of the firm will increase with the divestiture; otherwise, it will decrease.

- When a firm takes on a new project with a positive net present value, the market price of the firm will be affected depending upon whether the NPV meets expectations. For example, a firm like Microsoft is expected to take on high positive NPV projects and this expectation is built into value. Even if the new projects taken on by Microsoft have positive NPV, there may be a drop in price if the NPV does not meet the high expectations of financial markets.

- When a firm makes an acquisition and pays a price that exceeds the present value of the expected cash flows from the firm being acquired (plus synergy and other benefits), it is the equivalent of taking on a negative net present value project and will lead to a drop in value.

Assets in Place: These are the assets already owned by a firm, or projects that it has already taken on.

5.12   FIRM VALUE AND OVERPAYMENT ON ACQUISITIONS

Megatech Corporation, a large software firm with a market value for its equity of $100 million, announces that it will be acquiring FastMail Corporation, a smaller software firm, for $15 million. On the announcement, Megatech's stock price drops by 3%. Based upon these facts, estimate the amount which the market thinks Megatech should have paid for FastMail Corporation:

☐ $15 million
☐ $3 million
☐ $12 million

How does NPV additivity enter into your answer?

2. Intermediate Cash Flows Are Invested at the Hurdle Rate

Implicit in all present value calculations are assumptions about the rate at which intermediate cash flows get reinvested. The net present value rule assumes that intermediate cash flows on a projects (i.e., cash flows that occur between the initiation and the end of the project) get reinvested at the *hurdle rate,* which is the cost of capital if the cash flows are to the firm and the cost of equity if the cash flows are to equity investors. Given that both the cost of equity and capital are based upon the returns that can be made on alternative investments of equivalent risk, this assumption should be a reasonable one.

Hurdle Rate: This is the minimum acceptable rate of return that a firm will accept for taking on a given project.

3. NPV Calculations Allow for Expected Term Structure and Interest Rate Shifts

In all of the examples throughout in this chapter, we have assumed that the discount rate remains unchanged over time. This is not always the case, however; the net present value can be computed using time-varying discount rates. The general formulation for the NPV rule is as follows:

$$\text{NPV of Project} = \sum_{t=1}^{t=N} \frac{CF_t}{\prod_{j=1}^{j=t} (1 + r_t)} - \text{Initial Investment}$$

where

CF_t = Cash flow in period t

r_t = One-period discount rate that applies to period t

N = Life of the project

The discount rates may change for three reasons:

- The level of interest rates may be expected to change over time and the term structure may provide some insight on expected rates in the future.
- The risk characteristics of the project may be expected to change in a predictable way over time, resulting in changes in the discount rate.
- The financing mix on the project may change over time, resulting in changes in both the cost of equity and the cost of capital.

ILLUSTRATION 5.15   NPV Calculation with Time-Varying Discount Rates
Assume that you are analyzing a four-year project, investing in computer software development. Further, assume that the technological uncertainty associated with the software industry leads to higher discount rates in future years.

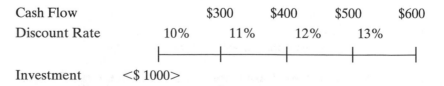

Cash Flow		$300	$400	$500	$600
Discount Rate	10%	11%	12%	13%	

Investment   <$ 1000>

The present value of each of the cash flows can be computed as follows:
PV of Cash Flow in year 1 = $ 300 / 1.10   = $272.72
PV of Cash Flow in year 2 = $ 400/ (1.10 * 1.11)   = $327.60

PV of Cash Flow in year 3 = $ 500/ (1.10 * 1.11 * 1.12)   = $365.63
PV of Cash Flow in year 4 = $ 600/ (1.10 * 1.11 * 1.12 * 1.13)   = $388.27
NPV of Project = $ 272.72 + $ 327.60 + $ 365.63 + $ 388.27 − $ 1000.00 = $354.22

5.13 CHANGING DISCOUNT RATES AND NPV

In the above analysis, assume that you had been asked to use one discount rate for all of the cash flows. Is there a discount rate that would yield the same NPV as the one above?

☐ Yes

☐ No

If yes, how would you interpret this discount rate?

Biases, Limitations, and Caveats
In spite of its advantages and its linkage to the objective of value maximization, the net present value rule continues to have its detractors, who point out some limitations:

- The net present value is stated in absolute rather than relative terms and does not, therefore, factor in the scale of the projects. Thus, project A may have a net present value of $200, while project B has a net present value of $100, but project A may require an initial investment that is ten or 100 times larger than project B. Proponents of the NPV rule argue that it is surplus value, over and above the hurdle rate, no matter what the investment.

- The net present value rule does not control for the life of the project. Consequently, when comparing mutually exclusive projects with different life-times, the NPV rule is biased toward accepting longer-term projects.

IN PRACTICE: COMPARING PROJECTS: NPV AND EQUIVALENT ANNUITIES

In general, a project with a higher net present value is better than one with a lower net present value, but only if they have the same lives. When comparing mutually exclusive projects with different lifetimes, it is no longer appropriate to compare the net present values; as a dollar value, it is biased towards longer term projects. To make net present values comparable across projects, they should be converted into annuities:

Equivalent Annuity = NPV of Project (Annuity factor given project life and discount rate)

To illustrate, assume that the net present value of a 5-year project is $ 100 and the net present value of a 10-year project is $ 200, the equivalent annuities, given a discount rate of 10% for both projects, would be as follows:

Equivalent Annuity of 5-year project = $ 100 (APV, 10%, 5 years) = $ 26.38

Equivalent Annuity of 10-year project = $ 200 (APV, 10%, 10 years) = $ 32.55

Given these equivalent annuities, the 10-year project is the better project. This approach implicitly assumes that these projects are replicable. To the degree that they are not, the assumptions about reinvestment opportunities have to be made explicit.

Internal Rate of Return

The internal rate of return is based on discounted cash flows. Unlike the net present value rule, however, it is a percentage rate of return. It is the discounted cash flow analog to the accounting rates of return. In general terms, the internal rate of return is that discount rate that makes the net present value of a project equal to zero. To illustrate, consider again the project described at the beginning of the net present value discussion:

Internal Rate of Return (IRR): The IRR of a project measures the rate of return earned by the project based upon cash flows, allowing for the time value of money.

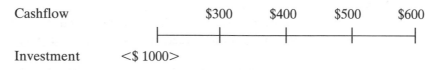

Internal Rate of Return = 24.89%

At the internal rate of return, the net present value of this project is zero. The linkage between the net present value and the internal rate of return is most visible when the net present value is graphed as a function of the discount rate in a *net present value profile*. A net present value profile for the project described is illustrated in Figure 5.4.

The net present value profile provides several insights on the project's viability. First, the internal rate of return is clear from the graph—it is the point at which the profile crosses the X axis. Second, it provides a measure of how sensitive the NPV— and, by extension, the project decision—is to changes in the discount rate. The slope of the NPV profile is a measure of the discount rate sensitivity of the project. Third, when mutually exclusive projects are being analyzed, graphing both NPV profiles together provides a measure of the break-even discount rate—the rate at which the decision maker will be indifferent between the two projects.

NPV Profile: This measures the sensitivity of the net present value to changes in the discount rate.

5.14 DISCOUNT RATES AND NPV

In the project described above, the NPV decreased as the discount rate was increased. Is this always the case?

☐ Yes

☐ No

If no, when might the NPV go up as the discount rate is increased?

Using the Internal Rate of Return

One advantage of the internal rate of return according to its proponents is that it can be used even in cases where the discount rate is unknown. While this is true for the calculation of the IRR, it is *not true* when the decision maker has to use the IRR to decide whether to take a project or not. At that stage in the process, the internal rate

Figure 5.4   NPV profile.

of return has to be compared to the discount rate—if the IRR is greater than the discount rate, the project is a good one; alternatively, the project should be rejected.

Like the net present value, the internal rate of return can be computed in one of two ways:

1. The IRR can be calculated based upon the free cash flows to the firm and the total investment in the project. In doing so, the IRR has to be compared to the cost of capital.
2. The IRR can be calculated based upon the free cash flows to equity and the equity investment in the project. If it is estimated with these cash flows, it has to be compared to the cost of equity, which should reflect the riskiness of the project.

DECISION RULE FOR IRR FOR INDEPENDENT PROJECTS

A. IRR is computed on cash flows to the firm

If the IRR > Cost of Capital   ⟹   Accept the project

If the IRR < Cost of Capital   ⟹   Reject the project

B. IRR is computed on cash flows to equity

If the IRR > Cost of Equity   ⟹   Accept the project

If the IRR < Cost of Equity   ⟹   Reject the project

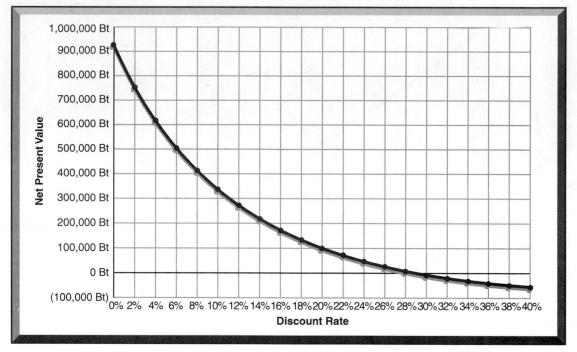

Figure 5.5   NPV profile of Disney theme park.

When choosing between projects of equivalent risk, the project with the higher IRR is viewed as the better project.

ILLUSTRATION 5.16   Estimating the IRR based on FCFF: Disney Theme Park in Thailand
The cash flows to the firm from the proposed theme park in Thailand are used to arrive at a NPV profile for the project in Figure 5.5.

The internal rate of return (in baht terms) on this project is 28.85%, which is *higher* than the cost of capital of 25.41%. These results are consistent with the findings from the NPV rule, which also recommended investing in the theme parks. (The internal rate of return in dollar terms is 15.40%, which exceeds the dollar cost of capital of 12.32%.)

ILLUSTRATION 5.17   Estimating IRR Based Upon FCFE: Aracruz Cellulose
The net present value profile depicted in Figure 5.6 is based upon the equity investment and the free cash flows to equity estimated for the paper plant for Aracruz.

The internal rate of return (in real terms) on this project is 13.87%, which is *higher* than the real cost of equity of 10.33%. Again, these results are consistent with the findings from the NPV rule, which also recommended accepting this investment.

Biases, Limitations, and Caveats
The internal rate of return is the most widely used discounted cash flow rule in investment analysis, but it does have some serious limitations.

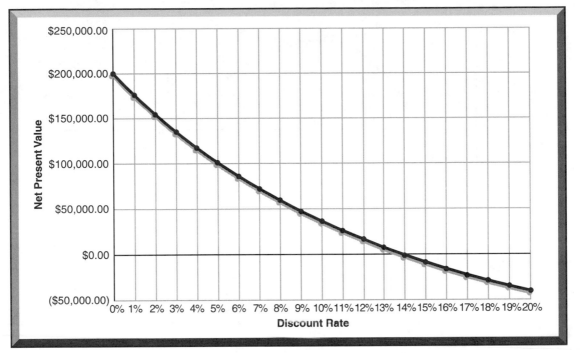

Figure 5.6   NPV profile on equity investment in paper plant: Aracruz.

- Since the IRR is a percent return measure, it tends to bias decision makers toward smaller projects, which are much more likely to yield high percentage returns, over larger ones.
- There are a number of scenarios where the internal rate of return cannot be computed or is not meaningful as a decision tool. The first is when there is either no investment or only a very small initial investment and the investment is spread over time. In such cases, the IRR cannot be computed, or, if computed, is likely to be meaningless. The second is when there is more than one internal rate of return for a project, and it is not clear which one the decision maker should use.

ILLUSTRATION 5.18   **Multiple IRR Projects**
Consider a project to manufacture and sell a consumer product, with a hurdle rate of 12%, that has a four-year life and the following cash flows over those four years (the project, which requires the licensing of a trademark, requires a large negative payment at the end of the fourth year):

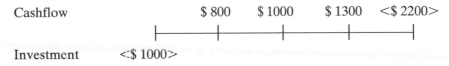

The net present value profile for this project (Figure 5.7) reflects the problems that arise with the IRR measure.

Figure 5.7 NPV profile for multiple IRR project.

As you can see, this project has two internal rates of return: 6.60% and 36.55%. Since the hurdle rate falls between these two IRRs, the decision on whether to take the project or not will change depending upon which IRR is used. In order to make the right decision in this case, the decision maker would have to look at the NPV profile. If, as in this case, the net present value is positive at the hurdle rate, the project should be accepted. If the net present value is negative at the hurdle rate, the project should be rejected.

IN PRACTICE: MULTIPLE IRRS: WHY THEY EXIST AND WHAT TO DO ABOUT THEM

The internal rate of return can be viewed mathematically as a root to the present value equation for cash flows. In the conventional project, where there is an initial investment and positive cash flows thereafter, there is only one sign change in the cash flows, and one root—that is, there is a unique IRR. When there is more than one sign change in the cash flows, there will be more than one internal rate of return.[5] In Figure 5.7, for example, the cash flow changes sign from negative to positive in year 1, and from positive to negative in year 4, leading to two internal rates of return.

Lest this be viewed as some strange artifact that is unlikely to happen in the real world, note that many long-term projects require substantial reinvestment at

---

[5]While the number of internal rates of return will be equal to the number of sign changes, some internal rates of return may be so far out of the realm of the ordinary (e.g., 10,000%) that they may not create the kinds of problems described here.

intermediate points in the project and that these reinvestments may cause the cash flows in those years to become negative. When this happens, the IRR approach may run into trouble.

There are a number of solutions suggested for the multiple IRR problems. One is to use the hurdle rate to bring the negative cash flows from intermediate periods back to the present. Another is to construct a NPV profile. In either case, it is probably much simpler to estimate and use the net present value.

Comparing NPV and IRR

While the net present value and the internal rate of return are viewed as competing investment decision rules, they generally yield similar conclusions in most cases. The differences between the two rules are most visible when decision makers are choosing between mutually exclusive projects.

Differences in Scale

The net present value of a project is stated in dollar terms and does not factor in the scale of the project. The internal rate of return, by contrast, is a percentage rate of return, which is standardized for the scale of the project. When choosing between mutually exclusive projects of different magnitudes, this can lead to very different results.

ILLUSTRATION 5.19   NPV and IRR for Projects of Different Scale

Assume that you are a small bank and that you are comparing two mutually exclusive projects. The first project, which is to hire four extra tellers at the branches that you operate, requires an initial investment of $1 million and produces the cash flow revenues shown below in Figure 5.8. The second project requires investment of $10 million in an automated teller machine, and is likely to produce the much higher cash flows shown in Figure 5.8, as well. The hurdle rate is 15% for both projects.

The two decision rules yield different results. The net present value rule suggests that Project B is the better project, while the internal rate of return rule leans toward Project A. This is not surprising, given the differences in scale.

Which rule yields the better decision? The answer depends on the capital rationing constraints faced by the business making the decision. When there are no capital rationing constraints (i.e., the firm has the capacity to raise as much capital as it needs to take prospective projects), the net present value rule provides the right answer—Project B should be picked over Project A. If there are capital rationing constraints, however, then taking Project B may lead to the rejection of good projects later on. In those cases, the internal rate of return rule may provide the better solution.

Capital Rationing: This refers to the scenario where the firm does not have sufficient funds—either on hand or in terms of access to markets—to take on all of the good projects it might have.

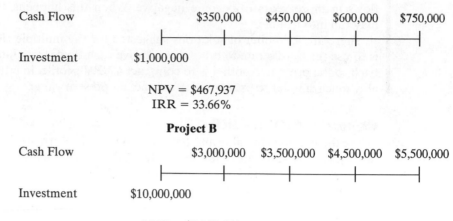

Figure 5.8   NPV and IRR—different scale projects.

AN APPROACH TO SCALING NPV: THE PROFITABILITY INDEX

Another way of scaling the net present value is to divide it by the initial investment in the project. Doing so provides the profitability index, which is another measure of project return:

$$\text{Profitability Index} = \frac{\text{Net Present Value}}{\text{Initial Investment}}$$

In Illustration 5.19, for instance, the profitability index can be computed as follows for each project:

Profitability Index for Project A = $467,937 / $1,000,000 = 46.79%

Profitability Index for Project B = $1,358,664 / $10,000,000 = 13.59%

Based on the profitability index, project A is the better project, after scaling for size.

In most cases, the profitability index and the internal rate of return will yield similar results. The differences between these approaches can be traced to differences in reinvestment assumptions.

Profitability Index (PI): The profitability index is the net present value of a project divided by the initial investment in the project—it is a scaled version of NPV.

Differences in Reinvestment Rate Assumption

While the differences between the NPV rule and the IRR rules due to scale are fairly obvious, there is a subtler, and much more significant difference between the two rules, relating to the reinvestment of intermediate cash flows. As pointed out earlier,

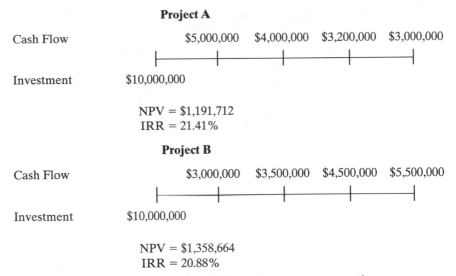

Figure 5.9   NPV and IRR—reinvestment assumption.

the net present value rule assumes that intermediate cash flows are reinvested at the discount rate, whereas the IRR rule assumes that intermediate cash flows are reinvested at the IRR. As a consequence, the two rules can yield different conclusions, even for projects with the same scale, as illustrated in Figure 5.9.

In this case, the net present value rule ranks Project B higher, while the IRR rule ranks Project A as the better project. The differences arise because the NPV rule assumes that intermediate cash flows get invested at the hurdle rate, which is 15%. The IRR rule assumes that intermediate cash flows get reinvested at the IRR of that project. While both projects are impacted by this assumption, it has a much greater effect for Project A, which has higher cash flows earlier on. The reinvestment assumption is made clearer if the expected end balance is estimated under each rule:

End Balance for Project A with IRR of 21.41% = $\$10,000,000*1.2141^4 = \$21,730,887$

End Balance for Project B with IRR of 20.88% = $\$10,000,000*1.2088^4 = \$21,353,673$

To arrive at these end balances, however, the cash flows in years 1, 2, and 3 will have to be reinvested at the IRR. If they are reinvested at a lower rate, the end balance on these projects will be lower than the values stated above, and the actual return earned will be lower than the IRR even though the cash flows on the project came in as anticipated.

The reinvestment rate assumption made by the IRR rule creates more serious consequences the longer the term of the project and the higher the IRR, since it implicitly assumes that the firm has and will continue to have a fountain of projects yielding returns similar to those earned by the project under consideration.

IN PRACTICE: A SOLUTION TO THE REINVESTMENT RATE PROBLEM: THE MODIFIED INTERNAL RATE OF RETURN

One solution that has been suggested for the reinvestment rate assumption is to assume that intermediate cash flows get reinvested at the hurdle rate—the cost of equity if the cash flows are to equity investors and the cost of capital if they are to the firm—and to calculate the internal rate of return from the initial investment and the terminal value. This approach yields what is called the modified internal rate of return (MIRR), as illustrated in Figure 5.10.

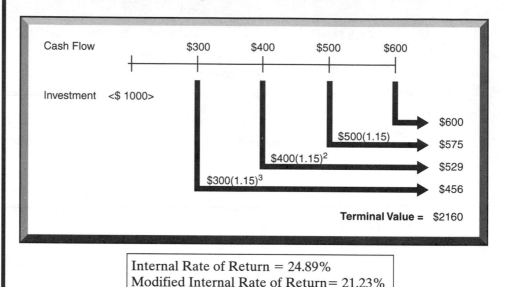

| Internal Rate of Return = 24.89% |
| Modified Internal Rate of Return = 21.23% |

Figure 5.10 IRR versus modified internal rate of return.

$$\text{Modified Internal Rate of Return} = (\$2160 / \$1000)^{1/4} - 1 = 21.23\%$$

The modified internal rate of return is lower than the internal rate of return because the intermediate cash flows are invested at the hurdle rate of 15% instead of the IRR of 24.89%.

There are many who believe that the MIRR is neither fish nor fowl, since it is a mix of the NPV rule and the IRR rule. From a practical standpoint, the MIRR becomes a weighted average of the returns on individual projects and the hurdle rates the firm uses, with the weights on each depending on the magnitude and timing of the cash flows—the larger and earlier the cash flows on the project, the greater the weight attached to the hurdle rate. Furthermore, the MIRR approach will yield the same choices as the NPV approach for projects of the same scale and lifetime.

■ **Modified Internal Rate of Return (MIRR):** This is the internal rate of return, computed on the assumption that intermediate cash flows are reinvested at the hurdle rate.

WHERE DO GOOD PROJECTS COME FROM?

In the process of analyzing new investments in the preceding chapters, we have contended that good projects have a positive net present value and earn an internal rate of return greater than the hurdle rate. While these criteria are certainly valid from a measurement standpoint, they do not address the deeper questions about good projects including the economic conditions that make for a "good" project and why it is that some firms have a more ready supply of "good" projects than others.

Implicit in the definition of a good project—one that earns a return that is greater than that earned on investments of equivalent risk—is the existence of super-normal returns to the business considering the project. In a competitive market for real investments, the existence of these excess returns should act as a magnet, attracting competitors to take on similar investments. In the process, excess returns should dissipate over time; how quickly they dissipate will depend on the ease with which competition can enter the market and provide close substitutes and on the magnitude of any differential advantages that the business with the good projects might possess. Take an extreme scenario, whereby the business with the good projects has no differential advantage in cost or project quality over its competitors, and new competitors can enter the market easily and at low cost to provide substitutes. In this case the super-normal returns on these projects should disappear very quickly.

An integral basis for the existence of a "good" project is the creation and maintenance of barriers to new or existing competitors taking on equivalent or similar projects. These barriers can take different forms, including

a. Economies of Scale: Some projects might earn high returns only if they are done on a "large" scale, thus restricting competition from smaller companies. In such cases, large companies in this line of business may be able to continue to earn super-normal returns on their projects because smaller competitors will not be able to replicate them.

b. Cost Advantages: A business might work at establishing a cost advantage over its competitors, either by being more efficient or by taking advantage of arrangements that its competitors cannot use. For example, in the late 1980s, Southwest Airlines was able to establish a cost advantage over its large competitors, such as American and United Airlines, by using non-union employees and having a less top-heavy cost structure.

c. Capital Requirements: Entry into some businesses might require such large investments that it discourages competitors from entering, even though projects in those businesses may earn above-market returns. For example, assume that Boeing is faced with a large number of high-return projects in the aerospace business. While this scenario would normally attract competitors, the huge initial investment needed to enter this business would enable Boeing to continue to earn these high returns.

d. Product Differentiation: Some businesses continue to earn excess returns by differentiating their products from those of their competitors, leading to either higher profit margins or higher sales. This differentiation can be created in a number of ways-through effective advertising and promotion (Coca Cola), technical expertise (Sony), better service (Nordstrom) and responsiveness to customer needs.

e. Access to Distribution Channels: Those firms that have much better access to the distribution channels for their products than their competitors are better able to earn excess returns. In some cases, the restricted access to outsiders is due to tradition or loyalty to existing competitors. In other cases, the firm may actually own the distribution channel, and competitors may not be able to develop their own distribution channels because the costs are prohibitive.

f. Legal and Government Barriers: In some cases, a firm may be able to exploit investment opportunities without worrying about competition because of restrictions on competitors from product patents the firm may own or due to government restrictions on competitive entry.

Quality of Management and Project Quality

In the preceding section we examined some of the factors that determine the attractiveness of the projects a firm will face. While some factors, such as government restrictions on entry, may largely be out of the control of incumbent management, there are other factors that can clearly be influenced by management.[6] Considering each of the factors discussed above, for instance, we would argue that a good management team can increase both the number of and the returns on available projects by

- *taking projects that exploit any economies of scale that the firm may possess.* In addition, management can look for ways it can create economies of scale in the firm's existing operations.

- *establishing and nurturing cost advantages over its competitors.* Some cost advantages may arise from labor negotiations, while others may result from long-term strategic decisions made by the firm. For instance, by owning and developing SABRE, the airline reservation system, American Airlines has been able to gain a cost advantage over its competitors.

- *taking actions that increase the initial cost for new entrants into the business.* One of the primary reasons Microsoft's was able to dominate the computer software market in the early 1990s was its ability to increase the investment needed to develop and market software programs.

- *increasing brand name recognition and value through advertising and by delivering superior products to customers.* A good example is the success that Snapple experienced in the early 1990s in promoting and selling its iced tea beverages.

- *nurturing markets in which the company's differential advantage is greatest, in terms of either cost of delivery or brand name value.* In some cases, this will involve expanding into foreign markets, as both Levi Strauss and McDonalds did in the 1980s in order to exploit their higher brand name recognition in those markets. In other cases, this may require concentrating on segments of an existing market as The Gap did, when it expanded its Banana Republic division, which sells upscale outdoor clothing.

- *improving the firm's reputation for customer service and product delivery.* This will enable the firm to increase both profits and returns. One of the primary fac-

---

[6]When government policy is influenced by lobbying by firms, it can be argued that even these factors may be affected by the management of a firm.

tors behind Chrysler's financial recovery in the 1980s was the company's ability to establish a reputation for producing quality cars and minivans.

- *developing distribution channels that are unique and cannot be easily accessed by competitors.* Avon, for instance, employed a large sales force to go door-to-door to reach consumers who could not be reached by other distribution channels.
- *getting patents on products or technologies that keep out the competition and earn high returns.* Doing so may require large investments in research and development over time. It can be argued that Intel's success in the market for semiconductors can be traced to the strength of its research and development efforts and the patents it consequently obtained on advanced chips, such as the Pentium.[7]

While the quality of management is typically related to the quality of projects a firm possesses, a good management team does not guarantee the existence of good projects. In fact, there is a rather large element of chance involved in the process. Even the best laid plans of the management team to create project opportunities may come to naught if circumstances conspire against them – a recession may upend a retailer, or an oil price shock may cause an airline to lose money.

The Role of Acquisitions

As firms mature and increase in size, they are often confronted with a quandary. Instead of being cash poor and project rich, they find that their existing projects generate far more cash than they have available projects in which to invest. This can be attributed partly to size and partly to competition. As they face up to their new status as cash-rich companies, with limited investment opportunities, acquiring other firms with a ready supply of high-return projects looks like an attractive option, but there is a catch. If these firms are publicly traded, the market price already reflects the expected higher returns not only on existing projects but also on expected future projects. In terms of present value, the value of a firm can be written as

$$\text{Value of Firm} = \begin{array}{l} \text{Present Value of Cash Flows from Existing Projects} \\ + \text{ Net Present Value of Cash Flows from Expected Future Projects} \end{array}$$

Thus, firms that are earning super-normal returns on their existing projects and are expected to maintain this status in the future will sell at prices that reflect these expectations. Accordingly, even if the cash-rich firm pays a "fair" price to acquire one of these firms, it has to earn more than the expected super-normal returns to be able to claim any premium from the acquisition. To put all this in perspective, assume that you are considering the acquisition of a firm that is earning 25% on its projects, when the hurdle rate on these projects is 12%, and that it is expected to maintain these high returns for the foreseeable future. A fair price attached to this acquisition will reflect this expectation. All this implies that an acquisition will earn super-normal returns for the acquirer if, and only if, one of the following conditions holds:

- The acquisition is done at a price below the fair price (i.e., the company is significantly undervalued).

---

[7]It is estimated that Intel spent between $3 billion and $5 billion developing the Pentium chip.

- The acquisition is done at a price that reflects the expectation that the firm will earn 25% but the acquirer manages to earn an even higher return, say 30%, on future projects.
- The acquisition enables the firm to take on projects that it would not have taken on as an independent firm; the net present value of these additional projects will then be a bonus that is earned by the acquiring firm. This is the essence of *synergy.*
- The acquisition lowers the discount rate on projects, leading to an increase in net present value, even though the returns may come in as expected.

Overall, it is clear that internally generated projects have better odds of success than do acquisitions since no premium is paid for market expectations up front.

Synergy: This is the increase in the value that results from combining two firms.

Corporate Strategy and Project Quality

At the lofty level of corporate strategy, there may seem to be little use for the mechanics of corporate finance. Consequently, corporate strategic decisions are often made with little or no corporate financial analysis to back them up. One way in which corporate strategy *can be* linked to corporate finance, however, is through investment policy. An objective of any corporate strategy should be to enable the firm to develop a long-term capacity to differentiate itself and earn higher returns than its competitors. Alternatively, the efficacy of a corporate strategic choice can be measured through its effect on the firm's capacity to earn excess returns on its projects. Many of the concepts that are popular in corporate strategy can be linked to the discussion in this section.

CONCLUSION

Investment analysis is arguably the most important part of corporate financial analysis. In this chapter, we have defined the scope of investment analysis and examined a range of investment analysis techniques, ranging from accounting rate of return measures, such as return of equity and return on assets, to discounted cash flow techniques, such as net present value and internal rate of return. In general, it can be argued that:

- Any decision that requires the use of resources is an investment decision; thus, investment decisions cover everything from broad strategic decisions at one extreme to decisions on how much inventory to carry at the other.
- There are two basic approaches to investment analysis; in the equity approach, the returns to equity investors from a project are measured against the cost of equity to decide whether to take on a project; in the firm approach, the returns to all investors (capital) in the firm are measured against the cost of capital to arrive at the same judgment.
- Accounting rate of return measures, such as return on equity or return on capital, generally work better for projects that have large initial investments, earnings that are roughly equal to the cash flows, and level earnings over time. For most projects, accounting returns will increase over time as the book value of the assets is depreciated.

- Payback, which looks at how quickly a project returns its initial investment in nominal cash flow terms, is a useful secondary measure of project performance or a measure of risk, but it is not a very effective primary technique because it does not consider cash flows after the initial investment is recouped.

- Discounted cash flow methods provide the best measures of true returns on projects because they are based on cash flows and consider the time value of money.

- Among discounted cash flow methods, net present value provides an unscaled measure while internal rate of return provides a scaled measure of project performance. Both methods require the same information and, for the most part, they yield the same conclusions when used to analyze independent projects. The internal rate of return does tend to overstate the return on good projects because it assumes that intermediate cash flows get reinvested at the internal rate of return. When analyzing mutually exclusive projects, the internal rate of return is biased toward smaller projects and may be the more appropriate decision rule for firms that have capital constraints.

- Firms seem much more inclined to use internal rate of return than net present value as an investment analysis tool; this can be partly attributed to the fact that IRR is a scaled measure of return, and partly to capital rationing constraints firms may face.

PROBLEMS AND QUESTIONS

1. A firm in Oklahoma is considering an investment project that needs an initial investment capital of $500,000. The project is to last 10 years with no salvage value. The EBIT is estimated to be $120,000 per year. What is the after-tax return on capital if the marginal tax rate is 34%?

2. A project calls for an initial investment of $1.2 million. This project will be completely depreciated over three years by the use of straight-line method, although its estimated market value at year 5 will be $400,000. It is estimated that the project will bring in $200,000 a year as EBIT for five years. The tax rate is 34%.
   a. Calculate after-tax ROC for each of the next five years.
   b. Find the geometric average return on capital.
   c. If the cost of capital is 25%, should the project be accepted?

3. Your company uses return on equity in the capital budgeting process. A project under evaluation needs an initial outlay of $1 million. Forty percent of the investment will be financed by bonds, with the balance of needed funding coming from equity. This project will generate an additional

$50,000 in net income a year. What is the return on equity if the salvage value is 0 when the project is terminated five years later?

4. A company's acceptable minimum return on capital is 12%. If the debt/equity ratio is 100%, and the after-tax interest rate is 5%. What is the corresponding acceptable minimum return on equity?

5. A company is considering building a hotel in Beijing, China. Because of the political risk involved, the company wants to have a small payback period. The cash flows are estimated to be as follows:

Year	Cash Flows
0	−3,000,000
1	250,000
2	500,000
3	750,000
4	750,000
5–20	750,000

   a. Find the payback period for the project.
   b. Find the NPV of this project if the discount rate is 10%.

6. A project under evaluation is estimated to generate free cash flow to the firm as follows:

Year	FCFF
0	−2,000,000
1	100,000
2–10 per year	300,000

Calculate the net present value if (1) the cost of capital is 10%; or (2) the cost of capital is 15%. Should the firm accept the project?

7. Your company is considering a project that will bring in annual free cash flow to equity in the amount of $50,000 for 10 years. If the cost of equity is 14%, what would be the maximum initial investment on the project below which the project would be accepted based on the NPV rule?

8. Your company has decided to invest in a project with estimated NPV of $2 million. The financing of the project is a combination of retained earnings and bonds. If the company has 1 million shares outstanding and the financial market seems to accept the management's estimate on the NPV of this project, what would be the impact of this project on the company's stock price per share?

9. It is sometimes argued that net present value should be based on time-varying discount rates. As an example, consider a project with projected cash flows as follows:

Year	Cash Flows	Appropriate Discount Rate
0	−500,000	
1	300,000	10%
2	350,000	12%

10. What is the NPV of this project?

11. There are two mutually exclusive projects with estimated cash flows to firm as follows:

Year	Project A	Project B
0	−500	−2,000
1–19	50	190
20	100	340

a. What is the IRR for Project A?
b. What is the IRR for Project B?
c. Which project should be accepted based on the IRR rule?

d. What are the NPVs of Project A and Project B if the cost of capital is 5%? Which project should be accepted on the NPV rule?
e. What are the NPVs of Project A and Project B if the cost of capital is 7.5%? Which project should be accepted based on the NPV rule?
f. Do the IRR rule and NPV rule always reach the same conclusion with regard to the selection of two mutually exclusive projects? Which method is more consistent with the objective of corporate finance to maximize shareholders' wealth?

12. You have acquired new equipment for a project costing $15 million. The equipment is expected to have a salvage value of $3 million and a depreciable life of 10 years. The cost of capital is 12%, and the firm faces a tax rate of 40%.
a. Estimate the present value and the nominal value of the tax benefits from depreciation, assuming that you use straight-line depreciation.
b. Estimate the present value and the nominal value of the tax benefits from depreciation, assuming that you use double-declining balance depreciation.
c. Why does double-declining balance depreciation yield a higher present value?

13. You are analyzing the depreciation tax benefits from acquiring an asset that cost $2.5 million and has a salvage value of $0.5 million. The asset is classified as an asset with a five-year depreciable life in the ACRS system. Using the depreciation rates provided in the ACRs table:
a. Estimate the depreciation tax benefits each year on this asset, assuming that the tax rate is 40%.
b. Estimate the present value of these tax benefits, assuming a cost of capital of 10%.
c. If you could expense this asset instead of using the ACRS rates, how much would you gain in present value terms from tax benefits?

14. In both examples above, there is an estimated salvage value. Assuming that you have to pay capital gains taxes at 20% on any excess of salvage value over book value, would you gain or lose by depreciating the assets down to zero and paying the capital gains taxes. Illustrate using straight-line depreciation in Problem 1 and ACRS depreciation in Problem 2.

15. You have just acquired equipment for $10 million, with a depreciable life of five years and no salvage value. You must decide whether you should be using the straight-line or double-declining balance method in estimating taxes and cash flows. Your tax rate is expected to increase over the five years.

Year	Tax Rate
1	20%
2	25%
3	30%
4	35%
5	40%

   a. Which depreciation method provides the larger nominal tax benefits?
   b. Which depreciation method provides the larger present value in tax benefits, assuming your cost of capital is 12%?

16. You are analyzing a project with a life of five years, which requires an initial investment in equipment and machinery of $10 million. The equipment is expected to have a five-year lifetime and no salvage value and to be depreciated straight line. The project is expected to generate revenues of $5 million each year for the five years and have operating expenses (not including depreciation) amounting to 30% of revenues. The tax rate is 40%, and the cost of capital is 11%.
   a. Estimate the after-tax operating cash flow each year on this project.
   b. Estimate the net present value for this project.
   c. How much of the net present value can be attributed to the tax benefits accruing from depreciation?
   d. Assume that the firm that takes this project is losing money currently and expects to continue losing money for the first three years. Estimate the net present value of this project.

17. You are considering a capital budgeting proposal to make glow-in-the-dark pacifiers for anxious first-time parents. You estimate that the equipment to make the pacifiers would cost you $50,000 (which you can depreciate straight line over the lifetime of the project, which is 10 years) and that you can sell 15,000 units a year at $2 a unit. The cost of making each pacifier would be $0.80, and the tax rate you would face would be

40%. You also estimate that you will need to maintain an inventory at 25% of revenues for the period of the project and that you can salvage 80% of this working capital at the termination of the project. Finally, you will be setting up the equipment in your garage, which means you will have to pay $2,000 a year to have your car garaged at a nearby private facility. (Assume that you can deduct this cost for tax purposes.) To estimate the discount rate for this project, you find that comparable firms are being traded on the financial markets with the following betas:

Company	Debt-Equity ratio	Tax rate	Beta
Nuk-Nuk	0.50	0.40	1.3
Gerber	1.00	0.50	1.5

You expect to finance this project entirely with equity, and the current Treasury Bond rate is 11.5%.
   a. What is the appropriate discount rate to use for this project?
   b. What is the after-tax operating cash flow each year for the lifetime of the project?
   c. What is the NPV of this project?

18. You are a financial analyst for a company that is considering a new project. If the project is accepted, it will use 40% of a storage facility that the company already owns but currently does not use fully. The project is expected to last 10 years, and the discount rate is 10%. You research the possibilities and find that the entire storage facility can be sold for $100,000 and a smaller facility can be acquired for $40,000. The book value of the existing facility is $60,000, and both the existing and new facilities (if it is acquired) would be depreciated straight line over 10 years. The ordinary tax rate is 40%, and the capital gains rate is 25%. What is the opportunity cost, if any, of using the storage capacity?

19. You have been observing the progressive gentrification of your city with interest. You realize that the time is ripe for you to open and run an aerobic exercise center. You find an abandoned warehouse that will meet your needs and rents for $48,000 a year. You estimate that it will initially cost $50,000 to renovate the place and buy Nautilus equipment for the center. (There will be no salvage and the entire initial cost is depreciable.) Your market research indicates that you can

expect to get 500 members, each paying $500 a year. You have also found five instructors you can hire for $24,000 a year each. Your tax rate, if you start making profits, will be 40%, and you choose to use straight-line depreciation on your initial investment. If your cost of capital is 15%, and you expect to retire to the Bahamas in 10 years, answer the following questions:

a.   Estimate the annual after-tax cash flows on this project.

b.   Estimate the net present value and internal rate of return for this investment. Would you take it?

20.   Brooks Brothers is thinking of investing in a new line of "punk rocker" clothes for the new executive. You have been hired to evaluate the project. You find that, if the project is accepted, you could use an abandoned warehouse already owned by Brooks Brothers, with a book value of $500,000. Your superior had been planning to rent this warehouse out to another firm for $100,000 a year. If your tax rate is 40%, your discount rate is 15%, your project lifetime is 10 years, and you use straight-line depreciation, what is the opportunity cost of using this warehouse?

21.   You are graduating in June and would like to start your own business manufacturing wine coolers. You collect the following information on the initial costs:

Cost of Plant and Equipment = $500,000
Licensing and Legal Costs = $50,000

You can claim an investment tax credit of 10% on plant and equipment. You also have been left a tidy inheritance that will cover the initial cost, and your estimated opportunity cost is 10%.

You estimate that you can sell 1 million bottles a year at $1 a bottle. You estimate your costs as follows:

Variable costs/bottle = 50 cents
Fixed Costs/year = $200,000

Adding up state, local, and federal taxes, you note that you will be in the 50% tax bracket. To be conservative, you assume that you will terminate the business in five years and that you will get nothing from the plant and equipment at salvage. (You also use straight-line depreciation.) As a final consideration, you note that starting this business will mean that you will not be able to take the investment banking job you have been offered (which offered $75,000 a year for the next five years). Should you take on the project?

22.   You are an expert at working with PCs and are considering setting up a software development business. To set up the enterprise, you anticipate that you will need to acquire computer hardware costing $100,000. (The lifetime of this hardware is five years for depreciation purposes, and straight-line depreciation will be used.) In addition, you will have to rent an office for $50,000 a year. You estimate that you will need to hire five software specialists at $50,000 a year to work on the software and that your marketing and selling costs will be $100,000 a year. You expect to price the software you produce at $100 per unit and to sell 6,000 units in the first year. The number of units sold is expected to increase 10% a year for the remaining four years, and the revenues and costs are expected to increase at 3% a year, reflecting inflation. The actual cost of materials used to produce each unit is $20, and you will need to maintain working capital at 10% of revenues. (Assume that the working capital investment is made at the beginning of each year.) Your tax rate will be 40%, and the cost of capital is 12%.

a.   Estimate the cash flows each year on this project.

b.   Should you accept the project?

23.   You are an analyst for a sporting goods corporation that is considering a new project that will take advantage of excess capacity in an existing plant. The plant has a capacity to produce 50,000 tennis racquets, but only 25,000 are being produced currently, although sales of the rackets are increasing 10% a year. You want to use some of the remaining capacity to manufacture 20,000 squash rackets each year for the next 10 years (which will use up 40% of the total capacity), and this market is assumed to be stable (no growth). An average tennis racquet sells for $100 and costs $40 to make. The tax rate for the corporation is 40%, and the discount rate is 10%. Is there an opportunity cost involved? If so, how much is it?

24.   You are examining the viability of a capital investment in which your firm is interested. The project will require an initial investment of $500,000 and the projected revenues are $400,000 a year for five years. The projected

cost-of-goods-sold is 40% of revenues, and the tax rate is 40%. The initial investment is primarily in plant and equipment and can be depreciated straight-line over five years. (The salvage value is zero.) The project makes use of other resources that your firm already owns:

- Two employees of the firm, each with a salary of $40,000 a year and who are currently employed by another division, will be transferred to this project. The other division has no alternative use for them, but they are covered by a union contract that will prevent them from being fired for three years (during which they would be paid their current salary).
- The project will use excess capacity in the current packaging plant. While this excess capacity has no alternative use now, it is estimated that the firm will have to invest $250,000 in a new packaging plant in year 4 as a consequence of this project using up excess capacity (instead of year 8 as originally planned).
- The project will use a van currently owned by the firm. Although the van is not currently being used, it can be rented out for $3,000 a year for five years. The book value of the van is $10,000, and it is being depreciated straight-line (with five years remaining for depreciation). The discount rate to be used for this project is 10%.

a. What (if any) opportunity cost is associated with using the two employees from another division?

b. What, if any, opportunity cost is associated with the use of excess capacity of the packaging plant?

c. What, if any, opportunity cost is associated with the use of the van?

d. What is the after-tax operating cash flow each year on this project?

e. What is the net present value of this project?

25. You have been hired as a capital budgeting analyst by a sporting goods firm that manufacturers

athletic shoes and has captured 10% of the overall shoe market. (The total market is worth $100 million a year.) The fixed costs associated with manufacturing these shoes is $2 million a year, and variable costs are 40% of revenues. The company's tax rate is 40%.

The firm believes that it can increase its market share to 20% by investing $10 million in a new distribution system (which can be depreciated over the system's life of 10 years to a salvage value of zero) and spending $1 million a year in additional advertising. The company proposes to continue to maintain working capital at 10% of annual revenues. The discount rate to be used for this project is 8%.

a. If working capital investments are made at the beginning of each year, what is the initial investment for this project?

b. What is the annual operating cash flow from this project?

c. What is the NPV of this project?

26. Your company is considering producing a new product. You have a production facility that is currently used to only 50% of capacity, and you plan to use some of the excess capacity for the new product. The production facility cost $50 million five years ago when it was built and is being depreciated straight-line over 25 years (in real dollars, assume that this cost will stay constant over time).

The new product has a life of 10 years, the tax rate is 40%, and the appropriate discount rate (real) is 10%.

a. If you take on this project, when will you run out of capacity?

b. When you run out of capacity, what will you lose if you choose to cut back production (in present value after-tax dollars)? You have to decide on which product you are going to cut back production.

c. What opportunity cost would be assigned to this new product if you chose to build a new facility when you ran out of capacity instead of cutting back on production?

Product Line	Capacity Used Currently	Growth Rate/Year	Current Revenues	Fixed Cost/Year	Variable Cost/Year
Old product	50%	5%/year	100 mil	25 mil	50 mil/yr
New product	30%	10%/year	80 mil	20 mil	44 mil/yr

27. You run a mail-order firm, selling upscale clothing. You are considering replacing your manual ordering system with a computerized system to make your operations more efficient and to increase sales. (All the cash flows given below are in real terms.)

- The computerized system will cost $10 million to install and $500,000 to operate each year. It will replace a manual order system that costs $1.5 million to operate each year.
- The system is expected to last 10 years and to have no salvage value at the end of the period.
- The computerized system is expected to increase annual revenues from $5 million to $8 million for the next 10 years.
- The cost of goods sold is expected to remain at 50% of revenues.
- The tax rate is 40%.
- As a result of the computerized system, the firm will be able to cut its inventory from 50% of revenues to 25% of revenues *immediately*. No change is expected in the other working capital components.

The real discount rate is 8%.
a. What is your expected cash flow at time = 0?
b. What is the expected incremental annual cash flow from computerizing the system?
c. What is the net present value of this project?

28. A multinational firm is considering a project which will generate net cash flows in five different countries. The marginal tax rates are all different in these countries.

Country	Cash flow before taxes	Marginal tax rate
A	$20 m	60%
B	$15 m	50%
C	$10 m	40%
D	$5 m	40%
E	$3 m	35%

a. Find the net combined after-tax cash flow generated by this project.
b. Find the weighted marginal tax rate.

29. Your company is considering a project proposal. The following information is gathered for analysis:

Year	Cash flow before taxes	Marginal tax rate
1	$10 m	25%
2	20 m	30%
3	50 m	30%
4	50 m	30%
5	100 m	40%

If the initial outlay is $120 m, and the cost of capital is 12%, should this project be accepted?

LIVE CASE STUDY

IV. MEASURING INVESTMENT RETURNS

Objective: To evaluate the quality of the projects that the company has already taken, and examine the potential for future projects.

Key Questions

- Is there a typical project for this firm? If yes, what would it look like in terms of life (long term or short term), investment needs and cash flow patterns?
- How good are the projects that the company has on its books currently?
- Are the projects in the future likely to look like the projects in the past? Why or why not?

Framework for Analysis

1. *Accounting Returns on Projects*

- What is the return on equity earned by the firm? Based upon this return, is the firm picking good projects?
- What is the return on capital earned by the firm? Based upon this return, is the firm picking good projects?
- Are there any trends in the accounting returns, and if so, what do they tell you about future projects?

2. *Economic Value Added*

- Compute the book value of equity invested in this company and compute the equity economic value added. What, if anything, does this tell you about this company?
- Compute the book value of capital invested in this company and compute the economic value added. What, if anything, does this tell you about this company?
- Why might a comparison based upon economic value added lead you to different conclusions than one based upon the return differences in the earlier section?

Getting Information on Investment Returns

Most of the information you need to estimate returns on capital and equity comes from the financial statements. You can obtain the complete financials for a firm from its annual report (**www.reportgallery.com**) or 10-K (**www.sec.gov/edgarhp.htm**), and you can get data from the previous years by visiting the morningstar data site or a comprehensive site maintained by daily stocks (**www.dailystocks.net**).

The net income and the operating income can be obtained from the income statement and the book values of equity and debt can be obtained from the balance sheet. The costs of equity and capital should already have been estimated in the risk and return section.

To get industry averages for returns on equity and capital (**indroe.xls**), as well as economic value added and equity economic value added, examine the data set on each on my web site (**indeva.xls**).

CHAPTER 6

ESTIMATING SIDE COSTS AND BENEFITS

While most of the cash flows on a project are a direct consequence of investing in the project, and can be estimated using the approaches described in the previous chapter, most projects create some costs and benefits to the business taking them that do not fit easily into this framework. In this chapter, we will explore some of these side costs and benefits, and examine how to consider them in estimating the returns on projects. In particular, we will examine the cost of using resources on a project which might be owned by the business already (opportunity costs) and the potential benefits to other projects from taking a new project (project synergy). We will also explore how best to value the numerous options that are embedded in some projects, including the option to abandon the project if it does not meet our requirements, the option to expand the project if it does better than expected, and the option to enter new markets that some projects may bestow on the firm.

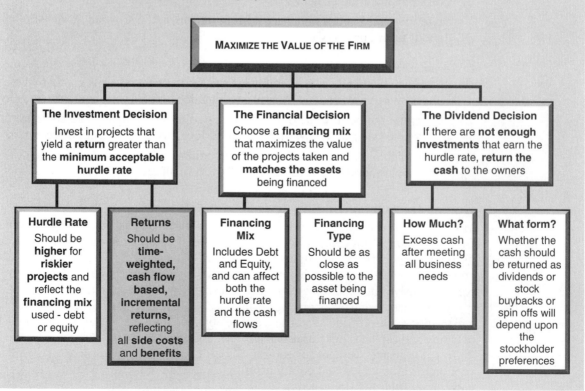

MAXIMIZE THE VALUE OF THE FIRM

The Investment Decision
Invest in projects that yield a **return** greater than the **minimum acceptable hurdle rate**

The Financial Decision
Choose a **financing mix** that maximizes the value of the projects taken and **matches the assets** being financed

The Dividend Decision
If there are **not enough investments** that earn the hurdle rate, **return the cash** to the owners

Hurdle Rate
Should be **higher** for **riskier projects** and reflect the **financing mix** used - debt or equity

Returns
Should be **time-weighted, cash flow based, incremental returns,** reflecting all **side costs and benefits**

Financing Mix
Includes Debt and Equity, and can affect both the hurdle rate and the cash flows

Financing Type
Should be as close as possible to the asset being financed

How Much?
Excess cash after meeting all business needs

What form?
Whether the cash should be returned as dividends or stock buybacks or spin offs will depend upon the stockholder preferences

OPPORTUNITY COSTS

In much of the project analyses that we present in this chapter, we assume that the resources needed for a project are newly acquired; this includes not only the building and the equipment, but also the personnel needed to get the project going. For most businesses considering new projects, this is an unrealistic assumption, however, since many of the resources used are already part of the business and will just be transferred to the new projects. When a business uses such resources, there is the potential for an opportunity cost—the cost created for the rest of the business as a consequence of this project. This opportunity cost may be a significant portion of the total investment needed on a project.

Opportunity Cost: This is the cost assigned to a project resource that is already owned by the firm. It is based upon the next best alternative use.

A General Framework for Analyzing Opportunity Costs
The general framework for analyzing opportunity costs begins by asking the question "Is there any other use for this resource right now?" For many resources, there will be an alternative use if the project being analyzed is not taken. For instance,

- The resource might be rented out, in which case the rental revenue is the opportunity lost by taking this project. For example, if the project is considering the use of a vacant building owned by the business already, the potential revenue from renting out this building to an outsider will be the opportunity cost.
- The resource could be sold, in which case the sales price, net of any tax liability and lost depreciation tax benefits, would be the opportunity cost from taking this project.
- The resource might be used elsewhere in the firm, in which case the cost of replacing the resource is considered the opportunity cost. Thus, the transfer of experienced employees from established divisions to a new project creates a cost to these divisions, which has to be factored into the decision making.

Sometimes, decision makers have to decide whether the opportunity cost will be estimated based on the lost rental revenue, the forgone sales price, or the cost of replacing the resource. When such a choice has to be made, it is the highest of the costs—that is, the best alternative forgone—that should be considered as an opportunity cost.

6.1   SUNK COSTS AND OPPORTUNITY COSTS

A colleague argues that resources that a firm already owns should not be considered in investment analysis, because the cost is a sunk cost. Do you agree?

☐ Yes

☐ No

How would you reconcile the competing arguments of sunk and opportunity costs?

◼ ▲
▼ ●   ILLUSTRATION 6.1   Estimating the Opportunity Cost for a Resource with a Current Alternative Use

Working again with the Bookscape On-line example, assume that the following additional information is provided:

- While Bookscape On-line will employ only two full-time employees, it is estimated that the additional business associated with on-line ordering and the administration of the service itself will add approximately 40 hours of work for the current general manager of the bookstore. As a consequence, the salary of the general manager will be increased from $100,000 to $120,000 next year; it is expected to grow 5% a year after that.

- It is also estimated that Bookscape On-line will utilize an office which is currently used to store financial records. The records will be moved to a bank vault, which will cost $1000 a year to rent.

The opportunity cost of the addition to the general manager's workload lies in the additional salary expenditure that will be incurred as a consequence. Taking the present value of the after-tax costs (using a 42% tax rate) over the next five years yields the following estimates:

	1	2	3	4
Increase in Salary	$20,000	$21,000	$22,050	$23,153
After-Tax	$11,600	$12,180	$12,789	$13,428
PV at 15.94%	$10,005	$9,061	$8,206	$7,431

The cumulated present value of the costs is $34,703.

Turning to the second resource—the storage space originally used for the financial records—if this project is taken, the opportunity cost is the cost of the bank vault:

$$\text{Additional Storage Expenses per Year} = \$1,000$$
$$\text{After-Tax Additional Storage Expenditure per Year} = \$1,000\,(1 - 0.42) = \$580$$
$$\text{PV of After-Tax Salary Expenditures for 4 Years} = \$580 * PV\,(A, 15.94\%, 4\text{ years})$$
$$= \$1,624$$

The opportunity costs estimated for the general manager's added workload ($34,702) and the storage space ($1,624) are in present value terms and can be added on to the initial investment in the on-line service—$1 million for capital investments and $150,000 million for working capital—and the net present value from Illustration 5.4 can be reestimated, as shown in Table 6.1. The net present value becomes more negative.

The cash flows associated with the opportunity costs could alternatively have been reflected in the years in which they occurred. Thus, the additional salary and storage expenses could have been added to the operating expenses of the store in each of the four years. As Table 6.2 indicates, this approach would yield the same net present value and would have clearly been the appropriate approach if the internal rate of return were to be calculated.

Table 6.1   NET PRESENT VALUE WITH OPPORTUNITY COSTS

Year	FCFF	PV of FCFF (at 15.94%)
0	($1,186,327)	($1,186,327)
1	$249,000	$214,762
2	$304,500	$226,517
3	$334,350	$214,522
4	$558,849	$309,259
NPV		($221,266)

Table 6.2   NET PRESENT VALUE WITH OPPORTUNITY COSTS—ALTERNATE APPROACH

Year	FCFF	PV of FCFF (at 15.94%)
0	($1,150,000)	($1,150,000)
1	$236,820	$204,256
2	$291,740	$217,025
3	$320,981	$205,945
4	$544,841	$301,507
NPV		($221,266)

Note that this net present value confirms our earlier finding—this project should not be taken.

IN PRACTICE: ESTIMATING THE COST OF EXCESS CAPACITY

Firms often use the excess capacity that they have in an existing plant, storage facility, or computer resource for a new project. When they do so, they often make one of two assumptions:

1. They assume that excess capacity is free, since it is not being used currently and cannot be sold off or rented, in most cases.

2. They allocate a portion of the book value of the plant or resource to the project. Thus, if the plant has a book value of $100 million and the new project uses 40% of it, $40 million will be allocated to the project.

We will argue that neither of these approaches considers the opportunity cost of using excess capacity, since the opportunity cost usually comes from costs that the firm will face in the future as a consequence of using up excess capacity today. By using up excess capacity on a new project, the firm will run out of capacity sooner than it would if it did not take the project. When it does run out of capacity, it has to take one of two paths:

• New capacity will have to be bought or built when capacity runs out, in which case the opportunity cost will be the higher cost in present value terms of doing this earlier rather than later. (or)

- Production will have to be cut back on one of the product lines, leading to a loss in cash flows that would have been generated by the lost sales.

Again, this choice is not random, since the logical action to take is the one that leads to the lower cost, in present value terms, for the firm. Thus, if it is cheaper to lose sales than to build new capacity, the opportunity cost for the project being considered should be based on the lost sales.

A general framework for pricing excess capacity for purposes of investment analysis asks three questions:

1. If the new project is not taken, when will the firm run out of capacity on the equipment or space that is being evaluated (as excess capacity)?

2. If the new project is taken, when will the firm run out of capacity on the equipment or space that is being evaluated? Presumably, with the new project using up some of the excess capacity, the firm will run out of capacity sooner than it would have otherwise.

3. What will the firm do when it does run out of capacity? The firm has two choices:

   - It can cut back on production of the less profitable product line and make less profits than it would have without a capacity constraint. In this case, the opportunity cost is the present value of the cash flows lost as a consequence.

   - It can buy or build new capacity, in which case the opportunity cost is the difference in present value between investing earlier rather than later.

PROJECT SYNERGY

When a project under consideration creates positive benefits (in the form of cash flows) for other projects that a firm may have, there are *project synergies*. For instance, assume that you are a clothing retailer considering whether to open an upscale clothing store for children in the same shopping center where you already own a store which caters to adult consumers. In addition to generating revenues and cash flows on its own, the children's store might increase the traffic into the adult store and increase profits at that store. That additional profit, and its ensuing cash flow, has to be factored into the analysis of the new store.

Project Synergy: This is the increase in cash flows that accrue to other projects, as a consequence of the project under consideration.

Sometimes the project synergies are not with existing projects but with other projects that are being considered contemporaneously. In such cases, the best way to analyze the projects is jointly, since examining each separately will lead to a much lower net present value. Thus, a proposal to open a children's clothing store and an adult clothing store in the same shopping center will have to be treated as a joint investment analysis, and the net present value will have to be calculated for both stores together. A positive net present value would suggest opening both stores, whereas a negative net present value would indicate that neither should be opened.

ILLUSTRATION 6.2   Cash Flow Synergies with Existing Projects

Assume that the Bookscape is considering adding a cafe to its bookstore. The cafe, it is hoped, will make the bookstore a more attractive destination for would-be shoppers. The following information relates to the proposed cafe:

- The initial cost of remodeling a portion of the store to make it a cafe and of buying equipment is expected to be $150,000. This investment is expected to have a life of five years, during which period it will be depreciated using straight line depreciation. None of the cost is expected to be recoverable at the end of the five years.
- The revenues in the first year are expected to be $60,000, growing at 10% a year for the next four years.
- There will be one employee, and the total cost for this employee in year 1 is expected to be $30,000, growing at 5% a year for the next four years.
- The cost of the material (food, drinks) needed to run the cafe is expected to be 40% of revenues in each of the five years.
- An inventory amounting to 5% of the revenues has to be maintained; investments in the inventory are made at the beginning of each year.
- The tax rate for Bookscape as a business is 42%.

Based upon this information, the estimated cash flows on the cafe are shown in Table 6.3. Note that the working capital is fully salvaged at the end of year 5, resulting in a cash inflow of $4,392.

Table 6.3   ESTIMATING CASH FLOWS FROM OPENING BOOKSCAPE CAFE

	0	1	2	3	4	5
Investment	$ 150,000					
Revenues		$ 60,000	$ 66,000	$ 72,600	$ 79,860	$ 87,846
Labor		$ 30,000	$ 31,500	$ 33,075	$ 34,729	$ 36,465
Materials		$ 24,000	$ 26,400	$ 29,040	$ 31,944	$ 35,138
Depreciation		$ 30,000	$ 30,000	$ 30,000	$ 30,000	$ 30,000
Operating Income		$ (24,000)	$ (21,900)	$ (19,515)	$ (16,813)	$ (13,758)
Taxes		$ (10,080)	$ (9,198)	$ (8,196)	$ (7,061)	$ (5,778)
AT Operating Income		$ (13,920)	$ (12,702)	$ (11,319)	$ (9,751)	$ (7,979)
+ Depreciation		$ 30,000	$ 30,000	$ 30,000	$ 30,000	$ 30,000
− Δ Working Capital	$ 3,000	$ 300	$ 330	$ 363	$ 399	$ (4,392)
Cash Flow to Firm	$ (153,000)	$ 15,780	$ 16,968	$ 18,318	$ 19,849	$ 26,413
PV at 11.75%	$ (153,000)	$ 14,121	$ 13,587	$ 13,126	$ 12,178	$ 15,156
Working Capital		$ 3,000	$ 3,300	$ 3,630	$ 3,993	$ 4,392

To compute the net present value, we will use Bookscape's cost of capital of 11.75%. In doing so, we recognize that this is the cost of capital for a bookstore, and that this is an investment in a cafe. It is, however, a cafe whose good fortunes rest with how well the bookstore is doing, and whose risk is, therefore, the risk associated with the bookstore. The present value of the cash inflows is less than the initial investment of $150,000, resulting in an NPV of −$84,282. This suggests that this is not a good investment, based on the cash flows it would generate.

Note, though, that this analysis is based upon looking at the cafe as a standalone entity, and that one of the benefits of the cafe is that it might attract more customers to the store and get those customers to buy more books. For purposes of our analysis, assume that the cafe will increase revenues at the store by $500,000 in year 1, growing at 10% a year for the following four years. In addition, assume that the pretax operating margin on these sales is 10%. The incremental cash flows from the "synergy" are shown in Table 6.4.

The present value of the incremental cash flows generated for the bookstore as a consequence of the cafe is $125,730. Incorporating this into the present value analysis yields the following:

$$\text{Net Present Value of Cafe} = -\$84,282 + \$125,753 = \$41,471$$

Incorporating the cash flows from the synergy into the analysis, the cafe is a good investment for Bookscape.

6.2 SYNERGY BENEFITS

In the analysis above, the cost of capital for both the cafe and the bookstore were identical at 11.75%. Assume that the cost of capital for the cafe had been 15%, while the cost of capital for the bookstore had stayed at 11.75%. Which discount rate would you use for estimating the present value of synergy benefits?

☐   15%

☐   11.75%

☐   An average of the two discount rates

☐   Could be 11.75% or 15% depending upon . . .

Explain.

Table 6.4 INCREMENTAL CASH FLOWS FROM SYNERGY

	1	2	3	4	5
Increased Revenues	$500,000	$550,000	$605,000	$665,500	$732,050
Operating Margin	10%	10%	10%	10%	10%
Operating Income	$50,000	$55,000	$60,500	$66,550	$73,205
Operating Income after Taxes	$29,000	$31,900	$35,090	$38,599	$42,459
PV of Additional Cash Flows	$25,951	$25,544	$25,144	$24,751	$24,363

IN PRACTICE: THE VALUE OF SYNERGY: DISNEY'S ANIMATED MOVIES

Disney has a well-deserved reputation for finding synergy in its movie operations, especially its animated movies. Consider, for instance, some of the spinoffs from its recent movies:

1. Plastic action figures and stuffed toys are produced and sold at the time the movies are released, producing profits for Disney both from its own stores and from royalties from sales of the merchandise at other stores.

2. Joint promotions of the movies with fast-food chains such as McDonald's and Burger King, where the chains give away movie merchandise with their kids' meals, and reduce Disney's own advertising costs for the movie by promoting it.

3. With its acquisition of Capital Cities, Disney now has a broadcasting outlet for cartoons based upon successful movies (*Aladdin, The Little Mermaid, 101 Dalmatians*), which produce production and advertising revenues for Disney.

4. Disney has also made a successful Broadway musical of its hit movies *Beauty and the Beast* and *The Lion King* and plans to use the theater that it now owns on Broadway to produce more such shows.

5. Disney's theme parks all over the world benefit indirectly since the characters from the latest animated movies and shows based upon these movies attract more people to the parks.

6. Finally, Disney has been extremely successful in promoting the video releases of its movies as must-have items for video collections.

In fact, for one of its best-known classics, *Snow White,* Disney released the movie in theaters dozens of times between the original release in 1937 and the eventual video release in 1985, making substantial profits each time.

Synergy in Acquisitions

Synergy is often a motive in acquisitions, but it is used as a way of justifying huge premiums and seldom analyzed objectively. The framework that we developed for valuing synergy in projects can be applied to valuing synergy in acquisitions. The key to the existence of synergy is that the target firm controls a specialized resource that becomes more valuable when combined with the bidding firm's resources. The specialized resource will vary depending upon the merger. Horizontal mergers occur when two firms in the same line of business merge. In that case, the synergy must come from some form of economies of scale, which reduce costs, or from increased market power, which increases profit margins and sales. Vertical integration occurs when a firm acquires a supplier of inputs into its production process or a distributor or retailer for the product it produces. The primary source of synergy in this case comes from more complete control of the chain of production. This benefit has to be weighed against the loss of efficiency from having a captive supplier who does not have any incentive to keep costs low and compete with other suppliers.

When a firm with strengths in one functional area acquires another firm with strengths in a different functional area, synergy may be gained by exploiting the strengths in these areas. Thus, when a firm with a good distribution network acquires a firm with a promising product line, value is gained by combining these two strengths. The argument is that both firms will be better off after the merger.

Most reasonable observers agree that there is a potential for operating synergy, in one form or the other, in many takeovers. Some disagreement exists, however, over whether synergy can be valued and, if so, how much that value should be. One school of thought argues that synergy is too nebulous to be valued and that any systematic attempt to do so requires so many assumptions that it is pointless. While this is debatable, it implies that a firm should not be willing to pay large premiums for synergy if it cannot attach a value to it.

While it is true that valuing synergy requires assumptions about future cash flows and growth, the lack of precision in the process does not mean that an unbiased estimate of value cannot be made. Thus we maintain that synergy can be valued by answering two fundamental questions:

1. *What form is the synergy expected to take?* Will it reduce costs as a percentage of sales and increase profit margins (e.g., when there are economies of scale)? Will it increase future growth (e.g., when there is increased market power)?

2. *When can the synergy be expected to start affecting cash flows—* instantaneously or over time?

Once these questions are answered, the value of synergy can be estimated using an extension of discounted cash flow techniques. First, the firms involved in the merger are valued independently, by discounting expected cash flows to each firm at the weighted average cost of capital for that firm. Second, the value of the combined firm, with no synergy, is obtained by adding the values obtained for each firm in the first step. Third, the effects of synergy are built into expected growth rates and cash flows, and the combined firm is revalued with synergy. The difference between the value of the combined firm with synergy and the value of the combined firm without synergy provides a value for synergy.

OPTIONS EMBEDDED IN PROJECTS

In Chapter 5, we examined the process for analyzing a project and deciding whether or not to accept the project. In particular, we noted that a project should be accepted *only if the returns on the project exceed the hurdle rate;* in the context of cash flows and discount rates, this translates into projects with positive net present values. The limitation with traditional investment analysis, which analyzes projects on the basis of expected cash flows and discount rates, is that it fails to consider fully the myriad options that are usually associated with many projects.

Real Option: A real option is an option on a nontraded asset, such as an investment project or a gold mine.

In this section, we will analyze three options that are embedded in capital budgeting projects. The first is the option to delay a project, especially when the firm has exclusive rights to the project. The second is the option to expand a project to cover new products or markets some time in the future. The third is the option to abandon a project if the cash flows do not measure up to expectations.

The Option to Delay a Project

Projects are typically analyzed based upon their expected cash flows and discount rates at the time of the analysis; the net present value computed on that basis is a measure of its value and acceptability at that time. Expected cash flows and discount rates change over time, however, and so does the net present value. Thus, a project that has a negative net present value now may have a positive net present value in the future. In a competitive environment, in which individual firms have no special advantages over their competitors in taking projects, this may not seem significant. In an environment in which a project can be taken by only one firm (because of legal restrictions or other barriers to entry to competitors), however, the changes in the project's value over time give it the characteristics of a call option.

In the abstract, assume that a project requires an initial investment of X (in real dollars) and that the present value of expected cash inflows computed right now is V. The net present value of this project is the difference between the two:

$$NPV = V - X$$

Now assume that the firm has exclusive rights to this project for the next n years, and that the present value of the cash inflows may change over that time because of changes in either the cash flows or the discount rate. Thus, the project may have a negative net present value right now, but it may still be a good project sometime in the future. Defining V as the present value of the cash flows as of now, the firm's decision rule on this project can be summarized as follows:

If $V > X$ Project has positive net present value
If $V < X$ Project has negative net present value

This relationship can be presented in a payoff diagram of cash flows on this project, as shown in Figure 6.1, assuming that the firm holds out until the end of the period for which it has exclusive rights to the project.

Note that this payoff diagram is that of a call option—the underlying asset is the project, the strike price of the option is the investment needed to take the project; and the life of the option is the period for which the firm has rights to the project. The present value of the cash flows on this project and the expected variance in this present value represent the value and variance of the underlying asset.

Obtaining the Inputs for Option Valuation

On the surface, the inputs needed to apply option pricing theory to valuing the option to delay are the same as those needed for any option: the value of the underlying asset; the variance in the value; the time to expiration on the option; the strike price; the riskless rate and the equivalent of the dividend yield. Actually estimating these inputs for valuation can be difficult, however.

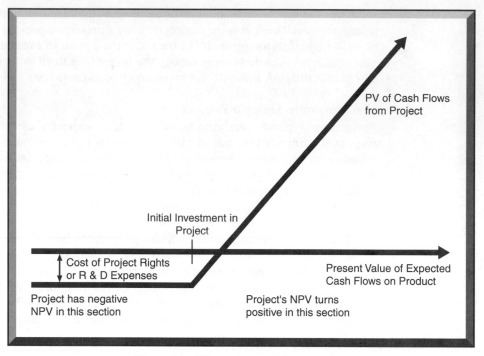

Figure 6.1 The option to delay a project.

Value Of The Underlying Asset

In the case of project options, the underlying asset is the project itself. The current value of this asset is the present value of expected cash flows from initiating the project now, which can be obtained by doing a standard capital budgeting analysis. There is likely to be a substantial amount of noise in the cash flow estimates and the present value, however. Rather than being viewed as a problem, this uncertainty should be viewed as the reason why the project delay option has value. If the expected cash flows on the project were known with certainty and were not expected to change, there would be no need to adopt an option pricing framework, since there would be no value to the option.

Variance in the Value of the Asset

As noted in the prior section, there is likely to be considerable uncertainty associated with the cash flow estimates and the present value that measures the value of the asset now, partly because the potential market size for the product may be unknown, and partly because technological shifts can change the cost structure and profitability of the product. The variance in the present value of cash flows from the project can be estimated in one of three ways. First, if similar projects have been introduced in the past, the variance in the cash flows from those projects can be used as an estimate. Second, probabilities can be assigned to various market scenarios, cash flows estimated under each scenario and the variance estimated across present values. Finally, the average variance in firm value of publicly traded companies which are in the business that the project will be in can be used. Thus, the average variance in firm value of biotechnology companies can be used as the variance for the option to delay a biotechnology project.

The value of the option is largely derived from the variance in cash flows—the higher the variance, the higher the value of the project delay option. Thus, the value of an option to do a project in a stable business will be less than the value of one in an environment where technology, competition, and markets are all changing rapidly.

 There is a data set on the Web that summarizes, by sector, the standard deviations in firm value and stock prices (**optvar.xls**).

Exercise Price on Option

A project option is exercised when the firm owning the rights to the project decides to invest in it. The cost of making this investment is equivalent to the exercise price of the option. The underlying assumptions are that this cost remains constant (in present value dollars) and that any uncertainty associated with the product is reflected in the present value of cash flows on the product.

Expiration of the Option and the Riskless Rate

The project delay option expires when the rights to the project lapse; investments made after the project rights expire are assumed to deliver a net present value of zero as competition drives returns down to the required rate. The riskless rate to use in pricing the option should be the rate that corresponds to the expiration of the option.

Dividend Yield

There is a cost to delaying taking a project, once the net present value turns positive. Since the project rights expire after a fixed period, and excess profits (which are the source of positive present value) are assumed to disappear after that time as new competitors emerge, each year of delay translates into one less year of value-creating cash flows.[1] If the cash flows are evenly distributed over time, and the life of the patent is n years, the cost of delay can be written as:

$$\text{Annual Cost of Delay} = \frac{1}{n}$$

Thus, if the project rights are for 20 years, the annual cost of delay works out to 5% of the value of the project a year.

6.3   COST OF DELAY AND EARLY EXERCISE

For typical listed options on financial assets, it is argued that early exercise is almost never optimal. Is this true for real options as well?

☐   Yes

☐   No

Explain.

---

[1]A value-creating cash flow is one that adds to the net present value because it is in excess of the required return for investments of equivalent risk.

Valuing the Option to Delay a Project: An Illustration

Assume that a pharmaceutical company has been approached by an entrepreneur who has patented a new drug to treat ulcers. The entrepreneur has obtained FDA approval and has the patent rights for the next 20 years. While the drug shows promise, it is still very expensive to manufacture and has a relatively small market. Assume that the initial investment to produce the drug is $500 million and the present value of the cash flows from introducing the drug now is only $350 million. The technology and the market are volatile, and the annualized variance in the present value estimated from a simulation is 0.05.[2]

While the net present value of introducing the drug is negative, the rights to this drug may still be valuable because of the variance in the present value of the cash flow. In other words, it is entirely possible that this drug may not only be viable but extremely profitable a year or two from now. To value this right, we first define the inputs to the option pricing model:

Value of the Underlying Asset (S) = PV of Cash Flows from Project if Introduced Now

= $ 350 million

Strike Price (K) = Initial Investment Needed to Introduce the Product = $ 500 million

Variance in Underlying Asset's Value = 0.05

Time to Expiration = Life of the Patent = 20 years

Dividend Yield = 1/Life of the Patent = 1/20 = 0.05

Assume that the 20-year riskless rate is 7%. The value of the option can be estimated as follows:

Call Value = 350 exp$^{(-0.05)(20)}$ (0.7065) − 500 exp$^{(-0.07)(20)}$ (0.3240) = $51.02 million

Thus, this ulcer drug, which has a negative net present value if introduced now, is still valuable to its owner.

6.4   HOW MUCH WOULD YOU PAY FOR THIS OPTION?

Assume that you are negotiating for a pharmaceutical company that is trying to buy this patent. Would you pay

☐ $51.02 million?

☐   more than $51.02 million?

☐   less than $51.02 million?

Explain.

Practical Considerations

While it is quite clear that the option to delay is embedded in many projects, there are several problems associated with the use of option pricing models to value these

---

[2]In a simulation, the present value is computed, allowing the key variables to change. The variance in the natural log of present values of cash inflows can be used in the option pricing model.

options. First, *the underlying asset in this option, which is the project, is not traded, making it difficult to estimate its value and variance.* We would argue that the value can be estimated from the expected cash flows and the discount rate for the project, albeit with error. The variance is more difficult to estimate, however, since we are attempting to estimate a variance in project value over time. One way of doing this is to run a series of simulations capturing as many scenarios for the future as possible and then calculating the variance in the present values derived from these simulations. An alternative is to use the variances in stock prices of firms involved in the same business; thus, the stock price variance of publicly traded biotechnology firms may be used as a proxy for the variance of a biotechnology project's cash flows. Table 6.5 summarizes standard deviation in firm value for firms in different industry groups in 1996.

Second, the *behavior of prices over time may not conform to the price path assumed by the option pricing models.* In particular, the assumption that value follows a diffusion process, and that the variance in value remains unchanged over time, may be difficult to justify in the context of a project. For instance, a sudden technological change may dramatically change the value of a project, either positively or negatively.

Third, *there may be no specific period for which the firm has rights to the project.* Unlike the example above, in which the firm had exclusive rights to the project for 20 years, often the firm's rights may be less clearly defined, both in terms of exclusivity and time. For instance, a firm may have significant advantages over its competitors, which may, in turn, provide it with virtually exclusive rights to a project for a period of time. The rights are not legal restrictions, however, and could erode faster than expected. In such cases, the expected life of the project itself is uncertain and only an estimate.

6.5 EXCLUSIVE RIGHTS AND THE OPTION FEATURE

A firm in an extremely competitive sector is faced with a project which has a negative net present value currently and wants to know how much the option to delay the project is worth. Which of the following would you think is the right response?

☐ It should be the value from the option pricing model.

☐ It should be zero.

☐ Neither.

Explain.

Implications of Viewing the Right to Delay a Project as an Option

Several interesting implications emerge from the analysis of the option to delay a project as an option. First, a project may have a negative net present value based upon expected cash flows currently, but it may still be a "valuable" project because of the option characteristics. Thus, while a negative net present value should encourage a firm to reject a project, it should not lead it to conclude that the rights to this project are worthless. Second, a project may have a positive net present value but still not be accepted right away because the firm may gain by waiting and accepting the project in a future period, for the same reasons that investors do not always exercise

Table 6.5   EQUITY AND FIRM VALUE STANDARD DEVIATIONS (SD) BY INDUSTRY

SIC Code	Industry	Debt Ratio	SD: Equity	SD: Firm
1	Agricultural—Crops	33.24%	29.75%	20.94%
2	Agricultural—Livestock	35.32%	49.52%	33.09%
7	Agricultural Services	26.93%	31.78%	24.04%
8	Forestry	46.58%	21.12%	13.24%
10	Fishing, Hunting and Trapping	20.75%	43.12%	34.75%
11	Metal Mining	26.93%	43.24%	32.38%
12	Coal Mining	62.39%	36.39%	16.40%
13	Oil and Gas Extraction	30.83%	46.29%	32.92%
14	Mining of Non-metals	25.06%	31.21%	24.14%
15	Building Contractors	37.73%	64.09%	41.02%
16	Heavy Construction	14.88%	46.09%	39.63%
17	Construction—Special Trade	25.01%	39.64%	30.45%
20	Food and Kindred Products	24.91%	29.22%	22.69%
21	Tobacco Products	45.70%	34.31%	20.26%
22	Textile Mill Products	37.68%	48.26%	31.23%
23	Apparel & Other Finished Products	21.10%	51.85%	41.48%
24	Lumber & Wood Products	24.54%	61.23%	46.88%
25	Furniture & Fixtures	20.02%	36.68%	29.90%
26	Paper & Allied Products	34.26%	33.14%	22.89%
27	Printing & Publishing	20.01%	36.47%	29.73%
28	Chemicals & Allied Products	14.40%	37.37%	32.38%
29	Petroleum Refining	42.23%	28.54%	18.02%
30	Rubber & Plastic Products	23.86%	37.36%	29.13%
31	Leather & Leather Products	19.81%	38.41%	31.36%
32	Stone, Clay, Glass & Concrete	34.94%	49.70%	33.38%
33	Primary Metal Industries	36.97%	38.74%	25.60%
34	Fabricated Metal Products	31.25%	39.90%	28.37%
35	Industrial & Commercial Machinery	19.73%	49.62%	40.37%
36	Electronic and Electrical Equipment	12.45%	48.62%	42.89%
37	Transportation Equipment	31.56%	41.15%	29.11%
38	Measuring, Analyzing & Controlling Instruments	12.88%	49.17%	43.17%
39	Miscellaneous Manufacturing	16.72%	44.77%	37.74%
40	Railroad Transportation	40.93%	26.19%	16.96%
41	Suburban Transit and Highway Transportation	42.89%	22.19%	14.36%
42	Motor Freight Transportation	32.91%	56.42%	38.81%
44	Water Transportation	48.34%	36.11%	20.40%
45	Air Transportation	48.81%	41.72%	23.07%
47	Transportation Services	34.31%	47.83%	32.45%
48	Communications	26.36%	40.19%	30.36%
49	Electric, Gas & Sanitary Services	48.24%	22.55%	13.70%
50	Wholesale trade - Durable goods	23.03%	52.81%	41.28%

Table 6.5   CONTINUED

SIC Code	Industry	Debt Ratio	SD: Equity	SD: Firm
51	Wholesale Trade—Nondurable Goods	26.22%	43.52%	32.86%
52	Building Materials, Hardware & Garden Dealers	37.73%	45.31%	29.39%
53	General Merchandise	40.93%	35.76%	22.50%
54	Food Stores	35.02%	31.64%	21.70%
55	Auto Dealers & Gas Service Stations	26.07%	47.64%	35.96%
56	Apparel & Accessory Stores	23.69%	45.70%	35.54%
57	Home Furniture, Furnishings & Equip Stores	27.18%	43.66%	32.58%
58	Eating & Drinking Establishments	22.18%	48.20%	38.12%
59	Miscellaneous Retail	18.91%	47.99%	39.43%
60	Depository Institutions	26.93%	57.73%	42.94%
61	Non-depository Institutions	12.44%	34.35%	30.41%
62	Security & Commodity Brokers, Dealers	8.90%	42.86%	39.28%
63	Insurance Carriers	10.58%	34.56%	31.18%
64	Insurance Agents, Brokers & Services	11.65%	27.12%	24.28%
65	Real Estate	43.42%	50.88%	30.17%
67	Holding & Other Investment Services	31.10%	33.06%	23.75%
70	Hotels, Rooming Houses & Lodging Places	44.27%	50.96%	29.81%
72	Personal Services	21.57%	35.12%	28.16%
73	Business Schools	9.54%	50.03%	45.50%
75	Auto Repair, Services & parking	37.89%	32.69%	21.57%
76	Miscellaneous Repair Services	76.22%	35.14%	12.64%
78	Motion Pictures	24.61%	60.26%	46.10%
79	Amusement & Recreation Services	32.52%	43.16%	30.10%
80	Health Services	20.51%	58.89%	47.37%
82	Educational Services	15.10%	50.79%	43.53%
87	Engineering, Accounting, Research Services	18.52%	45.68%	37.72%
89	Services not listed elsewhere	32.77%	36.54%	25.58%

STANDARD DEVIATION BY BOND RATING CLASS

Bond Rating	Annualized Std. Dev.	Correlation with Stock prices
AAA	5.50%	10%
AA	6.00%	10%
A	6.50%	10%
BBB	7.00%	15%
BB	8.50%	15%
B	9.50%	20%
CCC	12.00%	25%
CC	13.50%	30%
C	15.00%	40%

an option just because it is in the money. This is more likely to happen if the firm has the rights to the project for a long time, and the variance in project inflows is high. To illustrate, assume that a firm has the patent rights to produce a new type of disk drive for computer systems and that building a new plant will yield a positive net present value right now. If the technology for manufacturing the disk drive is in flux, however, the firm may delay taking the project in the hopes that the improved technology will increase the expected cash flows and consequently the value of the project.

The Option to Expand a Project

In some cases, firms take projects because doing so allows them either to take on other projects or to enter other markets in the future. In such cases, it can be argued that the initial projects are options allowing the firm to take other projects, and the firm should therefore be willing to pay a price for such options. A firm may accept a negative net present value on the initial project because of the possibility of high positive net present values on future projects.

To examine this option using the same framework developed earlier, assume that the present value of the expected cash flows from entering the new market or taking the new project is V, and the total investment needed to enter this market or take this project is X. Further, assume that the firm has a fixed time horizon, at the end of which it has to make the final decision on whether or not to take advantage of this opportunity. Finally, assume that the firm cannot move forward on this opportunity if it does not take the initial project. This scenario implies the option payoffs shown in Figure 6.2.

As you can see, at the expiration of the fixed time horizon, the firm will enter the new market or take the new project if the present value of the expected cash flows at that point in time exceeds the cost of entering the market.

ILLUSTRATION 6.3   Valuing an Option to Expand: Disney Entertainment

Assume that Disney is considering investing $100 million to create a Spanish version of the Disney channel to serve the growing Mexican market. Assume, also, that a financial analysis of the cash flows from this investment suggests that the present value of the cash flows from this investment to Disney will be only $80 million. Thus, by itself, the new channel has a negative NPV of $20 million.

One factor that does have to be considered in this analysis is that if the market in Mexico turns out to be more lucrative than currently anticipated, Disney could expand its reach to all of South America with an additional investment of $150 million any time over the next 10 years. While the current expectation is that the cash flows from having a Disney channel in South America is only $100 million, there is considerable uncertainty about both the potential for such a channel and the shape of the market itself, leading to significant variance in this estimate.

The value of the option to expand can now be estimated by defining the inputs to the option pricing model as follows:

Value of the Underlying Asset (S) = PV of Cash Flows from Expansion to Latin America, if Done Now = $ 100 Million

Strike Price (K) = Cost of Expansion into Latin America = $150 Million

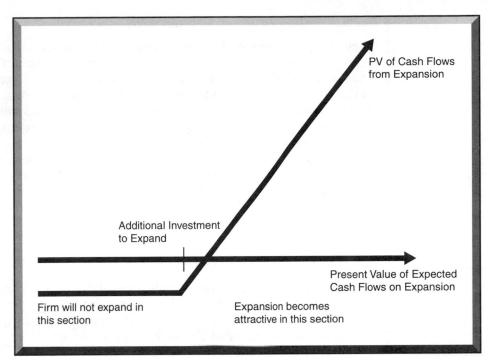

Figure 6.2 The option to expand a project.

We estimate the variance in the estimate of the project value by using the annualized variance in firm value of publicly traded entertainment firms in the Latin American markets, which is approximately 10%:

$$\text{Variance in Underlying Asset's Value} = 0.10$$

$$\text{Time to Expiration} = \text{Period for Which Expansion Option Applies} = 10 \text{ Years}$$

There is no cost of delay.

Assume that the ten-year riskless rate is 6.5%. The value of the option can be estimated as follows:

$$\text{Call Value} = 100\,(0.7915) - 150\,\exp^{(-0.065)(10)}\,(0.3400) = \$52.5 \text{ million}$$

This value can be added on to the net present value of the original investment in Mexico, which has a negative NPV of $20 million.

$$\text{NPV of Disney Channel in Mexico} = \$80 \text{ million} - \$100 \text{ million} = -\$20 \text{ million}$$

$$\text{Value of Option to Expand} = \$52.5 \text{ million}$$

$$\text{NPV of Project with Option to Expand} = -\$20 \text{ million} + \$52.5 \text{ million}$$

$$= \$32.5 \text{ million}$$

Disney should invest in the Mexican project because the option to expand into the Latin American market more than compensates for the negative net present value of the Mexican project.

IN PRACTICE: ARE STRATEGIC CONSIDERATIONS REALLY OPTIONS?

Many firms, faced with projects that do not meet their financial benchmarks, use the argument that these projects should be taken anyway because of "strategic considerations." In other words, it is argued that these projects will accomplish other goals for the firm or allow the firm to enter into other markets. While we are leery of how this argument is used to justify poor projects, there are cases where these strategic considerations are really referring to options embedded in projects—options to produce new products or expand into new markets.

Take the example of the Disney Channel project described above. The project, based upon conventional capital budgeting, has a negative net present value, but it should be taken nevertheless, because it gives Disney the option to enter a potentially lucrative market. Disney might well use the "strategic considerations" argument to take the project.

The differences between using option pricing and the "strategic considerations" argument are the following:

1. Option pricing assigns value to only some of the "strategic considerations" that firms may have. For instance, the option to enter the Latin American market has value because of the variance in the estimates of the value of entering the market, and the fact that Disney has to take the smaller project (the Mexican venture) first in order to get the option. However, strategic considerations that are not clearly defined or include generic terms such as "corporate image" or "growth potential" may not have any value from an option pricing standpoint.

2. Option pricing attempts to put a dollar value on the "strategic consideration" being valued. As a consequence, the existence of strategic considerations does not guarantee that the project will be taken. In the Disney example, the Mexican venture should not be taken if the value of the option to enter the Latin American market is less than $20 million.

Practical Considerations

The practical considerations associated with estimating the value of the option to expand are similar to those associated with valuing the option to delay. In most cases, firms with options to expand have no specific time horizon by which they have to make an expansion decision, making these open-ended options, or, at best, options with arbitrary lives. Even in those cases where a life can be estimated for the option, neither the size nor the potential market for the product may be known, and estimating either can be problematic. Furthermore, we have assumed that both the cost and the present value of expansion are known initially. In reality, the firm may not have good estimates for either before taking the first project since it does not have much information on the underlying market.

Implications

The option to expand is implicitly used by firms to rationalize taking projects that may have negative net present value but provide significant opportunities to tap into new markets or sell new products. While the option pricing approach adds rigor to this argument by estimating the value of this option, it also provides insight into those occasions when it is most valuable. In general, the option to expand is clearly more valuable for more volatile businesses with higher returns on projects (such as biotechnology or computer software) than for stable businesses with lower returns (such as housing, utilities, or automobile production).

It can also be argued that research and development (R&D) provides one immediate application for this methodology. Firms that expend large resources on research and development argue that they do so because it provides them with new products for the future. In recent years, however, more firms have stopped accepting this explanation at face value as a rationale for spending more money on R&D, and have started demanding better returns from their investments.

Research, Development, and Test Market Expenses

Firms that spend considerable amounts of money on research and development or test marketing are often stymied when they try to evaluate these expenses, since the payoffs are often in terms of future projects. At the same time, there is the very real possibility that after the money has been spent, the products or projects may turn out not to be viable; consequently, the expenditure is treated as a sunk cost. In fact, it can be argued that R&D has the characteristics of a call option—the amount spent on R&D is the cost of the call option, and the projects or products that might emerge from the research provide the options. If these products are viable (i.e., the present value of the cash inflows exceeds the needed investment), the payoff is the difference between the two; if not, the project will not be accepted, and the payoff is zero.

Several logical implications emerge from this view of R&D. First, research expenditures should provide much higher value for firms that are in volatile technologies or businesses, since the variance in product or project cash flows is positively correlated with the value of the call option. Thus, Minnesota Mining and Manufacturing (3M), which expends a substantial amount on R&D on basic office products, such as the Post-it pad, generally should receive less value for its research than does Intel, whose research primarily concerns semiconductor chips. Second, the value of research and the optimal amount to be spent on research will change over time as businesses mature. The best example is the pharmaceutical industry—pharmaceutical companies spent most of the 1980s investing substantial amounts in research and earning high returns on new products, as the health care business expanded. In the 1990s, however, as health care costs started leveling off and the business matured, many of these companies found that they were not getting the same payoffs on research and started cutting back.

6.6   R&D EXPENDITURES AND OPTION PRICING

If we perceive research and development expenses as the price of acquiring options (product patents), research and development expenditure will have most value if directed to

- ☐ areas where the technology is stable and the likelihood of success is high.
- ☐ areas where the technology is volatile, though the likelihood of success is low.
- ☐ neither.

Explain.

The Option to Abandon a Project

The final option to consider here is the option to abandon a project when its cash flows do not measure up to expectations. To illustrate this option, assume that V is the remaining value on a project if it continues to the end of its life, and L is the liquidation or abandonment value for the same project at the same point in time. If the project has a life of n years, the value of continuing the project can be compared to the liquidation (abandonment) value—if it is higher, the project should be continued; if it is lower, the holder of the abandonment option could consider abandoning the project

$$\text{Payoff from Owning an Abandonment Option} \quad = 0 \quad \text{if } V > L$$
$$= L \quad \text{if } V \le L$$

These payoffs are graphed in Figure 6.3 as a function of the expected stock price. Unlike the prior two cases, the option to abandon takes on the characteristics of a put option.

Valuing an Option to Abandon: An Illustration

Assume that Disney is considering taking a 25-year project which requires an initial investment on its part of $250 million in a real estate partnership to develop time share properties with a South Florida real estate developer, and where the present value of expected cash flows is $254 million. While the net present value of $4 million is small, assume that Disney has the option to abandon this project any time by selling its share back to the developer in the next five years for $150 million. The variance in the present value of the cash flows from being in the partnership is 0.09, and this is obtained from a simulation of the project cash flows.

The value of the abandonment option can be estimated by determining the characteristics of the put option:

$$\text{Value of the Underlying Asset (S)} = \text{PV of Cash Flows from Project}$$
$$= \$254 \text{ million}$$

Strike Price (K) = Salvage Value from Abandonment = $150 million

Variance in Underlying Asset's Value = 0.09

Time to Expiration = Life of the Project = 5 years

Dividend Yield = 1/Life of the Project = 1/25 = 0.04 (We are assuming that the project's present value will drop by roughly 1/n each year into the project.)

Assume that the five-year riskless rate is 7%. The value of the put option can be estimated as follows:

Call Value = $254 \exp^{(0.04)(5)} (0.9105) - 150 \exp^{(-0.07)(5)} (0.7496) = \$ 110.12$ million

Using put call parity, we get

Put Value = $\$110.12 - 254 \exp^{(0.04)(5)} + 150 \exp^{(-0.07)(5)} = \$ 7.86$ million

The value of this abandonment option has to be added on to the net present value of the project of $4 million, yielding a total net present value with the abandonment option of $11.86 million.

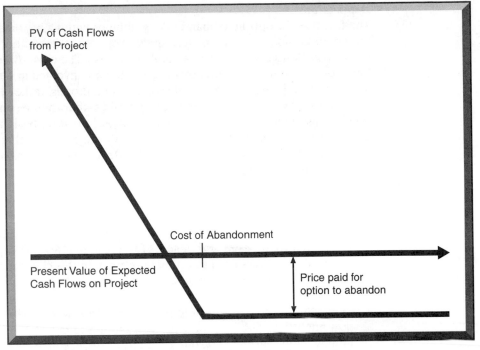

Figure 6.3   The option to abandon a project.

6.7   ABANDONMENT VALUE AND PROJECT LIFE

Consider the project described above. Assume that three years into the project, the cash flows are coming in 20% below expectations. What will happen to the value of the option to abandon?

☐   It will increase.

☐   It will decrease.

☐   It may increase or decrease, depending upon . . .

Explain.

Practical Considerations

In the above analysis we assumed, rather unrealistically, that the abandonment value was clearly specified up front and that it did not change during the life of the project. This may be true in some very specific cases, in which an abandonment option is built into the contract. More often, however, the firm has the option to abandon, and the salvage value from doing so can be estimated with noise up front. Further, the abandonment value may change over the life of the project, making it difficult to apply traditional option pricing techniques. Finally, it is entirely possible that abandoning a project may not bring in a liquidation value, but may create costs instead; a manufacturing firm may have to pay severance to its workers, for instance. In such cases, it would not make sense to abandon, unless the cash flows on the project are even more negative.

Implications

The fact that the option to abandon has value provides a rationale for firms to build the flexibility to scale back or terminate projects if they do not measure up to expectations. Firms can do this in a number of ways. The most direct way is to build in the option contractually with other parties that are involved in the project. Thus, contracts with suppliers may be written on an annual basis, rather than long term, and employees may be hired on a temporary basis, rather than permanently. The physical plant used for a project may be leased on a short-term basis, rather than bought, and the financial investment may be made in stages rather than as an initial lump sum. While there is a cost to building in this flexibility, the gains may be much larger, especially in volatile businesses.

CONCLUSION

Projects often create costs and benefits for a firm that are not captured in the initial estimates of cash flows used to estimate returns. In this chapter, we examined some of these indirect costs and benefits:

- Opportunity costs measure the costs of resources that the company already owns that might be used for a new project. While the business might not spend new money acquiring these resources, there are consequences in terms of the cash flows which have to be reflected in the returns.
- Projects may also provide synergistic benefits for other projects that a firm might have. These benefits, which also take the form of cash flows, should be reflected in the returns.
- Projects may also create options for the business which are valuable—options to expand into new markets and to produce new products, options to abandon and options on timing.

In summary, the project returns have to reflect all of the side costs and benefits.

PROBLEMS AND QUESTIONS

1. You have been hired as a capital budgeting analyst by a sporting goods firm that manufactures athletic shoes and has captured 10% of the overall shoe market. (The total market is worth $100 million a year.) The fixed costs associated with manufacturing these shoes is $2 million a year, and variable costs are 40% of revenues. The company's tax rate is 40%. The firm believes that it can increase its market share to 20% by investing $10 million in a new distribution system (which can be depreciated over the system's life of 10 years to a salvage value of zero) and spending $1 million a year in additional advertising. The company proposes to continue to maintain working capital at 10% of annual revenues. The discount rate to be used for this project is 8%.

   How much would the firm's market share have to increase for you to be indifferent to taking or rejecting this project?

2. You are considering the possibility of replacing an existing machine that has a book value of $500,000, a remaining depreciable life of five

years, with a new machine that will cost $2 million and have a 10-year life. The existing machine can be sold for $300,000 now, and the discount rate is 10%. Assuming that you use straight-line depreciation and that neither machine will have any salvage value at the end of the next 10 years, how much would you need to save each year to make the change (the tax rate is 40%)?

3. You are helping a bookstore decide whether it should open a coffee shop on the premises. The details of the investment are as follows:
   - The coffee shop will cost $50,000 to open; it will have a five-year life and be depreciated straight-line over the period to a salvage value of $10,000.
   - The sales at the shop are expected to be $15,000 in the first year and to grow 5% a year for the following five years.
   - The operating expenses will be 50% of revenues.
   - The tax rate is 40%.
   - The coffee shop is expected to generate additional sales of $20,000 next year for the book shop, and the pretax operating margin is 40%. These sales will grow 10% a year for the following four years.
   - The discount rate is 12%.
   a. Estimate the net present value of the coffee shop without the additional book sales.
   b. Estimate the present value of the cash flows accruing from the additional book sales.
   c. Would you open the coffee shop?

4. You are the owner of a small hardware store, and you are considering opening a gardening shop in a vacant area in the back of the store. You estimate that it will cost you $50,000 to set up the store and that you will generate $10,000 in after-tax cash flows for the life of the store (which is expected to be 10 years). The one concern you have is that you have limited parking; by opening the gardening shop you run the risk of not having enough parking for customers who shop at your hardware store. You estimate that the lost sales would amount to $3,000 a year and that your after-tax operating margin on sales at the hardware store is 40%. If your discount rate is 14%, would you open the gardening shop?

5. You are the manager of a grocery store and you are considering offering baby-sitting services to your customers. You estimate that the licensing and set-up costs will amount to $150,000 initially and that you will be spending about $60,000 annually to provide the service. As a result of the service, you expect sales at the store, which are $5 million currently, to increase by 20%; your after-tax operating margin is 10%. If your cost of capital is 12%, and you expect the store to remain open for 10 years, would you offer the service?

6. A company is considering delaying a project that has annual after-tax cash flows of $25 million but that costs $300 million to take. (The life of the project is 20 years, and the cost of capital is 16%.) A simulation of the cash flows leads you to conclude that the standard deviation in the present value of cash inflows is 20%. If you can acquire the rights to the project for the next 10 years, what are the inputs for the option pricing model? (The six-month Treasury bill rate is 8%, the 10-year bond rate is 12%, and the 20-year bond rate is 14%.)

7. You have been approached by a real estate conglomerate with a deal: You can buy 100,000 square feet of space in a mall at $50/square foot. Over the next 10 years, you expect to make an after-tax cash inflow of $500,000 a year. At the end of 10 years, you expect to be able to sell the space back at $5 million to other investors.
   a. From a standard capital budgeting analysis, would you take this project if your discount rate were 15%?
   b. Assume that, as an inducement, the promoters offer to give you the option to buy another 100,000 square feet at today's price anytime over the next five years. The five-year bond rate is 6%, and the prices per square foot for the last six years have been as follows:

Year	Price/Square Foot
−6	$20
−5	$30
−4	$55
−3	$70
−2	$55
−1	$50

   What is the value of this option?

8. You are examining the financial viability of investing in some abandoned copper mines in Chile, which still have significant copper deposits. A geology survey suggests that there might still be 10 million pounds of copper in the mines and that the cost of opening up the mines will be $3 million (in present value dollars). The capacity output rate is 400,000 pounds a year, and the price of copper is expected to increase 4% a year. The Chilean government is willing to grant a 25-year lease on the mine. The average production cost is expected to be 40 cents a pound, and the current price per pound of copper is 85 cents. (The production cost is expected to grow 3% a year, once initiated.) The annualized standard deviation in copper prices is 25%, and the 25-year bond rate is 7%.

   a. Estimate the value of the mine using traditional capital budgeting techniques.

   b. Estimate the value of the mine based on an option pricing model.

   c. How would you explain the difference between the two values?

9. You are analyzing a capital budgeting project that is expected to have a PV of cash inflows of $250 million and will cost $200 million (in present value dollars) initially. A simulation of the project cash flows yields a variance in present value of cash inflows of 0.04. You have to pay $12.5 million a year to retain the project rights for the next five years. The five-year Treasury bond rate is 8%.

   a. What is the value of the project, based on traditional NPV?

   b. What is the value of the project as an option?

   c. Why are the two values different? What factor (or factors) determine the magnitude of this difference?

10. Cyclops, Inc., a high-technology company specializing in state-of-the-art visual technology, is considering going public. The company has no revenues or profits yet on its products, but it has a 10-year patent to a product that will enable contact lens users to obtain maintenance-free lenses that will last for years. Although the product is technically viable, it is exorbitantly expensive to manufacture, and its immediate potential market will be relatively small. (A cash-flow analysis of the project suggests that the present value of the cash inflows on the project, if adopted now, would be $250 million, whereas the cost of the project would be $500 million.) The technology is evolving rapidly, and a simulation of alternative scenarios yields a wide range of present values, with an annualized standard deviation of 60%. To move toward this adoption, the company will have to continue to invest $10 million a year in research. The 10-year bond rate is 6%.

   a. Estimate the value of this company.

   b. How sensitive is this value estimate to the variance in project cash flows? What broader lessons would you draw from this analysis?

11. Answer true or false to the following statements:

   a. The right to pursue a project will not be valuable if there is a great deal of uncertainty about the viability of the project.

   b. A project can be viewed as an option only if there are some barriers to entry which prevent competitors from replicating it.

   c. A company that has valuable patents that do not yet generate cash flows and earnings will be undervalued using traditional discounted cashflow valuation.

   d. A company should take on a project as soon as it becomes financially viable (i.e., when its NPV exceeds zero).

   e. The value of a project will increase as the volatility of the industry and the technology underlying the project increase.

CHAPTER 7

CAPITAL STRUCTURE: AN OVERVIEW OF THE FINANCING DECISION

In the last few chapters, we have examined the investment principle and argued that projects that earn a return greater than the minimum acceptable hurdle rate are good projects. In coming up with the cost of capital, which we defined to be the minimum acceptable hurdle rate, however, we used the existing financing mix of the firm. In this chapter, we examine the choices that a firm has in terms of financing instruments and the basic trade-off between using debt and equity. In the process, we examine the following questions:

- What are the fundamental characteristics of debt and equity, and what are the different types of debt and equity securities? What are hybrid securities, and why do firms issue them?

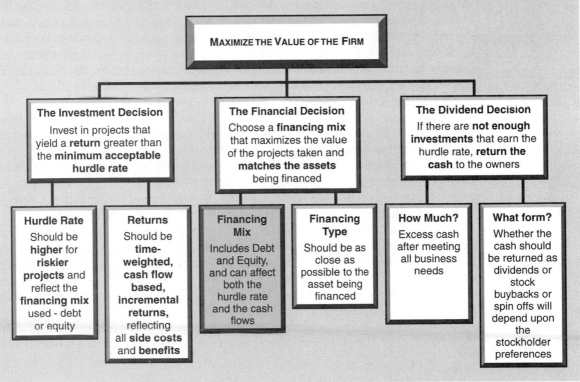

MAXIMIZE THE VALUE OF THE FIRM

The Investment Decision
Invest in projects that yield a **return** greater than the **minimum acceptable hurdle rate**

The Financial Decision
Choose a **financing mix** that maximizes the value of the projects taken and **matches the assets** being financed

The Dividend Decision
If there are **not enough investments** that earn the hurdle rate, **return the cash** to the owners

Hurdle Rate
Should be **higher** for **riskier projects** and reflect the **financing mix** used - debt or equity

Returns
Should be **time-weighted, cash flow based, incremental returns,** reflecting all **side costs** and **benefits**

Financing Mix
Includes Debt and Equity, and can affect both the hurdle rate and the cash flows

Financing Type
Should be as close as possible to the asset being financed

How Much?
Excess cash after meeting all business needs

What form?
Whether the cash should be returned as dividends or stock buybacks or spin offs will depend upon the stockholder preferences

- What is the basic trade-off between debt and equity? Why might more debt be good for some firms and not for others?
- Under what conditions does the financing mix not matter?

THE CHOICES: TYPES OF FINANCING

There are only two ways in which any business can raise money—debt or equity. This may seem simplistic, given the array of choices firms have in terms of financing vehicles. We will begin this section with a discussion of a broad distinction between debt and equity and then look at a range of financing vehicles available within each of these categories. We will then examine securities that share some characteristics with debt and some with equity and are therefore called *hybrid securities*.

Hybrid Security: This refers to any security that shares some of the characteristics of debt and some characteristics of equity.

The Continuum between Debt and Equity

While the distinction between debt and equity is often made in terms of bonds and stocks, its roots lie in the nature of the cash flow claims of each type of financing. The first distinction is that a *debt claim* entitles the holder to a contracted set of cash flows (usually interest and principal payments), whereas an *equity claim* entitles the holder to any residual cash flows left over after meeting all other promised claims. While this remains the fundamental difference, other distinctions have arisen, partly as a result of the tax code and partly as a consequence of legal developments.

The second distinction, which is a logical outgrowth of the nature of cash flow claims (contractual versus residual), is that debt has a prior claim on both cash flows on a period-to-period basis (for interest and principal payments) and on the assets of the firm (in the case of liquidation). Third, the tax laws have generally treated interest expenses, which accrue to debt holders, very differently and often much more advantageously than dividends or other cash flows that accrue to equity. In the United States, for instance, interest expenses are tax deductible, and thus create tax savings, whereas dividend payments have to be made out of after-tax cash flows. Fourth, usually debt has a fixed maturity date, at which point the principal is due, while equity generally has an infinite life. Finally, equity investors, by virtue of their claim on the residual cash flows of the firm, are generally given the bulk of or all of the control of the management of the firm. Debt investors, on the other hand, play a much more passive role in management, exercising, at most, veto power[1] over significant financial decisions. These differences are summarized in Figure 7.1.

To summarize, debt is defined as any financing vehicle that is a contractual claim on the firm (and not a function of its operating performance), creates tax-deductible

---

[1]The veto power is usually exercised through covenants in bond agreements.

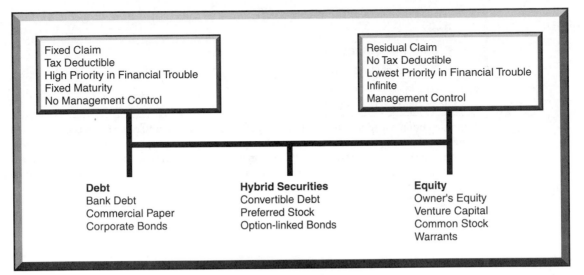

Figure 7.1   Debt Versus Equity.

payments, has a fixed life, and has priority claims on cash flows in both operating periods and in bankruptcy. Conversely, equity is defined as any financing vehicle that is a residual claim on the firm, does not create a tax advantage from its payments, has an infinite life, does not have priority in bankruptcy, and provides management control to the owner. Any security that shares characteristics with both is a hybrid security.

IN PRACTICE: A FINANCING CHECKLIST FOR CLASSIFYING SECURITIES

Some new securities, at first sight, are difficult to categorize as either debt or equity. To check where on the spectrum between straight debt and straight equity these securities fall, answer the following questions:

1. *Are the payments on the securities contractual or residual?*
   - If contractual, it is closer to debt.
   - If residual, it is closer to equity.
2. *Are the payments tax deductible?*
   - If yes, it is closer to debt.
   - If no, it is closer to equity.
3. *Do the cash flows on the security have a high priority or a low priority if the firm is in financial trouble?*
   - If it has high priority, it is closer to debt.
   - If it has low priority, it is closer to equity.
4. *Does the security have a fixed life?*
   - If yes, it is closer to debt.
   - If no, it is closer to equity.

5. *Does the owner of the security get a share of the control of management of the firm?*

- If no, it is closer to debt.
- If yes, it is closer to equity.

7.1 IS IT DEBT OR IS IT EQUITY?

You have been asked to classify a security as debt or equity, and have been provided the following characteristics for the security: It requires fixed monthly payments which are tax deductible and it has an infinite life. Its claims on the cash flows of the firm, during operation, and on the assets, if the firm goes bankrupt, come after all debt holders' claims (including unsecured debt) are met but prior to equity investors.

☐ It is debt.
☐ It is equity.
☐ It is a hybrid security.

Explain.

EQUITY

While most people think of equity in terms of common stock, the equity claim can take a variety of forms, depending partly upon whether the firm is privately owned or publicly traded, and partly upon the firm's growth and risk characteristics.

Private firms have fewer choices available than do publicly traded firms, since they cannot issue securities to raise equity. Consequently, they have to depend either upon the owner or a private entity, usually a venture capitalist, to bring in the equity needed to keep the business operating and expanding.

1. Owner's Equity

Most businesses, including the most successful companies of our time, such as Microsoft and Wal-Mart, started off as small businesses with one or a few individuals providing the seed money and plowing back the earnings of the firm into the businesses. These funds, brought in by the owners of the company, are referred to as the *owner's equity,* and provide the basis for the growth and eventual success of the business.

2. Venture Capital

As small businesses succeed and grow, they typically run into a funding constraint, where the funds that they have access to are insufficient to cover their investment and growth needs. A *venture capitalist* provides equity financing to small and often risky businesses in return for a share of the ownership of the firm.

Generally speaking, the capacity to raise funds from alternative sources and/or to go public will increase with the size of the firm and decrease with the uncertainty about its future prospects. Thus, smaller and riskier businesses are more likely to seek venture capital and are also more likely to be asked to give up a disproportionate share of the value of the firm when receiving the venture capital.

Venture Capital: This is usually equity capital provided to a private firm by an investor or investors, in exchange for a share of the ownership of the firm.

7.2   THE EFFECTS OF DIVERSIFICATION ON VENTURE CAPITALISM

You are comparing the required returns of two venture capitalists who are interested in investing in the same software firm. One venture capitalist has all of his capital invested in only software firms, whereas the other venture capitalist has invested her capital in small companies in a variety of businesses. Which of these two will have the higher required rate of return?

☐   The venture capitalist who is invested only in software companies

☐   The venture capitalist who is invested in a variety of businesses

☐   Cannot answer without more information

7.3   REQUIRED RETURN AND PROPORTIONAL OWNERSHIP

If both venture capitalists described above had the same expected cash flow estimates for the business, which one would demand a larger share of the ownership for the same capital investment?

☐   The venture capitalist with the higher required rate of return

☐   The venture capitalist with the lower required rate of return

3. Common Stock

The conventional way for a publicly traded firm to raise equity is to issue common stock at a price the market is willing to pay. For a newly listed company, this price is estimated by the issuing entity (such as an investment banker); for an existing company, it is based upon the current market price. In some cases, the common stock issued by a company is uniform; that is, each share receives a proportional share of both the cash flows (such as dividends) and the voting rights. In other cases, different classes of common stock will provide different cash flows and voting rights.

While existing firms do not use common stock very often to raise new financing for their projects and operations, it remains the most widely used approach to raising equity. Common stock is a simple security, and it is relatively easy to understand and value. In fact, it can be argued that common stock makes feasible all other security choices for a publicly traded firm, since a firm without equity cannot issue debt or hybrid securities. The accounting treatment of common stock follows well-established precedent and can be presented easily within the conventional format of financial statements.

4. Warrants

In recent years, firms have started looking at equity alternatives to common stock. One alternative used successfully by the Japanese companies in the late 1980s involved warrants, where the holders received the right to buy shares in the company at a fixed price in return for paying for the warrants up front. Since their value is derived from the price of the underlying common stock, warrants have to be treated as another form of equity.

Why might a firm use warrants rather than common stock to raise equity? We can think of several reasons. First, warrants are priced based upon the implied volatility assigned to the underlying stock; the greater the volatility, the greater the value. To the degree that the market overestimates the firm's volatility, the firm may gain by using warrants and option-like securities. Second, warrants, by themselves, create no financial obligations at the time of the issue. Consequently, issuing warrants is a good way for a high-growth firm to raise funds, especially when current cash flows are low or nonexistent. Third, for financial officers who are sensitive to the dilution created by issuing common stock, warrants seem to provide the best of both worlds—they do not create any new additional shares currently, while they raise equity investment funds for current use.

Warrants: A warrant is a security issued by a company that provides the holder with the right to buy a share of stock in the company at a fixed price during the life of the warrant.

7.4   STOCK PRICE VARIANCE AND WARRANT USE

Companies with high variance in their stock prices should use warrants more than companies with low variance in their stock prices, because warrant prices increase with variance.

☐   True
☐   False

Explain.

IN PRACTICE: VALUING WARRANTS

Warrants are long-term call options, but standard option pricing models are based upon the assumption that exercising an option does not affect the value of the underlying asset. This may be true for listed options on stocks, but it is not true for warrants, since their exercise increases the number of shares outstanding and brings fresh cash into the firm, both of which will affect the stock price. The expected negative impact (dilution) of exercise will make warrants less valuable than otherwise similar call options. The adjustment for dilution to the stock price in the Black-Scholes model involves three steps:

Step 1:   The stock price is adjusted for the expected dilution from warrant exercise:

$$\text{Dilution-adjusted } S = (S\, n_s + W\, n_w) / (n_s + n_w)$$

where

  S = Current value of the stock n_w = Number of warrants outstanding
  W = Market value of warrants outstanding n_s = Number of shares outstanding

When the warrants are exercised, the number of shares outstanding will increase, reducing the stock price. The numerator reflects the market value of equity, including both stocks and warrants outstanding.

Step 2:   The variance used in the option pricing formula is the variance in the value of the equity in the company (i.e., the value of stocks plus warrants, not just the stocks).

Step 3:   Once the call is valued using the option pricing model, the option value is adjusted to reflect dilution:

$$\text{Dilution-Adjusted Value} = \text{Call Value from Model} * n_s / (n_w + n_s)$$

5. Contingent Value Rights

Contingent value rights provide investors with the right to sell stocks for a fixed price, and thus derive their value from the volatility of the stock and the desire on the part of investors to hedge against losses. *Put options,* which are traded on the option exchanges, give their holders a similar right to sell the underlying stock at a fixed price. There are two primary differences between contingent value rights and puts. First, the proceeds from the contingent value rights sales go to the firm, whereas those from the sale of listed puts go to private parties. Second, contingent value rights tend to be much more long term than typical listed puts.

There are several reasons why a firm may choose to issue contingent value rights. The most obvious is that the firm believes it is significantly undervalued by the market. In such a scenario, the firm may offer contingent value rights to take advantage of its belief and to provide a signal to the market of the undervaluation. Contingent value rights are also useful if the market is overestimating volatility and the put price reflects this misestimated volatility. Finally, the presence of contingent value rights as insurance may attract new investors to the market for the common stock.

Contingent Value Rights: A contingent value right (CVR) provides the holder with the right to sell a share of stock in the underlying company at a fixed price during the life of the right.

DEBT

The clear alternative to using equity, which is a residual claim, is to borrow money. This option both creates a fixed obligation to make cash flow payments and provides the lender with prior claims if the firm is in financial trouble.

1. Bank Debt

Historically, the primary source of borrowed money for all private firms and many publicly traded firms have been commercial banks with the interest rates on the debt based upon the perceived risk of the borrower. Bank debt provides the borrower with several advantages. First, it can be used for borrowing relatively small amounts of money; in contrast, bond issues thrive on economies of scale, with larger issues having lower costs. Second, if the company is neither well known nor widely followed, bank debt provides a convenient framework to convey information to the lender that will help in both pricing and evaluating the loan. The presence of hundreds of investors in bond issues makes this both costly and infeasible if bonds are issued as the primary vehicle for debt. Finally, in order to issue bonds, firms have to submit to being rated. The added dynamic of dealing with ratings agencies, in addition to the equity investors, may create conflicts between the two, which the manager then has to resolve. In contrast, firms have to deal with only the lending bank when they take on bank debt, which may be simpler to do in some cases,[2] and minimizes the amount of information that they have to make public.

---

[2]This is especially true if the bank is a local bank and knows the firm well. This knowledge may allow the bank to grant more freedom to the borrowing firm.

7.5 CORPORATE BONDS AND BANK DEBT

If a company can issue corporate bonds, it should not use bank debt.

☐ True

☐ False

Explain.

2. Bonds

For larger publicly traded firms, an alternative to bank debt is to issue bonds. Generally speaking, bond issues have several advantages. One is that bonds usually carry more favorable financing terms than equivalent bank debt, largely because risk is shared by a larger number of financial market investors. A second advantage is that bond issues might provide a chance for the issuer to add on special features that could not be added on to bank debt. For instance, bonds can be convertible into common stock or have commodity options attached to them. In borrowing money, firms have to make a variety of choices including:

1. Whether the debt should be *short term* or *long term*
2. Whether the interest payments on the debt should be *fixed* for the lifetime of the borrowing or be a function of a market interest rate *(floating rate)*
3. Whether the debt should be *secured* using specific assets or the general cash flows of the firm
4. What *currency* the cash flows on the debt should be in
5. How the debt should be *repaid*
6. Any *special features* that should be added on to the debt

7.6 DEBT MATURITY AND INTEREST RATES

Assume that you have an upward-sloping yield curve, and that your investment banker advises you to issue short-term debt because it is cheaper than long-term debt. Is this true?

☐ Yes

☐ No

Why or why not?

IN PRACTICE: DEBT INNOVATIONS

The past two decades have seen an explosion in new features added on to bonds. Some, such as floating rates and caps and floors, arose as a consequence of the high inflation and interest rate volatility that characterized the late 1970s. Some of these features take advantage of the better understanding issuers (or their agents) have of how to price options. Table 7.1 summarizes some of the most important innovations, and the rationale for their introduction. While these innovations provide both companies and buyers with more options and the capacity to tailor bonds to their specific needs, they do carry a downside. The special features, especially when combined, become more and more difficult to value and to keep track of over time.

Innovation	Description/Year Introduced	Rationale for Innovation
Floating rate loans	Interest rate varies with index	Volatility in inflation and interest rates
Puttable bonds	Bondholders can put bond back to firm, and get face value, under specified events	Protection of bondholder interests
Convertible/exchangeable floating rate notes	Floating rate note can be converted into equity	Provide flexibility to buyer of bond
Extendable bonds	Life of the bond can be extended at the option of the issuer	Provide more flexibility to the issuer
Caps and floors	Limits interest rate movements on a floating rate loan	Limit risk to issuer and buyer
Swaps	Allows exchange of bonds for bonds with different characteristics (fixed to floating, different currency)	Allow firms to alter their financing mix
Reverse floating rate notes	Interest rate varies inversely with an index; as index rate goes up, rate on bond goes down	Increase duration and price sensitivity of bond
Swaptions	Option on a swap	Allows firms to buy options to do swaps

Table 7.1 INNOVATIONS IN BOND MARKET

HYBRID SECURITIES

Summarizing our analysis thus far, equity represents a residual claim on the cash flows and assets of the firm and is generally associated with management control. Debt, on the other hand, represents a fixed claim on the cash flows and assets of the firm and is usually not associated with management control. There are a number of securities that do not fall neatly into either of these two categories; rather, they share some characteristics with equity and some with debt. These securities are called *hybrid securities.*

1. Convertible Debt

A *convertible bond* is a bond that can be converted into a predetermined number of shares, at the discretion of the bondholder. While it generally does not pay to convert at the time of the bond issue, conversion becomes a more attractive option as stock prices increase. Firms generally add conversion options to bonds to lower the interest rate paid on the bonds.

In a typical convertible bond, the bondholder is given the option to convert the bond into a specified number of shares of stock. The *conversion ratio* measures the number of shares of stock for which each bond may be exchanged. Stated differently, the *market conversion value* is the current value of the shares for which the bonds can be exchanged. The *conversion premium* is the excess of the bond value over the conversion value of the bond.

Thus, a convertible bond with a par value of $1,000, which is convertible into 50 shares of stock, has a conversion ratio of 50. The conversion ratio can also be used to compute a conversion price—the par value divided by the conversion ratio— yielding a conversion price of $20. If the current stock price is $25, the market conversion value is $1,250 (50 * $25). If the convertible bond is trading at $1,300, the conversion premium is $50.

Convertible Debt: This is debt that can be converted into equity at a rate that is specified as part of the debt agreement (conversion rate).

IN PRACTICE: A SIMPLE APPROACH TO DECOMPOSING DEBT AND EQUITY

The value of a convertible debt can be decomposed into straight debt and equity components using a simple approach. Since the price of a convertible bond is the sum of the straight debt and the call option components, the value of the straight bond component in conjunction with the market price of the convertible bond should be sufficient to estimate the call option component, which is also the equity component:

Value of Equity Component = Market Price of Convertible Bond − Value of
Straight Bond
Component

The value of the straight bond component can be estimated using the coupon payments on the convertible bond, the maturity of the bond and the market interest rate the company would have to pay on a straight debt issue. This last input can be estimated directly if the company also has straight bonds in the market place, or it can be based upon the bond rating, if any, assigned to the company.

For instance, assume that you have a 10-year convertible bond, with a 5% coupon rate trading at $1,050, and that the company has a debt rating of BBB (with a market interest rate of 8%). The value of the straight bond and equity components can be estimated as follows:

Straight Bond Component = $ 50 (PVA, 10 years, 8%) + 1000/1.08^{10} = $ 798.69
Equity Component = $ 1,050 − $ 799 = $ 251

7.7   CONVERTIBLE DEBT AND YIELDS

The yields on convertible bonds are much lower than the yields on straight bonds issued by a company. Therefore, convertible debt is cheaper than straight debt.

☐ True
☐ False
Why or why not?

2. Preferred Stock

Preferred stock is another security that shares some characteristics with debt and some with equity. Like debt, preferred stock has a fixed dollar dividend; if the firm does not have the cash to pay the dividend, it is cumulated and paid in a period when there are sufficient earnings. Like debt, preferred stockholders do not have a share of control in the firm, and their voting privileges are restricted to issues that might affect their claims on the firm's cash flows or assets. Like equity, payments to preferred stockholders are not tax deductible and come out of after-tax cash flow. Also like equity, preferred stock does not have a maturity date when the face value is due. In terms of priority, in the case of bankruptcy, preferred stockholders have to wait until the debtholders' claims have been met before receiving any portion of the assets of the firm.

While accountants and ratings agencies continue to treat preferred stock as equity, it can be argued that the fixed commitments that preferred stock create are like debt obligations and have to be dealt with likewise. The obligations created by preferred stock are generally less onerous than those created by debt, however, since they are cumulated, cannot cause default, and do not have priority over debt claims in the case of bankruptcy.

Unlike convertible debt, which can be decomposed into equity and debt components, preferred stock cannot really be treated as debt because preferred dividends are not tax deductible and certainly cannot be viewed as the equivalent of equity because of the differences in cash flow claims and control. Consequently, preferred stock is treated as a third component of capital, in addition to debt and equity, for purposes of capital structure analysis and for estimating the cost of capital.

Preferred Stock: This is a hybrid security. Like debt, it has a promised payment (the preferred dividend) in each period. Like equity, its cash flows are not tax deductible and it has an infinite life.

7.8   PREFERRED STOCK AND EQUITY

Many ratings agencies and regulators treat preferred stock as equity in computing debt ratios because it does not have a finite maturity and firms cannot be forced into bankruptcy if they fail to pay preferred dividends. Do you agree with this categorization?

☐ Yes
☐ False
Why or why not?

3. Option-Linked Bonds

In recent years, firms have recognized the value of combining options with straight bonds to create bonds that more closely match the firm's specific needs. Consider two examples. In the first, commodity companies issued bonds linking the principal and/or interest payments to the price of the commodity. Thus interest payments would rise if the price of the commodity increased, and would fall if the commodity's price fell. The benefit for the company was that it tailored the cash flows on the bond to the cash flows from its assets and reduced the likelihood of default. These *commodity-linked bonds* can be viewed as a combination of a straight bond and a call option on the underlying commodity. In the second example, consider insurance companies that have recently issued bonds whereby the principal or interest on the bond is reduced in the case of a specified catastrophe, and remains unaffected in its absence. For instance, an insurance firm which has the bulk of its revenues coming from homeowners' insurance in California, might attach a provision that reduces principal and/or interest in the case of a major earthquake. Again, the rationale is to provide the firm with some breathing room when it needs it the most—when a catastrophe creates huge cash outflows for the firm.

Commodity Bonds: Commodity bonds are bonds where the interest and/or the principal payments are linked to the price of the commodity. In most cases, the payments will increase with the price of the commodity and decrease if it drops.

THE BENEFITS OF DEBT

In the broadest terms, debt provides two differential benefits over equity. The first is the *tax benefit:* interest payments on debt are tax deductible, while cash flows on equity are not. The second is the *added discipline imposed on management,* by having to make payments on debt. Both benefits can and should be quantified if firms want to make reasonable judgments on debt capacity.

Debt Has a Tax Advantage

The primary benefit of debt relative to equity is the tax advantage it confers on the borrower. In the United States, interest paid on debt is tax deductible, whereas cash flows on equity (such as dividends) have to be paid out of after-tax cash flows. For the most part, this is true in other countries as well, though some countries try to provide partial protection against the *double taxation* of dividends by providing a tax credit to investors who receive the dividends for the corporate taxes paid (Britain) or by taxing retained earnings at a rate higher than dividends (Germany).

Double Taxation: There is double taxation when the same income gets taxed twice, once at the entity level and once at the individual level. Thus, dividends, which are paid out of after-tax corporate profits, are double taxed when individuals have to pay taxes on them as well.

The tax benefits from debt can be presented in two ways. In the first approach, the present value of tax savings arising from interest payments are computed and added on to firm value. In the second approach, the savings from the tax deduction are shown as the difference between the pre-tax rate of borrowing and the after-tax rate.

The Dollar Tax Savings
Consider a firm that borrows $B to finance its operations, on which it faces an interest rate of r%, and assume that it faces a marginal tax rate of t on income. The annual tax savings from the interest tax deduction can be calculated as follows:

Annual Interest Expense Arising from the Debt = r B
Annual Tax Savings Arising from the Interest Payment = t r B

The present value of the annual tax savings can be computed by making three other assumptions. The first is that the debt is perpetual, which also means that the dollar savings are a perpetuity. The second is that the appropriate discount rate for this cash flow is the interest rate on the debt, since it reflects the riskiness of the debt. The third is that the expected tax rate for the firm will remain unchanged over time, and that the firm is in a tax-paying position. With these three assumptions, the present value of the savings can be computed as follows:

Present Value of Tax Savings from Debt   = t r B / r = t B
= Marginal Tax Rate * Debt

While the conventional view is to look at the tax savings as a perpetuity, the approach is general enough to be used to compute the tax savings over a shorter period (say, ten years). Thus, a firm which borrows $100 million at 8% for ten years, and has a tax rate of 40%, can compute the present value of its tax savings as follows:

Present Value of Interest Tax Savings = Annual Tax Savings (PV of Annuity)
= (.08* 0.4 * $ 100 million) (PV of Annuity, 8%, 10 years) = $ 21.47 million

In addition, the net tax benefit can be computed if dividends also provide a tax benefit, albeit one that is smaller than that conferred by debt. In such a case, the present value of the net tax savings from debt can be written as:

Present Value of Net Tax Savings from Debt
= PV of Tax Savings from Debt − PV of Tax Savings from Dividend Payments

To illustrate, consider the example of a country whose tax rate on cash paid out as dividends (t_{div}) is less than the tax rate on retained earnings (t_{re}). The present value of the tax savings arising from dividends can be written as follows, assuming a growth rate of g in dividends and a cost of equity of k_e:

Present Value of Tax Savings from Dividends = $(t_{re} - t_{div})$ Dividend $(1 + g) / (k_e - g)$

Note that this is the present value of a growing perpetuity.

When asked to analyze the effect of adding debt on value, some analysts use a shortcut and simply add the tax benefit from debt to the value of the firm with no debt:

Value of Levered Firm with Debt B = Value of Unlevered Firm + t B

The limitation of this approach is that it considers only the tax benefit from borrowing and none of the additional costs. It also yields the unrealistic conclusion that firm value increases monotonically with more debt.

Marginal Tax Rate: This is the tax rate that applies on the marginal dollar of income at a firm. In general, it will be higher than the average tax rate.

Pretax and After-Tax Costs

The tax benefit from debt can also be expressed in terms of the difference between the pre-tax and after-tax cost of debt. To illustrate, if r is the interest rate on debt, and t is the marginal tax rate, the after-tax cost of borrowing (k_d) can be written as follows:

$$\text{After-Tax Cost of Debt } (k_d) = r\,(1 - t)$$

This is the familiar formula used for calculating the cost of debt in the cost of capital calculation. In this formula, the after-tax cost of debt is a decreasing function of the tax rate. A firm with a tax rate of 40%, which borrows at 8%, has an after-tax cost of debt of 4.8%. Another firm with a tax rate of 70%, which borrows at 8%, has an after-tax cost of debt of 2.4%. There are two points to be emphasized in this calculation. First, the tax rate to be used is the *marginal rate* and not the average rate, since interest tax deductions are set off against the marginal dollar. Second, this calculation makes sense only if the firm is making money and paying taxes; a firm that has large accumulated losses and no taxable income may not get a tax benefit from debt.

7.9   NET OPERATING LOSS CARRYFORWARDS AND TAX BENEFITS

You have been asked to assess the after-tax cost of debt for a firm which has $2 billion in net operating losses to carry forward and operating income of roughly $2 billion this year. If the company can borrow at 8%, and the marginal corporate tax rate is 40%, the after-tax cost of debt this year is

☐ 8%.
☐ 4.8%.

What would your after-tax cost of debt be next year?

Implications for Optimal Capital Structure

Other things remaining equal, the benefits of debt are much greater when tax rates are higher. Consequently, there are four predictions that can be made about debt ratios across companies and across time.

1. The debt ratios of entities facing higher tax rates should be higher than the debt ratios of comparable entities facing lower tax rates. These differences in tax rates across entities are most commonly seen in U.S. real estate, where operations can be organized as Real Estate Investment Trusts (REITs) or Master Limited Partnerships (MLPs), whereby the income is taxed at the individual investor level rather than the entity level or as corporations where income is

taxed at both levels. We would expect REITs and MLPs to have lower debt ratios than real estate corporations.

2. Firms that have substantial non-debt tax shields, such as depreciation, should be less likely to use debt than firms that do not have these tax shields.

3. If tax rates increase over time, we would expect debt ratios to go up over time as well, reflecting the higher tax benefits of debt.

4. While it is always difficult to compare debt ratios across countries, we would expect debt ratios in countries where debt has a much larger tax benefit or whose tax rates are higher to be higher than debt ratios in countries where debt has a lower tax benefit.

Real Estate Investment Trusts (REITs) A real estate investment trust is an entity that owns real estate and is allowed to pass through its earnings to its investors without being taxed. In return, it is restricted to just real estate investments, and it has to pay 95% of its earnings as dividends.

The Discipline of Debt

In the 1980s, in the midst of the leveraged buyout boom, a group of practitioners and academics, led by Michael Jensen at Harvard, developed and expounded on a new rationale for borrowing, based upon improving firms' efficiency in the utilization of their free cash flows. *Free cash flows* represent cash flows made on operations over which managers have discretionary spending power—they may use them to take projects, pay them out to stockholders, or hold them as idle cash balances. The group argued that managers in firms that have substantial free cash flows and no or low debt have such a large cash cushion against mistakes that they have no incentive to be efficient in either project choice or project management. One way to introduce discipline into the process is to force these firms to borrow money, since borrowing creates the commitment to make interest and principal payments, increasing the risk of default on projects with substandard returns. It is this difference between the forgiving nature of the equity commitment and the inflexibility of the debt commitment that has led some to call equity a cushion and debt a sword.

The underlying assumptions in this argument are that there is a separation of ownership and management, and that managers will not maximize shareholder wealth without a prod (debt). From our discussion in Chapter 2, it is clear that both assumptions are grounded in fact. Most large U.S. corporations employ managers who own only a very small portion of the outstanding stock in the firm; they receive much of their income as managers rather than stockholders. Furthermore, evidence indicates that managers, at least sometimes, put their interests ahead of those of stockholders.

While conceding the need for discipline, we would also add that debt may have a beneficial effect *only up to a certain point*. At some point, the risk added by the leverage may be so great that managers become reluctant to take even the slightest risks, for fear of bankruptcy, and turn down even good projects.

7.10   Debt as a Disciplining Mechanism

Assume that you buy into this argument that debt adds discipline to management. Which of the following types of companies will most benefit from debt adding this discipline?

☐ Conservatively financed, privately owned businesses

☐ Conservatively financed, publicly traded companies, with a wide and diverse stock holding

☐ Conservatively financed, publicly traded companies, with an activist and primarily institutional holding

(By conservatively financed we mean primarily with equity.)

Free Cash Flows (Jensen's): The free cash flows referred to here are the operating cash flows after taxes, but before discretionary capital expenditures.

Management Considerations on Using Debt

The argument that debt adds discipline to the process also provides an interesting insight into management perspectives on debt. Based purely upon managerial incentives, the optimal level of debt may be much lower than that estimated based upon shareholder wealth maximization. Left to themselves, why would managers want to burden themselves with debt, knowing fully well that they will have to become more efficient and pay a larger price for their mistakes?

The corollary to this argument is that the debt ratios of firms in countries in which stockholder power to influence or remove managers is minimal will be much lower than optimal because managers enjoy a more comfortable existence by carrying less debt than they can afford to. Conversely, as stockholders acquire power, they will push these firms to borrow more money and, in the process, increase their stock prices.

There is a data set on the Web that summarizes, by sector, the percentage of stock that is closely held and debt ratios (**indcapst.xls**).

The Empirical Evidence

Do increases in leverage lead to improved efficiency? The answer to this question should provide some insight into whether the argument for added discipline has some basis. A number of studies have attempted to answer this question, though most have done so indirectly.

- Firms that are taken over in hostile takeovers are generally characterized by poor performance in both accounting profitability and stock returns. Bhide (1993), for instance, notes that the return on equity of these firms is 2.2% below their peer group, while the stock returns are 4% below the peer group's returns.

- While the poor performance, by itself, does not constitute support for the free cash flow hypothesis, Palepu (1986) presents evidence that target firms in acquisitions are underleveraged relative to similar firms that are not taken over.

- There is evidence that increases in leverage are followed by improvements in operating efficiency. Palepu (1990) presents evidence of modest improvements in operating efficiency at firms involved in leveraged buyouts. Kaplan (1989) and Smith (1990) also report improvements in operating efficiency at firms following leveraged buyouts. Denis and Denis (1993) present more direct evidence of improvements in operating efficiency after leveraged recapitalizations. In their study of 29 firms, which increased debt substantially, they report a median increase in the return on assets of 21.5%. Much of this gain seems to arise out of cutbacks in unproductive capital investments, since the median reduction in capital expenditures of these firms is 35.5%.

Of course, we must consider that the evidence presented above is consistent with a number of different hypotheses, among them the free cash flow hypothesis. Moreover, acquisitions, which often comprise the sample in most of these studies, are accompanied by a number of changes, in addition to leverage shifts, making it difficult to isolate the impact of leverage on firm performance.

Leveraged Recapitalization: In a leveraged recapitalization, a firm borrows money and either buys back stock or pays a dividend, thus increasing its debt ratio substantially.

THE COSTS OF DEBT

As any borrower will attest, debt certainly has disadvantages. In particular, borrowing money can expose the firm to default and eventual liquidation, increase the agency problems arising from the conflict between the interests of equity investors and lenders, and reduce the flexibility of the firm to take actions now or in the future.

A. Bankruptcy Costs

The primary concern when borrowing money is the increase in expected bankruptcy costs that typically follows. The expected bankruptcy cost can be written as a product of the probability of bankruptcy and the direct and indirect costs of bankruptcy.

The Probability of Bankruptcy

The *probability of bankruptcy* is the likelihood that a firm's cash flows will be insufficient to meet its promised debt obligations (interest and principal). While such a failure does not automatically imply bankruptcy, it does trigger default, with all its negative consequences. Using this definition, we find that the probability of bankruptcy is a function of the following:

1. *Size of operating cash flows relative to size of cash flows on debt obligations:* Other things remaining equal, the larger the operating cash flows relative to the cash flows on debt obligations, the smaller the likelihood of bankruptcy. Accordingly, the probability of bankruptcy increases marginally for all firms, as they borrow more money, irrespective of how large and stable their cash flows might be.
2. *Variance in operating cash flows:*   Given the same cash flows on debt, a firm with stable and predictable cash flows has a lower probability of bankruptcy than does another firm with a similar level of operating cash flows, but with far greater variability in these cash flows.

 There is a data set on the Web that summarizes, by sector, variances in operating earnings (**indcapst.xls**).

The Cost of Bankruptcy

The cost of going bankrupt is neither obvious nor easily quantified. It is true that bankruptcy is a disaster for all involved in the firm—lenders often get a fraction of what they are owed, and equity investors get nothing—but the overall cost of bankruptcy includes the indirect costs on operations of being perceived as having high default risk.

1. Direct Costs

The direct, or deadweight, cost of bankruptcy is that which is incurred in terms of cash outflows at the time of bankruptcy. These costs include the legal and administrative costs of a bankruptcy, as well as the present value effects of delays in paying out the cash flows. Warner (1977) estimated the legal and administrative costs of 11 railroads to be, on average, 5.3% of the value of the assets at the time of the bankruptcy. He also estimated that it took, on average, 13 years before the railroads were reorganized and released from the bankruptcy costs. These costs, while certainly not negligible, are not overwhelming, especially in light of two additional factors. First, the direct cost as a percentage of the value of the assets decreases to 1.4% if the asset value is computed five years before the bankruptcy. Second, railroads, in general, are likely to have higher bankruptcy costs than other companies, because of the nature of their assets (real estate and fixed equipment).

2. Indirect Costs

If the only costs of bankruptcy were the direct costs noted above, the low leverage maintained by many firms would be puzzling. There are, however, much larger costs associated with taking on debt and increasing default risk, which arise prior to the bankruptcy, largely as a consequence of the perception that a firm is in financial trouble. The first is the perception on the part of the *customers of the firm* that the firm is in trouble. When this happens, customers may *stop buying the product or service,* because of the fear that the company will go out of business. In 1980, for example, when car buyers believed that Chrysler was on the verge of bankruptcy, they chose to buy from Ford, GM, and other car manufacturers, largely because they were concerned about receiving service and parts for their cars after their purchases. Similarly, in the late 1980s, when Continental Airlines found itself in financial trouble, business travelers switched to other airlines because they were unsure about whether they would be able to accumulate and use their frequent flier miles on the airline. The second indirect cost is the stricter terms *suppliers start demanding* to protect themselves against the possibility of default, leading to an increase in working capital and a decrease in cash flows. The third cost is the difficulty the firm may experience trying *to raise fresh capital* for its projects—both debt and equity investors are reluctant to take the risk, leading to capital rationing constraints, and the rejection of good projects.

Shapiro (1986) points out that the indirect costs of bankruptcy are likely to be higher for the following types of firms:

- *Firms that sell durable products with long lives that require replacement parts and service:* Thus, a personal computer manufacturer would have higher indirect costs associated with bankruptcy than would a grocery store.

- *Firms that provide goods or services for which quality is an important attribute but is difficult to determine in advance:* Since the quality cannot be determined easily in advance, the reputation of the firm plays a significant role in whether the customer will buy the product in the first place. For instance, the perception that an airline is in financial trouble may scare away customers who worry that the planes belonging to the airline will not be maintained in good condition.

- *Firms producing products whose value to customers depends on the services and complementary products supplied by independent companies:* Returning to the example of personal computers, a computer system is valuable only insofar as there is software available to run it. If the firm manufacturing the computers is perceived to be in trouble, it is entirely possible that the independent suppliers that produce the software might stop providing it. Thus, as Apple Computers gets into financial trouble, many software manufacturers might stop producing software for its computers, leading to an erosion in its potential market.

- *Firms that sell products that require continuous service and support from the manufacturer:* A manufacturer of copying machines, for which constant service seems to be a necessary operating characteristic, would be affected more adversely by the perception of default risk than would a furniture manufacturer, for example.

7.11 DEBT AND BANKRUPTCY

Rank the following companies on the magnitude of bankruptcy costs from most to least, taking into account both explicit and implicit costs:

☐ Grocery store

☐ Airplane manufacturer

☐ High-technology company

Explain.

Implications for Optimal Capital Structure

If the expected bankruptcy cost is indeed the product of the probability of bankruptcy and the direct and indirect bankruptcy cost, interesting and testable implications emerge for capital structure decisions:

1. Firms operating in businesses with volatile earnings and cash flows should use debt less than should otherwise similar firms with stable cash flows. For instance, regulated utilities in the United States have high leverage because regulation and the monopolistic nature of their businesses result in stable earnings and cash flows. At the other extreme, toy manufacturing firms such as Mattel can have large shifts in income from one year to another, based upon the commercial success or failure of a single toy.[3] These firms should use leverage far less in meeting their funding needs.

2. If firms can structure their debt in such a way that the cash flows on the debt increase and decrease with their operating cash flows, they can afford to borrow

---

[3] In years past, a single group of toys, such as the Teenage Mutant Ninja Turtles or the Power Rangers, could account for a substantial proportion of a major toy manufacturer's profits.

more. This is because the probability of default is greatest when operating cash flows decrease, and the concurrent reduction in debt cash flows makes the default risk lower. Commodity companies, whose operating cash flows increase and decrease with commodity prices, may be able to use more debt if the debt payments are linked to commodity prices. Similarly, a company whose operating cash flows increase as interest rates (and inflation) go up and decrease when interest rates go down may be able to use more debt if the debt has a floating rate feature.

3. If an external entity provides protection against bankruptcy, by providing either insurance or bailouts, firms will tend to borrow more. To illustrate, the deposit insurance offered by the FSLIC and the FDIC enables savings and loans and banks to maintain higher leverage than they otherwise could. While one can argue for this insurance on the grounds of preserving the integrity of the financial system, undercharging for the insurance will accentuate this tendency and induce high-risk firms to take on too much debt, letting taxpayers bear the cost. Similarly, governments that step in and regularly bail out firms on social grounds (e.g., to save jobs) will encourage all firms to overuse debt.

4. Since the direct bankruptcy costs are higher, when the assets of the firm are not easily divisible and marketable, firms with assets that can be easily divided and sold should be able to borrow more than firms with assets that do not share these features. Thus, a firm, such as Weyerhauser, whose value comes from its real estate holdings should be able to borrow more money than a firm such as Coca Cola, which derives a great deal of its value from its brand name.

5. Firms that produce products that require long-term servicing and support generally should have lower leverage than similar firms whose products do not share this feature.

B. Agency Costs

Equity investors and lenders will not always agree on the best course of action for a firm, largely because they have very different cash flow claims to the firm. Equity investors, who receive a residual claim on the cash flows, tend to favor actions that increase the value of their holdings, even if that means increasing the risk that the bondholders (who have a fixed claim on the cash flows) will not receive their promised payments. Bondholders, on the other hand, want to preserve and increase the security of their claims. Since the equity investors generally control the firm's management and decision making, their interests will dominate bondholder interests, unless bondholders take some protective action. By borrowing money, a firm exposes itself to this conflict and its negative consequences, and pays the price in terms of both real costs and a loss of freedom in decision making.

The Conflict Between Stockholders and Bondholders

The conflict between bondholder and stockholder interests manifests itself in all three aspects of corporate finance: (1) deciding what projects to take (investment decisions), (2) how to finance these projects, and (3) how much to pay out as dividends.

Investment Decisions

Earlier, we emphasized that any project that earns a return that exceeds the hurdle rate, adjusted to reflect the riskiness of the project, is a good project that should increase firm value. It would seem logical that both stockholders and bondholders would be in favor of taking all such projects, but this is not always so. While stockholders may enthusiastically support this proposition, bondholders may find themselves worse off after some of these projects are taken. This is because bondholders lend money to the firm with the expectation that the projects taken will have a certain risk level and set the interest rate on the bonds accordingly. If the firm takes projects that are riskier than expected, however, the bondholder will lose on his or her existing holdings because the price of the holdings will decrease (and the interest rate increase) to reflect the higher risk. The bondholder's loss is the stockholder's gain. While the project may have a positive net present value, the stockholders not only gain the entire present value but they expropriate wealth from the bondholders, as well. This wealth expropriation can sometimes lead to perverse decision making, whereby stockholders take projects that do not earn the hurdle rate (i.e., have negative net present value) but the value of equity actually increases because the wealth transferred from bondholders exceeds the negative net present value.

Bondholders and lenders often attempt to protect themselves against the risk shifting that occurs with investment decisions by writing in covenants in lending agreements constraining the firm from increasing the riskiness of its investments. These constraints may range from mild limits on investments in new businesses to tighter limits, giving bondholders veto power over investment decisions.

Risk Shifting: Risk shifting refers to the tendency of stockholders in firms and their agents (managers) to take on much riskier projects than bondholders expect them to.

Financing Decisions

The conflict between stockholder and bondholder interests also comes to the fore when new projects have to be financed. The equity investors in a firm, left to their own devices, would like to take on new debt, using the assets of the firm as security and providing the new lenders with prior claims over existing lenders, since this reduces the interest rate on the new debt. The existing lenders in a firm obviously do not want to provide new lenders with priority over their claims, since it makes their debt riskier.

Similarly, a firm may adopt a conservative financial policy and borrow money at low rates, with the implicit expectation of keeping its default risk low. Once it has borrowed the money, however, the firm might choose to shift to a strategy of higher leverage and default risk, leaving the original lenders worse off. In 1988, for example, RJR Nabisco rocked the corporate bond markets by announcing its intention to do a leveraged buyout. The company's existing debt, which had enjoyed a high rating dropped dramatically in price upon the announcement, as shown in Figure 7.2.

The decline in the market value of the bonds can be seen as a transfer of wealth from existing bondholders to stockholders.

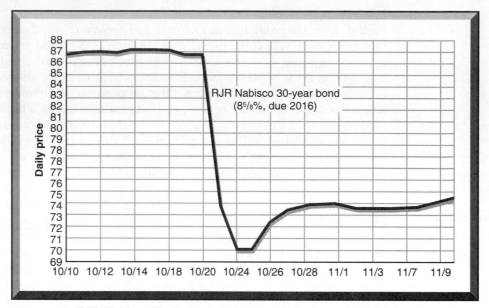

Figure 7.2 RJR Nabisco: Bond prices Around LBO announcement (October 20, 1988).

While bondholders cannot protect themselves against all such eventualities, they can protect themselves at least against a specified set of actions that stockholders might take by inserting a put clause in the bonds, allowing them to sell the bonds back to the firm at face value, if these actions are taken.

Protective Puts (in Bonds): A protective put in a bond allows a bondholder to return the bonds to the issuer before maturity and receive the face value, under a series of conditions which are enumerated in the bond covenants. For instance, the put may be triggered by an increase in the leverage.

Dividend Decisions

Dividend payments and equity repurchases also divide stockholders and bondholders. Consider a firm that has built up a large cash reserve but has very few good projects available. The stockholders in this firm may benefit if the cash is paid out as a dividend or used to repurchase stock. The bondholders, on the other hand, will prefer that the firm retain the cash, since it can be used to make payments on the debt, thereby reducing default risk.

It should come as no surprise that stockholders, if not constrained, will go ahead and pay the dividends or buy back stock, overriding bondholder concerns. In some cases, the payments are large and can increase the default risk of the firm dramatically. In 1989, for example, Colt Industries sold its most liquid assets and used the cash to pay a dividend that was 50% of the stock price. As a result, its bond rating dropped from investment grade to junk bond status.

If increases in dividends are indeed bad news for bondholders, bond prices should react negatively to the announcement of such increases. The empirical evidence supports this hypothesis. As illustrated in Figure 7.3, bond prices decrease following the

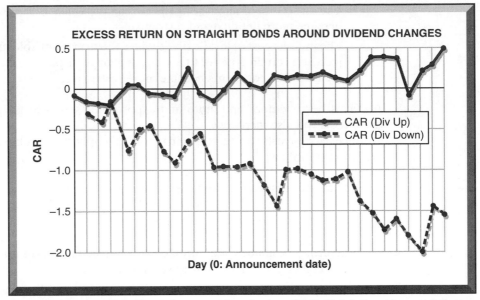

Figure 7.3   Effects of dividend changes on bond prices. CAR: Cululative Abnormal Return on the Stock.

announcement of dividend increases, while they are relatively unaffected by dividend decreases. At the same time, empirical evidence indicates that stock prices increase following the announcement of dividend increases.

Bondholders can protect themselves against such loss by restricting dividends in the bond covenants to a certain percentage of earnings or by limiting dividend increases to a specified amount. Hybrid securities also provide an appealing way of dealing with agency costs. Convertible bonds give bondholders some protection against expropriation by stockholders, for instance, because they can convert their holdings into equity.

7.12   RISK SHIFTING AND BONDHOLDERS

It is often argued that bondholders who plan to hold their bonds until maturity and collect the coupons and the face value are not affected by risk shifting that occurs after they buy the bonds, since the effect is only on market value. Do you agree?

☐ Yes

☐ No

Explain.

Where Does the Agency Cost Show Up?
The agency cost of this disagreement can show up in a couple of ways as real costs:

1. If bondholders believe that there is a significant chance that stockholder actions might make them worse off, they can build this expectation into bond prices by demanding much higher rates on debt.

2. If bondholders can protect themselves against such actions by writing in restrictive covenants, two costs follow:

- The direct cost of monitoring the covenants, which increases as the covenants become more detailed and restrictive.
- The indirect cost of lost flexibility since the firm is not able to take certain projects, use certain types of financing, or change its payout; this cost will also increase as the covenants become more restrictive.

As firms borrow more and more and expose themselves to greater agency costs, these costs will also increase.

Since agency costs can be substantial, several implications relating to optimal capital structure follow:

1. The agency cost arising from risk shifting is likely to be greatest in firms whose investments cannot be easily observed and monitored. For example, a lender to a firm that invests in real estate is less exposed to agency cost than is a lender to a firm that invests in intangible assets. Consequently, it is not surprising that manufacturing companies and railroads, which invest in substantial real assets, have much higher debt ratios than service companies.

2. The agency cost associated with monitoring actions and second-guessing investment decisions is likely to be largest for firms whose projects are long term, follow unpredictable paths, and may take years to come to fruition. Pharmaceutical companies in the United States, for example, which often take on research projects that may take years to yield commercial products, have historically maintained low debt ratios, even though their cash flows would support more debt.

C. Loss of Flexibility

As noted earlier, one of the byproducts of the conflict between stockholders and bondholders is the introduction of strict bond covenants that reduce the flexibility of firms to make investment, financing, or dividend decisions. It can be argued that this is part of a much greater loss of flexibility arising from taking on debt. One of the reasons firms do not use their debt capacity is that they like to preserve it for a rainy day, when they might need the debt to meet funding needs or specific contingencies. Firms that borrow to capacity lose this flexibility and have no fall-back funding if they do get into trouble.

Firms value flexibility for two reasons. First, the value of the firm may be maximized by preserving some flexibility to take on future projects as they arise. Second, flexibility provides managers with more breathing room and more power, and it protects them from the monitoring that comes with debt. Thus, while the argument for maintaining flexibility in the interests of the firm is based upon sound principles, it is sometimes used as camouflage by managers pursuing their own interests. There is also a trade-off between not maintaining enough flexibility (because a firm has too much debt) and having too much flexibility (by not borrowing enough).

Financial Flexibility: Financial flexibility refers to the capacity of firms to meet any unforeseen contingencies that may arise (such as recessions and sales downturns) and take advantage of unanticipated opportunities (such as great projects), using the funds they have on hand and any excess debt capacity that they might have available.

Valuing Flexibility

When making financial decisions, mangers consider the effects such decisions will have on their capacity to take new projects or meet unanticipated contingencies in future periods. Practically, this translates into firms maintaining excess debt capacity or larger cash balances than are warranted by current needs, to meet unexpected future requirements. While maintaining this financing flexibility has value to firms, it also has a cost; the large cash balances earn low returns, and excess debt capacity implies that the firm is giving up some value and has a higher cost of capital.

The value of flexibility can be analyzed using the option pricing framework; a firm maintains large cash balances and excess debt capacity in order to have the option to take projects that might arise in the future. The value of this option will depend upon two key variables:

1. *Quality of the firm's projects:* It is the excess return that the firm earns on its projects that provides the value to flexibility. Other things remaining equal, firms operating in businesses where projects earn substantially higher returns than their hurdle rates should value flexibility more than those that operate in stable businesses where excess returns are small.

2. *Uncertainty about future projects:* If flexibility is viewed as an option, its value will increase when there is greater uncertainty about future projects; thus, firms with predictable capital expenditures should value flexibility less than those with high variability in capital expenditures.

This option framework would imply that firms such as Compaq, which earn large excess returns on their projects and face more uncertainty about future investment needs, can justify holding large cash balances and excess debt capacity, whereas a firm with much smaller excess returns and more predictable investment needs should hold a much smaller cash balance and less excess debt capacity.

IN PRACTICE: USING OPTION PRICING MODEL TO VALUE FLEXIBILITY

The value of flexibility can be calculated as a percentage of firm value, with the following inputs for the option pricing model:

S = Annual Net Capital Expenditures as % of Firm Value (1 + Excess Return)

K = Annual Net Capital Expenditures as % of Firm Value

t = 1 year

σ^2 = Variance in ln (Net Capital Expenditures)

y = Annual Cost of Holding Cash or Maintaining Excess Debt Capacity as % of Firm Value

To illustrate, assume that a firm which earns 18% on its projects has a cost of capital of 13%, and that net capital expenditures are 10% of firm value; the variance in ln(net capital expenditures) is 0.04. Also assume that the firm could have a cost of capital of 12% if it used its excess debt capacity. The value of flexibility as a percentage of firm value can be estimated as follows:

S = 10% (1.05) = 10.50%   [Excess Return = 18% − 13% = 5%]
K = 10%
t = 1 year
σ^2 = 0.04
y = 13% − 12% = 1%

Based on these inputs and a riskless rate of 5%, the value of flexibility is 1.31% of firm value.

7.13   VALUE OF FLEXIBILITY AND FIRM CHARACTERISTICS

Both Chrysler and Microsoft have huge cash balances, and you are a stockholder in both firms. The management of each firm claims to hold the cash because they need the flexibility. Which of the two managements are you more likely to accept this argument from?

☐   Microsoft's management

☐   Chrysler's management

Explain.

Implications for Optimal Capital Structure

The above variables have implications for optimal capital structure:

- Firms that have large and unpredictable demands on their cash flows to take on projects with high excess returns will value flexibility more and borrow less than firms with stable investment requirements and low-return projects. Thus, even the most successful firms in the high-technology arena (which is characterized by high returns and uncertainty about investment requirements), such as Intel and Microsoft, use very little debt in their capital structure.

- As firms and industries mature, the returns on projects drop off and project requirements become more stable. These changes increase the capacity of firms to borrow money. Intel and Microsoft, by this reasoning, will find the value of flexibility decrease over time, increasing their debt capacities.

THE TRADE-OFF IN A BALANCE SHEET FORMAT

Bringing together the benefits and the costs of debt, we can present the trade-off in a balance sheet format:

ADVANTAGES OF BORROWING	DISADVANTAGES OF BORROWING
1. *Tax Benefit:* Higher tax rates → Higher tax benefit	1. *Bankruptcy Cost:* Higher business risk → Higher cost
2. *Added Discipline:* Greater the separation between managers and stockholders → Greater the benefit	2. *Agency Cost:* Greater the separation between stockholders and lenders → Higher the cost
	3. *Loss of Future Financing Flexibility:* Greater the uncertainty about future financing needs → Higher the cost

Table 7.2   FINANCIAL PRINCIPLES DETERMINING CAPITAL STRUCTURE DECISIONS

Planning Principle by Order of Importance	Percentage of Responses Within Each Rank[a]						
	Unimportant	2	3	4	Important	Not Ranked	Mean
1. Maintaining financial flexibility	0.6	0.0	4.5	33.0	61.4	0.6	4.55
2. Ensuring long-term survivability	4.0	1.7	6.8	10.8	76.7	0.0	4.55
3. Maintaining a predictable source of funds	1.7	2.8	20.5	39.2	35.8	0.0	4.05
4. Maximizing security prices	3.4	4.5	19.3	33.5	37.5	1.7	3.99
5. Maintaining financial independence	3.4	4.5	22.2	27.3	40.9	1.7	3.99
6. Maintaining a high debt rating	2.3	9.1	32.4	43.2	13.1	0.0	3.56
7. Maintaining comparability with other firms in the industry	15.9	36.9	33.0	10.8	2.8	0.6	2.47

Overall, if the marginal benefits of borrowing exceed the marginal costs, the firm should borrow money. Otherwise, it should use equity.

Survey Results

What do firms consider when they make capital structure decisions? To answer this question, Pinegar and Wilbricht (1989) surveyed financial managers at 176 firms in the United States. They concluded that the financial principles listed in Table 7.2 determine capital structure decisions, in the order of importance in which they were given.

The foremost principles the survey participants identified were maintaining financial flexibility and ensuring long-term survivability (which can be construed as avoiding bankruptcy). Surprisingly few managers attached much importance to maintaining comparability with other firms in their industries or maintaining a high debt rating.

THERE IS NO OPTIMAL CAPITAL STRUCTURE: THE MILLER-MODIGLIANI THEOREM

In spite of the arguments presented above, there is a large and influential school of thought that argues that capital structure decisions do not really affect the value of the firm. The seeds of this argument were sown in best a seminal paper written by Miller & Modigliani containing one of corporate finance's best-known theorems, the *Miller-Modigliani theorem.*

In their initial work, Miller and Modigliani (MM) operated in an environment void of taxes, transactions costs, and the possibility of default. In that environment, they concluded that the value of a firm was unaffected by its leverage and that investment and financing decisions could be separated. Their conclusion can be confirmed in several ways; we present two below.

The Irrelevance of Capital Structure: Balance Sheet Proof

Miller and Modigliani made the following assumptions about the markets in which they were working:

1. There are no taxes.
2. Markets are frictionless and there are no transactions costs.
3. There are no direct or indirect bankruptcy costs (the expected bankruptcy costs are zero).
4. There are no agency costs, either between stockholders and managers and between stockholders and bondholders.

In such an environment, reverting back to the balance sheet format developed earlier, it is quite clear that all of the advantages and disadvantages disappear, leaving debt with no marginal benefits and costs. Accordingly, we can conclude that debt does not affect value.

In a later paper, Miller and Modigliani preserved the environment they introduced above but made one change, allowing for a tax benefit for debt. In this scenario, where debt continues to have no costs, the optimal debt ratio for a firm is 100% debt. In fact, in such an environment the value of the firm increases by the present value of the tax savings for interest payments (See Figure 7.4).

$$\text{Value of Levered Firm} = \text{Value of Unlevered Firm} + t_c\,B$$

where t_c is the corporate tax rate and B is the dollar borrowing.

An Alternative Proof
Miller and Modigliani presented an alternative proof of the irrelevance of leverage, grounded in the notion that debt does not affect the underlying cash flows of the firm in the absence of taxes. Consider two firms that have the same cash flow (X) from operations. The first firm is an all-equity firm, while the second firm has both equity and debt. The interest rate on debt is r.

	FIRM A	FIRM B
Type of firm	All-equity firm: $(V_u = E)$	Has some equity and debt $(V_L = E_L + D_L)$
Actions now	Investor buys a fraction α of the firm: $(\alpha\,V_u)$	Investor buys a fraction α of both equity and debt of the firm: $\alpha\,E_L + \alpha\,D_L$
Next period	Investor receives a fraction α of the cash flow: $(\alpha\,X)$	Investor receives the following: $\alpha(X - rD_L) + \alpha\,r\,D_L = \alpha\,X$

Since the investor receives the same cash flows in both firms, the price he or she will pay for either firm has to be the same. This implies that leverage is irrelevant.

Note that this proof works only if the firm does not receive a tax benefit from debt; a tax benefit would give Firm B a higher cash flow than Firm A.

The Effect of Taxes: The Miller Proof of Irrelevance
It is clear in the Miller-Modigliani model that introducing the tax benefit of debt into the mix undercuts the conclusion that debt is irrelevant. In an address in 1976,

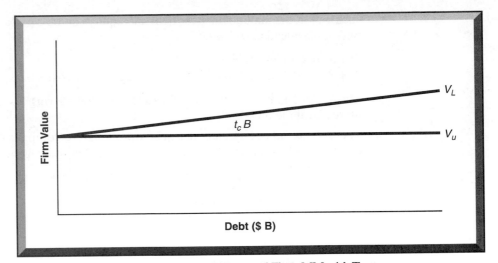

Figure 7.4   Value of Levered Firm: MM with Taxes.

however, Merton Miller argued that the debt irrelevance theorem could be resusci-
tated even in the presence of corporate taxes if taxes on the dividend and interest income individuals receive from firms were factored into the analysis.

To see the Miller proof of irrelevance, assume that investors face a tax rate of t_d
on interest income and a tax rate of t_c on equity income. Assume also that the firm
pays an interest rate of r on debt and faces a corporate tax rate of t_c. The after-tax return to the investor from owning debt can then be written as follows:

$$\text{After-Tax Return from Owning Debt} = r\,(1 - t_d)$$

The after-tax return to the investor from owning equity can be written after the double taxation—once at the corporate level and once at the equity level:

$$\text{After-Tax Return from Owning Equity} = k_e\,(1 - t_c)\,(1 - t_e)$$

The returns to equity can take two forms—dividends or capital gains; the equity tax
rate is a blend of the tax rates on both. In such a scenario, Miller noted that the value
of the firm, with leverage, could be written as:

$$V_L = V_u + [1 - (1 - t_c)\,(1 - t_e))/(1 - t_d)]B$$

where V_L is the value of the firm with leverage, V_U is the value of the firm without
leverage, and B is the dollar debt.

As Miller noted, there are several possible scenarios that can be considered here:

1. *The tax rate on equity is the same as the tax rate on debt:* If this were the case, the
   result reverts back to the original one—the value of the firm increases monotonically with the debt.

2. *The tax rate on debt is higher than the tax rate on equity:* In such a case, the differences in the tax rates may more than compensate for the double taxation of equity
   cash flows. To illustrate, assume that the tax rate on ordinary income is 70%, the tax
   rate on capital gains on stock is 28%, and the tax rate on corporations is 35%. In

such a case, the tax liabilities for debt and equity can be calculated for a firm that pays no dividend as follows:

Tax Rate on Debt Income = 70%
Tax Rate on Equity Income = $1 - (1 - 0.35)(1 - .28) = 0.532$ or 53.2%

This is not an implausible scenario, especially considering tax law in the United States until the mid-1980s.

3. The tax rate on equity income is just low enough to compensate for the double taxation: In this case, we are back to the original debt irrelevance theorem.

$$(1 - t_d) = (1 - t_c)(1 - t_e) \quad \text{Debt is irrelevant}$$

Miller's analysis brought investor tax rates into the analysis for the first time and provided some insight into the role of investor tax preferences on a firm's capital structure. As Miller himself notes, however, this analysis does not reestablish the irrelevance of debt under all circumstances; rather, it opens up the possibility that debt could still be irrelevant, despite its tax advantages.

The Consequences of Debt Irrelevance

If the financing decision is irrelevant, as posited by Miller and Modigliani, corporate financial analysis is simplified in a number of ways:

*   *The cost of capital, which is the weighted average of the cost of debt and the cost of equity, is unaffected by changes in the proportions of debt and equity.* This might seem unreasonable, especially since the cost of debt is much lower than the cost of equity. In the MM world, however, any benefits incurred by substituting cheaper debt for more expensive equity are offset by increases in both their costs, as shown in Figure 7.5.

*   *The value of the firm is unaffected by the amount of leverage it has.* Thus, if the firm is valued as an all-equity entity, its value will remain unchanged even if it is valued with any other debt ratio. (This actually follows from the implication that the cost of capital is unaffected by changes in leverage and from the assumption that the operating cash flows are determined by investment decisions rather than financing decisions.)

*   *The investment decision can be made independently of the financing decision.* In other words, if a project is a bad project when evaluated as an all-equity project, it will remain so using any other financing mix.

Some Closing Thoughts

It is unlikely that capital structure is irrelevant in the real world, given tax preferences for debt and default risk. In spite of this, Miller and Modigliani were pioneers in moving capital structure analysis from an environment in which firms picked their debt ratios based upon their peer group and management preferences to one that recognized the trade-offs. They also drew attention to the fact that good investment decisions comprise the core of value creation for firms. To be more precise, a firm that takes bad projects cannot hope to recoup the lost value by making better financing

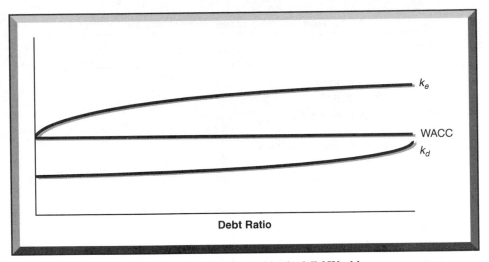

Figure 7.5   Cost of Capital in the MM World.

decisions; a firm that takes good projects will succeed in creating value, even if its capital structure choices are suboptimal. Finally, while the concept of a world with no taxes, default risk, or agency problems may seem a little far-fetched, there are some environments about which the description might hold. Assume, for instance, that the U.S. government decides to encourage small businesses to invest in urban areas by relieving them of their tax burden and providing a backup guarantee on loans (default protection). Firms that respond to these initiatives might find that their capital structure decisions do not affect their value.

Finally, surveys of financial managers indicate that, in practice, they do not attach as much weight to the trade-off mentioned earlier as we do in theory. In a survey by Pinegar and Wilbricht (1989), managers were asked to cite the most important inputs governing their financial decisions. Their responses are ranked in the order of the importance managers attached to them in Table 7.3.

Notice that, while the capital structure trade-off theory would predict that bankruptcy cost and tax-related variables would be the most important variables, this survey suggests that they are not actually given as much weight by financial managers making capital structure decisions as the theory suggests. Instead, financial managers seem to weigh financial flexibility and potential dilution much more heavily in their capital structure decisions.

IN PRACTICE: THE DILUTION BOGEY

The dilution effect refers to the possible decrease in earnings per share from any action that might lead to an increase in the number of shares outstanding. As evidenced in Table 7.3, managers, especially in the United States, weigh these potential dilution effects heavily in decisions on what type of financing to use, and how to fund projects. Consider, for instance, the choice between raising equity using a rights issue, where the stock is issued at a price below the current market price, and a public issue of stock at the market price. The latter is a much more expensive option, from the

Table 7.3 INPUTS INTO CAPITAL STRUCTURE DECISIONS

| Inputs/Assumptions by Order of Importance | Percentage of Responses Within Each Rank | | | | | | |
| | Least Important ....Most Important | | | | | Not Ranked | Mean |
	1	2	3	4	5		
1. Projected cash flow from asset to be financed	1.7%	1.1%	9.7%	29.5%	58.0%	0.0%	4.41
2. Avoiding dilution of common equity's claims	2.8%	6.3%	18.2%	39.8%	33.0%	0.0%	3.94
3. Risk of asset to be financed	2.8%	6.3%	20.5%	36.9%	33.0%	0.6%	3.91
4. Restrictive covenants on senior securities	9.1%	9.7%	18.7%	35.2%	27.3%	0.0%	3.62
5. Avoiding mispricing of securities to be issued	3.4%	10.8%	27.3%	39.8%	18.7%	0.0%	3.60
6. Corporate tax rate	4.0%	9.7%	29.5%	42.6%	13.1%	1.1%	3.52
7. Voting control	17.6%	10.8%	21.0%	31.2%	19.3%	0.0%	3.24
8. Depreciation & other tax shields	8.5%	17.6%	40.9%	24.4%	7.4%	1.1%	3.05
9. Correcting mispricing of securities	14.8%	27.8%	36.4%	14.2%	5.1%	1.7%	2.66
10. Personal tax rates of debt and equity holders	31.2%	34.1%	25.6%	8.0%	1.1%	0.0%	2.14
11. Bankruptcy costs	69.3%	13.1%	6.8%	4.0%	4.5%	2.3%	1.58

perspective of investment banking fees and other costs, but is chosen, nevertheless, because it results in fewer shares being issued (to raise the same amount of funds). The fear of dilution is misplaced for the following reasons:

1. Investors measure their returns in terms of total return and not just in terms of stock price. While the stock price will go down more after a rights issue, each investor will be compensated adequately for the price drop (by either receiving more shares or by being able to sell their rights to other investors). In fact, if the transaction costs are considered, stockholders will be better off after a rights issue than after an equivalent public issue of stock.

2. While the earnings per share will almost always drop in the immediate aftermath of a new stock issue, the stock price will not necessarily follow suit. In particular, if the stock issue is used to finance a good project (i.e., a project with a positive net present value), the increase in value should be greater than the increase in the number of shares, leading to a higher stock price.

Ultimately, the measure of whether a company should issue stock to finance a project should depend upon the quality of the investment. Firms that dilute their stockholdings to take good investments are making the right choice for their stockholders.

THERE IS AN OPTIMAL CAPITAL STRUCTURE

The counter to the Miller-Modigliani proposition is that the trade-offs on debt may work in favor of the firm, at least initially, and that borrowing money may lower the cost of capital and increase firm value. We will examine the mechanics of putting this argument into practice in the next chapter; here, we will make a case for the existence of an optimal capital structure, and look at some of the empirical evidence for and against it.

The Case for an Optimal Capital Structure

If the debt decision involves a trade-off between the benefits of debt (tax benefits and added discipline) and the costs of debt (bankruptcy costs, agency costs, and lost flexibility), it can be argued that the marginal benefits will be exactly offset by the marginal costs *only in exceptional cases,* and not always (as argued by Miller and Modigliani). In fact, under most circumstances, the marginal benefits will either exceed the marginal costs (in which case, debt is good and will increase firm value) or fall short of marginal costs (in which case, equity is better). Accordingly, there is an optimal capital structure for most firms at which firm value is maximized.

Of course, it is always possible that managers may be operating under an *illusion* that capital structure decisions matter when the reality might be otherwise. Consequently, we examine some of the empirical evidence to see if it is consistent with the theory of an optimal mix of debt and equity.

Empirical Evidence

The question of whether there is an optimal capital structure can be answered in a number of ways. The first is to see if differences in capital structure across firms can be explained systematically by differences in the variables driving the trade-offs. Other things remaining equal, we would expect to see the relationships listed in Table 7.4.

While this may seem like a relatively simple test to run, keeping all other things equal in the real world is often close to impossible. In spite of this limitation, attempts to see if the direction of the relationship is consistent with the theory have produced mixed results.

Bradley, Jarrell, and Kim (1984) analyzed whether differences in debt ratios can be explained by proxies for the variables involved in the capital structure trade-off. They noted that the debt ratio is:

- *Negatively correlated with the volatility in annual operating earnings,* as predicted by the bankruptcy cost component of the optimal capital structure trade-off.

- *Positively related to the level of non-debt tax shields,* which is counter to the tax hypothesis, which argues that firms with large non-debt tax shields should be less inclined to use debt.

- *Negatively related to advertising and R&D expenses used as a proxy for agency costs;* this is consistent with optimal capital structure theory.

Table 7.4 DEBT RATIOS AND FUNDAMENTALS	
Variable	**Effect on Debt Ratios**
Marginal tax rate	As marginal tax rates increase, debt ratios increase.
Separation of ownership and management	The greater the separation of ownership and management, the higher the debt ratio.
Variability in operating cash flows	As operating cash flows become more variable, the bankruptcy risk increases, resulting in lower debt ratios.
Debt holders' difficulty in monitoring firm actions, investments, and performance	The more difficult it is to monitor the actions taken by a firm, the lower the optimal debt ratio.
Need for flexibility	The greater the need for decision-making flexibility in future periods, the lower the optimal debt ratio.

Others who have attempted to examine whether cross-sectional differences in capital structure are consistent with the theory have come to contradictory conclusions.

A second test of whether differences in capital structure can be explained by differences in firm characteristics involves examining differences in debt ratios across industries. Table 7.5 summarizes debt ratios, by industry, on both book value and market value terms at the end of 1994. The table provides relevant information on average tax rates, variability in operating income, and investment needs for each industry.

An alternate test of the optimal capital structure hypothesis is to examine the stock price reaction to actions taken by firms either to increase or decrease leverage. In evaluating the price response, we have to make some assumptions about the motivation of the firms making these changes. If we assume that firms are rational and that they make these changes to get closer to their optimal, both leverage-increasing and -decreasing actions should be accompanied by positive excess returns, at least on average. In a study cited in the previous chapter, Smith (1988) notes that the evidence is *not* consistent with an optimal capital structure hypothesis, however, since leverage-increasing actions seem to be accompanied by positive excess returns while leverage-reducing actions seem to be followed by negative returns. The only way to reconcile this tendency with an optimal capital structure argument is by assuming that managerial incentives (desire for stability and flexibility) keep leverage below the optimal for most firms and that actions by firms to reduce leverage are seen as serving managerial interests rather than stockholder interests.

Table 7.5   DEBT RATIOS BY INDUSTRY-1995

Industry	Debt Ratio: MV	Debt Ratio: BV	Variances	Insider Holdings	Cap Ex/MV	ROE	FCF/Price
Agricultural Products	35.05%	47.05%	30.86%	30.16%	7.18%	24.35%	11.72%
Mining	26.33%	36.64%	34.50%	14.28%	6.55%	13.86%	6.70%
Petroleum Production & Refining	27.08%	39.88%	28.91%	26.00%	13.05%	16.11%	7.45%
Building Contractors & Related Areas	28.21%	36.16%	42.19%	33.34%	6.51%	15.16%	7.72%
Food Production	22.90%	39.89%	39.27%	28.38%	7.77%	24.12%	5.06%
Beverages	25.07%	40.19%	38.07%	33.20%	7.13%	17.52%	5.36%
Tobacco	31.42%	49.82%	37.59%	4.28%	3.48%	33.16%	6.98%
Textile & Clothing Manufacturers	21.89%	27.23%	46.01%	33.97%	5.98%	14.84%	7.12%
Furniture	16.66%	22.83%	47.80%	42.89%	7.59%	19.69%	7.85%
Paper & Plastic Production	30.41%	46.81%	42.48%	20.64%	8.74%	20.96%	5.96%
Publishing	16.29%	32.38%	42.39%	30.75%	6.92%	26.82%	6.28%
Chemicals	17.30%	31.57%	42.88%	21.66%	7.17%	37.80%	6.19%
Pharmaceuticals	8.52%	24.63%	39.12%	27.62%	10.35%	26.25%	2.76%
Consumer Products	18.62%	39.23%	44.38%	29.05%	6.94%	26.45%	4.36%
Autos & Related	26.91%	38.00%	47.17%	28.23%	6.67%	21.66%	7.71%
Miscellaneous Manufacturing	24.00%	37.75%	47.91%	26.05%	8.71%	21.10%	8.45%
Equipment Manufacturing	19.06%	29.57%	49.32%	25.60%	6.52%	18.45%	6.83%
Computers & Office Equipment	8.44%	17.29%	51.26%	25.84%	7.34%	18.89%	5.50%
Consumer Electronics	9.48%	15.79%	59.81%	23.96%	7.30%	14.22%	4.82%
Other Consumer Durables	15.89%	25.18%	41.72%	39.32%	6.71%	18.71%	5.02%
Transportation	33.57%	44.97%	41.62%	29.22%	8.64%	18.09%	7.26%
Telephone Utilities	19.83%	38.54%	25.24%	19.34%	12.28%	16.21%	3.37%
Entertainment (TV & Movies)	19.60%	39.83%	38.78%	41.59%	7.24%	26.68%	10.80%
Electric & Gas Utilities	43.22%	52.90%	32.25%	19.49%	6.51%	12.31%	5.29%
Wholesalers	19.16%	28.18%	46.94%	33.12%	4.79%	15.22%	6.95%
Retailers	21.65%	30.01%	45.21%	35.39%	9.24%	20.42%	5.49%
Restaurants & Eating Places	20.21%	32.28%	42.94%	29.45%	16.12%	18.19%	7.45%
Banks & Financial Service	17.23%	28.40%	67.01%	30.13%	2.07%	18.99%	11.39%

Industry	Debt Ratio: MV	Debt Ratio: BV	Variances	Insider Holdings	Cap Ex/MV	ROE	FCF/Price
Insurance	14.35%	31.71%	39.84%	34.15%	5.15%	19.11%	5.51%
Real Estate	30.85%	40.97%	39.49%	29.15%	3.08%	19.15%	7.75%
Other Services	20.17%	34.86%	39.92%	36.07%	7.18%	24.67%	6.99%
Computer Software & Services	3.48%	10.10%	43.58%	34.16%	9.28%	19.07%	3.80%
Health Services	17.30%	27.97%	44.72%	30.13%	5.83%	12.30%	6.12%
Average	**21.52%**	**33.90%**	**42.46%**	**28.69%**	**7.46%**	**20.32%**	**6.61%**

Table 7.5   CONTINUED

 This data set on the web that summarizes average debt ratios, by industry, for firms in the U.S.

HOW FIRMS CHOOSE THEIR CAPITAL STRUCTURES

While the theory suggests that firms should pick the mix of debt and equity that maximizes firm value, the most common approach is to set leverage close to that of the peer group to which the firm belongs. If firms in the peer group are similar on the fundamental characteristics (tax rates and cash flow variability) and tend to be right, at least on average, it can be argued that this approach provides a shortcut to arriving at the optimal. It is likely to fail, however, when firms differ on these characteristics.

A Financing Hierarchy

It can be argued that firms follow a financing hierarchy: retained earnings are the most preferred choice for financing, followed by debt; new equity, common and preferred, is the least preferred choice. The argument is supported as follows. First, managers value *flexibility and control*. To the extent that external financing reduces flexibility for future financing (especially if it is debt) and control (bonds have covenants; new equity attracts new stockholders into the company and may reduce insider holdings as a percentage of total holding), managers prefer retained earnings as a source of capital. Second, while it costs nothing in terms of flotation costs to use retained earnings, *it costs more* to use external debt and even more to use external equity.

Survey Results

There is some evidence to support a financing hierarchy. For instance, in the survey by Pinegar and Wilbricht (Table 7.6), managers were asked to rank six different sources of financing: from most preferred to least preferred, internal equity, external equity, external debt, preferred stock, and hybrids (convertible debt and preferred stock).

Retained earnings (internal equity) emerged as the clear first choice for financing projects. The survey yielded some other interesting conclusions as well:

Table 7.6 SURVEY RESULTS ON PLANNING PRINCIPLES

Ranking	Source	Planning Principle Cited	Score
1	Retained Earnings	None	5.61
2	Straight Debt	Maximize Security Prices	4.88
3	Convertible Debt	Cash Flow & Survivability	3.02
4	External Common Equity	Avoiding Dilution	2.42
5	Straight Preferred Stock	Comparability	2.22
6	Convertible Preferred	None	1.72

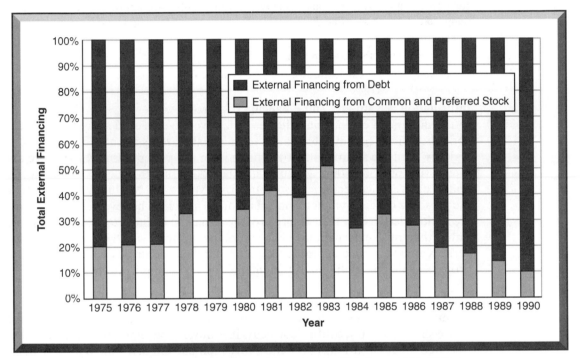

Figure 7.6 Breakdown of financing for U.S. firms: 1975–1990.

- External debt is strongly preferred over external equity as a way of raising funds. The values of external debt and external equity issued between 1975 and 1990 by U.S. corporations are shown in Figure 7.6.
- Given a choice, firms would much rather use straight debt than convertible debt, in spite of the lower interest cost on the latter. Managers perhaps have a much better sense of the value of the conversion option than is recognized, since the conventional wisdom holds that the lure of lower rates will result in more convertibles being issued than justified by theory.
- The primary reason for *not* issuing external equity seems to be the avoidance of dilution, and the main reason *for using* debt is the maximization of stock prices.

- A firm's choices may say a great deal about its financial strength. Thus, the decisions by RJR Nabisco and GM, in 1993, to raise new funds through convertible preferred stock were seen by markets as an admission by these firms of their financial weakness. Not surprisingly, the financial market response to the issue of the securities listed in Table 7.6 mirrors the preferences: the most negative responses are reserved for securities near the bottom of the list, the most positive (or at least the least negative) for those at the top of the list.

7.14 VALUE OF FLEXIBILITY AND FIRM CHARACTERISTICS

You are reading the *Wall Street Journal* and notice a tombstone ad for a company, offering to sell convertible preferred stock. What would you hypothesize about the health of the company issuing these securities?

☐ Nothing

☐ Healthier than the average firm

☐ In much more financial trouble than the average firm

Information Asymmetry and Financing Hierarchy

In the discussion of financing choices so far, we have steered away from questions about how firms convey information to financial markets about their future choices and how well the securities that the firms issue are priced. Firms know more about their future prospects than do the financial markets that they deal with; markets may under- or overprice securities issued by firms. Myers and Majluf (1984) note that, in the presence of this asymmetric information, firms which believe that their securities are underpriced, given their future prospects, may be inclined to reject good projects rather than raise external financing. Alternatively, firms which believe that their securities are overpriced are more likely to issue these securities, even if they have no projects available. In this environment, the following implications emerge:

- Managers prefer retained earnings to external financing, since it allows them to consider projects on their merits, rather than depending upon whether markets are pricing their securities correctly. It follows then that firms will be more inclined to retain earnings over and above their current investment requirements to finance future projects.

- When firms issue securities, markets will consider the issue a signal of whether these securities are overvalued. This signal is likely to be more negative for securities, such as stocks, where the asymmetry of information is greater, and smaller for securities, such as straight bonds, where the asymmetry is smaller. This would explain both the rankings in the financial hierarchy and the market reaction to these security issues.

CONCLUSION

In this chapter we have laid the groundwork for analyzing a firm's optimal mix of debt and equity by laying out the benefits and the costs of borrowing money. In particular, we made the following points:

- We differentiated between debt and equity, at a generic level, by pointing out that any financing approach that results in fixed cash flows and has prior claims in the case of default, has fixed maturity, and has no voting rights is debt, while a financing approach that provides for residual cash flows and has low or no priority in claims in the case of default, has infinite life, and has a lion's share of the control is equity.

- The primary benefit of debt is a tax benefit: Interest expenses are tax deductible, while cash flows to equity (dividends) are not. This benefit increases with the tax rate of the entity taking on the debt.

- A secondary benefit of debt is that it forces managers to be more disciplined in their choice of projects by increasing the costs of failure; a series of bad projects may create the possibility of defaulting on interest and principal payments.

- The primary cost of borrowing is an increase in the expected bankruptcy cost—the product of the probability of default and the cost of bankruptcy. The probability of default is greater for firms that have volatile cash flows. The cost of bankruptcy includes both the direct costs of bankruptcy and the indirect costs (lost sales, tighter credit, and less access to capital).

- Borrowing money exposes the firm to the possibility of conflicts between stock- and bondholders over investment, financing, and dividend decisions. The covenants that bondholders write into bond agreements to protect themselves against expropriation cost the firm in both monitoring costs and lost flexibility.

- The loss of flexibility that arises from borrowing money is more likely to be a problem for firms with substantial and unpredictable investment opportunities.

- In the special case where there are no tax benefits, default risk, or agency problems, the financing decision is irrelevant.

- In most cases, however, the trade-off between the benefits and costs of debt will result in an optimal capital structure, whereby the value of the firm is maximized.

PROBLEMS AND QUESTIONS

1. An income bondholder receives interest payments only if the firm makes income. If the firm does not make interest payments in a year, the interest is cumulated and paid in the first year that the firm makes income. A preferred stockholder receives preferred dividends only if the firm makes income. If a firm does not make preferred dividend payments in a year, the dividend is cumulated and paid in the first year that the firm makes income. Are income bonds really preferred stock? What are the differences? For purposes of analyzing debt, how would you differentiate between income bonds and regular bonds?

2. A commodity bond links interest and principal payments to the price of a commodity. Differentiate a commodity bond from a straight bond, and then from equity. How would you factor these differences into your analysis of the debt ratio of a company that has issued exclusively commodity bonds?

3. You are analyzing a new security that has been promoted as equity, with the following features:
   - The dividend on the security is fixed in dollar terms for the life of the security, which is 20 years.
   - The dividend is not tax deductible.

- In the case of default, the holders of this security will receive cash only after all debtholders, secured as well as unsecured, are paid.
- The holders of this security will have no voting rights.

Based on the description of debt and equity in the chapter, how would you classify this security? If you were asked to calculate the debt ratio for this firm, how would you categorize this security?

4. You are analyzing a convertible preferred stock, with the following characteristics for the security:
   - There are 50,000 convertible preferred shares outstanding, with a face value of $100 each and a 6% preferred dividend rate.
   - The firm has straight preferred stock outstanding, with a preferred dividend rate of 9%.
   - The convertible preferred stock is trading at $105.

   Estimate the preferred stock and equity components of this preferred stock.

5. You have been asked to calculate the debt ratio for a firm which has the following components to its financing mix:
   - The firm has 1 million shares outstanding, trading at $50 per share.
   - The firm has $25 million in straight debt, carrying a market interest rate of 8%.
   - The firm has 20,000 10-year convertible bonds outstanding, with a face value of $1,000, a market value of $1,100, and a coupon rate of 5%.

   Estimate the debt ratio for this firm.

6. You have been asked to estimate the debt ratio for a firm, with the following financing details:
   - The firm has two classes of shares outstanding; 50,000 shares of class A stock, with 2 voting rights per share, trading at $100 per share and 100,000 shares of class B stock, with 1/2 voting right per share, trading at $90 per share.
   - The firm has $5 million in bank debt, and the debt was taken on recently.

   Estimate the market debt ratio. Why does it matter when the bank debt was taken on?

7. You are the owner of a small and successful firm with an estimated market value of $50 million.

You are considering going public.
   a. What are the considerations you would have in choosing an investment banker?
   b. You want to raise $20 million in new financing which you plan to reinvest back in the firm. (The estimated market value of $50 million is based on the assumption that this $20 million is reinvested.) What proportion of the firm would you have to sell in the initial public offering to raise $20 million?
   c. How would your answer to (b) change if the investment banker plans to underprice your offering by 10%?
   d. If you wanted your stock to trade in the $20 to $25 range, how many shares would you have to create? How many shares would you have to issue?

8. U.S. firms are heavily dependent on debt for external financing, and they are overleveraged. Comment.

9. Convertible bonds are often issued by small, high-growth companies to raise debt. Why?

10. A manager of NoZone Inc., a company in urgent need of financing, is debating whether to issue straight debt at 11% or convertible debt at 7%. He is leaning toward the convertible debt because it is cheaper. Is it? How would you check this proposition?

11. A company is trying to estimate its debt ratio. It has 1 million shares outstanding, trading at $50 per share, and had $250 million in straight debt outstanding (with a market interest rate of 9%). It also has two other securities outstanding:
    a. It has 200,000 warrants outstanding, conferring on its holders the right to buy stock in the Complex Inc., at $65 per share. These warrants are trading at $12 each.
    b. It also has 10,000 20-year convertible bonds outstanding, with a coupon rate of 6% and 10 years to maturity (Face value is $1,000), trading at par.

    Estimate the debt ratio in market value terms.

12. Venture capitalists take advantage of small businesses by demanding a disproportionate share of the ownership of the company for their investment. Comment.

13. Firms generally can borrow money by using bank debt or by issuing bonds. Why might a firm choose one method over the other?

14. Preferred stock is often considered as equity, when analysts calculate debt ratios. Is this appropriate? Under what conditions would you consider it to be more like debt?

15. Debt will always be cheaper than preferred stock, because of the tax advantage that it confers on the firm. What is the source of the tax advantage? Is this statement true?

16. MVP Inc., a manufacturing firm with no debt outstanding and a market value of $100 million, is considering borrowing $40 million and buying back stock. Assuming that the interest rate on the debt is 9% and that the firm faces a tax rate of 35%, answer the following questions:
   a. Estimate the annual interest tax savings each year from the debt.
   b. Estimate the present value of interest tax savings, assuming that the debt change is permanent.
   c. Estimate the present value of interest tax savings, assuming that the debt will be taken on for 10 years only.
   d. What will happen to the present value of interest tax savings if interest rates drop tomorrow to 7% but the debt itself is a fixed rate debt?

17. A business in the 45% tax bracket is considering borrowing money at 10%.
   a. What is the after-tax interest rate on the debt?
   b. What is the after-tax interest rate if only half of the interest expense is allowed as a tax deduction?
   c. Will your answer change if the firm is losing money now and does not expect to have taxable income for the next three years?

18. WestingHome Inc. is a manufacturing company that has accumulated a net operating loss of $2 billion over time. It is considering borrowing $5 billion to acquire another company.
   a. Based on the corporate tax rate of 36%, estimate the present value of the tax savings that could accrue to the company.
   b. Does the existence of a net operating loss carryforward affect your analysis? (Will the tax benefits be diminished as a consequence?)

19. Answer true or false to the following questions relating to the free cash-flow hypothesis.
   a. Companies with high operating earnings have high free cash flows.
   b. Companies with large capital expenditures, relative to earnings, have low free cash flows.
   c. Companies that are committed to paying a large portion of their free cash flow as dividends do not need debt to add discipline.
   d. The free cash-flow hypothesis for borrowing money makes more sense for firms in which there is a separation of ownership and management.
   e. Firms with high free cash flows are run inefficiently.

20. Assess the likelihood that the following firms will be taken over, based on your understanding of the free cash-flow hypothesis.
   a. A firm with high growth prospects, good projects, low leverage, and high earnings.
   b. A firm with low growth prospects, poor projects, low leverage, and poor earnings.
   c. A firm with high growth prospects, good projects, high leverage, and low earnings.
   d. A firm with low growth prospects, poor projects, high leverage, and good earnings.
   e. A firm with low growth prospects, poor projects, low leverage, and good earnings.

   You can assume that earnings and free cash flows are highly correlated.

21. Nadir, Inc., an unlevered firm, has expected earnings before interest and taxes of $2 million per year. Nadir's tax rate is 40%, and the market value is $V = E = \$12$ million. The stock has a beta of 1, and the risk-free rate is 9%. (Assume that $E(R_m) - R_f = 6\%$.) Management is considering the use of debt; debt would be issued and used to buy back stock, and the size of the firm would remain constant. The default-free interest rate on debt is 12%. Because interest expense is tax deductible, the value of the firm would tend to increase as debt is added to the capital structure, but there would be an offset in the form of the rising cost of bankruptcy. The firm's analysts have estimated that the present value of any bankruptcy cost is $8 million and that the probability of bankruptcy will

increase with leverage according to the following schedule:

Value of Debt	Probability of Failure (%)
$2,500,000	0.0
5,000,000	8.0
7,500,000	20.5
8,000,000	30.0
9,000,000	45.0
10,000,000	52.5
12,500,000	70.0

a. What is the cost of equity and cost of capital at this time?

b. What is the optimal capital structure when bankruptcy costs are considered?

c. What will the value of the firm be at this optimal capital structure?

22. Agency costs arise from the conflict between stockholders and bondholders, but they do not impose any real costs on firms. Comment.

23. Two firms are considering borrowing. One firm has excellent prospects in terms of future projects and is in a business in which cash flows are volatile and future needs are difficult to assess. The other firm has more stable cash flows and fewer project opportunities and predicts its future needs with more precision. Other things remaining equal, which of these two firms should borrow more?

24. How would you respond to a claim by a firm that maintaining flexibility is always good for stockholders, although they might not recognize it in the short term?

25. A firm that has no debt has a market value of $100 million and a cost of equity of 11%. In the Miller-Modigliani world:

a. What happens to the value of the firm as the leverage is changed (assume no taxes)?

b. What happens to the cost of capital as the leverage is changed (assume no taxes)?

c. How would your answers to (a) and (b) change if there were taxes?

26. XYZ Pharma Inc. is a pharmaceutical company that traditionally has not used debt to finance its projects. Over the last 10 years, it has also reported high returns on its projects and growth rates, and has incurred substantial research and development expenses over the time period. The health-care business overall is growing much slower now, and the projects the firm is considering have lower expected returns.

a. How would you justify the firm's past policy of not using debt?

b. Do you think the policy should be changed now? Why or why not?

27. Stockholders can expropriate wealth from bondholders through their investment, financing, and dividend decisions. Explain.

28. Bondholders can always protect themselves against stockholder expropriation by writing bond covenants. Therefore, no agency cost is associated with the conflict between stockholders and bondholders. Do you agree?

29. Unitrode Inc., which makes analog/linear integrated circuits for power management, has not used debt in the financing of its projects. The managers of the firm contend that they do not borrow money because they want to maintain financial flexibility.

a. How does not borrowing money increase financial flexibility?

b. What is the trade-off you will be making if you have excess debt capacity and you choose not to use it because you want financial flexibility?

30. Consolidated Power is a regulated electric utility that has equity with a market value of $1.5 billion and debt outstanding of $3 billion. A consultant notes that this is a high debt ratio relative to the average across all firms, which is 27%, and suggests that the firm is overlevered.

a. Why would you expect an electric utility to be able to maintain a higher debt ratio than the average company?

b. Does the fact that the company is a regulated monopoly affect its capacity to carry debt?

31. Assume that legislators are considering a tax reform plan that will lower the corporate tax rate from 36% to 17%, while preserving the tax deductibility of internal expenses. What effect would this tax reform plan have on the optimal debt ratios of companies? Why? What if the tax deductibility of debt were removed?

32. Governments often step in to protect large companies that get into financial trouble and bail them out. If this is an accepted practice, what effect would you expect it to have on the debt ratios of firms? Why?

33. The Miller-Modigliani theorem proposes that debt is irrelevant. Under what conditions is this true? If debt is irrelevant, what is the effect of changing the debt ratio on the cost of capital?

34. Based on the financing hierarchy described in this chapter, what types of securities would you expect financially strong firms to issue? What about financially weak firms? Why?

35. In general, private firms tend to take on much less debt than publicly traded firms. Based on the discussion in this chapter, how would you explain this phenomenon?

36. There is a significant cost to bankruptcy because the stock price essentially goes to zero. Comment.

37. Studies indicate that the direct cost of bankruptcy is small. What are the direct costs? What are the indirect costs of bankruptcy? What types of firms are most exposed to these indirect costs?

38. When stockholders have little power over incumbent managers, firms are likely to be underlevered. Comment.

39. Debt is always cheaper than equity. Therefore, the optimal debt ratio is all debt. How would you respond to this statement?

LIVE CASE STUDY

V. CAPITAL STRUCTURE CHOICES

Objective: To examine the current financing choices of the firm, and analyze, from a qualitative standpoint, whether the firm is under or over leveraged.

Key Questions

- What are the different kinds or types of financing that this company has used to raise funds? Where do they fall in the continuum between debt and equity?

- How large, in qualitative or quantitative terms, are the advantages to this company from using debt?

- How large, in qualitative or quantitative terms, are the disadvantages to this company from using debt?

- From the qualitative trade-off, does this firm look like it has too much or too little debt?

Framework for Analysis

1. Benefits of Debt

- What marginal tax rate does this firm face and how does this measure up to the marginal tax rates of other firms? Are there other tax deductions that this company has (like depreciation) to reduce the tax bite?

- Does this company have high free cash flows (e.g., EBITDA/Firm Value)? Has it taken and does it continue to have good investment projects? How responsive are managers to stockholders? (Will there be an advantage to using debt in this firm as a way of keeping managers in line or do other (cheaper) mechanisms exist?)

2. Costs of Debt

- How high are the current cash flows of the firm (to service the debt) and how stable are these cash flows? (Look at the variability in the operating income over time.)

- How easy is it for bondholders to observe what equity investors are doing? Are the assets tangible or intangible? If not, what are the costs in terms of monitoring stockholders or in terms of bond covenants?

- How well can this firm forecast its future investment opportunities and needs? How much does it value flexibility?

Getting Information on Capital Structure Choices

To find out the breakdown on the types of securities and financing that your company has outstanding, check the footnotes on the 10-K report (**www.sec.gov/edgarhp.htm**). To get the other inputs needed for the analysis, you should check the historical financials on the firm. To get industry average numbers for these inputs, check the data set on my web page for capital structure variables (**indcapst.xls**).

CHAPTER 8

CAPITAL STRUCTURE: MODELS AND APPLICATIONS

In the last chapter, we examined the costs and benefits of borrowing, and noted that the trade-off favors debt for some firms and equity for others. In this chapter, we move beyond generalities to practical tools for analyzing the capital structure and choosing an optimal debt level for a firm. We explore two ways of doing so. The first approach is to choose the debt ratio that minimizes the cost of capital. Here, we revisit the cost of capital, explain its role in analysis and valuation, and discuss its relationship to the optimal debt ratio. The second approach also attempts to maximize firm value, but does so by adding the value of the unlevered firm to the present value of tax benefits, and then netting out the expected bankruptcy costs.

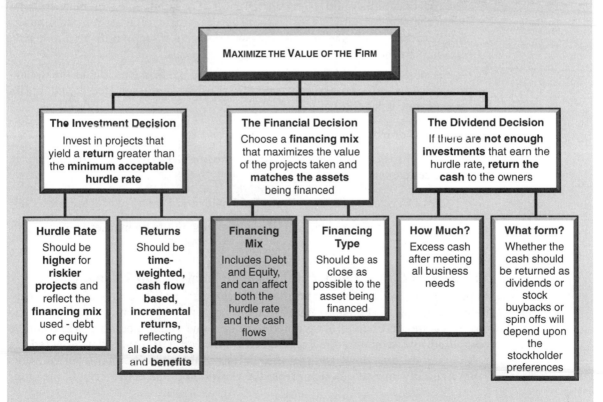

MAXIMIZE THE VALUE OF THE FIRM

The Investment Decision
Invest in projects that yield a **return** greater than the **minimum acceptable hurdle rate**

The Financial Decision
Choose a **financing mix** that maximizes the value of the projects taken and **matches the assets** being financed

The Dividend Decision
If there are **not enough investments** that earn the hurdle rate, **return the cash** to the owners

Hurdle Rate
Should be **higher** for **riskier projects** and reflect the **financing mix** used - debt or equity

Returns
Should be **time-weighted, cash flow based, incremental returns**, reflecting all **side costs** and **benefits**

Financing Mix
Includes Debt and Equity, and can affect both the hurdle rate and the cash flows

Financing Type
Should be as close as possible to the asset being financed

How Much?
Excess cash after meeting all business needs

What form?
Whether the cash should be returned as dividends or stock buybacks or spin offs will depend upon the stockholder preferences

257

COST OF CAPITAL APPROACH

In Chapters 3 and 4, we estimated the minimum acceptable hurdle rates for equity investors (the cost of equity), and for all investors in the firm (the cost of capital). We defined the *cost of capital* to be the weighted average of the costs of the different components of financing—including debt, equity, and hybrid securities—used by a firm to fund its financial requirements. By altering the weights of the different components, firms might be able to change their cost of capital.[1]

Definition of the Weighted Average Cost of Capital (WACC)

The *weighted average cost of capital* is defined as the weighted average of the costs of the different components of financing used by a firm:

$$WACC = k_e \, (E/(D + E + PS)) + k_d \, (D/(D + E + PS)) + k_{ps} \, (PS/(D + E + PS))$$

where WACC is the weighted average cost of capital, k_e, k_d, and k_{ps} are the costs of equity, debt, and preferred stock, and E, D, and PS are their respective market values.

The estimation of the costs of the individual components—equity, debt, and preferred stock—and of the weights in the cost of capital formulation are explored in detail in Chapter 4. To summarize:

- The cost of equity should reflect the riskiness of an equity investment in the company. The standard models for risk and return—the capital asset pricing model and the arbitrage pricing model—measure risk in terms of non-diversifiable risk, and convert the risk measure into an expected return.

- The cost of debt should reflect the default risk of the firm (the higher the default risk, the greater the cost of debt) and the tax advantage associated with debt (interest is tax deductible):

    Cost of Debt = Pretax Interest Rate on Borrowing (1 − tax rate)

- The cost of preferred stock should reflect the preferred dividend and the absence of tax deductibility:

    Cost of Preferred Stock = Preferred Dividend / Preferred Stock Price

- The weights used for the individual components should be market value weights rather than book value weights.

The Role of Cost of Capital in Investment Analysis and Valuation

In order to understand the relationship between the cost of capital and optimal capital structure, we first have to establish the relationship between firm value and the cost of capital. In Chapter 5, we noted that the value of a project to a firm could be computed by discounting the expected cash flows on it at a rate that reflected the riskiness of the cash flows, and that the analysis could be done either from the viewpoint of equity investors alone or from the viewpoint of the entire firm. In the latter

---

[1] If capital structure is irrelevant, the cost of capital will be unchanged as the capital structure is altered.

approach, we discounted the cash flows to the firm on the project (i.e., the project cash flows prior to debt payments but after taxes) at the project's cost of capital. Extending this principle, the value of the entire firm can be estimated by discounting the expected cash flows over time at the firm's cost of capital. The firm's aggregate cash flows can be estimated as cash flows after operating expenses, taxes, and any capital investments needed to create future growth in both fixed assets and working capital:

Free Cash Flow to Firm (FCFF) = EBIT (1 − t) − (Capital Expenditures − Depreciation) − Change in Non-cash Working Capital

The value of the firm can then be written as:

$$\text{Value of Firm} = \sum_{t=1}^{t=n} \frac{\text{CF to Firm}_t}{(1 + \text{WACC})^t}$$

The value of a firm is therefore a function of its cash flows and its cost of capital. In the specific case where the cash flows to the firm are unaffected by the debt/equity mix, and the cost of capital is reduced, the value of the firm will increase. If the objective in choosing the financing mix for the firm is the maximization of firm value, this can be accomplished, in this case, by *minimizing the cost of capital.* In the more general case where the cash flows to the firm are a function of the debt/equity mix, the optimal financing mix is the one *that maximizes firm value.*[2]

The optimal financing mix for a firm is simple to compute if one is provided with a schedule that relates the costs of equity and debt to the leverage of the firm.

WACC, Firm Value, and Leverage

Assume that you are given the costs of equity and debt at different debt levels for Jershey's, a leading manufacturer of chocolates and other candies, and that the cash flows to this firm are currently $200 million. Jershey's is in a relatively stable market, and these cash flows are expected to grow at 6% forever, and are unaffected by the debt ratio of the firm. The WACC schedule is provided in Table 8.1, along with the value of the firm at each level of debt. Note that the value of the firm = Cash flows to firm * (1 + g)/(WACC − g) = $200 * 1.06 / (WACC − .06).

The value of the firm increases (decreases) as the WACC decreases (increases), as illustrated in Figure 8.1.

While this illustration makes the choice of an optimal financing mix seem trivial, it obscures some real problems that may arise in its applications. First, an analyst typically does not have the benefit of having the entire schedule of costs of financing prior to an analysis. In most cases, the only level of debt about which there is any certainty about the cost of financing is the current level. Second, the analysis assumes implicitly that the level of cash flows to the firm is unaffected by the financing mix of the firm and, consequently, by the default risk (or bond rating) for the firm. While this may be reasonable in some cases, it might not in others. For instance, a firm that manufactures consumer durables (cars, televisions, etc.) might find that its sales drop if its default risk increases because investors are reluctant to buy its products.

---

[2]In other words, the value of the firm might not be maximized at the point that cost of capital is minimized, if firm cash flows are much lower at that level.

Table 8.1 WACC, FIRM VALUE, AND DEBT RATIOS				
D/(D + E)	Cost of Equity	Cost of Debt	WACC	Firm Value
0	10.50%	4.80%	10.50%	$4,711
10%	11.00%	5.10%	10.41%	$4,807
20%	11.60%	5.40%	10.36%	$4,862
30%	12.30%	5.52%	10.27%	$4,970
40%	13.10%	5.70%	10.14%	$5,121
50%	14.00%	6.30%	10.15%	$5,108
60%	15.00%	7.20%	10.32%	$4,907
70%	16.10%	8.10%	10.50%	$4,711
80%	17.20%	9.00%	10.64%	$4,569
90%	18.40%	10.20%	11.02%	$4,223
100%	19.70%	11.40%	11.40%	$3,926

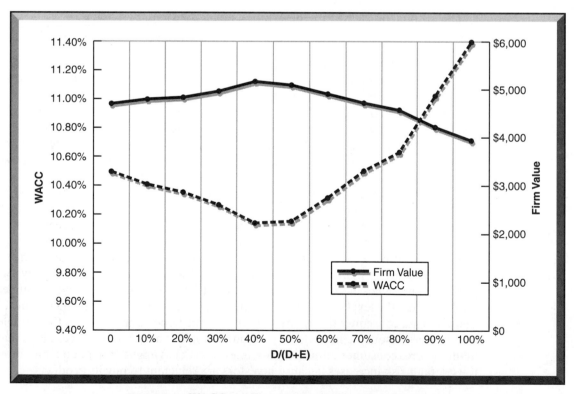

Figure 8.1   WACC and Firm Value as a Function of Leverage.

A PRACTICAL FRAMEWORK FOR ANALYZING CAPITAL STRUCTURE

As noted above, there are compromises that have to be made in order to apply the cost of capital approach to real-world problems. A general framework for analyzing these problems is provided in this section.

Cost of Equity

The primary task here is to estimate the cost of equity at different levels of debt. The approach described below applies if the CAPM is used to estimate cost of equity; the approach can be modified if the APM or a multi-factor model is used to estimate the cost of equity, instead.

Step 1: Obtain a current estimate of the equity beta and the debt/equity ratio. The current beta estimate can be estimated either with top-down (with a regression) approaches, or bottom-up (with sector betas) approaches.

Step 2: Estimate the unlevered beta (i.e., the beta that the firm would have had if it had no debt at all). If one uses the relationship between beta and leverage developed in Chapter 4, the unlevered beta can be written as:

$$\beta_u = \beta_{current}/[1 + (1 - t)D/E]$$

where β_u is the unlevered beta of the firm, $\beta_{current}$ is the current equity beta of the firm, t is the tax rate for the firm, and D/E is the average debt/equity ratio during the period of the regression.

Step 3: Reestimate the levered betas for different levels of debt:

$$\beta_{levered} = \beta_u [1 + (1 - t)D/E]$$

where $\beta_{levered}$ is the equity beta given new leverage and D/E is the new debt/equity ratio. At each level of leverage, measured using the debt/equity ratio, the equity beta is reestimated.

Step 4: Estimate the costs of equity using this levered beta:

$$k_e = R_f + \beta_{levered} [E(R_m) - R_f]$$

where k_e is the cost of equity, $E(R_m)$ is the expected return on the market index, and R_f is the current risk-free rate.

The definition of levered beta used in this table is based upon the assumption that all market risk is borne by the equity investors; this is unrealistic especially at higher levels of debt. An alternative estimate of levered betas apportions some of the market risk to the debt:

$$\beta_{levered} = \beta_u\,[1 + (1 - t)D/E] - \beta_{debt}\,(1 - t)\,D/E$$

The beta of debt is based upon the rating of the bond, and is estimated by regressing past returns on each rating class against returns on a market index. The levered betas estimated using this approach will generally be lower than those estimated with the conventional model.

8.2   BETAS OF DEBT, EQUITY, AND OPTIMAL DEBT RATIOS

When we assign a beta for debt, we are assuming that debt holders bear some market risk (as opposed to the assumption that equity investors will bear all the market risk). This assumption

☐   will increase the optimal debt ratio for a firm (relative to that calculated assuming that the beta of debt is 0).

☐   will decrease the optimal debt ratio for a firm.

☐   should not really affect the optimal debt ratio for a firm.

Explain.

Costs of Debt

Once again, the task is to estimate the cost of debt of the firm at different levels of debt. As background to estimating the cost of debt, two schedules have to be developed. The first lays out the relationship between default risk and a firm's underlying characteristics. For instance, if bond ratings are used to measure default risk, this schedule will describe the relationship between ratings and financial ratios, using either general information or information pertaining to a particular industry. The other schedule includes current market interest rates on corporate bonds in each ratings class. These default premiums will change over time and will have to be updated on a regular basis.

Given this background, the cost of debt for a firm can be estimated at different levels of debt by first estimating the bond rating for the firm at each debt level and then using the interest rate that corresponds to that rating:

Step 1:   Prepare the latest income statement showing the current operating income and relevant financial ratios.

Step 2:   Compute the current market value of the firm:

Market Value of Firm = Market Value of Equity + Market Value of Debt

Step 3:   As the debt ratio is changed, compute the dollar value of debt:

Dollar Value of Debt = [Debt/(Debt + Equity)] * Current Market Value of Firm

Step 4:   Compute the amount that will be paid as interest (Interest Rate * Dollar Value of Debt) and the financial ratios at each new debt ratio.

Step 5:   Using the schedule relating bond ratings to financial ratios, estimate what the firm's rating will be at each new debt ratio and the market interest rate that would correspond to that rating; this is the before-tax cost of debt.

Step 6: The after-tax cost of debt can then be computed using the firm's tax rate:

$$k_d = \text{After-Tax Cost of Debt} = \text{Before-Tax Cost of Debt} * (1 - \text{Tax Rate})$$

Cost of Capital

The costs of capital for different levels of debt can be estimated using the costs of equity and debt at each level. The debt ratio at which the cost of capital is minimized is the optimal debt ratio.

General Assumptions

The approach described above for estimating the cost of capital at different levels of debt rests on several assumptions. First, the effect on firm value of changing the capital structure is isolated by keeping the asset side fixed and changing the liability side. In practical terms, this implies that the debt ratio is increased (decreased) by issuing debt (equity) and repurchasing equity (debt). You may wonder if the optimal debt ratio obtained by doing this can be generalized to cases where the firm plans to invest the new funds in projects rather than in buying back securities. The answer is yes, on one condition: as long as the firm continues to make investments in the same line of business[3] in which it has operated in the past, the optimal debt ratio obtained from the above analysis can continue to be used. If the firm is planning to invest in new businesses, with different risk profiles, however, the optimal debt ratio calculated, keeping the asset side fixed, may no longer be appropriate.

The pretax operating income is assumed to be unaffected by the firm's financing mix and, by extension, its bond rating. If the operating income is a function of the firm's default risk, the basic framework will not change. Minimizing the cost of capital may not be the optimal course of action, however, since the value of the firm is determined by both the cash flows and the cost of capital. The value of the firm will have to be computed at each debt level, and the optimal debt ratio will be that which maximizes firm value.

ILLUSTRATION 8.1   Analyzing the Capital Structure for Disney—June 1997

The general framework can be used to find the optimal capital structure for a firm, as we did for Disney in June 1997. In 1997, Disney had debt outstanding of $12.342 billion, much of it as a consequence of financing the acquisition of Capital Cities in the previous year. This debt is estimated[4] to have a market value of $11.18 billion. In June 1997, there were 675.13 million shares outstanding trading at $75.38 per share. In Chapter 4, we used these inputs in conjunction with an estimated beta of 1.25 and a tax rate of 36% for Disney as a firm to arrive at a cost of capital of 12.22%:

Value of Equity = 675.13 million Shares * $ 75.38 = $ 50,888 million
Value of Debt = $ 11,180 million
Value of Disney as a Firm = $ 50,888 m + $ 11,180 m = $ 62,068 million
Cost of Equity = 7% + 1.25 (5.5%) = 13.85%

---

[3]The implicit assumption is that projects in the same business line have similar cash flow generating potential.

[4]This market value is estimated using an average maturity of three years for the debt, an interest expense of $478 million, and a pretax cost of debt, based upon Disney's current borrowing rate of 7.5%. The present value of the interest expenses and the book value are estimated using this borrowing rate.

After-Tax Cost of Debt = 7.50% (1 − .36) = 4.80%

Cost of Capital = (50,888/62,068)(13.85%) + 4.80% (11,180/62,068) = 12.22%

8.3   MARKET VALUE, BOOK VALUE, AND COST OF CAPITAL

Disney had a book value of equity of approximately $16.5 billion. Using the book value of debt of $12.342 billion, estimate the cost of capital for Disney using book value weights.

Disney's Cost of Equity and Leverage

In Chapter 4, we laid the groundwork for estimating cost of equity as leverage changes, by stating the beta as a function of the leverage. We estimated[5] Disney's unlevered beta by taking the weighted average of the unlevered betas of the businesses it was involved in to be 1.09. Using the equation for the levered beta,

Levered Beta = Unlevered Beta * [1 + (1 − tax rate) (Debt/ Equity)]

a long-term bond rate of 7%, and the historical premium of 5.5%, we estimate the cost of equity at different debt ratios for Disney in Table 8.2.

To examine how sensitive our assumptions are to this definition of levered betas, we also estimated the betas, apportioning some of the market risk to debt:

$$\beta_{levered} = \beta_u [1 + (1 − t)D/E] - \beta_{debt} (1 − t) D/E$$

The beta of debt is based upon the rating of the bond and is estimated by regressing past returns on each rating class against returns on a market index.

 This spreadsheet allows you to estimate the betas and costs of equity for a firm as the leverage changes (**unlev.xls**).

Disney's Cost of Debt and Leverage

A number of financial ratios are correlated with bond ratings, and ideally we would build a sophisticated model to predict ratings. For purposes of this illustration, however, we use a much simpler version: We assume that bond ratings are determined solely by the interest coverage ratio, which is defined as follows:

Interest Coverage Ratio = Earnings Before Interest & Taxes / Interest Expense

Interest Coverage Ratio: The interest coverage ratio is the earnings before interest and taxes divided by the interest expense. It is a measure of the firm's capacity to service its interest payments, with higher coverage ratios representing more safety.

We chose the interest coverage ratio for three reasons. First, it is a key ratio that is used by both Standard and Poor's and Moody's to determine ratings. Second, there is significant correlation not only between the interest coverage ratio and bond ratings, but

---

[5]The alternative approach would be to unlever the beta from the regression of Disney returns against market returns of 1.40 using the average debt/equity ratio of 14% for Disney during the regression period, which was 1992 to 1996.

Unlevered Beta = Current Beta / (1 + (1 − t) Average Debt/Equity)
= 1.40 / (1 + (1 − 0.36)) (0.14)) = 1.28

Table 8.2   LEVERAGE, BETAS, AND THE COST OF EQUITY

Debt Ratio	D/E Ratio	Beta	Cost of Equity
0%	0%	1.09	13.00%
10%	11%	1.17	13.43%
20%	25%	1.27	13.96%
30%	43%	1.39	14.65%
40%	67%	1.56	15.56%
50%	100%	1.79	16.85%
60%	150%	2.14	18.77%
70%	233%	2.72	21.97%
80%	400%	3.99	28.95%
90%	900%	8.21	52.14%

also between the interest coverage ratio and other ratios used in analysis, such as the debt coverage ratio and the funds flow ratios. Third, the interest coverage ratio changes as a firm changes its financing mix and decreases as the debt ratio increases.

The data in Table 8.3 was obtained based upon an analysis of the financial ratios of large manufacturing firms in different ratings classes. Using this table as a guideline, then, a firm with an interest coverage ratio of 2.55 would have a rating of BBB for its bonds.

The relationship between bond ratings and interest rates in June 1997 was obtained by looking at yields to maturity of long-term bonds in each ratings class and averaging these yields. Table 8.4 summarizes the interest rates/rating relationship and reports the spread for these bonds over treasury bonds (the treasury bond rate in June 1997 was 7%).

Table 8.5 summarizes Disney's projected operating income statement for the financial year 1996–97. It shows that Disney had earnings before interest, taxes, and depreciation of $6,693 million and paid out interest of only $479 million. The financial ratios provide evidence of the capacity of Disney to meet its debt obligations.

Default Spreads: This is the difference between the rate at which a firm with a specified default risk can borrow and the government bond rate on a bond of equivalent maturity.

Disney's actual earnings before interest and taxes were much lower than $5,559 million, because of the amortization charge that Disney took in 1996 to reflect its acquisition of Capital Cities. Since our intention is to measure "normalized operating income," and Disney has already paid[6] for this acquisition, we will not consider it in our analysis. Note that the interest coverage ratio is 11.61, but Disney's current rating is AA. Referring to Table 8.3, based upon the coverage ratio alone, Disney should command a AAA rating. Part of the reason for this is that Disney's interest expenses

[6]In contrast, the depreciation charges on existing assets will have to be reinvested back in these assets as capital maintenance expenditure to maintain the earning capacity of the assets.

Table 8.3   BOND RATINGS AND INTEREST COVERAGE RATIOS

Bond Rating	Interest Coverage Ratio	
	Low	High
AAA	8.50	∞
AA	6.50	8.50
A+	5.50	6.50
A	4.25	5.50
A−	3.00	4.25
BBB	2.50	3.00
BB	2.00	2.50
B+	1.75	2.00
B	1.50	1.75
B−	1.25	1.50
CCC	0.80	1.25
CC	0.65	0.80
C	0.20	0.65
D	−∞	0.20

Table 8.4   BOND RATINGS AND MARKET INTEREST RATES

Rating	Interest Rate	Spread Over Long Bond Rate
AAA	7.20%	0.20%
AA	7.50%	0.50%
A+	7.80%	0.80%
A	8.00%	1.00%
A−	8.25%	1.25%
BBB	8.50%	1.50%
BB	9.00%	2.00%
B+	9.50%	2.50%
B	10.25%	3.25%
B−	11.25%	4.25%
CCC	12.00%	5.00%
CC	13.00%	6.00%
C	14.50%	7.50%
D	17.00%	10.00%

for 1996 do not reflect the annualized interest expenses that the company is likely to face next year on its total book debt of slightly more than $12 billion.

Finally, to compute Disney's ratings at different debt levels, we redo the operating income statement at each level of debt, compute the interest coverage ratio at that level of debt, and find the rating that corresponds to that level of debt. For example, Table 8.6 provides operating income statements showing the debt ratio in-

Table 8.5 DISNEY'S INCOME STATEMENT IN 1996

Revenues	18,739
−Operating expenses	12,046
EBITDA	6,693
−Depreciation	1,134
EBIT	5,559
−Interest expense	479
Income before taxes	5,080
−Taxes	847
Income after taxes	4,233
Interest coverage ratio = 5,559/479 = 11.61	

Table 8.6 EFFECT OF MOVING TO HIGHER DEBT RATIOS

D/(D + E)	0.00%	10.00%
D/E	0.00%	11.11%
$ Debt	$0	$6,207
EBITDA	$6,693	$6,693
Depreciation	$1,134	$1,134
EBIT	$5,559	$5,559
Interest Expense	$0	$447
Taxable Income	$5,559	$5,112
Pretax Int. cov.	∞	12.44
Likely Rating	AAA	AAA
Interest Rate	7.20%	7.20%
Eff. Tax Rate	36.00%	36.00%
After-Tax Cost of Debt	4.61%	4.61%

creased to 10% of the overall value of the firm. The first step in the process is to estimate the dollar debt at 10%, which can be calculated as 10% of the value of Disney as a firm:

$$\text{Value of Disney} = \text{Market Value of Equity} + \text{Market Value of Debt}$$
$$= \$50,888 \text{ million} + \$11,180 \text{ million} = \$62,068 \text{ million}$$
$$\text{Dollar Debt at } 10\% = 10\% \text{ of } \$62,068 \text{ million} = \$6207 \text{ million}$$

Note that there is an element of circular reasoning involved here. The interest rate is needed to calculate the interest coverage ratio, and the coverage ratio is necessary to compute the interest rate. To get around the problem, we do a series of iterations until there is consistency between the rate used to calculate the interest expense and the rate that is obtained from the coverage ratio. (We start with a AAA rate).

This process is repeated for each level of debt from 20% to 90%, and the after-tax costs of debt are obtained at each level of debt, and reported in Table 8.7.

Table 8.7 COSTS OF DEBT AT DIFFERENT DEBT RATIOS

Debt Ratio	$ Debt	Interest Exp.	Interest Coverage Ratio	Bond Rating	Interest Rate	AT Cost of Debt
0%	$0	$0	∞	AAA	7.20%	4.61%
10%	$6,207	$447	12.44	AAA	7.20%	4.61%
20%	$12,414	$968	5.74	A+	7.80%	4.99%
30%	$18,621	$1,536	3.62	A−	8.25%	5.28%
40%	$24,827	$2,234	2.49	BB	9.00%	5.76%
50%	$31,034	$3,181	1.75	B	10.25%	6.56%
60%	$37,241	$4,469	1.24	CCC	12.00%	7.68%
70%	$43,448	$5,214	1.07	CCC	12.00%	7.68%
80%	$49,655	$5,959	0.93	CCC	12.00%	7.97%
90%	$55,862	$7,262	0.77	CC	13.00%	9.42%

Interest Coverage Ratio = EBIT/Interest Expense; EBIT for Disney = $ 5,559 million

8.4 MARKET VALUE, BOOK VALUE, AND COST OF CAPITAL

Using the framework developed in Table 8.6, estimate the bond rating and cost of debt for Disney at a 20% debt ratio.

D/(D+E)	0.00%	10.00%	20.00%
D/E	0.00%	11.11%	
$ Debt	$0	$6,207	
EBITDA	$6,693	$6,693	
Depreciation	$1,134	$1,134	
EBIT	$5,559	$5,559	
Interest Expense	$0	$447	
Taxable Income	$5,559	$5,112	
Pretax Int. cov.	∞	12.44	
Likely Rating	AAA	AAA	
Interest Rate	7.20%	7.20%	
Eff. Tax Rate	36.00%	36.00%	
After-tax Cost of Debt	4.61%	4.61%	

There is a dataset on the Web that summarizes bond ratings, interest coverage ratios, and spreads for U.S. firms (**ratings.xls**).

Disney: Effects of Leverage on Cost of Capital

Now that we have estimated the cost of equity and the cost of debt at each debt level, we are in a position to compute Disney's cost of capital. This is done for each debt level in Exhibit 8.1. The cost of capital, which is 13.00% when the firm is unlevered,

Exhibit 8.1   Cost of Capital Worksheet for Disney

	0.00%	10.00%	20.00%	30.00%	40.00%	50.00%	60.00%	70.00%	80.00%	90.00%
D/(D+E)	0.00%	10.00%	20.00%	30.00%	40.00%	50.00%	60.00%	70.00%	80.00%	90.00%
D/E	0.00%	11.11%	25.00%	42.86%	66.67%	100.00%	150.00%	233.33%	400.00%	900.00%
$ Debt	$0	$6,207	$12,414	$18,621	$24,827	$31,034	$37,241	$43,448	$49,655	$55,862
Beta	1.09	1.17	1.27	1.39	1.56	1.79	2.14	2.72	3.99	8.21
Cost of Equity	13.00%	13.43%	13.96%	14.65%	15.56%	16.85%	18.77%	21.97%	28.95%	52.14%
Operating Inc.	$6,693	$6,693	$6,693	$6,693	$6,693	$6,693	$6,693	$6,693	$6,693	$6,693
Depreciation	$1,134	$1,134	$1,134	$1,134	$1,134	$1,134	$1,134	$1,134	$1,134	$1,134
Interest	$0	$447	$968	$1,536	$2,234	$3,181	$4,469	$5,214	$5,959	$7,262
Taxable Income	$5,559	$5,112	$4,591	$4,023	$3,325	$2,378	$1,090	$345	($400)	($1,703)
Tax	$2,001	$1,840	$1,653	$1,448	$1,197	$856	$392	$124	($144)	($613)
Net Income	$3,558	$3,272	$2,938	$2,575	$2,128	$1,522	$698	$221	($256)	($1,090)
(+)Deprec'n	$1,134	$1,134	$1,134	$1,134	$1,134	$1,134	$1,134	$1,134	$1,134	$1,134
Funds from Op.	$4,692	$4,406	$4,072	$3,709	$3,262	$2,656	$1,832	$1,355	$878	$44
Pre-tax Int. Cov	∞	12.44	5.74	3.62	2.49	1.75	1.24	1.07	0.93	0.77
Funds Int. Cov	∞	9.86	4.21	2.41	1.46	0.83	0.41	0.26	0.15	0.01
Funds/Debt	∞	0.71	0.33	0.20	0.13	0.09	0.05	0.03	0.02	0.00
Likely Rating	AAA	AAA	A+	A−	BB	B	CCC	CCC	CCC	CC
Interest Rate	7.20%	7.20%	7.80%	8.25%	9.00%	10.25%	12.00%	12.00%	12.00%	13.00%
Eff. Tax Rate	36.00%	36.00%	36.00%	36.00%	36.00%	36.00%	36.00%	36.00%	33.59%	27.56%

Cost of Capital Calculations

	0.00%	10.00%	20.00%	30.00%	40.00%	50.00%	60.00%	70.00%	80.00%	90.00%
D/(D+E)	0.00%	10.00%	20.00%	30.00%	40.00%	50.00%	60.00%	70.00%	80.00%	90.00%
D/E	0.00%	11.11%	25.00%	42.86%	66.67%	100.00%	150.00%	233.33%	400.00%	900.00%
$ Debt	$0	$6,207	$12,414	$18,621	$24,827	$31,034	$37,241	$43,448	$49,655	$55,862
Cost of Equity	13.00%	13.43%	13.96%	14.65%	15.56%	16.85%	18.77%	21.97%	28.95%	52.14%
Cost of Debt	4.61%	4.61%	4.99%	5.28%	5.76%	6.56%	7.68%	7.68%	7.97%	9.42%
WACC	13.00%	12.55%	12.17%	11.84%	11.64%	11.70%	12.11%	11.97%	12.17%	13.69%
Firm Value (C)	$58,319	$60,435	$62,314	$64,054	$65,133	$64,800	$62,597	$63,372	$62,332	$55,393
Firm Value (G)	$53,172	$58,014	$62,705	$67,419	$70,542	$69,560	$63,445	$65,524	$62,751	$47,140

decreases as the firm initially adds debt, reaches a minimum of 11.64% at 40% debt, and then starts to increase again. This is illustrated in Table 8.8. The same information is presented in Figure 8.2.

To illustrate the robustness of this solution to alternative measures of levered betas, the costs of debt, equity, and capital were reestimated under the assumption that debt bears some market risk. If the debt holders bear some market risk, the cost of equity is lower at each level of debt and Disney's optimal debt ratio remains at 40%.

Table 8.8	COSTS OF DEBT, EQUITY, AND CAPITAL—DISNEY		
Debt Ratio	**Cost of Equity**	**AT Cost of Debt**	**Cost of Capital**
0.00%	13.00%	4.61%	13.00%
10.00%	13.43%	4.61%	12.55%
20.00%	13.96%	4.99%	12.17%
30.00%	14.65%	5.28%	11.84%
40.00%	15.56%	5.76%	11.64%
50.00%	16.85%	6.56%	11.70%
60.00%	18.77%	7.68%	12.11%
70.00%	21.97%	7.68%	11.97%
80.00%	28.95%	7.97%	12.17%
90.00%	52.14%	9.42%	13.69%

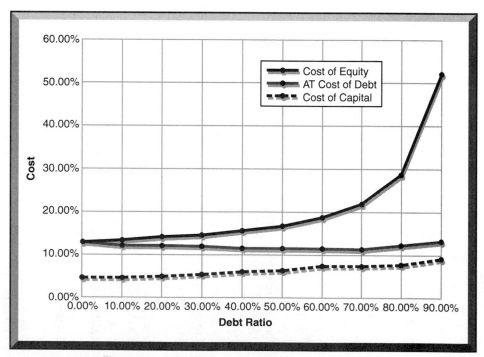

Figure 8.2   Disney: Cost of Debt, Equity, and Capital.

Firm Value and Cost of Capital

The rationale for minimizing the cost of capital is that it maximizes the value of the firm. To illustrate the effects of moving to the optimal on Disney's firm value, we start off with a simple formula:

$$\text{Firm Value} = \text{CF to Firm} (1 + g) / (\text{WACC} - g)$$

where

$$g = \text{Growth rate in the cash flow to the firm (steady state)}$$

The current value of the firm is \$62,068 million and the current weighted average cost of capital is 12.22%. The current cash flow to the firm is:

$$\text{Cash Flow to Firm} = \text{EBIT} (1 - \text{tax rate}) + \text{Depreciation} - \text{Capital Spending}$$
$$= 5,559 (1 - 0.36) + 1,134 - 1745 - = \$2,947 \text{ million}$$

(Working capital was ignored)
Solving for the implied growth rate:

$$\text{Growth Rate} = (\text{Firm Value} * \text{WACC} - \text{CF to Firm})/(\text{Firm Value} + \text{CF to Firm})$$
$$= (62,068 * .1222 - 2947)/(62,068 + 2,947) = .0713 \text{ or } 7.13\%$$

Now assume that Disney moves to 40% debt and a WACC of 11.64%. By moving to the lower cost of capital, the firm will save the following amount in annual financing costs:

$$\text{Annual Financing Costs with Existing WACC} = \$62,068m (.1222) = \$7,583$$
$$\text{Annual Financing Costs with New WACC} = \$62,068 (.1164) = \$7224$$
$$\text{Savings in Annual Financing Costs} = \$7,583 - \$7,227 = \$356 \text{ m}$$

(Differences in dollar values are due to rounding)
The present value of these savings, assuming it grows at the same rate as the cash flows to the firm, is:

$$\text{Present Value of Savings} = (\$356 * 1.0713)/(.1164 - .0713) = \$8,474 \text{ million}$$

The value of the firm[7] will increase by \$8,474 million by moving to the optimal debt ratio. With 675.13 million shares outstanding, assuming that stockholders can rationally evaluate the effect of this refinancing, the increase in the stock price can be calculated:

$$\text{Increase in Stock Price} = \text{Increase in Firm Value} / \text{Number of Shares Outstanding}$$
$$= 8474 /675.13 = \$12.55$$

Since the current stock price is \$75.38, the stock price can be expected to increase to \$87.93, which translates into a 16.65% increase in the price. Since the asset side of the balance sheet is kept fixed and changes in capital structure are made by borrowing funds and repurchasing stock, this implies that the stock price would increase to

---

[7]An alternative approach is to value the entire firm using the new cost of capital:

> Cash Flow to Firm = \$2,947 million
> WACC = 11.46%
> Growth Rate in Cash Flows to Firm − 7.13%
> Firm Value = \$2,947 * 1.0713 / (.1146 − .0713) = \$72,888 million

The difference between this value (\$72,888) and the value estimated in the text can be attributed to the fact that we kept firm value fixed at \$62,068 while estimating the annual financing savings.

Table 8.9	COSTS OF CAPITAL AND FIRM VALUE: DISNEY	
Debt Ratio	**Cost of Capital**	**Firm Value**
0.00%	13.00%	$53,172
10.00%	12.55%	$58,014
20.00%	12.17%	$62,705
30.00%	11.84%	$67,419
40.00%	11.64%	$70,542
50.00%	11.70%	$69,560
60.00%	12.11%	$63,445
70.00%	11.97%	$65,524
80.00%	12.17%	$62,751
90.00%	13.69%	$47,140

$87.93 on the announcement of the repurchase. The firm value and cost of capital at different debt ratios are summarized in Table 8.9.

8.5   RATIONALITY AND STOCK PRICE EFFECTS

This analysis assumes that the stock will be bought back at the higher estimated price of $87.93. Estimate the effect on the stock price of the capital structure change if you were able to buy stock back at the old price of $75.38.

IN PRACTICE: EFFECTIVE TAX RATES, INCOME, AND INTEREST EXPENSES

While it is conventional to leave the marginal tax rate unchanged as the debt ratio is increased, we adjust the tax rate to reflect the potential loss of the tax benefits of debt at higher debt ratios, where the interest expenses exceed the earnings before interest and taxes. To illustrate this point, note that the earnings before interest and taxes at Disney are $5,559 million. As long as interest expenses are less than $5,559 million, interest expenses remain fully tax deductible and earn the 36% tax benefit. For instance in Exhibit 8.1, even at a 70% debt ratio, the interest expenses are $5,214 million and the tax benefit is, therefore, 36% of this amount.

At an 80% debt ratio, however, the interest expenses balloon to $5,959 million, which is greater than the earnings before interest and taxes of $5,559 million. We consider the tax benefit on the interest expenses up to this amount:

$$\text{Tax Benefit} = \$5{,}559 \text{ million} * .36 = \$ 2{,}001 \text{ million}$$

As a proportion of the total interest expenses, the tax benefit is now less than 36%:

$$\text{Effective Tax Rate} = \$2{,}001/\$5.959 = 33.59\%$$

This, in turn, raises the after-tax cost of debt. This is a conservative approach, since losses can be carried forward. Given that this is a permanent shift in leverage, it does make sense to be conservative.

This spreadsheet allows you to compute the optimal debt ratio firm value for any firm, using the same information used for Disney. It has updated interest coverage ratios and default spreads built in (**capstr.xls**).

Caveat Emptor: Some Considerations in Using the Model

There are several considerations that need to be taken into account when using this approach to come up with an optimal debt ratio. First, the bond rating is assumed to be predictable, based upon financial ratios. The ratings agencies would argue, however, that subjective factors, such as the perceived quality of management, are part of the ratings process. One way to build these factors into the analysis would be to modify the ratings obtained from the financial ratio analysis across the board to reflect the ratings agencies' subjective concerns.[8] Second, it is assumed that at every debt level, all existing debt will be refinanced at the "new" interest rate that will prevail after the capital structure change. For instance, Disney's existing debt of approximately $12 billion, which has a AA rating, is assumed to be refinanced at the interest rate corresponding to a BB rating, which is our estimate of Disney's rating at the optimal debt level of 40%. This is done for two reasons. The first is that existing debt holders might have protective puts that enable them to put their bonds back to the firm and receive face value.[9] The second is that it gives us the value increment without "wealth expropriation" effects—the effects of stockholders expropriating wealth from bondholders, when debt is increased, and vice versa, when debt is reduced—from the value calculations. These wealth-transfer effects can be built in by locking in current rates on existing bonds and recalculating the optimal debt ratio.[10] Third, the assumption that the operating income is unaffected by the bond rating is a key one. If the operating income is adversely affected by the drop in the bond rating, the value of the firm may not be maximized where the weighted average cost of capital is minimized. Again, the analysis can be modified so that the operating income is a function of the bond rating, and by calculating the value of the firm at each debt level.[11] Finally, the unconstrained analysis leaves us with the uncomfortable finding that at its optimal debt ratio, Disney has a bond rating below investment grade. Since most financial managers would be troubled by this sudden increase in default risk and its implications for the long-term survival of the firm, we introduce constraints into the analysis.

Investment Grade Bonds: An investment grade bond is one with a rating greater than BBB. Some institutional investors, such as pension funds, are constrained from holding bonds with lower ratings.

---

[8]For instance, assume that a firm's current rating is AA, but that its financial ratios would result in an A rating. It can then be argued that the ratings agencies are, for subjective reasons, rating the company one notch higher than the rating obtained from a purely financial analysis. The ratings obtained for each debt level can then be increased by one notch across the board to reflect these subjective considerations.

[9]If they do not have protective puts, it is in the best interests of the stockholders not to refinance the debt (as in the leveraged buyout of RJR Nabisco) if debt ratios are increased.

[10]This will have the effect of reducing interest cost, when debt is increased, and thus interest coverage ratios. This will lead to higher ratings, at least in the short term.

[11]For example, we assumed that Boeing's operating income would drop 10% if its rating dropped below A− and another 10% if it dropped below BBB. Consequently, the optimal debt ratio is reduced to 20%.

Building Constraints into the Analysis

The simplest solution is a "bond rating constraint," whereby the debt level that has the lowest cost of capital subject to the constraint that the bond rating meets or exceeds a certain level is chosen. For example, in the previous illustration, if Disney insisted on preserving a bond rating of A− or above, the optimal debt ratio would be 30%.

While this approach is simple, it is essentially subjective and is therefore open to manipulation. For instance, the management at Disney could insist that it wants to preserve a AA rating and hence justify the existing debt policy. One way to make managers more accountable in this regard is to measure the cost of a rating constraint:

$$\text{Cost of Rating Constraint} = \text{Maximum Firm Value without Constraints} - \text{Maximum Firm Value with Constraints}$$

If Disney insisted on maintaining an A− rating, its constrained optimal debt ratio would be 30%. The cost of preserving the constraint can then be measured as the difference in firm value at 50% and at 30%:

$$
\begin{aligned}
\text{Cost of Rating Constraint for Disney} &= \text{Value at 40\% Debt} - \text{Value at 30\% Debt} \\
&= \quad\quad \$70{,}542 \quad\quad - \quad\quad \$67{,}419 \\
&= \$3{,}123 \text{ million}
\end{aligned}
$$

This does overstate the cost of the rating constraint, since operating income is being held constant as the rating drops from A- to BB. To the degree that operating income moves with ratings, this cost will drop.

The second approach to building in constraints is to analyze the effects of changes in operating income on the optimal debt ratio. In the base case described above, Disney's operating income in 1996 was used to find the optimal leverage. One could argue that Disney's operating income is volatile and could change, however, depending upon the health of the entertainment business (Table 8.10).

There are several ways of using historical data to modify the analysis. One approach is to look at the firm's performance during previous downturns. In Disney's case, the recession in 1991 resulted in a drop in operating income of almost 22% from $1,287 million to $1,004 million. A second approach is to obtain a statistical measure of the volatility in operating income, so that we can be more conservative in choosing debt levels for firms with more volatile earnings. In Disney's case, the standard deviation in percentage changes in operating income is 38.43%. Finally, it has to be noted that Disney's acquisition of Capital Cities has changed its risk exposure and made it more susceptible to the swings in income in the broadcasting business.

To examine the sensitivity of the conclusions to changes in operating income, we lowered EBITDA by 30% and examined the effect on the optimal debt ratio. The optimal debt ratio declines from 40% to 30%. Table 8.11 summarizes the effect on optimal debt ratios of lower earnings.

As you can see, the optimal debt ratio declines as the EBITDA decreases. It is striking to note, however, that Disney can afford to carry a significantly higher amount of debt even with dramatically lower operating income.

Table 8.10   DISNEY'S OPERATING INCOME HISTORY: 1981–1996

Year	Operating Income	Change in Operating Income
1981	$119.35	
1982	$141.39	18.46%
1983	$133.87	−5.32%
1984	$142.60	6.5%
1985	$205.60	44.2%
1986	$280.58	36.5%
1987	$707.00	152.0%
1988	$789.00	11.6%
1989	$1,109.00	40.6%
1990	$1,287.00	16.1%
1991	$1,004.00	−22.0%
1992	$1,287.00	28.2%
1993	$1,560.00	21.2%
1994	$1,804.00	15.6%
1995	$2,262.00	25.4%
1996	$3,024.00	33.7%

Table 8.11   EFFECTS OF OPERATING INCOME ON OPTIMAL DEBT RATIO: DISNEY

% Lower	$ EBITDA	Optimal Debt Ratio
10%	$6,271.20	40%
20%	$5,574.40	40%
30%	$4,877.60	30%
40%	$4,180.80	20%
50%	$3,484.00	20%
60%	$2,787.20	10%
70%	$2,090.40	10%
80%	$1,393.60	0%
90%	$696.80	0%

8.6   BANKRUPTCY COSTS AND DEBT RATIOS

The optimal debt ratio obtained by minimizing the cost of capital is too high because it does not consider bankruptcy costs.

☐ True

☐ False

Explain.

Determinants of Optimal Debt Ratio

The preceding analysis highlights some of the determinants of the optimal debt ratio.

(a) Firm's Tax Rate

In general, the tax benefits from debt increase as the tax rate goes up. In relative terms, firms with higher tax rates have higher optimal debt ratios than do firms with lower tax rates, other things being equal. It also follows that a firm's optimal debt ratio will increase as its tax rate increases.

(b) Pretax Returns on the Firm (in Cash Flow Terms)[EBITA/Firm Value]

This is defined as the EBITDA as a percentage of the market value of the firm. It follows that a firm with higher pretax returns can sustain much more debt as a proportion of the market value of the firm, since debt payments can be met much more easily from prevailing cash flows. Disney, for example, has EBITDA which is 10.78% of firm value in the base case, and an optimal debt ratio of 40%. Halving this to pretax return to 5.39% will reduce the optimal debt ratio to 10%.

(c) Variance in Operating Income

The variance in operating income enters the base case analysis in two ways. First, it plays a role in determining the current beta: firms with high (low) variance in operating income will tend to have high (low) betas. Second, the volatility in operating income can be one of the factors determining bond ratings at different levels of debt: ratings drop off much more dramatically for higher-variance firms as debt levels are increased. It follows that firms with higher (lower) variance in operating income will have lower (higher) optimal debt ratios. The variance in operating income also plays a role in the constrained analysis, since higher variance firms are much more likely to register significant drops in operating income. Consequently, the decision to increase debt should be made much more cautiously for these firms.

(d) Default Spreads

The default spreads commanded by different ratings classes tend to increase during recessions and decrease during recoveries. Keeping other things constant, as the spreads increase (decrease) optimal debt ratios decrease (increase), for the simple reason that higher spreads penalize firms which borrow more money and have lower ratings. In fact, the default spreads on corporate bonds have steadily declined since 1992, leading to higher optimal debt ratios for all firms.

8.7 LEVEL OF INTEREST RATES AND OPTIMAL DEBT RATIOS

As interest rates go down, the optimal debt ratios for all firms should go up since debt becomes much cheaper.

☐ True

☐ False

Explain.

Extending the Cost of Capital Approach

The cost of capital approach, which works so well for manufacturing firms that are publicly traded and rated and stay financially healthy, may have to be adapted in other cases, such as for private firms that might not be rated; financial service firms such as banks, and insurance companies; and firms in financial trouble.

Firms That Are Not Rated

There are two advantages to working with a publicly rated company like Disney. First, the current rating for the company provides information that can be used to assess its current default risk and how this risk might change as the debt ratio changes. Second, it provides a rationale for the process of estimating ratings and then using the ratings to estimate the interest rate on the debt. This does not imply that the approach cannot be used for unrated firms; however, there are at least two ways of dealing with this deficit. The first is to estimate a synthetic bond rating for the firm, based upon interest coverage or other financial ratios, and then use this rating to estimate an interest rate on debt. For private firms in the United States, this may provide a useful approximation of default risk. The second is to develop an alternative measure of default risk, which can then be used to estimate an interest rate on the debt. This measure can be based upon credit scoring approaches used by banks to determine default risk and interest rates; it can be as simple as classifying firms on a continuum from "very safe" to "very risky."

■▲
▼●   ILLUSTRATION 8.2   **Applying the Cost of Capital Approach to a Private Firm: Bookscape Books**

Bookscape, as a private firm, has neither a market value for its equity nor a rating for its debt. In order to estimate the optimal capital structure for Bookscape, we made the following assumptions:

- The operating income and depreciation estimates were obtained from the most recent income statement for the firm:

Revenues	$ 20,000,000
Operating Expenses	
Labor	$ 4,000,000
Material	$ 12,000,000
Lease Expenses	$ 500,000
Other Supplies	$ 1,000,000
Depreciation & Amortization	$ 500,000
EBIT	$ 2,000,000
Interest Expenses	$ 0
Taxable Income	$ 2,000,000
Taxes	$ 840,000
Net Income	$ 1,160,000

Since we consider the present value of operating lease expenses to be debt, we add back the lease expenses to the earnings before interest and taxes to arrive at an adjusted earnings before interest and taxes. For the rest of the analysis, operating lease expenses will be viewed as the equivalent of interest expenses:

$$\text{Adjusted EBIT} = \text{EBIT} + \text{Operating Lease Expenses}$$
$$= \$\,2{,}000{,}000 + \$\,500{,}000 = \$\,2{,}500{,}000$$

- While Bookscape has no debt outstanding, the present value of the operating lease expenses (see Chapter 4) of $ 3.36 million is considered as debt.

- To estimate the market value of equity, we use a multiple of 22.41 times net income. This multiple is the average multiple at which comparable firms which are publicly traded are valued:

$$\text{Estimated Market Value of Equity} = \text{Net Income} * \text{Average Multiple}$$
$$= 1{,}160{,}000 * 22.41 = 26{,}000{,}000$$

- The interest rates at different levels of debt will be estimated based upon a "synthetic" bond rating. This rating will be assessed using the following table, which summarizes ratings and default spreads over the long-term bond rate as a function of interest coverage ratios for small firms which are rated by S&P as of June 1997.

Interest Coverage Ratio	Rating	Spread over T Bond Rate
>12.5	AAA	0.20%
9.50–12.50	AA	0.50%
7.5–9.5	A+	0.80%
6.0–7.5	A	1.00%
4.5–6.0	A–	1.25%
3.5–4.5	BBB	1.50%
3.0–3.5	BB	2.00%
2.5–3.0	B+	2.50%
2.0–2.5	B	3.25%
1.5–2.0	B–	4.25%
1.25–1.5	CCC	5.00%
0.8–1.25	CC	6.00%
0.5–0.8	C	7.50%
< 0.5	D	10.00%

Note that smaller firms need higher coverage ratios than the larger firms to get the same rating. Based upon this table and Bookscape's current income statement, we can estimate a synthetic rating for it:

$$\text{Current Interest Coverage Ratio} = \text{Adjusted EBIT} / \text{Interest Expense (Lease Expense)}$$
$$= 2{,}500{,}000/500{,}000 = 5.00$$

Table 8.12   COSTS OF CAPITAL AND FIRM VALUE FOR BOOKSCAPE

Debt Ratio	Beta	Cost of Equity	Interest Coverage Ratio	Bond Rating	Interest Rate	AT Cost of Debt	Cost of Capital	Firm Value
0%	1.03	12.65%	∞	A+	7.80%	4.52%	12.65%	$26,781
10%	1.09	13.01%	8.79	A+	7.80%	4.52%	12.16%	$29,025
20%	1.18	13.47%	4.03	BBB	8.50%	4.93%	11.76%	$31,182
30%	1.28	14.05%	2.23	B	10.25%	5.95%	11.62%	$32,000
40%	1.42	14.83%	1.52	B−	11.25%	6.53%	11.51%	$32,679
50%	1.62	15.93%	1.05	CC	13.00%	7.54%	11.73%	$31,341
60%	2.00	18.00%	0.88	CC	13.00%	8.20%	12.12%	$29,250
70%	2.74	22.09%	0.68	C	14.50%	10.39%	13.90%	$22,267
80%	4.12	29.64%	0.59	C	14.50%	10.90%	14.65%	$20,184
90%	8.23	52.28%	0.53	C	14.50%	11.30%	15.40%	$18,434

This coverage ratio suggests that Bookscape will have a bond rating of A− and a pretax cost of debt of 8.25% at its current debt ratio. Note that this is close to the cost of debt of 8% that we used in Chapter 4 as Bookscape's cost of debt.

- The tax rate used in the analysis is 42%. The long-term bond rate at the time of this analysis was 7%.

Based upon this information and using the same approach that we used for Disney, the cost of capital and firm value were estimated for Bookscape at different debt ratios. The information is summarized in Table 8.12.

The firm value is maximized (and the cost of capital is minimized) at a debt ratio of 40%, though the firm value is relatively flat between 30% and 60%.

IN PRACTICE: OPTIMAL DEBT RATIOS FOR PRIVATE FIRMS

While the trade-off between the costs and benefits of borrowing remain the same for private and publicly traded firms, there are differences between the two that may result in private firms borrowing less money. A comparison of the costs and benefits of debt for private and public firms yields the following conclusions:

- Taking on debt increases default risk and expected bankruptcy cost much more substantially for small private firms than for larger publicly traded firms, partly because the owners of the former are exposed more frequently to unlimited (personal) liability, and partly because the perception of financial trouble can be much more damaging to small, private firms. This is partially reflected in the use of different interest coverage ratios to get ratings.

- Taking on debt yields a smaller advantage in terms of disciplining decision makers in the case of privately run firms, since there is no separation of ownership and management.

- Taking on debt generally exposes small private firms to more restrictive bond covenants and higher agency costs than it does large publicly traded firms.
- The loss of flexibility associated with using excess debt capacity is likely to weigh more heavily on small, private firms than large, publicly traded firms, due to the former's lack of access to public markets.

Barring the scenario in which the individual tax rate is substantially higher than the corporate tax rate and the tax benefits of debt are therefore substantially larger for small, private firms, all of the factors mentioned above would lead us to observe much lower debt ratios at small private firms.

Banks and Insurance Companies

There are several problems in applying the cost of capital approach to financial service firms, such as banks and insurance companies. The first is that the interest coverage ratio spreads, which are critical in determining the bond ratings, have to be estimated separately for financial service firms; applying manufacturing company spreads will result in absurdly low ratings for even the safest banks, and very low optimal debt ratios. The second is a measurement problem that arises partly from the difficulty in estimating the debt on a financial service company's balance sheet. Given the mix of deposits, repurchase agreements, short-term financing, and other liabilities that may show up on the balance sheet, one solution may be to focus only on long-term debt, defined tightly, and to use interest coverage ratios defined consistently. The third problem is that financial service firms may find their operating income affected by their bond rating; as the rating drops, the operating income might drop too. The final and most critical problem is that financial service firms operate under significant regulatory constraints on book capital that may restrict their capacity to change leverage.

 ILLUSTRATION 8.3   Applying the Cost of Capital Approach to Deutsche Bank
We analyze the optimal capital structure for Deutsche Bank, using data from 1996. To begin, we make the following assumptions:

- The earnings before long-term interest expenses and taxes amounted to 23,209 million DM.
- Deutsche Bank was ranked AAA and paid 7.70% on its long-term debt in 1994. It had 110,111 DM in long-term debt outstanding at the end of the year.
- Deutsche Bank had 526.847 million shares outstanding, trading at 119.2 DM per share, and had a beta of 0.94 (the German long bond rate at that time was 7.50%).
- The interest coverage ratios used to estimate the bond ratings were adjusted downward, based upon the ratings of banks.[12]
- The operating income for Deutsche Bank is assumed to drop if its rating drops. Table 8.13 summarizes the interest coverage ratios and estimated operating income drops for different ratings classes.

---

[12]U.S. banks were used to estimate the numbers in the table. Since there are no "junk bond" status banks in our sample, we extrapolated the table below BBB.

Table 8.13   INTEREST COVERAGE RATIOS, RATINGS, AND OPERATING INCOME DECLINES

Interest Coverage Ratio	Rating is	Spread is	Operating Income Decline
<0.05	D	10.00%	−50.00%
0.05–0.10	C	7.50%	−40.00%
0.10–0.20	CC	6.00%	−40.00%
0.20–0.30	CCC	5.00%	−40.00%
0.30–0.40	B−	4.25%	−25.00%
0.40–0.50	B	3.25%	−20.00%
0.50–0.60	B+	2.50%	−20.00%
0.60–0.80	BB	2.00%	−20.00%
0.80–1.00	BBB	1.50%	−20.00%
1.00–1.50	A−	1.25%	−17.50%
1.50–2.00	A	1.00%	−15.00%
2.00–2.50	A+	0.80%	−10.00%
2.50–3.00	AA	0.50%	−5.00%
> 3.00	AAA	0.20%	0.00%

Figure 8.14   DEBT RATIOS, WACC, AND FIRM VALUE: DEUTSCHE BANK

Debt Ratio	Cost of Equity	Cost of Debt	WACC	Firm Value
0%	10.13%	4.24%	10.13%	DM 124,288.85
10%	10.29%	4.24%	9.69%	DM 132,558.74
20%	10.49%	4.24%	9.24%	DM 142,007.59
30%	10.75%	4.24%	8.80%	DM 152,906.88
40%	11.10%	4.24%	8.35%	DM 165,618.31
50%	11.58%	4.24%	7.91%	DM 165,750.19
60%	12.30%	4.40%	7.56%	DM 162,307.44
70%	13.51%	4.57%	7.25%	DM 157,070.00
80%	15.92%	4.68%	6.92%	DM 151,422.87
90%	25.69%	6.24%	8.19%	DM 30,083.27

Thus, we assume that the operating income will drop 5% if Deutsche Bank's rating drops to AA and 20% if it drops to BBB.

Based upon these assumptions, the optimal long-term debt ratio for Deutsche Bank is estimated to be 50%, lower than the current debt ratio of 60%. Table 8.14 summarizes the cost of capital and firm values at different debt ratios for the firm. The actual long-term debt ratio for Deutsche Bank of 60% is slightly higher than the optimal. Going to the optimal will increase firm value by roughly 3.4 billion DM or 2%.

IN PRACTICE: SELF-IMPOSED, AND LENDER CONSTRAINTS

In most analyses of optimal capital structure, an analyst will be faced with a series of constraints, some of which come from regulatory requirements, some of which are self-imposed, and some of which are imposed by existing lenders to the firm. One very common constraint imposed by all three is a constraint that the book value debt ratio not exceed a specified number. Since the analysis we have done so far has focused on market value debt ratios, there is the risk that the book value constraint may be violated. There are two solutions:

1. The first is to do the entire analysis using book value of debt and equity, looking for the optimal debt ratio. Since the approach we have described is driven by cash flows, the optimal dollar debt that is computed should not be affected significantly by doing this.

2. The second and more general approach (since it can be used to analyze any kind of constraint) is to keep track of the book value debt ratio in the traditional analysis, and view the optimal capital structure as the one that minimizes the cost of capital subject to the book value debt ratio being lesser than the specified constraint.

Firms in Trouble

As we discussed earlier, a key input that drives the optimal capital structure is the current operating income. If this income is depressed, either because the firm is a cyclical one or due to firm-specific factors that are expected to be temporary, the optimal debt ratio that will emerge from the analysis will be much lower than the firm's true optimal. For example, automobile manufacturing firms would have had very low debt ratios if the optimal debt ratios had been computed based upon the operating income in 1991 and 1992, which were recession years. If the drop in operating income is permanent, however, this lower optimal debt ratio is, in fact, the correct estimate.

When faced with a firm with depressed current operating income, the first issue to address is whether the drop in income is temporary or permanent. If the drop is temporary, we must determine the normalized operating income for the firm. The *normalized operating income* is an estimate of how much the firm can be expected to earn in a normal year, that is, a year without the specific characteristics that depressed earnings this year. The optimal debt ratio arrived at using the normalized operating income has to be approached cautiously, since the analysis is based upon the assumption that earnings will recover to this level.

Normalized Income: This is a measure of the income that a firm can make in a normal year, where there are no extraordinary gains or losses either from firm-specific factors (such as write offs and onetime sales) or macroeconomic factors (such as the economic cycle).

■ ▲
▼ ●
ILLUSTRATION 8.4   Applying the Cost of Capital Approach to Aracruz Cellulose

Aracruz Cellulose, the Brazilian pulp and paper manufacturing firm, reported depressed revenues and earnings in 1996. We estimated the optimal debt ratio for Aracruz, based upon the following facts:

- In 1996, Aracruz had earnings before interest and taxes of only 15 million BR, and claimed depreciation of 190 million BR. Capital expenditures amounted to 250 million BR.
- Aracruz had gross debt outstanding of 1520 million BR. While the nominal rate on this debt, especially the portion that is in Brazilian Real, is high, we will continue to do the analysis in real terms, and use a current real cost of debt of 5.5%, which is based upon a real risk-free rate of 5% and a default spread of 0.5%.
- The corporate tax rate in Brazil is estimated to be 32%.
- Aracruz had 976.10 million shares outstanding, trading 2.05 BR per share. The beta of the stock is estimated, using comparable firms, to be 0.71.

In Chapter 4, we estimated Aracruz's current real cost of capital to be 7.48%:

Current Cost of Equity $= 5\% + 0.71\,(7.5\%) = 10.33\%$
Market Value of Equity $= 2.05\ \text{BR} * 976.1 = 2{,}001\ \text{million BR}$
Current Cost of Capital
$= 10.33\%\,(2001/(2001+1520)) + 5.5\%\,(1-.32)\,(1520/(2001+1520)) = 7.48\%$

Based upon 1996 operating income, the optimal debt ratio for Aracruz is 0%. It is worth noting, however, that 1996 was a poor year for Aracruz, both in terms of revenues and operating income. In 1995, Aracruz had earnings before interest and taxes of 271 million BR. In Table 8.15, the cost of capital and the firm value are estimated under this operating income for different debt ratios.

Table 8.15   ARACRUZ CELLULOSE: COST OF CAPITAL, FIRM VALUE, AND DEBT RATIOS

Debt Ratio	Beta	Cost of Equity	Rating	Cost of Debt	AT Cost of Debt	Cost of Capital	Firm Value
0.00%	0.47	8.51%	AAA	5.20%	3.54%	8.51%	2,720 BR
10.00%	0.50	8.78%	AAA	5.20%	3.54%	8.25%	2,886 BR
20.00%	0.55	9.11%	AA	5.50%	3.74%	8.03%	3,042 BR
30.00%	0.60	9.53%	A	6.00%	4.08%	7.90%	3,148 BR
40.00%	0.68	10.10%	A−	6.25%	4.25%	7.76%	3,262 BR
50.00%	0.79	10.90%	BB	7.00%	4.76%	7.83%	3,205 BR
60.00%	0.95	12.09%	B−	9.25%	6.29%	8.61%	2,660 BR
70.00%	1.21	14.08%	CCC	10.00%	6.80%	8.98%	2,458 BR
80.00%	1.76	18.23%	CCC	10.00%	6.92%	9.18%	2,362 BR
90.00%	3.53	31.46%	CCC	10.00%	7.26%	9.68%	2,149 BR

Table 8.16   OPTIMAL DEBT RATIO AND OPERATING INCOME

EBIT	Optimal Debt Ratio
$15 (1996 level)	0%
$100	10%
$150	20%
$200	30%
$271 (1995 level)	40%

The optimal debt ratio, with gross debt, is 40%. It is not clear whether Aracruz can earn as much as it did in 1995 in a normal year. Table 8.16 summarizes the optimal debt ratios for intermediate levels of operating income between 1995 and 1996 levels.

Using the normalized operating income, we find that the optimal debt ratio is lower than the existing debt ratio of 43.17%, suggesting that Aracruz is overlevered, especially at existing levels of earnings.

IN PRACTICE: NORMALIZING OPERATING INCOME

In estimating optimal debt ratios, it is always more advisable to use normalized operating income rather than current operating income. Most analysts normalize earnings by taking the average earnings over a period of time (usually five years). Since this holds the scale of the firm fixed, it may not be appropriate for firms which have changed in size over time. The right way to normalize income will vary across firms:

1. For cyclical firms, whose current operating income may be overstated (if the economy is booming) or understated (if the economy is in recession), the operating income can be estimated using the average operating margin over an entire economic cycle (usually 5 to 10 years):

    Normalized EBIT = Average Operating Margin (Cycle) * Current Sales

2. For firms which have had a bad year in terms of operating income, due to firm-specific factors (such as the loss of a contract), the operating margin for the industry in which the firm operates can be used to calculate the normalized operating income:

    Normalized EBIT = Average Operating Margin (Industry) * Current Sales

The normalized operating income can also be estimated using returns on capital across an economic cycle (for cyclical firms) or an industry (for firms with firm-specific problems), but returns on capital are much more likely to be skewed by mismeasurement of capital and accounting differences across firms.

 There is a dataset on the Web that summarizes operating margins by industry group in the United States for the most recent quarter (**margin.xls**).

ADJUSTED PRESENT VALUE

In the adjusted present value approach, the firm value and leverage are connected using the value of the firm without debt as the starting point and adding the positive and negative value effects of leverage to it. In particular, when the primary benefit of borrowing is a tax benefit and the most significant cost of borrowing is the risk of bankruptcy, the value of a levered firm can be written as follows:

$$\text{Value of Levered Firm} = \text{Value of Unlevered Firm} + \text{Present Value of Tax Benefits of Debt} - \text{Present Value of Expected Bankruptcy Costs}$$

The value of the levered firm can then be estimated at different levels of the debt, and the debt level that maximizes firm value is the optimal debt ratio.

Value of Unlevered Firm

The first step in this approach is the estimation of the value of the unlevered firm. This can be accomplished by valuing the firm as if it had no debt (i.e., by discounting the expected after-tax operating cash flows at the unlevered cost of equity). In the special case where cash flows grow at a constant rate in perpetuity,

$$\text{Value of Unlevered Firm} = \text{FCFF}_0 \, (1 + g)/(\rho_u - g)$$

where FCFF_0 is the current after-tax operating cash flow to the firm, ρ_u is the unlevered cost of equity, and g is the expected growth rate.

The inputs needed for this valuation are the expected cash flows, growth rates, and the unlevered cost of equity. To estimate the latter, we can draw on our earlier analysis and compute the unlevered beta of the firm:

$$\beta_{\text{unlevered}} = \beta_{\text{current}}/[1 + (1 - t)D/E]$$

where $\beta_{\text{unlevered}}$ is the unlevered beta of the firm, β_{current} is the current equity beta of the firm, t is the tax rate for the firm, and D/E is the average debt/equity ratio during the regression. This unlevered beta can then be used to arrive at the unlevered cost of equity.

Expected Tax Benefit from Borrowing

The second step in this approach is the calculation of the expected tax benefit from taking on a given level of debt. This tax benefit is a function of the tax rate of the firm, and is discounted back at the cost of debt to reflect the riskiness of this cash flow. If the tax savings are viewed as a perpetuity, we have the following:

$$
\begin{aligned}
\text{Value of Tax Benefits} &= [\text{Tax Rate} * \text{Cost of Debt} * \text{Debt}] / \text{Cost of Debt} \\
&= \text{Tax Rate} * \text{Debt} \\
&= t_c D
\end{aligned}
$$

The tax rate referred to here is the firm's marginal tax rate, and the approach is general enough to allow it to change over time.

Estimating Expected Bankruptcy Costs

The third step is to evaluate the effect of the given level of debt on the default risk of the firm and on expected bankruptcy costs. In theory, at least, this requires the estimation of the probability of default with the additional debt and the direct and indirect cost of bankruptcy. If π_a is the probability of default after the additional debt and BC is the present value of the bankruptcy cost, the present value of expected bankruptcy cost can be estimated as follows:

$$\text{PV of Expected Bankruptcy Cost} = \text{Probability of Bankruptcy} * \text{PV of Bankruptcy Cost}$$
$$= \pi_a \, BC$$

This component of the adjusted present value approach poses the most significant estimation problem, since neither the probability of bankruptcy nor the bankruptcy cost can be estimated directly.

There are two basic ways in which the probability of bankruptcy can be indirectly estimated. One is to estimate a bond rating, as we did in the cost of capital approach, at each level of debt and use the empirical estimates of default probabilities for each rating. For instance, Table 8.17, based upon a study by Altman and Kishore, summarizes the probability of default over ten years by bond rating class.[13]

The other approach is to use a statistical approach, such as a *probit,* to estimate the probability of default based upon the firm's observable characteristics at each level of debt.

The bankruptcy cost can be estimated, albeit with considerable noise, from studies that have looked at the magnitude of this cost in actual bankruptcies. Combining the results of Warner (1977) on direct bankruptcy cost and shapiro (1989a) on indirect bankruptcy cost may provide a measure of the total bankruptcy costs faced by firms.

Table 8.17   **DEFAULT RATES BY BOND RATING CLASSES**

Rating	Default Probability
AAA	0.01%
AA	0.28%
A+	0.40%
A	0.53%
A−	1.41%
BBB	2.30%
BB	12.20%
B+	19.28%
B	26.36%
B−	32.50%
CCC	50.00%
CC	65.00%
C	80.00%
D	100.00%

---

[13]This study estimated default rates over ten years only for some of the ratings classes. We extrapolated the rest of the ratings.

■ **Probit:** This is a statistical technique that allows the probability of an event to be estimated as a function of the observable characteristics.

■ **Bankruptcy Cost:** This is the cost associated with going bankrupt. It includes both direct costs (from a firm going bankrupt) and indirect costs (arising from the perception that a firm may go bankrupt).

IN PRACTICE: USING PROBITS TO ESTIMATE THE PROBABILITY OF BANKRUPTCY

It is possible to estimate the probability of default using statistical techniques, when there is sufficient data available. For instance, if we have a dataset that lists all firms that went bankrupt during a period of time, as well as firms that did not go bankrupt during the same period, together with descriptive characteristics on these firms, a probit analysis can be used to estimate the likelihood of bankruptcy as a function of these characteristics. The steps involved in a probit analysis are as follows:

1. Identify the event of interest: Probits work best when the event either occurs or it does not. For bankruptcy, the event might be the filing for bankruptcy protection under the law.

2. Over a specified time period, collect information on all the firms that were exposed to the event. In the bankruptcy case, this would imply collecting information on which firms that filed for bankruptcy over a certain period (say, 5 years).

3. Based upon your knowledge of the event, and other research on it, specify measurable and observable variables that are likely to be good predictors of that event. In the case of bankruptcy, these might include excessive debt ratios, declining income, poor project returns and small market capitalization.

4. Collect information on these variables for the firms that filed for bankruptcy, at the time of the filing. Collect the same information for all other firms that were in existence at the same time, and which have data available on these variables. (If this is too data intensive, a random sampling of the firms that were not exposed to the event can be used.) In the bankruptcy analysis, this would imply collecting information on debt ratios, income trends, project returns and market capitalization for the firms that filed for bankruptcy at the time of the filing, and for all other firms across the period.

5. In a probit, the dependent variable is the occurrence of the specified event (1 if it occurs, 0 if it does not) and the independent variables are the variables specified in step 3. The output from the probit looks very much like the output from a multiple regression, with statistical significance attached to each of the independent variables.

Once the probit has been done, the probability of a firm defaulting can be estimated by plugging in that firm's values for the independent variables into the probit. The predicted value that emerges from the probit is the probability of default.

The Net Effect

The net effect of adding debt can be calculated by aggregating the costs and the benefits at each level of debt:

$$\text{Value of Levered Firm} = \text{FCFF}_0\,(1 + g)/(\rho_u - g) + t_c\,D - \pi_a\,BC$$

The debt level that maximizes firm value is the optimal debt ratio.

Benefits and Limitations of This Approach

The advantage of this approach is that it separates out the effects of debt into different components and allows the analyst to use different discount rates for each component. It does not make the assumption that the debt ratio stays unchanged forever, which is an implicit assumption in the cost of capital approach. Instead, it allows the analyst the flexibility to keep the dollar value of debt fixed, and calculate the benefits and costs of the fixed dollar debt.

These advantages have to be weighed off against the difficulty of estimating probabilities of default and the cost of bankruptcy. In fact, many analysts that use the adjusted present value approach ignore the expected bankruptcy costs, leading them to the conclusion that firm value increases monotonically with leverage.

 ILLUSTRATION 8.5   Using the Adjusted Present Value Approach to Calculate Optimal Debt Ratio for Disney in 1997

This approach can be applied to estimate the optimal capital structure for Disney. The first step is to estimate the value of the unlevered firm. To make this estimate, we start with the value of Disney as a firm in 1997 and net the effect of the tax savings and bankruptcy costs arising from the existing debt.

Value of Disney as a Firm in 1997: (Value of Equity + Value of Debt)	$50,888 + $11,180 = $62,068
−PV of Tax Savings from Existing Debt: (Existing Debt * Tax Rate)	$11,180 * 0.36 = $4,025
+ PV of Expected Bankruptcy Cost (Probability of Bankruptcy * Cost)	$62,068 * .25 * .0028 = $41
= Value of Disney as Unlevered Firm	$62,068 − $4,025 + $41 = $58,084

The probability of bankruptcy is estimated using the bond rating for Disney in 1997, which was AA, and the default probabilities in Table 8.17. The bankruptcy cost is assumed to be 25% of the firm value, prior to the tax savings.[14]

The next step in the process is to estimate the tax savings at different levels of debt (Table 8.18). While we use the standard approach of assuming that the present value is calculated over a perpetuity, we reduce the tax rate used in the calculation, if interest expenses exceed the earnings before interest and taxes. The adjustment to the tax rate is described more fully in the preceding section on the cost of capital.

---

[14]This estimate is based upon the Warner study, which estimates bankruptcy costs for large companies to be 10% of the value, and upon the qualitative analysis of indirect bankruptcy costs in Cornell and Shapiro.

Table 8.18 TAX SAVINGS FROM DEBT ($\tau_c D$)			
Debt Ratio	**$ Debt**	**Tax Rate**	**Tax Benefits**
0%	$0	36.00%	$0
10%	$6,207	36.00%	$2,234
20%	$12,414	36.00%	$4,469
30%	$18,621	36.00%	$6,703
40%	$24,827	36.00%	$8,938
50%	$31,034	36.00%	$11,172
60%	$37,241	36.00%	$13,407
70%	$43,448	35.43%	$15,394
80%	$49,655	31.00%	$15,394
90%	$55,862	24.71%	$15,394

Table 8.19 EXPECTED BANKRUPTCY COST			
Debt Ratio	**Bond Rating**	**Probability of Default**	**Expected Bankruptcy Cost**
0%	AAA	0.01%	$2
10%	AAA	0.01%	$2
20%	A+	0.40%	$62
30%	A−	1.41%	$219
40%	BB	12.20%	$1,893
50%	B	26.36%	$4,090
60%	CCC	50.00%	$7,759
70%	CC	65.00%	$10,086
80%	CC	65.00%	$10,086
90%	C	80.00%	$12,414

Note that the tax benefits of debt are capped at the level of current earnings before interest and taxes, which is $5,559 million. Beyond the 60% debt level, the interest expenses exceed the earnings before interest and taxes. The final step in the process is to estimate the expected bankruptcy cost, based upon the bond ratings, probabilities of default, and the assumption that the bankruptcy cost is 25% of firm value. Table 8.19 summarizes these probabilities.

The value of the levered firm is estimated in Table 8.20 by aggregating the effects of the tax savings and the expected bankruptcy costs.

The firm value is optimized at between 40% and 50% debt, which is consistent with the findings from the other approach. These findings are, however, very sensitive to both the estimate of bankruptcy cost, as a percent of firm value, and the probabilities of default.

This spreadsheet allows you to compute the value of a firm, with leverage, using the adjusted present value approach (**apy.xls**).

Debt Ratio	Unlevered Firm Value	Tax Benefits	Expected Bankruptcy Cost	Value of Levered Firm
0%	$58,084	$0	$2	$58,083
10%	$58,084	$2,234	$2	$60,317
20%	$58,084	$4,469	$62	$62,491
30%	$58,084	$6,703	$219	$64,569
40%	$58,084	$8,938	$1,893	$65,129
50%	$58,084	$11,172	$4,090	$65,166
60%	$58,084	$13,407	$7,759	$63,732
70%	$58,084	$15,394	$10,086	$63,392
80%	$58,084	$15,394	$10,086	$63,392
90%	$58,084	$15,394	$12,414	$61,065

Table 8.20 VALUE OF DISNEY WITH LEVERAGE

COMPARATIVE ANALYSIS

The most common approach to analyzing the debt ratio of a firm is to compare its leverage to that of "similar" firms. A simple way of doing this analysis is to compare a firm's debt ratio to the average debt ratio for the industry in which the firm operates. The underlying assumptions here are that firms within the same industry are comparable, and that, on average, these firms are operating at or close to their optimal. Both assumptions can be contested, however. Firms within the same industry can have different product mixes, different amount of operating risk, different tax rates, and different project returns; in fact, most do. For instance, Disney is considered part of the entertainment industry, but its mix of business is very different from that of Time Warner or Viacom. Furthermore, Disney's size and risk characteristics are very different from those of King World, which is also considered part of the same industry group. There is also anecdotal evidence that since firms try to mimic the industry average, the average debt ratio across an industry might not be at or even close to its optimal.

There is a dataset on the Web that summarizes market value and book value debt ratios, by industry, in addition to other relevant characteristics (**indcapst.xls**).

ILLUSTRATION 8.6 Estimating Debt Ratio Based upon Comparable Firms
In the following table, we report the debt ratios and financial characteristics of the firms that were considered by Value Line to be part of the entertainment group in July 1997.

Based upon the average debt ratios, Disney can be considered to be slightly underlevered in market value terms, since its debt ratio at 18.17% is lower than the average of 23.79%. This comparison, however, would not factor in the significant differences in both market capitalization and other characteristics across firms in this sample.

COMPANY NAME	MARKET DEBT RATIO	BOOK DEBT RATIO	TAX RATE	EBITDA/ VALUE	STANDARD DEVIATION IN OPER. INCOME
Disney (Walt)	18.19%	43.41%	43.58%	8.37%	22.57%
Time Warner	29.39%	68.34%	40.00%	6.80%	24.46%
Westinghouse Electric	26.98%	51.97%	36.00%	4.93%	30.92%
Viacom Inc. "A"	48.14%	46.54%	61.50%	14.55%	33.22%
Clear Channel	11.95%	58.60%	39.89%	3.14%	33.70%
BHC Communic. "A"	0.00%	0.00%	36.00%	5.04%	13.02%
Gaylord Entertainm. "A"	13.92%	41.47%	36.00%	8.71%	29.70%
Belo (A.H.) "A" Corp.	23.34%	63.04%	39.25%	10.93%	21.89%
Evergreen Media "A"	16.77%	39.45%	36.00%	9.62%	0.00%
Tele-Communications Intl Inc	23.28%	34.60%	36.00%	4.29%	0.00%
King World Productions	0.00%	0.00%	36.00%	12.72%	21.73%
Jacor Communications	30.91%	57.91%	47.53%	3.97%	62.07%
LIN Television	19.48%	71.66%	36.30%	9.78%	0.00%
Regal Cinemas	4.53%	15.24%	39.43%	7.38%	0.00%
Westwood One	11.40%	60.03%	36.00%	4.53%	76.55%
United Television	4.51%	15.11%	39.72%	6.91%	15.48%
Amer Radio Sys "A"	26.27%	45.49%	48.49%	4.98%	0.00%
Cox Radio "A" Inc.	0.00%	0.00%	39.49%	6.44%	0.00%
Le Groupe Videotron Ltee	74.97%	88.69%	36.00%	14.36%	25.24%
Spelling Entmt Group	33.76%	49.63%	64.05%	22.03%	30.28%
Western Int'l Communications	27.94%	44.66%	63.38%	9.74%	23.00%
Cinar Films Inc.	0.61%	2.08%	36.00%	3.11%	0.00%
SFX Broadcasting "A"	55.61%	83.59%	36.00%	7.07%	0.00%
Baton Broadcasting Inc.	36.50%	63.40%	70.56%	9.46%	32.97%
EMMIS Broad. "A"	24.35%	76.99%	40.48%	10.57%	0.00%
Scandinavian Broadcasting Sys.	34.17%	83.93%	36.00%	−8.11%	0.00%
Carmike Cinemas	43.44%	60.12%	36.00%	17.94%	29.50%
GC Companies Inc.	1.16%	2.10%	41.00%	18.10%	0.00%
Cineplex Odeon	54.38%	60.96%	36.00%	15.05%	59.60%
Quintel Entmt Inc	0.00%	0.00%	36.00%	5.40%	0.00%
Moffat Communications Ltd.	10.88%	24.77%	40.39%	16.41%	24.82%
Sinclair Broadcast Group	85.77%	85.53%	86.00%	21.64%	0.00%
Seattle FilmWorks	0.00%	0.00%	36.00%	7.46%	34.41%
Tele-Metropole	23.71%	38.53%	47.50%	18.54%	34.47%
Telemundo Group	49.26%	81.23%	80.33%	14.84%	0.00%
Silicon Gaming	0.59%	2.75%	36.00%	0.46%	0.00%
Boston Celtics LP	31.99%	79.82%	36.00%	8.11%	19.08%
AMC Entertainment	57.58%	76.15%	41.35%	47.87%	41.16%
Jones Intercable Inv LP	19.37%	68.07%	36.00%	13.31%	24.22%

COMPANY NAME	MARKET DEBT RATIO	BOOK DEBT RATIO	TAX RATE	EBITDA/ VALUE	STANDARD DEVIATION IN OPER. INCOME
All Amer Communications	58.34%	67.05%	41.98%	16.61%	44.26%
Clark (Dick) Prods.	0.00%	0.00%	38.26%	8.93%	43.57%
Granite Broadcasting	77.89%	100.90%	36.00%	15.56%	0.00%
CHUM Ltd.	0.00%	0.00%	48.45%	40.09%	20.05%
Boston Acoustics	0.00%	0.00%	36.00%	11.53%	28.26%
Price Communications	0.00%	0.00%	36.00%	−1.59%	118.47%
Image Entertainment	0.54%	1.58%	36.00%	19.09%	36.96%
Rentrak Corp	9.07%	30.73%	38.61%	19.99%	42.06%
Box Worldwide	0.00%	0.00%	36.00%	−5.37%	116.72%
Cinergi Pictures Entmt	21.72%	13.48%	36.00%	−14.93%	0.00%
Lancit Media Prods.	0.00%	0.00%	36.00%	−1.56%	51.29%
Electrohome Ltd.	70.87%	42.50%	50.42%	45.15%	36.55%
Average	23.79%	40.04%	42.51%	10.98%	25.53%

One way of controlling for these differences is to regress debt ratios against the variables that we showed to affect optimal debt ratios—tax rates, the standard deviation in operating income, and the cash flow generating capacity (EBITDA/Firm Value):

$$\text{Debt Ratio} = -0.1067 + 0.69\ \text{Tax Rate} + 0.61\ \text{EBITDA/Value} - 0.07\ \text{Std Dev in OI}$$
$$\quad\quad (0.90)\quad (2.58)\quad\quad\quad (2.21)\quad\quad\quad\quad\quad (0.60)$$

The R-squared of the regression is 27.16%. This regression can be used to arrive at a predicted value for Disney of:

$$\text{Predicted Debt Ratio} = -0.1067 + 0.69\ (.4358) + 0.61\ (.0837) - 0.07\ (.2257) = .2314$$

Based upon the capital structure of other firms in the entertainment industry, Disney should have a market value debt ratio of 23.14%.

Extending to the Market

To ensure comparability on debt ratios, a firm with similar tax rates, pretax returns as a fraction of the market value of the firm, and variance in operating income has to be identified. Note, though, that the firm need not be in the same industry nor produce the same product. The difficulty of finding such a firm gives rise to a second approach, whereby differences on these variables are controlled for when debt ratios are compared across firms. The simplest way to control for these differences, while using the maximum information available in the cross-section of firms, is to run a cross-sectional regression, regressing debt ratios against these variables:

$$\text{Debt Ratio} = \alpha_0 + \alpha_1 \text{ Tax Rate} + \alpha_2 \text{ Pretax Returns} + \alpha_3 \text{ Variance in Operating Income}$$

There are several advantages to this approach. Once the regression has been run and the basic relationship established (i.e., the intercept and coefficients have been estimated), the predicted debt ratio for any firm can be computed quickly using the measures of the independent variables for this firm. If a task involves calculating the optimal debt ratio for a large number of firms in a short time period, this may be the only practical way of approaching the problem, since using the cost of capital approach is time intensive.[15]

There are also limitations to this approach. The coefficients tend to be unstable and shift over time. Besides some standard statistical problems and errors in measuring the variables, these regressions also tend to explain only a small portion of the differences in debt ratios between firms.[16] However, they provide significantly more information than does a naive comparison of a firm's debt ratio to the industry average.

 There is a dataset on the Web that summarizes the latest debt ratio regression across the entire market (**Regress.xls**).

ILLUSTRATION 8.7   An Illustration of the Cross-sectional Approach

A cross-sectional regression of debt ratios against a number of relevant variables uses 1996 data for 2929 firms listed on the NYSE, AMEX, and NASDAQ databases. The regression provides the following results:

$$\text{DFR} = 0.1906 - 0.0552 \text{ PRVAR} - .1340 \text{ CLSH} - 0.3105 \text{ CPXFR} + 0.1447 \text{ FCP}$$
$$(37.97^a) \quad (2.20^a) \qquad\qquad (6.58^a) \qquad (8.52^a) \qquad\qquad (12.53^a)$$

where

DFR = Book Value of Debt / (Book Value of Debt + Market Value of Equity)
PRVAR = Variance in firm value
CLSH = Closely held shares as a percent of outstanding shares
CPXFR = Capital Expenditures / (Book Value of Debt + Book Value of Equity)
FCP = Free Cash Flow to Firm / Market Value of Equity

While the coefficients all have the right sign and are statistically significant, the regression itself has an R-squared of only 9.38%.

SIC: This is a four-digit industry code used by most services in the United States to classify firms. For a broader aggregation, the classification is often done using the first two digits of the code.

---

[15]There are some who have hypothesized that underleveraged firms are much more likely to be taken over than firms that are overleveraged or correctly leveraged. If an analyst wants to find the 100 firms on the New York Stock Exchange that are most underleveraged, the cross-sectional regression and the predicted debt ratios that come out of this regression can be used to find this group.

[16]The independent variables are correlated with each other. This multicollinearity makes the coefficients unreliable and they often have signs that go counter to intuition.

One way to improve the predictive power of the regression is to aggregate the data first and then do the regression. To illustrate using 1996 data, the firms are aggregated into two-digit SIC codes, and the same regression is rerun:

$$DFR = 0.2370 - 0.1854 \; PRVAR + .1407 \; CLSH + 1.3959 \; CPXFR - .6483 \; FCP$$
$$(6.06^a) \quad (1.96^b) \qquad\qquad (1.05) \qquad\qquad (5.73^a) \qquad\qquad (3.89^a)$$

Note that while the regression coefficients all preserve their signs, the size of the coefficients has changed and the R-squared of the regression has increased to 42.47%.

The other way to improve the regression is to transform the variables to conform more closely to the regression ideal, which is that the variables should be normally distributed.

8.8 OPTIMAL DEBT RATIOS BASED UPON COMPARABLE FIRMS

The predicted debt ratio from the regression shown above will generally yield

☐ a debt ratio similar to the optimal debt ratio from the cost of capital approach.

☐ a debt ratio higher than the optimal debt ratio from the cost of capital approach.

☐ a debt ratio lower than the optimal debt ratio from the cost of capital approach.

☐ any of the above, depending upon . . .

Explain.

CONCLUSION

This chapter has provided background on three tools that can be used to analyze capital structure.

• The first approach uses the cost of capital—the weighted average of the costs of equity, debt, and preferred stock—where the weights are market value weights and the costs of financing are current costs. The objective is to minimize the cost of capital, which also maximizes the value of the firm. A general framework is developed to use this model in real-world applications and applied to find the optimal financing mix for Disney. We find that Disney, which had almost $12 billion in debt in 1996, would minimize its cost of capital at a debt level of 40%, leading to an increase in market value of the firm of about $8.5 billion. Even allowing for a much-diminished operating income, we find that Disney has excess debt capacity.

• The second approach estimates the value of the firm at different levels of debt by adding the present value of the tax benefits from debt to the unlevered firm's value, and then subtracting out the present value of expected bankruptcy costs. The optimal debt ratio is the one that maximizes firm value.

• The final approach is to compare a firm's debt ratio to "similar" firms. While comparisons of firm debt ratios to an industry average are commonly made, they are generally not very useful in the presence of large differences among firms within the same industry. A cross-sectional regression of debt ratios against underlying financial variables brings in more information from the general population of firms and can be used to predict debt ratios for a large number of firms.

PROBLEMS AND QUESTIONS

1. Rubbermaid Corporation, a manufacturer of consumer plastic products, is evaluating its capital structure. The balance sheet of the company is as follows (in millions):

Assets		Liabilities	
Fixed Assets	4000	Debt	2500
Current Assets	1000	Equity	2500

In addition, you are provided with the following information:

   a. The debt is in the form of long term-bonds, with a coupon rate of 10%. The bonds are currently rated AA and are selling at a yield of 12%. (The market value of the bonds is 80% of the face value).
   b. The firm currently has 50 million shares outstanding, and the current market price is $80 per share. The firm pays a dividend of $4 per share and has a price/earnings ratio of 10.
   c. The stock currently has a beta of 1.2. The six-month Treasury bill rate is 8%.
   d. The tax rate for this firm is 40%.
   (1) What is the debt/equity ratio for this firm in book value terms? in market value terms?
   (2) What is the debt/(debt+equity) ratio for this firm in book value terms? in market value terms?
   (3) What is the firm's after-tax cost of debt?
   (4) What is the firm's cost of equity?
   (5) What is the firm's current cost of capital?

2. Now assume that Rubbermaid Corporation has a project that requires an initial investment of $100 million and has the following projected income statement:

EBIT	$20 million
−Interest	$4 million
EBT	$16 million
Taxes	$6.40 million
Net Income	$9.60 million

(Depreciation for the project is expected to be $5 million a year forever.)

This project is going to be financed at the same debt/equity ratio as the overall firm and is expected to last forever. Assume that there are no principal repayments on the debt (it too is perpetual).

   (1) Evaluate this project from the equity investors' standpoint. Does it make sense?
   (2) Evaluate this project from the firm's standpoint. Does it make sense?
   (3) In general, when would you use the cost of equity as your discount rate/benchmark?
   (4) In general, when would you use the cost of capital as your hurdle rate?
   (5) Assume, for economies of scale, that this project is going to be financed *entirely* with debt. What would you use as your cost of capital for evaluating this project?

3. Rubbermaid is considering a major change in its capital structure. It has three options:

Option 1: Issue $1 billion in new stock and repurchase half of its outstanding debt. This will make it a AAA rated firm. (AAA rated debt is yielding 11% in the marketplace.)

Option 2: Issue $1 billion in new debt and buy back stock. This will drop its rating to A−. (A− rated debt is yielding 13% in the marketplace.)

Option 3: Issue $3 billion in new debt and buy back stock. This will drop its rating to CCC. (CCC rated debt is yielding 18% in the marketplace.)

   (1) What is the cost of equity under each option?
   (2) What is the after-tax cost of debt under each option?
   (3) What is the cost of capital under each option?
   (4) What would happen to (a) the value of the firm; (b) the value of debt and equity; and (c) the stock price under each option, if you assume rational stockholders?
   (5) From a cost of capital standpoint, which of the three options would you pick, or would you stay at your current capital structure?
   (6) What role (if any) would the variability in Rubbermaid's income play in your decision?

(7) How would your analysis change (if at all) if the money under the three options listed above were used to make new investments (instead of repurchasing debt or equity)?

(8) What other considerations (besides minimizing the cost of capital) would you bring to bear on your decision?

(9) Intuitively, why doesn't the higher rating in option 1 translate into a lower cost of capital?

4. Rubbermaid Corporation is interested in how it compares with its competitors in the same industry.

	Rubbermaid Corporation	Other Competitors
Debt/Equity Ratio	50%	25%
Variance in EBITDA	20%	40%
EBITDA/MV of firm	25%	15%
Tax rate	40%	30%
R&D/sales	2%	5%

a. Considering each of these variables, explain at an intuitive level whether you would expect Rubbermaid to have more or less debt than its competitors and why.

b. You have also run a regression of debt/equity ratios against these variables for all the firms on the New York Stock Exchange and have come up with the following regression equation:

$$D/E = .10 - .5 \text{ (Variance in EBITDA)} + 2.0 \text{ (EBITDA/MV)} + .4 \text{ (Tax rate)} + 2.5 \text{ (R\&D/sales)}$$

(All inputs to the regression were in decimals; that is, 20% was input as .20 . . . .)

Given this cross-sectional relationship, what would you expect Rubbermaid's debt/equity ratio to be?

5. As CEO of a major corporation, you have to make a decision on how much you can afford to borrow. You currently have 10 million shares outstanding, and the market price per share is $50. You also currently have about $200 million in debt outstanding (market value). You are rated as a BBB corporation now.

a. Your stock has a beta of 1.5 and the Treasury bond rate is 8%.

b. Your marginal tax rate is 46%.

c. You estimate that your rating will change to a B if you borrow $100 million. The BBB rate now is 11%. The B rate is 12.5%.

(1) Given the marginal costs and benefits of borrowing the $100 million, should you go ahead with it?

(2) What is your best estimate of the weighted average cost of capital with and without the $100 million in borrowing?

(3) If you do borrow the $100 million, what will the price per share be after the borrowing?

(4) Assume that you have a project that requires an investment of $100 million. It has expected before-tax revenues of $50 million and costs of $30 million a year in perpetuity. Is this a desirable project by your criteria? Why or why not?

(5) Does it make a difference in your decision if you are told that the cash flows from the project in (4) are certain?

6. You have been hired as a management consultant by AD Corporation to evaluate whether it has an appropriate amount of debt. (The company is worried about a leveraged buyout.) You have collected the following information on AD's current position:

a. There are 100,000 shares outstanding, at $20 a share. The stock has a beta of 1.15.

b. The company has $500,000 in long-term debt outstanding and is currently rated as a "BBB." The current market interest rate is 10% on BBB bonds and 6% on Treasury bills.

c. The company's marginal tax rate is 40%.

You proceed to collect the data on what increasing debt will do to the company's ratings:

Additional Debt*	New Rating	Interest Rate
$500,000	BB	10.5
$1,000,000	B	11.5
$1,500,000	B−	13.5
$2,000,000	C	15

*In addition to the existing debt of $500,000:

(1) How much additional debt should the company take on?

(2) What will the price per share be after the company takes on new debt?

(3) What is the weighted average cost of capital before and after the additional debt?

(4) Assume that you are considering a project that has the following earnings in perpetuity, and is of comparable risk to existing projects.

Revenues/year	$1,000,000
Cost of goods sold	$400,000 (includes depreciation of $100,000)
EBIT	$600,000
Debt payments	$100,000 (all interest payments)
Taxable income	$500,000
Tax	$200,000
After-tax profit	$300,000

If this project requires an investment of $3 million, what is its NPV?

7. UB Inc. is examining its capital structure with the intent of arriving at an optimal debt ratio. It currently has no debt and has a beta of 1.5. The riskless interest rate is 9%. Your research indicates that the debt rating will be as follows at different debt levels.

D/(D+E)	Rating	Interest Rate
0%	AAA	10%
10%	AA	10.5%
20%	A	11%
30%	BBB	12%
40%	BB	13%
50%	B	14%
60%	CCC	16%
70%	CC	18%
80%	C	20%
90%	D	25%

The firm currently has 1 million shares outstanding at $20 per share (tax rate = 40%).

a. What is the firm's optimal debt ratio?

b. Assuming that the firm restructures by repurchasing stock with debt, what will the value of the stock be after the restructuring?

8. GenCorp, an automotive parts manufacturer, currently has $25 million in outstanding debt and has 10 million shares outstanding. The book value per share is $10, while the market value is $25. The company is currently rated A, and its bonds have a yield to maturity of 10%, and the current beta of the stock is 1.06. The six-month Treasury bond rate is 8% now, and the company's tax is 40%.

a. What is the company's current weighted average cost of capital?

b. The company is considering a repurchase of 4 million shares at $25 per share with new debt. It is estimated that this will push the company's rating down to a B (with a yield to maturity of 13%). What will the company's weighted average cost of capital be after the stock repurchase?

9. You have been called in as a consultant for Herbert's Inc., a sporting goods retail firm, which is examining its debt policy. The firm currently has a balance sheet that looks as follows:

Liability		Assets	
LT bonds	$100	Fixed Assets	300
Equity	$300	Current assets	100
Total	$400	Total	400

The firm's income statement is as follows:

Revenues	250
COGS	175
Depreciation	25
EBIT	50
LT interest	10
EBT	40
Taxes	16
Net income	24

The firm currently has 100 shares outstanding, selling at a market price of $5 per share, and the bonds are selling at par. The firm's current beta is 1.12, and the Treasury bond rate is 7%.

a. What is the firm's current cost of equity?

b. What is the firm's current cost of debt?

c. What is the firm's current weighted average cost of capital?

Assume that management of Herbert's Inc. is considering doing a debt equity swap (i.e., borrowing enough money to buy back 70 shares of stock at $5 per share). It is believed that this swap will lower the firm's rating to C and raise the interest rate on the company's debt to 15%.

    d. What is the firm's new cost of equity?
    e. What is the effective tax rate (for calculating the after-tax cost of debt) after the swap?
    f. What is the firm's new cost of capital?

10. Terck Inc., a leading pharmaceutical company, currently has a balance sheet as follows:

Liability		Assets	
LT Bonds	$1000	Fixed assets	1700
Equity	$1000	Current assets	300
Total	$1000	Total	1000

The firm's income statement looks as follows:

Revenues	1000
COGS	400
Depreciation	100
EBIT	500
LT interest	100
EBT	400
Taxes	200
Net income	200

The firm's bonds are all 20-year bonds with a coupon rate of 10% and are selling at 90% of face value. (The yield to maturity on these bonds is 11%.) The stocks are selling at a PE ratio of 9 and have a beta of 1.25. The Treasury bond rate is 6%. [Cost of debt = 10%; tax rate = 40%]

    a. What is the firm's current cost of equity?
    b. What is the firm's current after-tax cost of debt?
    c. What is the firm's current weighted average cost of capital?

Assume that management of Terck Inc., which is very conservative, is considering doing an equity-for-debt swap (i.e., issuing $200 more of equity to retire $200 of debt). This action is expected to lower the firm's interest rate by 1%.

    d. What is the firm's new cost of equity?
    e. What is the new WACC?
    f. What will the value of the firm be after the swap?

11. You have been asked to analyze the capital structure of DASA Inc., an environmental waste disposal firm, and to make recommendations on a future course of action. DASA Inc. has 40 million shares outstanding, selling at $20 per share, and a debt equity ratio (in market value terms) of 0.25. The beta of the stock is 1.15 and the firm currently has a AA rating, with a corresponding market interest rate of 10%. The firm's income statement is as follows:

EBIT	$150 million
Interest exp.	$20 million
Taxable income	$130 million
Taxes	$52 million
Net income	$78 million

The current Treasury bond rate is 8%. Tax rate = 40%.

    a. What is the firm's current weighted average cost of capital?
    b. The firm is proposing borrowing an additional $200 million in debt and repurchasing stock. If it does so, its rating will decline to A, with a market interest rate of 11%. What will the weighted average cost of capital be if the firm makes this move?
    c. What will the new stock price be if the firm borrows $200 million and repurchases stock (assuming rational investors)?

12. You have been asked by JJ Corporation, a California-based firm that manufactures and services digital satellite television systems, to evaluate its capital structure. They currently have 70 million shares outstanding trading at $10 per share. In addition, it has 500,000 ten-year convertible bonds, with a coupon rate of 8%, trading at $1000 per bond. JJ Corporation is rated BBB, and the interest rate on BBB straight bonds is currently 10%. The beta for the company is 1.2, and the current risk-free rate is 6%. The tax rate is 40%.

    a. What is the firm's current debt/equity ratio?

b. What is the firm's current weighted average cost of capital?

JJ Corporation is proposing to borrow $250 million to use for the following purposes:

> Buy back $100 million worth of stock.
>
> Pay $100 million in dividends.
>
> Invest $50 million in a project with a NPV of $25 million.

The effect of this additional borrowing will be a drop in the bond rating to B, which currently carries an interest rate of 11%.

c. What will the firm's cost of equity be after this additional borrowing?

d. What will the firm's weighted average cost of capital be after this additional borrowing?

e. What will the value of the firm be after this additional borrowing?

13. Pfizer, one of the largest pharmaceutical companies in the United States, is considering its debt capacity. In March 1995, Pfizer had an outstanding market value of equity of $24.27 billion, debt of $2.8 billion, and a AAA rating. Its beta was 1.47, and it faced a marginal corporate tax rate of 40%. The Treasury bond rate at the time of the analysis was 6.50%, and AAA bonds trade at a spread of 0.30% over the Treasury rate.

a. Estimate the current cost of capital for Pfizer.

b. It is estimated that Pfizer will have a BBB rating if it moves to a 30% debt ratio and that BBB bonds have a spread of 2% over the Treasury rate. Estimate the cost of capital if Pfizer moves a 30% debt ratio.

c. Assuming a constant growth rate of 6% in the firm value, how much will firm value change if Pfizer moves its optimal? What will the effect be on the stock price?

d. Pfizer has considerable research and development expenses. Will this fact affect whether Pfizer takes on the additional debt?

14. Upjohn, another major pharmaceutical company, is also considering whether it should borrow more. It has $664 million in book value of debt outstanding and 173 million shares outstanding at $30.75 per share. The company has a beta of 1.17 and faces a tax rate of 36%. The Treasury bond rate is 6.50%.

a. If the interest expense on the debt is $55 million, the debt has an average maturity of 10 years, and the company is currently rated AA− (with a market interest rate of 7.50%), estimate the market value of the debt.

b. Estimate the current cost of capital.

c. It is estimated that if Upjohn moves to its optimal debt ratio, and no growth in firm value is assumed, the value per share will increase by $1.25. Estimate the cost of capital at the optimal debt ratio.

15. Bethlehem Steel, one of the oldest and largest steel companies in the United States, is considering the question of whether it has any excess debt capacity. The firm has $527 million in market value of debt outstanding and $1.76 billion in market value of equity. The firm has earnings before interest and taxes of $131 million, and faces a corporate tax rate of 36%. The company's bonds are rated BBB, and the cost of debt is 8%. At this rating, the firm has a probability of default of 2.30%, and the cost of bankruptcy is expected to be 30% of firm value. The T. Bond rate is 6.5%.

a. Estimate the unlevered value of the firm.

b. Estimate the levered value of the firm, using the adjusted present value approach, at a debt ratio of 50%. At that debt ratio, the firm's bond rating will be CCC, and the probability of default will increase to 46.61%.

16. Kansas City Southern, a railroad company, had debt outstanding of $985 million and 40 million shares trading at $46.25 per share in March 1995. It earned $203 million in earnings before interest and taxes and faced a marginal tax rate of 36.56%. The firm was interested in estimating its optimal leverage using the adjusted present value approach. The following table summarizes the estimated bond ratings and probabilities of default at each level of debt from 0% to 90%.

Debt Ratio (%)	Bond Rating	Probability of Default (%)
0	AAA	0.28
10	AAA	0.28
20	A−	1.41
30	BB	12.20
40	B−	32.50
50	CCC	46.61
60	CC	65.00
70	C	80.00
80	C	80.00
90	D	100.00

(Assume marginal tax rate does not change) The direct and indirect bankruptcy cost is estimated to be 25% of the firm value. Estimate the optimal debt ratio of the firm, based on levered firm value. The T. Bond rate is 7%.

17. In 1995, an analysis of the capital structure of Reebok provided the following results on the weighted average cost of capital and firm value.

	Actual	Optimal	Change
Debt ratio	4.42%	60.00%	55.58%
Beta for the stock	1.95	3.69	1.74
Cost of equity	18.61%	28.16%	9.56%
Bond rating	A−	B+	
After-tax cost of debt	5.92%	6.87%	0.95%
WACC	18.04%	15.38%	−2.66%
Firm value (with no growth)	$3,343 mil	$3,921 mil	$578 mil
Stock price	$39.50	$46.64	$7.14

This analysis was based on the 1995 earnings before interest and taxes of $420 million and a tax rate of 36.90%.

   a. Why is the optimal debt ratio for Reebok so high?

   b. What might be some of your concerns in moving to this optimal?

18. Timberland Inc., a manufacturer and retailer of footwear and sportswear, is considering its highly levered status. In 1995, the firm had $237 million in market value of debt outstanding and 11 million shares outstanding at $19.88 per share. The firm had earnings before interest and taxes of $44 million, a book value of capital of $250 million, and a tax rate of 37%. The Treasury bond rate is 7.88%, and the stock has a beta of 1.26. The following table summarizes the estimated bond ratings and interest rates at different levels of debt for Timberland:

Debt Ratio (%)	Bond Rating	Interest Rate on Debt (%)
0	AAA	8.18
10	AAA	8.18
20	A+	8.88
30	A	9.13
40	A−	9.38
50	BB	10.38
60	BB	10.38
70	B	11.88
80	B−	12.88
90	CCC	13.88

   a. Estimate the optimal debt ratio, using the cost of capital approach.

19. You are trying to evaluate whether United Airlines has any excess debt capacity. In 1995, UAL had 12.2 million shares outstanding at $210 per share and debt outstanding of approximately $3 billion (book as well as market value). The debt had a rating of B and carried a market interest rate of 10.12%. In addition, the firm had leases outstanding, with annual lease payments anticipated to be $150 million. The beta of the stock is 1.26, and the firm faces a tax rate of 35%. The Treasury bond rate is 6.12%.

   a. Estimate the current debt ratio for UAL.

   b. Estimate the current cost of capital.

   c. Based on 1995 operating income, the optimal debt ratio is computed to be 30%, at which point the rating will be BBB, and the market interest rate is 8.12%. Estimate the cost of capital and firm value at the optimal.

   d. Would the fact that 1995 operating income for airlines was depressed alter your analysis in any way? Explain why.

20. Intel has earnings before interest and taxes of $3.4 billion and faces a marginal tax rate of 36.50%. It currently has $1.5 billion in debt outstanding and a market value of equity of $51 billion. The beta for the stock is 1.35, and the pretax cost of debt is 6.80%. The Treasury bond rate is 6%. Assume that the firm is considering a massive increase in leverage to a 70% debt ratio, at which level the bond rating will be C (with a pretax interest rate of 16%).

a. Estimate the current cost of capital.

b. Assuming that all debt is refinanced at the new market interest rate, what would your interest expenses be at 70% debt? Would you be able to get the entire tax benefit? Why or why not?

c. Estimate the beta of the stock at 70% debt, using the conventional levered beta calculation. Reestimate the beta, on the assumption that C rated debt has a beta of 0.60. Which one would you use in your cost of capital calculation?

d. Estimate the cost of capital at 70% debt.

e. What will happen to firm value if Intel moves to a 70% debt ratio?

f. What general lessons on capital structure would you draw for other growth firms?

21. NYNEX, the phone utility for the New York Area, has approached you for advice on its capital structure. In 1995, NYNEX had debt outstanding of $12.14 billion and equity outstanding of $20.55 billion. The firm had earnings before interest and taxes of $1.7 billion, and faced a corporate tax rate of 36%. The beta for the stock is 0.84, and the bonds are rated A− (with a market interest rate of 7.5%). The probability of default for A− rated bonds is 1.41%, and the bankruptcy cost is estimated to be 30% of firm value. The T. Bond rate is 6.5%.

a. Estimate the unlevered value of the firm.

b. Value the firm if it increases its leverage to 50%. At that debt ratio, its bond rating would be BBB, and the probability of default would be 2.30%.

c. Assume now that NYNEX is considering a move into entertainment, which is likely to be both more profitable and riskier than

the phone business. What changes would you expect in the optimal leverage?

22. A small, private firm has approached you for advice on its capital structure decision. It is in the specialty retailing business, and it had earnings before interest and taxes last year of $500,000.

- The book value of equity is $1.5 million, but the estimated market value is $6 million.
- The firm has $1 million in 5-year debt outstanding and paid an interest expense of $80,000 on the debt last year. (Based on the interest coverage ratio, the firm would be rated AA and would be facing an interest rate of 8.25%.)
- The equity is not traded, but the average beta for comparable traded firms is 1.05, and their average debt/equity ratio is 25%. The T. Bond rate is 7%.

a. Estimate the current cost of capital for this firm.

b. Assume now that this firm doubles its debt from $1 million to $2 million, and that the interest rate at which it can borrow increases to 9%. Estimate the new cost of capital, and the effect on firm value.

c. You also have a regression that you have run of debt ratios of publicly traded firms against firm characteristics:

$$DBTFR = 0.15 + 1.05 \, (EBIT/FIRM \ VALUE) - 0.10 \, (BETA)$$

Estimate the debt ratio for the private firm, based on this regression.

d. What are some of the concerns you might have in extending the approaches used by large publicly traded firms to estimate optimal leverage to smaller firms?

23. XCV Inc., which manufactures automobile parts for assembly, is considering the costs and the benefits of leverage. The CFO notes that the return on equity of the firm, which is only 12.75% now, based on the current policy of no leverage, could be increased substantially by borrowing money. Is this true? Does it follow that the value of the firm will increase with leverage? Why or why not?

24. You have been provided the information on the after-tax cost of debt and cost of capital that a company will have at a 10% debt ratio, and asked to estimate the after-tax cost of debt and cost of capital at 20%. The long term treasury bond rate is 7%.

Debt Ratio	10%	20%	Extra Column
$ Debt	$1,500		
EBIT	$1,000		
Interest Expenses	$120		
Interest Coverage Ratio	8.33		
Bond Rating	AA		
Interest Rate	8.00%		
After-tax Cost of Debt	4.80%		
Beta	1.06		
Cost of Equity	12.83%		
Cost of Capital	12.03%		

The interest coverage ratios, ratings and spreads are as follows:

Coverage Ratio	Rating	Spread over Treasury
> 10	AAA	0.30%
7–10	AA	1.00%
5–7	A	1.50%
3–5	BBB	2.00%
2–3	BB	2.50%
1.25–2	B	3.00%
0.75–1.25	CCC	5.00%
0.50–0.75	CC	6.50%
0.25–0.50	C	8.00%
< 0.25	D	10.00%

25. CSL Corporation is a mid-sized transportation firm with 10 million shares outstanding, trading at $25 per share and debt outstanding of $50 million. It is estimated that the cost of capital, which is currently 11%, will drop to 10%, if the firm borrows $100 million and buys back stock. Estimate the expected change in the stock price if the expected growth rate in operating earnings over time is 5%.

26. You have run a regression of changes in firm value against changes in long term bond rates and arrived at the following regression:

Change in Firm Value = 0.16 − 5.00 Change in Long Term Bond Rate

The firm has $100 million in zero-coupon two-year notes outstanding, and plans to borrow another $150 million using zero-coupon securities. If your objective is to match the duration of the financing to those of the assets, what should the maturity of these zero-coupon notes be?

27. You have been asked to assess analyze the financial mix for ServiStar, a privately owned chain of hardware stores, and have been provided with the following information on the firm:
   a. The firm has $4.5 million in bank debt outstanding on its books, and it had interest payments of $300,000 in the most recent year. The book value of equity was $2 million.
   b. The firm had a return on equity of 21% in the most recent year, and the average PE ratio of publicly traded hardware firms is 20.
   c. The firm faces a tax rate of 40%, and was able to claim $250,000 in depreciation in the most recent year.

   Estimate the following inputs for this firm:
   Estimated Market Value of Firm =
   Estimated EBITDA =
   Current Market Value Debt Ratio =

————— LIVE CASE STUDY

VI. OPTIMAL CAPITAL STRUCTURE

Objective: To estimate the optimal mix of debt and equity for this firm, based upon its characteristics and constraint.

Key Questions

- Based upon the cost of capital approach, what is the optimal debt ratio for your firm?
- Bringing in reasonable constraints into the decision process, what would your recommended debt ratio be for this firm?
- Does your firm have too much or too little debt relative to the sector? relative to the market?

Framework for Analysis

1. Cost of Capital Approach

- What is the current cost of capital for the firm?
- What happens to the cost of capital as the debt ratio is changed?
- At what debt ratio is the cost of capital minimized and firm value maximized? (If they are different, explain)
- What will happen to the firm value if the firm moves to its optimal?
- What will happen to the stock price if the firm moves to the optimal, and stockholders are rational?

2. Building Constraints into the Process

- What rating does the company have at the optimal debt ratio? If you were to impose a rating constraint, what would it be? Why? What is the optimal debt ratio with this rating constraint?
- How volatile is the operating income? What is the "normalized" operating income of this firm and what is the optimal debt ratio of the firm at this level of income?

3. Relative Analysis

- Relative to the sector to which this firm belongs, does it have too much or too little in debt? (Do a regression, if necessary)
- Relative to the rest of the firms in the market, does it have too much or too little in debt? (Use the market regression, if necessary)

Getting Information on Optimal Capital Structure

To get the inputs needed to estimate the optimal capital structure, examine the 10-K report (**www.sec.gov/edgarhp.htm**) or the annual report. The ratings, interest coverage ratios and default spreads come from the ratings table on my web site (**ratings.xls**).

The market regression for debt ratios is available on my web site (**regress.xls**). You can download information on other firms in the sector individually or look at the Value Line pages corresponding to each of these firms. You can get a list of the comparable firms on the web site (**www.dailystocks.com**—enter a symbol and pick the industry comparison).

To estimate the optimal capital structure for your firm, you can use the excel spreadsheet on my web site titled **capstr.xls,** and enter the inputs for your firm. The ratings and coverage ratios are built into the spreadsheet.

CHAPTER 9

CAPITAL STRUCTURE—
THE FINANCING DETAILS

In this chapter, we complete our analysis of the financing decision by building on the discussion of optimal capital structure initiated in the previous chapter. In particular, we examine the following questions:

- When the actual and optimal debt ratios differ, what is the best path for moving from the actual to the optimal?
- When and how should firms increase or decrease leverage *quickly*?
- When and how should firms increase or decrease leverage *gradually*?
- What is the appropriate financing mix for a firm? In particular, how should firms decide on the maturity, currency mix, and special features for their debt issues?
- How do tax, agency cost, and information asymmetry affect the financing mix?

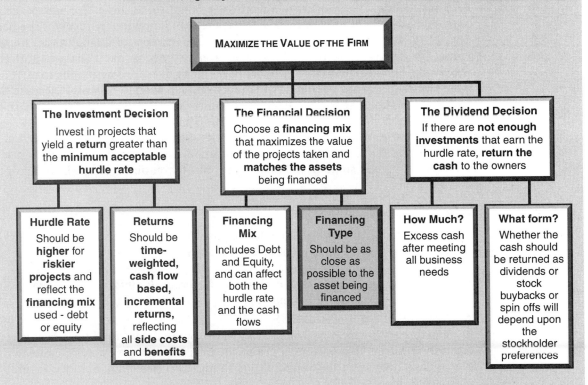

MAXIMIZE THE VALUE OF THE FIRM

The Investment Decision
Invest in projects that yield a **return** greater than the **minimum acceptable hurdle rate**

The Financial Decision
Choose a **financing mix** that maximizes the value of the projects taken and **matches the assets** being financed

The Dividend Decision
If there are **not enough investments** that earn the hurdle rate, **return the cash** to the owners

Hurdle Rate
Should be **higher** for **riskier projects** and reflect the **financing mix** used - debt or equity

Returns
Should be **time-weighted, cash flow based, incremental returns**, reflecting all **side costs** and **benefits**

Financing Mix
Includes Debt and Equity, and can affect both the hurdle rate and the cash flows

Financing Type
Should be as close as possible to the asset being financed

How Much?
Excess cash after meeting all business needs

What form?
Whether the cash should be returned as dividends or stock buybacks or spin offs will depend upon the stockholder preferences

A FRAMEWORK FOR CAPITAL STRUCTURE CHANGES

A firm whose actual debt ratio is very different from its optimal has several choices to make. First, it has to decide *whether to move toward the optimal or preserve the status quo.* Second, once it decides to move toward the optimal, the firm has to choose *between changing its leverage quickly or moving more deliberately.* This decision may also be governed by pressure from external sources, such as impatient stockholders or bond ratings agency concerns. Third, if the firm decides to move gradually to the optimal, it has to decide whether to use new financing *to take new projects, or to shift its financing mix on existing projects.*

In the previous chapter, we presented the rationale for moving toward the optimal in terms of the value that could be gained for stockholders by doing so. Conversely, the cost of preserving the status quo is the loss of this potential value increment. While managers make this decision, they will often find themselves under some pressure from stockholders, if they are underlevered, or under threat of bankruptcy, if they are overlevered, to move toward their optimal debt ratios.

IMMEDIATE OR GRADUAL CHANGE

When firms are significantly underlevered or overlevered, they have to decide whether to adjust their leverage quickly or gradually over time. The advantage of a prompt movement to the optimal is that the firm immediately receives the benefits of the optimal leverage, which include a lower cost of capital and a higher value. The disadvantage of a sudden change in leverage is that it changes both the way and the environment in which managers make decisions within the firm. If the optimal debt ratio has been misestimated, a sudden change may also increase the risk that the firm may have to backtrack and reverse its financing decisions. To illustrate, assume that a firm's optimal debt ratio has been calculated to be 40% and that the firm moves to this optimal from its current debt ratio of 10%. A few months later, the firm discovers that its optimal debt ratio is really 30%. It will then have to repay some of the debt that it has taken on to get back to the optimal leverage.

Underlevered Firms

For underlevered firms, the decision to increase the debt ratio to the optimal quickly or gradually is determined by a number of factors:

1. *Degree of Confidence in the Optimal Leverage Estimate:*   The greater the noise in the estimate of optimal leverage, the more likely the firm will choose to move gradually to the optimal.

2. *Comparability to Peer Group:*   When the optimal debt ratio for a firm is very different from that of its peer group, the firm is much less likely to move to the optimal quickly because analysts and ratings agencies might not look favorably on the change.

3. ***Likelihood of a Takeover:***   Empirical studies of the characteristics of target firms in acquisitions have noted that underleveraged firms are much more likely to be acquired than are overlevered firms.[1] Often, the acquisition is financed at least partially by the target firm's unused debt capacity. Consequently, firms with excess debt capacity which delay increasing debt run the risk of being taken over; the greater this risk, the more likely the firm will choose to take on additional debt quickly.

    A number of factors may determine the likelihood of a takeover. One is the prevalence of antitakeover laws (at the state level) and amendments (at the firm level) designed specifically to prevent the possibility of hostile acquisitions. Another is the size of the firm; the larger the firm, the more protected it may feel from hostile takeovers. The third is the extent of holdings by insiders and managers in the company; insiders and managers with substantial stakes may be able to preempt hostile acquisitions.

4. ***Need for Financing Slack:***   On occasion, firms may require financial slack to meet unanticipated needs for funds, either to keep existing projects going, or to take on new ones. Firms that need and value financial slack will be less likely to move quickly to their optimal debt ratios and use up their excess debt capacity.

Financing Slack: The financing slack is the difference between the debt that a firm chooses to carry and the optimal debt that it could carry, when the former is less than the latter.

ILLUSTRATION 9.1   Debt Capacity and Takeovers

The Disney acquisition of Capital Cities, while a friendly acquisition, illustrates some of the advantages to the acquiring firm of acquiring an underlevered firm. Capital Cities at the time of the acquisition had $657 million in outstanding debt, and 154.06 million shares outstanding trading at $100 per share; its market value debt ratio was only 4.07%. With a beta of 0.95, a borrowing rate of 7.70%, and a corporate tax rate of 43.50%, this yielded a cost of capital of 11.90%. (The Treasury bond rate at the time of the analysis was 7%.)

$$\text{Cost of Capital} = 12.23\% \ (15{,}406/(15{,}406 + 657)) + 7.70\% \ (1 - .435) \ (657/(15{,}406 + 657))$$
$$= 11.90\%$$

The following table summarizes the costs of equity, debt, and capital, as well as the estimated firm values and stock prices at different debt ratios for Capital Cities:

Debt Ratio	Beta	Cost of Equity	Interest Coverage Ratio	Bond Rating	Interest Rate	Cost of Debt	Cost of Capital	Firm Value	Stock Price
0.00%	0.93	12.10%	∞	AAA	7.30%	4.12%	12.10%	$15,507	$96.41
10.00%	0.99	12.42%	10.73	AAA	7.30%	4.12%	11.59%	$17,007	$106.15

[1]Palepu (1986) notes that one of the variables that seems to predict a takeover is a low debt ratio, in conjunction with poor operating performance.

Debt Ratio	Beta	Cost of Equity	Interest Coverage Ratio	Bond Rating	Interest Rate	Cost of Debt	Cost of Capital	Firm Value	Stock Price
20.00%	1.06	12.82%	4.75	A	8.25%	4.66%	11.19%	$18,399	$115.19
30.00%	1.15	13.34%	2.90	BBB	9.00%	5.09%	10.86%	$19,708	$123.69
40.00%	1.28	14.02%	1.78	B	11.00%	6.22%	10.90%	$19,546	$122.63
50.00%	1.45	14.99%	1.21	CCC	13.00%	7.35%	11.17%	$18,496	$115.81
60.00%	1.71	16.43%	1.00	CCC	13.00%	7.35%	10.98%	$19,228	$120.57
70.00%	2.37	20.01%	0.77	CC	14.50%	9.63%	12.74%	$13,939	$86.23
80.00%	3.65	27.08%	0.61	C	16.00%	11.74%	14.81%	$10,449	$63.58
90.00%	7.30	47.16%	0.54	C	16.00%	12.21%	15.71%	$9,391	$56.71

Note that the firm value is maximized at a debt ratio of 30%, leading to an increase in the stock price of $23.69.

While debt capacity was never stated as a rationale for Disney's acquisition of Capital Cities, it is worth noting that Disney borrowed about $10 billion for this acquisition and paid $125 per share. Capital Cities stockholders could well have achieved the same premium, if management at the company had borrowed the money and repurchased stock. While in this case it can be argued that Capital Cities stockholders did not lose as a result of the acquisition, they would have (at least based on our numbers) if Disney had paid a smaller premium on the acquisition.

Overlevered Firms

Similar considerations apply to overlevered firms that are considering how quickly they should lower their debt ratio. As in the case of underlevered firms, the precision of the estimate of the optimal leverage will play a role, with more precise estimates leading to quicker adjustments. The other factor, in the case of overlevered firms, is *the possibility of default*—the primary risk of having too much debt. Too much debt results in higher interest rates and lower ratings on the debt. Thus, the greater the chance of bankruptcy, the more likely the firm is to move quickly to reduce debt and move to its optimal.

9.1   INDIRECT BANKRUPTCY COSTS AND LEVERAGE

In Chapter 7, we talked about indirect bankruptcy costs, where the perception of default risk affected sales and profits. Assume that a firm with substantial indirect bankruptcy costs has too much debt. Is the urgency to get back to an optimal debt ratio for this firm greater or lesser than it is for a firm without such costs?

☐   Greater

☐   Lesser

Explain.

THE PROCESS OF CHANGE

The process by which firms adjust their leverage will depend upon two factors: (1) the speed with which they want to change their financing mix, and (2) the availability of new projects that can be financed with the new debt or equity.

Increasing Leverage Quickly

When underlevered firms need to increase leverage quickly, they can do so in a number of ways: borrowing money and buying back stock; replacing equity with debt of equal market value; or selling assets and repurchasing stock.

- *Borrowing money and buying back stock (or paying a special dividend)* increases leverage because the borrowing increases the debt, while the equity repurchase or dividend payment concurrently reduces the equity. A number of companies have used this approach to increase leverage quickly, largely in response to takeover attempts. For example, in 1985, to stave off a hostile takeover, Atlantic Richfield borrowed $4 billion and repurchased stock to increase its leverage from 12% to 34%.

- In a *debt-for-equity swap,* a firm replaces equity with debt of equivalent market value by swapping the two securities. Here, again, the simultaneous increase in debt and the decrease in equity causes the debt ratio to increase substantially. In many cases, as can be seen in Table 9.1, firms offer equity investors a combination of cash and debt in lieu of equity. In 1986, for example, Owens Corning gave its stockholders $52 in cash and debt with a face value of $35, for each outstanding share, thereby increasing its debt and reducing equity.

- Finally, when firms currently have debt outstanding, and want to change their debt ratio, they can do so by *selling a portion of their assets and using the proceeds to repurchase stock.*

In each of these cases, the firm may be stymied by bond covenants that explicitly prohibit these actions or impose large penalties on the firm. The firm will have to weigh these restrictions against the benefits of the higher leverage and the increased value that flows from it.

In the last few years, several firms have gone through *leveraged recapitalizations,* whereby one or more of the above strategies has been used to increase leverage quickly. Table 9.1 lists some of the firms and the strategies they used.

Note that nearly every one of these restructurings was motivated by a desire to prevent a hostile takeover. Managers seldom initiate large increases in leverage since the leverage puts added pressure on them to perform.

Debt-for-Equity Swaps: This is a voluntary exchange of outstanding equity for debt of equal market value.

9.2 INSIDER HOLDINGS AND LEVERAGE

Closely held firms (where managers and insiders hold a substantial portion of the outstanding stock) are less likely to increase leverage quickly than firms with widely dispersed stockholdings.

☐ True

☐ False

Explain.

ILLUSTRATION 9.2 Changing Leverage Quickly: Nichols Research

In 1994, Nichols Research, a firm that provides technical services to the defense industry, had debt outstanding of $6.8 million and market value of equity of $120

Table 9.1   A SELECTIVE SAMPLE OF LEVERAGED RECAPITALIZATIONS

Company	Date	Trigger for Recap	Strategy Used
CBS Inc.	1985	Hostile takeover bid by Ted Turner	Acquisition of 21% of common stock.
Caeser's World	1987	Hostile bid by Martin Sosnoff	Borrow $1 billion and pay special dividend of $26.25.
Carter Hawley Hale	1986	Hostile bid by The Limited	Spin off division and pay special dividend of $325 mil.
Colt Industries	1986		Borrow $1.5 billion and pay special dividend of $85.
FMC	1986	Potential hostile takeover	Pay special dividend of $80.
GenCorp	1987	Hostile takeover by AFG	Borrow $1.6 billion and buy back stock.
Gillette Corp.	1986	Hostile bid by Revlon	Repurchase 7 million shares in the open market.
Goodyear Tire & Rubber Co.	1986	Hostile bid by James Goldsmith	Sell three units and buy back 20 million shares of stock.
HBO & Co.	1986	Maintain stockholder value	Purchase 26% of the outstanding stock.
Harcourt Brace Jovanovich	1987	Hostile bid by British Painting	Borrow money and pay special dividend.
Holiday Corp.	1986	Hostile takeover bid by Donald Trump	Pay special dividend of $65 per share.
Inco Ltd.	1988	Potential for hostile takeover	Pay $1 billion in special dividends.
Interco Ltd.	1988	Hostile takeover bid by Rales Brothers	Borrow $2.8 billion and pay special dividend of $14 per share.
Kroger	1988	Hostile takeover bid by Haft Brothers	Pay special dividend.
Multimedia	1988	LBO proposal from management	Borrow money and buy back stock.
Newmont Mining	1987	Hostile bid by Ivanhoe Partners	Pay special dividend of $33 per share.
Optical Coating Laboratories	1988		Pay special dividend of $13 per share.
Owens Corning	1986	Hostile bid by Wickes	Debt-for-equity swap + special dividend ($52 + $35 of debt for equity).
Phillips Petroleum	1984	Hostile takeover by Pickens	Double firm's debt and buy back stock.
Quantum Chemical	1988		Pay special dividend of $50 per share.
Santa Fe Southern Pacific	1987	Potential for hostile takeover	Pay $4 billion to the stockholders.
Shoney's	1988		Special dividend + debt-for-equity swap.
Standard Brand Paints	1987	Hostile bid for Entregrowth	Buy back 53% of the outstanding shares.
Swank Inc.	1987	Hostile takeover	Pay special dividend of $17.
UAL	1987	Potential for hostile takeover	Borrow money and repurchase 63% of outstanding shares.
USG Corp.	1988	Potential for hostile bid from Desert Partners	Special dividend + debt-for-equity swap.
Union Carbide	1985	Hostile bid by GAF Inc.	Special dividend + debt-for-equity swap.
Unocal	1985	Hostile bid by T. Boone Pickens	Repurchase 49% of the outstanding shares.

million. Based upon its EBITDA of $12 million, Nichols had an optimal debt ratio of 30%, which would lower the cost of capital to 12.07% (from the current cost of capital of 13%) and increase the firm value to $146 million (from $126.8 million). There are a number of reasons for arguing that Nichols should increase its leverage quickly:

- Its small size, in conjunction with its low leverage and large cash balance ($25.3 million), makes it a prime target for an acquisition.
- While 17.6% of the shares are held by owners and directors, this amount is unlikely to hold off a hostile acquisition, since institutions own 60% of the outstanding stock.
- The firm has been reporting steadily decreasing returns on its projects, due to the shrinkage in the defense budget. In 1994, the return on capital was only 10%, which is much lower than the cost of capital.

If Nichols decides to increase leverage, it can do so in a number of ways:

- It can borrow enough money to get to 30% of its overall firm value ($146 million at the optimal debt ratio) and buy back stock. This would require $37 million in new debt.
- It can borrow $37 million and pay a special dividend of that amount.
- It can use its current cash balance of $25 million to buy back stock or pay dividends, and increase debt to 30% of the remaining firm value (30% of $121 million).[2] This would require approximately $29.5 million in new debt, which can be used to buy back stock.

Decrease Leverage Quickly

Firms that have to decrease leverage quickly face a more difficult problem, since the perception that they might not survive affects their capacity to raise new financing. Optimally, such firms would like to issue equity and use it to pay off some of the outstanding debt, but their equity issues might not be well received in the market. Consequently, they have to consider two options—they can either renegotiate debt agreements or sell their assets to pay off the debt.

- *When firms renegotiate debt agreements,* they try to convince some of the lenders to take an equity stake in the firm in lieu of some or all of their debt in the firm. The best bargaining chip the firm possesses is the possibility of default, since lenders faced with default are more likely to agree to these terms. In the late 1980s, for example, many U.S. banks were forced to trade in their Latin American debt for equity stakes or receive little or nothing on their loans.
- The firm may choose to *sell assets and use the proceeds to retire some of the outstanding debt.* Many firms that had taken on too much debt in the course of leveraged buyouts in the 1980s, and wanted to pay off some of it, adopted this approach.

---

[2]We are assuming that the optimal debt ratio will be unaffected by the paying out of the special dividend. It is entirely possible that the paying out of the cash will make the firm riskier (leading to a higher unlevered beta) and lower the optimal debt ratio.

9.3 ASSET SALES TO REDUCE LEVERAGE

Assume that a firm has decided to sell assets to pay off its debt. In deciding which assets to sell, the firm should

☐ sell its worst-performing assets to raise the cash.

☐ sell its best-performing assets to raise the cash.

☐ sell its most liquid assets to raise the cash.

☐ Other . . .

Explain.

Increasing Leverage Gradually

Firms that have the luxury of increasing their leverage gradually over time begin by analyzing the availability of good projects that can be financed with the debt. If there are good projects available, borrowing the money to take on these projects will provide firms with an added benefit: The firm not only gets the increase in value of moving to the optimal debt ratio, it also gets the additional increment in value from the positive net present value of new projects.

In the earlier chapters on investment analysis, we defined good projects as those that earn a return greater than the hurdle rate. The return can be measured in either cash flow terms (as the internal rate of return) or accounting terms (as the return on equity or the return on capital), and must be compared to an appropriate benchmark (cost of equity for equity returns, and cost of capital for return on capital).

Firms that have excess debt capacity but do not have good projects to choose from will be better off increasing the debt capacity by repurchasing stock and/or increasing dividends over time.

IN PRACTICE: DEBT CAPACITY AND ACQUISITIONS

It is sometimes argued that firms with excess debt capacity use it to acquire other firms. This makes sense only if the acquisition can be justified on a standalone basis, without the benefit of the added value from moving to the optimal debt ratio. To illustrate, assume that a firm is currently underleveraged but could increase its value by $50 million if it moves to its optimal debt ratio by borrowing $200 million. The firm proceeds to borrow $200 million and buy a target firm worth $175 million; it then argues that it is in fact better off overall because it has a net gain in value of $25 million ($50 million in increased value from moving to the optimal reduced by the overpayment of $25 million on the acquisition). This argument does not hold up, however, because the firm could have increased its value by $50 million if it had borrowed the money and bought back stock. Excess debt capacity cannot be used, therefore, to justify bad investment or acquisition decisions.

ILLUSTRATION **9.3**   **Charting a Framework for Changing Leverage: Disney**

Reviewing the capital structure analysis done for Disney in Chapter 8, Disney had a debt ratio of approximately 18% in July 1997, with $11.18 billion in debt (estimated market value) and $50.89 billion in equity. Its optimal debt ratio, based upon minimizing cost of capital, was 40%. Table 9.2 summarizes the debt ratios, costs of capital, and firm value at debt ratios ranging from 0% to 90%.

Table 9.2	DEBT RATIO, WACC, AND FIRM VALUE: DISNEY	
Debt Ratio	**Cost of Capital**	**Firm Value**
0.00%	13.00%	$53,172
10.00%	12.55%	$58,014
20.00%	12.17%	$62,705
30.00%	11.84%	$67,419
40.00%	11.64%	$70,542
50.00%	11.70%	$69,560
60.00%	12.11%	$63,445
70.00%	11.97%	$65,524
80.00%	12.17%	$62,751
90.00%	13.69%	$47,140

The optimal debt ratio for Disney is 40%, since the cost of capital is minimized and the firm value is maximized at this debt level. Assuming that Disney operates under an investment grade rating constraint (of BBB), the optimal debt ratio is 30%.

Disney is not under any immediate pressure to increase its leverage, partly because of its size ($62 billion) and partly because it has done well for its stockholders over the previous years.[3] Let us assume, however, that Disney decides to increase its leverage over time toward its optimal for two reasons:

1. It is embarking on international expansion, which will require extensive external financing.

2. Its stockholders are restive due to a series of management missteps[4] and compensation issues, and its stock price has stagnated for the last year.

The question of how to increase leverage over time can be best answered by looking at the quality of the projects that Disney had available to it in 1996. To make this judgment, we estimate the return on capital earned by Disney in 1996:

$$\text{Return on Capital} = \text{EBIT} (1 - \text{tax rate}) / (\text{BV of Debt} + \text{BV of Equity})$$
$$= 5559 (1 - .36)/(7663 + 11368)$$
$$= 18.69\%$$

This is higher than the cost of capital[5] of 12.22% that Disney faced in 1997 and the 11.84% it will face if it moves to the optimal. Assuming that the returns on capital will be higher than the cost of capital in the future, Disney should finance its new pro-

---

[3]See Jensen's alpha calculation in Chapter 4. Over the 1992-96 time period, Disney has earned an excess return of 1.81% a year.

[4]Disney and its chief operating officer, Michael Ovitz, parted company after Mr. Ovitz and Disney's CEO, Mr. Eisner could not get along. The parting was expensive, costing Disney an estimated $90 million.

[5]The correct comparison should be to the cost of capital that Disney will have at its optimal debt ratio. It is, however, even better if the return on capital also exceeds the current cost of capital, since it will take time to get to the optimal.

jects with debt. Over time, we would expect to see an increase in the debt ratio, though the value of equity will itself increase as earnings are reinvested back in the company. To make forecasts of changes in leverage over time, we made the following assumptions:

- Revenues, operating earnings, capital expenditures, and depreciation are expected to grow 10% a year for the next five years (based upon analyst estimates of growth). The current values for each of these is provided in Table 9.3.
- Non-cash working capital is assumed to be 5% of revenues, and to stay at that level through the entire five-year period.
- The interest rate on new debt is expected to be 7.5%.
- The dividend payout ratio is currently 22.32%.
- The current beta for Disney is 1.25.
- The Treasury bond rate is 7%, and the risk premium is assumed to be 5.5%.

The values of debt and equity, over time, are estimated as follows:

$$\text{Equity}_t = \text{Equity}_{t-1} (1 + \text{Cost of Equity}_{t-1}) - \text{Dividends}_t$$

The rationale is simple: The cost of equity measures the expected return on the stock, inclusive of price appreciation and the dividend yield, and the payment of dividends reduces the value of equity outstanding at the end of the year.[6] The value of debt is estimated by adding the new debt taken on to the debt outstanding at the end of the previous year.

We begin this analysis by looking at what would happen to the debt ratio if Disney maintains its existing payout ratio of 22.32%, does not buy back stock, and applies excess funds to pay off debt. Table 9.3 uses the expected capital expenditures and non-cash working capital needs over the next five years, in conjunction with external financing needs, to estimate the debt ratio in each year.

Disney produces a cash surplus every year, since internal cash flows (net income + depreciation) are well in excess of capital expenditures and working capital needs. If this is applied to paying off debt, the increase in the market value of equity over time will cause the debt ratio to drop from 18.01% to 7.23% by the end of year 5. If Disney wants to increase its debt ratio to 30%, it will need to do one or a combination of the following:

1. *Increase its dividend payout ratio:* The higher dividend increases the debt ratio in two ways. It increases the need for debt financing in each year, and it reduces the expected price appreciation on the equity. In Table 9.4, for instance, increasing the dividend payout ratio to 50% results in a debt ratio of 9.67% at the end of the fifth year (instead of 7.23%).

   In fact, increasing dividend payout alone is unlikely to increase the debt ratio substantially.

---

[6]The effect of dividends on the market value of equity can best be captured by noting the effect the payment on dividends has on stock prices on the ex-dividend day. Stock prices tend to drop on ex-dividend day by about the same amount as the dividend paid.

Table 9.3	ESTIMATED DEBT RATIO WITH EXISTING PAYOUT RATIOS: DISNEY					
	Current Year	**1**	**2**	**3**	**4**	**5**
Equity	$50,888	$57,651	$65,251	$73,793	$83,393	$94,183
Debt	$11,180	$10,908	$10,599	$10,246	$9,844	$9,386
Debt/(Debt + Equity)	18.01%	15.91%	13.97%	12.19%	10.56%	9.06%
Revenues	$18,739	$20,613	$22,674	$24,942	$27,436	$30,179
Capital Expenditures	$1,745	$1,920	$2,111	$2,323	$2,555	$2,810
+ Chg in Work. Cap.	$15	$94	$103	$113	$125	$137
− Depreciation	$1,134	$1,247	$1,372	$1,509	$1,660	$1,826
− Net Income	$1,214	$1,335	$1,483	$1,647	$1,830	$2,033
+ Dividends	$271	$298	$331	$368	$408	$454
= New Debt	($317)	($272)	($309)	($353)	($402)	($458)
Beta	1.25	1.23	1.21	1.19	1.18	1.17
Cost of Equity	13.88%	13.76%	13.65%	13.56%	13.48%	13.41%
Growth Rate		10.00%	10.00%	10.00%	10.00%	10.00%
Dividend Payout Ratio	22.32%	22.32%	22.32%	22.32%	22.32%	22.32%

[a] $\text{Net Income}_t = \text{Net Income}_{t-1} (1+g) - \text{Interest Rate} (1-t) * (\text{Debt}_t - \text{Debt}_{t-1})$

Table 9.4	ESTIMATED DEBT RATIO WITH HIGHER DIVIDEND PAYOUT RATIO					
	Current Year	**1**	**2**	**3**	**4**	**5**
Equity	$50,888	$57,281	$64,446	$72,479	$81,486	$91,587
Debt	$11,180	$11,278	$11,389	$11,513	$11,653	$11,810
D/(Debt + Equity)	18.01%	16.45%	15.02%	13.71%	12.51%	11.42%
Revenues	$18,739	$20,613	$22,674	$24,942	$27,436	$30,179
Capital Expenditures	$1,745	$1,920	$2,111	$2,323	$2,555	$2,810
Chg in Work. Cap.	$15	$94	$103	$113	$125	$137
− Depreciation	$1,134	$1,247	$1,372	$1,509	$1,660	$1,826
− Net Income	$1,214	$1,335	$1,464	$1,605	$1,759	$1,927
+ Dividends	$271	$668	$732	$802	$879	$964
= New Debt	($317)	$98	$110	$124	$140	$157
Beta	1.25	1.23	1.22	1.21	1.20	1.19
Cost of Equity	13.88%	13.79%	13.71%	13.64%	13.58%	13.52%
Growth Rate		10.00%	10.00%	10.00%	10.00%	10.00%
Payout Ratio	22.32%	50.00%	50.00%	50.00%	50.00%	50.00%

2. *Repurchase stock each year:*   This affects the debt ratio in much the same way as does increasing dividends, because it increases debt requirements and reduces equity. For instance, if Disney bought back 5% of the stock outstanding each year, the debt ratio at the end of year 5 would be significantly higher as shown in Table 9.5.

	Table 9.5 ESTIMATED DEBT RATIO WITH EQUITY BUYBACK OF 5% A YEAR					
	Current Year	**1**	**2**	**3**	**4**	**5**
Equity	$50,888	$54,768	$59,030	$63,717	$68,875	$74,561
Debt	$11,180	$13,791	$16,703	$19,958	$23,604	$27,697
Debt/(Debt + Equity)	18.01%	20.12%	22.06%	23.85%	25.52%	27.09%
Revenues	$18,739	$20,613	$22,674	$24,942	$27,436	$30,179
Capital Expenditures	$1,745	$1,920	$2,111	$2,323	$2,555	$2,810
+ Chg in Work. Cap.	$15	$94	$103	$113	$125	$137
− Depreciation	$1,134	$1,247	$1,372	$1,509	$1,660	$1,826
− Net Income	$1,214	$1,335	$1,335	$1,320	$1,285	$1,227
+ Dividends	$271	$298	$298	$295	$287	$274
+ Stock Buyback		$2,883	$3,107	$3,354	$3,625	$3,924
= New Debt	($317)	$2,611	$2,912	$3,255	$3,646	$4,092
Beta	1.25	1.27	1.29	1.32	1.34	1.36
Cost of Equity	13.88%	14.00%	14.12%	14.24%	14.35%	14.46%
Growth Rate		10.00%	10.00%	10.00%	10.00%	10.00%
Dividend Payout Ratio	22.32%	22.32%	22.32%	22.32%	22.32%	22.32%

Note that the debt ratio increases to 25.64% by the end of year 5.

3. ***Increase capital expenditures each year:*** While the first two approaches increase the debt ratio by shrinking the equity, the third approach increases the scale of the firm. It does so by increasing the capital expenditures, which incidentally includes acquisitions of other firms, and financing these expenditures with debt. Disney could increase its debt ratio fairly significantly by embarking on a series of acquisitions. In Table 9.6, we estimate the debt ratio for Disney if it triples its capital expenditures and meets its external financing needs with debt.

   This is the riskiest strategy of the three, since it presupposes the existence of enough good investments (or acquisitions) to cover $35 billion in new investments over the next five years. It may, however, be the strategy that seems most attractive to management that is intent on building a global entertainment empire.

9.4 CASH BALANCES AND CHANGING LEVERAGE

Companies with excess debt capacity often also have large cash balances. Which of the following actions by a company with a large cash balance and debt on its books will increase its debt ratio? (You can pick more than one.)

☐ Using the cash to acquire another company

☐ Paying a large special dividend

☐ Paying off debt

☐ Buying back stock

Explain.

	Current Year	1	2	3	4	5
			Table 9.6			
Equity	$50,888	$57,637	$65,573	$74,725	$85,283	$97,465
Debt	$11,180	$14,445	$18,167	$22,408	$27,243	$32,753
Debt/(Debt + Equity)	18.01%	20.04%	21.69%	23.07%	24.21%	25.15%
Revenues	$18,739	$20,613	$22,674	$24,942	$27,436	$30,179
Capital Expenditures	$1,745	$5,759	$6,334	$6,968	$7,665	$8,431
Chg in Work. Cap.	$15	$94	$103	$113	$125	$137
− Depreciation	$1,409	$1,550	$1,705	$1,875	$2,063	$2,269
− Net Income	$1,214	$1,335	$1,302	$1,241	$1,148	$1,016
+ Dividends	$271	$298	$291	$277	$256	$227
= New Debt	($592)	$3,265	$3,721	$4,241	$4,834	$5,510
Beta	1.25	1.32	1.34	1.36	1.37	1.38
Cost of Equity	13.85%	14.27%	14.38%	14.47%	14.55%	14.62%
Growth Rate		10.00%	10.00%	10.00%	10.00%	10.00%
Dividend Payout Ratio	22.32%	22.32%	22.32%	22.32%	22.32%	22.32%

Decreasing Leverage Gradually

The benefits overlevered firms gain by lowering their debt ratios gradually over time include the residual cash flows that can be used to take on new projects and the increase in equity over time, leading to lower debt ratios. For this to work, however, firms must have access to good projects, which can be financed either with the internal equity or with new stock issues, leading to higher equity and lower debt ratios. If firms do not have access to good projects, the residual cash flows of the firms will have to be utilized to pay off outstanding debt and lower the debt ratio. It goes without saying that firms should desist from paying dividends or repurchasing stock during the course of this adjustment.

Internal Equity: Internal equity usually is that portion of the earnings that gets reinvested back into the company (i.e., the retained earnings).

IN PRACTICE: HYBRID SECURITIES AND CHANGING FINANCING MIX

In some cases, overlevered firms can gain from issuing hybrid securities, such as convertible debt, where the mix of debt and equity changes over time as the stock price changes. As the firm's fortunes improve, the equity component in convertible debt increases as a proportion of the convertible bond's value, leading to lower debt ratios.

ILLUSTRATION 9.4   A Framework for Changing Leverage: Time Warner

In 1994, Time Warner had 379.3 million shares outstanding, trading at $44 per share, and $9.934 billion in outstanding debt, left over from the leveraged acquisition of Time by Warner Communications in 1989. The EBITDA in 1994 was $1.146 billion, and Time Warner had a beta of 1.30. The optimal debt ratio for Time Warner, based upon this operating income, is only 10%. Table 9.7 examines the effect on leverage of cutting dividends to zero and using operating cash flows to take on projects and repay debt.

	Current Year	1	2	3	4	5
Table 9.7	**ESTIMATED DEBT RATIOS: TIME WARNER**					
Equity	$16,689	$19,051	$21,694	$24,651	$27,960	$31,663
Debt	$9,934	$9,745	$9,527	$9,276	$8,988	$8,655
Debt/(Debt + Equity)	37.31%	33.84%	30.52%	27.34%	24.33%	21.47%
Capital Expenditures	$300	$330	$363	$399	$439	$483
− Depreciation	$437	$481	$529	$582	$640	$704
− Net Income	$35	$39	$52	$68	$88	$112
− Dividends	$67	$0	$0	$0	$0	$0
= New Debt	($105)	($189)	($218)	($251)	($289)	($332)
Beta	1.30	1.25	1.21	1.17	1.14	1.11
Cost of Equity	14.15%	13.87%	13.63%	13.42%	13.24%	13.08%
Growth Rate		10.00%	10.00%	10.00%	10.00%	10.00%
Payout Ratio	11%	0%	0%	0%	0%	0%

Allowing for a growth rate of 10% in operating income, Time Warner repays $189 million of its outstanding debt in the first year. By the end of the fifth year, the growth in equity and the reduction in debt combine to lower the debt ratio to 21.47%.

Figure 9.1 summarizes the framework that we have developed in the last few pages.

This spreadsheet allows you to estimate the effects of changing dividend policy or capital expenditures on debt ratios over time (**chgfin.xls**).

9.5   INVESTING IN OTHER BUSINESS LINES

In the analysis above, we have argued that firms should invest in projects as long as the return on equity is greater than the cost of equity. Assume that a firm is considering acquiring another firm with its debt capacity. In analyzing the return on equity the acquiring firm can make on this investment, we should compare the return on equity to

☐   the cost of equity of the acquiring firm.

☐   the cost of equity of the acquired firm.

☐   a blended cost of equity of the acquired and acquiring firm.

☐   none of the above.

Explain.

Security Innovation and Capital Structure Changes

While the changes in leverage discussed so far in this chapter have been accomplished using traditional securities such as straight debt and equity, firms that have specific objectives on leverage may find certain products that are designed to meet those objectives. Consider a few examples:

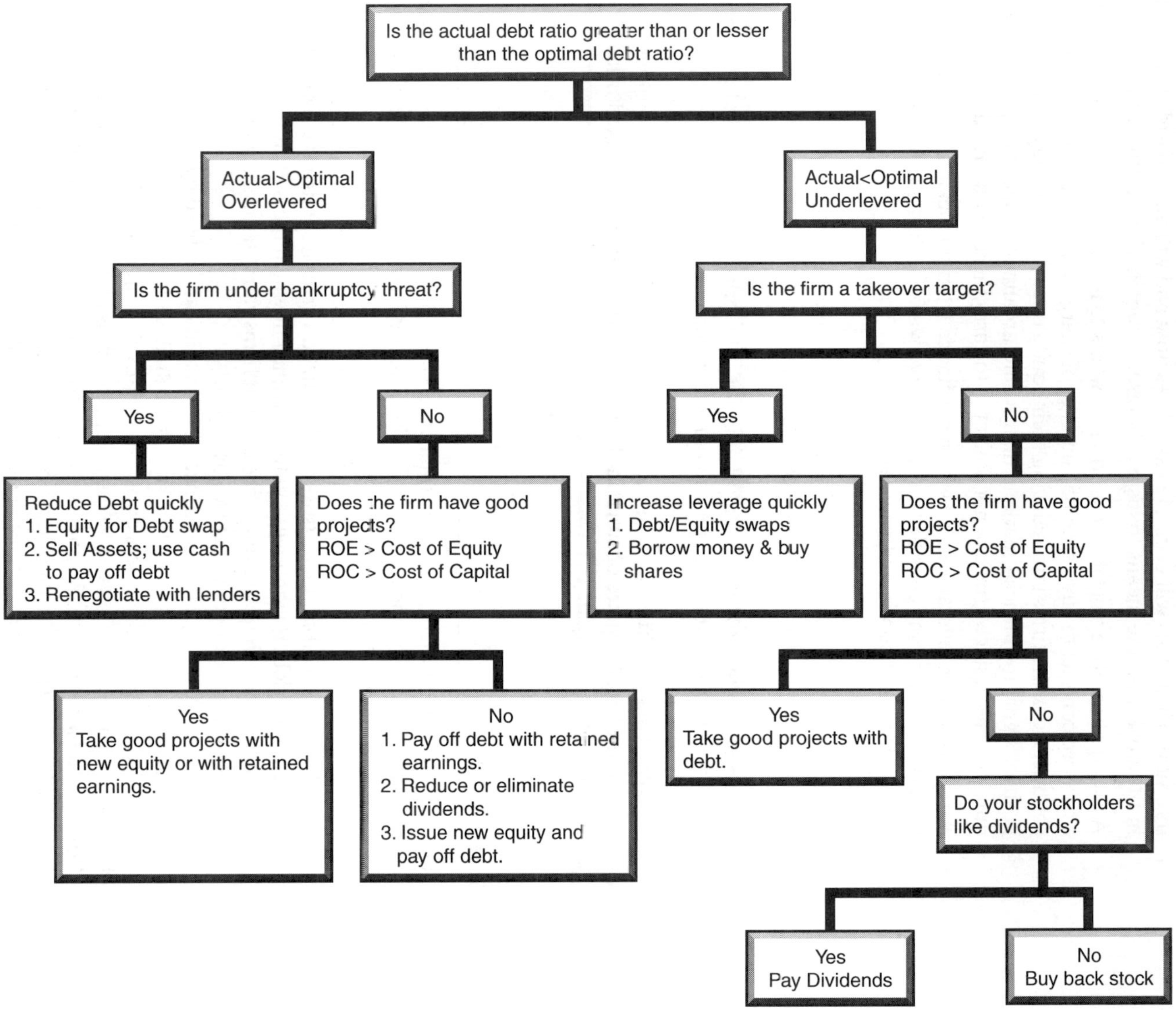

Figure 9.1 A Framework for Analyzing Capital Structure.

The diagram reads as follows:

Is the actual debt ratio greater than or lesser than the optimal debt ratio?

This branches into two paths:

Actual>Optimal / Overlevered

Is the firm under bankruptcy threat?

- **Yes**: Reduce Debt quickly
  1. Equity for Debt swap
  2. Sell Assets; use cash to pay off debt
  3. Renegotiate with lenders

- **No**: Does the firm have good projects?
  ROE > Cost of Equity
  ROC > Cost of Capital

  - **Yes**: Take good projects with new equity or with retained earnings.
  - **No**:
    1. Pay off debt with retained earnings.
    2. Reduce or eliminate dividends.
    3. Issue new equity and pay off debt.

Actual<Optimal / Underlevered

Is the firm a takeover target?

- **Yes**: Increase leverage quickly
  1. Debt/Equity swaps
  2. Borrow money & buy shares

- **No**: Does the firm have good projects?
  ROE > Cost of Equity
  ROC > Cost of Capital

  - **Yes**: Take good projects with debt.
  - **No**: Do your stockholders like dividends?
    - **Yes**: Pay Dividends
    - **No**: Buy back stock

319

- A firm that intends to raise its debt ratio over time may do so by selling *puts* on its equity. These puts will generate cash flows now, and will also provide investors in the stock with the means to insure themselves against stock price downturns.

- Another alternative available to a firm that wants to increase leverage over time is a forward contract to buy a specified number of shares of equity in the future. These contracts lock the firms into reducing their equity over time and may carry a more positive signal to financial markets than would an announcement of plans to repurchase stock, since firms are not obligated to carry through on the latter.

- A firm with high leverage, faced with a resistance from financial markets to common stock issues, may consider more inventive ways of raising equity, such as using warrants and contingent value rights.

Forward Contract: A forward contract is an agreement to buy or sell the underlying asset at a fixed price at a future point in time.

Puts: This is the right to buy an underlying asset at a price that is fixed at the time the right is issued and during a specified time period.

Contingent Value Rights: A contingent value right (CVR) provides the holder with the right to sell a share of stock in the underlying company at a fixed price during the life of the right.

WORKING OUT THE DETAILS

Once a firm has decided to use new financing, either debt or equity, it has to decide on the details of the financing. As we saw in Chapter 7, firms can raise debt and equity in a variety of ways, and they have to make a series of choices on the design of the new financing. In the case of debt, they have to make decisions on the maturity of the debt, any special characteristics (such as fixed versus floating rates, conversion options, etc.) the debt might have, and the currency in which the debt is to be issued. In the case of equity, there are fewer choices, but firms can still raise equity from common stock, warrants, or contingent value rights.

In this section, we lay out a sequence of steps that can be used by a firm to devise an appropriate finance mix. The first step in the analysis is an examination of the cash flow characteristics of the assets or projects that will be financed; the objective is to try and match the cash flows on the liability stream as closely as possible to the cash flows on the asset stream. We then superimpose a series of considerations that may lead the firm to deviate from or modify this financing mix. First, we consider the tax savings that may accrue from using different financing vehicles, and weigh the tax benefits against the costs of deviating from the mix. Next, we examine the influence that equity research analysts and ratings agency views have on the choice of financing vehicle; instruments that are looked on favorably by either or, better still, both groups will clearly be preferred to those that evoke strong negative responses from them. We also factor in the difficulty that some firms might have in conveying information to markets; in the presence of asymmetric information, firms may have to make financing choices that do not reflect their asset mix. Finally, we allow for the possibility that firms may want to structure their financing to reduce agency conflicts between stockholders and bondholders.

Step 1: Examine the Cash Flow Characteristics of Assets

The first and most important factor that a firm has to consider in the design of the securities it will use to raise funds is the *cash flow patterns of the assets* that are to be financed with these securities. We will argue that firms should begin with the premise that the cash flows on their liability streams should match up with the cash flows on the assets that they own.

Why Match Asset Cash Flows to Cash Flows on Liabilities?

To see why firms should match up cash flows on assets to cash flows on liabilities, let us begin by defining firm value as the present value of the cash flows generated by the assets owned by the firm. This firm value will vary over time, not only as a function of firm-specific factors such as project success but also as a function of broader macroeconomic variables—interest rates, inflation rates, economic cycles, and exchange rates. Figure 9.2 provides the time series of predicted firm value for a hypothetical firm, where all of the changes in firm value are assumed to occur as a result of changes in macroeconomic variables.

This firm can choose to finance these assets with any financing mix it wants. The value of equity at any point in time is the difference between the value of the firm and the value of outstanding debt. Assume, for instance, that the firm chooses to

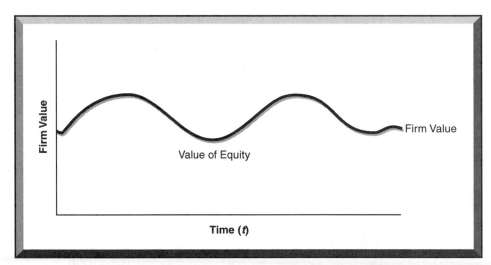

Figure 9.2   Firm Value Over Time with Short-Term Debt.

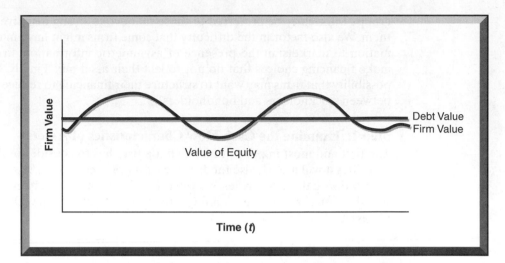

Figure 9.3 Firm Value Over Time with Short-Term Debt.

finance the assets shown in Figure 9.2 using very-short-term debt, and that this debt is unaffected by changes in macroeconomic variables. Figure 9.3 provides the firm value, debt value, and equity value over time for the firm. Note that there are periods when the firm value drops below the debt value, which would suggest that the firm is flirting with bankruptcy in those periods. Firms that weigh this possibility into their financing decision will therefore borrow much less.

Now consider a firm which finances the assets described in Figure 9.2 with debt that matches up exactly to the assets, in terms of cash flows, and also in terms of the sensitivity of debt value to changes in macroeconomic variables. Figure 9.4 provides the firm value, debt value, and equity value for this firm. Since debt value and firm value move together here, the possibility of default is significantly reduced. This, in turn, will allow the firm to carry much more debt, and the added debt should provide tax benefits that make the firm more valuable. Thus, matching liability cash flows to asset cash flows allows firms to have higher optimal debt ratios.

9.6   The Rationale for Asset and Liability Matching

In Chapter 4, we argued that firms should focus on only market risk, since firm-specific risk can be diversified away. By the same token, it should not matter if firms use short-term debt to finance long-term assets, since investors in these firms can diversify away this risk anyway.

☐   True
☐   False
Comment.

Financing Maturity

Notwithstanding the discussion above, it is difficult and expensive to match individual cash flows on assets perfectly with individual cash flows on liabilities. However,

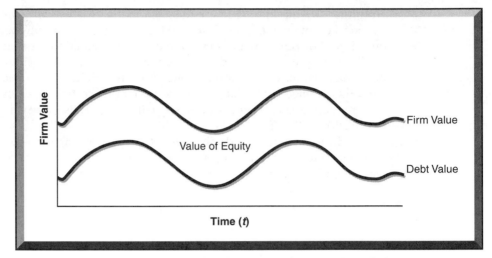

Figure 9.4   Firm Value Over Time with Long-Term Debt.

firms can often obtain a significant portion of the benefits listed in the previous section by matching the duration of their assets to the duration of their liabilities. The *duration of an asset or a liability* is a weighted maturity of all the cash flows on that asset or liability, where the weights are based upon both the timing and the magnitude of the cash flows. In general, larger and earlier cash flows are weighted more than are smaller and later cash flows. By incorporating the magnitude and timing of all the cash flows, duration encompasses all the variables that affect the interest rate sensitivity of an asset or liability. The higher the duration of an asset or liability, the more sensitive it is to changes in interest rates.

Duration of a Firm's Debt

The duration of a straight bond or loan issued by a company can be written in terms of the coupons (interest payments) on the bond (loan) and the face value of the bond, as follows (N is the bond maturity):

$$\text{Duration of Bond} = dP/dr = \frac{\left[\displaystyle\sum_{t=1}^{t=N} \frac{t*\text{Coupon}_t}{(1+r)^t} + \frac{N*\text{Face Value}}{(1+r)^N}\right]}{\left[\displaystyle\sum_{t=1}^{t=N} \frac{\text{Coupon}_t}{(1+r)^t} + \frac{\text{Face Value}}{(1+r)^N}\right]}$$

Where r is the yield to maturity.

Holding other factors constant, the duration of a bond will increase with the maturity of the bond and decrease with the coupon rate on the bond. For example, the duration of a 7%, 30-year coupon bond, when interest rates are 8%, can be written as follows:

$$\text{Duration of Bond} = dP/dr = \frac{\left[\displaystyle\sum_{t=1}^{t=30} \frac{t*\$70}{(1.08)^t} + \frac{30*\$1000}{(1.08)^{30}}\right]}{\left[\displaystyle\sum_{t=1}^{t=30} \frac{\$70}{(1.08)^t} + \frac{\$1000}{(1.08)^N}\right]} = 12.41$$

Note that the duration is lower than the maturity. This will generally be true for coupon-bearing bonds, though special features in the bond may sometimes increase duration.[7] For zero-coupon bonds, the duration is equal to the maturity.

The measure of duration estimated above is called *Macaulay duration,* and it does make some strong assumptions about the yield curve; specifically, the yield curve is assumed to be flat and move in parallel shifts. Other duration measures change these assumptions. For purposes of our analysis, however, a rough measure of duration will suffice.

The duration of the bond will be affected by any changes made to the bond's cash flow characteristics. Table 9.8 summarizes the direct impact of a couple of widely used bond features on duration and the indirect impact on interest rate risk.

Macaulay Duration: This is a specific measure of duration which is estimated on the assumption of a flat term structure and parallel shifts in the yield curve.

Duration of a Firm's Assets

This measure of duration can be extended to any asset with expected cash flows. Thus, the duration of a project or asset can be estimated in terms of its predebt operating cash flows:

$$\text{Duration of Project/Asset} = dPV/dr = \frac{\left[\sum_{t=1}^{t=N} \frac{t*CF_t}{(1 + r)^t} + \frac{N*\text{Terminal Value}}{(1 + r)^N}\right]}{\left[\sum_{t=1}^{t=N} \frac{CF_t}{(1 + r)^t} + \frac{\text{Terminal Value}}{(1 + r)^N}\right]}$$

where

CF_t = After-tax operating cash flow on the project in year t
Terminal value = Value at the end of the project lifetime
N = Life of the project
r = Discount rate for project (Cost of Equity or Capital)

The duration of any asset provides a measure of the interest rate risk embedded in that asset.

One of the limitations of traditional duration analysis is that it keeps cash flows fixed, while interest rates change. On real projects, however, the cash flows will be adversely affected by the increases in interest rates, and the degree of the effect will vary from business to business—more for cyclical firms (automobiles, housing) and less for noncyclical firms (food processing). Thus the actual duration of most projects will be higher than the estimates obtained by keeping cash flows constant.

---

[7]For instance, in reverse floater bonds, the coupon rate varies inversely with the interest rate, rising when interest rates drop and dropping when interest rates rise. This will increase bond duration.

Table 9.8   EFFECTS OF SPECIAL FEATURES ON DURATION

Special Feature	Effect on Duration/Interest Rate Risk
Interest rate is floating instead of fixed	• Duration is lowered. If the floating rate has no caps or floors, the floating rate loan will have the same duration as the rate to which it is pegged (e.g., 6-month LIBOR). • The value of the bond is not sensitive to interest rate changes.
Bond is callable	• Duration is lowered. As interest rates go down and the likelihood of a call increases, the duration of these bonds decreases. • The value of a callable bond becomes less sensitive to interest rate changes as interest rates go down. It will look more like a non-callable bond as interest rates go up.

One way of estimating duration without depending upon the traditional bond duration measures is to use historical data. If the duration is, in fact, the sensitivity of asset values to interest rate changes, and a time series of data of asset value and interest rate changes is available, a regression of the former on the latter should yield a measure of duration:

$$\Delta \text{ Asset Value}_t = a + b \, \Delta \text{ Interest Rate}_t$$

In this regression, the coefficient b on interest rate changes should be a measure of the duration of the assets. For firms with publicly traded stocks and bonds, the firm value is the sum of the market values of the two over time. For a private company, the regression can be run, using changes in operating income as the dependent variable:

$$\Delta \text{ Operating Income}_t = a + b \, \Delta \text{ Interest Rate}_t$$

Here again, the coefficient b is a measure of the duration of the assets.

9.7   PROJECT LIFE AND DURATION

In investment analyses, analysts often cut off project lives at an arbitrary point and estimate a salvage or a terminal value. If these cash flows are used to estimate project duration, we will tend to

☐ understate duration.

☐ overstate duration.

☐ not affect the duration estimate.

Explain.

IN PRACTICE: CALCULATING DURATION FOR THE DISNEY THEME PARK

In this application, we will calculate duration using the traditional measures for the Disney Theme Park in Thailand. The cash flows for the project are summarized in Table 9.9, together with the present value estimates, calculated using the cost of capital.

Table 9.9 CALCULATING A PROJECT'S DURATION

Year	Total FCFF	PV of FCFF	PV*t
1	($39,078 Bt)	(31,161 Bt)	−31160.969
2	($36,199 Bt)	(23,017 Bt)	−46034.931
3	($11,759 Bt)	(5,962 Bt)	−17886.497
4	16,155 Bt	6,532 Bt	26128.0524
5	21,548 Bt	6,947 Bt	34736.1086
6	33,109 Bt	8,512 Bt	51073.1332
7	46,692 Bt	9,572 Bt	67005.9744
8	58,169 Bt	9,509 Bt	76074.0372
9	902,843 Bt	117,694 Bt	1059242.66
NPV		98,626 Bt	1219177.57

Duration of the Project = 1,219,178 / 98,626 = 12.36 years

This duration is understated, however, because the project is arbitrarily cut off after nine years. Using the true life for the project should yield a higher duration estimate. (In fact, the duration of a perpetuity is $\frac{1+r}{r}$.)

Duration and Financing Choices
Once the duration of the assets is known, the duration of the financing can be set in one of two ways: by matching individual assets and liabilities, or by matching the assets of the firm with its collective liabilities. In the first approach, the cash flows on the financing can be matched up as closely as possible to the individual project being financed. Alternatively, the duration of the financing can be matched up to the duration of the asset it funds. While this approach provides a precise matching of each asset's characteristics to those of the financing used for it, it has several limitations. First, it is expensive to arrange separate financing for each project, given the fixed costs associated with raising funds. Second, this approach ignores interactions and correlations between projects which might make project-specific financing suboptimal for the firm. Consequently, this approach works only for companies that have very large, independent projects.

When it is difficult or costly to pair up financing to the specific projects being financed, the duration of all assets can be estimated in one of two ways:

1. By taking a weighted average of the duration of individual assets

2. By estimating the duration of all assets from the cumulated operating cash flows to the firm or the cumulated firm value.

The duration of liabilities can be estimated collectively as well and matched up as closely as possible to the duration of the assets. This approach saves on transactions costs.

9.8 PROJECT AND FIRM DURATION

Which of the following types of firms should be most likely to use project-specific financing (as opposed to financing the portfolio of projects)?

☐ Firms with a few large homogeneous projects

☐ Firms with a large number of small homogeneous projects

☐ Firms with a few large heterogeneous projects

☐ Firms with a large number of small heterogeneous projects

Explain. (Homogeneous and heterogeneous refer to similarities or differences in cash flow patterns across projects)

The Fixed/Floating Rate Choice

In recent years, firms have been provided far more choices in the design of their debt. One of the most common choices firms have to make is whether to make the coupon rate a fixed rate or a floating rate, pegged to an index rate such as the LIBOR. In making this decision, we once again examine the characteristics of the projects being financed with the debt.

Uncertainty About Future Projects

The assumption that the duration of assets and liabilities can be matched up to arrive at the "right" maturity mix for financing is predicated on the belief that the assets and projects of a firm are well identified and that the interest rate sensitivity of these assets can therefore be estimated easily. For some firms, this may be difficult to do, however. The firm may be in transition (it could be restructuring), or the industry may be changing. In such cases, the firm may use a financing mix that is easy to change (short-term or floating rate loans) until it feels more certain about its future investment plans.

An Alternative: The presence of derivatives provides an alternative for firms that are faced with this uncertainty. They can use the financing mix that is most appropriate given their current asset mix and use derivatives to manage changes in their risk characteristics.

Cash Flows and Inflation

If a firm has assets whose earnings increase as interest rates go up, and decrease as interest rates go down, it should finance those assets with floating rate loans. While not too many manufacturing projects have these characteristics in low-inflation economies, more do in high-inflation economies, since increase in inflation results in increases in both earnings/revenues and in interest rates.

Floating Rate Debt: The interest rate on floating rate debt varies from period to period and is linked to a specified short-term rate; for instance, many floating rate bonds have coupon rates that are tied to the London Interbank Borrowing Rate (LIBOR).

9.9   INFLATION UNCERTAINTY AND FLOATING RATE DEBT

Assume that the inflation rate increases and becomes more volatile. You would expect the use of floating rate debt to

☐   increase substantially.

☐   decrease substantially.

☐   be unaffected.

Explain.

Currency Risk and Financing Mix

Many of the points made about interest rate risk exposure also apply to currency risk exposure. If any of a firm's assets or projects create cash flows that are in a currency other than the one in which the equity is denominated, there is a currency risk. The liabilities of a firm can be issued in these currencies to reduce the currency risk. A firm that expects 20 percent of its cash flows to be in Deutsche Marks, for example, would attempt to issue DM-denominated debt, in the same proportion, to mitigate the currency risk.

In recent years, firms have used more sophisticated variations on traditional bonds to manage foreign exchange risk. For instance, Philip Morris issued a dual currency bond in 1985—coupon payments were made in Swiss Francs, while the principal payment was in U.S. Dollars. In 1987, Westinghouse issued Principal Exchange Rate Linked Securities (PERLS), whereby the principal payment was the U.S. dollar value of 70.13 New Zealand dollars. Finally, firms have issued bonds embedded with foreign currency options called Indexed Currency Option Notes (ICON), which combine a fixed-rate bullet repayment bond with an option on foreign exchange. This approach is likely to work only for firms that have fairly predictable currency flows, however. For firms that do not, currency derivatives may be a cheaper way to manage currency risk, since the currency exposure changes from period to period.

PERLS: This is a bond, denominated in the domestic currency, where the principal payment at maturity is based upon the domestic currency equivalent of a fixed foreign currency amount. For instance, this could be a dollar denominated bond with the payment at maturity set equal to the dollar value of 1600 Deutsche Marks. Thus, if the dollar strengthens against the DM during the life of the bond, the principal payment will decrease.

Other Features

As we noted in Chapter 7, several special features have been added to corporate bonds. In this section, we examine how the cash flows on assets may help determine whether any of these special features should be included in new debt issued by a firm.

Business Risk

The most controversial type of risk, in terms of whether and how it should be managed, is *business risk*. Business risk arises from changes in the underlying business that a firm operates in and its exposure to macroeconomic factors; an automobile manufacturing firm, for instance, is exposed to the risk of an economic recession. Some firms have attempted to add special features to their liabilities to reduce their exposure to business risk.

- Insurance companies, for instance, have issued bonds whose payments can be drastically curtailed if there is a catastrophe that requires payouts by the insurance company. By doing so, they reduce their debt payments in those periods when their overall cash flows are most negative, thereby reducing their likelihood of default.

- Companies in commodity businesses have issued bonds whose principal and interest payments are tied to the price of the commodity. Since the operating cash flows in these firms are also positively correlated with commodity prices, adding this feature to debt decreases the likelihood of default, and allows the firm to use more debt. In 1980, for instance, Sunshine Mining issued 15-year silver-linked bond issues, which combined a debt issue with an option on silver prices.

IN PRACTICE: CATASTROPHE BONDS

As an example of a catastrophe bond issue, consider the bond issue made by USAA Insurance Company. The company privately placed $477 million of these bonds, backed up by reinsurance premiums, in June 1997. The company was protected in the event of a hurricane that created more that $1 billion in damage to the East Coast anytime before June 1998. The bonds came in two classes; in the first class, called principal-at-risk, the company could reduce the principal on the bond in the event of a hurricane; in the second class, which was less risky to investors, the coupon payments would be suspended in the event of a hurricane, but the principal would be protected. In return, the investors in these bonds, in October 1997, were earning an extra yield of almost 1.5% on the principal-at-risk bonds and almost 0.5% on the principal-protected bonds.

9.10 SPECIAL FEATURES AND INTEREST RATES

Adding special features to bonds, such as linking coupon payments to commodity prices or catastrophes, will reduce their attractiveness to investors and make the interest rates paid on them higher. It follows then that

☐ companies should not add these special features to bonds.

☐ adding these special features cannot create value for the firm if the bonds are fairly priced.

☐ adding special features can still create value even if the bonds are fairly priced.

Explain.

Growth Characteristics

Firms vary in terms of how much of their value comes from projects or assets already in place and how much comes from future growth. Firms that derive the bulk of their value from future growth use different types of financing and design their financing differently than do those that derive most of their value from assets in place. This is because the current cash flows on "high-growth" firms will be low, relative to the market value. Accordingly, the financing approach used should not create large cash outflows early; it can create substantial cash outflows later, however, reflecting the cash flow patterns of the firm. In addition, the financing should exploit the value that the perception of high growth adds to securities, and it should put relatively few constraints on investment policies.

Straight bonds do not quite fit the bill, because they create large interest payments and do not gain much value from the high-growth perceptions. Furthermore, they are likely to include covenants designed to protect the bondholders, which restrict investment and future financing policy. Convertible bonds, by contrast, create much lower interest payments, impose fewer constraints, and gain value from higher growth perceptions. They might be converted into common stock, but only if the firm is successful.

Convertible Debt: This is debt that can be converted into equity at a rate that is specified as part of the debt.

Zero-coupon Bond: A zero-coupon bond pays no interest during the life of the bond and pays the face value of the bond at maturity. It has a duration equal to its maturity.

Step 2: Examine the Tax Implications of the Financing Mix

A firm's financing choices have tax consequences. It is possible, therefore, that the favorable tax treatment of some financing choices may encourage firms to use them more than others, even if it means deviating from the choices that would be dictated by the asset characteristics. Consider the rationale used by some companies for the use of zero-coupon bonds. Since the IRS allows firms to impute interest payment on the bonds, the firms using the zeros are able to claim a tax deduction for a non-cash expense, decreasing their tax liability in the near periods. While the imputed interest income to the buyers of these bonds may create a tax liability that affects bond prices and rates, that can be avoided by placing these bonds with tax-exempt institutions.

The danger of structuring financing with the intention of saving on taxes is that changes in the tax law can very quickly render the benefit moot and leave the firm with a financing mix that is unsuited to its asset mix.

Step 3: Consider How Ratings Agencies and Equity Research Analysts Will React

Firms are rightfully concerned about the views of equity research analysts and ratings agencies on the actions they take, though they often overestimate the influence of both groups. Analysts represent stockholders, and ratings agencies represent bondholders; consequently they take very different views of the same actions. For instance, analysts may view a stock repurchase by a company with limited project opportunities as a positive action, while ratings agencies may view it as a negative action and lower ratings in response. Analysts and ratings agencies also measure the impact of actions using very different criteria. In general, analysts view a firm's actions through the prism of higher earnings per share and by looking at the firm relative to comparable firms, using multiples such as PE or PBV ratios. Ratings agencies, on the other hand, measure the effect of actions on the financial ratios, such as debt ratios and coverage ratios, which they then use to assess risk and assign ratings.

Given the weight attached to the views of both these groups, firms sometimes design securities with the intent of satisfying both groups. In some cases, they find ways of raising funds that seem to make both groups happy, at least on the surface. To illustrate, consider the use of leasing, before generally accepted accounting principles required capitalizing of leases. Leasing increased the real leverage of the company, and thus, the earnings per share, but it did not affect the measured leverage of the company because it was not viewed as debt. To the degree that analysts and ratings agencies rely on imperfect measures and do not properly factor in the effects of firm actions, firms can exploit their limitations. In a more recent example, insurance companies in the United States have issued *surplus notes,* which are considered debt for tax purposes and equity by insurance regulators, enabling them to have the best of both worlds—they could issue debt, while counting it as equity.[8]

When securities are designed in such a way, the real question is whether the markets are fooled and if so, for how long. A firm that substitutes leases for debt may fool the ratings agency and even the debt markets for some period of time, but it cannot evade the reality that it is much more levered and hence much riskier than it seems.

Finally, ratings agencies and analysts are but two players in a game that involves many more, including stockholders and bondholders themselves, and the firm's managers. Table 9.10 summarizes the different objectives, criteria, and measurement devices used by each. It is extremely unlikely, given the conflicts in interest between some of these groups, that any one financing action will result in unanimous acceptance.

Step 4: Examine the Effects of Asymmetric Information

Firms generally have more information about their future prospects than do financial markets. This *asymmetry in information* creates friction when firms try to raise funds. In particular, firms with good prospects try to distinguish themselves from firms without such prospects by taking actions that are costly and difficult to imitate. Firms also try to reduce the effect of uncertainty in future cash flows by

---

[8]In 1994 and 1995, insurance companies issued a total of $6 billion of surplus notes in the private placement market. Surplus notes are bonds where the interest payments are made only if the firm has a profit (surplus), and are suspended in periods of losses.

Table 9.10 Objective Functions for Different Groups

	Ratings Agencies	Equity Research Analysts	Existing Bondholders	Managers	Stockholders
Objective	Measure risk of default in company's bond issues (existing and new)	Evaluate whether the stock is a good buy for clients (make recommendations)	Ensure that their loans to the firm (or bonds) are protected	Maximize managerial interests without arousing too much stockholder dissatisfaction	Maximize stock price
Measurement device	Financial ratios measuring • cash flow generating capacity • degree of leverage • risk • profitability	Multiples (PE, PBV) relative to comparable firms * EPS effects * EPS growth	Financial ratios specified in covenants	EPS Effects Earnings growth Earnings stability Remuneration systems	Discounted cash flow valuation Multiples
Questions raised in analysis	How will this action affect the company's ability to meet its debt payments?	How will this action affect the company's multiples and its standing relative to comparables?	How will this action affect the security and safety of the company's existing debt?	How will this action affect • flexibility? • remuneration? • relationships with large stockholders?	How will this action affect the stock price?
What makes them happy?	1. High coverage ratios 2. Low leverage ratios 3. High profitability ratios	1. Low multiples relative to comparable firms 2. Increases in EPS 3. Increases in growth	1. Protection of cash flows and ratings on existing debt (or) 2. Capacity to cash out without loss	1. High flexibility 2. More stability 3. Increase in EPS and growth 4. Higher stock price	1. Higher stock prices

designing their securities to minimize this effect. Firms may therefore issue securities that may not be optimal from the standpoint of matching up to their asset cash flows but are specifically designed to convey information to financial markets.

A number of researchers have used this information asymmetry argument to draw very different conclusions about the debt structure firms should use. Myers (1977) argued that firms tend to underinvest as a consequence of the asymmetry of information. One proposed solution to the problem is to issue short-term debt, even if the assets being financed are long-term assets. Flannery (1986) and Kale and Noe (1990) note that while both short- and long-term debt will be mispriced in the presence of asymmetric information, long-term debt will be mispriced more. Consequently, they argue that high-quality firms will issue short-term debt, while low-quality firms will issue long-term debt.

Goswami, Noe, and Rebello (1995) analyze the design of securities and relate it to uncertainty about future cash flows. They conclude that if the asymmetry of information concerns uncertainty about long-term cash flows, firms should issue coupon-bearing long-term debt, with restrictions on dividends. In contrast, firms with uncertainty about near-term cash flows and significant refinancing risk should issue long-term debt, without restrictions on dividend payments. When uncertainty about information is uniformly distributed across time, firms should finance with short-term debt.

Information Asymmetry: Information asymmetry arises any time one party to a transaction or agreement has more or better information than the other. Thus, managers may know more about their firms than their stockholders, and stockholders may know more than do bondholders.

Step 5: Consider the Implications of Financing Mix for Agency Costs

The final consideration in designing securities is the provision of features intended to reduce agency conflicts between stockholders and bondholders. As we noted in Chapter 7, differences between bondholders and stockholders on investment, financing, and dividend policy decisions can have an impact on the capital structure either by increasing the costs of borrowing or by increasing the constraints associated with borrowing. In some cases, firms design securities with the specific intent of reducing this conflict and its associated costs:

- We argued earlier that convertible bonds are a good choice for growth companies because of their cash flow characteristics. It can also be argued that convertible bonds reduce the anxiety of bondholders about equity investors taking on riskier projects and expropriating wealth, by allowing them to become stockholders if the stock price increases enough.
- More corporate bonds today include put options that allow bondholders to put the bonds back at face value if the firm takes a specified action (such as

increasing leverage) or if its rating drops. In a variation, in 1988, Manufacturers Hanover issued floating rate, rating-sensitive notes promising bondholders higher coupons if the firm's rating deteriorated over time.

- Merrill Lynch introduced LYONs (Liquid Yield Option Notes), which incorporated put and conversion features to protect against both the risk shifting and claim substitution to which bondholders are exposed.

LYONS: Liquid yield option notes are notes whose holders have the right either to put them back to the firm under specified circumstances or to convert them into equity.

In Summary

In deciding on the optimal financing mix, firms should begin by examining the characteristics of the assets that they own (Are they long term or short term? How sensitive are they to economic conditions and inflation? What currencies are the cash flows in?) and trying to match up the maturity, interest rate and currency mix, and special features of their financing to these characteristics. They can then superimpose tax considerations, the views of analysts and ratings agencies, agency costs, and the effects of asymmetric information to modify this financing mix. Figure 9.5 summarizes the discussion on the preceding pages.

 ILLUSTRATION **9.5** Coming Up with the Financing Details: Disney
In the following extended illustration, we come up with the financing details for Disney, using two approaches. First, we use a subjective analysis of Disney's project characteristics to define the appropriate debt mix for the company. Then we use a more quantitative approach for analyzing project characteristics, and use it to come up with the financing details for the firm. Both approaches should be considered in light of the analysis done in the previous chapter, which suggested that Disney had untapped debt potential that could be used for future projects.

Intuitive Approach

In the intuitive approach, we begin with an analysis of the characteristics of a typical project taken on by Disney and use it to make recommendations for Disney's new financing. Given the significant differences between Disney's different business lines, our recommendations would vary by business:

Business	Project Cash Flow Characteristics	Type of Financing
Creative content	Projects are likely to 1. Be short term 2. Have cash outflows primarily in dollars (since Disney makes most of its movies and TV programs in the United States) but cash inflows could have a substantial foreign currency component (because of overseas revenues)	Debt should be 1. Short term 2. Primarily U.S. dollar 3. If possible, tied to the success of movies (*Lion King* Bonds?)

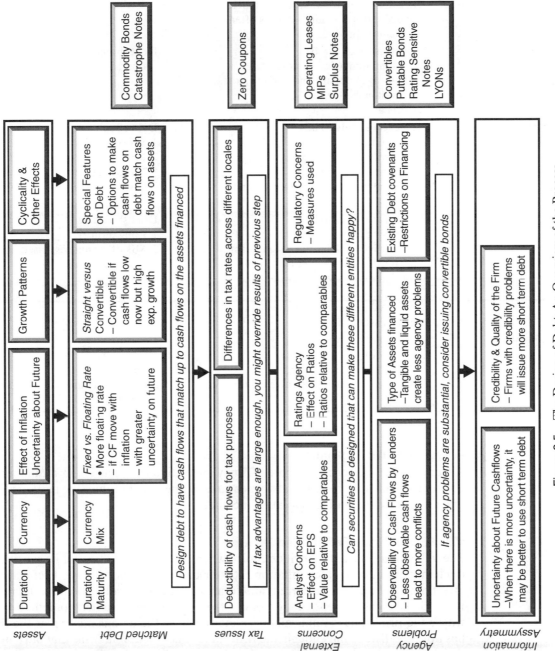

Figure 9.5 The Design of Debt: An Overview of the Process.

335

Business	Project Cash Flow Characteristics	Type of Financing
	3. Have net cash flows which are heavily driven by whether the movie or TV series is a "hit," which is often difficult to predict.	
Retailing	Projects are likely to be 1. Medium term (tied to store life) 2. Primarily in dollars (most of the stores are still in the United States) 3. Cyclical	Debt should be in the form of operating leases.
Broadcasting	Projects are likely to be 1. Short term 2. Primarily in dollars, though foreign component is growing 3. Driven by advertising revenues and show success	Debt should be 1. Short term 2. Primarily dollar debt 3. If possible, linked to network ratings
Theme parks	Projects are likely to be 1. Very long term 2. Primarily in dollars, but a significant proportion of revenues come from foreign tourists, who may be impacted by exchange rate movements 3. Affected by success of movie and broadcasting divisions	Debt should be 1. Long term 2. Mix of currencies, based upon tourist makeup
Real Estate	Projects are likely to be 1. Long term 2. Primarily in dollars 3. Affected by real estate values in the area	Debt should be 1. Long term 2. Dollars 3. Real-estate linked (mortgage bonds)

■▲▼● A Quantitative Approach

A quantitative approach estimates Disney's sensitivity to changes in a number of macroeconomic variables, using two measures: Disney's firm value (the market value of debt and equity) and its operating income.

Value Sensitivity to Factors: Past Data

The value of a firm is the obvious choice when it comes to measuring its sensitivity to changes in interest rates, inflation rates, or currency rates, because it reflects the effect of these variables on current and future cash flows as well as on discount rates. It is a viable measurement, though, only if the firm has been publicly traded. In cases where the firm value is not available, either because the data is missing or the firm has not been listed long enough, the firm values of comparable firms that have been listed for a longer period can be used in the regression. This will provide a measure of the industry characteristics.

We begin by collecting past data on firm value, operating income, and the macro-economic variables against which we want to measure its sensitivity. In the case of Disney, we chose four broad measures (see Table 9.11):

- *Long-term Treasury bond rate,* since the sensitivity of firm value to changes in interest rates provides a measure of the duration of the projects. It also provides insight into whether the firm should be using fixed or floating rate debt; a firm whose operating income moves with interest rates should consider using floating rate loans.
- *Real GNP,* since the sensitivity of firm value to this variable provides a measure of the cyclicality of the firm.
- *Currency rate,* since the sensitivity of firm value to the currency rate provides a measure of the exposure to currency rate risk, and thus helps determine what the currency mix for the debt should be.
- *Inflation rate,* since the sensitivity of firm value to the inflation rate helps determine whether the interest rate on the debt should be fixed or floating rate debt.

This is not intended to be an all-encompassing analysis. An extended analysis might include other variables, such as industry-specific variables that may affect firm value and operating income.

Once this data has been collected, we can then estimate the sensitivity of firm values to changes in the macroeconomic variables by regressing changes in firm value each year against changes in each of the individual variables.

Sensitivity to Changes in Interest Rates

As we discussed earlier, the duration of a firm's projects provides useful information for determining the maturity of its debt. While bond-based duration measures may provide some answers, they will understate the duration of assets/projects if the cash flows on these assets/projects themselves vary with interest rates. Regressing changes in firm value against changes in interest rates over this period yields the following result (T statistics in brackets):

$$\text{Change in Firm Value} = \underset{(3.09)}{0.22} \quad \underset{(1.69)}{- 7.43} \, (\text{Change in Interest Rates})$$

Based upon this regression, the duration of Disney's assets collectively is about 7.43 years. In designing its debt, Disney should try to keep the duration of its debt to about 7.43 years.

9.11 REGRESSION R-SQUARED

The R-squared of the regression shown above is only 10%. This would suggest that

- ☐ this regression is not very useful, since good regressions have high R-squared values.
- ☐ this regression is useful only if it backs up your intuition.
- ☐ the coefficient on the regression is a noisy estimate, and you should look at longer periods or sector averages.

Explain.

Year	Firm Value	Operating Income	Long Bond Rate	Real GNP	Weighted Dollar	Inflation Rate
1981	$1,707	$119.35	13.98%	3854	115.65	8.90%
1982	$2,108	$141.39	10.47%	3792	123.14	3.80%
1983	$1,817	$133.87	11.80%	4047	128.65	3.80%
1984	$2,024	$142.60	11.51%	4216	138.89	4.00%
1985	$3,655	$205.60	8.99%	4350	125.95	3.80%
1986	$5,631	$280.58	7.22%	4431	112.89	1.20%
1987	$8,371	$707.00	8.86%	4633	95.88	4.40%
1988	$9,195	$789.00	9.14%	4789	95.32	4.40%
1989	$16,015	$1,109.00	7.93%	4875	102.26	4.60%
1990	$14,963	$1,287.00	8.07%	4895	96.25	6.10%
1991	$17,122	$1,004.00	6.70%	4894	98.82	3.10%
1992	$24,771	$1,287.00	6.69%	5061	104.58	2.90%
1993	$25,212	$1,560.00	5.79%	5219	105.22	2.70%
1994	$26,506	$1,804.00	7.82%	5416	98.6	2.70%
1995	$33,858	$2,262.00	5.57%	5503	95.1	2.50%
1996	$39,561	$3,024.00	6.42%	5679	101.5	3.30%

Table 9.11 DISNEY'S FIRM VALUE AND MACROECONOMIC VARIABLES

(We have not considered the operating income from the Capital Cities acquisition.)

Sensitivity to Changes in the Economy

Is Disney a cyclical firm? One way of answering this question is to measure the sensitivity of firm value to changes in economic growth. Regressing changes in firm value against changes in the GNP over this period yields the following result (T statistics in brackets):

$$\text{Change in Firm Value} = 0.31 + 1.71 \text{ (GNP Growth)}$$
$$(2.43) \quad (0.45)$$

Disney is only mildly sensitive to cyclical movements in the economy (The T statistic is not statistically significant). This may be because it derives so much of its revenues from overseas visitors to its theme parks, and from its strong brand name, and because of its dependency on big movie hits for financial success.

Sensitivity to Changes in the Inflation Rates

We earlier made the argument, based upon asset/liability matching, that firms whose firm value tends to move with inflation should be more likely to issue floating rate debt. To examine whether Disney fits this bill, we regressed changes in firm value against changes in the GNP over this period with the following result:

$$\text{Change in Firm Value} = 0.26 - 0.22 \text{ (Change in Inflation Rate)}$$
$$(3.36) \quad (0.05)$$

Disney's firm value is unaffected by changes in the inflation rate. Other things held equal, we would argue that Disney should be using fixed rate debt rather than floating rate debt. Since interest payments have to be made out of operating cash flows, we will also have to look at how operating income moves with inflation before we can pass final judgment on this issue.

Sensitivity to Changes in the Dollar

The question of how sensitive Disney's value is to currency rates can be answered by looking at how the firm value changes as a function of changes in currency rates. Regressing changes in firm value against changes in the weighted dollar over this period yields the following regression (T statistics in brackets):

$$\text{Change in Firm Value} = 0.26 \quad \textbf{-1.01} \text{ (Change in Weighted Dollar)}$$
$$(3.46) \quad (0.98)$$

Disney's value has not been very sensitive to changes in the dollar over the last fifteen years. If this pattern continues, its debt should be primarily dollar debt. If it had been very sensitive to exchange rate changes, Disney might have considered issuing some debt denominated in other currencies to insulate itself against some of the currency risk.

Cash Flow Sensitivity to Factors: Past Data

In some cases, it is more reasonable to estimate the sensitivity of operating cash flows directly against changes in interest rates, inflation, and other variables. This is particularly the case when designing interest payments on debt, which have to be made out of operating cash flows. For instance, while the regression of firm value on inflation rates showed no relationship and led to the conclusion that Disney should not issue floating rate debt, this conclusion might be overridden if operating income turns out to be correlated with inflation rates. For Disney, we repeated the analysis using operating income as the dependent variable, rather than firm value. Since the procedure for the analysis is similar, we summarize the conclusions below (T statistics are in brackets):

- Regressing changes in operating cash flow against changes in interest rates over this period yields the following result:

$$\text{Change in Operating Income} = 0.31 - 4.99 \text{ (Change in Interest Rates)}$$
$$(2.90) \quad (0.78)$$

Disney's operating income, like its firm value, has been very sensitive to interest rates, which confirms our conclusion to use long-term debt. It yields a lower estimate of duration than the firm value measure, for two reasons—income tends to be smoothed out relative to value, and current operating income does not reflect the effects of changes in interest rates on discount rates.

- Regressing changes in operating cash flow against changes in GNP over this period yields the following regression:

$$\text{Change in Operating Income} = 0.17 + \textbf{4.06} \text{ (GNP Growth)}$$
$$(1.04) \quad (0.80)$$

Disney's operating income is more sensitive to economic cycles than is the firm value, but the relationship is not statistically significant.

- Regressing changes in operating cash flow against changes in the dollar over this period yields the following regression:

$$\text{Change in Operating Income} = 0.26 - \textbf{3.03} \text{ (Change in Dollar)}$$
$$(3.14) \quad (2.59)$$

Disney's operating income is much more sensitive to changes in the dollar than is Disney's firm value. In particular, a stronger dollar seems to hurt Disney's operating income, which we would attribute to its effect on tourist revenues at the theme parks.

- Regressing changes in operating cash flow against changes in inflation over this period yields the following result:

$$\text{Change in Operating Income} = 0.32 + 10.51 \text{ (Change in Inflation Rate)}$$
$$(3.61) \quad (2.27)$$

This is the regression where there is the biggest difference between firm value and operating income. The operating income, unlike the firm value, tends to move with inflation. Since interest payments have to be made from operating income, this would argue for the use of floating rate debt.

The question of what to do when operating income and firm value give different results can be resolved fairly simply. For issues relating to the overall design of the debt, the firm value regression should be relied on more; for issues relating to the design of interest payments on the debt, the operating income regression should be used more. Thus, for the duration measure, the regression of firm value on interest rates should, in general, give a more precise estimate. For the inflation rate sensitivity, since it affects the choice of interest payments (fixed or floating), the operating income regression should be relied on more.

Overall Recommendations

Based upon the analyses of firm value and operating income, our recommendations would essentially match those we would have given using the intuitive approach, but they would have more depth to them because of the additional information we have acquired from the quantitative analysis:

- The debt issued should be long term and should have duration of approximately 7.43 years.
- The debt should be a mix of floating rate and fixed rate debt, since operating income tends to move with inflation.

- The debt should be a mix of currencies; the exact choice of currencies will depend upon the makeup of tourist revenues at the theme parks, and Disney's overall business mix.

While this type of analysis yields useful results, those results should be taken with a grain of salt. They make sense only if the firm has been in its current business for a long time and expects to remain in it for the foreseeable future. In today's environment, in which firms find their business mixes changing dramatically from period to period as they reorganize, acquire, divest, or restructure, it may be dangerous to base too many conclusions on a historical analysis. In such cases, it might make more sense to look at the characteristics of the industry in which a firm plans to expand, rather than using past earnings or firm value as a basis for the analysis.

 There is a dataset on the Web that summarizes the results of regressing firm value against macroeconomic variables, by sector, for U.S. companies (**macro.xls**).

 ILLUSTRATION 9.5   **Estimating the Right Financing Mix for Bookscape, Aracruz, and Deutsche Bank**
While we will not examine the right financing type for Bookscape, Aracruz, and Deutsche Bank in the same level of detail as we did for Disney, we will summarize, based upon our understanding of their businesses, what we think will be the best kind of financing for each of these firms:

- *Bookscape:* Given Bookscape's dependency on revenues at its New York bookstores, we would design the debt to be
  - Fairly long term, since it is a long-term investment
  - Dollar-denominated, since all the cash flows are in dollars
  - Fixed rate debt, since Bookscape's lack of pricing power makes it unlikely that it can keep pace with inflation

  It is worth noting that operating leases fulfill all of these conditions, making them the right debt for Bookscape.
- *Aracruz:* Aracruz operates most of its paper plants in Brazil, but sells a significant proportion of its products overseas. More than eighty percent of its revenues in 1995 and 1996 were from outside Brazil, and the bulk of these revenues were dollar-denominated. Given this structure, we would design debt to be
  - Long term, since a typical paper plant has a life in excess of twenty years
  - Predominantly dollar-denominated, since the cash inflows are primarily in dollars
  - Floating rate debt, since paper and pulp prices are likely to reflect inflation

  The last recommendation is shaky partly because the overall inflation rate and paper/pulp inflation rates may not move together. It would be better if we could modify the debt to link coupon payments to the price of paper and pulp (similar to the silver-and gold-linked bonds described earlier).

- *Deutsche Bank:* In the case of Deutsche Bank, the recommendation is made simpler by the fact that the debt ratio we are analyzing is the long-term debt ratio. In addition to being long term, however, the debt should reflect

  - The mix of currencies in which Deutsche Bank gets its cash flows, which should lead to significant dollar (from its U.S. holdings) and British Pound (from its Morgan Grenfell subsidiary) debt issues. In future years, this would expand to include more emerging market debt issues to reflect Deutsche Bank's greater dependency on cash flows from these markets.

  - The changing mix of Deutsche Bank's business to reflect its increasing role in investment banking.

It is possible that Deutsche Bank's reputation in Europe may allow it to borrow more cheaply in some markets (say, Germany) than in others. If that is the case, it can either issue its dollar-denominated or pound-denominated debt in those markets, or issue debt in the currency of those markets (say, DM) and then swap the debt into dollar or pound debt.

IN PRACTICE: Firm Reputation, Interest Rates and the Role of Swaps

Firms should try to match the currencies in which they raise financing to the currencies of their projects' cash flows. Generally, firms should raise financing in each country to fund projects in that country. In some cases, however, firms may have a much better reputation among investors in one country (usually, the domestic market in which they operate) than in other markets. In such cases, firms may choose to raise their funds domestically, even for foreign projects, because they get better terms on their financing. This creates a mismatch between cash inflows and outflows, which can be resolved using currency swaps, where a firm's liabilities in one currency can be swapped for liabilities in another currency. This may enable the firm to take advantage of its reputation effect and match cash flows at the same time.

Generally speaking, swaps can be used to take advantage of any "market" imperfections that a firm might observe. Thus, if floating rate debt is attractively priced relative to fixed rate debt, a firm which does not need floating rate debt can issue floating rate debt, and then swap it for fixed rate debt at a later date.

CONCLUSION

In this chapter, we have completed our analysis of capital structure by looking at the ways in which firms can go from identifying their optimal debt ratios to actually devising the right financial mix for themselves. In particular, we noted that:

- Some firms have to change their leverage quickly to respond to external pressure brought on by the likelihood of an acquisition (if a firm is underlevered) or the chance of bankruptcy (if a firm is overlevered). Those firms that want to increase leverage quickly can do so by borrowing money and repurchasing stock, conducting debt-for-equity swaps, or selling assets and paying large special dividends. Those firms that want to decrease leverage quickly can do so by renegotiating their debt agreements to have more of an equity component or by selling assets and paying off debt.

- Some firms have the luxury of moving to their desired leverage gradually over time. They have to decide whether to take on new projects with the financing or to change the financing mix on their existing projects. That decision should be based upon the quality of projects; firms with good projects should finance them with new debt, if they want to increase leverage, or with new equity, if they want to decrease leverage.

- Once firms have decided on new financing, they still have to decide on the maturity, interest rate structure, currency, and special features for their financing. In making these decisions, they should first look at the cash flow characteristics of the assets that will be funded by the new financing and use other factors (such as taxes, the views of analysts and ratings agencies, agency conflicts, and information factors) to modify the financing to meet their specific objectives.

PROBLEMS AND QUESTIONS

1. BMD Inc. is a firm with no debt on its books currently and a market value of equity of $2 billion. Based upon its EBITDA of $200 million, it can afford to have a debt ratio of 50%, at which level the firm value should be $300 million higher.
   a. Assuming that the firm plans to increase its leverage instantaneously, what are some of the approaches it could use to get to 50%?
   b. Is there a difference between repurchasing stock and paying a special dividend? Why or why not?
   c. If BMD has a cash balance of $250 million at this time, will it change any of your analysis?

2. MiniSink Inc. is a manufacturing company that has $100 million in debt outstanding and 9 million shares trading at $100 per share. The current beta is 1.10, and the interest rate on the debt is 8%. In the latest year, MiniSink reported a net income of $7.50 per share, and analysts expect earnings growth to be 10% a year for the next five years. The firm faces a tax rate of 40% and pays out 20% of its earnings as dividends (the Treasury bond rate is 7%).
   a. Estimate the debt ratio each year for the next five years, assuming that the firm maintains its current payout ratio.
   b. Estimate the debt ratio each year for the next five years, assuming that the firm doubles its dividends and repurchases 5% of the outstanding stock every year.

3. IOU Inc. has $5 billion in debt outstanding (carrying an interest rate of 9%), and 10 million shares trading at $50 per share. Based upon its current EBIT of $500 million, its optimal debt ratio is only 30%. The firm has a beta of 1.20, the tax rate is 40%, and the current Treasury bond rate is 7%. Assuming that the operating income will increase 10% a year for the next five years and that the firm's depreciation and capital expenditures both amount to $100 million

annually for each of the five years, estimate the debt ratio for IOU if

a. It maintains its existing policy of paying $50 million a year in dividends for the next five years.

b. It eliminates dividends.

4. DGF Corporation has come to you for some advice on how best to increase its leverage over time. In the most recent year, DGF had EBIT of $300 million, owed $1 billion in both book value and market value terms, and had a net worth of $2 billion. (The market value was twice the book value). It had a beta of 1.30, and the interest rate on its debt is 8% (the Treasury bond rate is 7%). If it moves to its optimal debt ratio of 40%, the cost of capital is expected to drop by 1%. The tax rate is 40%.

a. How should the firm move to its optimal? In particular, should it borrow money and take on projects, or should it pay dividends/repurchase stock?

b. Are there any other considerations that may affect your decision?

5. STL Inc. has asked you for advice on putting together the details of the new debt issues it is planning to make. What information would you need to obtain to provide this advice?

6. Assume now that you have uncovered the following facts about the types of projects STL takes:

a. The projects are primarily infrastructure projects, requiring large initial investments and long gestation periods.

b. Most of the new projects will be in emerging markets, and the cash flows are expected to be in the local currencies, when they do occur.

c. The magnitude of the cash flows will, in large part, depend upon how quickly the economies of the emerging markets grow in the long term.

How would you use this information in the design of the debt?

7. You are attempting to structure a debt issue for Eaton Corporation, a manufacturer of automotive components. You have collected the following information on the market values of debt and equity for the last 10 years:

Year	Market Value of Equity	Debt
1985	1,824.9	436
1986	2,260.6	632
1987	2,389.6	795
1988	1,960.8	655
1989	2,226	836
1990	1,875.9	755
1991	2,009.7	795
1992	2,589.3	833
1993	3,210	649
1994	3,962.7	1053

In addition, you have the following information on the changes in long-term interest rates, inflation rates, GNP, and exchange rates over the same period.

Year	Long Bond Rate (%)	GNP Growth (%)	Weighted Dollar	Inflation Rate (%)
1985	11.40	6.44	125.95	3.50
1986	9.00	5.40	112.89	1.90
1987	9.40	6.90	95.88	3.70
1988	9.70	7.89	95.32	4.10
1989	9.30	7.23	102.26	4.80
1990	9.30	5.35	96.25	5.40
1991	8.80	2.88	98.82	4.20
1992	8.10	6.22	104.58	3.00
1993	7.20	5.34	105.22	3.00
1994	8.00	5.97	98.6	2.60

a. Estimate the duration of this firm's projects. How would you use this information in designing the debt issue?

b. How cyclical is this company? How would that affect your debt issue?

c. Estimate the sensitivity of firm value to exchange rates. How would you use this information in designing the debt issue?

d. How sensitive is firm value to inflation rates? How would you use this information in designing the debt issue?

e. What factors might lead you to override the results of this analysis?

8. Repeat the analysis in Problem 7 for a private firm that has provided you with the following estimates of operating income for the 10 years for which you have the macroeconomic data:

Year	Operating Income
1985	463.05
1986	411.696
1987	483.252
1988	544.633
1989	550.65
1990	454.875
1991	341.481
1992	413.983
1993	567.729
1994	810.968

9. Assuming that you do the regression analysis with both firm value and operating income, what are the reasons for the differences you might find in the results, using each? When would you use one over the other?

10. Pfizer, a major pharmaceutical company, has a debt ratio of 10.30% and is considering increasing its debt ratio to 30%. Its cost of capital is expected to drop from 14.51% to 13.45%. Pfizer had earnings before interest and taxes of $2 billion in 1995 and a book value of capital (debt + equity) of approximately $8 billion. It also faced a tax rate of 40% on its income. The stock in the firm is widely held, but the corporate charter includes significant anti-takeover restrictions.
   a. Should Pfizer move to its desired debt ratio quickly or gradually? Explain.
   b. Given the choice in part (a), explain how you would move to the optimal.
   c. Pfizer is considering using the excess debt capacity for an acquisition. What are some of the concerns it should have?

11. Upjohn, another major pharmaceutical company, is considering increasing its debt ratio from 11% to 40%, which is its optimal debt ratio. Its beta is 1.17, and the current Treasury bond rate is 6.50%. The return on equity was 14.5% in the most recent year, but it is dropping, as health care matures as a business. The company has also been mentioned as a possible takeover target and is widely held.
   a. Would you suggest that Upjohn move to the optimal ratio immediately? Explain.
   b. How would you recommend that Upjohn increase its debt ratio?

12. U.S. steel companies have generally been considered mature, in terms of growth, and often take on high leverage to finance their plant and equipment. Steel companies in some emerging markets often have high risk and good growth prospects. Would you expect these companies also to have high leverage? Why or why not?

13. You are trying to decide whether the debt structure that Bethlehem Steel has currently is appropriate, given its assets. You regress changes in firm value against changes in interest rates and arrive at the following equation:

Change in Firm Value = 0.20% − 6.33
(Change in Interest Rates)

   a. If Bethlehem Steel has primarily short-term debt outstanding, with a maturity of one year, would you deem it appropriate?
   b. Why might Bethlehem Steel be inclined to use short-term debt to finance longer term assets?

14. Railroad companies in the United States tend to have long-term, fixed rate, dollar-denominated debt. Explain why.

15. The following table summarizes the results of regressing changes in firm value against changes in interest rates for six major footwear companies:

Change in Firm Value = a + b
(Change in Long Term Interest Rates)

Company	Intercept (a)	Slope Coefficient (b)
LA Gear	−0.07	−4.74
Nike	0.05	−11.03
Stride Rite	0.01	−8.08
Timberland	0.06	−22.50
Reebok	0.04	−4.79
Wolverine	0.06	−2.42

   a. How would you use these results to design debt for each of these companies?
   b. How would you explain the wide variation across companies? Would you use the average across the companies in any way?

16. You have run a series of regressions of firm value changes at Motorola, the semiconductor company, against changes in a number of macroeconomic variables. The results are as follows:

Change in Firm Value = 0.05 − 3.87
(Change in Long-Term Interest Rate)
Change in Firm Value = 0.02 + 5.76
(Change in Real GNP)
Change in Firm Value = 0.04 − 2.59
(Inflation Rate)
Change in Firm Value = 0.05 − 3.40 ($/DM)

(Assume that all coefficients are statistically significant.)

a. Based on these regressions, how would you design Motorola's financing?

b. Motorola, like all semiconductor companies, is sensitive to the health of the high-technology sector. Is there any special feature you can add to the debt to reflect this dependence?

17. Assume that you are designing the debt that will be issued by Compaq Computer. Knowing what you do about the business—it is high-growth, high-risk and extremely volatile—what type of debt would you suggest that Compaq use? Why?

18. Heavily regulated companies in the United States, such as power and phone utilities, are governed by regulatory agencies that grant them rate increases based upon inflation. They are also restricted in terms of investment policy and cannot diversify into other businesses. What type of debt would you expect these firms to issue? Why?

19. ACM Inc. is a mining company that holds large stakes in copper, zinc, and magnesium mines around the world. Historically, its revenues and earnings have gone up in periods of high inflation and down during periods of deflation or low inflation. What type of debt would you recommend for ACM Inc.? What special features would you consider adding to this debt?

20. In this chapter, we have argued that firms with substantial cash flows in foreign currencies should consider using debt denominated in those currencies. Can you think of good reasons for such firms to continue to issue debt denominated in the local currency and in local markets?

21. A CFO of a small manufacturing firm with long-term assets argues that it is better to use short-term debt because it is cheaper than long-term debt. This in turn, he notes, reduces the cost of capital. Do you agree? Why or why not?

22. GF Technology Inc. is in the business of manufacturing disk drives for computers. While the underlying business is risky, the managers of GF Technology believe that their cash flows are much more stable than perceived by the market, largely because of several long-term contracts that the firm has with major computer manufacturers. They are considering the use of convertible bonds to raise funds for the firms. Would you concur? Why or why not?

23. VisiGen Inc. is a biotechnology firm involved in gene therapy. It is trying to raise funds to finance its research and is weighing the pluses and minuses of issuing stock versus warrants. What would your advice be?

LIVE CASE STUDY

VII. MECHANICS OF MOVING TO THE OPTIMAL

Objective: To develop a plan to get from the firm's current leverage to its optimal, and to examine the "right type" of financing for the firm.

Key
Questions

- If your firm's actual debt ratio is different from its "recommended" debt ratio, how should they get from the actual to the optimal? In particular,
    a) should they do it gradually over time or should they do it right now?
    b) should they alter their existing mix (by buying back stock or retiring debt) or should they take new projects with debt or equity?
- What type of financing should this firm use? In particular,
    c) should it be short term or long term?
    d) what currency should it be in?
    e) what special features should the financing have?

Framework
for Analysis

1. The Immediacy Question
- If the firm is under levered, does it have the characteristics of a firm that is a likely takeover target? (Target firms in hostile takeovers tend to be smaller, have poorer project and stock price performance than their peer groups and have lower insider holdings.)
- If the firm is over levered, is it in danger of bankruptcy? (Look at the bond rating, if the company is rated. A junk bond rating suggests high bankruptcy risk.)

2. Alter Financing Mix or Take Projects
- What kind of projects does this firm expect to have? Can it expect to make excess returns on these projects? (Past project returns is a reasonable place to start—see the section under investment returns.)
- What type of stockholders does this firm have? If cash had to be returned to them, would they prefer dividends or stock buybacks? (Again, look at the past. If the company has paid high dividends historically, it will end up with investors who like dividends.)

3. Financing Type
- How sensitive has this firm's value been to changes in macroeconomic variables such as interest rates, currency movements, inflation and the economy?
- How sensitive has this firm's operating income been to changes in the same variables?

- How sensitive is the sector's value and operating income to the same variables?
- Intuitively, what is a typical project for this firm and what financing will best fit this project?

Getting Information on Mechanics of Capital Structure

To get the inputs needed to estimate the capital structure mechanics, you can get the information on macroeconomic variables such as interest rates, inflation, GNP growth and exchange rates from my web site (**macro.xls**). You can get historical information on your own firm by looking at the Value Line page for your firm, which has information for the last 15 years on revenues and operating income.

You can get information on sector sensitivity to macroeconomic variables in the data set on my web site (**indfin.xls**).

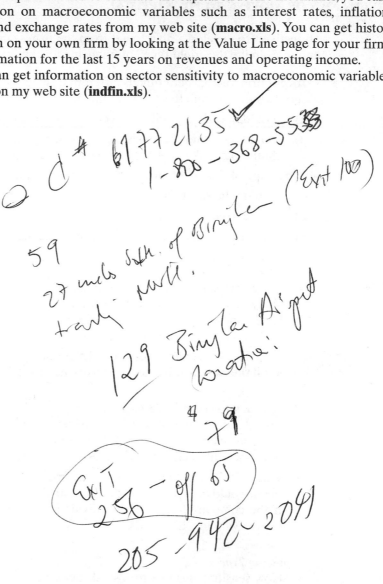

CHAPTER 10

THE DETERMINANTS OF DIVIDEND POLICY

As a firm starts receiving cash flows from its current operations it is faced with a decision. Should it reinvest the cash back into the business, or should it pay it out to equity investors? The decision may seem simple enough, but it evokes a surprising amount of controversy. In this chapter, we look at three very different schools of thought on dividend policy. The first argues that dividends do not really matter, since they do not affect value. The second vehemently argues that dividends are bad for the average stockholder, because of the tax disadvantage they create, which results in lower value. The third argues that dividends are clearly good because stockholders like them. We will probe a series of questions to provide a groundwork for analyzing dividend policy:

- What are the ways in which a firm can return cash to its stockholders?

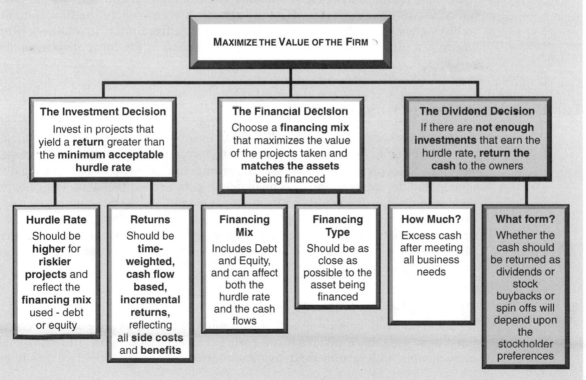

349

- What are some of the historical patterns that emerge from an examination of dividend policy over time (for U.S. firms)? How different is dividend policy across countries?
- What is the basis for the argument that dividend policy is irrelevant and does not affect value?
- What are the basis and evidence for the argument that dividends create a tax disadvantage?
- What is behind the notion that some stockholders like dividends?
- What do firms actually look at when they set dividend policy?
- What are the alternatives to paying dividends, and how should firms pick among these alternatives?

WAYS OF RETURNING CASH TO STOCKHOLDERS

While dividends have traditionally been considered the primary approach for publicly traded firms to return cash or assets to their stockholders, they comprise only one of many ways available to the firm to accomplish this objective. In particular, firms can return cash to stockholders through *equity repurchases,* where the cash is used to buy back outstanding stock in the firm and reduces the number of shares outstanding, or through *forward contracts,* where the firm commits to buying back its own stock in future periods at a fixed price. In addition, firms can return some of their assets to their stockholders in the form of spinoffs and splitoffs.

THE HISTORICAL EVIDENCE ON DIVIDENDS

Several interesting findings emerge from an examination of the dividend policies practiced by firms in the United States in the last 50 years. First, dividends tend to lag behind earnings; that is, increases in earnings are followed by increases in dividends, and decreases in earnings by dividend cuts. Second, firms are typically reluctant to change dividends; this hesitancy is magnified when it comes to cutting dividends, making for "sticky" dividend policies. Third, dividends tend to follow a much smoother path than do earnings. Finally, there are distinct differences in dividend policy over the life cycle of a firm, driven by changes in growth rates, cash flows, and project availability.

Dividends Tend to Follow Earnings

It should not come as a surprise that earnings and dividends are positively correlated over time, since dividends are paid out of earnings. Figure 10.1 shows the movement in both earnings and dividends between 1960 and 1996. Two trends are

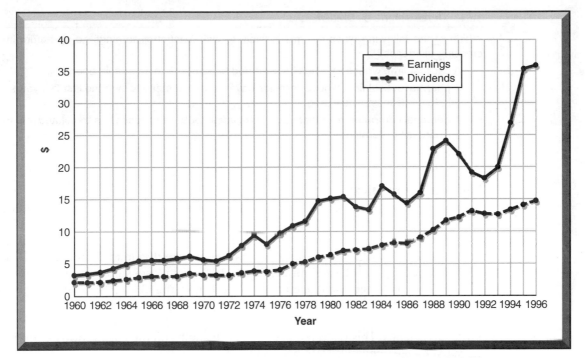

40

35

30

25

$

20

15

10

5

0
1960 1962 1964 1966 1968 1970 1972 1974 1976 1978 1980 1982 1984 1986 1988 1990 1992 1994 1996

Year

— Earnings
-- Dividends

Figure 10.1   Aggregate earnings and dividends: S & P 500—1960–96.

visible in this graph. First, dividend changes tend to lag behind earnings changes over time. Second, the dividend series is much smoother than is the earnings series.

In 1956, John Lintner conducted an extensive analysis of how firms set dividends and concluded that firms have three important concerns. First, they set *target dividend payout ratios,* whereby they decide on the fraction of earnings they are willing to pay out as dividends in the long term. Second, they change dividends to match long-term and sustainable shifts in earnings, but they increase dividends only if they feel they can maintain these higher dividends. As a consequence of this concern over having to cut dividends, dividends lag earnings and have a much smoother path. Finally, managers are much more concerned about changes in dividends, rather than levels of dividends. Fama and Babiak (1968) noted the lagged effect that earnings have on dividends, by regressing changes in dividends against changes in earnings in both current and prior periods. They confirmed Lintner's findings that dividend changes tend to follow earnings changes.

■ **Target Dividend Payout Ratio:** This is the desired proportion of earnings that a firm wants to pay out in dividends.

10.1   DETERMINANTS OF DIVIDEND LAG

Which of the following types of firms is likely to wait *least* after earnings go up before increasing dividends?

☐   A cyclical firm, whose earnings have surged because of an economic boom

☐   A pharmaceutical firm, whose earnings have increased steadily over the last five years, due to a successful new drug

☐   A personal computer manufacturer, whose latest laptop's success has translated into an increase in earnings

Explain.

Dividends Are Sticky

Firms generally do not change their dollar dividends frequently. This reluctance to change dividends, which results in "sticky dividends," is rooted in several factors. One is the firm's concern about its capability to maintain higher dividends in future periods. Another is the negative market view of dividend decreases and the consequent drop in the stock price. Figure 10.2 provides a summary of the number of firms that increased, decreased, or left unchanged their annual dividends from 1981 to 1990.

Sticky Dividends   This is a reference to the reluctance on the part of firms, empirically, to change dividends from period to period.

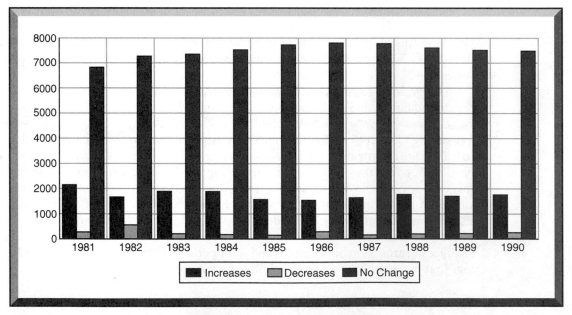

Figure 10.2 Dividend changes: Publicly owned firm—1981–90.

As you can see, in most years, the number of firms that do not change their dollar dividends far exceeds the number that do. Among the firms that change dividends, five times as many, on average, increase dividends as decrease them.

10.2 DIVIDEND CUTS AND CYCLICAL FIRMS

When the earnings of cyclical firms dip during recessions, you would expect to see

☐ dividends to be cut to reflect the drop in earnings.

☐ dividends to be increased to compensate for the drop in earnings.

☐ dividends to remain unchanged.

☐ dividends to be cut only if earnings drop more than expected.

Dividends Follow a Smoother Path Than Earnings

As a result of the reluctance of firms to raise dividends until they feel able to maintain them, and to cut dividends unless they absolutely have to, dividends follow a much smoother path than earnings. This stability of dividends is supported by a couple of measures. First, the variability in historical dividends is significantly lower than the variability in historical earnings. Using annual data on aggregate earnings and dividends from 1960 to 1994, for instance, the standard deviation of dividends is 5.13% while the standard deviation in earnings is 14.09%. Second, the standard deviation in earnings yields across companies is 18.57%, which is significantly higher than the standard deviation in dividend yields, which is only 3.15%. In other words, the variation in earnings yields across firms is much greater than the variation in dividend yields.

Dividend Yield This is the dollar dividend per share divided by the current price per share.

There is a dataset on the Web that summarizes dollar earnings and dividends for U.S. companies going back to 1960 (**spearn.xls**).

A Firm's Dividend Policy Tends to Follow the Life Cycle of the Firm

A firm's life cycle can generally be graphed in terms of investment opportunities and growth. Not surprisingly, firms generally adopt dividend policies that best fit where they currently are in their life cycles. For instance, high-growth firms with great investment opportunities do not usually pay dividends, whereas stable firms with larger cash flows and fewer projects tend to pay out more of their earnings as dividends. Figure 10.3 graphs the typical path dividend payouts follow over a firm's life cycle.

This intuitive relationship between dividend policy and growth is reemphasized when payout ratios are correlated with expected growth rates. For instance, looking at all NYSE firms in 1995 and classifying them on the basis of expected growth rates, we estimated the dividend payout ratios and dividend yields by growth class; these are reported in Figure 10.4.

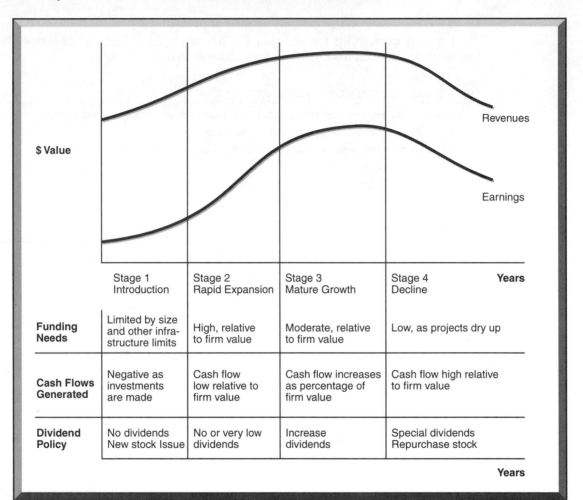

Figure 10.3 Life cycle analysis of dividend policy.

As expected growth rates increase, the dividend yields and payout ratios decrease.[1]

10.3 DIVIDEND POLICY AT GROWTH FIRMS

Assume that you are following a growth firm whose growth rate has begun easing. Which of the following would you most likely observe in terms of dividend policy at the firm?

☐ An immediate increase of dividends to reflect the lower reinvestment needs

☐ No change in dividend policy and an increase in the cash balance

☐ No change in dividend policy and an increase in acquisitions of other firms

Explain.

---

[1]These are growth rates projected by Value Line for firms in October 1995.

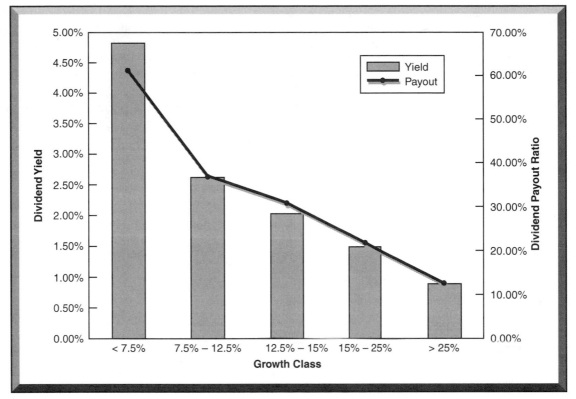

Figure 10.4   Dividend yields and payout ratios, by growth class.

DIFFERENCES IN DIVIDEND POLICY ACROSS COUNTRIES

While all of the discussion so far has focused on dividend policy in the United States, there are both commonalities and differences in dividend policy across countries. As in the United States, dividends in other countries are sticky and follow earnings. However, there are differences in dividend payout ratios across countries. Figure 10.5 summarizes the proportion of earnings paid out in dividends in the G-7 countries in 1982–84 and again in 1989–91. These differences can be attributed to a number of factors.

1. **Differences in Stage of Growth:**   Just as higher-growth companies tend to pay out less in dividends (see Figure 10.3), countries with higher growth pay out less in dividends. For instance, Japan had much higher expected growth in 1982–84 than the other G-7 countries and paid out a much smaller percentage of its earnings as dividends.

2. **Differences in Tax Treatment:**   Unlike the United States, where dividends are double-taxed, some of these countries provide at least partial protection against the double taxation of dividends. For instance, Germany taxes corporate retained earnings at a higher rate than corporate dividends.

3. ***Differences in Corporate Control:***   When there is a separation between ownership and management, as there is in many large publicly traded firms, and stockholders have little control over incumbent managers, the dividends paid by firms will be lower. Managers, left to their own devices, have a much greater incentive to accumulate cash than do stockholders.

Not surprisingly, the dividend payout ratios of companies in emerging markets are much lower than the dividend payout ratios in the G-7 countries. The higher growth and relative power of incumbent management in these countries contribute to keeping these payout ratios low.

10.4   FORCED DIVIDEND PAYOUTS

Some countries, such as Brazil, require all companies to pay out a minimum dividend (say 35% of earnings). Which of the following types of companies will be hurt most by such a policy?

☐ Stable-growth companies with substantial cash and low investment needs

☐ High-growth companies with significant investment needs

☐ All companies equally

Explain.

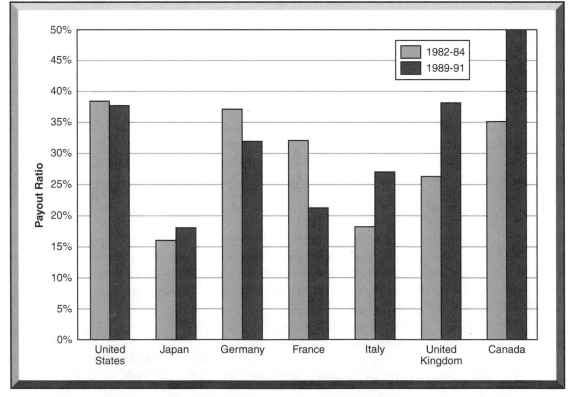

Figure 10.5   Dividend payout ratios in G-7 countries.

Measures of Dividend Policy

There are two widely used measures of dividend policy. The first is the *dividend yield,* which relates the dividend paid to the price of the stock:

Dividend Yield = Annual Dividends per Share/Price per Share

The dividend yield is significant for several reasons. First, it provides a measure of that component of the total return that comes from dividends, with the balance coming from price appreciation.

Expected Return on Stock = Dividend Yield + Price Appreciation

Second, some investors use the dividend yield as a measure of risk and as an investment screen, that is, they invest in stocks with high dividend yields. Studies indicate that stocks with high dividend yields earn excess returns, after adjusting for market performance and risk.

Figure 10.6 tracks dividend yields on stocks listed on the New York Stock Exchange in September 1997. It reveals wide differences across stocks on the exchange on dividend policy, with a large subset of stocks not paying dividends at all.

The median dividend yield of 1.76% and the average dividend yield of 2.11% are low by historical standards, as evidenced by Figure 10.7, which reports average dividend yields by year from 1960 to 1996.

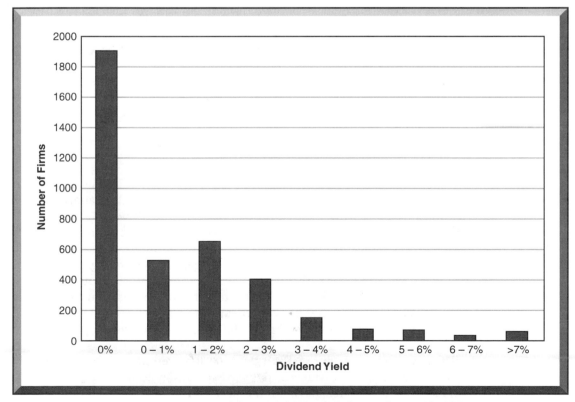

Figure 10.6   Dividend yields for U.S. firms—September 1997.

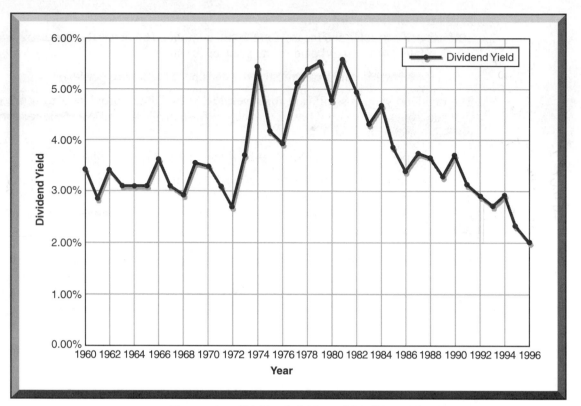

Figure 10.7 Dividend yields on S&P 500—1960–96.

The second widely used measure of dividend policy is the *dividend payout ratio,* which relates dividends paid to the earnings of the firm:

$$\text{Dividend Payout Ratio} = \text{Dividends/Earnings}$$

The payout ratio is used in a number of different settings. It is used in valuation as a way of estimating dividends in future periods, since most analysts estimate growth in earnings rather than dividends. Second, the retention ratio—the proportion of the earnings reinvested back into the firm (Retention Ratio = 1 − Dividend Payout Ratio)—is useful in estimating future growth in earnings; firms with high retention ratios (low payout ratios) generally have higher growth rates in earnings than do firms with lower retention ratios (higher payout ratios). Third, the dividend payout ratio tends to follow the life cycle of the firm, starting at zero when the firm is in high growth and gradually increasing as the firm matures and its growth prospects decrease. Figure 10.8 graphs the dividend payout ratios of U.S. firms in 1997.

The payout ratios that are greater than 100% represent firms that paid out more than their earnings as dividends. The median dividend payout ratio in 1994 was 24.93%, while the average payout ratio was 27.58%.

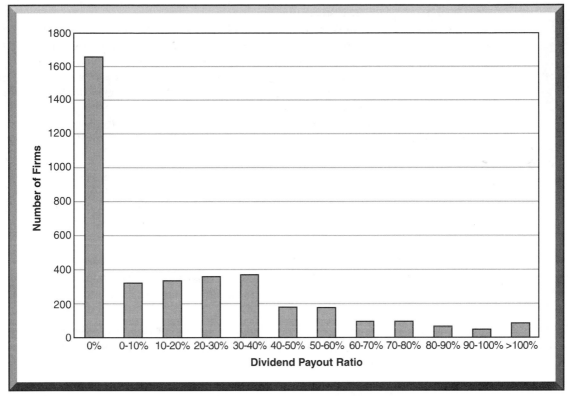

Figure 10.8   Dividend payout ratios for U.S. firms—September 1997.

 There is a dataset on the Web that summarizes dividend yields and payout ratios for U.S. companies, categorized by sector **(divend.xls)**.

 10.5   DIVIDENDS THAT EXCEED EARNINGS

Companies should never pay out more than 100% of their earnings as dividends.

☐   True
☐   False

Explain.

WHEN ARE DIVIDENDS IRRELEVANT?

There is a school of thought that argues that what a firm pays in dividends is irrelevant and that stockholders are indifferent about receiving dividends. Like the capital structure irrelevance proposition, the dividend irrelevance argument has its roots in a paper crafted by Miller and Modigliani (1961).

The Underlying Assumptions

The underlying intuition for the dividend irrelevance proposition is simple. Firms that pay more dividends offer less price appreciation but must provide the same total return to stockholders, given their risk characteristics and the cash flows from their investment decisions. Thus, if there are no taxes, or if dividends and capital gains are taxed at the same rate, investors should be indifferent to receiving their returns in dividends or price appreciation.

For this argument to work, in addition to assuming that there is no tax advantage or disadvantage associated with dividends, we also have to assume the following:

(handwritten note in left margin: have gone down)

- There are no transactions costs associated with converting price appreciation into cash, by selling stock. If this were *not* true, investors who need cash urgently might prefer to receive dividends. *(handwritten: — takes months... (18 m avg.))*

- Firms that pay too much in dividends can issue stock, again with no flotation or transactions costs, to take on good projects. There is also an implicit assumption that this stock is fairly priced.

(handwritten note in left margin: MM: make invstmt dec. first then payout dividends...)

- The investment decisions of the firm are unaffected by its dividend decisions, and the firm's operating cash flows are the same no matter which dividend policy is adopted.

- Managers of firms that pay too little in dividends do not waste the cash pursuing their own interests (i.e., managers with large free cash flows do not use them to take on bad projects). *(handwritten: WILL DO THIS WITH or WITHOUT DIVIDENDS !)*

Under these assumptions, neither the firms paying the dividends nor the stockholders receiving them will be adversely affected by firms paying either too little or too much in dividends.

10.6 DIVIDEND IRRELEVANCE

Based upon the Miller-Modigliani assumptions, dividends are least likely to affect value for the following types of firms:

☐ Small companies with substantial investment needs

☐ Large companies with significant insider holdings

☐ Large companies with significant holdings by pension funds (which are tax exempt).

Explain.

A Proof of Dividend Irrelevance

To provide a formal proof of irrelevance, assume that LongLast Corporation, an *unlevered* firm manufacturing furniture, has a net operating income after taxes of $100 million, growing at 5% a year, and a cost of capital of 10%. Further assume that this firm has net capital expenditure needs (capital expenditures in excess of depreciation) of $50 million, also growing at 5% a year, and that there are 105 million shares outstanding. Finally, assume that this firm pays out residual cash flows as dividends each year. The value of LongLast Corporation can be estimated as follows:

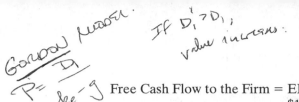

Free Cash Flow to the Firm = EBIT (1 − tax rate) − Net Capital Expenditures
= $100 million − $50 million = $50 million
Value of the Firm = Free Cash Flow to Firm (1 + g) / (WACC - g)
= $ 50 (1.05) / (.10 − .05) = $1,050 million
Price per Share = $1,050 million / 105 million = $10.00

Based upon its cash flows, this firm could pay out $50 million in dividends.

Dividend per Share = $50 million/105 million = $0.476
Total Value per Share = $10.00 + $0.476 = $10.476

To examine how the dividend policy affects firm value, assume that LongLast Corporation is told by an investment consultant that its stockholders would gain if the firm paid out $100 million in dividends, instead of $50 million. It now has to raise $50 million in new financing to cover its net capital expenditure needs. Assume that LongLast Corporation can issue new stock with *no flotation cost* to raise these funds. If it does so, the firm value will remain unchanged, since the value is determined not by the dividend paid but by the cash flows generated on the projects. The stock price will decrease, because there are more shares outstanding, but stockholders will find this loss offset by the increase in dividends per share. In order to estimate the price per share at which the new stock will be issued, note that after the dividend payment, the old stockholders in the firm will own only $1,000 million of the total firm value of $1,050 million.

Value of the Firm = $1,050 million
Dividends per Share = $100 million/105 million Shares = $0.953
Value of the Firm for Existing Stockholders after Dividend Payment =
$1,000 million
Price per Share = $1,000 million / 105 million = $9.523
Value Accruing to Stockholder = $9.523 + $0.953 = $10.476

Another way of seeing this is to divide the stockholders into existing and new stockholders. When dividends are increased by $50 million, and new stock is issued for an equivalent amount, the existing stockholders now own only $1,000 million out of the firm value of $1,050 million, but their loss in firm value is offset by their gain in dividends. In fact, if the operating cash flows are unaffected by dividend policy, we can show that the firm value will be unaffected by dividend policy and that the average stockholder will be indifferent to dividend policy since he or she receives the same total value (price + dividends) under any dividend payment.

To consider an alternate scenario, assume that LongLast Corporation pays out no dividends and retains the residual $50 million as a cash balance. The value of the firm to existing stockholders can then be computed as follows:

Value of Firm = Present Value of After-Tax Operating CF + Cash Balance
= $50 (1.05) / (.10 − .05) + $50 million = $1,100 million
Value per Share = $1,100 million / 105 million shares = $10.476

Note that the total value per share is unchanged from the previous two scenarios, as shown in Table 10.1, though all of the value comes from price appreciation.

When LongLast Corporation pays less than $50 million in dividends, the cash accrues in the firm and adds to its value. The increase in the stock price again is offset by the loss of cash flows from dividends.

It is important to note though that the irrelevance of dividend policy is grounded on the following assumptions.

- The issue of new stock is assumed to be costless and can therefore cover the cash shortfall created by paying excess dividends.

- It is assumed that firms that face a cash shortfall do not respond by cutting back on projects and thereby affecting future operating cash flows.

- Stockholders are assumed to be indifferent between receiving dividends and price appreciation.

- Any cash remaining in the firm is invested in projects that have zero net present value (such as financial investments) rather than used to take on poor projects.

Implications of Dividend Irrelevance

If dividends are, in fact, irrelevant, firms are spending a great deal of time pondering an issue about which their stockholders are indifferent. A number of strong implications emerge from this proposition. Among them, the value of equity in a firm should not change as its dividend policy changes. This does not imply that the price per share will be unaffected, however, since larger dividends should result in lower stock prices and more shares outstanding. In addition, in the long term, there should be no correlation between dividend policy and stock returns. Later in this chapter, we will examine some studies that have attempted to examine whether dividend policy is in fact irrelevant in practice.

Table 10.1   VALUE PER SHARE TO EXISTING STOCKHOLDERS FROM DIFFERENT DIVIDEND POLICIES

Value of Firm (Operating CF)	Dividends	Value to Existing Stockholders	Price per Share	Dividends per Share	Total Value per Share
$1,050	$ -	$1,100	$10.48	$ -	$10.48
$1,050	$10.00	$1,090	$10.38	$0.10	$10.48
$1,050	$20.00	$1,080	$10.29	$0.19	$10.48
$1,050	$30.00	$1,070	$10.19	$0.29	$10.48
$1,050	$40.00	$1,060	$10.10	$0.38	$10.48
$1,050	$50.00	$1,050	$10.00	$0.48	$10.48
$1,050	$60.00	$1,040	$9.90	$0.57	$10.48
$1,050	$70.00	$1,030	$9.81	$0.67	$10.48
$1,050	$80.00	$1,020	$9.71	$0.76	$10.48
$1,050	$90.00	$1,010	$9.62	$0.86	$10.48
$1,050	$100.00	$1,000	$9.52	$0.95	$10.48

The assumptions needed to arrive at the dividend irrelevance proposition may seem so onerous that many reject it without testing it. That would be a mistake, however, because the argument does contain a valuable message: A firm that has invested in bad projects cannot hope to resurrect its image with stockholders by offering them higher dividends. In fact, the correlation between dividend policy and total stock returns is weak.

THE TAXATION OF DIVIDENDS

The second school of thought on dividends argues that they create a tax disadvantage for the investors who receive them because they are taxed much more heavily than the alternative—capital gains. Carrying this rationale forward, dividend payments should decrease firm value and reduce the returns to stockholders after personal taxes. Consequently, firms will be better off either retaining the money they would have paid out as dividends or repurchasing stock.

Some History on Tax Rates

In the eyes of the Internal Revenue Service, dividends and capital gains have always been considered different types of income and, for the most part, are taxed differently (See Fig. 10.9). For several decades, until 1986, capital gains in the United States were taxed at a rate that was only 40% of the ordinary tax rate for individuals. Thus, an investor who would have paid a tax rate of 30% on ordinary income would have paid only 12% on capital gains. Under this setup, the differential advantage of capital gains is clearly a function of the investor's tax rate, with the advantage increasing with the tax rate. In 1979, for example, when the highest marginal tax rate was 70%, some investors were paying 28% on their capital gains (a tax rate differential of 42%). In 1981, a change in the tax law brought the highest marginal tax rate down to 50%, dropping the differential tax advantage to 30%.

The Tax Reform Act of 1986 was designed to simplify the tax code. One of the actions it took was to set the same tax rate on dividends and capital gains, capping the highest marginal tax rate at 28%. This simplification did not survive long in practice, however; subsequent changes in the tax law raised the highest marginal tax rate on ordinary income (dividends) to 39.6%, while leaving the capital gains tax rate at 28%. The latest changes in the tax laws, contained in the 1997 Tax Reform Act, propose to lower the capital gains tax rate even further to 20%.

The tax advantage associated with capital gains for corporations has always been lower than that associated with individuals, even though, for much of the last two decades, the capital gains tax rate has generally been lower than the ordinary tax rate. Obviously, there are no tax differences between dividends and capital gains for pension funds because their income is tax exempt.

In summary, there is a strong factual basis for the argument that historically, in the United States, capital gains have been treated more favorably under tax law than have dividends. The double taxation of dividends—once at the corporate level and once at the investor level—has never been addressed directly in U.S. tax law, but it has been dealt with in other countries in a couple of ways. In some countries, like Britain, individual

encourages charitable giving: Give' a $1, only pay 60c

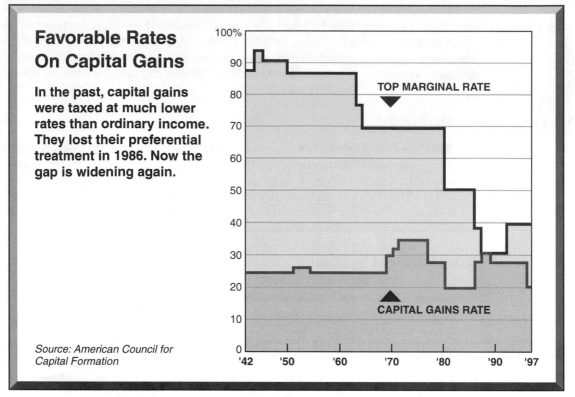

Favorable Rates On Capital Gains

In the past, capital gains were taxed at much lower rates than ordinary income. They lost their preferential treatment in 1986. Now the gap is widening again.

TOP MARGINAL RATE

CAPITAL GAINS RATE

Source: American Council for Capital Formation

Figure 10.9   Tax rates on ordinary income and capital gains.

investors are allowed a tax credit for the corporate taxes paid on cash flows paid to them as dividends. In other countries, like Germany, the portion of the earnings paid out as dividends is taxed at a lower rate than the portion reinvested back into the firm.

Capital Gains (Losses)   This is the portion of the return that an investor earns on an asset that can be attributed to the increase (decrease) in price of that asset.

10.7   TAX RATES, DOUBLE TAXATION, AND DIVIDEND POLICY

Assume now that the highest marginal tax rate for individuals is lowered to 15%. Would you expect companies to

☐   pay more in dividends?

☐   pay less in dividends?

☐   pay the same amount in dividends?

Explain.

The Tax Timing Option

When the 1986 tax law was signed into law, equalizing tax rates on ordinary income and capital gains, some believed that all the tax disadvantages associated with dividends had disappeared. Others noted that, even with the same tax rates, dividends carried a tax disadvantage because the investor had no choice on when to show the dividend as income; taxes were due when the firm paid out the dividends. In contrast, investors retained discretionary power over when to show and pay taxes on capital gains, since such taxes were not due until the asset was sold. This option allowed the investor to reduce the tax liability in one of two ways. First, by taking capital gains in periods when he or she has low income or capital losses to offset against the gain, the investor may be able to reduce the taxes paid. Second, deferring an asset's sale until an investor's death may result in tax savings.

IN PRACTICE: ESTIMATING THE TAX DISADVANTAGE/ADVANTAGE OF DIVIDENDS

The exact magnitude of the tax disadvantage associated with receiving dividends is often difficult to measure simply because different investors have different tax rates; thus, a pension fund, which does not pay any taxes, may not see any tax differences between dividends and capital gains, whereas individual investors may face different marginal tax rates on dividends and capital gains, depending upon their wealth and income levels. One simple way of estimating the differential between the tax rates of dividends and capital gains, at least to the marginal investor in a stock, is to look at the behavior of stock prices on the ex-dividend day.

If dividends and capital gains are viewed as equivalent from the investor's tax standpoint, the stock price should drop by about the same amount as the dollar dividend on the ex-dividend day to prevent arbitrage. To the degree that dividends are viewed as less attractive (because of the tax differential) than capital gains, investors will settle for a smaller capital gain, in pretax terms, as the equivalent of a dollar dividend. In other words, the price drop on the ex-dividend day will be smaller than the dollar dividend, and the magnitude of the difference will reflect the tax differential. Finally, if capital gains are taxed more heavily than dividends, the price drop on the ex-dividend day will be greater than the dollar dividend. In fact, the following relationship applies between differential tax rates and ex-dividend day price behavior:

$$\frac{P_B - P_A}{D} = \frac{(1 - t_o)}{(1 - t_{cg})}$$

where P_B is the price before the ex-dividend day, P_A is the price after the ex-dividend day, D is the dollar dividend, t_o is the tax rate on dividends and t_{cg} is the tax rate on capital gains.

Implications

There can be no argument that dividends have historically been treated less favorably than capital gains by the tax authorities. In the United States, the double taxation of dividends, at least at the level of individual investors, should create a strong disincentive to pay or to increase dividends. Other implications of the tax disadvantage argument include the following:

- Firms with an investor base composed primarily of individuals typically should have lower dividends than do firms with investor bases predominantly made up of tax-exempt institutions.

- The higher the income level (and hence the tax rates) of the investors holding stock in a firm, the lower the dividend paid out by the firm.

- As the tax disadvantage associated with dividends increases, the aggregate amount paid in dividends should decrease. Conversely, if the tax disadvantage associated with dividends decreases, the aggregate amount paid in dividends should increase. For instance, the change in the tax law in 1986 should have caused a surge in dividend payments by firms, because it eliminated the distinction between dividends and capital gains.

10.8   CORPORATE TAX STATUS AND DIVIDEND POLICY

Corporations are exempt from paying taxes on 70% of the dividends they receive from their stockholdings in other companies, whereas they face a capital gains tax rate of 20%. If all the stock in your company is held by other companies, and the ordinary tax rate for companies is 36%,

☐   dividends have a tax advantage relative to capital gains.

☐   capital gains have a tax advantage relative to dividends.

☐   dividends and capital gains are taxed at the same rate.

Explain.

SOME REASONS FOR PAYING DIVIDENDS THAT DO NOT MEASURE UP

Notwithstanding the tax disadvantages, firms continue to pay dividends and typically view such payments positively. There are a number of reasons for paying dividends, but only a few of them stand up to rational scrutiny, as we discuss below.

The Bird-in-the-Hand Fallacy

One rationalization given for why dividends are better than capital gains is that dividends are certain, whereas capital gains are uncertain; risk-averse investors, it is argued, will therefore prefer the former. This argument is severely flawed, however. The simplest counterresponse is to point out that the choice is not between certain dividends today and uncertain capital gains at some unspecified point in the future, but between dividends today and an almost equivalent amount in price appreciation today. This follows from our earlier discussion, where we noted that the stock price dropped by slightly less than the dividend on the ex-dividend day. By paying the dividend, the firm causes its stock price to drop today.

   Another response to this argument is that a firm's value is determined by the cash flows from its projects. If a firm increases its dividends, but its investment policy remains unchanged, it will have to replace the dividends with new stock issues. Investors who receive the higher dividend will therefore find themselves losing, in present value terms, an equivalent amount in price appreciation.

Temporary Excess Cash

In some cases, firms are tempted to pay or initiate dividends in years in which their operations generate excess cash. While it is perfectly legitimate to return excess cash to stockholders, firms should also consider their own long-term investment needs. If the excess cash is a temporary phenomenon, resulting from having an unusually good year or a nonrecurring action (such as the sale of an asset), and the firm expects cash shortfalls in future years, it may be better off retaining the cash to cover some or all of these shortfalls. Another option is to pay the excess cash as a dividend in the current year and issue new stock when the cash shortfall occurs. This is not very practical, since the substantial expense associated with new security issues makes this a costly strategy in the long term. Table 10.2 summarizes the cost of issuing bonds, preferred stock, and common stock, by size of issue.

This said, it is important to note that some companies do pay dividends and issue stock during the course of the same period, mostly out of a desire to maintain their dividends. Figure 10.10 summarizes new stock issues by firms as a percentage of firm value, classified by their dividend yields.

Table 10.2 ISSUANCE COST FOR SECURITIES			
	Cost of Issuing Securities		
Size of Issue	Bonds	Preferred Stock	Common Stock
Under $1 mil	14.0%	—	22.0%
$1.0–1.9 mil	11.0%	—	16.9%
$2.0–4.9 mil	4.0%	—	12.4%
$5.0–$9.9 mil	2.4%	2.6%	8.1%
$10–19.9 mil	1.2%	1.8%	6.0%
$20–49.9 mil	1.0%	1.7%	4.6%
$50 mil and over	0.9%	1.6%	3.5%

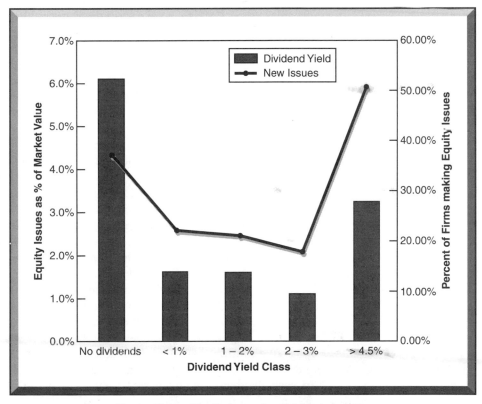

Figure 10.10   Equity issues by dividend class.

While it is not surprising that stocks that pay no dividends are most likely to issue stock, it is surprising that firms in the highest dividend yield class also issue significant proportions of new stock (approximately half of all the firms in this class also make new stock issues). This suggests that many of these firms are paying dividends, on the one hand, and issuing stock, on the other.

SOME GOOD REASONS FOR PAYING DIVIDENDS

There are several reasons why firms continue to pay dividends, ranging from investor preferences to clientele effects, to information signaling.

Some Investors Like Dividends

Many in the "dividends are bad" school of thought argue that rational investors should reject dividends due to the tax disadvantage they carry. Whatever one might think of the merits of that argument, there are some investors who have a strong preference for dividends and view large dividends positively. The most striking empirical evidence for this comes from studies of companies that have two classes of shares: one that pays cash dividends, and another that pays an equivalent amount of stock dividends; thus, investors are given a choice between dividends and capital gains.

John Long (1978) studied the price differential on Class A and B shares traded on Citizens Utility. Class B shares paid a cash dividend, while Class A shares paid an equivalent stock dividend. Moreover, Class A shares could be converted at little or no cost to Class B shares at the option of its stockholders. Thus, an investor could choose to buy Class B shares to get cash dividends, or Class A shares to get an equivalent capital gain. During the period of this study, the tax advantage was clearly on the side of capital gains; thus, we would expect to find Class B shares selling at a discount on Class A shares. The study found, surprisingly, that the Class B shares sold at a premium over Class A shares. Figure 10.11 summarizes the price differential between the two share classes over the period of the analysis.

While it may be easy to ascribe this phenomenon to irrational investors, this is not the case. Not all investors like dividends—many see its tax burden as onerous—but there are also many who view it positively, for a number of reasons. These investors may not be paying much in taxes, and consequently, do not care about the tax disadvantage associated with dividends. Or they might need and value the cash flow generated by the dividend payment. There are some who argue that the same amount can be raised in cash by selling stock, but the transactions costs and the difficulty of breaking up small holdings and selling unit shares may make this infeasible.

Bailey (1988) extended Long's study to examine Canadian utility companies that also offered dividend and capital-gains shares, and had similar findings. Table 10.3 summarizes the price premium at which the dividend shares sold. Note, once again, that, on average, the cash dividend shares sell at a premium of 7.5% over the stock dividend shares. We caution that while these findings do not indicate that *all* stockholders like dividends, they do indicate that the stockholders in these specific companies liked cash dividends so much that they were willing to overlook the tax disadvantage and pay a premium for shares that offered them.

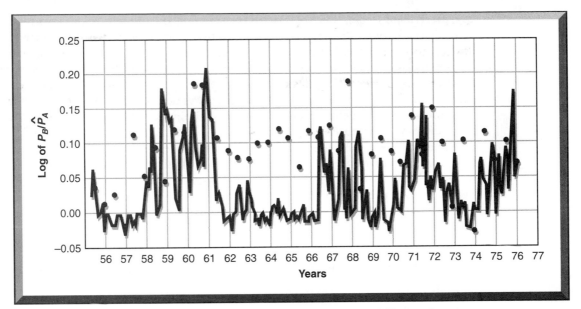

Figure 10.11   Price differential on Citizens Utility stock.

The natural log of $P_B/\hat{P}_A$ (the connected monthly observations) for the period 1956–1976. $\hat{P}_B$ is the price per share of Series B stock with dividends reinvested during each half-year prior to payment of the semi-annual Series A dividend.

Table 10.3   **PRICE DIFFERENTIAL BETWEEN CASH AND STOCK DIVIDEND SHARES**

Company	Premium on Cash Dividend Shares over Stock Dividend Shares
Consolidated Bathurst	19.30%
Donfasco	13.30%
Dome Petroleum	0.30%
Imperial Oil	12.10%
Newfoundland Light & Power	1.80%
Royal Trustco	17.30%
Stelco	2.70%
TransAlta	1.10%
Average	**7.54%**

The Clientele Effect

Stockholders in the companies covered by the studies mentioned above clearly like cash dividends. At the other extreme are companies that pay no dividends, such as Microsoft, whose stockholders seem perfectly content with that policy. Given the vast diversity of stockholders, it is not surprising that, over time, stockholders tend to invest in firms whose dividend policies match their preferences. Stockholders in high tax brackets, who do not need the cash flow from dividend payments, tend to invest in companies that pay low or no dividends. By contrast, stockholders in low tax brackets, who need the cash from dividend payments, and tax-exempt institutions that need current cash flows will usually invest in companies with high dividends. This clustering of stockholders in companies with dividend policies that match their preferences is called the *clientele effect.*

The existence of a clientele effect is supported by empirical evidence. One study looked at the portfolios of 914 investors to see if their portfolio positions were affected by their tax brackets. Not surprisingly, the study found that older and poorer investors were more likely to hold high-dividend-paying stocks than were younger and wealthier investors. In another study (see Table 10.4), dividend yields were regressed against the characteristics of the investor base of a company (including age, income, and differential tax rates):

$$\text{Dividend Yield}_t = a + b\,\beta_t + c\,\text{Age}_t + d\,\text{Income}_t + e\,\text{Differential Tax Rate}_t + \epsilon_t$$

Not surprisingly, this study found that safer companies, with older and poorer investors, tended to pay more in dividends than companies with wealthier and younger investors. Overall, dividend yields decreased as the tax disadvantage of dividends increased.

Dividend Clientele Effect This refers to the tendency of investors to buy stock in firms which have dividend policies that meet their preferences for high, low, or no dividends.

10.9   DIVIDEND CLIENTELE AND TAX EXEMPT INVESTORS

Pension funds are exempt from paying taxes on either ordinary income or capital gains, and also have substantial ongoing cash flow needs. What types of stocks would you expect these funds to buy?

☐ Stocks that pay high dividends
☐ Stocks that pay low or no dividends

Explain.

Table 10.4 DIVIDEND YIELDS AND INVESTOR CHARACTERISTICS		
Variable	**Coefficient**	**Implies**
Constant	4.22%	
Beta Coefficient	−2.145	Higher beta stocks pay lower dividends.
Age/100	3.131	Firms with older investors pay higher dividends.
Income/1000	−3.726	Firms with wealthier investors pay lower dividends.
Differential Tax Rate	−2.849	If ordinary income is taxed at a higher rate than capital gains, the firm pays less dividends.

Implications of the Clientele Effect

The existence of a clientele effect has some important implications. First, it suggests that firms get the investors they deserve, since the dividend policy of a firm attracts investors who like it. Second, it means that firms will have a difficult time changing an established dividend policy, even if it makes complete sense to do so. For instance, U.S. telephone companies have traditionally paid high dividends and acquired an investor base that liked these dividends. In the 1990s, many of these firms turned toward multimedia businesses, with much larger reinvestment needs and less stable cash flows. While the need to cut dividends in the face of the changing business mix might seem obvious, it was nevertheless a hard sell to stockholders, who had become used to the dividends.

The clientele effect also provides an alternative argument for the irrelevance of dividend policy, at least when it comes to valuation. In summary, if investors migrate to firms that pay the dividends that most closely match their needs, it can be argued that the value of any firm should not be determined by dividend policy. Thus, a firm that pays no or low dividends should not be penalized for doing so, because its investors *do not* want dividends. Conversely, a firm that pays high dividends should not have a lower value, since its investors like dividends. This argument assumes that there are enough investors in each dividend clientele to allow firms to be fairly valued, no matter what their dividend policy.

Empirical Evidence

The question of whether the clientele effect is strong enough to divorce the value of stocks from dividend policy is an empirical one. If the effect is strong enough, the returns on stocks, over long periods, should not be affected by their dividend policies. If there is a tax disadvantage associated with dividends, the returns on stocks that pay high dividends should be higher than the returns on stocks that pay low dividends, to compensate for the tax differences. Finally, if there is an overwhelming preference for dividends, these results should be reversed.

Black and Scholes (1974) examined this question by creating 25 portfolios of NYSE stocks, classifying firms into five quintiles based upon dividend yield, and then subdividing each group into five additional groups based upon risk (beta), each year for 35 years, from 1931 and 1966. When they regressed total returns on these portfolios against the dividend yields, the authors found no statistically significant relationship between the two. These findings were contested in a later study by Litzenberger and Ramaswamy (1979), who used updated dividend yields every month and examined whether the total returns in ex-dividend months were correlated with dividend yields. They found a strong *positive* relationship between total returns and dividend yields, supporting the hypothesis that investors are averse to dividends. They also estimated that the implied tax differential between capital gains and dividends was approximately 23%. Miller and Scholes (1981) countered by arguing that this finding was contaminated by the information effects of dividend increases and decreases. In response, they removed from the sample all cases in which the dividends were declared and paid in the same month and concluded that the implied tax differential was only 4%, which was not significantly different from zero.

In the interests of fairness, we must point out that most studies of this phenomenon have concluded that total returns and dividend yields are positively correlated.

While many of them contend that this is because the implied tax differential between dividends and capital gains is significantly different from zero, there are alternative explanations for the phenomenon. In particular, while one may disagree with the conclusions arrived at by Miller and Scholes, their argument that the higher returns on stocks that pay high dividends might have nothing to do with the tax disadvantages associated with dividends but may in fact be a reflection of the price increases associated with unexpected dividend increases, has both a theoretical and an empirical basis, as discussed below.

10.10   DIVIDEND CLIENTELE AND CHANGING DIVIDEND POLICY

Telephone companies in the United States have long had the following features—they are regulated, have stable earnings and low reinvestment needs, and pay high dividends. Many of these telephone companies are now considering entering the multimedia age and becoming entertainment companies, which requires more reinvestment and creates more volatility in earnings. If you were the CEO of a telephone company, which of the following would you do?

☐   Announce an immediate cut in dividends as part of a major capital investment plan.

☐   Continue to pay high dividends, and use new stock issues to finance the expansion.

☐   Something else.

Explain.

Information Signaling

Financial markets examine every action a firm takes for implications for future cash flows and firm value. When firms announce changes in dividend policy, they are conveying information to markets, whether or not they intend to. There are a couple of stories that can be told about what information dividend changes *signal* to financial markets.

Dividends as a Positive Signal

Financial markets tend to view announcements made by firms about their future prospects with a great deal of skepticism, since firms routinely make exaggerated claims. At the same time, there are some firms, with good projects, that are undervalued by markets. How do such firms convey information credibly to markets? *Signaling theory* suggests that these firms need to take actions that cannot be easily imitated by firms without good projects. Increasing dividends can be viewed as one such action. By increasing dividends, firms create a cost to themselves, since they commit to paying these dividends in the long term. The fact that they are willing to make this commitment indicates to investors that they believe that they have the capacity to generate these cash flows in the long term. This positive signal should therefore lead to a reevaluation of the cash flows and firm values and an increase in the stock price.

Decreasing dividends operates as a negative signal, largely because firms are reluctant to cut dividends. Thus, when firms take this action, markets see it as an indication that these firms are in substantial and long-term financial trouble. Consequently, such actions lead to a drop in stock prices.

The empirical evidence concerning price reactions to dividend increases and decreases is consistent, at least on average, with these stories. Figure 10.12 summarizes the average excess returns around dividend changes for firms.

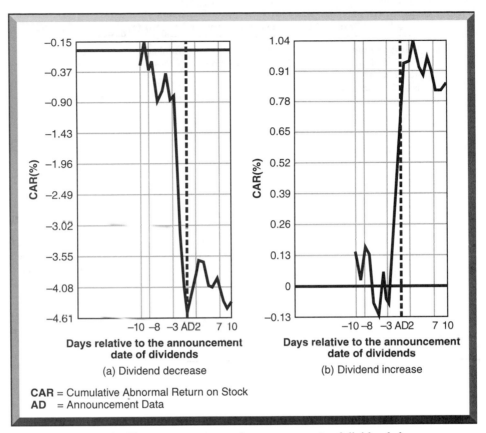

Figure 10.12   Excess returns around announcements of dividend changes.

   This explanation for why firms increase dividends has to be considered with some caution, however. While it is true that firms with good projects may use dividend increases as a way of conveying information to financial markets, given the substantial tax liability that it may create for stockholders, is it the most efficient way? For smaller firms, which have relatively few signals available to them, the answer might be yes. For larger firms, which have many ways of conveying information to markets, dividends might not be the least expensive or the most effective signal. For instance, the information may be more effectively and economically conveyed through an analyst report on the company.

Dividends as a Negative Signal
An equally plausible story can be told about how an increase in dividends sends a negative signal to financial markets. Consider a firm that has never paid dividends in the past, but has registered extraordinary growth and high returns on its projects. When this firm first starts paying dividends, its stockholders may consider this an indication that the firm's projects are neither as plentiful nor as lucrative as they used to be.
   Table 10.5, reproduced from Palepu and Healy (1986), reports the earnings growth around dividend initiations for 151 firms from 1970 to 1979. As you can see, the earnings growth rate increases significantly after dividends are initiated,

Table 10.5 EARNINGS GROWTH AROUND DIVIDEND INITIATIONS

Earnings Growth Rates in Years Surrounding First-Time Dividend Payments by 131 Firms in the Period 1970 to 1979*

Year Relative to Dividend Initiation	Number of Firms	Mean Earnings Growth Rate	Median Earnings Growth Rate
−4	130	14.9%	17.4%
−3	129	−7.1	7.6
−2	128	12.9	10.5
−1	131	42.7**	28.0
1	130	55.0**	40.2
2	130	22.0**	35.9
3	130	35.0**	28.2
4	128	3.5	19.5

*In the original research, earnings performance was computed as earnings changes standardized by stock prices. Here these values were converted to earnings growth rates by assuming that the average price earnings ratio for the sample firms is ten.
**Significantly different from zero at the 10% level or lower.
(Palepu and Healy)

Median Earnings Growth Rates in Years Surrounding First-Time Dividend Payments*

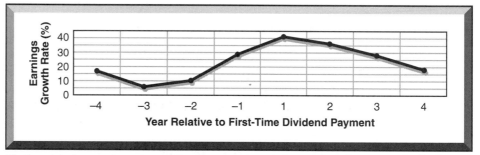

*In the original research earnings performance was computed as earnings changes standardized by stock prices. Here these values were converted to earnings growth ratios by assuming that the average price-earnings ratio for the sample firms is ten.
(Palepu and Healy)

suggesting that they operate as positive signals of future earnings growth even for these firms.

10.11 DIVIDENDS AS SIGNALS

Silicon Electronics, a company with a history of not paying dividends, high earnings growth, and reinvestment back into the company, announces that it will be initiating dividends. You would expect

☐ the stock price to go up.

☐ the stock price to go down.

☐ the stock price to remain unchanged.

Explain.

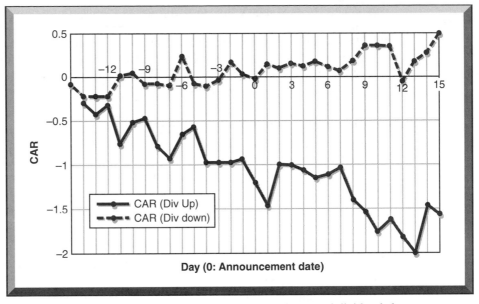

Figure 10.13   Excess returns on straight bonds around dividend changes.

STOCKHOLDERS, BONDHOLDERS, AND DIVIDENDS

The question of how much to pay in dividends is intimately connected to the financing decisions made by the firm, that is, how much debt the firm should carry. In Chapter 9, we examined how firms that want to increase or decrease leverage can do so by changing their dividend policy: Increasing dividends increases leverage, and decreasing dividends reduces leverage. In the previous chapters, we also outlined the interests of bondholders in dividend policy. Firms that increase dividends may harm bondholders by increasing their default risk, thus reducing the market value of bonds. Figure 10.13 shows the reaction of bond prices to dividend increases and decreases.

In response to this threat to their interests, bondholders often write in specific covenants into bond agreements on dividend policy, restricting the payment of dividends. These restrictions often play a role in determining a firm's dividend policy.

STOCKHOLDERS, MANAGERS, AND DIVIDENDS

In examining debt policy, we noted that one reason for taking on more debt was to induce managers to be more disciplined in their project choice. Implicit in this free cash flow argument is the assumption that cash accumulations, if left to the discretion of the managers of the firm, would be wasted on poor projects. If this is true, we can argue that forcing a firm to make a commitment to pay dividends reduces cash available to managers. This, in turn, forces managers to be disciplined in project choice.

If this is the reason stockholders want managers to commit to paying larger dividends, firms in which there is a clear separation between ownership and management should pay larger dividends than should firms with substantial insider ownership and involvement in managerial decisions.

10.12   CORPORATE GOVERNANCE AND DIVIDEND POLICY

In countries where stockholders have little or no control over incumbent managers, you would expect dividends paid by companies

☐   to be lower than dividends paid by similar companies in other countries.

☐   to be higher than dividends paid by similar companies in other countries.

☐   to be about the same as dividends paid by similar companies in other countries.

Survey Results

Given the pros and cons for paying dividends, and the lack of a consensus on the effect of dividends on value, it is worth considering what managers factor in when they make dividend decisions. Baker, Farrelly, and Edelman (1985) surveyed managers on their views on dividend policy and reported the level of agreement with a series of statements. Table 10.6 summarizes their findings.

It is quite clear from this survey that, rightly or wrongly, managers believe that their dividend payout ratios affect firm value and operate as signals of future prospects. They also operate under the presumptions that investors choose firms with dividend policies that match their preferences and that management should be responsive to their needs.

Table 10.6   MANAGEMENT BELIEFS ABOUT DIVIDEND POLICY

Statement of Management Beliefs	Agree	No Opinion	Disagree
1. A firm's dividend payout ratio affects the price of the stock.	61%	33%	6%
2. Dividend payments provide a signaling device of future prospects.	52%	41%	7%
3. The market uses dividend announcements as information for assessing firm value.	43%	51%	6%
4. Investors have different perceptions of the relative riskiness of dividends and retained earnings.	56%	42%	2%
5. Investors are basically indifferent with regard to returns from dividends and capital gains.	6%	30%	64%
6. A stockholder is attracted to firms that have dividend policies appropriate to the stockholder's tax environment.	44%	49%	7%
7. Management should be responsive to shareholders' preferences regarding dividends.	41%	49%	10%

OTHER APPROACHES TO RETURNING CASH TO STOCKHOLDERS

Dividends represent just one way of returning cash to stockholders. There are other approaches that may provide more attractive options to firms, depending upon their stockholder characteristics and their objectives. These include *equity repurchases,* whereby the cash is used to buy back outstanding stock in the firm, reducing the number of shares outstanding; and *forward contracts* to buy equity in future periods, whereby the price at which the shares will be bought back is fixed.

While not strictly representing the return of cash to stockholders, we will also consider four other options: *stock dividends* and *stock splits,* which, though used by many firms to supplement cash dividends, just change the number of shares outstanding, and *spinoffs* and *splitoffs,* which can be viewed as a return of assets (rather than cash) to stockholders.

EQUITY REPURCHASES

The most widely used alternative to paying dividends is to use the cash to repurchase outstanding stock. Such *equity repurchases,* while returning cash to stockholders, provide some advantages to firms, but they also have some limitations relative to dividends.

The Process of Equity Repurchase

The process of repurchasing equity will depend largely upon whether the firm intends to repurchase stock in the open market, at the prevailing market price, or to make a more formal tender offer for its shares. There are three widely used approaches to buying back equity:

- *Repurchase Tender Offers:*   In a repurchase tender offer, a firm specifies a price at which it will buy back shares, the number of shares it intends to repurchase, and the period of time for which it will keep the offer open, and invites stockholders to submit their shares for the repurchase. In many cases, firms retain the flexibility to withdraw the offer if an insufficient number of shares are submitted or to extend the offer beyond the originally specified time period. This approach is used primarily for large equity repurchases.

- *Open Market Purchases:*   In the case of open market repurchases, firms buy shares in the market at the prevailing market price. While firms do not have to disclose publicly their intent to buy back shares in the market, they have to comply with SEC requirements to prevent price manipulation or insider trading. Finally, open market purchases can be spread out over much longer time periods than tender offers and are much more widely used for smaller repurchases. In terms of flexibility, an open market repurchase affords the firm much more freedom in deciding when to buy back shares and how many shares to repurchase.

- *Privately Negotiated Repurchases:*   In privately negotiated repurchases, firms buy back shares from a large stockholder in the company at a negotiated price. This method is not as widely used as the first two and may be employed by managers or owners as a way of consolidating control and eliminating a troublesome stockholder.

Repurchase Tender Offer   This is an offer by a firm to buy back a specified number of shares at a fixed price during the offer period.

Open Market Purchases   This is an offer to buy shares in the market at the prevailing market price.

The Rationale

In the last decade, more and more firms have used equity repurchases as an alternative to paying dividends. Figure 10.14 summarizes new equity issues and equity repurchases at U.S. corporations between 1981 and 1990.

There are several advantages to using equity repurchases as an alternative to dividend payments to return cash to stockholders:

1. Unlike regular dividends, which imply a commitment to continue payment in future periods, equity repurchases are viewed primarily as onetime returns of cash. Consequently, firms with excess cash flows that are uncertain about their ability to continue generating these cash flows in future periods should repurchase stocks rather than pay dividends. These firms could choose to pay special dividends instead of repurchasing stock, however, since special dividends also do not imply a commitment to making similar payments in the future.

2. The decision to repurchase stock affords firms much more flexibility to reverse themselves and/or to spread the repurchases over a longer period than does the decision to pay an equivalent special dividend. In fact, there is substantial evidence that many firms that announce ambitious stock repurchase plans do not carry them through to completion.

3. Equity repurchases may offer tax advantages to stockholders, since dividends are taxed at ordinary tax rates, while the price appreciation that flows from equity repurchases is taxed at capital gains rate. Furthermore, stockholders have the option not to sell their shares back to the firm and therefore do not have to realize the capital gains in the period of the equity repurchases.

4. Equity repurchases are much more focused in terms of paying out cash only to those stockholders who need it. This benefit flows from the voluntary nature of stock buybacks: Those who need the cash can tender their shares back to the firm, while those who do not can continue to hold on to them.

5. Equity repurchases may provide a way of increasing insider control in firms, since they reduce the number of shares outstanding. If the insiders do not tender their shares back, they will end up holding a larger proportion of the firm and, consequently, having greater control.

6. Finally, equity repurchases may provide firms with a way of supporting their stock prices when they are under assault. For instance, in the aftermath of the crash of 1987, many firms initiated stock buyback plans to keep stock prices from falling further.

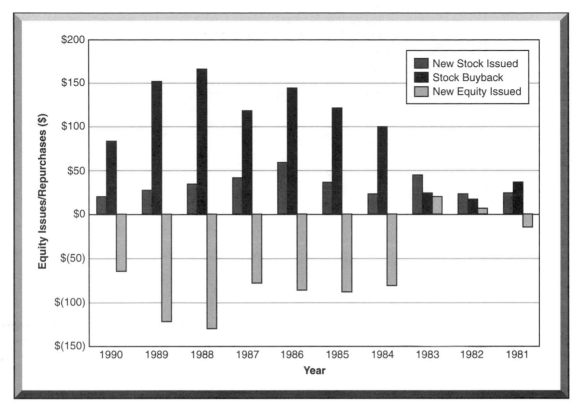

Figure 10.14   Net equity issues—1981–90.

In summary, equity repurchases allow firms to return cash to stockholders and still maintain flexibility in future periods.

IN PRACTICE: EQUITY BUYBACKS AND DILUTION

Some equity repurchases are motivated by the desire to reduce the number of shares outstanding and therefore increase the earnings per share. This argument is buttressed by assuming that the firm's price earnings ratio will remain unchanged, leading to a higher price. While the reduction in the number of shares might increase earnings per share, the effect is usually a consequence of higher leverage and not of the stock buyback per se. In other words, a special dividend of the same amount would have resulted in the same returns to stockholders. Furthermore, the increase in leverage should increase the riskiness of the stock and lower the price/earnings ratio. Whether this will increase or decrease the price per share will depend on whether the firm is moving to its optimal by repurchasing stock, in which case the price will increase, or moving away from it, in which case the price will drop.

    To illustrate the effect on EPS of stock buybacks, assume that an all-equity firm in the specialty retailing business with 100 shares outstanding has $100 in earnings after taxes and a market value of $1,500. Assume that this firm borrows $300 and buys back 20 shares, using the funds. As long as the after-tax interest expense on the borrowing is less than $20, this firm will report higher earnings per share after the repurchase. If the firm's tax rate is 50%, for instance, the effect on earnings per share will be as follows:

| | BEFORE Repurchase | AFTER REPURCHASE | |
		Interest Expense = $30	Interest Expense = $55
EBIT	$200	$200	$200
- Interest	$0	$30	$55
= Taxable Inc.	$200	$170	$145
- Taxes	$100	$85	$72.50
= Net Income	$100	$85	$72.50
# Shares	100	80	80
EPS	$1.00	$1.125	$0.91

If we assume that the price/earnings ratio remains at 15, the price per share will increase in proportion to the earnings per share. In this case, however, we should expect to see a drop in the price/earnings ratio, as the increase in leverage will make the firm riskier. Whether the drop will be sufficient to offset or overwhelm the increase in earnings per share will depend upon whether the firm has excess debt capacity and whether, by going to 20%, it is moving closer to its optimal debt mix.

10.13   STOCK BUYBACKS AND EPS EFFECTS

In the example above, the earnings per share increased when the firm borrowed money to buy back stock. Will this always be the case?

☐ Yes

☐ No

Explain.

Limitations of Equity Repurchases

Many critics of dividend policy would argue that equity repurchases are clearly preferable to both regular dividends (because of the tax advantages and the flexibility of the former) and special dividends (because of the tax benefits). There is a downside to this flexibility, however. To the degree that actions taken by firms signal their assurance about future cash flows, it can be argued that a firm that repurchases stock rather than instituting dividends is signaling a greater uncertainty about future cash flows. If this is the case, the increase in value that follows an equity repurchase would be smaller than the increase in value following an equivalent regular dividend payment. And if the firm fails to carry out equity repurchase plans to completion, markets will become increasingly skeptical of these plans and respond accordingly.

The Empirical Evidence

Several studies have examined the stock (and bond) price reaction to equity repurchases; most of them indicate a strong positive stock price reaction, with increases ranging from 10% to 20% around the announcements. Furthermore, this increase seems to be permanent rather than transitory, suggesting that the price increase is not just the result of liquidity effects, but of something deeper. It is not clear, however, which of the hypotheses best explains these results:

1. The increase in value seems too large to be explained away in terms of the tax benefits of equity repurchase relative to dividends. Since the typical repurchase in this sample involved a buyback of 15 to 20% of the outstanding shares, the tax savings should be roughly 5–6%, at the maximum.[2] Unless firms are expected to continue repurchasing large proportions of their equity every year—a very unlikely scenario—it is difficult to arrive at price increases of the magnitude observed in most of these studies.

2. It is also not clear that the price increase can be explained purely in terms of leverage, that is, that these firms were underleveraged to begin with and that buying back stock brings them closer to their optimal debt ratios (and higher firm values). For instance, Vermaelen (1981) reports that firms that do not issue debt to repurchase equity actually have higher price increases than firms that do.

3. The final possibility is that the increase in stock prices as a consequence of equity repurchases is the result of the information conveyed to financial markets by such buybacks; in particular, the equity repurchase may be viewed as a signal that the firm believes that its stock is significantly undervalued. Dann and DeAngelo (1983) tested this hypothesis by categorizing equity repurchases into privately negotiated buybacks (in which the motivation is usually control) and open market repurchases/tender offers (in which the motivation may include undervaluation), and concluded that stock prices actually declined slightly for the first group. This suggests that at least some of the price increase can be attributed to information effects.

It is unfair to compare the price increase associated with equity repurchases in these studies with the price increases associated with dividend increases noted in the previous chapter, because of the difference in dollar values between the two. Rather, a more appropriate comparison would look at the impact on stock prices of a given dollar change in regular dividends as opposed to the price impact an equivalent equity repurchase. In that case, we would expect the former to have a much larger impact, because dividends imply a much larger commitment on the part of the firm.

?

10.14   STOCK BUYBACKS AND STOCK PRICE EFFECTS

For which of the following types of firms would a stock buyback be most likely to lead to a drop in the stock price?

☐   Companies with a history of poor project choice

☐   Companies which borrow money to buy back stock

☐   Companies which are perceived to have great investment opportunities

Explain.

---

[2]A simple approximation of the tax benefit can be estimated by multiplying the equity repurchase proportion by the differential tax rate. Even taking the highest tax differential during the period (about 40%) yields a tax benefit of only 6% on an equity repurchase of 15% of the outstanding equity.

A Framework for Deciding on Equity Repurchases

While this signaling argument has some merit, it can be argued that, for most firms, the flexibility and the tax arguments will outweigh this concern. In general, however, the net benefit of equity repurchases, as opposed to dividends, will depend upon the following:

1. *Sustainability and Stability of Excess Cash Flow:*   To the degree that both equity repurchases and increased dividends are triggered by excess cash flows, the question of which course of action to take cannot be answered without looking at the sustainability of cash flows. If the excess cash flows are temporary or unstable, firms should repurchase stock; if they are stable and predictable, the signaling argument may tilt firms toward increasing dividends.

2. *Stockholder Tax Preferences:*   When capital gains and dividends are taxed at different rates, the tax preferences of the stockholders will determine whether a firm should repurchase stock or pay dividends. If stockholders are taxed at much higher rates on dividends and, consequently, are averse to dividends, the firm will be better off repurchasing stock. If, on the other hand, stockholders prefer dividends, the firm may gain by paying a special dividend.

3. *Predictability of Future Investment Needs:*   Firms that are uncertain about the magnitude of future investment opportunities are much more likely to use equity repurchases as a way of returning cash to stockholders.

4. *Undervaluation of the Stock:*   An equity repurchase makes even more sense when managers perceive their stock to be undervalued. By buying back the stock, managers can accomplish two objectives. First, if the stock remains undervalued, the remaining stockholders will benefit if managers buy back stock at less than true value. Alternatively, the stock buyback may send a signal to financial markets that the stock is undervalued, and the market will react accordingly by pushing up the price.

■ ▲　ILLUSTRATION 10.1　**Examining Disney's Choices**
▼ ●　To illustrate the choice between dividends and equity repurchases, let us consider the example of Disney. Assume, for the moment, that Disney generates $1 billion in excess cash in 1997 and that its regular dividend is only $250 million. We would argue that the excess cash should be used to buy back stock because:

1. Disney, as an entertainment company, has volatile earnings and cash flows. If Disney commits to paying higher regular dividends, it might be unable to maintain those dividends if it has a poor year.

2. Disney's stockholders have generally bought the stock for price appreciation rather than dividend yield. It is reasonable to assume, therefore, that they would much rather have the option to sell their shares back and make a capital gain, rather than receive a larger dividend (or a special dividend).

3. Disney has ambitious plans to expand its entertainment empire into Latin America and Asia. These plans create uncertainty about future investment needs; if overseas expansion goes well, future investment needs will be much higher. This uncertainty tilts the scales in favor of an equity repurchase.

FORWARD CONTRACTS TO BUY EQUITY

Many firms that announce equity repurchase plans fail to carry these plans to fruition. While this flexibility in implementation can be viewed as a benefit, it reduces the signaling benefit (and the concurrent price increase) of buying back stock. An alternative strategy, which may preserve the tax advantages of equity repurchases while also increasing the signaling benefit, is to enter into *forward contracts* to acquire stock at a fixed price. Since these contracts are commitments, the firm is forced to repurchase the shares at that price. Consequently, the market will likely view the action as concrete act and react accordingly.

Another advantage of forward contracts is that unlike regular equity repurchases, in which the number of shares that will be bought back in future periods is unknown because the stock price will be different, the number of shares that will be bought back in a forward contract is known because the purchases are at a fixed price. Consequently, the effects of the equity repurchase plans on earnings per share and related multiples can be estimated more precisely.

This certainty comes at a price, however. By agreeing to buy back shares at a fixed price, the firm increases its risk exposure, since it commits to paying this price even if the stock price drops. While it may gain an offsetting advantage if stock prices go up, the commitment to pay a higher price to buy stocks when stock prices are lower can be a burden, especially if the stock price dropped as a consequence of lower earnings or cash flows.

To summarize, the decision to cement the commitment to buying back stocks by entering into a forward contract will depend, in large part, on whether the signaling benefits are large enough to offset the higher risk and lost flexibility associated with the forward contract. The choice between paying an increased dividend or entering into a forward contract involves a tradeoff between the tax savings that may accrue from the forward contract and the increased risk associated with the forward contract.

Forward Contract   This is a contract to acquire an asset (like stock) at a fixed price at a specified time in the future.

STOCK DIVIDENDS AND STOCK SPLITS

A stock dividend involves issuing to existing stockholders additional shares in the company at no cost. Thus, in a 5% stock dividend, every existing stockholder in the firm receives new shares equivalent to 5% of the number of shares currently owned. Many firms use stock dividends to supplement cash dividends; others view them as an alternative. A *stock split,* in some ways, is just a large stock dividend, since it too increases the number of shares outstanding, but it does so by a much larger factor. Thus, a firm may have a two-for-one stock split, whereby the number of shares in the firm is doubled.

The mechanics of a stock split or dividend are simple: The firm issues additional shares in the firm and distributes them to existing stockholders in proportion to their original holdings in the firm. Thus, stock splits and dividends should not alter the proportional ownership of the firm on the part of existing stockholders.

Stock Dividend (Split) These are additional shares issued at no cost to existing stockholders, in proportion to their current holdings.

Effect on Value

Since stock dividends and stock splits have no real effect on cash flows but change only the number of shares outstanding, they should not affect the cash flows of the firm, and thus should not increase the value of equity, in the aggregate. Rather, the share price will decline to reflect the increased number of shares. To illustrate, assume that a small manufacturing firm with an aggregate value of equity of $110 million and 10 million shares outstanding declares a 10% stock dividend. The aggregate value of equity will remain $110 million, but the price per share will drop from $11 per share ($110 million/10 million) to $10 per share ($110 million / 11 million). Note, though, that the stockholders in this firm are no worse off after the stock dividend, the stock price drop notwithstanding, because they receive a compensatory increase in the number of shares outstanding.

The Rationale

If the effect on stockholder wealth is in fact neutral, why do firms pay stock dividends or announce stock splits in the first place? Some firms view stock dividends as a way of fooling stockholders; thus, a firm that is in trouble and unable to pay its regular cash dividend may announce that it is "substituting" an equivalent stock dividend. It is possible that some stockholders may actually believe that these are substitutes, but it is extremely unlikely that financial markets will not see through this deception. Other firms view stock dividends as a supplement to cash dividends and use them in periods in which they have posted good results. This rationale is more defensible, because the announcement of a stock dividend may convey information to financial markets about future prospects. In fact, the use of both stock dividends and stock splits as signals of better cash flows in the future may increase the firm value.

An additional reason given (especially) for stock splits is the desire on the part of some firms to keep their stock prices within a specified trading range. Consequently, if the stock price rises above the range, a stock split may be used to bring the price back down. To illustrate, assume that a firm wants its stock to trade in the $20 to $40 range, and that the stock price rises to $45. With a two-for-one stock split, the number of shares will double and the stock price will drop back down to roughly $22.50.

The remaining question is why would a firm have a desired trading range in the first place. Firms that do argue that given restrictions on buying shares in even lots (e.g., 100 shares), a price that is too high reduces the potential market for the stock to wealthier investors and institutional investors. Bringing the price down increases the number of potential buyers for the stock, leading to a higher stock price. Furthermore, there is a control benefit to the stock being more widely held. Both of these arguments are dubious, however. The transactions costs, if one counts the bid–ask spread as one component, actually increase as a percentage of the stock price as the price drops. Thus, the firm may lose more investors than it gains by cutting the price. There is a cost to being widely held, as well, since it increases the gulf between stockholders and managers and leads to higher agency costs.

The empirical evidence on stock splits suggests that while the initial price reaction to stock splits is positive, these excess returns are not sustained if the firm cannot maintain or increase its dividends per share in following periods.

10.15 STOCK DIVIDENDS

A company which has a history of paying cash dividends announces that it will be doubling its dividend but paying it in the form of stock instead. As an investor, would you view this as

☐   neutral news, since stock dividends do not create value anyway?

☐   good news, since dividends were doubled?

☐   bad news, since the cash dividends were cut?

Explain.

DIVESTITURES, SPINOFFS, SPLITUPS, AND SPLITOFFS

Divestitures, spinoffs, splitups and splitoffs are other options for returning non-cash assets to stockholders. Consider a company with operations in multiple business lines, some of which are being systematically undervalued; the whole firm is therefore worth less than its parts. This firm has four options:

1. ***Divest the undervalued business and pay a liquidating dividend:***   One way in which this firm can deal with its predicament is through *divestiture,* which involves selling those parts that are being undervalued by the market for their true market value and then paying out the cash to stockholders in the form of either equity repurchases or dividends.

2. ***Spin off the undervalued businesses:***   An alternative is to spin off or create a new class of shares in the undervalued business line and to distribute these shares to the existing stockholders. Since the shares are distributed in proportion to the existing share ownership, it does not alter the proportional ownership in the firm.

3. ***Split up the entire firm:***   In a *splitup,* the firm splits itself off into different business lines, distributes these shares to the original stockholders, in proportion to their original ownership in the firm, and then ceases to exist.

4. ***Split off the undervalued business:***   A *splitoff* is similar to a spinoff, insofar as it creates new shares in the undervalued business line. In this case, however, the existing stockholders are given the option to exchange their parent company stock for these new shares, which changes the proportional ownership in the new structure.

Divestiture A divestiture is the sale of a portion or portions of a firm for cash.

Spinoff In a spinoff, shares in an asset or assets of a firm are created and distributed to stockholders in proportion to their holdings.

Splitoff In a splitoff, shares in an asset or assets of a firm are created, but existing stockholders are then given the option to exchange their parent company shares for these new shares.

The Mechanics

In terms of the mechanics, divestitures are the most straightforward to understand. The firm sells the assets to the highest bidder and then uses the cash generated by the sale to pay a special dividend or to buy back stock. In the case of spinoffs and splitups, the existing stockholders receive the new shares of stock in proportion to their existing holdings, while in the case of splitoffs, the firm offers stockholders the option to convert their existing shares for the new shares in the subsidiary. The SEC also requires that stock issued in spinoffs be registered, to prevent abuses of the process.

Spinoffs may be taxed as dividends if firms do not meet certain requirements under the tax code, which is designed to ensure that there is a business purpose for the divestiture rather than, tax avoidance. First, the parent and the subsidiary must be engaged in business for the five years preceding the spinoff, and the subsidiary must be at least 80% owned by the parent. Second, the parent has to distribute the shares in the subsidiary without a prearranged plan for these securities to be resold.

The Rationale

Firms may choose to divest or spin off assets for a number of reasons and may choose one approach over the others:

1. *Source of Undervaluation:* The initial rationale for divestitures, spinoffs, splitoffs, and splitups is the perceived undervaluation of some or all of the firm's components. The firm may be undervalued for a number of different reasons, each of which lends itself to a different response.

   • If the poor quality of incumbent management at the division or business level is one of the reasons for the low value assigned to a business, the firm will probably gain the most by selling the business, severing its connection to incumbent management. If, on the other hand, the problem lies in the quality of the management at the corporate level, a spinoff may be all that is needed.

   • If there is a broad perception that sections of the business are undervalued because of the pall created by other sections of the business, the appropriate response would be a spinoff, if only one business line is involved, or a splitup, if multiple business lines are involved. As an example of a spinoff, consider the pressure brought to bear on the tobacco firms, such as Philip Morris and RJR Nabisco, to spin off their food businesses, because of the perception that the lawsuits overhanging the tobacco businesses were weighing down the values of their food businesses as well. An example of a splitup comes from AT&T, which has split up into three business lines, each trading separate shares.

- If there is a perception on the part of some stockholders that a section of the firm is undervalued, a splitoff may make more sense because it allows these stockholders the option to exchange their shares for the new shares, maximizing the value increment to the firm.

  In the case of spinoffs, splitoffs, and splitups, the division or assets can continue to operate relatively smoothly. A sale or breakup of the assets might have a disruptive influence, however, which in turn might lower their value.

2. *Tax and Regulatory Concerns:*   One or another of these options may provide a tax benefit, making it more favorable. For instance, Marriott spun off its real estate operations into a Real Estate Investment Trust (REIT) in the late 1980s. One reason for the spinoff might have been the perception of undervaluation. An even stronger reason might have been the tax advantages accruing from the REIT status, since REITs do not pay taxes at the entity level. A second factor is that the spun off entity might be under fewer regulatory constraints than the parent company. For instance, AT&T may have decided to spin off its non-telephone businesses in part because the regulatory burden under which the phone business operated was constraining its other business pursuits as well.

3. *Expropriation of Bondholder Wealth:*   Some divestitures or spinoffs are motivated by the desire to transfer wealth from bondholders to stockholders. In a divestiture, the sale of an existing asset and the payment of a liquidating dividend clearly leave bondholders worse off. In a spinoff or splitup, the results are more ambiguous, since the spun-off entities often take a share of the debt with them.

Real Estate Investment Trusts (REITs): A real estate investment trust is a real estate holding firm with traded securities, which is entitled to special tax treatment in return for restrictions on dividends and investment policy.

10.16 SPINOFF, SPLITOFF, OR DIVESTITURE?

MegaCorp is a conglomerate; one of its divisions, MegaOil, an oil service business, has reported declining earnings over the last five years and has underperformed other oil service companies. The other divisions of MegaCorp have all outperformed their peer groups and reported healthy earnings. The management of the company is considering a restructuring. Which of the following actions would you recommend to MegaCorp?

☐ Sell the oil service subsidiary to the highest bidder.

☐ Spin off the oil service subsidiary.

☐ Split off the oil service subsidiary.

Explain.

Empirical Evidence

Linn and Rozeff (1984) examined the price reaction to announcements of divestitures by firms and reported an average excess return of 1.45% for 77 divestitures between 1977 and 1982. Their results have been confirmed by a number of other studies of selloffs. They also note an interesting contrast between firms that announce the

Table 10.7   MARKET REACTION TO DIVESTITURE
ANNOUNCEMENTS

Price Announced	Motive Announced	
	Yes	No
Yes	3.92%	2.30%
No	0.70%	0.37%

sale price and motive for the divestiture at the time of the divestiture, and those that do not: In general, markets react much more positively to the first group than to the second, as shown in Table 10.7. It appears that financial markets view firms that are evasive about the reasons for and the use of proceeds from divestitures with skepticism.

Schipper and Smith (1983) examined 93 firms that announced spinoffs between 1963 and 1981 and reported an average excess return of 2.84% in the two days surrounding the announcement. Similar results are reported in Hite and Owens (1983) and Miles and Rosenfeld (1983). Further, there is evidence that the excess returns increase with the magnitude of the spun-off entity. Finally, Schipper and Smith find evidence that the excess returns are greater for firms in which the spinoff is motivated by tax and regulatory concerns.

CHOOSING AMONG THE ALTERNATIVES

As you can see, firms have a variety of options available to them when it comes to returning cash to stockholders. They can pay out the cash as dividends—either regular or special—repurchase stock, enter into forward contracts to buy stock, or spin off businesses and distribute shares in these businesses to their stockholders. In this section, we will attempt to develop a general framework that brings together all these factors.

The Determinants

The broad determinants of which approach a firm should use to return cash to stockholders include the tax implications of each approach, the effect on a firm's flexibility on future actions, and the signaling benefits (or price effect) that may accrue from each of the actions. In addition, firms often consider how ratings agencies and analysts will view these actions, and the restrictions imposed by existing bond covenants, in making their final decisions.

Information Effects and Signaling Incentives

There is a clear information effect associated with each of the actions described above. The signaling benefit from each action will vary, however, depending upon the degree of commitment associated with it. Thus, increases in regular dividends convey a larger commitment than do equity repurchases, for example, since the former have to be maintained in future periods. Table 10.8 ranks the actions described above in terms of the commitment associated with each and the associated signaling benefit.

Table 10.8   COMMITMENT AND SIGNALING BENEFIT ASSOCIATED WITH ACTIONS

Action	Commitment	Signaling Benefit
Regular Dividend	To continue payment at the same level in future periods	High
Special Dividend	None	None
Equity Repurchase	Generally low, unless the company has a practice of buying back stock; it may, however, operate as a signal that the stock is currently undervalued	Low–Moderate
Forward Equity Contracts	To buy stock at the forward price	High
Stock Splits/Dividends	Generally none, but some firms may be expected to maintain the same dollar dividend per share (which would be an increase in dividends)	Low
Spinoffs/Splitups	May operate as a signal that the business being spun off is undervalued	Low–Moderate

Stockholder Tax Preferences

Each of the actions described above has tax consequences, in terms of both the rate at which stockholders will be taxed and the time these taxes are due. These tax consequences will vary across different types of stockholders—individual versus institutional, taxable versus tax-exempt, and wealthy versus poor. Thus, a firm needs to know who its stockholders are in order to choose an optimal approach to returning cash to stockholders. Table 10.9 summarizes the tax consequences of each action for stockholders.

Effect on Flexibility

Firms value flexibility in making investment, financing, and dividend decisions in the future. To the degree that some of the actions described above reduce flexibility more than others, firms may avoid taking them. The tradeoff, however, is between preserving flexibility and increasing the signaling benefits from a given action. Increasing dividends has a large positive signaling benefit precisely because it requires a commitment on the part of the firm and because it reduces flexibility.

Bond Covenants

In some cases, bond covenants may restrict a firm's flexibility in setting or changing dividends. In particular, these covenants may specify that no more than a specified percentage of earnings can be paid out as dividends (to prevent firms from paying out liquidating dividends) and that either equity repurchases have to be approved by bondholders, or the bonds must be puttable if the equity repurchase goes through. In fact, bond covenant restrictions on financing policy may also constrain the firm when it comes to deciding how and how much to return to stockholders.

In an interesting twist on this same principle, it can be argued that firms that do not use the freedom bond covenants grant them to set dividends may be transferring wealth to bondholders, especially if bond prices are set on the assumption that

Table 10.9 TAX CONSEQUENCES OF ACTIONS

Action	Tax Consequences to Individual Investors
Regular Dividend	• Individual investors are taxed at ordinary tax rate. • Corporate investors are exempt from paying taxes on 70% of dividends received.
Special Dividend	• Individual investors are taxed at ordinary tax rate. • Corporate investors are exempt from paying taxes on 85% of dividends received.
Equity Repurchase	• Both individual and corporate investors are taxed at capital gains tax rate.
Forward Equity Contracts	• Both individual and corporate investors are taxed at capital gains tax rate.
Stock Splits/Dividends	• Generally no tax consequences for investors.
Spinoffs/Splitups	• Not taxable if it fulfills the conditions laid out in the tax law.

they will. To illustrate, if the bond covenant restricts dividend payments to 50% of earnings, and bond prices are set on the assumption that they will be paid, a firm that pays out only 20% of its earnings as dividends may be enriching the bondholders at the expense of the stockholders.

Ratings Agency/Analyst Views

When it comes to choosing among alternative approaches to returning cash or assets to stockholders, firms often consider the views of investors and equity research analysts, on the one hand, and of rating agencies and other representatives of bondholders, on the other. To the degree that the interests of the groups do not coincide, the firm may have to choose between them. To illustrate, a firm might be under pressure to spin off its most valuable assets if stockholders feel that the value of these assets is being dragged down by a negative perception of the rest of the firm. At the same time, the firms' bondholders may be averse to a spinoff, especially if it reduces their claim on these assets.

10.17 STOCK DIVIDENDS

Can a spinoff ever be viewed as good news by both bondholders and stockholders?

☐ Yes

☐ No

Explain.

A General Framework

In a general framework, firms will consider *all* of these determinants in deciding how to return cash to stockholders. Based upon the above discussion, for instance, we can draw the following conclusions:

1. Firms that want to derive the maximum signaling benefit from the return of the cash, and whose stockholders like or are indifferent to cash dividends, will likely increase regular dividends. Firms that want to derive the signaling benefit but whose stockholders are more resistant to dividends might have to enter into forward contracts to repurchase equity.

2. Firms that are unsure about their capacity to keep generating excess cash in future periods are more inclined to use special dividends, if their stockholder base likes dividends, or equity repurchases, if it does not.

3. Firms that do not have excess cash flows in the current period, but believe in their capacity to generate higher cash flows in the future may use stock splits and stock dividends, with the implicit understanding that they will be increasing dividends in future periods.

4. Firms that have assets they believe to be significantly undervalued can sell the assets and return the cash to stockholders (special dividends or equity repurchases), if the assets are liquid and the perceived quality of incumbent management is one of the reasons for the undervaluation. If the assets are not liquid, however, and it is desirable for incumbent management to stay in place, firms should consider spinoffs, whereby existing stockholders get stock in the undervalued assets.

?   **10.18   STOCK BUYBACKS, DIVIDENDS, OR CASH RETENTION?**

Immunotech, Inc. is a small electronics firm whose earnings and stock price have climbed 100% over the last two years. A large one-year contract from the Defense Department has created a large cash inflow in the current year, and Immunotech does not have the capacity to take on more investments this year (due to a shortage of skilled employees). Immunotech has never paid a dividend before. Which of the following actions would you recommend?

☐ Hold the cash for projects in future years.
☐ Initiate a regular dividend to attract new investors to the company and signal.
☐ Pay a special dividend.
☐ Buy back stock.
☐ Other:

Explain.

CONCLUSION

Like investment and financing decisions, dividend decisions involve tradeoffs. Unlike the former, however, there seems to be little consensus on where the tradeoffs should lead us in terms of the "right" dividend policy. On the one hand, some believe that due to the tax disadvantages associated with receiving dividends, relative to price appreciation, firms should reduce or even eliminate dividends and consider alternative ways of returning cash to stockholders. On the other hand, many argue that dividend increases operate as positive financial signals and that there are investors who like dividends, notwithstanding the tax disadvantages. Finally, there is the school of thought that argues that dividend policy should not really affect value, as long as it does not affect the firm's investment policy. This argument maintains that, as long as there are enough investors in each dividend clientele, firms should not be penalized for adopting a particular dividend policy.

In summary, there is some truth to all of these viewpoints, and it may be possible to develop a consensus around the points on which they agree. The reality is that dividend policy requires a tradeoff between the additional tax liability it may create for some investors against the potential signaling and free cash flow benefits of making the dividend commitment. In some cases, the firm may choose not to increase or initiate dividends, because its stockholders are in high tax brackets and are particularly averse to dividends. In other cases, dividend increases may result.

Finally, firms should consider the range of alternatives to returning cash to stockholders, such as equity buybacks, forward contracts, spinoffs and splitoff, and choose the "right" way based on their own characteristics.

PROBLEMS AND QUESTIONS

1. Based on the empirical evidence that you have been presented with in this chapter, state whether the following statements are true or false.
   a. Firms are reluctant to change dividends.

   True   False
   b. Stock prices generally go up on the ex-dividend date by less than the amount of the dividend.

   True   False
   c. Increasing dividend payments to stockholders generally makes bondholders in the firm better off.

   True   False

2. Dividend policy is often described as "sticky." What is meant by this description? What might explain the sticky nature of dividends?

3. Companies are far more reluctant to cut dividends than to increase them. Why might this be the case? What are the implications for financial markets when firms announce that they will be cutting dividends?

4. Under what assumptions can the Miller–Modigliani argument that dividends are irrelevant be made? What types of firms are most likely to fit these assumptions?

5. Dividends create a tax disadvantage for investors. Is this statement true for all investors and all markets? Under what conditions is it *not* true?

6. A company that historically has had low capital investments and paid out high dividends is entering a new industry, in which capital expenditure requirements are much higher. What should the firm do to its dividends? What practical problems might it run into?

7. "An increase in dividends operates as a positive financial signal." Explain this statement. Is there empirical evidence to support it?

8. Can a dividend increase ever be a negative financial signal? Explain. Is there any evidence to support this hypothesis?

9. If Consolidated Power is priced at $50 with dividend, and its price falls to $46.50 when a dividend of $5 is paid, what is the implied marginal rate of personal taxes for its stockholders? Assume that the tax on capital gains is 40% of the personal income tax.

10. Show that, if companies are excluded from paying taxes on 85% of the dividends they receive from other corporations and if the marginal investor is a corporation, then the ex-dividend day equality becomes

$$\frac{P_B - P_A}{D} = \frac{(1 - .15t_o)}{(1 - t_{cg})}$$

11. You are comparing the dividend policies of three dividend-paying utilities. You have collected the following information on the ex-dividend behavior of these firms.

	NE Gas	SE Bell	Western Electric
Price before	$50	$70	$100
Price after	48	67	95
Dividends/share	4	4	5

If you were a tax-exempt investor, which company would you use to make "dividend arbitrage" profits? How would you go about doing so?

12. Southern Rail has just declared a dividend of $1. The average investor in Southern Rail faces an ordinary tax rate of 50%. Although the capital gains rate is also 50%, it is believed that the investor gets the advantage of deferring this tax until future years. (The effective capital gains rate will therefore be 50% discounted back to the present.) If the price of the stock before the ex-dividend day is $10 and it drops to $9.20 by the end of the ex-dividend day, how many years is the average investor deferring capital gains taxes? (Assume that the opportunity cost used by the investor in evaluating future cash flows is 10%.)

13. LMN Corporation, a real estate corporation, is planning to pay a dividend of $0.50 per share. Most of the investors in LMN Corporation are other corporations, who pay 40% of their ordinary income and 28% of their capital gains as taxes. However, they are allowed to exempt 85% of the dividends they receive from taxes. If the shares are selling at $10 per share, how much would you expect the stock price to drop on the ex-dividend day?

14. UJ Gas is a utility that has followed a policy of increasing dividends every quarter by 5% over dividends in the prior year. The company announces that it will increase quarterly dividends from $1.00 to $1.02 next quarter. What price reaction would you expect to the announcement? Why?

15. Microsoft Corporation, which has had a history of high growth and no dividends, announces that it will start paying dividends next quarter. How would you expect its stock price to react to the announcement? Why?

16. JC Automobiles is a small auto parts manufacturing firm, which has paid $1.00 in annual dividends each year for the last five years. It an-nounces that dividends will increase to $1.25 next year. What would you expect the price reaction to be? Why? If your answer is different from the prior problem, explain the reasons for the difference.

17. Would your answer be different for the previous problem if JC Automobiles were a large firm followed by 35 analysts? Why or why not?

18. WeeMart Corporation, a retailer of children's clothes, announces a cut in dividends following a year in which both revenues and earnings dropped significantly. How would you expect its stock price to react? Explain.

19. RJR Nabisco, in response to stockholder pressure in 1996, announced a significant increase in dividends paid to stockholders, financed by the sale of some of its assets. What would you expect the stock price to do? Why?

20. RJR Nabisco also had $10 billion in bonds outstanding at the time of the dividend increase. How would you expect Nabisco's bonds to react to the announcement? Why?

21. A recent innovation in managerial incentive schemes is for the shareholders of a corporation to partially compensate management with stock options. How could such a scheme affect management's decisions concerning optimal dividend policy?

22. If the next tax reform act were to impose a flat tax of 23% on all income, how do you think this would affect corporations' dividend policies? Why?

23. This chapter has demonstrated the consequences of differential taxation of dividends and capital gains: firms have weakened incentives to pay dividends. Why would the U.S. government (acting through the tax code) want these consequences?

24. A company that has excess cash on hand is trying to decide whether to pay out the cash as a regular dividend or a special dividend or to repurchase stock with it. What are some of the considerations that would enter into this decision?

25. An equity repurchase will always provide a lesser signaling benefit than will an equivalent dollar increase in regular dividends. Explain this statement. Does it hold true if the comparison is to special dividends?

26. Suppose that a firm's management is anticipating having to make future cuts in dividends when

they unexpectedly get awarded a large cash set-
tlement in a court decision. Could the firm conceivably reduce total dividend payments by using the surplus to repurchase shares? If so, would
this be the optimal way to use the windfall?

27. In many cases, firms have offered to repurchase
shares from one of their shareholders in what is
called a "targeted" repurchase. In a targeted repurchase, only the shareholder named is allowed
to tender shares, and the purchase price is often
well above the current market price. Such repurchases are generally used to "buy off" someone
who has announced the intention to take over the
firm. Would such an arrangement benefit or hurt
the sharcholders who aren't allowed to tender
shares? Why?

28. A firm is planning to borrow money to make an
equity repurchase to increase its stock price. It is
basing its analysis on the fact that there will be
fewer shares outstanding after the repurchases,
and higher earnings per share.
   a. Will earnings per share always increase af-
      ter such an action? Explain.
   b. Will the higher earnings per share always
      translate into a higher stock price? Explain.
   c. Under what conditions will such a
      transaction lead to a higher price?

29. Stock repurchases can send different signals to
the marketplace depending on whether or not
management is allowed to tender any shares they
own for repurchase. Suppose that JCL Steel has 1
million shares outstanding at a market price of $42
per share. The firm's current debt to capital ratio is
0.5 and interest payments are 10% of debt. JCL has
just had a very good year and has $10 million of
"extra" cash available. Management owns 5% of
outstanding shares, and the firm has just announced that it will reduce debt by $5 million and
buy back 100,000 shares at $50 per share. Managers
will not be allowed to tender their shares, and earnings before interest and taxes are expected to be
$15 million next year.
   a. If the firm's tax rate is 40%, what effect will
      the combined debt and equity repurchase
      have on EPS?
   b. Calculate JCL's current P/E ratio and
      determine the post-split price assuming
      that the P/E stays the same. Compare it to
      the $50 tender offer. Do you think

management agrees with your assumption?
Why or why not?
   c. Could management have caused the stock
      market to reevaluate its assumption about
      the "correct" price for JCL stock by buying
      back the 100,000 shares at the current
      market price? Why or why not?
   d. Would your answers to (b) and (c) have
      changed if management had been allowed
      to tender shares for repurchase?

30. ABT Trucking has excess cash of $300,000 and
100,000 shares outstanding. The firm is contem-
plating paying this $300,000 out as an extra divi-
dend to shareholders. Post-dividend, the price is
expected to be $27 per share. Alternatively, the
company is considering using the excess cash to
repurchase 10,000 shares at $30 per share.
   a. If shareholders' ordinary income is taxed at
      40% and their capital gains are taxed at
      28%, how should the firm disburse the
      money?
   b. If the shareholders consist mainly of other
      corporations, how should the firm disburse
      the money?

31. JR Computers, a firm that manufactures and
sells personal computers, is an all-equity firm
with 100,000 shares outstanding, $10 million in
earnings after taxes, and a market value of $150
million. Assume that this firm borrows $60 mil-
lion at an interest rate of 8% and buys back
40,000 shares using the funds. If the firm's tax rate
is 50%, estimate
   a. The effect on earnings per share of the
      action.
   b. What the interest rate on the debt would
      have to be for the earnings per share effect
      to disappear.

32. JK Tobacco, a diversified firm in food and tobacco is concerned about its stock price, which
has dropped almost 25% over the previous two
years. The managers of the firm believe that the
price drop has occurred because the tobacco division is the target of lawsuits, which may result
in a large liability for the firm. What action would
you recommend to the firm? What might be some
of the barriers to such an action?

33. The stock price of GenChem Corporation, a
chemical manufacturing firm with declining earnings, has dropped from $50 to $35 over the course

of the last year, largely as a consequence of the market perception that the current management is incompetent. The management is planning to split off the firm into three businesses but plans to continue running all of them. Do you think the splitoff will cause the stock price to increase? Why or why not? What would you recommend?

34. The stock prices of firms generally increase when they announce spinoffs. How would you explain this phenomenon? On which types of firms would you expect spinoffs to have the largest positive impact, and why?

35. WeeKids, a firm that operates play arenas for children, has paid $1 as a dividend per share each year for the last five years. Because of a decline in revenues and increased competition, their earnings have plummeted this year. They substitute a $1 stock dividend for the cash dividend. What would you expect the market reaction to the stock dividend to be? Why?

36. In 1995, the Limited, a specialty retailing firm, announced that it was splitting up its businesses into three separate businesses—the Limited stores forming one business, Victoria's Secret and lingerie becoming the second business, and its other holdings forming the third business. The Limited had been struggling over the previous four years with lackluster sales and operating profits overall, and the market reacted positively to the announcement. What might be some of the explanations for this reaction?

37. JW Bell, a regulated company, also has extensive holdings in nonregulated businesses and reports consolidated income from all segments. There are severe restrictions on investment and financing policy in the regulated component of the business. Can you provide a rationale for spinning off the nonregulated businesses?

38. An article in a business periodical recently argued that the only reason for spinoffs and splitoffs was to make it easier for Wall Street to value firms. Why would a spinoff or a splitoff make it easier to value a firm? Do you agree that this is the only reason for spinoffs and splitoffs? If so, what types of firms would you expect to take these actions?

39. JC Conglo Corporation is a firm that was founded in the 1960s and grew to become a conglomerate through acquisitions. It has substantial corporate costs that get allocated over the different divisions of the firm. Analysts argue that divesting the firm of these divisions will increase value, since the buyer will not have to pay the corporate costs. Under what conditions would spinning off the divisions of the firm add to the value of the firm? Conversely, under what conditions would a spinoff have a neutral or negative effect on value?

40. RJR Nabisco, the food and tobacco giant, is waging a battle against dissident stockholders who want it to divest itself of its food division and pay a large dividend to the stockholders. RJR Nabisco offers to spin off the food division, while keeping it under incumbent management. Are stockholders likely to be satisfied? Why or why not?

LIVE CASE STUDY

VIII. DIVIDEND POLICY

Objective: To examine the firm's current dividend policy in light of its current characteristics

Key Questions

- How has this company returned cash to its owners? Has it paid dividends, bought back stock, or spun off assets?
- Given this firm's characteristics today, how would you recommend that they return cash to stockholders (assuming that they have excess cash)?

Framework for Analysis

1. Historical Dividend Policy

- How much has this company paid in dividends over the last few years?
- How much stock has this company bought back over the last few years?

2. Firm Characteristics

- How easily can the firm convey information to financial markets? In other words, how necessary is it for them to use dividend policy as a signal?
- Who is the average stockholder in this firm? Does he or she like dividends or would they prefer stock buybacks?
- How well can this firm forecast its future financing needs? How valuable is preserving flexibility to this firm?
- Are there any significant bond covenants that you know of that restrict the firm's dividend policy?
- How does this firm compare with other firms in the sector in terms of dividend policy?

Getting Information on Dividend Policy

You can get information on dividends paid and stock bought back over time from the financials of the firm. (The statement of changes in cash flows is usually the best source for both.) To see typical dividend payout ratios and yields for the sector in which this firm operates, examine the data set on industry averages on my Web site (**inddiv.xls**)

CHAPTER 11

A FRAMEWORK FOR ANALYZING DIVIDEND POLICY

In the previous chapter, we examined three schools of thought on dividends which came to very different conclusions. Here, we provide a framework that considers points raised by all three schools of thought and provides specific answers to the following questions:

- When should a firm be pressured to increase its payouts to stockholders, and how can such a firm defend itself?
- When should a firm be pressured to reduce its payouts to stockholders, and what are the consequences of excessive dividends?
- What types of firms have the most flexibility in setting dividend policy?
- How should firms measure their dividend policies against others firms?

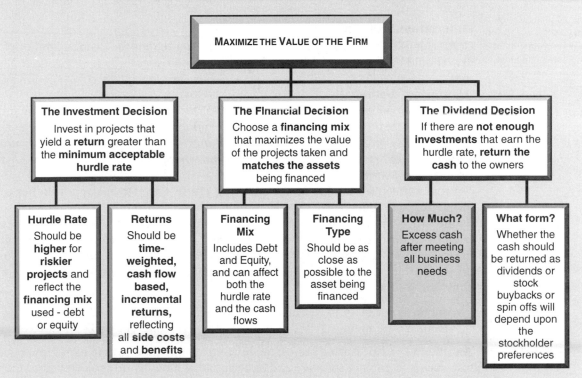

MAXIMIZE THE VALUE OF THE FIRM

The Investment Decision
Invest in projects that yield a **return** greater than the **minimum acceptable hurdle rate**

The Financial Decision
Choose a **financing mix** that maximizes the value of the projects taken and **matches the assets** being financed

The Dividend Decision
If there are **not enough investments** that earn the hurdle rate, **return the cash** to the owners

Hurdle Rate
Should be **higher** for **riskier projects** and reflect the **financing mix** used - debt or equity

Returns
Should be **time-weighted, cash flow based, incremental returns**, reflecting all **side costs** and **benefits**

Financing Mix
Includes Debt and Equity, and can affect both the hurdle rate and the cash flows

Financing Type
Should be as close as possible to the asset being financed

How Much?
Excess cash after meeting all business needs

What form?
Whether the cash should be returned as dividends or stock buybacks or spin offs will depend upon the stockholder preferences

BRINGING IT ALL TOGETHER

The three schools of thought on dividend policy each raise some legitimate points. The "dividend irrelevancy" school emphasizes that firm value cannot be changed by dividend decisions, and that firms get stockholders who like their dividend policy. The "dividends are good" school is also grounded on the notion of investor clienteles, but it assumes that stockholders for the most part like dividends and view dividend increases as a positive signal. The "dividends are bad" school is predicated on the tax disadvantages that accrue when dividends are paid.

The Tradeoffs

A firm has to walk a tightrope when it comes to setting dividend policy. On the one hand, paying too much in dividends creates several problems: The firm may find itself short of funds for new investments and may have to incur the cost associated with new security issues or capital rationing, and the investors receiving the dividends may face a much larger tax liability. On the other hand, paying too little in dividends can also create problems. For one, the firm will find itself with a cash balance that increases over time, which can lead to investments in "bad" projects, especially when the interests of management in the firm are different from those of the stockholders. In response, some argue for leverage as a way of inducing discipline in the firm. In addition, paying too little in dividends may transfer wealth from stockholders to bondholders, especially if bond prices are set on the assumption that the firm will maintain a reasonable dividend payout.

Determinants of Dividend Policy

Concerning the tradeoff noted above, we would argue that the dividend policy of a firm should be determined by the following characteristics.

Investment Opportunities

Since the payment of dividends reduces the cash available to the firm to take on projects, the dividend policy of a firm should be influenced strongly by both the availability and the returns on its projects. *Other things remaining equal, a firm with more investment opportunities should pay a lower fraction of its earnings as dividends than should a stable firm.*

From a practical standpoint, the quality of a firm's investment opportunities can be measured in a number of ways. One approach is to look at the actual return made by the firm on its current projects and to compare it to the hurdle rate—the cost of equity, if returns are measured in equity terms, or the cost of capital, if returns are measured prior to debt. Since it is difficult to compute market returns on individual projects, project returns are usually measured in accounting terms as the return on equity or the return on capital:

$$\text{Return on Equity} = \text{Net Income} / \text{Book Value of Equity}$$
$$\text{Return on Capital} = \text{EBIT} (1 - \text{Tax Rate}) / (\text{BV of Debt} + \text{BV of Equity})$$

Another way of measuring project quality is to assume that firms in high-growth sectors, such as computer software and biotechnology, have "good projects," since there is a positive correlation between growth and investment opportunities.

11.1   Use of Book Value in Return on Equity (Capital) Calculations

In an apparent deviation from the general rule of using market value, wherever available, the returns on equity and capital are computed based upon book value. The reason we do this is:

☐   Book value is not as volatile as market value.

☐   Book value provides a more conservative estimate of returns than market value.

☐   Book value is a proxy for market value of existing assets.

Explain.

Stability in Earnings

In the previous chapter, we noted the reluctance of firms to cut dividends, even in the face of lower earnings. As a result, *firms with unstable earnings tend to pay out a much lower fraction of their earnings as dividends* because they are concerned about their ability to maintain these dividends. Conversely, *firms with stable and predictable earnings typically pay out a much larger proportion of their earnings as dividends.*

The stability of earnings is largely determined by three variables—the kind of business the firm is in, the operating leverage (fixed costs) it employs to run its business, and the amount of financial leverage it has taken on. In general, firms in cyclical businesses (e.g., automobiles and housing) and businesses with volatile earnings (e.g., technology) are more likely to have lower payout ratios than are firms in stable businesses (such as utilities, which are regulated). Firms that operate with high operating leverage are likely to pay a lower fraction of their earnings as dividends than are firms with low operating leverage. And firms that have higher financial leverage tend to pay out lower dividends than do firms with lower financial leverage. From an empirical standpoint, there should be an inverse relationship between the variance in earnings and the dividend payout ratio.

Alternative Sources of Capital

One of the consequences of paying too high a dividend is that the firm has to raise external financing to cover the shortfall and to take on new projects. To the degree that a firm can do this at low cost, it can afford to pay out a much larger proportion of its earnings as dividends. There are several costs associated with issuing external financing, however. One is the actual flotation cost associated with the issue, including investment banking commissions and transactions costs. As we noted in earlier chapters, this cost varies inversely with the size of the issue and is likely to be smaller for larger firms. Another cost arises from the credibility of the firm—firms run the risk of being unable to convince markets of the quality of their projects and thus end up either issuing new securities at too low a value or rejecting good projects. This cost is also generally lower for larger and more established firms, though small firms with good track records for taking good projects may also be able to raise external financing. Other things remaining equal, a firm that can issue new stock or bonds at low cost is more likely to pay high dividends.

From an empirical standpoint, this suggests a positive relationship between the size of the firm and the dividend payout ratio: Larger firms should pay out a higher proportion of their earnings as dividends than do smaller firms.

11.2   FLOTATION COSTS AND DIVIDEND POLICY

In the last few years, firms have acquired far more power to raise capital in markets them-selves, with lower costs, by using techniques like shelf registration. What effect, if any, would you expect these developments to have on the cash paid out to stockholders?

☐ I would expect an increase in the cash returned to the stockholders.

☐ I would expect a decrease in the cash returned to the stockholders.

☐ I would expect no change in the cash returned to the stockholders.

Degree of Financial Leverage

We noted earlier that a firm with higher financial leverage is likely to pay a lower proportion of its earnings as dividends than is one with lower leverage; this is because the variability in earnings increases with leverage. Higher financial leverage may reduce dividends for two other reasons, as well. First, as firms borrow more, they are much more likely to face constraints on dividend policy, restricting not only the dollar dividends but also the proportion of earnings that can be paid out as dividends. Second, taking on debt creates a commitment to making interest payments, which reduces the free cash flow available to managers. Since increasing dividends accomplishes the same goal, it can be argued that high financial leverage and high dividends are alternative approaches to keeping managers disciplined.

Empirically, we would expect firms with high financial leverage to pay out a lower proportion of their earnings as dividends than otherwise similar firms with low financial leverage.

Signaling Incentives

As we discussed in the previous chapter, firms often use dividend changes as a way of conveying information to financial markets. Increases in dividends generally operate as positive signals of future cash flows, resulting in increases in value, while cuts in dividends operate as negative signals and are associated with negative returns. To the extent that dividends are costly to the firm (by increasing their dependence on external financing) and to its stockholders (by creating a tax liability), it can be argued that there may be alternative signals available to the firm which convey the same information at much less cost. For instance, a firm that is covered by dozens of analysts should have a lesser need to use dividend increases to convey information to markets than should one that garners little or no attention.

Stockholder Characteristics

Finally, a firm's dividend policy should be strongly influenced by the type of stockholders it attracts. A firm whose stockholders like dividends will generally pay a much higher proportion of its earnings as dividends than will one without such stockholders. But how does a firm end up with such stockholders in the first place? The clientele effect argues that stockholders choose firms that adopt dividend policies that match their preferences. Thus, a firm that institutes high dividends will find itself trapped into maintaining such a policy, even if the circumstances under which the policy was initiated change. Empirically, this suggests a strong and positive relationship between past dividend payout and current dividend payout. Firms are unlikely to voluntarily shift from paying very high proportions of their earnings as dividends to paying very low proportions or vice versa.

There is a dataset that summarizes the latest averages, by sector, of proxies for each of the above mentioned variables relating to dividend policy (**inddiv.xls**).

A FRAMEWORK FOR ANALYZING DIVIDEND POLICY

In applying a rational framework for analyzing dividend policy, a firm will attempt to answer two questions:

1. How much cash is available to be paid out as dividends, after meeting capital expenditure and working capital needs to sustain future growth, and how much of this cash is actually paid out to stockholders?

2. How good are the projects that are available to the firm?

In general, firms that have good projects will have much more leeway on dividend policy, since stockholders will expect that the cash accumulated in the firm will be invested in these projects and eventually earn high returns. By contrast, firms that do not have good projects will find themselves under pressure to pay out all or most of the cash that is available as dividends.

How Much Can a Firm Afford to Pay Out or Return to Its Stockholders?

To estimate how much cash a firm can afford to return to its stockholders, we begin with the net income—the accounting measure of the stockholders earnings during the period—and convert it to a cash flow as follows. First, any capital expenditures are subtracted from the net income, since they represent a cash outflow. Depreciation, on the other hand, is added back in because it is a non-cash charge. The difference between capital expenditures and depreciation is referred to as *net capital expenditures* and is usually a function of the growth characteristics of the firm. High-growth firms tend to have high net capital expenditures relative to earnings, whereas low-growth firms may have low net capital expenditures. Second, increases in working capital drain a firm's cash flows, while decreases in working capital increase the cash flows available to equity investors. Firms that are growing fast in industries with high working capital requirements (retailing, for instance) typically have large increases in working capital. Since we are interested in the cash flow effects, we consider only changes in *non-cash working capital* in this analysis. Finally, equity investors also have to consider the effect of changes in the levels of debt on their cash flows. Repaying the principal on existing debt represents a cash outflow, but it may be fully or partially financed by the issue of new debt, which is a cash inflow. Again, netting out the repayment of old debt against the new debt issues provides a measure of the cash flow effects of changes in debt.

Allowing for the cash flow effects of net capital expenditures, changes in working capital, and net changes in debt on equity investors, we can define the cash flows left over after these changes as the *free cash flow to equity:*

Free Cash Flow to Equity (FCFE) = Net Income
- (Capital Expenditures − Depreciation)
- (Change in Non-Cash Working Capital)
+ (New Debt Issued − Debt Repayments)

This is the cash flow available to be paid out as dividends.

This calculation can be simplified if we assume that the net capital expenditures and working capital changes are financed using a specified mix of debt and equity.[1] If δ is the proportion of the net capital expenditures and working capital changes that is raised from debt financing, the effect on cash flows to equity of these items can be summarized as follows:

Equity Cash Flows Associated with Capital Expenditure Needs =
− (Capital Expenditures − Depreciation) $(1 - \delta)$

Equity Cash Flows Associated with Working Capital Needs =
− (Δ Non-Cash Working Capital) $(1-\delta)$

Accordingly, the cash flow available for equity investors after meeting capital expenditure and working capital needs is:

Free Cash Flow to Equity = Net Income
− (Capital Expenditures − Depreciation) $(1 - \delta)$
− (Δ Non-Cash Working Capital) $(1-\delta)$

The new debt issues cover principal repayments.

Assuming that a specified proportion of net capital expenditures and working capital needs will be financed with debt is particularly useful in two cases. First, the target or optimal debt ratio of the firm can be used to forecast the free cash flow to equity that will be available in future periods. Second, in examining past periods, the firm's average debt ratio over the period can be used to arrive at approximate free cash flows to equity.

■ **Net Capital Expenditure:** This is the difference between capital expenditures and depreciation. It is a measure of the financing needed, from internal or external sources, to meet capital investment needs.

■ **Free Cash Flow to Equity:** This is the cash flow left over for equity investors after meeting all needs—debt payments, capital expenditures, and working capital.

IN PRACTICE: ESTIMATING THE FCFE AT A FINANCIAL SERVICE FIRM

The standard definition of free cash flows to equity is straightforward to put into practice for most manufacturing firms, since the net capital expenditures, non-cash working capital needs, and debt ratio can be estimated from the financial statements. In contrast, the estimation of free cash flows to equity is difficult for financial service firms, due to several reasons. First, estimating net capital expenditures and non-cash working capital for a bank or insurance company is difficult to do, since all of the assets and liabilities are in the form of financial claims. Second, it is difficult to define

---

[1]When we refer to working capital from this point on, we are focusing only on non-cash working capital.

short-term debt for financial service firms, again due to the complexity of their balance sheets.

To estimate the FCFE for a bank, we began by categorizing the income earned into three categories—*net interest income* from taking deposits and lending them out at a higher interest rate, *arbitrage income* from buying financial claims (at a lower price) and selling financial claims (of equivalent risk) at a higher price, and *advisory and fee income* from providing financial advice and services to firms. For each of these sources of income, we traced the equity investment that would be needed:

Type of Income	Net Investment Needed
Net Interest Income	Net Loans − Total Deposits
Arbitrage Income	Investments in Financial Assets − Corresponding Financial Liabilities
Advisory Income	Training Expenses

(Net Loans = Total Loans − Bad Debt Provisions)

The first two categories of net investment can usually be obtained from the balance sheet, and changes in these net figures from year to year can be treated as the equivalent of net capital expenditures. While, in theory, training expenses should be capitalized and treated as tax-deductible capital expenditures, they are seldom shown in enough detail at most firms for this to be feasible.

11.3   Defining Free Cash Flows to Equity

The reason that the net income is not the amount that a company can afford to pay out in dividends is because

☐   Earnings are not cash flows.

☐   Some of the earnings have to be reinvested back in the firm to create growth.

☐   There may be cash inflows or outflows associated with the use of debt.

☐   All of the above.

Explain.

Illustration **11.1**   Estimating Free Cash Flows to Equity for Disney, Aracruz, Bookscape, and Deutsche Bank

In the following analysis, we estimate the free cash flows to equity for each of the four firms that we are analyzing in this book. We begin with an analysis of the free cash flows to equity at Disney from 1992 to 1996 (Table 11.1).

In 1996, the numbers are heavily skewed by the $10 billion issued in new debt to finance the acquisition of Capital Cities for $18.5 billion. The negative FCFE of $7.914 billion was financed with the new stock issued for the Capital Cities acquisition. Without considering this acquisition, the FCFE in 1996 would have been $1,086 million.

The net debt issued during the period averaged $130 million, and the average net capital expenditure and working capital needs amounted to $545 million ($1001 − $539 + $82), resulting in a debt ratio of approximately 23.81%. Using the approximate formulation for FCFE, and ignoring the Capital Cities acquisition, Table 11.2 yields the following results for FCFE for Disney for the same period.

Table 11.1 ESTIMATES OF FCFE FOR DISNEY: 1992 TO 1996

Year	Net Income	Capital Expenditures	Depreciation	Change in Working Capital	Net Debt Issued	FCFE
1992	$817	$544	$317	($106)	($54)	$642
1993	$889	$794	$364	$211	$68	$316
1994	$1,110	$1,026	$410	$654	$686	$526
1995	$1,380	$897	$470	$271	$82	$764
1996	$1,214	$20,246	$1,134	($617)	$9,367	($7,914)
1996[a]	$1,214	$1,746	$1,134	($617)	($133)	$1,086
Average[a]	$1,082	$1,001	$539	$82	$130	$667

[a]Without the Capital Cities acquisition.

Table 11.2 ESTIMATES OF APPROXIMATE FCFE FOR DISNEY: 1992 TO 1996

Year	Net Income	(Cap Ex − Depr)$(1-\delta)$	Change in Working Capital $(1-\delta)$	FCFE
1992	$817	$173	($81)	$725
1993	$889	$328	$160	$402
1994	$1,110	$469	$498	$143
1995	$1,380	$325	$206	$849
1996	$1,214	$466	($470)	$1,218
Average	$1,082	$352	$63	$667

DR = Debt Ratio

While the year-to-year FCFE are different, the average FCFE over the period remains $667 million.

We follow up with an analysis of the FCFE at Aracruz from 1994 to 1996. We begin our analysis after the Real Plan of 1994, since many of the numbers prior to 1994 are not comparable to post-1994 numbers and are heavily influenced by the hyperinflation of the early 1990s.

As Table 11.3 indicates, Aracruz had an average FCFE of 140 million BR during the three-year period, even though the FCFE in 1996 were negative.

The free cash flows to equity for Bookscape are estimated as well just for 1996 in Table 11.4. Note that the operating lease is the only debt that the firm has, and the calculation of FCFE is therefore straightforward with the following assumptions:

1. The capital expenditures in 1996 were $700,000 and depreciation was $500,000 for Bookscape as a firm.

2. The revenues in 1996 increased by $2.5 million over 1995 revenues, leading to an increase in non-cash working capital of $250,000.

3. The net income for the year was $1.16 million.

		Table 11.3	ESTIMATES OF FCFE FOR ARACRUZ: 1994–1996			
Year	Net Income	Capital Expenditures	Depreciation	Change in Working Capital	Net Debt Issued	FCFE
1994	BR 248	BR 450	BR 193	BR 70	BR 253	BR 174
1995	BR 326	BR 455	BR 165	(BR 23)	BR 425	BR 484
1996	BR 47	BR 212	BR 190	BR 35	(BR 228)	(BR 238)
Average	BR 207	BR 372	BR 183	BR 27	BR 150	BR 140

Table 11.4 ESTIMATED FCFE FOR BOOKSCAPE: 1996	
Net Income	$1,160,000
+ Depreciation	$500,000
− Capital Expenditure	$700,000
− Change in Working Capital	$250,000
FCFE	$710,000

Bookscape had FCFE of $710,000 in 1996.

To estimate the FCFE for Deutsche Bank, we used the categories developed earlier for banks—*net interest income, arbitrage income,* and *advisory and fee income* from providing financial advice and services to firms. To estimate the net investment made in 1996 for each source of income, and ignoring training expenses, we used the balance sheet numbers for 1995 and 1996:

	1995	1996	Change
Interbank Assets	128,508	212,269	83,761
Net Loans	395,215	370,598	(24,617)
ST Investments	88,566	175,492	86,926
LT Investments	65,735	78,154	12,419
Net Fixed Assets	9,062	10,375	1,313
Other Assets	11,474	14,365	2,891
Total Non-Cash Assets	*698,560*	*861,253*	*162,693*
Total Deposits	301,386	375,629	74,243
ST Borrowings	211,320	254,197	42,877
LT Borrowings	97,536	110,111	12,575
ST Liabilities	52,702	82,114	29,412
LT Liabilities	24,936	32,064	7,128
Liabilities	*687,880*	*854,115*	*166,235*

We then categorized these changes into the "interest income" investments, "arbitrage income" investments, and "other" investments, considering interbank investments as interest income investments.

Interest Income Investments = (Net Loans + Interbank Investments − Deposits)$_{1996}$ − (Net Loans + Interbank Investments − Deposits)$_{1995}$

Arbitrage Investments = (Short Term and Long Term Investments − ST Borrowings − LT Borrowings − ST Liabilities − LT Liabilities)$_{1996}$ − (Short-Term and Long Term Investments − ST Borrowings − LT Borrowings − ST Liabilities − LT Liabilities)$_{1995}$

Other Investments = (Net Fixed Assets + Other Assets)$_{1996}$ − (Net Fixed Assets + Other Assets)$_{1995}$

With these definitions, and based upon Deutsche's Bank's net income of 2,134 million DM in 1996, we estimated the FCFE in 1996:

Net Income	2134
− Interest Income Investments	−15099
− Arbitrage Income Investments	7,353
− Other Investments	4,204
FCFE	5,676

This analysis would suggest that Deutsche Bank had 5.676 billion DM available to be returned to stockholders in 1996.

 This spreadsheet allows you to estimate the free cash flows to equity for a firm over a period for up to 10 years and compare it to dividends paid (**dividend.xls**).

Relationship to Dividend Payout Ratio

The conventional measure of dividend policy—the dividend payout ratio—evaluates dividends as a proportion of earnings. In contrast, our approach estimates dividends as a proportion of the free cash flow to equity:

$$\text{Dividend Payout Ratio} = \text{Dividends}/\text{Earnings}$$
$$\text{Dividend to FCFE Ratio} = \text{Dividends}/\text{FCFE}$$

The ratio of dividends to FCFE provides a measure of how much of the cash that is available to be paid out to stockholders is actually returned to them in the form of dividends. In fact, this definition can be expanded to include equity repurchases:

Cash to Stockholders to FCFE Ratio = (Dividends + Equity Repurchases) / FCFE

If this ratio, over time, is equal or close to 1, the firm is paying out all that it can to its stockholders. If it is significantly less than 1, the firm is paying out less than it can afford to and is using the difference to increase its cash balance or to invest in marketable securities. If it is significantly over 1, the firm is paying out more than it can afford and is either drawing on an existing cash balance or issuing new securities.

Table 11.5   DIVIDEND PAYOUT RATIOS AND FCFE FOR PUBLICLY TRADED FIRMS

Company	Period Analyzed	Dividends	Dividends + Stock Buybacks	Earnings	FCFE	Payout Ratio	Cash Returned/ FCFE
Disney	1992–1996	168	450	1082	667	15.53%	67.47%
Aracruz	1994–1996	73	73	207	140	35.27%	52.14%
Deutsche Bank	1996	1354	1354	2134	5676	63.45%	23.85%

■▲ ▼● ILLUSTRATION **11.2**   Comparing Dividend Payout Ratios to FCFE Payout Ratios—Disney, Aracruz, Bookscape, and Deutsche Bank

In Table 11.5, we compare the dividend payout ratios to the cash returned as a percent of FCFE for the publicly traded firms in our analysis.

Aracruz Cellulose and Deutsche Bank did not buy back any stock during the periods analyzed, but Disney did buy back, on average, $282 million worth of stock each year between 1992 and 1996. The dividend payout ratio is clearly very different from the dividends as a percent of FCFE. Disney, for instance, pays out about two-thirds of its FCFE as dividends, while its payout ratio is much lower. Aracruz seems to have stayed fairly close to the statutory dividend payout ratio mandated for Brazilian firms of 35%, while its dividends comprised, on average, around 52.14% of FCFE. Deutsche Bank offers the largest deviation between dividend payout ratios (63.45%) and dividends as a percent of FCFE (which is only 23.85%). All of these firms, on average, accumulated cash during the period. Disney did use a substantial portion of the cash it accumulated during the period to partly finance its acquisition of Capital Cities.

For the only private firm in our sample, Bookscape, there are no public dividends, but the owner of the firm can withdraw the FCFE without hurting the future prospects of the firm.

Why Dividends May Be Less Than FCFE

Firms pay out less in dividends than they have available in free cash flows to equity for a number of reasons. While the reasons may vary from firm to firm, they can be categorized as follows:

- The managers of a firm may gain by retaining cash rather than paying it out as a dividend. The desire for empire building may make increasing the size of the firm an objective on its own. Or, management may feel the need to build up a cash cushion to tide over periods when earnings may dip; in such periods, the cash cushion may reduce or obscure the earnings drop and may allow managers to remain in control.

- The firm may be unsure about its future financing needs and may choose to retain some cash to take on unexpected projects or meet unanticipated needs.

- The firm may have volatile earnings and may retain cash to help smooth out dividends over time.

- Bondholders may impose restrictions on cash payments to stockholders, which may prevent the firm from returning available cash flows to its stockholders.

11.4 WHAT HAPPENS TO THE FCFE THAT ARE NOT PAID OUT?

In 1996, Microsoft had free cash flows to equity of roughly $2.5 billion, paid no dividends, and bought back no stock. Where would you expect to see the difference of $2.5 billion show up in Microsoft's financials?

☐ It will be invested in new projects.

☐ It will be retained earnings, increasing the book value of equity.

☐ It will increase the cash balance of the company.

☐ None of the above.

Explain.

Cross-sectional Evidence on Dividends and FCFE

The tendency of firms to pay out less in dividends than they have available in free cash flow to equity is brought home when we examine the cross-sectional differences across firms on dividends paid as a percentage of free cash flow to equity. In 1994, for instance, the average dividend to free cash flow to equity ratio across all firms on the NYSE was 61.22%. Figure 11.1 shows the distribution of dividends to FCFE across all firms.

A percentage less than 100% indicates that the firm is paying out less in dividends than it has available in cash flows and that it is generating surplus cash. For those firms that did not make net debt payments (debt payments in excess of new debt issues) during the period, this cash surplus shows up as an increase in the cash balance. A percentage greater than 100% indicates that the firm is paying out more in dividends than it has available in cash flow. These firms have to finance these dividend payments either out of existing cash balances or by making new stock and debt issues.

This data set on the Web summarizes dividend payout and FCFE ratios, by industry, for U.S. companies (**divfcfe.xls**).

What Kind of Projects Does the Firm Have?

The alternative to returning cash to stockholders is reinvesting the funds back into the firm. Consequently, a firm's investment opportunities provide the other dimension for analyzing dividend policy. Other things remaining equal, a firm with better projects typically has more flexibility in setting dividend policy and defending it against stockholder demands for more dividends. How do we define a "good" project? Returning to our earlier discussions of investment policy, a good project is one that earns at least the hurdle rate, which is the cost of equity, if cash flows are estimated on an equity basis, or the cost of capital, if cash flows are on a predebt basis.

Conceivably, we could estimate the expected cash flows on every project available to the firm and calculate the internal rates of return or net present value of each project to evaluate project quality. There are several practical problems with this, however. First, the analyst has to be able to obtain the detailed cash flow es-

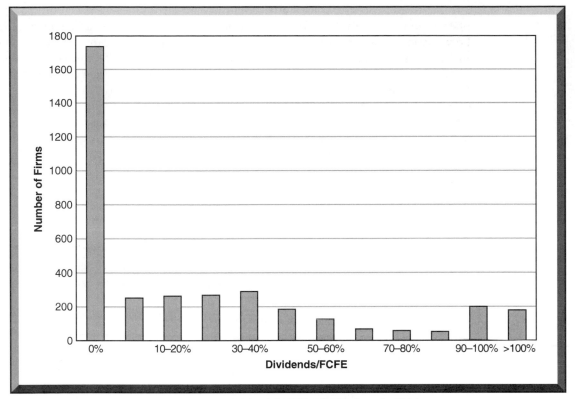

Figure 11.1   Dividends/FCFE: NYSE firms in 1996.

timates and hurdle rates for all available projects, which can represent a great deal of information. This problem is worse for outside analysts, because much of this information is not public. The second problem is that, even if these cash flows are available for existing projects, they will not be available for projects that will be taken in future years.

An alternative approach to measuring project quality involves using accounting measures of return on past projects; we can assume that these measures are not only good proxies for the cash flow returns on these projects, but that they are indicative of the project choice available to the firm in both the current and future periods. The accounting measures of return can be compared to the cost of equity (if the measure is the return on equity) or the cost of capital (if the measure is the return on capital), to determine if the projects are making more than the hurdle rate:

ACCOUNTING MEASURE	HURDLE RATE
Return on Equity$_t$ = Net Income$_t$ / BV of Equity$_{t-1}$	Cost of Equity
Return on Capital$_t$ = EBIT$_t$ (1−t) / (BV of Debt$_{t-1}$ + BV of Equity$_{t-1}$)	Cost of Capital

Critics of this approach argue that accounting income is not always a good measure of cash flow. While this is undoubtedly true, there is nevertheless a high correlation between levels of accounting income and levels of cash flows. Another criticism of this approach is the implicit assumption it makes that the book value of capital is a good measure of the market value of assets in place. Note that the return on the total market value—obtained, for instance, by dividing net income by the market value of equity or the after-tax operating income by the total market value of the firm—is not a good measure of the quality of existing projects, because the market value includes a premium for expected growth. Thus, a high-growth firm will have low returns on market value of equity or capital, but this does not mean that the firm's project choices or returns have been substandard.

Relying on past project returns may indeed be dangerous, especially when a firm is making a transition from one stage in its growth cycle to the next, or if it is in the process of restructuring. Under these and other scenarios, it is entirely possible that the expected returns on new projects are very different from past project returns. In such cases, it is worthwhile scrutinizing past returns for trends that may carry over into the future. The average return on equity or capital for a firm may not reveal these trends very well, because they are slow to reflect the effects of new projects, especially at large firms. An alternative measure, which better captures year-to-year shifts, is the *marginal return on equity or capital,* which is defined as follows:

$$\text{Marginal Return on Equity}_t = (\text{Net Income}_t - \text{Net Income}_{t-1}) / (\text{BV Equity}_{t-1} - \text{BV of Equity}_{t-2})$$

While the marginal return on equity (capital) and the average return on equity (capital) will move in the same direction, the marginal returns typically change much more than do the average returns, the difference being a function of the size of the firm.

Finally, accounting income and returns may fluctuate year to year, not only because of changes in project quality, but also because of broader macroeconomic factors, such as economic cycles and interests. Consequently, the comparisons between accounting returns and hurdle rates should be done across long enough periods, say five to ten years, to average out these other effects.

11.5   HISTORICAL, AVERAGE, AND PROJECTED RETURNS ON CAPITAL

You have been asked to judge the quality of the projects available at Super Meats, a meat processing company. It has earned an average return on capital of 10% over the last five years, but its marginal return on capital last year was 14%. The industry average return on capital is 12%, and it is expected that Super Meats will earn this return on its projects over the next five years. If the cost of capital is 12.5%, which of the following conclusions would you draw about Super Meat's projects?

☐   It invested in good projects over the last five years.

☐   It invested in good projects last year.

☐   It does not expect to invest in good projects over the next five years.

☐   All of the above.

In terms of setting dividend policy, which of these conclusions matter the most?

■ ▲
▼ ● ILLUSTRATION **11.3**   Evaluating Project Quality at Disney, Aracruz, Deutsche Bank, and Bookscape

In Chapter 5, we analyzed the quality of projects taken at these companies over the last year by comparing the returns on equity and capital to the costs of equity and capital. We reproduce the results in Table 11.6.

Using the accounting rates of return, Disney and Bookscape earned excess returns on their projects in 1996. Aracruz and Deutsche Bank earned returns lower than their required returns, though Aracruz's performance could be partly attributed to a poor earnings year in 1996.

We also analyzed the stock price performance of the publicly traded firms in our sample in Chapter 4, using the intercept from the regression and comparing to the expected intercept:

$$\text{Excess Return} = \text{Intercept} - \text{Risk-Free Rate} (1 - \text{Beta})$$

The results from this comparison are summarized in Table 11.7. They are consistent with Table 11.6. Disney's stock outperformed expectations, while Aracruz and Deutsche Bank underperformed.

Since the average returns over time can be deceptive at hiding trends in the estimates, it is sometimes useful to compute these numbers on an annual basis. The graph in Figure 11.2 summarizes returns on equity, returns on the stock, and required returns at Disney each year from 1992 to 1996.

While Disney earned a return on equity that exceeded its cost of equity in the first three years, the trend seems to have been reversed in 1995 and 1996. In terms of stock price performance, almost all of the excess returns over the period can be attributed to Disney's returns in 1992. In 1995 and 1996, the returns on the stock fell below the

Table 11.6   ACCOUNTING MEASURES OF PROJECT QUALITY

Company	ROE	Cost of Equity	ROE − Cost of Equity	ROC	Cost of Capital	ROC − WACC
Disney	24.95%	13.85%	11.10%	18.69%	12.20%	6.49%
Bookscape	21.09%	13.05%	8.04%	16.71%	11.75%	4.96%
Aracruz	2.22%	10.33%	−8.11%	0.29%	7.48%	−7.19%
Deutsche Bank	7.25%	12.67%	−5.42%	5.52%	7.30%	−1.78%

Table 11.7   STOCK PRICE PERFORMANCE MEASURES OF PROJECT QUALITY

Company	Period	Intercept	Monthly Risk-Free Rate	Beta	Rf (1−Beta)	Intercept − Rf(1−Beta)	Annualized Excess Return
Disney	1992–96	−0.01%	0.40%	1.40	−0.16%	0.15%	1.81%
Aracruz	1994–96	−0.26%	2.20%	0.68	0.70%	0.96%	−10.97%
Deutsche Bank	1992–96	−0.67%	0.45%	0.80	0.09%	−0.76%	−8.75%

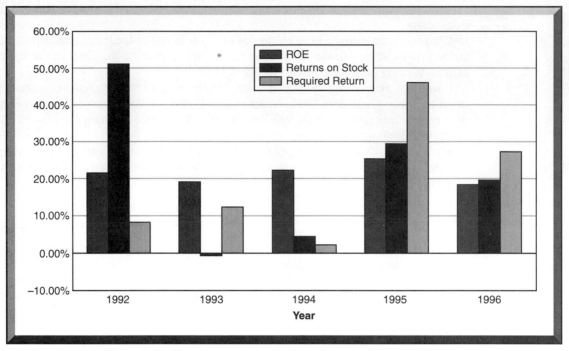

Figure 11.2   Returns on equity, stock, and required returns—Disney.

required returns. What this analysis suggests is a downward trend in performance that is hidden when one looks at five-year averages.

Overall, the past performance of Aracruz and Deutsche should expose them to significant pressure from stockholders to return more cash to stockholders. The fact that the Brazilian and German corporate governance systems protect incumbent management against such pressure may allow them to continue with their existing dividend policy. Disney, on the other hand, has bought itself time, largely due to its high return on equity and superior stock price performance especially early in the decade. This flexibility, however, will be threatened if it does not improve stock price performance and arrest the decline in accounting returns. Finally, Bookscape, as a privately owned firm, is not exposed to external pressure, but the owner of the bookstore is clearly benefiting from a high return on existing investments.

 This spreadsheet allows you to analyze project quality, using both returns on equity and returns on the stock, over a period of up to 10 years for a firm (**dividend.xls**).

IN PRACTICE: CORRECTING ACCOUNTING RETURNS

Accounting rates of return, such as return on equity and capital, are subject to abuse and manipulation. For instance, decisions on how to account for acquisitions (purchase or pooling), choice of depreciation methods (accelerated versus straight line), and whether to expense or capitalize an item (research and development) can all affect reported income and book value. In addition, in any specific year, the return on equity and capital can be biased upward or downward depending on whether the firm had an unusually good or bad year. To estimate a fairer measure of returns on existing projects, we would recommend the following:

1. Normalize the income before computing returns on equity or capital. For Aracruz, in the above analysis, using the average income over the last three years instead of the depressed income in 1996, provides returns on equity or capital that are much closer to the required returns.

2. Back out the cosmetic earnings effects caused by accounting decisions, such as the one on pooling versus purchase. This is precisely why we should consider Disney's income prior to the amortization of the Capital Cities acquisition in computing returns on equity and capital.

3. If there are operating expenses designed to create future growth rather than current income, capitalize those expenses and treat them as part of book value, while computing operating income prior to those expenses. This is what we did with Bookscape, when we capitalized operating leases and treated them as part of the capital base and looked at earnings before interest, taxes, and operating leases in computing return on capital.

Dividend Policy, FCFE, and Project Quality: Some Generalizations

Once a firm's capacity to pay dividends and its project quality have been measured, a framework for analyzing dividend policy emerges. Using the first measure, either a firm can be paying out more in dividends than it can afford to (FCFE), or it is paying out less. Using the second measure, a firm can either have good projects (those with returns greater than the hurdle rate) or not. Combining these two measures yields four combinations:

1. *A firm may have good projects and may be paying out more than its free cash flow to equity as a dividend.* In this case, the firm is losing value on two grounds. First, by paying too much in dividends, it is creating a cash shortfall that has to be met by issuing securities. Second, the cash shortfall often creates capital rationing constraints; as a result, the firm may reject good projects it otherwise would have taken.

2. *A firm may have good projects and may be paying out less than its free cash flow to equity as a dividend.* While it will accumulate cash as a consequence, the firm can legitimately argue that it has good projects in which it will invest the cash in the future, though investors may wonder why it did not take the projects in the current period.

3. *A firm may have poor projects and may be paying out less than its free cash flow to equity as a dividend.* This firm will also accumulate cash, but it will find itself under pressure from stockholders to distribute the cash, because of their concern that the cash will be used to finance poor projects.

4. *A firm may have poor projects and may be paying out more than its free cash flow to equity as a dividend.* This firm first has to deal with its poor project

choices, possibly by cutting back on those that make returns below the hurdle rate. Since the reduced capital expenditure will increase the free cash flow to equity, this may take care of the dividend problem. If it does not, the firm will have to cut dividends as well.

Figure 11.3 illustrates the potential combinations of these possibilities.

While historical data may provide the basis for estimating the parameters for making these comparisons, the entire analysis can and should be forward-looking. The objective is not to estimate return on equity on past projects, but to forecast expected returns on future projects. To the degree that past information is useful in making these forecasts, it is an integral part of the analysis.

11.6 STOCKHOLDER PRESSURE AND DIVIDEND POLICY

Which of the following companies would you expect to see under greatest pressure from its stockholders to buy back stock or pay large dividends? (All of the companies have costs of capital of 12%.)

☐ A company with a historical return on capital of 25% and a small cash balance

☐ A company with a historical return on capital of 6% and a small cash balance

☐ A company with a historical return on capital of 25% and a large cash balance

☐ A company with a historical return on capital of 6% and a large cash balance

The managers at the company argue that they need the cash to do acquisitions. Would this make it more or less likely that stockholders will push for stock buybacks?

☐ More likely

☐ Less likely

The Effects of Financial Leverage

In the above analysis, we emphasized the interaction of investment and dividend policy. This analysis is further enriched—and complicated—if we bring in the firm's financing decisions as well. In Chapter 9, we noted that one of the ways a firm can increase leverage over time is by increasing dividends or repurchasing stock; at the same time, it can decrease leverage by cutting or not paying dividends. Thus, the question of how much a firm should pay in dividends cannot really be answered without analyzing whether it is under- or overlevered and whether it intends to close this leverage gap.

An underlevered firm may be able to pay more than its FCFE as dividends and may do so intentionally to increase its debt ratio. An overlevered firm, on the other hand, may have to pay less than its FCFE as dividends because of its desire to reduce leverage. In some of the cases described above, leverage can be used to strengthen the suggested recommendations. For instance, an underlevered firm with poor projects and a cash flow surplus has an added incentive to raise dividends and to reevaluate investment policy, since it will be able to increase its leverage by doing so. In some cases, however, the imperatives of moving to an optimal debt ratio may act as a barrier to carrying out changes in dividend policy. Thus, an overlevered firm with poor projects and a cash flow surplus may find the cash better spent reducing debt rather than paying out dividends.

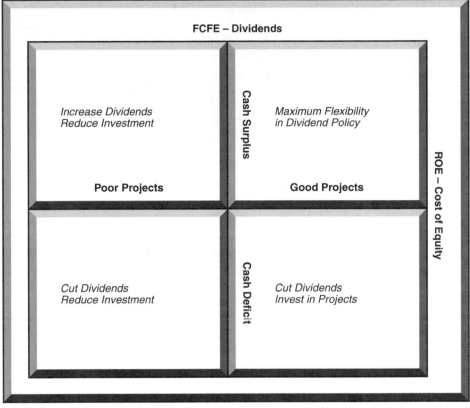

Figure 11.3   Analyzing dividend policy.

POOR PROJECTS AND LOW PAYOUT

In this section, we examine the consequences of paying out much less in dividends than a firm has available in cash flows, while facing poor investment opportunities. We also discuss stockholder reaction and management response to the dividend policy.

Consequences of Low Payout

When a firm pays out less than it can afford to in dividends, it accumulates cash. If a firm does not have good projects (now or in the future) in which to invest this cash, it faces several possibilities: In the most benign case, the cash accumulates in the firm and is invested in financial assets. Assuming that these financial assets are fairly priced, these investments are zero net present value projects and should not negatively affect value. There is the possibility, however, that the firm may find itself the target of an acquisition, financed in part by its large holding of liquid assets.

As the cash in the firm accumulates, the managers may be tempted to take on projects that do not meet their hurdle rate requirements, either to reduce the likelihood of a takeover or because of the desire to earn higher returns than on financial assets.[2] These actions will clearly lower the value of the firm. Another possibility, and one fraught with even more danger for the firm, is that the management may decide to use the cash to finance an acquisition and that such an acquisition will result in a transfer of wealth to the stockholders of the acquired firms. While managers will argue that such acquisitions make sense from a strategic and synergistic viewpoint, history is replete with cases of firms that used large cash balances, acquired over years of paying low dividends while generating high free cash flows to equity, to finance takeovers that detract from stockholder value.

Stockholder Reaction

Given the range of possible outcomes described above, it is not surprising that the stockholders of firms that pay insufficient dividends and do not have "good" projects put pressure on managers to return more of the cash back to them. In fact, this is the scenario that originally led to the development of the "free cash flow" hypothesis. Under this hypothesis, which is described more fully in Chapter 7, managers cannot be trusted with large cash flows which they can spend at their discretion. Consequently, it is argued, firms should borrow more and create the commitment to making interest and principal payments, thereby forcing managers to be more disciplined in their investment choices. An alternative to taking on debt is to force firms to disgorge more of these cash flows as dividends.

Management's Defense

Not surprisingly, managers of firms that pay out less in dividends than they can afford to argue that this policy is in the best long-term interest of the firm. They maintain that while the current project returns may be poor, future projects will be both more plentiful and lucrative (in terms of returns). While this argument may work initially when presented, it will become progressively more difficult to sustain if the firm continues to post poor returns on its projects. Managers may also argue that the cash accumulation is needed to meet demands arising from future contingencies. For instance, cyclical firms will often argue that large cash balances are needed to tide them over the next recession. Again, while there is a kernel of truth to the argument, the "reasonableness" of the cash balance has to be measured against the experience of the firm in terms of cash requirements in prior recessions. Finally, in some cases, managers will justify a firm's cash accumulation and low dividend payout based upon the behavior of comparable firms. Thus, a firm may argue that it is essentially copying the dividend policy of its closest competitors and that it has to continue to do so to remain competitive. The argument that "every one else does it" cannot be used to justify a bad dividend policy, however.

While all of these justifications are presented in terms of stockholder wealth maximization or the best long-term interests of the firm, they may really be just smoke screens designed to hide the fact that this dividend policy serves managerial rather than stockholder interests. Maintaining large cash balances and low dividends provides incumbent

---

[2]This is especially likely if the cash is invested in Treasury bills or other low-risk, low-return investments. On the surface, it may seem better for the firm to take on risky projects that earn, say 7%, rather than invest in T. Bills and make 3%, though this clearly does not make sense after adjusting for the risk.

managers with two advantages. They increase the funds that are directly under their control, and thus increase their power to direct future investments; and they increase the margin for safety for these managers, stabilizing earnings and increasing their tenure.

11.7 ANTITAKEOVER AMENDMENTS AND DIVIDEND POLICY

A large number of companies in the United States have added antitakeover amendments to their corporate charters. What would you expect to happen to dividend policy after these charter amendments are approved?

☐ I would expect dividends and stock buybacks to increase.

☐ I would expect dividends and stock buybacks to decrease.

☐ I would expect them to remain unchanged.

This data set of firms on the U.S. stock markets that are most likely to feel under pressure to raise dividends is created by applying the following screens (**poorlow.xls**):

- The return on equity was at least 5% lower than their cost of equity.
- The dividends were less than 50% of free cash flows to equity.
- The cash balance for the firm was greater than 5% of the market value of the firm.

GOOD PROJECTS AND LOW PAYOUT

While the outcomes for stockholders in firms with poor projects and low dividend payout ratios range from neutral to terrible, the results may be more positive for firms that have a better selection of projects, and whose incumbent management has had a history of earning high returns for the stockholders.

Consequences of Low Payout

The immediate consequence of paying out less in dividends than is available in free cash flow to equity is the same for these firms as it is for firms with poor project choice: The cash balance of the firm increases to reflect the cash surplus. The long-term effects of cash accumulation are generally much less negative for these firms, however, for the following reasons:

1. The presence of projects that earn returns greater than the hurdle rate increases the likelihood that the cash will be productively invested in the long term.

2. The high returns earned on internal projects reduces both the pressure and the incentive to invest the cash in poor projects or in acquisitions.

3. Firms that earn high returns on their projects are much less likely to be targets of takeovers, limiting the need to reduce the cash balance quickly.

To summarize, firms that have a history of taking good projects and that expect to continue to have a ready supply of such projects may be able to sustain a policy of retaining cash rather than paying out dividends; in fact, they can actually create value in the long term by using this cash productively.

Stockholders' Reaction

Stockholders are much less likely to feel a threat to their wealth in firms that have historically shown good judgment in picking projects. Consequently, they are more likely to acquiesce when managers in those firms withhold cash rather than pay it out. This suggests that, while the free cash flow hypothesis has a solid basis for arguing that managers cannot be trusted with large cash balances, it does not apply equally across all firms. The managers of some firms earn the trust of their stockholders because of their capacity to deliver extraordinary returns on both their projects and their stock over long periods of time. These managers will generally have much more flexibility in determining dividend policy.

This discussion helps resolve the tradeoff firms face between satisfying their long-term prospects and paying dividends or repurchasing stock. The notion that greedy stockholders force firms with good projects to return too much cash too quickly is not based in fact. Rather, stockholder pressure for dividends or stock repurchases is greatest in firms whose projects yield marginal or poor returns, and least in firms whose projects have high returns.

Management Responses

Managers in firms that have posted stellar records in projects and stock returns clearly have a much easier time convincing stockholders of the desirability of withholding cash rather than paying it out. The strongest argument for doing this is that the cash will be used productively in the future and earn above-market returns for the stockholders. Not all stockholders will buy this argument, however; some will argue that future projects may be less attractive than past projects, especially when the industry in which the firm is operating is maturing. For example, many specialty retail firms, such as The Limited, found themselves under pressure to return more cash to stockholders in the early 1990s as margins and growth rates in the business declined.

Thus far, we have assumed that good returns on projects and good returns on stocks go hand in hand. While this may be true in general, there are some companies that post good records in terms of returns in projects but will find their stock price declining. One explanation for this is that the firm's project returns, while higher than the hurdle rate, were actually lower than expected, resulting in a drop in the stock price. Thus, a firm that reports a return on equity of 22%—much higher than its cost of equity of 15%—may still see its stock price drop if the market expectation was a return on equity of 25%.

 This data set of firms on the U.S. stock exchange that are least likely to feel under pressure to raise dividends is created by applying the following screens (**goodlow.xls**):

- The return on equity in the most recent year was at least 5% higher than their cost of equity.

- To eliminate those cases in which the most recent year was an outlier, the average return on equity in the last five years had to be at least 5% higher than the cost of equity.

- The dividends were less than 50% of free cash flow to equity.

POOR PROJECTS AND HIGH PAYOUT

In many ways, the most troublesome combination of circumstances occurs when firms pay out much more in dividends than they can afford, while posting less-than-stellar returns on their projects. These firms have problems with both their investment and their dividend policies, and the latter cannot be solved adequately without addressing the former.

Consequences of High Payout

When a firm pays out more in dividends than it has available in free cash flow to equity, it is creating a cash deficit that has to be funded by drawing on the firm's cash balance, issuing stock to cover the shortfall, or borrowing money to fund its dividends. If the firm uses the first approach, it will reduce equity and raise its debt ratio. The second approach allows the firm to neutralize the drop in equity created by the excess dividends with new stock issues; the downside is the issuance cost of the stock. The third approach enables the firm to increase its debt, while reducing equity, accentuating the increase in the debt ratio.

Since the free cash flows to equity are after capital expenditures, it can be argued that this firm's real problem is not that it pays out too much in dividends, but that it is earning too little on its projects. Cutting back on low-return projects would therefore increase the free cash flow to equity and could eliminate the cash shortfall created by paying too much in dividends.

Stockholder Reaction

The stockholders of a firm that pays much more in dividends than it has available in free cash flow to equity are faced with a quandary: On the one hand, they may want the firm to reduce its dividends to eliminate the need for additional borrowing or equity issues each year. On the other hand, the firm's record in picking projects does not evoke much trust that the management is using funds wisely, and it is entirely possible that the funds saved by not paying the dividends will be used on other poor projects as well. Consequently, these firms will have to address their investment problems and then cut back on poor projects, which, in turn, will increase the free cash flow to equity. If the cash shortfall persists, the firm should then cut back on dividends.

It is therefore entirely possible, especially if the firm is underleveraged to begin with, that the stockholders will not push for lower dividends but will try to get managers to improve project quality instead. It is also possible that they will push the firm to eliminate enough poor projects so that the free cash flow to equity covers the expected dividend payment.

Management Responses

The managers of firms with poor projects and dividends that exceed free cash flows to equity may contest the notion that they have investment problems rather than dividend problems. They may also disagree with the notion that the most efficient way of dealing with these problems is to eliminate some of the capital expenditures. In general, their arguments will mirror those used by any firm with a poor investment track record: The period used to analyze project returns was not representative; it was an industrywide problem that will pass; and/or the projects have long gestation periods.

Overall, it is unlikely that these managers will convince the stockholders of their good intentions on future projects. Consequently, there will be a strong push toward cutbacks in capital expenditures, especially if the firm is borrowing money to finance the dividends and does not have much excess debt capacity.

 This data set of firms that best fit the criteria of poor projects and high payouts is created by applying the following screens (**poorhigh.xls**):

- The return on equity in the most recent year was at least 5% lower than their cost of equity.
- The dividends were greater than free cash flows to equity, and the dividend yield exceeded 2%.
- The new stock issues made in the most recent year were at least 2% of the market value of equity in that year.

GOOD PROJECTS AND HIGH PAYOUT

The costs of trying to maintain unsustainable dividends are most evident in firms that have a selection of good projects to choose from. The cash that is paid out as dividends could well have been used to invest in some of these projects, and could have yielded a much higher return for stockholders and higher stock prices for the firm.

Consequences of High Payout

When a firm pays out more in dividends than it has available in free cash flow to equity, it is creating a cash shortfall. If this firm also has good projects currently available that are not being taken because of capital rationing constraints, it can be argued that the firm is paying a hefty price for its dividend policy. Even if the projects are passed up for other reasons, it can be argued that the cash this firm is paying out as dividends would earn much better returns for it if left to accumulate in the firm.

Dividend payments also create a cash deficit that now has to be met by issuing new securities. On the one hand, issuing new stock carries a potentially large issuance cost, which reduces firm value. On the other hand, if the firm issues new debt, it might become overleveraged, and this may reduce value.

Stockholder Reaction

Rationally, the best thing for stockholders to do in this case is to insist that the firm pay out less in dividends and take on better projects. This may not happen, however, if the firm has paid high dividends for an extended period of time and has acquired stockholders who value high dividends even more than they value the firm's long-term health. Even so, stockholders may be much more amenable to cutting dividends, and reinvesting the cash in the firm, if the firm has a ready supply of good projects at hand.

11.8 DIVIDEND POLICY AND HIGH-GROWTH FIRMS

High-growth firms are often encouraged to start paying dividends to expand their stockholder base, since there are stockholders who will not or cannot hold stock that do not pay dividends. Do you agree with this rationale?

☐ Yes

☐ No

Explain.

Management Responses

The managers of firms that have good projects while paying out too much in dividends have to figure out a way to cut dividends, while differentiating themselves from those firms that are cutting dividends due to declining earnings. The initial suspicion with which markets view dividend cuts can be overcome, at least partially, by providing markets with information on project quality at the time of the dividend cut. If the dividends have been paid for a long time, however, the firm may have acquired stockholders who like the high dividends and may not be particularly interested in the projects that the firm has available. If this is the case, the initial reaction to the dividend cut, no matter how carefully packaged, will be negative. However, as disgruntled stockholders sell their holdings, the firm will acquire new stockholders who may be more willing to accept the lower dividend and the new investment policy.

 This data set of firms that best fit the criteria of good projects and high payouts is created by applying the following screens (**goodhigh.xls**):

- The return on equity in the most recent year was at least 5% higher than their cost of equity.
- The dividends were greater than free cash flows to equity, and the dividend yield exceeded 2%.
- The new stock issues made in the most recent year were at least 2% of the market value of equity in that year.

ILLUSTRATION 11.4   **Analyzing Dividend Policy at Disney, Aracruz, and Deutsche Bank**
Using the framework devised above, we are now in a position to analyze the dividend policy at each of the three publicly traded firms in our sample. Table 11.8 summarizes the recommendations for each of the firms (see also Figure 11.4).

For Disney, with its combination of low dividends relative to FCFE and high returns on equity, allowing cash to accumulate seemed initially to be the right solution. The recent acquisition of Capital Cities, the declining returns on equity, and the poor stock returns in the last few years lead us to believe, however, that Disney will come under pressure to return more cash to its stockholders. This recommendation is given added weight by our finding in Chapter 8 that the firm is

Table 11.8 RECOMMENDATIONS FOR FIRMS: DISNEY, ARACRUZ, AND DEUTSCHE BANK

Company	Dividends versus FCFE	Project Quality	Leverage	Dividend Recommendations
Disney	Dividends were 67.47% of FCFE between 1992 and 1996. In 1996, the acquisition of Capital Cities led to a very large negative FCFE.	1. Average project quality between 1992–96 was good, but the trends are negative. 2. Excess cash was used for Capital Cities acquisition.	Underlevered	Given trends in returns, and recent stock price performance, return more cash to owners. Since the firm has historically maintained a low dividend payout, it should buy back stock.
Aracruz	Dividends were 52.14% of FCFE between 1994 and 1996. The drop in net income in 1996 also led to a drop in FCFE.	Returns have lagged required returns, both on accounting and market basis between 1994 and 1996.	Overlevered, significantly at 1996 earnings levels, and marginally at normalized earnings levels.	Wait to see if 1996 performance was an outlier. If income is normalized, the FCFE generated should be used initially to pay down debt and then to buy back stock.
Deutsche Bank	Dividends were 23.85% of FCFE between 1992 and 1996. The acquisition of Morgan Grenfell still has not paid off in terms of returns.	Returns have lagged required returns, both on accounting and market basis between 1992 and 1996.	Close to optimal leverage.	Since stock buybacks are still not allowed in Germany, increase dividends paid or pay a special dividend.

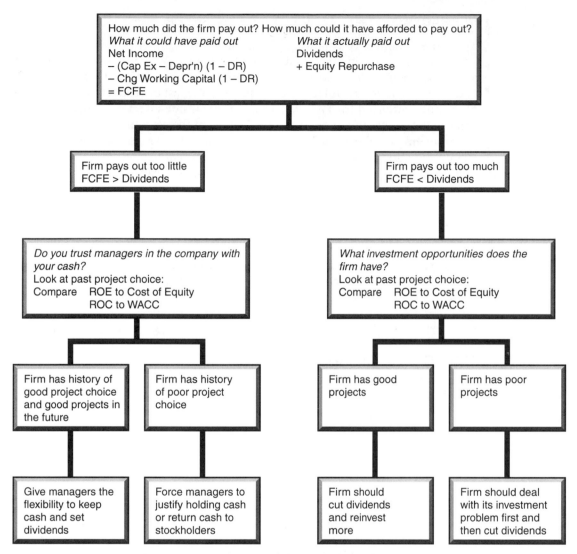

Figure 11.4   A framework for analyzing dividend policy.

underlevered. Given its history of paying low dividends, buying back stock should be a more palatable option to stockholders. Both Aracruz and Deutsche Bank pay less in dividends than they have available as FCFE and have had a history of poor returns in terms of projects and dividends to their stockholders. For Aracruz, which we consider overlevered, we would recommend that the FCFE be used to pay down the debt initially and that the company initiate stock buybacks after that, given its volatility in income. For Deutsche Bank, which is fairly close to optimal leverage, the restrictions on buying back stock faced by German companies imply that the only way to return cash to stockholders is to pay higher dividends.

IN PRACTICE: THE EFFECT OF RESTRICTIONS ON STOCK BUYBACKS

There are a number of countries, like Germany, that either do not allow stock buy-backs or restrict companies from buying back stock. While these restrictions often are based upon noble reasons—keeping control of corporations from being monop-olized by a few groups and forcing companies to invest in productive projects—they have the unintended (or intended, in some cases) side effect of providing cover for firms without investment opportunities that want to accumulate cash.

While individual stockholders might not be able to change this policy, they should still push companies with poor projects and excess cash to return cash to the stock-holders by paying special dividends and increasing regular dividends.

AN ALTERNATIVE APPROACH TO ANALYZING DIVIDEND POLICY

So far, we have examined the dividend policy of a firm by looking at its fundamen-tals. There are many managers who would argue that their dividend policies are judged relative to their competitors, however, and many analysts would agree. This "comparable-firm" approach to analyzing dividend policy can be defined narrowly, by looking only at firms that are similar in size and business mix, for example, or more broadly, by looking at the determinants of dividend policy across all firms.

Using Comparable Firms

In the simplest form of this approach, a firm's dividend yield and payout are com-pared to its peer group and judged to be adequate, excessive, or inadequate, accord-ingly. Thus, a utility stock with a dividend yield of 3.5% may be criticized for paying out an inadequate dividend if utility stocks on average pay a much higher dividend, whereas a computer software firm that has a dividend yield of 1.0% may be viewed as paying too high a dividend, if software firms on average pay a much lower divi-dend. Table 11.9 summarizes dividend yield and payout ratios across different in-dustry groups as well as the ratio of dividends to FCFG.

While comparing a firm's dividend yield and payout to comparable firms may pro-vide some intuitive appeal, it can be misleading for a number of reasons. First, it as-sumes that all firms within the same industry group have the same net capital expenditure and working capital needs, which may not be true, depending on their stage in the life cycle. Second, even if the firms are at the same stage in the life cycle, it is entirely possible that the entire industry is adopting a dividend policy that is un-sustainable or suboptimal.

11.9   PEER GROUP ANALYSIS

Assume that you are advising a small high-growth bank that is concerned about the fact that its dividend payout and yield are much lower than other banks. The CEO of the bank is con-cerned that investors will punish the bank for its dividend policy. What do you think?

☐   The bank will be punished for its errant dividend policy.

☐   Investors are sophisticated enough for the bank to be treated fairly.

☐   The bank will not be punished for its low dividends as long as it tries to convey informa-tion to its investors about the quality of its projects and growth prospects.

Table 11.9 Dividend Ratios by industry			
Industry	**Dividend Yield**	**Dividend Payout**	**Dividends/FCFE**
Advertising	0.66%	36.04%	32.62%
Air Transport	0.34%	27.21%	50.71%
Alcoholic Beverages	1.75%	45.73%	56.97%
Aluminum	1.13%	49.61%	66.58%
Apparel	0.52%	29.76%	27.70%
Appliances	1.41%	40.47%	46.80%
Auto & Truck	1.40%	39.49%	47.88%
Auto Parts (OEM)	1.56%	31.85%	37.73%
Auto Parts (Replacement)	1.13%	26.60%	38.98%
Bank	1.99%	38.60%	38.60%
Bank (Canadian)	2.28%	37.33%	37.33%
Bank (Midwest)	1.98%	38.74%	38.74%
Beverage (Soft Drink)	0.85%	44.43%	53.38%
Brokerage Houses	0.85%	16.21%	16.66%
Building Materials	0.92%	21.83%	31.86%
Building Supplies	0.32%	11.63%	54.04%
Cable TV	0.37%	NA	NA
Canadian Energy	2.13%	49.99%	120.88%
Cement & Aggregates	0.98%	21.48%	28.51%
Chemical (Diversified)	1.74%	41.28%	64.71%
Chemical (Basic)	1.73%	40.58%	49.21%
Chemical (Specialty)	1.13%	37.25%	49.85%
Coal/Alternate Energy	0.74%	3.48%	6.91%
Computer & Peripherals	0.06%	14.94%	18.17%
Computer Software	0.16%	9.03%	9.18%
Copper	1.89%	36.03%	97.40%
Cosmetics	0.60%	47.43%	64.96%
Defense	0.50%	29.36%	28.08%
Diversified Co.	0.95%	30.78%	33.21%
Drug	0.17%	126.94%	142.58%
Drugstore	0.76%	35.47%	75.05%
Electrical Equipment	0.77%	49.64%	55.56%
Electric (Foreign)	0.55%	22.83%	37.48%
Electronics	0.30%	20.24%	29.66%
Entertainment	0.48%	12.76%	11.97%
Environmental	0.54%	43.69%	49.42%
European	0.45%	56.16%	56.16%
Foreign Utilitics	5.04%	32.84%	18.39%
Financial Services	1.25%	22.57%	22.76%
Food Processing	1.26%	48.60%	56.87%

Table 11.9   (CONTINUED)

Industry	Dividend Yield	Dividend Payout	Dividends/FCFE
Food Wholesalers	1.12%	26.24%	55.63%
Furn./Home Furnishings	1.38%	22.90%	24.48%
Natural Gas Distributors	4.40%	91.86%	207.93%
Natural Gas Diversified	1.85%	41.56%	116.89%
Gold/Silver Mining	0.68%	232.62%	115.12%
Grocery	1.07%	22.22%	59.33%
Healthcare Information	0.22%	15.83%	14.21%
Homebuilding	0.74%	25.01%	26.17%
Home Services	1.26%	12.73%	17.64%
Hotel/Gaming	0.49%	17.47%	70.35%
Household Products	1.25%	45.89%	54.15%
Industrial Services	0.58%	27.32%	32.56%
Insurance (Diversified)	1.45%	21.86%	23.92%
Insurance (Life)	1.02%	32.69%	33.94%
Insurance (Prop/Casualty)	1.64%	25.69%	27.02%
Precision Instruments	0.38%	29.10%	39.41%
Machinery	1.02%	24.64%	26.75%
Maritime	1.59%	48.36%	142.86%
Medical Services	0.17%	12.42%	13.69%
Medical Supplies	0.32%	51.75%	57.77%
Metal Fabricating	1.26%	19.67%	23.43%
Metals & Mining (Div.)	0.96%	69.21%	NA
Newspaper	1.30%	35.54%	33.61%
Office Equip & Supplies	1.42%	37.98%	39.68%
Oilfield Services/Equip.	0.32%	25.59%	40.07%
Petroleum (Integrated)	2.22%	64.58%	101.24%
Petroleum (Producers)	0.50%	24.90%	NA
Packaging & Container	0.84%	34.19%	52.58%
Paper & Forest Products	1.74%	121.48%	90.89%
Publishing	1.05%	78.84%	71.84%
Railroad	1.53%	30.01%	74.35%
Recreation	0.59%	55.84%	72.50%
REIT	5.92%	3.83%	3.86%
Restaurant	0.65%	15.88%	88.82%
Retail Stores	0.48%	36.02%	48.91%
Retail (Special Lines)	0.37%	22.25%	43.54%
Semiconductor Equipment	0.19%	0.40%	0.80%
Semiconductor	0.05%	9.47%	19.62%
Shoe	0.93%	15.09%	20.96%

Industry	Dividend Yield	Dividend Payout	Dividends/FCFE
Steel (General)	1.77%	31.71%	180.39%
Steel (Integrated)	1.39%	54.37%	66.74%
Telecom Foreign	1.59%	52.31%	46.02%
Telecom Equipment	0.25%	5.99%	9.97%
Telecom Services	1.07%	88.16%	150.61%
Textile	1.06%	21.92%	24.09%
Thrift	1.56%	31.58%	31.58%
Tire & Rubber	1.13%	23.91%	35.40%
Tobacco	3.12%	71.46%	71.58%
Trucking	0.93%	24.72%	101.67%
Utilities (Central)	5.68%	75.49%	73.37%
Utilities (East)	5.81%	82.22%	76.78%
Utilities (West)	4.67%	69.11%	72.54%
Water Utilities	4.95%	71.65%	91.33%

Table 11.9   (CONTINUED)

 ILLUSTRATION **11.5**   **Analyzing Disney's Dividend Policy Using Comparable Firms**
In comparing Disney's dividend policy to its peer group, we analyze the dividend yields and payout ratios of comparable firms in 1997, as shown in Table 11.10.[3]

We would expect companies with less predictable earnings and higher expected growth rates to have lower dividend yields and payout ratios than firms with more predictable earnings and lower growth. The problem with this comparison is that there is very little variability in dividend policy across firms in this group. They all have low dividend yields and payout ratios, with Disney's yield and payout ratio being close to the average for the industry. We did try regressing dividend yield and payout ratios against expected growth rates:

Dividend Payout Ratio = 0.24 − 0.89 (Expected growth rate) $R^2 = 21.37\%$
                             (1.28)

Dividend Yield = 0.0107 − 0.043 (Expected growth rate) $R^2 = 33.65\%$
                             (1.74)

(T statistics are in parentheses)

Using Disney's expected growth rate of 15% in these regressions yields the following predicted values for the dividend measures:

   Predicted Dividend Payout for Disney = 0.24 − 0.89 (.15) = 0.1066 or 10.66%
   Predicted Dividend Yield for Disney = 0.0107 − 0.043(.15) = 0.0044 or .44%

---

[3]The Value Line classification of firms into industry groups was used to put together the comparable firm list. The earnings predictability estimates and forecasted growth rates are also from Value Line.

Table 11.10   PAYOUT RATIOS AND DIVIDEND YIELDS: ENTERTAINMENT FIRMS

Company Name	Price	Dividend Yield	Dividend Payout	Earnings Stability	Expected Growth
Belo (A.H.)	$44.50	0.99%	22.11%	55.00	2.50%
King World	$40.13	0.00%	0.00%	95.00	6.50%
Gaylord 'A'	$23.50	1.70%	45.98%	40.00	9.50%
Disney (Walt)	$79.56	0.67%	19.78%	80.00	15.00%
Chris-Craft	$50.00	0.00%	0.00%	30.00	19.00%
Clear Channel	$68.25	0.00%	0.00%	55.00	24.00%
Viacom "A"	$31.63	0.00%	0.00%	5.00	24.00%
Westinghouse	$26.31	0.76%	10.50%	20.00	4.85%
Average		0.51%	12.30%	47.50	13.17%

These predicted values suggest that, given its expected growth rate, Disney's payout ratio of 19.73% and dividend yield of 0.67% is too high relative to other firms in the sector.

It is important to note, however, that the use of comparable firms is limited by the difficulty in identifying truly comparable firms and in controlling for differences across these firms. The regressions shown above have limited power because of the small number of observations used in each case.

IN PRACTICE: DEALING WITH EQUITY RESEARCH ANALYSTS AND INVESTORS

One of the concerns that many firms have, when their dividend policy is different from that of their peer groups, is that they will be punished by investors and equity research analysts for deviating from the norm. This is particularly true when a company belongs to an industry where high dividends are the norm (for instance, utilities and financial service firms, in the United States), and the company wants to follow a policy of paying low dividends, because it has good investment opportunities.

While there is no direct evidence on whether outliers in terms of dividend policy are punished by investors, a limited study of stock returns and price multiples (such as PE ratios) within each sector seems to indicate no support for this notion.

For firms which decide to pay low dividends in a high-dividend sector, we would recommend that as much information as possible be provided to investors about investment opportunities. A history of good project choice will make its sales pitch much more credible.

Using the Entire Cross-Section

The alternative to using only comparable firms in the same industry is to study the entire population of firms and to try to estimate the fundamentals that cause differences in dividend payout across firms. We outlined some of the determinants of dividend policy earlier in this chapter and suggested some empirical relationships that should hold between dividend payout and proxies for these determinants. In particular, we argued that:

- Dividend payout ratios and earnings variability are negatively correlated with each other.
- Dividend payout ratios and project returns (return on equity, return on capital) are negatively correlated with each other.
- Dividend payout ratios and size (market capitalization) are positively correlated with each other.
- Dividend payout ratios and insider holdings are negatively correlated with each other.
- Dividend payout ratios and debt ratios are negatively correlated with each other.

Using data from 1996, we regressed dividend yields and payout ratios against all of these variables and arrived at the following regression equations:

PAYOUT = 0.3410 − 0.2109 BETA + 0.0000033 MKTCAP + 0.0274 DBTRATIO + 0.1825 ROE − 0.0167 NCEX/TA R^2 = 7.04%

YIELD = 0.0189 − 0.0121 BETA + 0.00000016 MKTCAP + 0.0056 DBTRATIO + 0.0094 ROE − 0.0028 NCEX/TA R^2 = 10.02%

where

        BETA − Beta of the stock
        MKTCAP = Market Value of Equity + Book Value of Debt
        DBTRATIO = Book Value of Debt / MKTCAP
        ROE = Return on Equity in 1996
        NCEX/TA = (Capital Expenditures − Depreciation) / Total Assets

The regression does not have very good explanatory power, however, since it explains only 7% to 10% of the differences in dividend measures. It is also troubling that some of the variables in these regressions have the wrong signs (the debt ratio, for instance, has a positive instead of a negative coefficient).

 ILLUSTRATION **11.6**   Analyzing Disney's Dividend Payout Using the Cross-Section
To illustrate the applicability of the cross-sectional regression in analyzing the dividend policies of Disney, we estimate the values of the independent variables in the regression for the firm, as shown in Table 11.11.

Substituting into the regression equation for the dividend payout ratio, we predicted the following payout ratio for Disney:

For Disney's Payout = 0.3410 − 0.2109 (1.25) + 0.0000033 (62,068) + 0.0274 (.1952) + 0.1825 (.2495) − 0.0167 (.0117) = 33.29%

Substituting into the regression equation for the dividend yield, we predict the following dividend yield for Disney:

For Disney's Yield = 0.0189 − 0.0121 (1.25) + 0.00000016 (62,068) + 0.0056 (.1952) + 0.0094 (.2495) − 0.0028 (.0117) = 1.71%

Both measures suggest that Disney is not paying enough in dividends, with a dividend payout ratio of 19.73% and a dividend yield of 0.67%, given its growth, risk and capital investment characteristics. This is in contrast to our conclusions from

Table 11.11 DISNEY'S FINANCIAL CHARACTERISTICS	
	Disney
ROE	24.95%
Beta	1.25
Market Capitalization	$62,068
Cap Exp/Total Assets	1.17%
Debt Ratio	19.52%

comparing Disney to other firms in the entertainment industry, and suggest that the firms in the entertainment industry, in general, pays much lower dividends than similar firms in other industries.

 There is a dataset that summarizes the latest dividend yield and payout regressions across the entire market **(divveg.xls)**.

CONCLUSION

In this chapter we expanded on many of the concepts introduced in the previous one, and developed a general framework for analyzing dividend policy. We emphasized the link between investment, financing, and dividend policy by noting that firms with a history of taking on good projects and the potential for more good projects in the future acquire much more control over their dividend policy. In particular, they can pay much less in dividends than they have available in cash flows and hold onto the surplus cash, because stockholders trust them to invest the cash wisely. In contrast, stockholders in firms with a history of poor project choice may be much less sanguine about retention of cash because of the fear that the cash will be invested in poor projects.

Some firms set dividends based upon the actions of comparable firms. We examined an analysis based upon a narrow definition of comparable firms (firms in the same line of business), and one based upon a broader definition (the determinants of dividend policy were examined in the entire population).

There is one point worth reemphasizing here. In this chapter, we have developed a framework designed to answer the question of how much cash should be returned to stockholders. While dividends may be the most widely used approach to returning cash to stockholders, there are alternatives available to most firms which were described in the previous chapter.

PROBLEMS AND QUESTIONS

1. JL Chem Corporation, a chemical manufacturing firm with changing investment opportunities, is considering a major change in dividend policy. It currently has 50 million shares outstanding and pays an annual dividend of $2 per share. The firm's current and projected income statement are provided below (in millions):

	Current	Projected for next year
EBITDA	$1200	$1350
− Depreciation	200	250
EBIT	1000	1100
− Interest Expenses	200	200
EBT	800	900
− Taxes	320	360
Net Income	480	540

The firm's current capital expenditure is $500 million. It is considering five projects for the next year:

Project	Investment	Beta	IRR (using cash flows to equity)
A	$190 mil	0.6	12.0%
B	$200 mil	0.8	12.0%
C	$200 mil	1.0	14.5%
D	$200 mil	1.2	15.0%
E	$100 mil	1.5	20.0%

The firm's current beta is 1.0, and the current Treasury bond rate is 8.5%. The firm expects working capital to increase $50 million both this year and next. The firm plans to finance its net capital expenditures and working capital needs with 30% debt.

a. What is the firm's current payout ratio?

b. What proportion of its current free cash flow to equity is it paying out as dividends?

c. What would your projected capital expenditure be for next year? (i.e., which of the five projects would you accept and why?)

d. How much cash will the company have available to pay out as dividends next year? (What is the maximum amount the company should pay out as dividends?)

e. Would you pay out this maximum amount as dividends? Why or why not? What other considerations would you bring to this decision?

f. JKL Corporation currently has a cash balance of $100 million (after paying the current year's dividends). If it pays out $125 million as dividends next year, what will its projected cash balance be at the end of the next year?

2. SASS is a small, closely held corporation that sells statistical software to brokerage houses and investment banks on CD-ROM. SASS will soon buy new, inexpensive "recordable" CD-ROM drives to enable them to produce software for distribution to their customers "in house." This is not only expected to reduce annual production costs by $20,000 per year, but will also enable the company to reduce inventory by $15,000 per year. The new drives will cost $12,000 (including shipping and installation) and will increase next year's depreciation by $2,400 (using MACRS depreciation). SASS finances all net capital expenditures and working capital requirements out of retained earnings and is in the 40% tax bracket.

a. How will the purchase of the new drives affect the company's FCFE for the coming year?

b. How permanent will this effect be?

3. In the problem above, assume that SASS is owned by a couple who currently pay 35% in combined state and federal taxes on personal income. These owners have decided to keep their company focused on the current product line and, hence, will not invest in any future capital expenditures except those needed to replace existing assets (i.e., no new projects).

a. Should they use any increase in FCFE to increase the dividends paid to them by the company?

b. Would your answer change if you learned that the owners intended to sell the business within the next few years?

4. GL Corporation, a retail firm, is making a decision on how much it should pay out to its stockholders. It has $100 million in investable funds. The following information is provided about the firm:

a. It has 100 million shares outstanding, each share selling for $15. The beta of the stock is 1.25, and the T. Bond rate is 8%.

b. The firm has $500 million of debt outstanding. The interest rate on the debt is 12%.

c. The corporation's tax rate is 50%.

d. The firm has the following investment projects:

Project	Investment Requirement	After-Tax Return on capital
A	$15 million	27%
B	10 million	20%
C	25 million	16%
D	20 million	14%
E	30 million	12%

The firm plans to finance all its investment needs at its current debt ratio.
- Should the company return money to its stockholders?
- If so, how much should be returned to stockholders?

5. LimeAide Corporation, a large soft drink manufacturing firm, is faced with the decision of how much to pay out as dividends to its stockholders. It expects to have a net income of $1,000 (after deprecation of $500), and it has the following projects:

Project	Initial Investment	Beta	IRR (to equity investors)
A	$500	2.0	21%
B	$600	1.5	20%
C	$500	1.0	12%

The firm's beta is 1.5, and the current T-Bond rate is 9%. The firm plans to finance net capital expenditures (cap ex-depreciation) and working capital with 20% debt. The firm also has current revenues of $5,000, which it expects to grow at 8%. Working capital will be maintained at 25% of revenues. How much should the firm return to its stockholders as a dividend?

6. InTech Corporation, a computer software firm that has never paid dividends before, is considering whether it should start doing so. This firm has a cost of equity of 16% and a cost of debt of 10%. (The tax rate is 40%.) The firm has $100 million in debt outstanding and 50 million shares outstanding, selling for $10 per share. The firm currently has net income

of $90 million and depreciation charges of $10 million. It also has projects available as shown below: The firm plans to finance its future capital investment needs using 20% debt.
- **a.** Which of these projects should the firm accept?
- **b.** How much (if any) should the firm pay out as dividends?

7. Triple J is a publicly traded tobacco company that is expecting to experience a 10% annual decrease in revenues, expenses, working capital, and depreciation for each of the next three years. The company paid off all outstanding debt at the beginning of last year and had net income of $48 million in the year just ended. Management has decided to dramatically change the focus of the company to specialize in the telecommunications industry. Toward that end, the managers have decided to forego any additional capital expenditures in the tobacco business for the next three years in order to build a "war chest" to be used to acquire a presence in the target industry. Using the information shown below, determine how large the war chest will be at the end of three years if management keeps the payout ratio at its current level. (You may assume that Triple J will invest any retained earnings in Government securities that will earn 10% per year. Furthermore, the current balance of the cash account is earmarked for maintaining the existing lines of business, so it shouldn't be included in your calculations.)

Income Statement for Year Just Ended

Revenues	$500,000,000
− Expenses	$350,000,000
− Depreciation	$70,000,000
EBIT	$80,000,000
− Taxes	$32,000,000
Net Income	$48,000,000
Dividends Paid	$24,000,000

Pertinent Balance Sheet Information
Net Working Capital = $70,000,000

Project	Initial Investment	EBIT	Annual Depreciation	Lifetime	Salvage
1	$10 million	$1 mil	$500,000	5 years	$2.5 mil
2	$40 million	$5 mil	$1 million	10 years	$10 mil
3	$50 million	$5 mil	$1 million	10 years	$10 mil

8. Is the strategy of Triple J's management described in the last problem in the shareholders' best interests? Why or why not?

9. NoLone Corporation, an all-equity manufacturing firm, has net income of $100 million currently and expects this number to grow at 10% a year for the next three years. The firm's working capital increased by $10 million this year and is expected to increase by the same dollar amount each of the next three years. The depreciation is $50 million and is expected to grow 8% a year for the next three years. Finally, the firm plans to invest $60 million in capital expenditure for each of the next three years. The firm pays 60% of its earnings as dividends each year. RYBR has a cash balance currently of $50. Assuming that the cash does not earn any interest, how much would you expect to have as a cash balance at the end of the third year?

10. Boston Turkey is a publicly traded firm, with the following income statement and balance sheet from its most recent financial year:

Income Statement

Revenues	$1,000,000
− Expenses	$400,000
− Depreciation	$100,000
EBIT	$500,000
− Interest Expense	$100,000
Taxable Income	$400,000
− Tax	$160,000
Net Income	$240,000

Balance Sheet

Assets		Liabilities	
Property, Plant, and Equipment	$1,500,000	Accounts Payable	$500,000
Land and Buildings	$500,000	Long-term Debt	$1,000,000
Current Assets	$1,000,000	Equity (100,000 shares)	$1,500,000
Total	$3,000,000	Total	$3,000,000

Boston Turkey expects its revenues to grow 10% next year and its expenses to remain at 40% of revenues. The depreciation and interest expenses

will remain unchanged at $100,000 next year. The working capital, as a percentage of revenue, will also remain unchanged next year.

The managers of Boston Turkey claim to have several projects available to choose from next year, in which they plan to invest the funds from operations, and they suggest that the firm really should not be paying dividends. The projects have the following characteristics: (You can assume that the projects are perpetuities)

Project	Equity Investment	Expected Annual CF to Equity	Beta
A	$100,000	12,500	1.00
B	$100,000	14,000	1.50
C	$50,000	8,000	1.80
D	$50,000	12,000	2.00

The Treasury bond rate is 6.25%. The firm plans to finance 40% of its future net capital expenditures (cap ex-depreciation) and working capital needs with debt.

a. How much can the company afford to pay in dividends next year?

b. Now assume that the firm actually pays out $1 per share in dividends next year. The current cash balance of the firm is $150,000. How much will the cash balance of the firm be at the end of next year, after the payment of the dividend?

11. Z-Tec Corporation, a firm providing Internet services, reported net income of $10 million in the most recent year, while making $25 million in capital expenditures (depreciation was $5 million). The firm had no working capital needs and uses no debt.

a. Can the firm afford to pay out dividends right now? Why or why not?

b. Assuming that net income grows 40% a year and that net capital expenditures grow 10% a year, when will the firm be in a position to pay dividends?

12. You are analyzing the dividend policy of Conrail, a major railroad, and you have collected the following information from the last five years:

The average debt ratio during this period was 40%, and the total noncash working capital at the end of 1990 was $10 million.

a. Estimate how much Conrail could have paid in dividends during this period.

Year	Net Income	Capital Expenditure	Depreciation	Noncash Working Capital	Dividends
1991	$240	$314	$307	$35	$70
1992	282	466	295	(110)	80
1993	320	566	284	215	95
1994	375	490	278	175	110
1995	441	494	293	250	124

b. If the average return on equity during the period was 13.5% and Conrail had a beta of 1.25, what conclusions would you draw about Conrail's dividend policy? (The average Treasury bond rate during the period was 7%, and the average return on the market was 12.5% during the period.)

13. Assume now that you have been asked to forecast cash flows that you will have available to repurchase stock and pay dividends during the next five years for Conrail. In making these forecasts, you can assume the following:
   - Net Income is anticipated to grow 10% a year from 1995 levels for the next five years.
   - Capital expenditures and depreciation are expected to grow 8% a year from 1995 levels.
   - The revenues in 1995 were $3.75 billion and are expected to grow 5% each year for the next five years. The working capital as a percentage of revenues is expected to remain at 1995 levels.
   - The proportion of net capital expenditures and depreciation that will be financed with debt will drop to 30%.
   a. Estimate how much cash Conrail will have available to pay dividends or repurchase stocks over the next five years.
   b. How will the perceived uncertainty associated with these cash flows affect your decision on dividends and equity repurchases?

14. Cracker Barrel, which operates restaurants and gift stores, is reexamining its policy of paying minimal dividends. In 1995, Cracker Barrel reported net income of $66 million; it had capital expenditures of $150 million in that year and claimed depreciation of only $50 million. The working capital in 1995 was $43 million on sales of $783 million. Looking forward, Cracker Barrel expects the following:
   - Net Income is expected to grow 17% a year for the next five years.

   - During the five years, capital expenditures are expected to grow 10% a year, and depreciation is expected to grow 15% a year.
   - The working capital as a percentage of revenues is expected to remain at 1995 levels, and revenues are expected to grow 10% a year during the period.
   - The company has not used debt to finance its net capital expenditures and does not plan to use any for the next five years.
   a. Estimate how much cash Cracker Barrel would have available to pay out to its stockholders over the next five years.
   b. How would your answer change if the firm plans to increase its leverage by borrowing 25% of its net capital expenditure and working capital needs?

15. Assume that Cracker Barrel wants to continue with its policy of not paying dividends. You are the CEO of Cracker Barrel and have been confronted by dissident stockholders, demanding to know why you are not paying out your FCFE (estimated in the previous problem) to your stockholders. How would you defend your decision? How receptive will stockholders be to your defense? Would it make any difference that Cracker Barrel has earned a return on equity of 25% over the previous five years, and that its beta is only 1.2? (The T Bond rate was 7%.)

16. Manpower Corporation, which provides nongovernment employment services in the United States, reported net income of $128 million in 1995. It had capital expenditures of $50 million and depreciation of $24 million in 1995, and its working capital was $500 million (on revenues of $5 billion). The firm has a debt ratio of 10% and plans to maintain this debt ratio.
   a. Estimate how much Manpower Corporation will have available to pay out as dividends next year, if all these items are expected to grow 10%.

b. The current cash balance is $143 million. If Manpower Corporation is expected to pay $12 million in dividends next year and repurchase no stock, estimate the expected cash balance at the end of the next year.

17. How would your answers to the previous problem change if Manpower Corporation plans to pay off its outstanding debt of $100 million next year and become a debt-free company?

18. You are an institutional investor and have collected the following information on five maritime firms in order to assess their dividend policies:

Company	FCFE	Dividends Paid	ROE	Beta
Alexander & Brown	$55	$35	8%	0.80
American President	$60	$12	14.5%	1.30
OMI Corporation	−$15	$5	4.0%	1.25
Overseas Shipholding	$20	$12	1.5%	0.90
Sea Containers	−$5	$8	14%	1.05

The average risk-free rate during the period was 7%, and the average return on the market was 12%.

a. Assess which of these firms you would pressure to pay more in dividends.

b. Which of the firms would you encourage to pay less in dividends?

c. How would you modify this analysis to reflect your expectations about the future of the entire sector?

19. You are analyzing the dividend policy of Black and Decker, a manufacturer of tools and appliances. The following table summarizes the dividend payout ratios, yields, and expected growth rates of other firms in the waste disposal business.

a. Compare Black and Decker's dividend policy to those of its peers, using the average dividend payout ratios and yields.

b. Do the same comparison, controlling for differences in expected growth.

Company	Payout Ratio (%)	Dividend Yield (%)	Exp. Growth (%)
Fedders Corporation	11	1.2	22.0
Maytag Corporation	37	2.8	23.0
National Presto	67	4.9	13.5
Toro Corporation	15	1.5	16.5
Whirlpool Corp.	30	2.5	20.5
Black & Decker	24	1.3	23.0

20. The following regression was run using all NYSE firms in 1995:

$$YIELD = 0.0478 - 0.0157\ BETA - 0.0000008$$
$$MKTCAP + 0.006797\ DBTRATIO + 0.0002\ ROE$$
$$- 0.09\ NCEX/TA \qquad R^2 = 12.88\%$$

where BETA = Beta of the stock
MKTCAP = Market Value of Equity
DBTRATIO = Book Value of Debt / MKTCAP
ROE = Return on Equity in 1994
NCEX/TA = (Capital Expenditures − Depreciation) / Total Assets

The corresponding values for Black and Decker, in 1995, were as follows:

Beta = 1.30
MKTCAP = $5,500 million
DBTRATIO = 35%
ROE = 14.5%
NCEX/TA = 4.00%

Black and Decker had a dividend yield of 1.3% and a dividend payout ratio of 24% in 1995.

a. Estimate the dividend yield for Black & Decker, based on the regression.

b. Why might your answer be different, using this approach, than the answer to the prior question, where you used only the comparable firms?

21. Handy and Harman, a leading fabricator of precious metal alloys, pays out only 23% of its earnings as dividends. The average dividend payout ratio for metal fabricating firms is 45%. The average growth rate in earnings for the entire sector is 10% (Handy and Harman is expected to grow 23%). Should Handy and Harman pay more in dividends just to get closer to the average payout ratio? Why or why not?

22. Is there any situation where a high payout/poor projects combination may actually be to the benefit of the shareholders? (*Hint:* Think about why we have bond covenants.)

LIVE CASE STUDY

IX. A FRAMEWORK FOR ANALYZING DIVIDENDS

Objective: To examine the firm's policy on returning cash to its owners, and to make judgments about whether that policy should be changed.

Key
Questions

- How much could this firm have returned to its stockholders over the last few years? How much did it actually return?
- Given this dividend policy and the current cash balance of this firm, would you push the firm to change its dividend policy (return more or less cash to its owners)?
- How does this firm's dividend policy compare to those of its peer group and to the rest of the market?

Framework
for Analysis

1. *Affordable Dividends*
- What were the free cash flows to equity that this firm had over the last few years?
- How much cash did the firm actually return to its owners over the last few years?
- What is the current cash balance for this firm?

2. *Management Trust*
- How well have the managers of the firm picked investments, historically? (Look at the investment return section.)
- Is there any reason to believe that future investments of this firm will be different from the historical record?

3. *Changing Dividend Policy*
- Given the relationship between dividends and free cash flows to equity, and the trust you have in the management of this firm, would you change this firm's dividend policy?

4. *Comparing to Sector and Market*
- Relative to the sector to which this firm belongs, does it pay too much or too little in dividends? (Do a regression, if necessary.)
- Relative to the rest of the firms in the market, does it pay too much or too little in dividends? (Use the market regression, if necessary.)

Getting Information on analyzing dividend policy

You can get the information that you need to estimate free cash flows to equity and returns on equity from past financials. You will also need a beta (see risk and return section) and a debt ratio (see risk and return section) to estimate the free cash flows to equity. To see what returns you would have made on your stock over the last 5 years examine the calendar returns portion of the page on your firm at the morningstar site under your firm (**www.morningstar.net**).

To compare dividends to free cash flows to equity for up to 10 years for your firm, you can use the spreadsheet on my web site titled **dividend.xls.** It will compute FCFE and dividends, and analyze project and stock returns over the period analyzed.

CHAPTER 12

BASICS OF VALUATION

In this chapter, we examine the basic principles of discounted cash flow valuation and lay the groundwork for linking valuation to the corporate financial decisions discussed thus far. In the process, we attempt to answer the following questions:

- What is the difference between valuing the firm and valuing equity?
- When valuing equity, what is the distinction between the dividend discount model and cash flow to equity model? When will the two models yield similar results? When are the results likely to be different?
- Will firm valuation and equity valuation provide consistent results? When should we use one approach over the other?
- What are some of the approaches available to estimating expected growth? How is expected growth related to the fundamentals of the firm and to its investment, financing, and dividend policy?

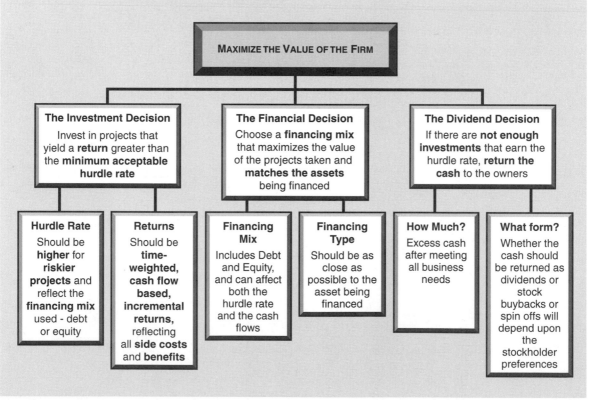

- How sensitive is firm or equity value to changes in assumptions about discount rates and expected growth?
- What are some of the multiples used by analysts to value firms? Why are they so popular? How are they related to discounted cash flow valuation?

VALUATION APPROACHES

There are two basic approaches to valuation that we will examine in this chapter. In the first, discounted cash flow valuation, the value of any asset is estimated by computing the present value of the expected cash flows on that asset, discounted back at a rate that reflects the riskiness of the cash flows. In a sense, it is a measure of the intrinsic value of an asset. In the second, the value of an asset is computed relative to how similar assets are priced in the market place. It is therefore a measure of relative rather than intrinsic value.

DISCOUNTED CASH FLOW VALUATION

Intuitively, the value of any asset should be a function of three variables: how much it generates in cash flows, when these cash flows are expected to occur, and the uncertainty associated with these cash flows. Discounted cash flow valuation brings all three of these variables together by computing the value of any asset to be the present value of its expected future cash flows:

$$\text{Value} = \sum_{t=1}^{t=n} \frac{CF_t}{(1+r)^t}$$

where

n = Life of the asset
CF_t = Cash flow in period t
r = Discount rate reflecting the riskiness of the estimated cash flows

The cash flows will vary from asset to asset: dividends for stocks; coupons (interest) and face value for bonds; and after-tax cash flows for real projects. The discount rate is a function of the riskiness of the estimated cash flows: riskier assets carry higher rates; safer projects carry lower rates.

Equity Valuation versus Firm Valuation

There are two paths to discounted cash flow valuation: the first is to value just the equity stake in the business; the second is to value the entire firm, including equity and any other claimholders in the firm (bondholders, preferred stockholders, etc.). While both approaches discount expected cash flows, the relevant cash flows and discount rates are different for each.

The *value of equity* is obtained by discounting expected cash flows to equity (the residual cash flows after meeting all expenses, tax obligations, investment needs, and interest and principal payments) at the cost of equity (the rate of return required by equity investors in the firm).

$$\text{Value of Equity} = \sum_{t=1}^{t=n} \frac{\text{CF to Equity}_t}{(1 + k_e)^t}$$

where

$$\text{CF to Equity}_t = \text{Expected Cash flow to Equity in Period t}$$
$$k_e = \text{Cost of Equity}$$

The dividend discount model is a specialized case of equity valuation, whereby the value of a stock is the present value of expected future dividends.

The *value of the firm* is obtained by discounting expected cash flows to the firm, (residual cash flows after meeting all operating expenses, investment needs, and taxes but prior to debt payments) at the weighted average cost of capital (the cost of the different components of financing used by the firm, weighted by their market value proportions).

$$\text{Value of Firm} = \sum_{t=1}^{t=n} \frac{\text{CF to Firm}_t}{(1 + \text{WACC})^t}$$

where

$$\text{CF to Firm}_t = \text{Expected Cash flow to Firm in Period t}$$
$$\text{WACC} = \text{Weighted Average Cost of Capital}$$

While the two approaches use different definitions of cash flow and discount rates, they will yield consistent estimates of value as long as consistent assumptions are made for both. It is important to avoid mismatching cash flows and discount rates, since discounting cash flows to equity at the weighted average cost of capital will lead to an upwardly biased estimate of the value of equity, while discounting cash flows to the firm at the cost of equity will yield a downward-biased estimate of the value of the firm.

Value of Equity: This is the value of the equity stake in a business; in the context of a publicly traded firm, it is the value of the common stock in the firm.

Value of Firm: The value of the firm is the value of all investors who have claims on the firm; thus, it includes lenders and debtholders, who have fixed claims and equity investors, who have residual claims.

12.1   FIRM VALUATION AND LEVERAGE

It is often argued that equity valuation requires more assumptions than firm valuation, because cash flows to equity require explicit assumptions about changes in leverage whereas cash flows to the firm are pre-debt cash flows and do not require assumptions about leverage. Is this true?

☐ Yes

☐ No

Explain.

ILLUSTRATION 12.1:   Effects of Mismatching Cash Flows and Discount Rates

Assume that you are analyzing a small manufacturing company with the following cash flows for the next five years (Table 12.1). Assume also that the cost of equity is 13.625% and the firm can borrow long term at 10%. The tax rate for the firm is 50%. The current market value of equity is $1,073 and the value of debt outstanding is $800.

	Table 12.1	ESTIMATED CASH FLOWS TO EQUITY AND THE FIRM		
Year	CF to Equity	Interest(1-t)	CF to Firm	
1	$50	$40	$90	
2	$60	$40	$100	
3	$68	$40	$108	
4	$76.2	$40	$116.2	
5	$83.49	$40	$123.49	
Terminal Value	$1603.01		$2363.01	

Cost of Equity = 13.625%
Cost of Debt = Pretax Rate (1 - Tax Rate) = 10% (1 - .5) = 5%
Value of Equity = $1073   Value of Debt = 800
WACC = Cost of Equity (Equity / (Debt + Equity)) + Cost of Debt
(Debt/(Debt+Equity))
= 13.625% (1073/1873) + 5% (800/1873) = 9.94%

Method 1: Discount CF to equity at cost of equity to get value of equity

PV of Equity $= 50/1.13625 + 60/1.13625^2 + 68/1.13625^3 + 76.2/1.13625^4$
$+ (83.49+1603)/1.13625^5 = \$1073$

Method 2: Discount CF to firm at cost of capital to get value of firm

PV of Firm $= 90/1.0994 + 100/1.0994^2 + 108/1.0994^3 + 116.2/1.0994^4$
$+ (123.49+2363)/1.0994^5 = \$1873$
PV of Equity   = PV of Firm − Market Value of Debt
= $ 1873 − $ 800 = $1073

X Method 1: Discount CF to equity at cost of capital to get too high a value for equity

PV of Equity $= 50/1.0994 + 60/1.0994^2 + 68/1.0994^3 + 76.2/1.0994^4$
$+ (83.49+1603)/1.0994^5 = \$1248$

X Method 2: Discount CF to firm at cost of equity to get too low a value for the firm

PV of Firm $= 90/1.13625 + 100/1.13625^2 + 108/1.13625^3 + 116.2/1.13625^4$
$+ (123.49+2363)/1.13625^5 = \$1613$
PV of Equity   = PV of Firm − Market Value of Debt
= $1612.86 − $800 = $813

The effects of using the wrong discount rate are clearly visible in the last two calculations. When the cost of capital is mistakenly used to discount the cash flows to equity, the value of equity increases by $175 over its true value ($1,073). When the cash flows to the firm are erroneously discounted at the cost of equity, the value of the firm is understated by $260.

The Choices in Discounted Cash Flow Models

All discounted cash flow models ultimately boil down to estimating three inputs: current cash flows, an expected growth rate in these cash flows, and a discount rate to use in discounting these cash flows. In this section, we will examine the choices available in terms of each of these inputs.

In terms of cash flows, there are three choices: either dividends or free cash flows to equity for equity valuation models, and free cash flows to the firm for firm valuation models. Discounting dividends usually provides the most conservative estimate of value for the equity in any firm, since most firms pay less in dividends than they can afford to. In Chapter 11, we noted that the free cash flow to equity (i.e., the cash flow left over after meeting all investment needs and making debt payments) is the amount that a firm can pay in dividends. The value of equity, based upon the free cash flow to equity, will therefore yield a more realistic estimate of value for firms, especially in the context of takeovers. Even if a firm is not the target of a takeover, it can be argued that the value of equity has to reflect the possibility of a takeover, and hence the expected free cash flows to equity. The choice between free cash flows to equity and free cash flows to the firm is really a choice between equity and firm valuation. As noted in the previous section, when done consistently, both approaches should yield the same values for the equity in a business. As a practical concern, however, cash flows to equity are after net debt issues or payments and become much more difficult to estimate when leverage is changing over time, whereas cash flows to the firm are pre-debt cash flows and are unaffected by changes in the leverage. Ease of use dictates that firm valuation will be more straightforward under this scenario.

The choice of discount rates will be dictated by the choice in cash flows. If the cash flow that is being discounted is dividends or free cash flows to equity, the appropriate discount rate is the cost of equity. If the cash flow being discounted is the cash flow to the firm, the discount rate has to be the cost of capital.

The final choice that all discounted cash flow models have to make relates to expected growth patterns. Since firms have infinite lives, the way in which we apply closure in valuation is to estimate a terminal value at a point in time and dispense with estimating cash flows beyond that point. To do this in the context of discounted cash flow valuation, we have to assume that cash flows beyond this point in time are constant forever, an assumption that we refer to as "stable" growth. If we do this, the present value of these cash flows can be estimated as the present value of a growing perpetuity. There are three questions that every valuation then has to answer:

1. How long into the future will a company be able to grow at a rate higher than the stable growth rate?

2. How high will the growth rate be during the high-growth period and what pattern will it follow?

3. What will happen to the firm's fundamentals (risk, cash flow patterns, etc.) as the expected growth rate changes?

At the risk of being simplistic, we can broadly classify growth patterns into three categories: firms which are in stable growth already, firms which expect to maintain a high growth rate for a period and then drop abruptly to stable growth, and firms which will have high growth for a specified period and then go through a transition phase to reach stable growth at a point in time in the future. As a practical point, it is important that as the growth rate changes, the firm's risk and cash flow characteristics change as well. In general, as expected growth declines toward stable growth,

Choose a			
Cash Flow	*Dividends*	*Cash flows to Equity*	*Cash flows to Firm*
	Expected Dividends to Stockholders	Net Income $-(1-\delta)$ (Capital Exp. $-$ Deprc'n) $-(1-\delta)$ Change in Non-Cash WC $=$ Free Cash Flow to Equity (FCFE) $[\delta =$ Debt Ratio]	EBIT $(1-$ tax rate) $-$ (Captial Exp. $-$ Deprec'n) $-$ Change in Non-Cash WC $=$ Free Cash Flow to Firm (FCFF)
& A Discount Rate	*Cost of Equity* • *Basis:* The riskier the investment, the greater should be the cost of equity. • *Models:* CAPM: Riskfree Rate + Beta (Risk Premium) (or) APM: Riskfree Rate $- \Sigma\text{Beta}_j$ (Risk Premium)$_j$: *n factors*		*Cost of Capital* $\text{WACC} = k_e(E/(D+E))$ $\quad + k_d(D/(D+E))$ $k_d =$ Current Borrowing Rate $(1-t)$ E,D: Market Values of Equity and Debt
& A Growth Pattern	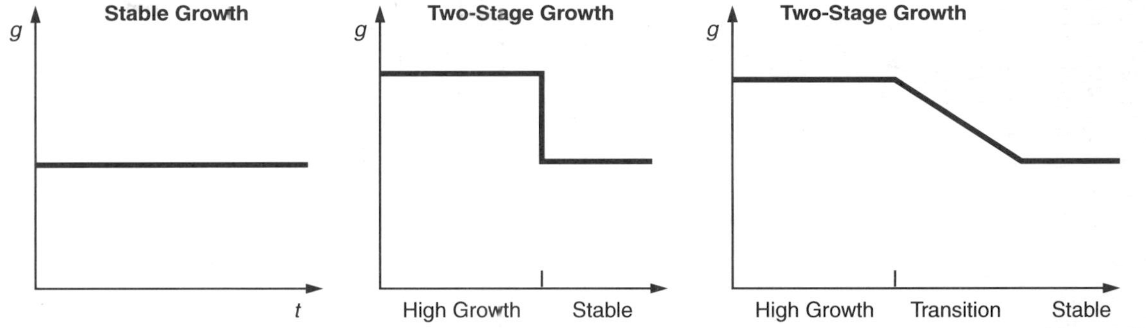 **Stable Growth**	**Two-Stage Growth**	**Two-Stage Growth**

Stable Growth: g vs t

Two-Stage Growth: g vs High Growth | Stable

Two-Stage Growth: g vs High Growth | Transition | Stable

Figure 12.1   Choices in discounted cash flow valuation.

firms should see their risk approach the "average" and reinvestment needs decline. These choices are summarized in Figure 12.1. We will now examine each of these valuation models in more detail.

 This spreadsheet allows you to pick the right discounted cash flow valuation model for your needs, given the characteristics of the business that you are valuing (**model.xls**).

IN PRACTICE: NOMINAL VERSUS REAL VALUATIONS

In practice, the value of the equity or the firm can be done in either real terms (with real cash flows and real discount rates) or nominal terms (with nominal cash flows and discount rates). Since taxes are based upon nominal earnings, it is usually better to employ nominal valuation. This advantage, however, is rapidly lost as inflation rates climb, since the noise induced by inflation estimates drowns out the effects of the other inputs to the valuation. As a rule of thumb, when the inflation rate reaches double digits, it is prudent to either switch to real valuation or do the valuation in another (more stable) currency. Note that switching to another currency does not really eliminate the need to forecast inflation, since future exchange rates will be affected by inflation estimates.

EQUITY VALUATION MODELS

As noted above, equity valuation models attempt to estimate the value of equity in a firm by discounting cash flows to equity at the rate of return required by equity investors (cost of equity). In this section, we consider two versions of equity valuation models: One narrowly defines cash flows to equity as dividends, and the other uses a more expansive definition of cash flows to equity.

Dividend Discount Model

When an investor buys stock, he generally expects to get two types of cash flows: dividends during the holding period and an expected price at the end of the holding period. Since this expected price is itself determined by future dividends, the value of a stock is the present value of dividends through infinity:

$$\text{Value per Share of Stock} = \sum_{t=1}^{t=\infty} \frac{DPS_t}{(1 + r)^t}$$

where

$$DPS_t = \text{Expected dividends per share}$$
$$r = \text{Required rate of return on stock (Cost of Equity)}$$

The rationale for the model lies in the present value rule: The value of any asset is the present value of expected future cash flows, discounted at a rate appropriate to the riskiness of the cash flows being discounted.

In the general version of the dividend discount model, we allow for two stages in growth—an initial period of extraordinary growth, followed by stable growth forever.

Extraordinary growth period   Stable growth: g_n forever

Value of the Stock = PV of Dividends During Extraordinary Phase + PV of Terminal Price

$$P_0 = \sum_{t=1}^{t=n} \frac{DPS_t}{(1 + r)^t} + \frac{P_n}{(1 + r)^n} \text{ where } P_n = \frac{DPS_{n+1}}{(r - g_n)}$$

where

DPS_t = Expected dividends per share in year t
r = Required rate of return
P_n = Price at the end of year n
g_n = Growth rate forever after year n

There are four basic inputs in this model. First, the *length of the high-growth period* is defined; the longer the high-growth period, the more valuable the stock is. Second, the *dividends per share* each period, during the growth period, is specified; since payout ratios change with growth rates, earnings growth rates and payout ratios must be estimated each year for the high-growth period. Third, the *rate of return* stockholders will demand for holding the stock is estimated, based upon the risk and return model used by the analyst. Finally, the *terminal price at the end of the high-growth period* is estimated, using the estimates of stable growth, the dividend payout, and required return after the high growth ends.

Terminal Price: This is the expected price of a stock (or equity) at the end of a specified holding period.

What Is a Stable Growth Rate?

It is difficult to talk about extraordinary growth without first defining what we mean by a *stable growth rate.* There are two insights to keep in mind when estimating a "stable" growth rate. First, since the growth rate in the firm's dividends is expected to last forever, the firm's other measures of performance (including earnings) can be expected to grow at the same rate. Consider the long-term consequences of a firm whose earnings grow 6% a year forever, while its dividends grow at 8%. Over time, the dividends will exceed earnings. Similarly, if a firm's earnings grow at a faster rate than its dividends in the long term, the payout ratio will converge toward zero, which is also not a steady state. Thus, though the model's requirement is for the expected growth rate in dividends, if the firm is truly in a steady state, analysts should be able to substitute in the expected growth rate in earnings and get the same result.

The second issue relates to what growth rate is reasonable as a "stable" growth rate. Again, the assumption that this growth rate will last forever establishes rigorous constraints on "reasonableness." A firm cannot in the long term grow at a rate significantly greater than the growth rate in the economy in which it operates. Thus, a firm that grows at 12% forever in an economy growing at 6% will eventually become larger than the economy. In practical terms, the stable growth rate cannot be larger than the nominal (real) growth rate in the economy in which the firm operates, if the valuation is done in nominal (real) terms.

Can a stable growth rate be much *lower* than the growth rate in the economy? There are no logical or mathematical limits on the downside. Firms that have a stable growth rate much lower than the growth rate in the economy will become smaller in proportion to the economy over time. Since there is no economic basis for arguing that this *cannot* happen, there is no reason to prevent analysts from using a stable growth rate much lower than the nominal growth rate in the economy.

The assumption that the growth rate in dividends has to be constant over time is a difficult assumption to meet, especially given the volatility of earnings. If a firm has an average growth rate that is close to a stable growth rate, the model can be used with little real effect on value. Thus, a cyclical firm that can be expected to have year-to-year swings in growth rates, but has an average growth rate of 6%, can be assumed to be in stable growth without a significant loss of generality. This is because dividends are smoothed even when earnings are volatile; they are less likely to be affected by year-to-year changes in earnings growth. In addition, the present value effects of using an average growth rate rather than a constant growth rate are small.

 Stable Growth Rate: This is a growth rate that a firm can sustain forever in both earnings, dividends and cash flows.

ILLUSTRATION 12.2   Estimating Stable Growth for Disney, Deutsche Bank, Aracruz, and Bookscape
We estimated the ceilings for stable growth rates for Disney, Deutsche Bank, Aracruz, and Bookscape by analyzing both the economies in which these firms operate and the businesses in which each operates (Table 12.2).

Table 12.2   ESTIMATES OF STABLE GROWTH: DISNEY, ARACRUZ, DEUTSCHE, AND BOOKSCAPE

Company	Valuation Approach	Estimated Stable Growth
Disney and Bookscape	Nominal U.S. dollars	5–6%: Set equal to long-term nominal growth rate in the U.S. economy
Aracruz	Real BR	5%: Based upon expected long-term real growth rate for Brazilian economy
Deutsche Bank	Nominal DM	5–6%: Set equal to nominal growth rate in the world economy

 This spreadsheet allows you to estimate the value of the stock in a firm using a stable-growth dividend discount model (**ddmst.xls**).

Length of High-Growth Period
The length of the high-growth period is a key input to this valuation model, and it does not lend itself easily to a rigid framework. Let us consider the easy cases first. First, if the firm is growing at a rate close to the stable growth rate right now, there is no extraordinary growth anticipated and it can be assumed that the firm is in stable growth already. Second, if the firm is growing at a rate higher than the stable growth rate, but the higher growth is coming from a single product or service for which the firm has a protected position, the extraordinary growth can be expected to last as long as the protection lasts. Thus, a pharmaceutical firm that is generating high

growth because of a single patent-protected product, whose patent is expected to expire in four years, can be expected to have a four-year high-growth period.

In other cases, the estimation is much more difficult. In general, we can make the following assumptions about the length of the high-growth period:

1. The greater the current growth rate in earnings of a firm, relative to the stable growth rate, the longer the high-growth period, though the growth rate may drop off during the period. Thus, a firm that is growing at 40% currently should have a longer high-growth period than one growing at 14%.

2. The larger the current size of the firm—both in absolute terms and relative to the market it serves—the shorter the high-growth period. Size remains one of the most potent forces that push firms toward stable growth; the larger a firm, the less likely it is to maintain an above-normal growth rate.

3. The magnitude of the barriers to entry in a business, either because of legal mechanisms such as patents or marketing mechanisms such as strong brand names, should affect the length of the high-growth period for a firm.

At the risk of sounding arbitrary, we suggest the following guidelines for defining the length of the high-growth period as a function of current growth rates:

CURRENT GROWTH RATE	LENGTH OF HIGH GROWTH PERIOD
≤ 1% higher than stable growth rate	No high growth
1–10% higher than stable growth rate	5 years
> 10% higher than stable growth rate	10 years

Again, the sensitivity of value to changes in the length of the high-growth period can always be estimated. While some analysts use growth periods greater than 10 years, the combination of high expected growth and long growth periods creates a potent mix in terms of increasing the size of the firm, in many cases well beyond the realm of reasonableness.

High-Growth Periods: This is a period during which a company's earnings or cash flows are expected to grow at a rate much higher than the overall growth rate of the economy.

12.2   LENGTH OF HIGH-GROWTH PERIOD AND BARRIERS TO ENTRY

Assume that you are analyzing two firms, both of which are enjoying high growth. The first firm is Earthlink Network, an Internet service provider, which operates in an environment with few barriers to entry and extraordinary competition. The second firm is Biogen, a biotechnology firm which is enjoying growth from two drugs for which it owns patents for the next decade. Assuming that both firms are well managed, which of the two firms would you expect to have a longer high-growth period?

☐ Earthlink Network

☐ Biogen

☐ Both are well managed and should have the same high-growth period.

Required Return on Stock—Discount Rates

The dividends and terminal price should be discounted back at a rate that reflects their riskiness to stockholders to arrive at the dividend discount model value. To arrive at this rate, we first have to arrive at a measure of the riskiness using a risk and return model. If the CAPM is used, for instance, the beta of the stock is the measure of risk; if the APM is used, the betas of the stock relative to the factors are the measures of risk. We then have to arrive at an expected return based upon the risk measure. In the CAPM, this requires an estimate for the riskless rate and the risk premium.

$$\text{Required Return on Equity} = \text{Riskless Rate} + \text{Beta (Risk Premium)}$$

A similar estimate can be made using the APM.

While the mechanics of estimating required returns have been examined fully in earlier chapters, a couple of points relate specifically to valuation. First, empirically there is a positive correlation between high growth and high risk. High-growth firms tend to have higher betas than do low-growth firms. Building on this point, it is important that as we change growth rates over time we also adjust risk accordingly. Thus, when a firm goes from high growth to low growth, it is important that its beta be reduced to reflect the lower growth.

12.3 BETAS AND GROWTH RATES

We will make the argument that the beta of a stock should converge on 1 as the expected growth rate in earnings converges on the stable growth rate. The reason for this convergence is (you can choose more than one):

☐ As growth rate declines, the risk of the firm should also decline.

☐ As firms become larger, they tend to become more diversified in their product, clientele, and geographical bases.

☐ As firms grow, they accumulate larger cash balances.

☐ All of the above.

Explain.

Expected Dividends During High-Growth Period

The first step in estimating expected dividends during the high-growth period is to estimate the expected earnings for each year. This is done using the current earnings and the expected growth rates in earnings, which may either be constant or vary each year across the high-growth period. These expected earnings are paired with estimated dividend payout ratios in each year, which again may change over the high-growth period. This may seem like an awkward procedure, since expected dividends could well be estimated using the current dividends and applying a dividend growth rate, but it is used for two reasons. First, most analyst projections for growth are stated in terms of earnings rather than dividends. Second, separating earnings growth from dividend payout provides more flexibility in terms of changing dividend payout ratios as earnings growth rates change. In particular, it allows us to raise dividend payout ratios as earnings growth rates decline.

Estimating Earnings Growth

The key input in this model is the *earnings growth rate*. It can be estimated using one of three approaches:

1. *Historical Growth:* The growth rate in earnings per share over past periods can be used to estimate future growth. In doing so, we assume that firms whose earnings have grown rapidly in the past will continue to do so in the future. There are two considerations in using this measure. The first is how far back to go; the growth rate will be different for different time periods, but it is important that some consistency be maintained across valuations. The other relates to the measurement of the growth rate itself; since earnings growth compounds over time, the geometric average growth rate in earnings, rather than the arithmetic average, should be used:

$$\text{Geometric Average Growth Rate in Earnings} = (\text{EPS}_0/\text{EPS}_{0-t})^{1/t} - 1$$

2. *Analyst Projections:* The easiest solution is to use an analyst projection of growth in earnings for the company being valued. For most U.S. companies, such projections are widely available and disseminated by a number of services, including Zacks and IBES. They are less widely available for non-U.S. companies, because there are far fewer equity research analysts in other markets.

3. *Fundamentals of the Firm:* The most complex—and the richest—approach relates expected growth to the fundamentals of the firm. In particular, the expected growth rate should be a function of the proportion of the earnings that are reinvested back into the firm and the returns earned on the projects taken with the money:

$$\text{Expected Growth Rate} = \text{Retention Ratio} * \text{Return on Equity}$$

The return on equity is itself affected by the leverage of the firm, and we expanded it to include this effect:

$$\text{Return on Equity} = \text{ROC} + \text{D/E}\,(\text{ROC} - i\,(1 - t))$$

where

$\text{ROC} = \text{Return on Capital} = \text{EBIT}\,(1 - t)\,/\,(\text{BV of Debt} + \text{BV of Equity})$
$\text{D/E} = \text{Debt/equity ratio}$
$i = \text{Interest rate on debt}$
$t = \text{Marginal tax rate}$

The advantage of this formulation is that it allows the analyst valuing the firm to bring in the effect of the investment, financing, and dividend decisions of the firm, not only in current periods but also in future periods.

Historical Growth Rate (in Earnings): This is the growth rate over the past few years in earnings; it can be calculated either by averaging the year-specific growth rates (arithmetic average) or by estimating the compounded growth rate over the whole period.

Fundamental Growth Rate: This is the growth rate in earnings estimated from the company's reinvestment rate and the quality of its projects.

12.4 DIFFERENCES IN GROWTH RATES

The growth rates from historical earnings, analyst projections, and fundamentals can often be very different. These differences can be best explained by

- ☐ firms becoming larger over time, as they grow.
- ☐ analyst biases in estimating growth.
- ☐ the inputs in the fundamental growth formula being current-year numbers rather than projections of the future.
- ☐ all of the above.

Earnings Growth Patterns

The earnings growth rate *during the high-growth period* can also take one of many paths, ranging from a constant growth rate to one that changes each year:

1. *Constant growth rate during the high-growth period:* From a purely mechanical standpoint, the simplest assumption is that the earnings growth rate is constant for the high-growth period, after which the growth rate drops to the stable level, as shown in Figure 12.2.

    The limitation of this formulation is obvious. It assumes that the growth rate is high during the initial period and is transformed overnight to a lower, stable rate at the end of the period. While these sudden transformations in growth can happen, it is much more realistic to assume that the shift from high growth to stable growth happens gradually over time. The assumption that the growth rate drops precipitously from its level in the initial phase to a stable rate also implies that this model is more appropriate for firms with modest growth rates in the initial phase. For instance, it is more reasonable to assume that a firm growing at 12% in the high-growth period will see its growth rate drop to 6% than it is for a firm growing at 40% in the high-growth period. If we assume that the growth rate and payout ratio are fixed for the high-growth period, the present value of the dividends during the high-growth period can be estimated as follows:

$$\text{PV of Dividends in High Growth Phase} = \frac{DPS_0 * (1 + g) * \left(1 - \frac{(1 + g)^n}{(1 + r)^n}\right)}{r - g}$$

This spreadsheet allows you to estimate the value of the stock in a firm using a two-stage dividend discount model (**ddm2st.xls**).

2. *Constant growth for initial part of high-growth period, followed by gradual reduction to stable growth:* In this case, the growth rate does not drop precipitously at the end of the high-growth period to the stable rate; rather, it adjusts more gradually to it, as shown in Figure 12.3.

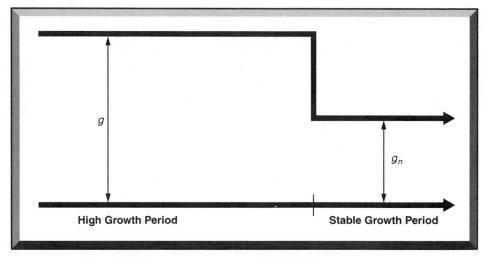

Figure 12.2   Constant growth rate during high-growth period.

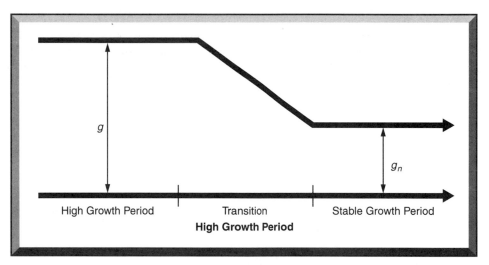

Figure 12.3   High growth followed by transition.

This model allows for growth rates and payout ratios to change gradually during the transition period. Thus, it may be more appropriate for firms that are expected to grow at very high rates, say 30 to 40% for the next few years. The present value of dividends during the high-growth phase can then be estimated as follows:

$$
\begin{array}{c}
\text{PV of Dividends} \\
\text{in High Growth}
\end{array}
=
\underbrace{\sum_{t=1}^{t=n1} \frac{\text{EPS}_0 * (1 + g_a)^t * \Pi_a}{(1 + r)^t}}_{\text{High-growth phase}}
+
\underbrace{\sum_{t=n1+1}^{t=n2} \frac{\text{DPS}_t}{(1 + r)^t}}_{\text{Transition}}
$$

where

$$EPS_t = \text{Earnings per share in year t}$$
$$DPS_t = \text{Dividends per share in year t}$$
$$g_a = \text{Growth rate in high-growth phase (lasts n1 periods)}$$
$$\Pi_a = \text{Payout ratio in high-growth phase}$$
$$r = \text{Required rate of return on equity}$$

 This spreadsheet allows you to estimate the value of the stock in a firm using a three-stage dividend discount model (**ddm3st.xls**).

3. ***Growth rates that change every year for the high-growth period:*** In the most general formulation, the growth rates and payout ratios can be different in each year of the high-growth period, reflecting changes in investment opportunities and firm size. The value of a stock, under this scenario, is the present value of the dividends each year during the high-growth period added to the present value of the terminal price at the end of the high-growth period.

 12.5 CYCLICAL FIRMS AND CONSTANT GROWTH RATES

Models that are built on the assumption of an expected constant growth rate over time cannot be used for cyclical firms, whose earnings growth is likely to be very volatile over time—high during economic booms and very low or negative during recessions.

☐ True

☐ False

Explain.

 ILLUSTRATION 12.3 Estimating EPS Growth at Disney, Aracruz, Deutsche Bank, and Bookscape

We begin by applying the fundamental approach to estimating earnings per share growth for the companies in our analysis. We initially use the returns on equity estimated for 1996 and the retention ratios in 1996 to arrive at the expected growth rate (Table 12.3).

Table 12.3 ESTIMATES OF EXPECTED GROWTH IN EARNINGS: DISNEY, ARACRUZ, DEUTSCHE BANK, AND BOOKSCAPE

Company	Based upon 1996 Estimates			Based upon Forecasted Estimates		
	ROE	Retention Ratio	Expected Growth Rate	Adjusted ROE	Retention Ratio	Expected Growth Rate
Disney	24.95%	77.68%	19.38%	25%	77.68%	19.42%
Bookscape	21.09%	38.79%	8.18%	21.09%	38.79%	8.18%
Aracruz	2.22%	65.00%	1.44%	13.91%	65.00%	9.04%
Deutsche Bank	7.25%	39.81%	2.89%	14.00%	45.00%	6.30%

Note that both Aracruz and Deutsche Bank have very low expected growth rates, due to their low returns on equity in 1996. We reestimated the expected growth rates, using forecasted returns on equity. For Deutsche Bank, the forecasted return on equity was assumed to be equal to the average return on equity across European commercial banks, which was 14% in 1996. For Disney and Bookscape, the current return on equity is assumed to be the forecasted return on equity. For Aracruz, we estimated the forecasted real return on equity in two steps. We first computed the average real return on capital of 9.91% for Aracruz between 1994 and 1996, by dividing the average after-tax operating income by the average book value of capital.[1] We then used the real cost of debt of 5.50% that we estimated for Aracruz earlier in the book, in conjunction with the existing debt/equity ratio of 62.90% and a tax rate of 32% to arrive at a return of equity of 13.91%:

$$\text{Normalized ROE}_{\text{Aracruz}} = \text{ROC} + \text{D/E} (\text{ROC} - i (1 - t))$$
$$= 9.91\% + 0.6290 (9.91\% - 5.50\%(1 - .32)) = 13.91\%$$

We adjusted the payout ratio for Deutsche Bank to reflect the average payout ratio over the last five years of 55%. For Bookscape, which does not pay dividends, we used the free cash flows to equity that we estimated in Chapter 11, of $710,000 in 1996 as a proxy for dividends. Since the net income in 1996 at Bookscape was $1,160,000, the retention ratio is then estimated as follows:

$$\text{Estimated Retention Ratio} = 1 - (710/1160) = 38.79\%$$

For Disney and Aracruz, we assumed that existing payout ratios were normal.

Estimating Dividend Payout Ratios
The other input needed to estimate expected dividends during the high-growth phase is the *dividend payout ratio*, since the expected dividends in period t can be written as:

$$\text{Expected Dividends in Period t} = \text{Expected Earnings}_t * \text{Payout Ratio}_t$$

The payout ratio should reflect changes in expected growth. As growth declines, the payout ratio should increase. Figure 12.4 graphs out payout ratio patterns under the two-stage and three-stage earnings growth formulations, and illustrates the linkage between growth rates and payout ratios.

12.6   PAYOUT RATIOS AND EXPECTED GROWTH
The dividend discount model cannot be used to value stock in a company with high growth that does not pay dividends.
☐ True
☐ False
Explain.

---

[1] The book values in Brazil are inflation adjusted. Consequently, dividing the earnings by the book value yields the real return. If the book values were not adjusted, the inflation rate would have to be subtracted from this estimate.

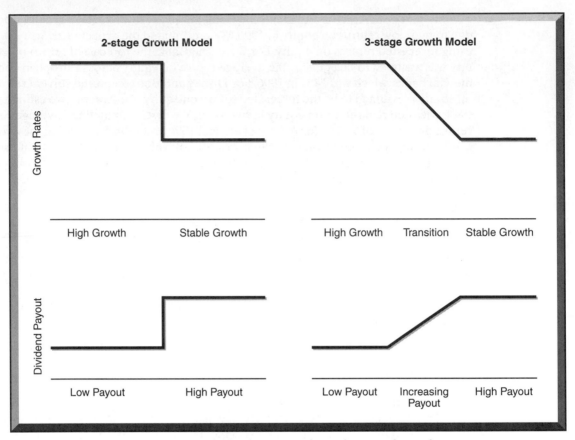

Figure 12.4   Dividend payout ratios and expected growth.

Estimating Terminal Price

The *terminal price*—the price at the end of the high-growth period—can be estimated from expected dividends in the first time period following the high-growth period, the required rate of return on the stock in the stable phase, and the expected stable growth rate in dividends as follows:

$$\text{Value of Stock} = \frac{DPS_{n+1}}{r - g_n}$$

where

DPS_{n+1} = Expected dividends one year after end of high-growth period
r_n = Required rate of return for equity investors in stable phase
g_n = Growth rate in dividends forever

As discussed earlier, a stable growth rate is assumed to be fairly close to the growth rate of the economy in which the firm operates. In addition, the payout ratio and risk should reflect the stable growth assumed for the firm, since stable firms pay out more of their earnings as dividends and have lower risk. One way of estimating this new payout ratio is to use the fundamental growth model described earlier in this chapter:

$$g = b\,[ROC + D/E\,(ROC - i\,(1 - t)\,)]$$

Manipulating this growth rate equation yields the payout ratio as a function of the expected growth rate:

$$\text{Payout Ratio} = 1 - b = 1 - [g\,/\,(ROC + D/E\,(ROC - i\,(1 - t)))]$$

where the inputs for this equation will be those for the stable-growth period. Once estimated, the terminal price has to be discounted back to the present and added back to the present value of dividends.

To illustrate, assume a firm has the following parameters for the ROC, debt/equity ratios, payout ratios, and interest rates in the initial high-growth phase and in the stable-growth phase:

	INITIAL GROWTH PHASE	STABLE PERIOD
ROC	20%	16%
Payout ratio	20%	?
D/E	1.00	1.00
i	10%	8%
Growth rate	?	8%

The tax rate for the firm is 40%.

Growth rate in first five years = $(1-0.2)\,[\,20\% + 1\,(20-10*(1-0.4))] = 27.2\ \%.$
Payout ratio after year five = $1 - [8\,/\,(16 + 1\,(16-8*(1-0.4)))] = 70.59\ \%.$

As the growth rate drops in the stable-growth period, the payout ratio increases from 20% to 70.59%.

IN PRACTICE: ESTIMATING FUNDAMENTALS FOR EXPECTED GROWTH

While the estimates for the fundamentals used to estimate growth (such as return on capital, debt/equity ratios, and interest rates) are often drawn from current estimates, the objective in valuation is to estimate these numbers for the future. Thus, the final estimate should draw on other information that is useful in making these estimates, including:

1. What are the averages for these fundamentals across all companies in the industry in which the firm operates? (A return on capital of 25% in a sector with an average return on capital of 12% might not be sustainable.)

2. Has the management of the firm changed or has the firm itself restructured? (When firms restructure by acquiring or divesting businesses or changing leverage, these changes should be built into future forecasts.)

As firms approach stable growth, using industry averages may yield more consistent estimates than preserving current levels for these fundamentals.

This file on the Web contains, by sector, the industry averages for returns on equity and retention ratios (**fundgr.xls**).

 12.7 TERMINAL VALUE AND PRESENT VALUE

The bulk of the present value in most discounted cash flow valuations comes from the terminal value. Therefore, it is reasonable to conclude that the assumptions about growth during the high-growth period do not affect value as much as assumptions about the terminal price.

☐ True

☐ False

Explain.

Bringing It All Together

Once the expected dividends and the terminal price have been estimated and the discount rate obtained from the risk measure for the firm, the present value of the dividends and terminal price is calculated, providing a measure of the value of the stock using the dividend discount model. The cash flows and interactions in the two-stage dividend discount model are represented in Figure 12.5.

IN PRACTICE: CORPORATE FINANCIAL DECISIONS AND VALUE

Figure 12.5 also illustrates the relationship between the corporate financial decisions that we discussed earlier in the the book and the value of the stock. In particular, the investment decisions made by a firm affect the expected growth rate in earnings of the firm through the return on capital and the discount rate through the beta. The financial leverage decisions affect the expected growth, through the debt/equity ratio, and the discount rate, through the beta (note that the equity beta is a levered beta). Finally, the decision made by a firm on how much cash to return to the stockholders affects the expected growth through the retention ratio and the expected cash flows through the projected dividends. The effects of even the most complex restructuring decisions made by firms can be traced to the value through this process.

ILLUSTRATION 12.4 Valuing a Firm in Stable Growth Using the DDM: Deutsche Bank

In Illustration 12.3, we estimated the sustainable growth at Deutsche Bank to be 6.30%, based upon a normalized return on equity of 14% and a retention ratio of 55%. In 1996, the earnings per share at Deutsche Bank was 4.27 DM, and the dividend payout ratio was 61.09%. Our earlier analysis of the risk at Deutsche Bank provided us with an estimate of beta of 0.94, which, used in conjunction with the German long bond rate of 7.50% and a risk premium of 5.5%, yielded a cost of equity of 12.67%. Based upon these inputs, the value of a share of stock in Deutsche Bank can be estimated as follows, using the stable growth DDM:

Expected Dividends per Share Next Year = 4.27 DM (1.063) (0.6109) = 2.73 DM

Value per Share = 2.73 DM / (.1267 − .063) = 42.89 DM

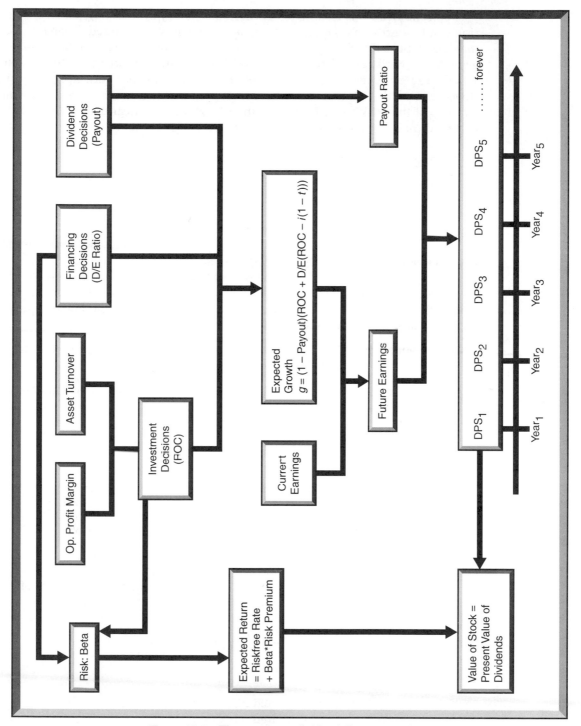

Figure 12.5   The two-stage dividend discount model.

Deutsche Bank was trading for 119 DM on the day of this analysis. This valuation would suggest that Deutsche Bank is significantly overvalued, given our estimates of expected growth and risk. It is also possible that we have underestimated growth or overestimated risk in the model, thus reducing our estimate of value. Finally, the difference could be attributed to dividends not reflecting the cash flows generated by Deutsche Bank, an argument that is given more weight by our analysis of the bank's FCFE in 1996; the FCFE was significantly higher than the dividends paid. (See Chapter 11 for details on FCFE calculation)

FCFE Valuation Model

In Chapter 11, while developing a framework for analyzing dividend policy, we estimated the free cash flow to equity as the cash flow that the firm can afford to pay out as dividends, and contrasted it with the actual dividends. We noted that many firms do not pay out their FCFE as dividends; thus, the dividend discount model may not capture their true capacity to generate cash flows for stockholders. A more appropriate model is the *free cash flow to equity model.*

Quickly recapping, the FCFE is the residual cash flow left over after meeting interest and principal payments and providing for capital expenditures to maintain existing assets and create new assets for future growth. The free cash flow to equity is measured as follows (Working capital refers to non-cash working capital):

$$\text{FCFE} = \text{Net Income} + \text{Depreciation} - \text{Capital Spending} - \Delta \text{Working Capital} - \text{Principal Repayments} + \text{New Debt Issues}$$

In the special case where the capital expenditures and the working capital are expected to be financed at the target debt ratio δ, and principal repayments are made from new debt issues, the FCFE is measured as follows:

$$\text{FCFE} = \text{Net Income} + (1 - \delta)(\text{Capital Expenditures} - \text{Depreciation}) + (1 - \delta)\Delta \text{Working Capital}$$

In the general version of the FCFE model, we allow for two stages in growth: an initial period of extraordinary growth followed by stable growth forever.

Extraordinary growth period   Stable growth: g_n forever

Value of the Stock = PV of FCFE During Extraordinary Phase + PV of Terminal Price

$$P_0 = \sum_{t=1}^{t=n} \frac{\text{FCFE}_t}{(1 + r)^t} + \frac{P_n}{(1 + r)^n} \text{ where } P_n = \frac{\text{FCFE}_{n+1}}{(r - g_n)}$$

where

$$\text{FCFE}_t = \text{Expected FCFE per share in year t}$$
$$r = \text{Required rate of return}$$

P_n = Price at the end of year n

g_n = Growth rate forever after year n

Just as in the dividend discount model, there are four basic inputs needed for this model to be usable. First, the *length of the high-growth period* is defined. Second, the *free cash flow to equity* each period during the growth period is specified; this means that net capital expenditures, working capital needs, and the debt financing mix are all estimated for the high-growth period. Third, the *rate of return* stockholders will demand for holding the stock is estimated. Finally, the *terminal price at the end of the high-growth period is* estimated, based upon the estimates of stable growth, the free cash flows to equity, and required return after the high growth ends.

Of the four inputs, the length of the high-growth period and the rate of return required by stockholders are the same for the dividend discount and FCFE valuation models. The differences in the other two inputs are minor but still worth emphasizing.

FCFE Model: This model estimates the value of equity to be the present value of the expected free cash flow to equity over time.

Estimating FCFE During the High-Growth Period

As in the dividend discount model, we start with the earnings per share and estimate expected growth in earnings. Thus, the entire discussion about earnings growth in the dividend discount model applies here as well. Once the earnings are estimated, the net capital expenditures, working capital needs, and debt financing needs have to be specified in order to arrive at the FCFE. Just as the dividend payout ratio was adjusted to reflect changes in expected growth, the net capital expenditure and working capital needs should change as the growth rate changes. In particular, high-growth companies will have relatively high net capital expenditures and working capital needs. As the growth rate changes, these requirements should also decline. Figure 12.6 depicts changes in these variables under different earnings growth formulations.

A similar point can be made about leverage. High growth, high-risk firms generally do not use much leverage to finance investment needs; as the growth tapers off, however, the firm will be much more willing to use debt, suggesting that debt ratios will increase as growth rates drop.

Net Capital Expenditures: This is the difference between capital expenditures and depreciation.

This file on the Web contains, by sector, the industry averages for net capital expenditures and working capital as a percent of revenues (**cap.ex.xls; wcdata.xls**).

This spreadsheet allows you to estimate the value of the stock in a firm using a stable growth FCFE discount model (**fcfest.xls**).

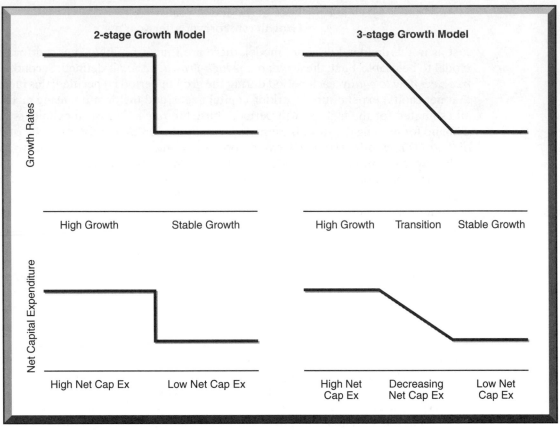

Figure 12.6 Net capital expenditures and expected growth

 This spreadsheet allows you to estimate the value of the stock in a firm using a two-stage FCFE discount model (**fcfe2st.xls**).

 This spreadsheet allows you to estimate the value of the stock in a firm using a three-stage FCFE discount model (**fcfe3st.xls**).

Estimating the Terminal Price
The terminal price in the FCFE model is also determined by the stable growth rate and the required return. The difference between this model and the dividend discount model lies primarily in the cash flow used to calculate the terminal price: The latter uses expected dividends in the period after the high-growth period, whereas the former uses the free cash flow to equity in that period:

$$\text{Value of Stock}_n = \frac{\text{FCFE}_{n+1}}{r - g_n}$$

In estimating that cash flow, the net capital expenditures and working capital needs should be consistent with the definition of stability. Many analysts assume that stable-growth firms have no net capital expenditures, an assumption which is consistent only if one stable growth rate is zero.

12.8 NET CAPITAL EXPENDITURES, FCFE, AND STABLE GROWTH

As firms approach stable growth, which of the following is likely to occur to net capital expenditures?

☐ Net capital expenditures should become zero.

☐ Net capital expenditures should increase as firms approach stable growth.

☐ Net capital expenditures should decrease as firms approach stable growth.

☐ None of the above.

FCFE Valuation versus Dividend Discount Model Valuation

The FCFE discounted cash flow model can be viewed as an alternative to the dividend discount model. Since the two approaches sometimes provide different estimates of value, however, it is worth a comparison.

There are two conditions under which the value obtained from using the FCFE in discounted cash flow valuation will be the same as the value obtained from using the dividend discount model. The first is obvious: When the dividends are equal to the FCFE, the value will be the same. The second condition is more subtle: When the FCFE is greater than dividends, but the excess cash (FCFE − Dividends) is invested in projects with net present value of zero, the values will also be similar. For instance, investing in financial assets that are fairly priced should yield a net present value of zero.

More often, the two models will provide different estimates of value. First, when the FCFE is greater than the dividend and the excess cash either earns below-market interest rates or is invested in negative net present value projects, the value from the FCFE model will be greater than the value from the dividend discount model. This is not as unusual as it might seem. There are numerous case studies of firms that, having accumulated large cash balances by paying out low dividends relative to FCFE, have chosen to use this cash to finance unwise takeovers (the price paid is greater than the value received). Second, the payment of smaller dividends than the firm can afford lowers debt/equity ratios; accordingly the firm may become underleveraged, reducing its value.

In those cases where dividends are greater than FCFE, the firm will have to issue either new stock or new debt to pay these dividends, leading to at least three possible negative consequences for value. One is the flotation cost on these security issues, which can be substantial for equity issues. Second, if the firm borrows the money to pay the dividends, the firm may become overleveraged (relative to the optimal), leading to a loss in value. Finally, paying too much in dividends can lead to capital rationing constraints whereby good projects are rejected, resulting in a loss of wealth.

When the two models yield different values, two questions remain: (1) What does the difference between the two models tell us? (2) Which of the two models is the appropriate one to use in evaluating the market price?

More often, the value from the FCFE model exceeds the value from the dividend discount model. The difference between the value obtained from the FCFE model and the value obtained from the dividend discount model can be considered one component of the value of controlling a firm (that is, it measures the value of controlling dividend policy). In a hostile takeover, the bidder can expect to control the firm and change the dividend policy (to reflect FCFE), thus capturing the higher FCFE value. In the more infrequent case—the value from the dividend discount model exceeds the value from the FCFE—the difference has less economic meaning but can be considered a warning on the sustainability of expected dividends.

As for which of the two values is more appropriate for evaluating the market price, the answer lies in the openness of the market for corporate control. If there is a significant probability that a firm can be taken over or its management changed, the market price will reflect that likelihood; in that case, the value from the FCFE model would be a more appropriate benchmark. As changes in corporate control become more difficult, because of a firm's size and/or legal or market restrictions on takeovers, the value from the dividend discount model will provide a more appropriate benchmark for comparison.

12.9 FCFE AND DDM VALUE

Most firms can be valued using FCFE and DDM valuation models. Which of the following statements would you most agree with on the relationship between these two values?

☐ The FCFE value will always be higher than the DDM value.

☐ The FCFE value will usually be higher than the DDM value.

☐ The DDM value will usually be higher than the FCFE value.

☐ The DDM value will generally be equal to the FCFE value.

IN PRACTICE: VALUING CONTROL

In many acquisitions, control is a stated rationale and a control premium is paid. The FCFE and DDM models presented should yield some insight into the value of control. In particular, the difference between the DDM value and the FCFE value can be viewed as the value of controlling dividend policy. Returning to our construct that relates expected growth to investment returns (return on capital) and financing policy (debt/equity ratios), the values of controlling investment and financing policy can be estimated. In sum, the value of control is the sum of these values.

By extension, the value of control should be greatest in badly managed firms and least in well-managed firms, since it is the difference between the value of the equity, assuming optimal policy, and the status quo value of equity. To value control, do the following:

1. Value the equity in the firm, using the DDM, assuming the status quo.

2. Value the equity in the firm, using the FCFE model, assuming that investment and financing policy is optimal. (Use the optimal debt ratio from Chapter 8, and use industry average returns on capital.)

3. The difference between the two values is the value of control.

The value of control should also yield some insight into the relative values of voting and nonvoting shares, since it is the former that will be targeted in a hostile takeover.

IN PRACTICE: Valuing Firms with Negative or Depressed Earnings

There are a number of reasons why a firm might have negative earnings, and the response will vary depending upon the reason:

- If the earnings of a cyclical firm are depressed due to a recession, the best response is to normalize earnings by taking the average earnings over an entire business cycle. (A good example would be Ford or Chrysler in 1991, when both companies had negative earnings as a consequence of the recession.)

  Normalized Net Income = Average ROE * Current Book Value of Equity
  Normalized After-Tax Operating Income = Average ROC * Current Book Value of Assets

  Once earnings are normalized, the growth rate used should be consistent with the normalized earnings and should reflect the real growth potential of the firm rather than the cyclical effects.

- If the earnings of a firm are depressed due to a onetime charge, the best response is to estimate the earnings without the onetime charge and value the firm based upon these earnings. (This would apply to firms such as ITT and Eastman Kodak, which had significant restructuring charges in the mid-1990s.)

- If the earnings of a firm are depressed due to poor management (i.e., the firm is a poor performer in a sector with healthy earnings), the average return on equity or capital for the industry can be used to estimate normalized earnings for the firm. The implicit assumption is that the firm will recover back to industry averages, once management has been removed.

  Normalized Net Income = Industry-Average ROE * Current Book Value of Equity
  Normalized After-Tax Operating Income = Industry-Average ROC * Current Book Value of Assets

- If the negative earnings over time have caused the book value to decline significantly, use the average operating or profit margins for the industry in conjunction with revenues to arrive at normalized earnings. Note that in the context of a discounted cash flow valuation, this normalization will occur over time, rather than instantaneously. Thus, a firm with negative operating income today could be assumed to converge on the normalized earnings five years from now. (This would be the approach to use for a firm like Digital Equipment, which had low earnings in 1996 while other firms in the sector were reporting record profits.)

- If the earnings of a firm are depressed or negative because it operates in a sector which is in the early stages of its life cycle, the discounted cash flow valuation will be driven by the perception of what the margins and returns on equity (capital) will be when the sector matures. (This would apply for firms in the cellular technology business in the mid-1990s.)

- If the equity earnings are depressed due to high leverage, the best solution is to value the firm rather than just the equity, factoring in the reduction in leverage over time. (This would be the choice when valuing a firm right after a leveraged buyout.)

ILLUSTRATION **12.5**   Valuing a Firm Using Two-Stage Growth: FCFE Model—Bookscape
In Illustration 12.3, we estimated the expected growth in equity earnings at
Bookscape bascd upon its return on equity of 21.09% and retention ratio of 38.79%
to be 8.18%. This moderate growth rate, and the fact that the leverage comes from
operating leases and is unlikely to change significantly, makes this firm a good can-
didate for a two-stage FCFE model. Table 12.4 summarizes the inputs used for
Bookscape in each stage.

The current net income for Bookscape is $1,160,000. In estimating the value of the
equity at Bookscape,

The first component of value is the present value of the expected FCFE during the
high-growth period, as shown in Table 12.5. Note that there is no leverage used in financing capital expenditure and working capital needs in this firm, since all of the
leverage takes the form of operating leases, which are already subtracted out to get
to net income.

Table 12.4   SUMMARY OF ASSUMPTIONS TO VALUE BOOKSCAPE

	High-Growth Phase	Stable-Growth Phase
Length	Five years	Forever, after year 5
Expected Growth Rate	Retention Ratio * ROE = .3879* 21.09% = 8.18%.	6% (set equal to nominal growth rate in economy).
Cost of Equity	7% + 1.1 (5.5%) = 13.05% (beta =1.1; T bond rate =7%).	7% + 1(5.5%) = 12.5% (assumes beta moves toward one).
Net Capital Expenditures	Net capital expenditures grows at same rate as earnings. In 1996, the capital expenditures were $700,000 and depreciation was $500,000.	Capital expenditures are assumed to be 110% of depreciation.
Non-Cash Working Capital	10% of Revenues; current revenue is $20,000,000; revenues grow at same rate as earnings.	10% of Revenues; revenues grow at same rate as earnings.

Table 12.5   FCFE OF BOOKSCAPE: HIGH-GROWTH PERIOD

Year	1	2	3	4	5
Net Income	$1,254.91	$1,357.57	$1,468.64	$1,588.80	$1,718.79
−Net Cap Ex	$216.36	$234.06	$253.21	$273.93	$296.34
− Δ Work. Cap.	$163.63	$177.02	$191.50	$207.17	$224.12
FCFE	$874.91	$946.49	$1,023.93	$1,107.70	$1,198.33
PV at 13.05%	$773.92	$740.59	$708.69	$678.17	$648.97
Revenues	$21,636.29	$23,406.46	$25,321.45	$27,393.12	$29,634.27
Working Capital	$2,163.63	$2,340.65	$2,532.15	$2,739.31	$2,963.43
Change in WC	$163.63	$177.02	$191.50	$207.17	$224.12

PV of FCFE During High-Growth Phase = $773.92 + $740.59 + $708.69 + $678.17 + $648.97 = $3,550.34

The price at the end of the high-growth phase (end of year 5) can be estimated using the constant-growth model:

Terminal Price = Expected $FCFE_{n+1} / (r - g_n)$
Expected Net $Income_6$ = $1,718.79 (1.06) = $1,821.92
Expected Net^2 Capital $Expenditures_6$ = $78.53
Expected $Change^3$ in Working $Capital_6$ = $177.81
Expected $FCFE_6$ = $1,821.92 − $78.53 − $177.81 = $1,565.58
Terminal Price = $1,565.58 /(.125 −.06) = $24,085.83

The present value of the terminal price can be then written as

$$PV \text{ of Terminal Price } = \frac{\$24,085.83}{(1.1305)^5} = \$13,043.94$$

Note that the terminal price is discounted back at the high-growth cost of equity. The cumulated present value of dividends and the terminal price can then be calculated as follows:

PV Today = PV of FCFE During High-Growth Phase + PV of Terminal Price
= $3,550.34 + $13,043.94 − $16,594.28

Based upon our analysis, we would estimate the value of equity at Bookscape today to be $16.594 million.

12.10   NET CAPITAL EXPENDITURES AND VALUE

In the valuation above, we assumed that capital expenditures would drop in stable growth to 110% of depreciation. What would the terminal value have been if, instead, we had assumed that net capital expenditures were zero? What if we had assumed that the net capital expenditures had continued at current levels?

IN PRACTICE: VALUING PRIVATE FIRMS

Unlike the valuation of stock in a publicly traded firm, the valuation of a private firm presents significant challenges. In particular,

1.   The information available on private firms will be sketchier than the information available on publicly traded firms.

2.   Past financial statements, even when available, might not reflect the true earnings potential of the firm. Many private businesses understate earnings to reduce their tax liabilities, and the expenses at many private businesses often reflect the blurring of lines between private and business expenses.

---

[2]To estimate net capital expenditures in year 6, we first estimate depreciation in year 6:
Depreciation in Year 6 − $500,000 $(1.0818)^5$ (1.06) = $785.31
Capital Expenditures in Year 6 = 110% of $785.31

[3]To estimate the change in working capital in year 6, estimate the revenues in year 6 (6% higher than revenues in year 5) and revenues in year 5. Then, take 10% of that change.

3. The owners of many private businesses, who are taxed on both the salary that they make and the dividends they take out of the business at the same rate, often do not try to distinguish between the two.

None of these limitations, by itself, creates an insurmountable problem. The limited availability of information does make the estimation of cash flows much more noisy, past financial statements will need to be restated to make them reflect the true earnings of the firm, and a reasonable opportunity cost will have to be charged for the owner's contribution to the business. Once the cash flows are estimated, however, the choice of a discount rate might be affected by the identity of the potential buyer of the business. If the potential buyer of the business is a publicly traded firm, the valuation should be done using the discount rates based upon market risk, as we have in the Bookscape valuation above. (Thus, if the buyer is Barnes and Noble, the value of $16.59 million would be the right value estimate.) If the potential buyer is another individual, who is not well diversified, the discount rate will have to be higher to reflect the total risk in the business. In the earlier chapter on capital budgeting, we estimated a total beta of 3.30 and a cost of equity for Bookscape of 25.05%. Using this cost of equity in the valuation would have yielded a value for the equity of only $10.8 million. Since the objective is to find the bidder who will pay the highest price for a business, it can be reasonably argued that diversified investors will pay higher prices for the same asset than nondiversified investors, assuming that they have the same expectations of cash flows.

ILLUSTRATION 12.6   Valuing a Firm Using Two-Stage Growth: FCFE Model—Aracruz Cellulose

We will apply the same process that we used to value Bookscape to value Aracruz Cellulose, with two major differences. First, we will use normalized earnings instead of 1996 earnings, since the latter is depressed below what we consider normal levels. Second, we will do the entire valuation in real terms instead of nominal terms. The inputs that we used to value Aracruz are summarized in Table 12.6.

The current earnings per share for Aracruz Cellulose is 0.044 BR. Consistent with the way we normalized return on equity in Illustration 12.3, we use the average earnings per share between 1994 and 1996 of 0.204 BR per share as a measure of the normalized earnings per share. Table 12.7 summarizes free cash flows to equity for the high-growth period, and the free cash flow to equity in the terminal year.

The terminal value at the end of year 5 is estimated using the FCFE in year 6 as follows:

$$\text{Terminal Value} = 0.269/(.125 - .05) = 3.59 \text{ BR}$$

The present values of the free cash flows to equity are then added to the present value of the terminal value of equity per share:

Value per Share = $0.154 + 0.152 + 0.150 + 0.149 + 0.147 + 3.59/1.10335 = 2.95$ BR

Note that this value is higher than the current price of 2.40 BR per share, but it is based upon the assumption that earnings are normalized. To the extent that this will take some time, the true value will be lower than this estimate. Thus, if it will take two years for earnings to approach normalcy, this estimate can be discounted back two years at 10.33% to arrive at a current value.

Table 12.6 SUMMARY OF ASSUMPTIONS TO VALUE ARACRUZ

Length	High-Growth Phase Five years	Stable-Growth Phase Forever, after year 5
Expected Growth Rate	Retention Ratio * ROE = 0.65% * 13.91% = 9.04% (see Illustration 12.3).	5% (set equal to estimated long-term real growth rate in Brazilian economy).
Cost of Equity	5% + 0.71 (7.5%) = 10.33% (beta =0.71; T bond rate =5%: risk premium = 7.5%).	5% + 1(7.5%) = 12.5% (assumes beta moves toward one).
Net Capital Expenditures	Net capital expenditures grow at same rate as earnings. In 1996, the capital expenditures were 0.24 BR and depreciation was 0.18 BR.	Capital expenditures are assumed to be 120% of depreciation.
Non-Cash Working Capital	32.15% of revenues; current revenue is 0.56 BR; revenues grow at same rate as earnings.	32.15% of Revenues; revenues grow at same rate as earnings.
Debt Ratio	39.01% of net capital expenditures and working capital investments come from debt.	39.01% of net capital expenditures and working capital investments come from debt.

Table 12.7 ESTIMATED REAL FCFE AT ARACRUZ FOR HIGH-GROWTH PERIOD

	1	2	3	4	5	Terminal Year
Earnings	BR 0.222	BR 0.243	BR 0.264	BR 0.288	BR 0.314	BR 0.330
− (CapEx−Depreciation)*(1−DR)	BR 0.042	BR 0.046	BR 0.050	BR 0.055	BR 0.060	BR 0.052
−Chg. Working Capital*(1−DR)	BR 0.010	BR 0.011	BR 0.012	BR 0.013	BR 0.014	BR 0.008
Free Cashflow to Equity	BR 0.170	BR 0.186	BR 0.202	BR 0.221	BR 0.241	BR 0.269
Present Value	BR 0.154	BR 0.152	BR 0.150	BR 0.149	BR 0.147	

FCFF Valuation

The free cash flow to the firm (FCFF) is the sum of the cash flows to all claimholders in the firm, including stockholders, bondholders, and preferred stockholders. There are two ways of measuring the free cash flow to the firm. One is to add up the cash flows to the claim holders:

FCFF = Free Cash Flow to Equity
+ Interest Expense (1 − Tax Rate) + Principal Repayments − New Debt Issues
+ Preferred Dividends

The other involves using earnings before interest payments and taxes (EBIT) as a base for the calculation:

FCFF = EBIT (1 - Tax Rate) + Depreciation − Capital Expenditure − Δ Working Capital

Both approaches should provide the same estimates of the cash flow.

The differences between FCFF and FCFE arise primarily from cash flows associated with debt (interest payments, principal repayments, and new debt issues) and other nonequity claims, such as preferred dividends. In general, FCFF will exceed FCFE.

One widely used measure in valuation is the earnings before interest, taxes, depreciation, and amortization (EBITDA). The free cash flow to the firm is a closely related concept, but it takes into account the potential tax liability from the earnings as well as capital expenditures and working capital requirements. Another common measure is the *net operating income* (NOI)—the income from operations, prior to taxes and nonoperating expenses. If nonoperating expenses are deducted, the resulting figure is the earnings before interest and taxes (EBIT). Each of these measures is used in valuation models, and each is a variant of the free cash flow to the firm. Each, however, makes some assumptions about the relationship between depreciation and capital expenditures that might not be consistent with the growth assumptions made in valuation.

Net Operating Income: This is the income from operations prior to taxes, debt payments, and nonoperating expenses.

IN PRACTICE: DISCOUNTING EARNINGS TO VALUE A FIRM

There are some analysts who believe that the value of equity of a firm can be obtained by just discounting the earnings—net income in the case of equity and after-tax operating earnings in the case of the firm. While the notion that the earnings belong to the stockholders and other claimholders of the firm has some allure, this can be done only if it is assumed that there is no growth in earnings. Note that both the growth in earnings per share and operating income are a function of the reinvestment rate. If earnings are being discounted, the reinvestment rate is assumed to be zero, which also implies that the growth rate is zero.

Growth in FCFE versus Growth in FCFF

In the section on estimating growth in earnings per share, we noted that this growth rate is the product of the amount reinvested (measured by the retention ratio) and the quality of those reinvestments (measured by the return on equity). While operating income growth cannot be estimated using the same equation, it can be estimated using similar variables. It is the product of the *reinvestment rate,* defined to be the proportion of after-tax operating income reinvested in net capital expenditures and working capital needs, and the quality of those investments, measured by the return on capital:

$$g_{EBIT} = \frac{\text{Net Capital Expenditure} + \text{Change in Non-Cash WC}}{\text{EBIT}(1 - t)} * \text{Return on Capital}$$

This equation does suggest that assumptions about expected growth, reinvestment, and project quality are all interrelated. In particular, there are two propositions that emerge from this equation. The first is that companies that do not reinvest cannot grow. The second is that companies that choose good investments (earning a higher return on capital) can either grow faster than companies that have similar reinvestment rates, or reinvest less (leading to higher free cash flows to the firm) than companies with similar growth rates.

12.11   DIFFERENCES IN GROWTH RATES

Hitherto, we have talked about three different expected growth rates: the growth rate in earnings per share, the growth rate in net income, and the growth rate in operating income. In general, which of the three expected growth rates is likely to be highest?

☐ Earnings per share

☐ Net income

☐ Operating income

Which is likely to be the lowest? Explain.

ILLUSTRATION 12.7   Estimating Growth in EBIT at Disney, Aracruz, Deutsche Bank, and Bookscape

For each firm in our sample, we use the return on capital and the reinvestment rate to estimate expected growth in operating income. Table 12.8 summarizes the estimates.

As in our earlier analyses, for Aracruz we use the average after-tax operating income from 1994 to 1996 to estimate a forecasted real return on capital of 9.91%. For Disney, note that the reinvestment rate is low only because we did not consider the acquisition of Capital Cities in our analysis. Assuming that there will be other such large capital expenditures or acquisitions in the future, we will assume that the reinvestment rate going forward will be 50% of after-tax operating income. The expected growth in operating income, assuming the return on capital remains around 20% is:

$$\text{Expected Growth in Operating Income} = \text{ROC} * \text{Reinvestment Rate}$$
$$= 20\% * .5 = 10\%$$

Note that this assumption, while increasing expected growth, will also reduce the cash flows each year.

The General Model

In the general version of the FCFF model, we allow for two stages in growth: an initial period of extraordinary growth followed by stable growth forever.

Extraordinary growth period   Stable growth: g_n forever

$$\text{Value of the Stock} = \text{PV of FCFF During Extraordinary Phase} + \text{PV of Terminal Price}$$

Table 12.8   ESTIMATES OF EXPECTED GROWTH IN OPERATING INCOME

Company	Based upon 1996 Earnings			Based upon Forecasted Levels		
	ROC	Reinvestment Rate	EBIT Growth	ROC	Reinvestment Rate	EBIT Growth
Disney	18.69%	20.94%	3.91%	20.00%	50%	10.00%
Bookscape	16.71%	31.03%	5.18%	16.71%	31.03%	5.18%
Aracruz	0.29%	333.33%	0.98%	9.91%	25%	2.48%

$$\text{Value of Firm}_0 = \sum_{t=1}^{t=n} \frac{FCFF_t}{(1 + r)^t} + \frac{P_n}{(1 + r)^n} \text{ where } P_n = \frac{FCFF_{n+1}}{(r - g_n)}$$

where

$FCFF_t$ = Expected FCFF in year t

   r = Cost of capital, which can vary across time, as risk and leverage change.

P_n = Value of firm at the end of year n

g_n = Growth rate forever after year n

Just as in the dividend discount model, there are four basic inputs in this model. First, the *length of the high-growth period* is defined. Second, the *free cash flow to the firm* each period during the growth period is specified; this requires estimating net capital expenditures and working capital needs for the high-growth period. Third, the *cost of capital* investors demand for holding stock, debt, and other securities is estimated, based upon their market value weights. Finally, the *terminal value of the firm at the end of the high-growth period* is estimated, based upon the estimates of stable growth, the dividend payout, and required return after the high growth ends.

The FCFF model therefore uses much of the same information needed for the FCFE model, but it differs in three respects. First, the free cash flow to the firm is before cash flows to debtholders and is thus based upon operating income growth rather than net income growth. Second, the discount rate is the cost of capital rather than the cost of equity. Third, the present value of the cash flows provides an estimate of the value of the firm, rather than just the equity.

That said, all of the caveats relating to FCFE valuation apply here as well. The assumptions about net capital expenditures and working capital should be consistent with assumptions about growth. The debt ratios matter here, not because they affect the cash flows, but because they help determine the cost of capital, and should be changed to reflect the changing characteristics of the firm.

FCFF Model: The FCFF model estimates the value of the firm to be the present value of the expected FCFF, discounted back at the cost of capital.

12.12   FIRM VALUATION AND LEVERAGE

A standard critique of the use of cost of capital in firm valuation is that it assumes that leverage stays stable over time (through the weights in the cost of capital). Is this true?

☐ Yes

☐ No

This spreadsheet allows you to estimate the value of a firm using a stable-growth FCFF discount model (**fcffst.xls**).

This spreadsheet allows you to estimate the value of a firm using a two-stage FCFF discount model (**fcff2st.xls**).

This spreadsheet allows you to estimate the value of a firm using a three-stage FCFF discount model (**fcff3st.xls**).

Firm Valuation versus Equity Valuation

Unlike the dividend discount model or the FCFE model, the FCFF model values the firm rather than equity. The value of equity, however, can be extracted from the value of the firm by subtracting out the market value of outstanding debt. Since this model can be viewed as an alternative way of valuing equity, two questions arise: (1) Why value the firm rather than equity? (2) Will the values for equity obtained from the firm valuation approach be consistent with the values obtained from the equity valuation approaches described in the previous chapter?

The advantage of using the firm valuation approach is that cash flows relating to debt do not have to be considered explicitly, since the FCFF is a pre-debt cash flow; by contrast, they have to be taken into account in estimating FCFE. In cases where the leverage is expected to change significantly over time, this can be a significant saving. At the same time, the firm valuation approach requires information about debt ratios and interest rates to estimate the weighted average cost of capital.

The value for equity obtained from the firm valuation and equity valuation approaches will be the same in two cases:

1. *If consistent assumptions are made about growth in the two approaches:* This does not mean that the same growth rate is used in both approaches, but it may require that the growth rates in earnings be adjusted for the effect of leverage. This is especially true for the calculation of the terminal value, whereby a stable growth rate is assumed in both FCFE and FCFF.

2. *If bonds are correctly priced:* The value of equity in the FCFF approach is obtained by subtracting out the market value of the debt from the value of the firm. If the firm's debt is overvalued, the value of equity obtained from the FCFF model will be lower than the value obtained from the equity valuation approaches. Similarly, the value of equity will be higher if the firm's debt is undervalued.

 ### 12.13 FIRM VALUE, DEBT, AND EQUITY VALUE

To obtain the value of equity from the value of the firm, we need to subtract out the following:

☐ Current long-term debt outstanding
☐ Current total debt outstanding
☐ Current debt + present value of expected new debt issues
☐ Current total debt outstanding as well as other nonequity claims
☐ Other

 ILLUSTRATION **12.8** Valuing a Firm with the Three-Stage FCFF Model: Disney

Disney, given the growth rate of 10% in operating income estimated for it in Illustration 12.8, might not seem like a good case study for a firm to value in a three-stage growth model. There are, however, mitigating circumstances. The first is that a growth rate of 10% in operating income is deceptively low since it translates into a growth rate of almost 20% in earnings per share. The second is that Disney has an extraordinary brand name, a barrier to entry which should allow it to grow for a longer period of time at above-normal growth rates. The assumptions we made to value Disney in each of the three stages are summarized in Table 12.9. Note that the total capital expenditures in each period can be estimated using the reinvestment rate, depreciation, and working capital estimates.

$$\text{Capital Expenditures}_t = \text{Reinvestment Rate}_t * \text{EBIT}_t(1 - t) + \text{Depreciation}_t - \text{Change in WC}_t$$

These inputs are used to estimate free cash flows to the firm, the cost of capital, and the present values during the high-growth and transition period in Table 12.10. The terminal value at the end of year 10 is estimated based upon the free cash flows to the firm in year 11 and the cost of capital in year 11:

$$\begin{aligned} \text{FCFF}_{11} &= \text{EBIT}(1-t) - \text{EBIT}(1-t)\text{ Reinvestment Rate} \\ &= \$13,539(1.05)(1-.36) + \$13,539(1.05)(1-.36)(.3125) = \$6,255 \text{ million} \end{aligned}$$

Table 12.9 SUMMARY OF ASSUMPTIONS ON DISNEY THREE-STAGE FCFF VALUATION

	High-Growth Phase	Transition Phase	Stable-Growth Phase
Length of Period	Five years	Five years	Forever after 10 years
Revenues	Current revenues: $18,739; expected to grow at same rate as operating earnings.	Continues to grow at same rate as operating earnings.	Grows at stable growth rate.
Pretax Operating Margin	29.67% of revenues, based upon 1996 EBIT of $5,559 million.	Increases gradually to 32% of revenues, due to economies of scale.	Stable margin is assumed to be 32%.
Tax Rate	36%	36%	36%
Return on Capital	20% (approximately 1996 level)	Declines linearly to 16%	Stable ROC of 16%
Working Capital	5% of revenues	5% of revenues	5% of revenues
Reinvestment Rate (Net Cap Ex + Working Capital Investments/EBIT)	50% of after-tax operating income; depreciation in 1996 is $1,134 million, and is assumed to grow at same rate as earnings.	Declines to 31.25% as ROC and growth rates drop: Reinvestment rate = g/ROC.	31.25% of after-tax operating income. This is estimated from the growth rate of 5%: reinvestment rate = g/ROC.
Expected Growth Rate in EBIT	ROC * reinvestment rate = 20% * .5 = 10%.	Linear decline to stable growth rate.	5%, based upon overall nominal economic growth.
Debt/Capital Ratio	18%	Increases linearly to 30%	Stable debt ratio of 30%
Risk Parameters	Beta = 1.25, k_e = 13.88% Cost of debt = 7.5% (Long-term bond rate = 7%)	Beta decreases linearly to 1.00; cost of debt stays at 7.5%.	Stable beta is 1.00; cost of debt stays at 7.5%.

Equity Valuation Models 473

Table 12.10 ESTIMATES OF FCFF, TERMINAL VALUE, AND COSTS OF CAPITAL FOR DISNEY

	Base	1	2	3	4	5	6	7	8	9	10
Expected Growth		10%	10%	10%	10%	10%	9%	8%	7%	6%	5%
Revenues	$18,739	$20,613	$22,674	$24,942	$27,436	$30,179	$32,895	$35,527	$38,014	$40,295	$42,310
Oper. Margin	29.67%	29.67%	29.67%	29.67%	29.67%	29.67%	30.13%	30.60%	31.07%	31.53%	32.00%
EBIT	$5,559	$6,115	$6,726	$7,399	$8,139	$8,953	$9,912	$10,871	$11,809	$12,706	$13,539
EBIT (1−t)	$3,558	$3,914	$4,305	$4,735	$5,209	$5,730	$6,344	$6,957	$7,558	$8,132	$8,665
+Depreciation	$1,134	$1,247	$1,372	$1,509	$1,660	$1,826	$2,009	$2,210	$2,431	$2,674	$2,941
− Capital Exp.	$1,754	$3,101	$3,411	$3,752	$4,128	$4,540	$4,847	$5,103	$5,313	$5,464	$5,548
− Change in WC	$94	$94	$103	$113	$125	$137	$136	$132	$124	$114	$101
= FCFF	$1,779	$1,966	$2,163	$2,379	$2,617	$2,879	$3,370	$3,932	$4,552	$5,228	$5,957
Terminal Value (in yr 10)											$120,521
Present Value		$1,752	$1,717	$1,682	$1,649	$1,616	$1,692	$1,773	$1,849	$1,920	$42,167
Cost of Equity		13.88%	13.88%	13.88%	13.88%	13.88%	13.60%	13.33%	13.05%	12.78%	12.50%
After-tax Cost of Debt		4.80%	4.80%	4.80%	4.80%	4.80%	4.80%	4.80%	4.80%	4.80%	4.80%
Debt Ratio		18.00%	18.00%	18.00%	18.00%	18.00%	20.40%	22.80%	25.20%	27.60%	30.00%
Cost of Capital		12.24%	12.24%	12.24%	12.24%	12.24%	11.80%	11.38%	10.97%	10.57%	10.19%
ROC	20%	20%	20%	20%	20%	20%	19.2%	18.4%	17.6%	16.8%	16%
Reinv. Rate		50%	50%	50%	50%	50%	46.875%	43.48%	39.77%	35.71%	31.25%

Note that the reinvestment rate is estimated from the return of capital of 16% and the expected growth rate of 5%.

$$\text{Cost of Capital in Terminal Year} = 10.19\%$$
$$\text{Terminal Value} = \$6{,}255/(.1019 - .05) = \$120{,}521 \text{ million}$$

The present values[4] of the free cash flows to the firm and the present value of the terminal value are computed, and the sum is reported below:

$$\text{Value of Disney} = \$57{,}817 \text{ million}$$

If we subtract out the market value of existing debt of \$11,180 million from this firm value, we arrive at the value of equity for Disney of \$46,637 million. The value of equity per share is computed by dividing by the number of shares outstanding:

$$\text{Value of Equity per Share} = \$46{,}637/\,675.13 = \$69.08$$

Thus, the valuation suggests that Disney was overvalued at \$75.38 per share.

IN PRACTICE: FROM VALUE OF EQUITY TO PER SHARE VALUE

In valuing equity for Disney, we subtracted out the value of the debt from the value of the firm to arrive at the value of equity. Implicit in this calculation is the assumption that the shares outstanding are the only equity claim on the firm. When firms have significant numbers of warrants, options, and convertible bonds outstanding, this assumption is no longer appropriate. To get from the value of the equity to the equity value per share, the following steps have to be followed:

1. Value the non-stock equity claims on the firm. Since many of these claims are options, they can be valued using standard option pricing models, allowing for dilution (see Appendix 4).
2. Subtract the value of the non-stock equity claims from the total value of the equity.
3. Divide by the number of shares outstanding.

IN PRACTICE: VALUING CASH

In many discounted cash flow valuations, it is common practice to value a firm and add the cash balance that the firm has to this value. This is a dangerous practice, and there are several risks:

1. If the earnings being discounted include the interest income from the cash balance, the cash is being counted twice, once in the discounted cash flow valuation and once when it is added on.

---

[4] As an issue of mechanics, the changing cost of capital makes it necessary is discount the cash flows at the cumulated cost of capital. Thus, the cash flow in year 6, for instance, is discounted as follows:

$$\text{PV of CF in Year 6} = \$\,3{,}370/\,(1.1224)^5\,(1.118) = \$\,1{,}692 \text{ million}$$

2. The risk characteristics, and by extension, the costs of equity and capital are affected by the cash balance. Hence, even if the earnings are cleansed of the interest income effects, the discount rates are lower because of the cash balance. Consequently, the value of cash is overstated.

The correct procedure to valuing cash, especially when cash is a significant proportion of the value of the firm (10% or greater) is to do the following:

1. Value the non-cash assets of the firm by discounting the earnings from the non-cash asset by the cost of capital of the non-cash assets—the beta used for the cost of equity is the beta of the non-cash assets.

2. Add the cash balance to this value to arrive at the total value of the firm.

ILLUSTRATION 12.9   Valuing a Division Using FCFF Model: Disney's Creative Content Division

The value of any of Disney's divisions can be estimated using the same process that we used to value Disney as a firm. There are a couple of special problems associated with valuing divisions that are similar to the problems that we faced in valuing a private firm. The first is that, while many firms do break out the operating income by division, this breakout is before the allocation of corporate general and administrative expenses and reflects other allocation decisions made by the firm. This results in a misstatement of the operating income. The second is the absence of market data on divisional value, which can pose a problem when it comes to estimating betas and debt ratios. We can overcome this problem by looking at the operating income for each division after the allocation of general and administrative expenses, and using the costs of capital we estimated for each division, based upon comparable firms, in Chapter 4.

To provide an illustration of the valuation of a division, consider the value of the theme parks division of Disney. The theme parks had a pretax operating income of $990 million in 1996. Assume that the operating income at the theme parks is in stable growth, growing at 5% a year, and that the return on capital on theme park investments is 25%. The free cash flow to the firm next year can be estimated as follows:

$$\text{FCFF} = \text{EBIT} (1-t) \text{ Next Year} - \text{Reinvestment Rate} * \text{EBIT} (1-t) \text{ Next Year}$$
$$= \$990 (1-.36)(1.05) - (5\%/25\%) * \$990 (1-.36)(1.05) = \$532.22 \text{ million}$$

$$\text{Value of Theme Parks Divisions} = \$532.22 \text{ million}/(.1225-.05) = \$7,341 \text{ million}$$

A similar valuation can be done for the other divisions at Disney as well.

IN PRACTICE: THE SUM OF THE PARTS

Firms like Disney, which are made up of operations in different businesses, can also be valued as the sum of each of these parts, though that sum might be different from the valuation done of the whole firm. To value a firm based upon its different parts, the following steps need to be followed:

1. Estimate the operating income for each division, as we did for Disney's theme park business.

2. Estimate the free cash flow to the firm for each division, after net capital expenditures and working capital needs.

3. Discount these cash flows back to the present, using the cost of capital for the division. In some cases, the sum of the parts will be less than the value of the firm, especially when there are economies of scale or brand name benefits associated with being part of the larger corporate entity. In other cases, the sum of the parts can be greater than the value obtained for the firm. This can occur either because investor perceptions of individual divisions are colored by their perceptions of the firm (as is the case with tobacco firms), or because the operating performance of some of the divisions is negatively affected by their connection to the firm (reverse synergy). This would then provide a rationale for divestitures, spinoffs, and splitoffs.

RELATIVE VALUATION

In intrinsic valuation the objective is to find assets that are priced below what they should be, given their cash flow, growth, and risk characteristics. In relative valuation, the philosophical focus is on finding assets that are cheap or expensive relative to how "similar" assets are being priced by the market right now. It is therefore entirely possible that an asset that is expensive on an intrinsic value basis may be cheap on a relative basis.

A. Standardized Values and Multiples

To compare the valuations of "similar" assets in the market, we need to standardize the values in some way. They can be standardized relative to the earnings that they generate, the book value or replacement value of the assets themselves, or relative to the revenues that they generate. Each approach is used widely and has strong adherents.

1. Earnings Multiples

One of the more intuitive ways to think of the value of any asset is as a multiple of the earnings generated by it. When buying a stock, it is common to look at the price paid as a multiple of the earnings per share generated by the company. This *price/earnings ratio* can be estimated using current earnings per share (which is called a trailing PE) or expected earnings per share in the next year (called a forward PE). When buying a business (as opposed to just the equity in the business) it is common to examine the value of the business as a multiple of the operating income (EBIT) or the operating cash flow (EBITDA). While a lower multiple is better than a higher one, these multiples will be affected by the growth potential and risk of the business being acquired.

2. Book Value or Replacement Value Multiples

While markets provide one estimate of the value of a business, accountants often provide a very different estimate of the value of the same business in their books.

This latter estimate, which is the *book value,* is driven by accounting rules and is heavily influenced by what was originally paid for the asset and any accounting adjustments (such as depreciation) made since. Investors often look at the relationship between the price they pay for a stock and the book value of equity (or net worth) as a measure of how over- or undervalued a stock is; the price/book value ratio that emerges can vary widely across sectors, depending again upon the growth potential and the quality of the investments in each. When valuing businesses, this ratio is estimated using the value of the firm and the book value of all assets (rather than just the equity). For those who believe that book value is not a good measure of the true value of the assets, an alternative is to use the replacement cost of the assets; the ratio of the value of the firm to replacement cost is called *Tobin's Q.*

3. Revenue Multiples

Both earnings and book value are accounting measures and are affected by accounting rules and principles. An alternative approach, which is far less affected by these factors, is to look at the relationship between value of an asset and the revenues it generates. For equity investors, this ratio is the *price/sales ratio,* where the market value per share is divided by the revenues generated per share. For firm value, this ratio can be modified as the *value/sales ratio,* where the numerator becomes the total value of the firm. This ratio, again, varies widely across sectors, largely as a function of the profit margins in each. The advantage of these multiples, however, is that it becomes far easier to compare firms in different markets, with different accounting systems at work.

B. The Fundamentals Behind Multiples

One reason commonly given for relative valuation is that it requires far fewer assumptions than does discounted cash flow valuation. This is a misconception. The difference between discounted cash flow valuation and relative valuation is that the assumptions that an analyst makes have to be made explicit in the former and they can remain implicit in the latter. It is important that we know what the variables are that drive multiples, since these are the variables we have to control for when comparing these multiples across firms.

To look under the hood, so to speak, of equity and firm value multiples, we will go back to fairly simple discounted cash flow models for equity and firm value and use them to derive our multiples. Thus, the simplest discounted cash flow model for equity which is a stable-growth dividend discount model would suggest that the value of equity is:

$$\text{Value of Equity} = P_0 = \frac{DPS_1}{k_e - g_n}$$

where DPS_1 is the expected dividend in the next year, k_e is the cost of equity, and g_n is the expected stable growth rate. Dividing both sides by the earnings, we obtain the discounted cash flow model for the PE ratio for a stable-growth firm:

$$\frac{P_0}{EPS_0} = PE = \frac{\text{Payout Ratio} * (1 + g_n)}{k_e - g_n}$$

Dividing both sides by the book value of equity, we can estimate the price/book value (PBV) ratio for a stable-growth firm:

$$\frac{P_0}{BV_0} = PBV = \frac{ROE * Payout\ Ratio * (1 + g_n)}{k_e - g_n}$$

where ROE is the return on equity. Dividing by the sales per share, the price/sales (PS) ratio for a stable-growth firm can be estimated as a function of its profit margin, payout ratio, and expected growth.

$$\frac{P_0}{Sales_0} = PS = \frac{Profit\ Margin * Payout\ Ratio * (1 + g_n)}{k_e - g_n}$$

We can do a similar analysis from the perspective of firm valuation. The value of a firm in stable growth can be written as:

$$Value\ of\ Firm\ =\ V_0 = \frac{FCFF_1}{k_c - g_n}$$

Where FCFF is the free cashflow to the firm and k_c is the cost of capital. Dividing both sides by the expected free cash flow to the firm yields the Value/FCFF multiple for a stable-growth firm:

$$\frac{V_0}{FCFF_1} = \frac{1}{k_e - g_n}$$

Since the free cash flow to the firm is the after-tax operating income netted against the net capital expenditures and working capital needs of the firm, the multiples of EBIT, after-tax EBIT, and EBITDA can also be similarly estimated. The Value/EBITDA multiple, for instance, can be written as follows:

$$\frac{Value}{EBITDA} = \frac{(1 - t)}{k_c - g} + \frac{Depr\ (t)/EBITDA}{k_c - g} - \frac{CEx/EBITDA}{k_c - g} - \frac{\Delta\ Working\ Capital/EBITDA}{k_c - g}$$

The point of this analysis is not to suggest that we go back to using discounted cash flow valuation but to get a sense of the variables that may cause these multiples to vary across firms in the same sector. An analyst who is blind to these variables might conclude that a stock with a PE of 8 is cheaper than one with a PE of 12, when the true reason may be that the latter has higher expected growth, or that a stock with a PBV ratio of 0.7 is cheaper than one with a PBV ratio of 1.5, when the true reason may be that the latter has a much higher return on equity. Table 12.11 lists the multiples that are widely used and the variables driving each; the variable that is the most significant is italicized for each multiple. This is what I would call the *companion variable* for this multiple (i.e., the one variable I would need to know in order to use this multiple to find under- or overvalued assets).

 This spreadsheet allows you to estimate the equity multiples for a firm based upon its fundamentals (**eqmult.xls**).

This spreadsheet allows you to estimate the firm value multiples for a firm based upon its fundamentals (**firmmult.xls**).

Multiple	Determining Variables
Price/Earnings Ratio	*Growth,* Payout, Risk
Price/Book Value Ratio	Growth, Payout, Risk, *ROE*
Price/Sales Ratio	Growth, Payout, Risk, *Net Margin*
Value/EBIT Value/EBIT (1 − t) Value/EBITDA	Growth, *Net Capital Expenditure needs,* Leverage, Risk
Value/Sales	Growth, Net Capital Expenditure Needs, Leverage, Risk, *Operating Margin*
Value/Book Capital	Growth, Leverage, Risk, and *ROC*

Table 12.11   MULTIPLES AND COMPANION VARIABLES

Companion variables are in bold type.

 There is a dataset on the Web that summarizes, by sector, price/book value and value/book value ratios and returns on equity and capital **(pbv.xls)**.

 There is a dataset on the Web that summarizes, by sector, price/sales and value/sales ratios and profit margins **(ps.xls)**.

 There is a dataset on the Web that summarizes, by sector, value/EBIT, value/EBITDA multiples, and capital expenditure ratios **(vebitda.xls)**.

C. The Use of Comparables

Most analysts who use multiples use them in conjunction with "comparable" firms to form conclusions about whether firms are fairly valued. At the risk of being simplistic, the analysis begins with two decisions: the multiple that will be used in the analysis and the group of firms that will comprise the comparable firms. The multiple is computed for each of the comparable firms, and the average is computed. To evaluate an individual firm, the analyst then compares its multiple to the average computed; if it is significantly different, the analyst makes a subjective judgment on whether the firm's individual characteristics (growth, risk. . .) may explain the difference. Thus, a firm may have a PE ratio of 22 in a sector where the average PE is only 15, but the analyst may conclude that this difference can be justified by the fact that the firm has higher growth potential than the average firm in the sector. If, in the analysts' judgment, the difference on the multiple cannot be explained by the fundamentals, the firm will be viewed as overvalued (if its multiple is higher than the average) or undervalued (if its multiple is lower than the average).

1. Choosing Comparables

The heart of this process is the selection of the firms that comprise comparable firms. From a valuation perspective, a comparable firm is one with similar cash flows, growth potential, and risk. If valuation were simple, the value of a firm would be analyzed by looking at how an identical firm—in terms of risk, growth, and cash flows—is priced. In most analyses, however, a comparable firm is defined to be one in the same business as the firm being analyzed. If there are enough firms in the sector to allow for it, this list will be pruned further using other criteria; for instance, only firms of similar size may be considered. Implicitly, the assumption being made here is that firms in the same sector have similar risk, growth, and cash flow profiles and therefore can be compared with much more legitimacy. This approach becomes more difficult to apply under two conditions:

1. ***There are relatively few firms in a sector.*** In most markets outside the United States, the number of publicly traded firms in a particular sector, especially if it is narrowly defined, is small.

2. ***The differences on risk, growth, and cash flow profiles across firms within a sector are large.*** Thus, there may be hundreds of computer software companies listed in the United States, but the differences across these firms are also large.

The tradeoff is therefore a simple one. Defining a sector more broadly increases the number of firms that enter the comparable firm list, but it also results in a more diverse group.

12.14 UNDERLYING ASSUMPTIONS IN COMPARABLE VALUATION

Assume that you are reading an equity research report where a buy recommendation for a company is being based upon the fact that its PE ratio is lower than the average for the industry. Implicitly, what is the underlying assumption or assumptions being made by this analyst?

☐ The sector itself is, on average, fairly priced.
☐ The earnings of the firms in the group are being measured consistently.
☐ The firms in the group are all of equivalent risk.
☐ The firms in the group are all at the same stage in the growth cycle.
☐ The firms in the group have similar cash flow patterns.
☐ All of the above.

2. Controlling for Differences Across Firms

Since it is impossible to find firms identical to the one being valued, we have to find ways of controlling for differences across firms. The advantage of the discounted cash flow models introduced in the previous section is that we have a clear idea of what the fundamental determinants of each multiple are, and therefore what we should be controlling for; Table 12.11 provides a summary of the variables. The process of controlling for the variables can range from very simple approaches, which modify the multiples to take into account differences on one key variable, to more complex approaches that allow for differences on more than one variable.

Let us start with the simple approaches. Here, the basic multiple is modified to take into account the most important variable determining that multiple. Thus, the PE ratio is divided by the expected growth rate in EPS for a company to come up with what is called a growth-adjusted PE ratio or PEG ratio. Similarly, the PBV ratio is divided by the ROE to come up with a value ratio, and the price/sales ratio by the net margin. These modified ratios are then compared across companies in a sector. Implicitly, the assumption made is that these firms are comparable on all the other dimensions of value, besides the one being controlled for.

ILLUSTRATION 12.10   Comparing PE Ratios and Growth Rates Across Firms:
Entertainment Companies

In Table 12.12, we have listed the PE ratios and expected analyst consensus growth rates over five years for a selected list of entertainment companies. The average ratio of PE to expected growth is 1.20. Disney, which has a PE ratio to growth ratio of 1.55 could be considered overvalued. This conclusion holds only if these firms are of equivalent risk, however.

Table 12.12   PE RATIOS, EXPECTED GROWTH, AND PEG RATIOS FOR
ENTERTAINMENT FIRMS

Company	PE	Expected Growth	PEG
King World Productions	10.4	7.00%	1.49
Aztar	11.9	12.00%	0.99
Viacom	12.1	18.00%	0.67
Vaughn Communication	14.2	15.00%	0.95
Todd-AO A	14.3	20.00%	0.72
Carmike Cinemas	15.1	15.00%	1.01
All American Communications	15.8	20.00%	0.79
GC Companies	20.2	15.00%	1.35
Circus Circus Enterprises	20.8	17.00%	1.22
Polygram NV ADR	22.6	13.00%	1.74
Regal Cinemas	25.8	23.00%	1.12
Walt Disney	27.9	18.00%	1.55
AMC Entertainment	29.5	20.00%	1.48
Premier Parks	32.9	28.00%	1.18
Family Golf Centers	33.1	36.00%	0.92
CINAR Films	48.4	25.00%	1.94
Average	*27.44*	*18.56%*	*1.20*

When firms vary on more than one dimension, it becomes difficult to modify the multiples to take into account the differences across firms. It is, however, feasible to run regressions of the multiples against the variables and then use these regressions to get predicted values for each firm. This approach works reasonably well when the number of comparable firms is large and the relationship between the multiple and variables is strong. When these conditions do not hold, a few outliers can cause the coefficients to change dramatically and make the predictions much less reliable.

There is a dataset on the Web that summarizes, by sector, PE ratios, expected growth rates, and PEG ratios (**pedata.xls**).

ILLUSTRATION 12.11   PBV Ratios and ROE: The Financial Services Sector

Table 12.13 summarizes price/book value ratios of European banks and reports on their returns on equity.

Table 12.13 PBV Ratios and ROE of European Financial Service Firms		
Bank	**PBV Ratio**	**ROE**
Abbey National	3.25	18.77%
Barclays	3.45	22.93%
BHW Holding	2.12	8.38%
Commerzbank	2.04	9.26%
Credit Lyonnais	0.734	0.81%
Credit Suisse	3.65	18.96%
Deutsche Bank	2.12	7.39%
Hamburgische Landesbank	1.18	1.89%
Lloyds TSB	8.46	33.93%
National Westminster	2.23	5.80%
Royal Bank of Scotland	2.22	18.80%
Schroeders	4.19	20.02%
Societe Generale	1.42	8.50%
Standard Chartered	3.66	29.47%

There is generally a strong relationship between price/book value ratios and returns on equity, with high ROE banks having high P/BV ratios. To make this relationship more explicit, we ran a regression of PBV ratios on ROE:

$$PBV = 0.56 + 16.05 \,(ROE) \qquad R^2 = 73.28\%$$
$$(2.15) \quad (5.74)$$

The numbers in brackets are t-statistics and suggest that the relationship between PBV ratios and the ROE in the regression is statistically significant. The R-squared indicates the percentage of the differences in PBV ratios that is explained by the ROE. Finally, the regression itself can be used to get predicted PBV ratios for the companies in the list. Thus, the predicted PBV ratio for Deutsche Bank would be:

$$\text{Predicted PBV}_{\text{Deutsche Bank}} = 0.56 + 16.05 \,(.0739) = 1.75$$

Since the actual PBV ratio for Deutsche Bank was 2.12, this would suggest that the stock was overvalued by roughly 16%.

3. Expanding the Comparable Firm Universe

Searching for comparable firms within the sector in which a firm operates is fairly restrictive, especially when there are relatively few firms in the sector or when a firm operates in more than one sector. Since the definition of a comparable firm is not one that is in the same business but one that has the same growth, risk, and cash flow characteristics as the firm being analyzed, it is not clear why we have to stay sector specific. A software firm should be comparable to an automobile firm if we can control for differences in the fundamentals.

The regression approach that we introduced in the previous section allows us to control for differences on those variables that we believe cause differences in multiples across firms. Using the minimalist version of the regression equations here, we should be able to regress PE, PBV, and PS ratios against the variables that should affect them:

$$PE = a + b\,(\text{Growth}) + c\,(\text{Payout Ratios}) + d\,(\text{Risk})$$
$$PBV = a + b\,(\text{Growth}) + c\,(\text{Payout Ratios}) + d\,(\text{Risk}) + e\,(\text{ROE})$$
$$PS = a + b\,(\text{Growth}) + c\,(\text{Payout Ratios}) + d\,(\text{Risk}) + e\,(\text{Margin})$$

It is, however, possible that the proxies that we use for risk (beta), growth (expected growth rate), and cash flow (payout) may be imperfect and that the relationship may not be linear. To deal with these limitations, we can add more variables to the regression (e.g., the size of the firm may operate as a good proxy for risk) and use transformations of the variables to allow for nonlinear relationships.

We ran these regressions for PE, PBV, and PS ratios across publicly listed firms in the United States in March 1997 twice—once with individual firms as our observations and once with the firms aggregated into sectors (which reduces the noise in the estimates). The sample, which had 4527 firms in it, yielded the regressions reported in Table 12.14. These regressions can then be used to get predicted PE, PBV, and PS ratios for each firm, which, in turn, can be compared to the actual multiples to find under- and overvalued firms.

The first advantage of this approach over the "subjective" comparison across firms in the same sector described in the previous section is that it does quantify, based upon actual market data, the degree to which higher growth or risk should affect the multiples. It is true that these estimates can be noisy, but this noise is a reflection of the reality that many analysts choose not to face when they make subjective judgments. Second, by looking at all firms in the universe, it allows analysts operating in sectors with relatively few firms in them to make more powerful comparisons. Finally, it gets analysts past the tunnel vision induced by comparing firms within a sector, when the entire sector may be under- or overvalued.

This file on the Web contains the latest cross-sectional regressions of multiples against fundamentals (**MReg97.xls**).

ILLUSTRATION 12.12　**Estimating Multiples for a Private Firm: Bookscape**
The regressions reported in Table 12.14, while based upon publicly traded firms, can be used to estimate the multiples for a private firm. For instance, we estimate the inputs for Bookscape into the price/book value regression as follows:

Beta = 1.10 (based upon comparable firms)

ROE = 21.09% (current ROE)

Expected growth = 8.18% (based upon the return on equity and retention ratio)

Payout ratio = 61.21% (based upon FCFE as a percentage of net income)

Table 12.14 Regressions of Multiples on Fundamentals: Marketwide

Individual Firms (Approximately 1400 firms)	Aggregated Regression (89 industries)
PE = 11.07 + 27.82 g + 0.7328 Payout + 2.9465 Beta (R² = 0.0957) (9.29) (10.27) (0.85) (2.98)	PE = 22.73 + 45.01 g − 9.28 Payout − 7.4870 Beta (R² = 0.3847) (6.35) (3.00) (1.69) (1.69)
PBV = −1.50 + 6.51 g + 0.61 Payout + 0.3292 Beta + 16.54 ROE (R² = 0.67) (6.67) (11.71) (3.96) (1.80) (50.93)	PBV = −0.35 + 6.32 g − 0.06 Payout + 0.1666 Beta + 11.60 ROE (R² = 0.53) (0.50) (3.54) (0.11) (0.33) (9.10)
PS = −1.44 + 7.55 g − 0.22 Payout − 0.2166 Beta + 30.86 MGN (R²=0.72) (6.96)(16.31) (1.52) (1.28) (53.14)	PS = 0.02 + 5.76 g − 0.82 Payout − 0.6755 Beta + 20.76 MGN (R² = 0.61) (0.04) (3.74) (1.69) (1.60) (11.21)

(T statistics are in brackets)
g = Expected growth in earnings over the next five years (enter as decimals, i.e., 15% is .15).
PE = Price/current EPS: Companies with negative earnings were eliminated from the sample.
PBV = Price/book value per share: Companies with negative BV were eliminated.
PS = Price/sales per share.
Payout = DPS/EPS: From most recent year; if negative, it is set to 100% (enter as decimals).
Beta = Betas based upon five years of monthly data.
MGN = Net income/sales (enter as decimals).
ROE = Net income/BV of equity (enter as decimals).

Plugging these variables into the market regression:

PBV= −1.50 + 6.51 (.0818) + 0.61 (.6121) + 0.3292 (1.10) + 16.54 (.2109) = 3.26

This multiple could then be applied to the book value of equity for Bookscape, which was $5.5 million in 1996, to yield the following market value for equity:

Market Value of Equity = $5.5 million (3.26) = $17.93 million

This can be compared to the earlier discounted cash flow valuation of Bookscape of $16.6 million from Illustration 12.5.

 ILLUSTRATION **12.13** Estimating Aracruz's Multiples Based upon Market Regressions

To estimate Aracruz's multiples, we ran the regression of multiples against fundamentals on Brazilian firms. Using data obtained from 1997 for 137 Brazilian companies, we ran the regression of PBV ratios against returns on equity and obtained the following:

$$PBV = \quad 1.06 + \quad 2.16 \text{ ROE} \quad R^2 = 15.49\%$$
$$(11.30) \quad (4.84)$$

Substituting Aracuz's normalized return on equity of 13.91% into the regression, we obtained an estimated PBV ratio:

$$PBV = 1.06 + 2.16 (.1391) = 1.36$$

Using data on 148 Brazilian companies from 1997, we regressed PS ratios against profit margins:

$$PS = \quad 0.95 + \quad 2.26 \text{ Margin} \quad R^2 = 15.17\%$$
$$(8.91) \quad (2.82)$$

Substituting in the net margin of 30% for Aracruz into this regression, we obtain the following:

$$PS = 0.95 + 2.26 (.30) = 1.63$$

Based on its current price/book value ratio of 0.96, Aracruz would be considered undervalued. However, based on its current price/sales ratio of 4.48, it would be considered overvalued. The noisiness in these regressions, as evidenced in the low R-squared values on the regressions, would make us cautious in accepting these recommendations.

 12.15 VALUING AN INITIAL PUBLIC OFFERING

If you were an investment banker pricing an initial public offering, would you primarily use discounted cash flow valuation, relative valuation, or a combination of the two?

☐ Relative valuation, because the buyers of the IPO will look at comparables

☐ Discounted cash flow valuation, because it reflects intrinsic value

☐ The higher of the two values, since it is my job to get the highest price I can for my client

☐ None of the above

Explain.

OPTION PRICING APPROACHES TO EQUITY VALUATION

While discounted cash flow and relative valuation models remain the standard approaches to valuation, there are some scenarios where a more realistic estimate of value can be obtained by using option pricing models. There are at least three specific cases where equity in a firm or business can be viewed as an option.

1. **Equity in a Deeply Troubled Firm:**   The first is the case of equity in a firm with negative earnings, few prospects of a turnaround, and large amounts of debt outstanding. In such a case, the equity investors in the firm can be viewed as holding an option to liquidate the firm. The assets of the firm comprise the underlying asset for the option; the duration of the debt outstanding yields the maturity of the option and the face value of the debt is the strike price. The value of this option derives from the variance in the value of the firm and the fact that the debt does not come due immediately.

2. **Natural Resource Firms:**   A substantial portion of the value of a natural resource firm comes from the reserves that the firm owns. Since the firm has the right to exploit these reserves and has flexibility in deciding when and how much of the reserves to extract, it can be argued that undeveloped reserves, at least, should be viewed as options. The value of this option derives from the variability in the price of the commodity, with increases in commodity price variance making reserves more valuable.

3. **Product Patents:**   Companies which own product patents can be viewed as owning options, since they have the "exclusive" right to develop and market these products during the life of the patents. When valuing a company which derives all or the bulk of its value, not from its earnings and cash flows on its existing projects, but from a patent that it owns (often untested and undeveloped), option pricing is a more effective tool in valuation than traditional discounted cash flow valuation or multiples. Chapter 6 contains an example of such an application.

These applications are discussed in more depth in Damodaran (1994).

IN PRACTICE: VALUING EQUITY AS AN OPTION

In valuing equity in a firm with negative earnings and large financial obligations, there are four key inputs that need to be estimated.

1. Liquidation value of the assets of the firm: There are two basic approaches to estimating the liquidation value. The first is to obtain the market values of the assets in an external market if these assets are traded (as would be the case with real estate), and add up these values. The second is to estimate the cash flows on assets-in-place, and discount them back at the cost of capital, to arrive at a value for the assets.

2. Variance in the firm value: The variance in firm value can also be estimated in one of two ways. The first approach, which can be used if both the equity and debt are traded, is to estimate the variance in past prices in both, and compute the variance

of a portfolio composed of the two, weighted by their relative market values. The second approach is to use the variance of the sector in which the firm operates as the variance in option pricing. (This was provided in Chapter 6 in Table 6.5.)

3. Duration of the Debt: Since firms often have multiple debt issues outstanding, the simplest way to deal with the duration issue is to estimate the durations of the debt separately and take a face-value weighted average of these durations. (We are, in a sense, converting multiple debt issues into one zero coupon bond, for simplicity.)

4. Face Value of the Debt: The cumulated face value of all of the debt represents the equivalent of the strike price of the option.

The fifth and final input to the option pricing model is the riskless rate, which should be set equal to the government bond rate (for the estimated duration of the option). Plugging these values into an option pricing model will yield the value of equity as a call option.

CONCLUSION

There are three basic approaches to valuation. The first is discounted cash flow valuation, where the value of any asset is estimated by computing the present value of the expected cash flows on it. This can be done either from the perspective of just the equity investors in the firm, by discounting cash flows to equity (defined strictly as dividends or expansively as free cash flows to equity) at the cost of equity or from the perspective of all claimholders in the firm, by discounting cash flows to the firm (cash flows prior to debt payments) at the cost of capital. The actual process of estimation, in either case, generally requires four inputs: the length of the period for which a firm or asset can be expected to generate growth greater than the stable growth rate (which is constrained to be close to the growth rate of the economy in which the firm operates), the cash flows during the high-growth period, the terminal value at the end of the high-growth period, and a discount rate. The expected growth potential will vary across firms, with some firms already growing at a stable growth rate and with others where the expectation, at least, is that growth will last for some period into the future.

The second approach to valuation is relative valuation, where the value of any asset is estimated by looking at how "similar" assets are priced in the market. The key steps in this approach are defining "comparable" firms or assets and choosing a standardized measure of value (usually value as a multiple of earnings, cash flows, or book value) to compare the firms. It is worth emphasizing that the multiples can also be stated in terms of the same variables—growth, risk, and payout—that determine discounted cash flow values. Finally, since this approach is based upon how comparable assets are priced, it will build in existing market biases—positive or negative—into the valuation.

The last approach to valuation is option pricing models, which can be particularly useful in valuing equity in deeply troubled firms, natural resource firms, and firms that derive the bulk of their value from product patents.

PROBLEMS AND QUESTIONS

1. Respond true or false to the following statements relating to the dividend discount model.
   a. The dividend discount model cannot be used to value a high-growth company that pays no dividends.
   b. The dividend discount model will undervalue stocks because it is too conservative.
   c. The dividend discount model will find more undervalued stocks when the overall stock market is depressed.
   d. Stocks that are undervalued using the dividend discount model have generally made significant positive excess returns over long periods (five years or more).
   e. Stocks that pay high dividends and have low price/earnings ratios are more likely to be undervalued using the dividend discount model.

2. Ameritech Corporation paid dividends per share of $3.56 in 1992, and dividends are expected to grow 5.5% a year forever. The stock has a beta of 0.90, and the Treasury bond rate is 6.25%.
   a. What was the value per share, using the Gordon Growth Model?
   b. The stock was trading for $80 per share. What would the growth rate in dividends have to be to justify this price?

3. A key input for the Gordon Growth Model is the expected growth rate in dividends over the long term. How, if at all, would you factor in the following considerations in estimating this growth rate?
   a. There is an increase in the inflation rate.
   b. The economy in which the firm operates is growing very rapidly.
   c. The growth potential of the industry in which the firm operates is very high.
   d. The current management of the firm is of very high quality.

4. Newell Corporation, a manufacturer of do-it-yourself hardware and housewares, reported earnings per share of $2.10 in 1993, on which it paid dividends per share of $0.69. Earnings are expected to grow 15% a year from 1994 to 1998, during which period the dividend payout ratio is expected to remain unchanged. After 1998, the earnings growth rate is expected to drop to a stable 6%, and the payout ratio is expected to in-crease to 65% of earnings. The firm has a beta of 1.40 currently, and it is expected to have a beta of 1.10 after 1998. The Treasury bond rate is 6.25%.
   a. What is the expected price of the stock at the end of 1998?
   b. What is the value of the stock, using the two-stage dividend discount model?

5. Church & Dwight, a large producer of sodium bicarbonate, reported earnings per share of $1.50 in 1993 and paid dividends per share of $0.42. In 1993, the firm also reported the following:

$$\text{Net Income} = \$30 \text{ million}$$
$$\text{Interest Expense} = \$0.8 \text{ million}$$
$$\text{Book Value of Debt} = \$7.6 \text{ million}$$
$$\text{Book Value of Equity} = \$160 \text{ million}$$

The firm faced a corporate tax rate of 38.5%. The market value debt-to-equity ratio is 5%. The Treasury bond rate is 7%.

The firm expects to maintain these financial fundamentals from 1994 to 1998, at which time it is expected to become a stable firm, with an earnings growth rate of 6%. The firm's financial characteristics will approach industry averages after 1998. The industry averages are as follows:

$$\text{Return on Assets} = 12.5\%$$
$$\text{Debt/Equity Ratio} = 25\%$$
$$\text{Interest Rate on Debt} = 7\%$$

Church & Dwight had a beta of 0.85 in 1993, and the unlevered beta is not expected to change over time.
   a. What is the expected growth rate in earnings, based on fundamentals, for the high-growth period (1994 to 1998)?
   b. What is the expected payout ratio after 1998?
   c. What is the expected beta after 1998?
   d. What is the expected price at the end of 1998?
   e. What is the value of the stock, using the two-stage dividend discount model?
   f. How much of this value can be attributed to extraordinary growth? to stable growth?

6. Medtronic Inc., the world's largest manufacturer of implantable biomedical devices, reported earnings per share in 1993 of $3.95 and paid dividends per share of $0.68. Its earnings are expected to grow 16% from 1994 to 1998, but the growth rate

is expected to decline each year after that to a stable growth rate of 6% in 2003. The payout ratio is expected to remain unchanged from 1994 to 1998, after which it will increase each year to reach 60% in steady state. The stock is expected to have a beta of 1.25 from 1994 to 1998, after which the beta will decline each year to reach 1.00 by the time the firm becomes stable (the Treasury bond rate is 6.25%).

a. Assuming that the growth rate declines linearly (and the payout ratio increases linearly) from 1999 to 2003, estimate the dividends per share each year from 1994 to 2003.

b. Estimate the expected price at the end of 2003.

c. Estimate the value per share, using the three-stage dividend discount model.

7. Kimberly-Clark, a household product manufacturer, reported earnings per share of $3.20 in 1993 and paid dividends per share of $1.70 in that year. The firm reported depreciation of $315 million in 1993 and capital expenditures of $475 million. (There were 160 million shares outstanding, trading at $51 per share.) This ratio of capital expenditures to depreciation is expected to be maintained in the long term. The working capital needs are negligible. Kimberly-Clark had debt outstanding of $1.6 billion and intends to maintain its current financing mix (of debt and equity) to finance future investment needs. The firm is in a steady state, and earnings are expected to grow 7% a year. The stock had a beta of 1.05 (the Treasury bond rate is 6.25%).

a. Estimate the value per share, using the dividend discount model.

b. Estimate the value per share, using the FCFE model.

c. How would you explain the difference between the two models, and which one would you use as your benchmark for comparison to the market price?

8. Ecolab Inc. sells chemicals and systems for cleaning, sanitizing, and maintenance. It reported earnings per share of $2.35 in 1993 and expected earnings growth of 15.5% a year from 1994 to 1998, and 6% a year after that. The capital expenditure per share was $2.25, and depreciation was $1.125 per share in 1993. Both are expected to grow at the same rate as earnings from 1994 to 1998. Working capital is expected to remain at 5% of revenues, and revenues that were $1,000 million in 1993 are expected to increase 6% a year from 1994 to 1998 and 4% a year after that. The firm currently has a debt ratio [D/(D+E)] of 5% but plans to finance future investment needs (including working capital investments) using a debt ratio of 20%. The stock is expected to have a beta of 1.00 for the period of the analysis, and the Treasury bond rate is 6.50%. There are 63 million shares outstanding.

a. Assuming that capital expenditures and depreciation offset each other after 1998, estimate the value per share.

b. Assuming that capital expenditures continue to be 200% of depreciation even after 1998, estimate the value per share.

c. What would the value per share have been if the firm had continued to finance new investments with its old financing mix (5%)? Is it fair to use the same beta for this analysis?

9. Dionex Corporation, a leader in the development and manufacture of ion chromography systems (used to identify contaminants in electronic devices), reported earnings per share of $2.02 in 1993 and paid no dividends. These earnings are expected to grow 14% a year for five years (1994 to 1998) and 7% a year after that. The firm reported depreciation of $2 million in 1993 and capital spending of $4.20 million and had 7 million shares outstanding. The working capital is expected to remain at 50% of revenues, which were $106 million in 1993 and are expected to grow 6% a year from 1994 to 1998 and 4% a year after that. The firm is expected to finance 10% of its capital expenditures and working capital needs with debt. Dionex had a beta of 1.20 in 1993, and this beta is expected to drop to 1.10 after 1998. The Treasury bond rate is 7%.

a. Estimate the expected free cash flow to equity from 1994 to 1998, assuming that capital expenditures and depreciation grow at the same rate as earnings.

b. Estimate the terminal price per share (at the end of 1998). Stable firms in this industry have capital expenditures that are 150% of revenues and maintain working capital at 25% of revenues.

c. Estimate the value per share, based on the FCFE model.

10. Biomet Inc. designs, manufactures, and markets reconstructive and trauma devices. It reported earnings per share of $0.56 in 1993, on which it paid no dividends. It had revenues per share in 1993 of $2.91. It had capital expenditures of $0.13 per share in 1993 and depreciation in the same year of $0.08 per share. The working capital was 60% of revenues in 1993 and will remain at that level from 1994 to 1998, whereas earnings and revenues are expected to grow 17% a year. The earnings growth rate is expected to decline linearly over the following five years to a rate of 5% in 2003. During the high-growth and transition periods, capital spending and depreciation are expected to grow at the same rate as earnings, but they are expected to offset each other when the firm reaches steady state. Working capital is expected to drop from 60% of revenues during the 1994–1998 period to 30% of revenues after 2003. The firm has no debt currently, but it plans to finance 10% of its net capital investment and working capital requirements with debt.

The stock is expected to have a beta of 1.45 for the high-growth period (1994–1998), and it is expected to decline to 1.10 by the time the firm goes into steady state (in 2003). The Treasury bond rate is 7%.

a. Estimate the value per share, using the FCFE model.

b. Estimate the value per share, assuming that working capital stays at 60% of revenues forever.

c. Estimate the value per share, assuming that the beta remains unchanged at 1.45 forever.

11. Omnicare, Inc., which provides pharmacy management and drug therapy to nursing homes, reported earnings per share of $0.85 in 1993 on revenues per share of $12.50. It had negligible capital expenditures, which were covered by depreciation, but had to maintain working capital at 40% of revenues. Revenues and earnings are expected to grow 20% a year from 1994 to 1998, after which the growth rate is expected to decline linearly over three years to 5% in 2001. The firm has a debt ratio of 15%, which it intends to maintain in the future. The stock has a beta of 1.10, which is expected to remain unchanged for the period of the analysis. The Treasury bond rate is 7%.

a. Estimate the value per share, using the free cash flow to equity model.

b. Assume now that you find out that the way that Omnicare is going to create growth is by giving easier credit terms to its clients. How would that affect your estimate of

value? (Will it increase or decrease?)

c. How sensitive is your estimate of value to changes in the working capital assumption?

12. Which of the following firms is likely to have a higher value from the dividend discount model, a higher value from the FCFE model, or the same value from both models?

a. A firm that pays out less in dividends than it has available in FCFE but that invests the balance in Treasury bonds.

b. A firm that pays out more in dividends than it has available in FCFE and then issues stock to cover the difference.

c. A firm that pays out, on average, its FCFE as dividends.

d. A firm that pays out less in dividends than it has available in FCFE, but uses the cash at regular intervals to acquire other firms, with the intent of diversifying.

e. A firm that pays out more in dividends than it has available in FCFE, but borrows money to cover the difference (the firm is already overlevered).

13. Union Pacific Railroad reported net income of $770 million in 1993, after interest expenses of $320 million (the corporate tax rate was 36%). It reported depreciation of $960 million in that year, and capital spending was $1.2 billion. The firm also had $4 billion in debt outstanding on the books, rated AA (carrying a yield to maturity of 8%), trading at par (up from $3.8 billion at the end of 1992). The beta of the stock is 1.05, and there were 200 million shares outstanding (trading at $60 per share), with a book value of $5 billion. Union Pacific paid 40% of its earnings as dividends, and working capital requirements are negligible. The Treasury bond rate is 7%.

a. Estimate the free cash flow to the firm in 1993.

b. Estimate the value of the firm at the end of 1993.

c. Estimate the value of equity at the end of 1993 and the value per share, using the FCFF approach.

14. Lockheed Corporation, one of the largest defense contractors in the United States, reported EBITDA of $1,290 million in 1993, prior to interest expenses of $215 million and depreciation charges of $400 million. Capital Expenditures in 1993 amounted to $450 million, and working cap-

ital was 7% of revenues (which were $13,500 million). The firm had debt outstanding of $3.068 billion (in book value terms), trading at a market value of $3.2 billion and yielding a pretax interest rate of 8%. There were 62 million shares outstanding, trading at $64 per share, and the most recent beta is 1.10. The tax rate for the firm is 40%. The Treasury bond rate is 7%.

The firm expects revenues, earnings, capital expenditures, and depreciation to grow at 9.5% a year from 1994 to 1998, after which time the growth rate is expected to drop to 4%. (Capital spending will offset depreciation in the steady-state period.) The company also plans to lower its debt/equity ratio to 50% for the steady state (which will result in the pretax interest rate dropping to 7.5%).
a. Estimate the value of the firm.
b. Estimate the value of the equity in the firm and the value per share.

15. In the face of disappointing earnings results and increasingly assertive institutional stockholders, Eastman Kodak considered a major restructuring in 1993. As part of this restructuring, it considered the sale of its health division, which earned $560 million in earnings before interest and taxes in 1993, on revenues of $5.285 billion. The expected growth in earnings was expected to moderate to 6% between 1994 and 1998 and to 4% after that. Capital expenditures in the health division amounted to $420 million in 1993, whereas depreciation was $350 million. Both are expected to grow 4% a year in the long term. Working capital requirements are negligible.

The average beta of firms competing with Eastman Kodak's health division is 1.15. Although Eastman Kodak has a debt ratio [D/(D+E)] of 50%, the health division can sustain a debt ratio [D/(D+E)] of only 20%, which is similar to the average debt ratio of firms competing in the health sector. At this level of debt, the health division can expect to pay 7.5% on its debt, before taxes. The tax rate is 40%, and the Treasury bond rate is 7%.
a. Estimate the cost of capital for the division.
b. Estimate the value of the division.
c. Why might an acquirer pay more than this estimated value?

16. National City Corporation, a bank holding company, reported earnings per share of $2.40 in 1993 and paid dividends per share of $1.06. The earnings had grown 7.5% a year over the prior

five years and were expected to grow 6% a year in the long term (starting in 1994). The stock had a beta of 1.05 and traded for 10 times earnings. The Treasury bond rate was 7%.
a. Estimate the P/E ratio for National City Corporation.
b. What long-term growth rate is implied in the firm's current PE ratio?

17. The following were the P/E ratios of firms in the aerospace/defense industry at the end of December 1993, with additional data on expected growth and risk:

Company	P/E Ratio	Expected Growth	Beta	Payout
Boeing	17.3	3.5%	1.10	28%
General Dynamics	15.5	11.5%	1.25	40%
General Motors— Hughes	16.5	13.0%	0.85	41%
Grumman	11.4	10.5%	0.80	37%
Lockheed Corporation	10.2	9.5%	0.85	37%
Logicon	12.4	14.0%	0.85	11%
Loral Corporation	13.3	16.5%	0.75	23%
Martin Marietta	11.0	8.0%	0.85	22%
McDonnell Douglas	22.6	13.0%	1.15	37%
Northrop	9.5	9.0%	1.05	47%
Raytheon	12.1	9.5%	0.75	28%
Rockwell	13.9	11.5%	1.00	38%
Thiokol	8.7	5.5%	0.95	15%
United Industrial	10.4	4.5%	0.70	50%

a. Estimate the average and median P/E ratios. What, if anything, would these averages tell you?
b. An analyst concludes that Thiokol is undervalued because its P/E ratio is lower than the industry average. Under what conditions is this statement true? Would you agree with it here?
c. Using a regression, control for differences across firms on risk, growth, and payout. Specify how you would use this regression to spot under- and overvalued stocks. What are the limitations of this approach?

18. NCH Corporation, which markets cleaning chemicals, insecticides, and other products, paid

dividends of $2 per share in 1993 on earnings of $4 per share. The book value of equity per share was $40, and earnings are expected to grow 6% a year in the long term. The stock has a beta of 0.85 and sells for $60 per share. The Treasury bond rate is 7%.

a. Based on these inputs, estimate the price/book value ratio for NCH.

b. How much would the return on equity have to increase to justify the price/book value ratio at which NCH sells for currently?

19. Longs Drug, a large U.S. drugstore chain operating primarily in northern California, had sales per share of $122 in 1993, on which it reported earnings per share of $2.45 and paid a dividend per share of $1.12. The company is expected to grow 6% in the long term and has a beta of 0.90. The current Treasury bond rate is 7%.

a. Estimate the appropriate price/sales multiple for Longs Drug.

b. The stock is currently trading for $34 per share. Assuming the growth rate is estimated correctly, what would the profit margin need to be to justify this price per share?

20. You are trying to estimate a price per share on an initial public offering of a company involved in environmental waste disposal. The company has a book value per share of $20 and earned $3.50 per share in the most recent time period. Although it does not pay dividends, the capital expenditures per share were $2.50 higher than depreciation per share in the most recent period, and the firm uses no debt financing. Analysts project that earnings for the company will grow 25% a year for the next five years. The data on other companies in the environment waste disposal business is shown below:

The average debt/equity ratio of these firms is 20%, and the tax rate is 40%.

a. Estimate the average price/book value ratio for these comparable firms. Would you use this average P/BV ratio to price the initial public offering?

b. What subjective adjustments would you make to the price/book value ratio for this firm and why?

21. You have been asked to assess whether Walgreen Company, a drugstore chain, is correctly priced relative to its competitors in the drugstore industry at the end of 1993. The following are the price/sales ratios, profit margins, and other relative details of the firms in the drugstore industry.

Company	P/S Ratio	Profit Margin (%)	Payout (%)	Expected Growth (%)	Beta
Arbor Drugs	0.42	3.40	18	14.0	1.05
Big B Inc.	0.30	1.90	14	23.5	0.70
Drug Empor.	0.10	0.60	0	27.5	0.90
Fay's Inc.	0.15	1.30	37	11.5	0.90
Geno vese	0.18	1.70	26	10.5	0.80
Longs Drug	0.30	2.00	46	6.0	0.90
Perry Drugs	0.12	1.30	0	12.5	1.10
Rite Aid	0.33	3.20	37	10.5	0.90
Walgreen	*0.60*	*2.70*	*31*	*13.5*	*1.15*

Based entirely on a subjective analysis, do you think that Walgreen is overpriced because its price/sales ratio is the highest in the industry? If it is not, how would you rationalize its value?

Company	Price	BV/Share	EPS	DPS	Beta	Expected Growth (%)
Air & Water	$9.60	$8.48	$0.40	$0.00	1.65	10.5
Allwaste	5.40	3.10	0.25	0.00	1.10	18.5
Browning Ferris	29.00	11.50	1.45	0.68	1.25	11.0
Chemical Waste	9.40	3.75	0.45	0.15	1.15	2.5
Groundwater	15.00	14.45	0.65	0.00	1.00	3.0
Intn'l Tech.	3.30	3.35	0.16	0.00	1.10	11.0
Ionics Inc.	48.00	31.00	2.20	0.00	1.00	14.5
Laidlaw Inc.	6.30	5.85	0.40	0.12	1.15	8.5
OHM Corp.	16.00	5.65	0.60	0.00	1.15	9.50
Rollins	5.10	3.65	0.05	0.00	1.30	1.0
Safety-Kleen	14.00	9.25	0.80	0.36	1.15	6.50

————————**LIVE CASE STUDY**

X. VALUATION

Objective: To estimate the value for the firm, identify one key "value driven" and come up with a plan to increase the value.

Key
Questions

- What type of cash flow (dividends, FCFE, or FCFF) would you choose to discount for this firm?
- What growth pattern (stable, 2-stage, 3-stage) would you pick for this firm? How long will high growth last?
- What is your estimate of value of equity in this firm? How does this compare to the market value?
- What is the "key variable" (risk, growth, leverage, profit margins . . .) driving this value?
- If you were hired to enhance value at this firm, what would be the path you would choose to increase value?

Framework
for Analysis

1. Cash Flow Choice
- How does this company's dividends compare to its free cash flow to equity?
- How stable is leverage expected to be at this firm?

    (If leverage is expected to change → use FCFF, if leverage is stable and dividends are equal to FCFE → use Dividends, if leverage is stable and dividends are not equal to FCFE → use FCFE. If you cannot estimate FCFE or FCFF, use dividends.)
- How high is inflation in the local currency?

2. Growth Pattern Choice
- How much have this company's earnings grown historically?
- How much do analysts expect this company's earnings to grow in the future?
- What do the fundamentals suggest about earnings growth at this company? (How much is being reinvested and at what rate of return?)
- If there is anticipated high growth, what are the barriers to entry that will allow this high growth to continue? For how long?

3. Valuation
- What is the value of this firm, based upon a discounted cash flow model?
- How much of this value comes from the expected growth?
- How sensitive is this value to changes in the different assumptions?

4. Value Enhancement

- In what aspect of corporate finance (investment, financing or dividend policy) does this firm lag? (You can build on the intrinsic analysis that you have done so far, or use industry averages.)

- If you fixed the problem areas (i.e., take better projects, move to the optimal debt ratio, return more or less cash to owners), what would happen to the value of the equity in this firm?

- What is the value of control in this firm?

Getting Information for Valuation

Most of the information that you need for valuation come from your current or past financial statements. You will also need a beta (see risk and return section) and a debt ratio (see risk and return section) to estimate the free cash flows to equity. To get an analyst estimate of expected growth in earnings per share over the next 5 years, check the morningstar web site (**www.morningstar.net**) that provides the consensus estimate for analyst projections for your firm.

To see industry averages for betas, fundamentals and other inputs, you might want to check the industry averages on my web site.

To examine how your firm ranks relative to the industry on the basis of multiples such as PE, PBV or PS ratios check out the valuation section of the morningstar web site (**www.morningstar.net**). You can also check the industry averages for these and other multiples in my web site.

To do the valuation, you can use the valuation spreadsheet that best meets your needs—dividends, FCFE or FCFF—stable, 2-stage or 3-stage. They are available on my web site.

Appendix 1:

Basics of Statistics: Means, Variances, Covariances, and Regressions

There are a number of ways in which large amounts of data can be presented. One approach breaks the numbers down into individual values (or ranges of values) and provides probabilities for each value or range. This is called a *distribution*. Another approach is to estimate "summary statistics" for the data. For a data series, $X_1, X_2, X_3, \ldots X_n$, where n is the number of observations in the series, the most widely used summary statistics are as follows:

- The mean (μ), which is the average of all of the observations in the data series.

$$\text{Mean} = \mu_x = \frac{\sum_{j=1}^{j=n} X_j}{n}$$

- The median, which is the midpoint of the series; half the data in the series are higher than the median and half are lower.
- The variance, which is a measure of the spread in the distribution around the mean, and is calculated by first summing up the squared deviations from the mean, and then dividing by either the number of observations (if the data represent the entire population) or by this number, reduced by one (if the data represent a sample).

$$\text{Variance} = \sigma_x^2 = \frac{\sum_{j=1}^{j=n} (X_j - \mu)^2}{n} \quad \text{(if population; divide by n − 1 if sample)}$$

When there are two series of data, there are a number of statistical measures that can be used to capture how the two series move together over time. The two most widely used are the correlation and the covariance. For two data series, $X\ (X_1, X_2, \ldots)$ and $Y\ (Y, Y \ldots)$, the covariance provides a nonstandardized measure of the degree to which they move together, and is estimated by taking the product of the deviations from the mean for each variable in each period.

$$\text{Covariance} = \sigma_{XY} = \sum_{j=1}^{j=n} \frac{(X_j - \mu_X)(Y_j - \mu_Y)}{n} \quad \text{(if population; divide by n − 1 if sample)}$$

The sign on the covariance indicates the type of relationship that the two variables have. A positive sign indicates that they move together and a negative that they move in opposite directions. While the covariance increases with the strength of the relationship, it is still relatively difficult to draw judgments on the strength of the relationship between two variables by looking at the covariance, since it is not standardized.

The correlation is the standardized measure of the relationship between two variables. It can be computed from the covariance:

$$\text{Correlation} = \rho_{XY} = \sigma_{XY} / \sigma_X \sigma_Y = \frac{\sum_{j=1}^{j=n}(X_j - \mu_X)(Y_j - \mu_Y)}{\sqrt{\sum_{j=1}^{j=n}(X_j - \mu_X)^2}\sqrt{\sum_{j=1}^{j=n}(Y_j - \mu_Y)^2}}$$

The correlation can never be greater than 1 or less than minus 1. A correlation close to zero indicates that the two variables are unrelated. A positive correlation indicates that the two variables move together, and the relationship is stronger the closer the correlation gets to 1. A negative correlation indicates the two variables move in opposite directions, and that relationship also gets stronger the closer the correlation gets to minus 1. Two variables that are perfectly positively correlated ($r = 1$) essentially move in perfect proportion in the same direction, while two assets which are perfectly negatively correlated move in perfect proportion in opposite directions.

A simple regression is an extension of the correlation/covariance concept. It attempts to explain one variable, which is called the dependent variable, using the other variable, called the independent variable. Keeping with statistical tradition, let Y be the dependent variable and X be the independent variable. If the two variables are plotted against each other on a scatter plot, with Y on the vertical axis and X on the horizontal axis, the regression attempts to fit a straight line through the points in such a way as to minimize the sum of the squared deviations of the points from the line. Consequently, it is called ordinary least squares (OLS) regression. When such a line is fit, two parameters emerge—one is the point at which the line cuts through the Y axis, called the intercept of the regression, and the other is the slope of the regression line:

$$\text{OLS Regression:} \quad Y = a + bX$$

The slope (b) of the regression measures both the direction and the magnitude of the relation. When the two variables are positively correlated, the slope will also be positive, whereas when the two variables are negatively correlated, the slope will be negative. The magnitude of the slope of the regression can be read as follows—for every unit increase in the dependent variable (X), the independent variable will change by b (slope). The close linkage between the slope of the regression and the correlation/covariance should not be surprising since the slope is estimated using the covariance:

$$\text{Slope of the Regression} = b = \frac{\text{Covariance}_{YX}}{\text{Variance of } X} = \frac{\sigma_{YX}}{\sigma_X^2}$$

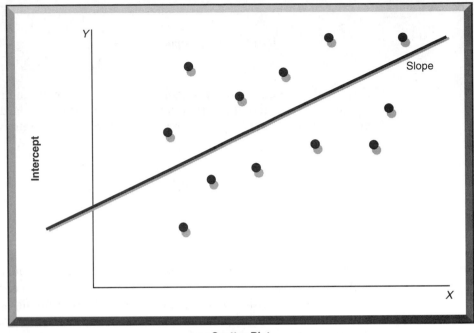

Scatter Plot

The intercept a of the regression can be read in a number of ways. One interpretation is that it is the value that Y will have when X is zero. Another is more straightforward, and is based upon how it is calculated. It is the difference between the average value of Y, and the slope adjusted value of X.

$$\text{Intercept of the Regression} = a = \mu_Y - b * (\mu_X)$$

Regression parameters are always estimated with some noise, partly because the data are measured with error and partly because we estimate them from samples of data. This noise is captured in a couple of statistics. One is the R-squared of the regression, which measures the proportion of the variability in Y that is explained by X. It is a direct function of the correlation between the variables:

$$\text{R-Squared of the Regression} = \text{Correlation}^2_{YX} = \rho^2_{YX} = \frac{b^2 \sigma^2_X}{\sigma^2_Y}$$

An R-squared value closer to 1 indicates a strong relationship between the two variables, though the relationship may be either positive or negative. Another measure of noise in a regression is the standard error, which measures the "spread" around each of the two parameters estimated—the intercept and the slope. Each parameter has an associated standard error, which is calculated from the data:

$$\text{Standard Error of Intercept} = SE_a = \sqrt{\frac{\left(\sum_{j=1}^{j=n} X_j^2\right)\left(\sum_{j=1}^{j=n} (Y_j - bX_j)^2\right)}{(n-1)\sum_{j=1}^{j=n} (X_j - \mu_X)^2}}$$

$$\text{Standard Error of Slope} = SE_b = \sqrt{\frac{\left(\sum\limits_{j=1}^{j=n}(Y_j - bX_j)^2\right)}{(n-1)\sum\limits_{j=1}^{j=n}(X_j - \mu_X)^2}}$$

If we make the additional assumption that the intercept and slope estimates are normally distributed, the parameter estimate and the standard error can be combined to get a "t statistic" that measures whether the relationship is statistically significant:

$$\text{T statistic for intercept} = a/SE_a$$
$$\text{T statistic from slope} = b/SE_b$$

For samples with more than 120 observations, a t statistic greater than 1.66 indicates that the variable is significantly different from zero with 95% certainty, while a statistic greater than 2.36 indicates the same with 99% certainty. For smaller samples, the t statistic has to be larger to have statistical significance.[1]

The regression that measures the relationship between two variables becomes a multiple regression when it is extended to include more than one independent variable ($X1, X2, X3, X4\ldots$) in trying to explain the dependent variable Y. While the graphical presentation becomes more difficult, the multiple regression yields a form that is an extension of the simple regression:

$$Y = a + b\,X1 + c\,X2 + dX3 + eX4$$

The R-squared still measures the strength of the relationship, but an additional R-squared statistic called the adjusted R-squared is computed to counter the bias that will induce the R-squared to keep increasing as more independent variables are added to the regression. If there are k independent variables in the regression, the adjusted R-squared is computed as follows:

$$\text{Adjusted R-Squared} = 1 - (1 - R^2)\frac{(n-1)}{(n-k)}$$

---

[1]The actual values that t statistics need to take on can be found in a table for the t distribution.

APPENDIX 2:

FINANCIAL STATEMENTS

There are three basic financial statements—the income statement that measures the revenues and expenses of the firm, the balance sheet that reports on the assets and liabilities of the firm, and the statement of cash flows that examines the sources and the uses of cash.

INCOME STATEMENT

An income statement provides information about a firm's operating activities over a specific time period. The net income of a company is equal to the revenues minus expenses, where revenues arise from selling goods or services, and expenses measure the costs associated with generating these revenues.

Classification—A Typical Income Statement

Since income can be generated from a number of different sources, generally accepted accounting principles (GAAP) requires that income statements be classified into four sections—income from continuing operations, income from discontinued operations, extraordinary gains or losses, and adjustments for changes in accounting principles. A typical income statement starts with revenues, and adjusts for the cost of the goods sold, depreciation on assets used to produce the revenues, and any selling or administrative expenses to arrive at an operating profit. The operating profit, when reduced by interest expenses, yields the taxable income, which when reduced by taxes yields net income.

Accrual versus Cash Basis—Income Statements

Firms often expend resources to acquire materials or manufacture goods in one period, but do not sell them until the following period. Alternatively, they often provide services in one period but do not get paid until the following period. In accrual-based accounting, the revenue from selling a good or service is recognized in the period in which the good is sold or the service is performed (in whole or substantially). A corresponding effort is made on the expense side to match[1] expenses to revenues. Under a cash-based system of accounting, revenues are recognized when payment is received, while expenses are recorded when paid. Since there is no matching of revenues and expenses, GAAP requires that firms use accrual-based accounting in income statements.

---

[1] If a cost (such as an administrative cost) cannot be easily linked with a particular revenue, it is usually recognized as an expense in the period in which it is consumed.

INCOME STATEMENT

Revenues
- Cost of Goods Sold
- Depreciation
- Selling expenses
- Administrative expenses
= Earnings before interest and taxes (EBIT)
- Interest expenses
= Earnings before taxes
- Taxes
= Net income before extraordinary items
+ Gains (Losses) from discontinued operations
+ Extraordinary gains (losses)
+ Net income changes caused by changes in accounting methods
= Net income after extraordinary items
- Preferred dividends
= Profit to common stockholders

GAAP—Recognizing Income

Generally accepted accounting principles require the recognition of revenues when the service for which the firm is getting paid has been performed in full or substantially, and has received in return either cash or a receivable that is both observable and measurable. For expenses which are directly linked to the production of revenues (like labor and materials), expenses are recognized in the same period in which revenues are recognized. Any expenses which are not directly linked to the production of revenues are recognized in the period in which the firm consumes the services.

While accrual accounting is straightforward in firms which produce goods and sell them, there are special cases where accrual accounting can be complicated by the nature of the product or service being offered.

- *Long-term contracts:* Long-term contracts span several accounting periods, and customers often make periodic payments as the contract progresses (example: a new home or commercial building). When a long-term contractor has a contract with a buyer with an agreed-upon price, revenue during the period of construction is recognized on the basis of the percentage of the contract that is completed. As the revenue is recognized on a percentage of completion basis, a corresponding proportion of the expense is also recognized. An alternative is to wait until the contract is completed, and recognize the total revenue and expense on completion. Since this delays the payment of income taxes, it is not permitted under the Internal Revenue Code for tax purposes.

- *Uncertainty about cash collections:* When there is considerable uncertainty about the capacity of the buyer of a good or service to pay for a service, the firm providing the good or service may recognize the income only when it collects portions of the selling price under the installment method. While this is similar to revenue recognition in the cash method, the expenses under the installment method are recognized only when the cash is collected, even though payment may be made in the period of the initial sale. An alternative to this approach is the cost-recovery-first method, where cash receipts and expenses are matched dollar for dollar (thus generating no profits) until all the expenses are covered, after which any additional revenues are reported as profits.

Generally Accepted Accounting Principles (GAAP): These are the principles that govern the construction of financial statements and help determine accounting rules.

BALANCE SHEET

Unlike the income statement, which measures flows over a period of time, the balance sheet provides a summary of what the firm owns in terms of assets and what it owes to both its lenders and its equity investors. The balance sheet is built around the equality:

$$\text{Assets} = \text{Liabilities} + \text{Shareholders' Equity}$$

Assets and liabilities can be further broken down into current and noncurrent portions.

Assets	Liabilities & Equity
Current assets	Current liabilities
Cash and marketable securities	Accounts payable
Accounts receivable	Short-term borrowing
Inventories	Other current liabilities
Other current assets	Long-term debt
Investments	Other Noncurrent liabilities
Property, plant & equipment (fixed assets)	Stockholders' equity
Intangible assets	Preferred stock
	Common stock
	Retained earnings
	Treasury stock

Assets

An asset is any resource that has the potential to either generate future cash inflows or reduce future cash outflows. For a resource to be an asset, therefore, a firm has to have acquired it in a prior transaction and be able to quantify future benefits with reasonable precision. Assets can be classified on several bases—fixed and current assets, monetary assets (like cash and notes receivable), and nonmonetary assets—and the GAAP principles on valuation vary from asset to asset.

Fixed Assets: Generally accepted accounting principles in almost all countries require the valuation of fixed assets at historical costs, adjusted for any depreciation charges on these assets. The rationale that is often provided for this practice is that:

(a) Book value is easier to obtain than market value for most assets, since an active secondary market does not exist for most assets.

(b) Book value can be more objectively valued than market value, and is less likely to be manipulated by firms to suit their purposes.

(c) Book value is a more conservative estimate of true value than market value.

All these arguments are open to challenge, and it is quite clear that the book value of many fixed assets bears little resemblance to the market value.

Since fixed assets are valued at book value, and are adjusted for depreciation provisions, the value of a fixed asset is strongly influenced by both its depreciable life and the depreciation method used. Since firms estimate the depreciable life, and lengthening the depreciable life can increase[2] reported earnings, it provides an opportunity for firms to manage reported earnings. Firms are also offered an opportunity to manage earnings through the choice of a depreciation method, since GAAP allows firms to use either straight line depreciation (where depreciation is spread evenly over the life of the asset) or accelerated depreciation methods (where more depreciation is taken in the initial years, and less later on). Most U.S. firms use straight line depreciation for financial reporting, while they use accelerated depreciation for tax purposes, since firms can report better earnings with the former, at least in the years right after the asset is acquired. In contrast, Japanese and German firms often use accelerated depreciation for both tax and financial reporting purposes, leading to income which is understated relative to their US. counterparts.

Inventory: There are three basic approaches to valuing inventory that are allowed by GAAP:

(a) *First-in, first-out (FIFO):*   Under FIFO, the cost of goods sold is based upon the cost of material bought earliest in the period, while the cost of inventory is based upon the cost of material bought later in the year. This results in inventory being valued close to current replacement cost. During periods of inflation, the use of FIFO will result in the lowest estimate of cost of goods sold among the three approaches, and the highest net income.

(b) *Last-in, first-out (LIFO):*   Under LIFO, the cost of goods sold is based upon the cost of material bought toward the end of the period, resulting in costs that closely approximate current costs. The inventory, however, is valued on the basis of the cost of material bought earlier in the year. During periods of inflation, the use of LIFO will result in the highest estimate of cost of goods sold among the three approaches, and the lowest net income.

(c) *Weighted average:*   Under the weighted average approach, both inventory and the cost of goods sold are based upon the average cost of all units bought during the period.

---

[2]It has the opposite effect on cash flows, since lengthening the depreciable life reduces depreciation and increases both taxable income and taxes.

Firms often adopt the LIFO approach for tax benefits during periods of high inflation, and studies indicate that firms with the following characteristics are more likely to adopt LIFO—rising prices for raw materials and labor, more variable inventory growth, an absence of other tax loss carryforwards, and large size. When firms switch from FIFO to LIFO in valuing inventory, there is likely to be a drop in net income and a concurrent increase in cash flows (because of the tax savings). The reverse will apply when firms switch from LIFO to FIFO.

Given the income and cash flow effects of inventory valuation methods, it is often difficult to compare the earnings of firms which use different methods. There is, however, one way of adjusting for these differences. Firms that choose to use the LIFO approach to value inventories have to specify in a footnote the difference in inventory valuation between FIFO and LIFO, and this difference is termed the LIFO reserve. This can be used to adjust the beginning and ending inventories, and consequently the cost of goods sold, and to restate income based upon FIFO valuation.

Intangible Assets: Intangible assets include a wide array of assets ranging from patents and trademarks to goodwill. GAAP requires that intangible assets be accounted for in the following way:

(a) The costs incurred in developing the intangible asset are expensed in that period, even though the asset might have a life of several accounting periods. Thus, the research and development expenditure that creates the patent (the intangible asset) is nevertheless expensed in the period it is incurred.

(b) When an intangible asset is acquired from an external party, the expenditure is treated as an asset, in contrast to the treatment of expenditures incurred in internally developing the same asset.

(c) Intangible assets have to be amortized over their expected lives, with a maximum amortization period of 40 years. The standard practice is to use straight-line amortization. For tax purposes, however, firms are not allowed to amortize goodwill and other intangible assets with no specific lifetime.

Intangible assets are often by-products of acquisitions. When a firm acquires another firm, the purchase price is first allocated over tangible assets, and the excess price is then allocated to any intangible assets such as patents or trade names. Any residual becomes goodwill. While accounting principles suggest that goodwill captures the value of any intangibles that are not specifically identifiable, it is really a reflection of the difference between the book value of assets and their market value.

Intangible Assets: Intangible assets are those assets that do not have a physical presence, and include assets such as patents, trademarks and goodwill.

Liabilities
For an obligation to be recognized as a liability, it must meet three requirements—it must be expected to lead to a future cash outflow or the loss of a future cash inflow

at some specified or determinable date, the firm cannot avoid the obligation, and the transaction giving rise to the obligation has happened.

1. Degree of Certitude

Liabilities vary in the degree to which they create a future obligation. At one extreme, a straight bond creates an obligation to make fixed payments on fixed dates and results in a very specific and certain obligation. At the other extreme, an option contract entered into by the firm creates a contingent obligation, where the amount and the timing of the obligation are unclear. Along the continuum, GAAP recognizes as accounting liabilities those obligations that create future payments that can be both quantified and timed, even if the amount and the timing have to be estimated by the firm. It does not recognize purchase or employment commitments or contingent contracts as accounting liabilities.

As firms enter into more and more complex arrangements to manage their financial and operating risk, a number of gray areas are emerging, where generally accepted accounting principles do not provide sufficient guidance on the right path to take. On example is the use of hybrid securities by firms, possessing some of the properties of debt and some of equity, making a classification into liabilities and stockholders' equity very difficult. Another is the use of off-balance sheet financing by firms, where a liability is created but not recognized. The evolving attitude toward this phenomenon is that firms must disclose information[3] about the off-balance sheet risk of any financial instruments or agreements that they have entered into.

2. Dealing with Leases

Firms often choose to lease long-term assets rather than buy them for a variety of reasons—the tax benefits are greater to the lessor than the lessee, and leases offer more flexibility in terms of adjusting to changes in technology and capacity needs. Lease payments create the same kind of obligation that interest payments on debt create, and have to be viewed in a similar light. If a firm is allowed to lease a significant portion of its assets and keep it off its financial statements, a perusal of the statements will give a very misleading view of the company's financial strength. Consequently, accounting rules have been devised to force firms to reveal the extent of their lease obligations on their books.

There are two ways of accounting for leases. In an operating lease, the lessor (or owner) transfers only the right to use the property to the lessee. At the end of the lease period, the lessee returns the property to the lessor. Since the lessee does not assume the risk of ownership, the lease expense is treated as an operating expense in the income statement and the lease does not affect the balance sheet. In a capital lease, the lessee assumes some of the risks of ownership and enjoys some of the benefits. Consequently, the lease, when signed, is recognized both as an asset and as a liability (for the lease payments) on the balance sheet. The firm gets to claim

---

[3]FASB 105 requires that the following be disclosed—the face value or notional principal amount, the terms of the instrument and the credit and market risk involved, and the accounting loss that the firm would incur if any party to the agreement did not perform.

depreciation each year on the asset and also deducts the interest expense component of the lease payment each year. In general, capital leases recognize expenses sooner than equivalent operating leases.

Since firms prefer to keep leases off the books, and sometimes prefer to defer expenses, there is a strong incentive on the part of firms to report all leases as operating leases. Consequently the Financial Accounting Standards Board has ruled that a lease should be treated as a capital lease if it meets any one of the following four conditions:

(a) If the lease life exceeds 75% of the life of the asset

(b) If there is a transfer of ownership to the lessee at the end of the lease term

(c) If there is an option to purchase the asset at a "bargain price" at the end of the lease term

(d) If the present value of the lease payments, discounted at an appropriate discount rate, exceeds 90% of the fair market value of the asset

The lessor uses the same criteria for determining whether the lease is a capital or operating lease and accounts for it accordingly. If it is a capital lease, the lessor records the present value of future cash flows as revenue and recognizes expenses. The lease receivable is also shown as an asset on the balance sheet, and the interest revenue is recognized over the term of the lease as paid.

From a tax standpoint, the lessor can claim the tax benefits (such as depreciation) of the leased asset only if it is an operating lease, though the revenue code uses slightly different criteria[4] for determining whether the lease is an operating lease.

3. Employee Benefits

Employers provide pension and health care benefits to their employees. In many cases, the obligations created by these benefits are extensive and a failure by the firm to adequately fund these obligations needs to be revealed in financial statements.

a. Pension Plans

In a pension plan, the firm agrees to provide certain benefits to their employees, either by specifying a "defined contribution" (where a fixed contribution is made to the plan each year by the employer, without any promises on the benefits which will be delivered in the plan) or a "defined benefit" (where the employer promises to pay a certain benefit to the employee). Under the latter, the employer has to put sufficient money into the plan each period, such that the amounts with reinvestment are sufficient to meet the defined benefits.

---

[4]The requirements for an operating lease in the revenue code are as follows: (a) The property can be used by someone other than the lessee at the end of the lease term, (b) the lessee cannot buy the asset using a bargain purchase option, (c) the lessor has at least 20% of its capital at risk, (d) the lessor has a positive cash flow from the lease independent of tax benefits, and (e) the lessee does not have an investment in the lease.

Under a defined contribution plan, the firm meets its obligation once it has made the prespecified contribution to the plan. Under a defined benefit plan, the firm's obligations are much more difficult to estimate, since they will be determined by a number of variables including the benefits that employees are entitled to, which will change as their salaries and employment status change, the prior contributions made by the employer and the returns they have earned, and the rate of return that the employer expects to make on current contributions. As these variables change, the value of the pension fund assets can be greater than, less than, or equal to pension fund liabilities (which include the present value of promised benefits). A pension fund whose assets exceed its liabilities is an overfunded plan, whereas one whose assets are less than its liabilities is an underfunded plan, and disclosures to that effect have to be included in financial statements, generally in the footnotes.

When a pension fund is overfunded, the firm has several options—it can withdraw the excess assets from the fund or it can discontinue contributions to the plan or it can continue to make contributions on the assumption that the overfunding is a transitory phenomenon that could well disappear by the next period. When a fund is underfunded, the firm has a liability, though the FASB rule requires that firms reveal only the excess of accumulated[5] pension fund liabilities over pension fund assets on the balance sheet.

b. Health Care Benefits

A firm can provide health care benefits in one of two ways—by making a fixed contribution to a health care plan, without promising specific benefits (analogous to a defined contribution plan), or by promising specific health benefits, and setting aside the funds to provide these benefits (analogous to a defined benefit plan). The accounting for health care benefits is very similar to the accounting for pension obligations. The key difference between the two is that firms do not have to report[6] the excess of their health care obligations over the health care fund assets as a liability on the balance sheet, though a footnote to that effect has to be added to the financial statement.

4. Income Taxes

Firms often use different methods of accounting for tax and financial reporting purposes, leading to a question of how tax liabilities should be reported. Since the use of accelerated depreciation and favorable inventory valuation methods for tax accounting purposes leads to a deferral of taxes, the taxes on the income reported in the financial statements will be much greater than the actual tax paid. The same principles of matching expenses to income that underlie accrual accounting suggest that the "deferred income tax" be recognized in the financial statements. Thus a company which pays $55,000 on its taxable income based upon its tax accounting, and which would have paid $75,000 on the income reported in its financial statements, will be

---

[5]The accumulated pension fund liability does not take into account the projected benefit obligation, where actuarial estimates of future benefits are made. Consequently, it is much smaller than the total pension liabilities.

[6]While companies might not have to report the excess of their health care obligations over assets as a liability, some firms choose to do so anyway. Boeing, in 1993, for instance reported an accrued retiree health care obligation of $2.158 billion as a liability.

forced to recognize the difference ($20,000) as deferred taxes. Since the deferred taxes will be paid in later years, they will be recognized as paid.

The question of whether the deferred tax liability is really a liability is an interesting one. Firms do not owe the amount categorized as deferred taxes to any entity, and treating it as a liability makes the firm look more risky than it really is.

5. Reserves in Financial Statements

Reserves can appear in financial statements as a deduction from an asset, as a liability, or as a reduction of stockholders' equity. While reserves have to be for specific purposes in the United States, firms in Germany and Japan are allowed to create general reserves to equalize income across time periods. Reserve accounts are created for at least two reasons:

(a) *To match expenses with benefits:*   A firm can create a reserve for an expense that is expected to arise from an activity from the current period, and reduce the income in the current period by the expense. When the expense actually occurs, the reserve is reduced by the amount and the net income in the future period is not affected by the expense. Thus, a bank which expects 1% of its loans to go uncollected may create a reserve for bad debts in the period the loan is made, and charge income in that period with a charge transferring funds to the reserve. Any subsequent loan defaults will be charged to the reserve.

(b) *To keep expenses out of income statements:*   Firms can keep some expenses out of the income statement, by directly reducing the stockholders' equity by a reserve created to meet the expense. While the net effect on stockholders' equity is the same as if the expense had been shown in the income statement, it results in an overstatement of net income for that period.

The varied uses to which reserves are put, and the wide diversity of accounting standards relating to reserves in different countries, suggest that analysts should be careful about how they factor in reserves when comparing the profitability of companies in different countries using different accounting standards.

STATEMENT OF CASH FLOWS

The statement of cash flows is based upon a reformulation of the basic equation relating assets to liabilities:

$$\text{Assets} \ = \ \text{Liabilities} \ + \ \text{Stockholders' Equity}$$

If each of these variables is measured in terms of changes (Δ), this equation can be rewritten as follows:

$$\Delta \, \text{Assets} \ = \ \Delta \, \text{Liabilities} \ + \ \Delta \, \text{Stockholders' Equity}$$

If assets are broken out on the basis of whether they are cash assets or non-cash assets, this works out to:

$$\Delta \, \text{Cash} \ + \ \Delta \, \text{Non-cash Assets} \ = \ \Delta \, \text{Liabilities} + \Delta \, \text{Stockholders' Equity}$$

Rearranging terms:

$$\Delta \text{ Cash } = \Delta \text{ Liabilities } + \Delta \text{ Stockholders' Equity } - \Delta \text{ Non-cash Assets}$$

Changes in cash flows can be traced to the following reasons:

- An increase in non-cash assets will decrease cash flows; increases in both current assets (such as inventory and accounts receivable), financial assets (through the purchase of securities), and fixed assets (through capital expenditures) will result in a drain on cash flows.

- Net profit will increase cash flows; this cash flow will be further increased if there are any non-cash charges (such as depreciation and amortization).

- Any payment of dividends or stock repurchases will decrease cash flows, as will the principal payment on debt; an issue of stock or debt will increase cash flows.

A statement of changes in cash flows classifies all changes into one of three categories—operating, investing, or financing activities. The final step in preparing a statement of changes in cash flows is to classify changes in liabilities, stockholders' equity, and noncash assets into one of these three categories, though some items will not fit easily into one or another of the categories. Once categorized, the statement of cash flows provides a breakdown of the changes in the cash balance over the period.

OTHER ISSUES IN ANALYZING FINANCIAL STATEMENTS

There are two more issues that bear consideration before concluding this appendix on financial statements—the first relates to differences in accounting standards and practices and how these differences may color comparisons across companies, and the second relates to accounting for acquisitions and how this can affect both the acquisition method and price.

Differences in Accounting Standards and Practices

There are differences in accounting standards across countries that affect the measurement of earnings. These differences, however, are not as great as they are made out to be, and cannot be used to explain away radical departures from fundamental principles of valuation.[7] Choi and Levich (1990), in a survey of accounting standards across developed markets, note that most countries subscribe to basic accounting notions of consistency, realization, and historical cost principles in preparing accounting statements. Table A2.1 summarizes accounting standards in eight major financial markets, and reveals that the common elements vastly outnumber those areas where there are differences.

---

[7]At the peak of the Japanese market, there were many investors who explained away the price-earnings multiples of sixty and greater in the market by noting that Japanese firms were conservative in measuring earnings. Even after taking into account the general provisions and excess depreciation used by many of these firms to depress current earnings, the price-earnings multiples were greater than fifty for many firms, suggesting either extraordinary expected growth in the future or overvaluation.

Table A2.1 COMPARISON OF ACCOUNTING PRINCIPLES

Accounting Principle	UK	USA	France	Germany	Netherlands	Sweden	Switzerland	Japan
1. Consistency—accounting principles and methods are applied on the same basis from period to period.	Yes	Yes	Yes	Yes	Yes	PP	PP	Yes
2. Realization—revenue is recognized when realization is reasonably assured.	Yes	Yes	Yes	Yes	Yes	Yes	PP	Yes
3. Fair presentation of the financial statement is required.	Yes	Yes	Yes	Yes	Yes	Yes	Yes	Yes
4. Historical cost convention—departures from the historical cost convention are disclosed.	Yes	Yes	Yes	Yes	Yes	Yes	RF	Yes
5. Accounting policies—a change in accounting principles and methods without a change in circumstances is accounted for by a prior year adjustment.	Yes	No	Yes	MP	RF	MP	MP	No
6. Fixed assets—revaluation—in historical cost statements, fixed assets are stated at an amount in excess of cost which is determined at irregular intervals.	MP	No	Yes	No	RF	PP	No	No
7. Fixed assets—revaluation—when fixed assets are stated, in historical cost statements, at an amount in excess of cost, depreciation based on the revaluation amount is charged to income.	Yes	No	Yes	No	Yes	Yes	No	No
8. Goodwill amortized.	MP	Yes	Yes	Yes	M	Yes	MP	Yes
9. Finance leases capitalized.	Yes	Yes	No	No	No	Yes	RF	No
10. Short-term marketable securities at the lower of cost or market value.	Yes	Yes	Yes	Yes	Yes	Yes	Yes	Yes
11. Inventory values at the lower of cost or market value.	Yes	Yes	Yes	Yes	Yes	Yes	Yes	Yes
12. Manufacturing overhead allocated to year-end inventory.	Yes	Yes	Yes	Yes	Yes	Yes	Yes	Yes

Table A2.1   CONTINUED

Accounting Principle	UK	USA	France	Germany	Netherlands	Sweden	Switzerland	Japan
13. Inventory costed using FIFO.	PP	M	M	M	M	PP	PP	M
14. Long-term debt includes maturities longer than one year.	Yes	Yes	Yes	No	Yes	Yes	Yes	Yes
15. Deferred tax recognized where accounting income and taxable income arise at different times.	Yes	Yes	Yes	No	Yes	No	No	Yes
16. Total pension fund assets and liabilities excluded from a company's financial statements.	Yes	Yes	Yes	No	Yes	Yes	Yes	Yes
17. Research and development expensed.	Yes	Yes	Yes	Yes	Yes	Yes	Yes	Yes
18. General purpose (purely discretionary) reserves allowed.	No	No	Yes	Yes	Yes	Yes	Yes	Yes
19. Offsetting assets and liabilities are offset against each other in the balance sheet only when a legal right of offset exists.	Yes	Yes	Yes	Yes	Yes	Yes	PP	Yes
20. Unusual and extraordinary gains and losses are taken in the income statement.	Yes	Yes	Yes	Yes	Yes	Yes	Yes	Yes
21. Closing rate method of foreign currency translation employed.	Yes	Yes	Yes	Yes	Yes	No	Yes	No
22. Currency translation gains or losses arising from trading are reflected in current income.	Yes	Yes	MP	MP	MP	MP	MP	No
23. Excess depreciation permitted.	Yes	No	Yes	Yes	Yes	Yes	Yes	Yes
24. Basic statements reflect a historical cost valuation (no price level adjustment).	Yes	Yes	Yes	Yes	M	Yes	Yes	Yes
25. Supplementary inflation—adjusted financial statements adjusted.	MP	MP	No	No	MP	Yes	No	No

Table A2.1 CONTINUED

Accounting Principle	UK	USA	France	Germany	Netherlands	Sweden	Switzerland	Japan
26. Accounting for long-term investments:								
(a) less than 20% ownership—cost method	Yes	Yes	Yes	Yes	No	Yes	Yes	Yes
(b) 20–50% ownership—equity method	Yes	Yes	Yes	No	Yes	MP	M	Yes
(c) More than 50% full consolidation	Yes	Yes	Yes	Yes	Yes	Yes	Yes	Yes
27. Both domestic and foreign subsidiaries consolidated.	Yes	Yes	Yes	M	Yes	Yes	MP	Yes
28. Acquisition accounted for under the purchase cost method.	PP	PP	Yes	Yes	Yes	PP	Yes	Yes
29. Minority interest excluded from consolidation income.	Yes	Yes	Yes	Yes	Yes	Yes	Yes	Yes
30. Minority interest excluded from consolidated owners' equity.	Yes	Yes	Yes	Yes	Yes	Yes	Yes	Yes

PP = Predominant practice
MP = Minority practice
M = Mixed practice
RF = Rarely or not found

The two countries which offer the strongest contrast to the United States are Germany and Japan. The key differences and their implications are as follows. First, companies in the United States generally maintain separate tax and financial reporting books, which in turn generates items like deferred taxes to cover differences between the two books, and two different depreciation methods—straight line in the financial reports, and accelerated in the tax reports. Companies in Germany and Japan do not maintain separate books. Consequently, depreciation methods in financial reports are much more likely to be accelerated and hence reduce stated income. Second, the requirement that leases be capitalized and shown as a liability is much more tightly enforced in the United States. In Japan, leases are generally treated as operating leases, and do not show up as liabilities in the balance sheet. In Germany, firms can capitalize leases, but have more leeway in classifying leases as operating and capital leases than U.S. companies. Third, goodwill once created can be amortized over 40 years in the United States and over much shorter time periods in Germany and Japan, again depressing stated income. Fourth, reserves in the United States can be created only for specific purposes, whereas German and Japanese companies can use general reserves to equalize income across periods, leading to income being understated during the good years, and overstated during bad years.

Most of these differences can be accounted and adjusted for when comparisons are made of companies in the U.S. and companies in other financial markets. Statistics such as price earnings ratios, which use stated and unadjusted earnings, can be misleading when accounting standards vary widely across the companies being compared.

Accounting for Acquisitions

There are two basic approaches of accounting for acquisitions. In the purchase method, the acquiring firm records the assets and liabilities of the acquired firm at market value, with goodwill capturing the difference between market value and the value of the assets acquired. This goodwill will then be amortized, though the amortization is not tax deductible. If a firm pays cash on an acquisition, it has to use the purchase method to record the transaction.

In a pooling of interest, the book values of the assets and liabilities of the merging firms are added up to arrive at the values for the combined firm. Since the market value of the transaction is not recognized, there is no goodwill created or amortized. This approach is allowed only if the acquiring firm exchanges its common stock for common stock of the acquired firm. Since earnings are not affected by the amortization of goodwill, the reported earnings per share under this approach will be greater than the reported earnings per share in the purchase approach, after the acquisition.

APPENDIX 3:

PRESENT VALUE

Present value is a concept that is intuitively appealing, simple to compute, and has a wide range of applications. It allows us to compare and aggregate cash flows that occur at different points in time.

TIMELINES AND NOTATION

Dealing with cash flows that are at different points in time is made easier using a *timeline* that shows both the timing and the amount of each cash flow in a stream. Thus, a cash flow stream of $100 at the end of each of the next four years can be depicted on a timeline like the one depicted in Figure A3.1.

In the figure, 0 refers to right now. A cash flow that occurs at time 0 is therefore already in present value terms and does not need to be adjusted for time value. A distinction must be made here between a *period of time* and a *point in time*. The portion of the timeline between 0 and 1 refers to *period* 1, which, in this example, is the first year. The cash flow that occurs at the *point* in time "1" refers to the cash flow that occurs at the end of period 1. Finally, the discount rate, which is 10% in this example, is specified for each period on the timeline and may be different for each period. Had the cash flows been at the beginning of each year instead of at the end of each year, the timeline would have been redrawn as it appears in Figure A3.2.

Note that in present value terms, a cash flow that occurs at the beginning of year 2 is the equivalent of a cash flow that occurs at the end of year 1.

Cash flows can be either positive or negative; positive cash flows are called *cash inflows* and negative cash flows are called *cash outflows*. For notational purposes, we will assume the following for this appendix and through this book:

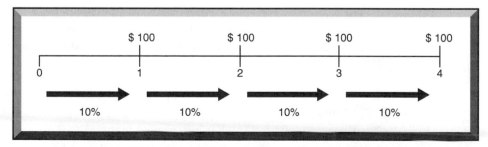

Figure A3.1   A timeline for cash flows: End of each period.

513

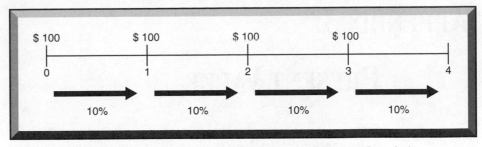

Figure A3.2   A timeline for cash flows: Beginning of each period.

NOTATION	STANDS FOR
PV	Present value
FV	Future value
CF_t	Cash flow at the end of period t
A	Annuity—constant cash flows over several periods
r	Discount rate
g	Expected growth rate in cash flows
n	Number of years over which cash flows are received or paid

THE INTUITIVE BASIS FOR PRESENT VALUE

There are three reasons why a cash flow in the future is worth less than a similar cash flow today:

1. Individuals *prefer present consumption to future consumption.* People would have to be offered more in the future to give up present consumption.

2. When there is *monetary inflation,* the value of currency decreases over time. The greater the inflation, the greater the difference in value between a dollar today and a dollar in the future.

3. Any *uncertainty (risk)* associated with the cash flow in the future reduces the value of the cash flow.

The process by which future cash flows are adjusted to reflect these factors is called *discounting,* and the magnitude of these factors is reflected in the *discount rate.*

The discount rate is a rate at which present and future cash flows are traded off. It incorporates:

1. The preference for current consumption (greater preference . . . higher discount rate)

2. Expected inflation (higher inflation . . . higher discount rate)

3. The uncertainty in the future cash flows (higher risk . . . higher discount rate)

A higher discount rate will lead to a lower present value for future cash flows.

THE MECHANICS OF PRESENT VALUE

The process of discounting future cash flows converts them into cash flows in present value terms. Conversely, the process of compounding converts present cash flows into future cash flows.

Cash flows at different points in time cannot be compared and aggregated. All cash flows have to be brought to the same point in time before comparisons and aggregations can be made.

There are five types of cash flows—simple cash flows, annuities, growing annuities, perpetuities, and growing perpetuities—which we discuss below.

Simple Cash Flows

A *simple cash flow* is a single cash flow in a specified future time period; it can be depicted on a timeline (Figure A3.3) where CF_t = the cash flow at time t.

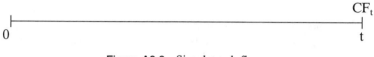

Figure A3.3   Simple cash flow.

This cash flow can be discounted back to the present using a discount rate that reflects the uncertainty of the cash flow. Concurrently, cash flows in the present can be compounded to arrive at an expected future cash flow.

I. Discounting a Simple Cash Flow

Discounting a cash flow converts it into present value dollars and enables the user to do several things. First, once cash flows are converted into present value dollars, they can be aggregated and compared. Second, if present values are estimated correctly, the user should be indifferent between the future cash flow and the present value of that cash flow. The present value of a cash flow can be written as follows:

$$\text{Present Value of Simple Cash Flow} = \frac{CF_t}{(1 + r)^t}$$

where

CF_t = Cash flow at the end of time period t
r = Discount rate

Other things remaining equal, the present value of a cash flow will decrease as the discount rate increases and continue to decrease the further into the future the cash flow occurs.

Discounting: This is the process of moving a cash flow that is expected to occur in the future back to today's terms.

II. Compounding a Cash Flow

Current cash flows can be moved to the future by compounding the cash flow at the appropriate discount rate.

$$\text{Future Value of Simple Cash Flow} = CF_0 (1 + r)^t$$

where

$$CF_0 = \text{Cash flow now}$$
$$r = \text{Discount rate}$$

Again, the compounding effect increases with both the discount rate and the compounding period.

━━━━━━━━━━ ▪ **Compounding:** Compounding is the process by which cash flows are moved from right now to some point in time in the future.

III. The Frequency of Discounting and Compounding

The frequency of compounding affects both the future and present values of cash flows. In the examples above, the cash flows were assumed to be discounted and compounded annually (i.e., interest payments and income were computed at the end of each year based on the balance at the beginning of the year). In some cases, however, the interest may be computed more frequently, such as on a monthly or semiannual basis. In these cases, the present and future values may be very different from those computed on an annual basis; the stated interest rate, on an annual basis, can deviate significantly from the effective or true interest rate. The effective interest rate can be computed as follows:

$$\text{Effective Interest Rate} = \left(1 + \frac{\text{Stated Annual Interest Rate}}{n}\right)^n - 1$$

where

n = number of compounding periods during the year (2 = semiannual; 12 = monthly)

For instance, a 10% annual interest rate, if there is semiannual compounding, works out to an effective interest rate of:

$$\text{Effective Interest Rate} = 1.05^2 - 1 = .10125 \text{ or } 10.25\%$$

As compounding becomes continuous, the effective interest rate can be computed as follows:

$$\text{Effective Interest Rate} = \exp^r - 1$$

where

$$\exp = \text{Exponential function}$$
$$r = \text{Stated annual interest rate}$$

Table A3.1 provides the effective rates as a function of the compounding frequency. As you can see, as compounding becomes more frequent, the effective rate increases, and the present value of future cash flows decreases.

━━━━━━━━━━ ▪ **Effective Interest Rate:** This is the true rate of interest, taking into account the compounding effects of more frequent interest payments.

Frequency	Rate	t	Formula	Effective Annual Rate
		Table A3.1	EFFECT OF COMPOUNDING FREQUENCY ON EFFECTIVE INTEREST RATES	
Annual	10%	1	.10	10%
Semiannual	10%	2	$(1 + .10/2)^2 - 1$	10.25%
Monthly	10%	12	$(1 + .10/12)^{12} - 1$	10.47%
Daily	10%	365	$(1 + .10/365)^{365} - 1$	10.5156%
Continuous	10%		$\exp^{10} - 1$	10.5171%

Annuities

An *annuity* is a constant cash flow that occurs at regular intervals for a fixed period of time. Defining A to be the annuity, the timeline for an annuity may be drawn as follows:

```
        A       A       A       A
 _____|_____|_____|_____|
 0       1       2       3       4
```

An annuity can occur at the end of each period, as in this timeline, or at the beginning of each period.

I. Present Value of an End-of-the-Period Annuity

The present value of an annuity can be calculated by taking each cash flow and discounting it back to the present and then adding up the present values. Alternatively, a formula can be used in the calculation. In the case of annuities that occur at the end of each period, this formula can be written as:

$$\text{PV of an Annuity} = PV(A,r,n) = A \left[\frac{1 - \dfrac{1}{(1 + r)^n}}{r} \right]$$

where

$$A = \text{Annuity}$$
$$r = \text{Discount rate}$$
$$n = \text{Number of years}$$

Accordingly, the notation we will use in the rest of this book for the present value of an annuity will be PV(A,r,n).

ILLUSTRATION A3.1 Estimating the Present Value of Annuities

Suppose you run an advertising agency and you have a choice of buying a copier for $10,000 cash down or paying $ 3,000 a year for five years for the same copier. If the opportunity cost is 12%, which would you rather do?

$$PV \text{ of } \$3000 \text{ Each Year for Next 5 Years} = \$3000 \left[\frac{1 - \dfrac{1}{(1.12)^5}}{.12} \right] = \$10,814$$

The present value of the installment payments exceeds the cash-down price; therefore you would want to pay the $10,000 in cash now.

Alternatively, the present value could have been estimated by discounting each of the cash flows back to the present and aggregating the present values as illustrated in Figure A3.4.

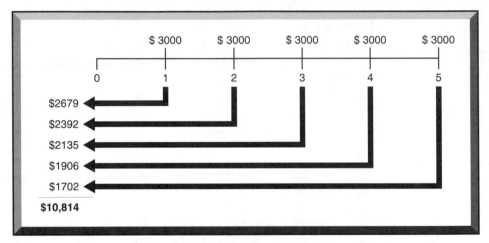

Figure A3.4 A timeline for cash flows.

II. Amortization Factors—Annuities Given Present Values

In some cases, the present value of the cash flows is known and the annuity needs to be estimated. This is often the case with home and automobile loans, for example, where the borrower receives the loan today and pays it back in equal monthly installments over an extended period of time. This process of finding an annuity when the present value is known is as follows:

$$\text{Annuity Given Present Value} = A(PV,r,n) = PV \left[\frac{r}{1 - \dfrac{1}{(1 + r)^n}} \right]$$

ILLUSTRATION **A3.2** Calculating the Monthly Payment on a House Loan

Suppose you are trying to borrow $200,000 to buy a house on a conventional 30-year mortgage with monthly payments. The annual percentage rate on the loan is 8%. The monthly payments on this loan can be estimated using the annuity due formula:

$$\text{Monthly Interest Rate on Loan} = APR/12 = 0.08/12 = 0.0067$$

$$\text{Monthly Payment on Mortgage} = \$200,000 \left[\frac{0.0067}{1 - \dfrac{1}{(1.0067)^{360}}} \right] = \$1473.11$$

This monthly payment is an increasing function of interest rates. When interest rates drop, homeowners usually have a choice of refinancing, though there is an up-front cost to doing so.

III. Future Value of End-of-the-Period Annuities

In some cases, an individual may plan to set aside a fixed annuity each period for a number of periods and will want to know how much he or she will have at the end of the periods. The future value of an end-of-the-period annuity can be calculated as follows:

$$\text{FV of an Annuity} = FV(A,r,n) = A \left[\frac{(1 + r)^n - 1}{r} \right]$$

Thus, the notation we will use throughout this book for the future value of an annuity will be $FV(A,r,n)$.

ILLUSTRATION A3.3   Individual Retirement Accounts (IRA)

Individual retirement accounts (IRAs) allow some tax payers to set aside $2,000 a year for retirement and exempts the income earned on these accounts from taxation. If an individual starts setting aside money in an IRA early in her working life, the value at retirement can be substantially higher than the nominal amount actually put in. For instance, assume that this individual sets aside $2,000 at the end of every year, starting when she is 25 years old, for an expected retirement at the age of 65, and that she expects to make 8% a year on her investments. The expected value of the account on her retirement date can be estimated as follows:

$$\text{Expected Value of IRA contributions at } 65 = \$2,000 \left[\frac{(1.08)^{40} - 1}{.08} \right] = \$518,113$$

The tax exemption adds substantially to the value because it allows the investor to keep the pre-tax return of 8% made on the IRA investment. If the income had been taxed at say 40%, the after-tax return would have dropped to 4.8%, resulting in a much lower expected value:

$$\text{Expected Value of IRA set} - \text{aside at 65 if taxed} = \$2,000 \left[\frac{(1.048)^{40} - 1}{.048} \right] = \$230,127$$

As you can see, the available funds at retirement drops by more than 55% as a consequence of the loss of the tax exemption.

IV. Annuity Given Future Value

Individuals or businesses who have a fixed obligation to meet or a target to meet (in terms of savings) some time in the future need to know how much they should set aside each period to reach this target. If you are given the future value and are looking for an annuity $- A(FV,r,n)$ in terms of notation:

$$\text{Annuity given Future Value} = A(FV,r,n) = FV \left[\frac{r}{(1 + r)^n - 1} \right]$$

ILLUSTRATION A3.4   Sinking Fund Provision on a Bond

In any *balloon payment loan,* only interest payments are made during the life of the loan, while the principal is paid at the end of the period. Companies that borrow money using balloon payment loans or conventional bonds (which share the same features) often set aside money in *sinking funds* during the life of the loan to ensure that they have enough at maturity to pay the principal on the loan or the face value of the bonds. Thus, a company with bonds with a face value of $10 million coming due in 10 years would need to set aside the following amount each year (assuming an interest rate of 8%):

$$\text{Sinking Fund Provision Each Year} = \$10,000,000 \left[\frac{.08}{(1.08)^{10} - 1} \right] = \$690,295$$

The company would need to set aside $690,295 at the end of each year to ensure that there are enough funds ($10 million) to retire the bonds at maturity.

Balloon Payment Loan: A balloon payment loan refers to a loan where only interest is paid for the life of the loan, and the entire principal is paid at the end of the loan's life.

Sinking Fund: A sinking fund is a fund that firms make annual contributions to in order to have enough funds to make a large principal payment on a loan.

V. Effect of Annuities at the Beginning of Each Year

The annuities considered thus far in this chapter are end-of-the-period cash flows. Both the present and future values will be affected if the cash flows occur at the beginning of each period instead of the end. To illustrate this effect, consider an annuity of $100 at the end of each year for the next four years, with a discount rate of 10%.

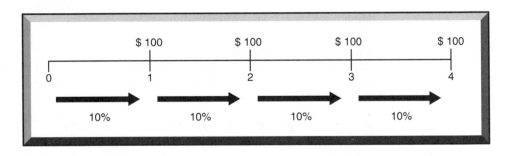

Contrast this with an annuity of $100 at the beginning of each year for the next four years, with the same discount rate:

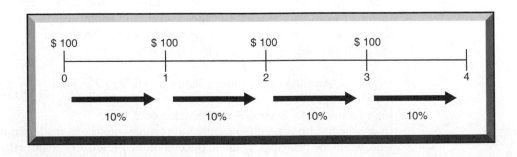

Since the first of these annuities occurs right now, and the remaining cash flows take the form of an end-of-the-period annuity over three years, the present value of this annuity can be written as follows:

$$\text{PV of \$100 at Beginning of Each of Next 4 Years} = \$100 + \$100 \left[\frac{1 - \frac{1}{(1.10)^3}}{.10} \right]$$

In general, the present value of a beginning-of-the-period annuity over n years can be written as follows:

$$\text{PV of Beginning of Period Annuities over n Years} = A + A \left[\frac{1 - \frac{1}{(1 + r)^{n-1}}}{r} \right]$$

This present value will be higher than the present value of an equivalent annuity at the end of each period.

The future value of a beginning-of-the-period annuity typically can be estimated by allowing for one additional period of compounding for each cash flow:

$$\text{FV of a Beginning-of-the-Period Annuity} = A (1 + r) \left[\frac{(1 + r)^n - 1}{r} \right]$$

This future value will be higher than the future value of an equivalent annuity at the end of each period.

ILLUSTRATION **A3.5** **IRA—Saving at the Beginning of Each Period Instead of the End**
Consider again the example of an individual who sets aside $2,000 at the end of each year for the next 40 years in an IRA account at 8%. The future value of these deposits amounted to $518,113 at the end of year 40. If the deposits had been made at the *beginning* of each year instead of the end, the future value would have been higher:

$$\text{Expected Value of IRA (beginning of year)} = \$2,000 (1.08) \left[\frac{(1.08)^{40} - 1}{.08} \right] = \$559,562$$

As you can see, the gains from making payments at the beginning of each period can be substantial.

Growing Annuities

A *growing annuity* is a cash flow that grows at a constant rate for a specified period of time. If A is the current cash flow, and g is the expected growth rate, the timeline for a growing annuity appears as follows:

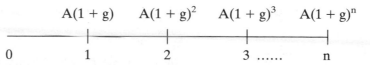

Note that, to qualify as a growing annuity, the growth rate in each period has to be the same as the growth rate in the prior period.

Growing Annuity: A growing annuity is a cash flow growing at a constant rate and paid at regular intervals of time.

The Process of Discounting

In most cases, the present value of a growing annuity can be estimated by using the following formula:

$$\text{PV of a Growing Annuity} = A(1 + g)\left[\frac{1 - \dfrac{(1 + g)^n}{(1 + r)^n}}{r - g}\right]$$

The present value of a growing annuity can be estimated in all cases but one—where the growth rate is equal to the discount rate. In that case, the present value is equal to the nominal sums of the annuities over the period, without the growth effect:

$$\text{PV of a Growing Annuity for n Years (when } r = g) = n\,A$$

Note also that this formulation works even when the growth rate is greater than the discount rate.[1]

ILLUSTRATION A3.6   The Value of a Gold Mine

Suppose you have the rights to a gold mine for the next 20 years, over which period you plan to extract 5,000 ounces of gold every year. The current price per ounce is $300, but it is expected to increase 3% a year. The appropriate discount rate is 10%. The present value of the gold that will be extracted from this mine can be estimated as follows:

$$\text{PV of Extracted Gold} = \$300 * 5000 * (1.03)\left[\frac{1 - \dfrac{(1.03)^{20}}{(1.10)^{20}}}{.10 - .03}\right] = \$16,145,980$$

The present value of the gold expected to be extracted from this mine is $16.146 million; it is an increasing function of the expected growth rate in gold prices. Figure A3.5 illustrates the present value as a function of the expected growth rate.

Perpetuities

A *perpetuity* is a constant cash flow at regular intervals *forever.* The present value of a perpetuity can be written as:

$$\text{PV of Perpetuity} = \frac{A}{r}$$

where A is the perpetuity. The future value of a perpetuity is infinite.

Perpetuity: A perpetuity is a constant cash flow paid at regular time intervals forever.

---

[1]Both the denominator and the numerator in the formula will be negative, yielding a positive present value.

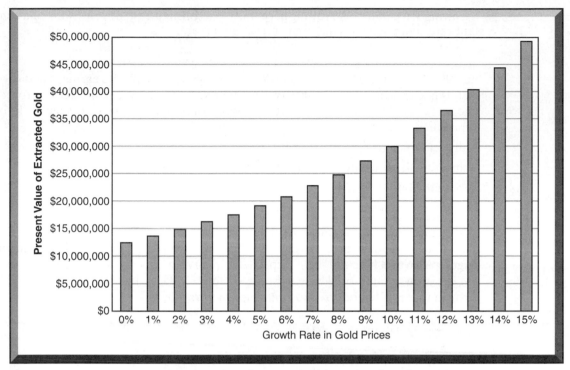

Figure A3.5   Present value of extracted gold as a function of growth rate.

ILLUSTRATION **A3.7   Valuing a Consol Bond**

A *console bond* is a bond that has no maturity and pays a fixed coupon. Assume that you have a 6% coupon consol bond. The value of this bond, if the interest rate is 9%, is as follows:

$$\text{Value of Consol Bond} = \$60 \ / \ .09 = \$667$$

The value of a consol bond will be equal to its face value (which is usually $1000) only if the coupon rate is equal to the interest rate.

Growing Perpetuities

A *growing perpetuity* is a cash flow that is expected to grow at a *constant rate* forever. The present value of a growing perpetuity can be written as:

$$\text{PV of Growing Perpetuity} = \frac{CF_1}{(r - g)}$$

where CF_1 is the expected cash flow next year, g is the constant growth rate, and r is the discount rate.

While a growing perpetuity and a growing annuity share several features, the fact that a growing perpetuity lasts forever puts constraints on the growth rate. It has to be less than the discount rate for this formula to work.

Growing Perpetuity: A growing perpetuity is a constant cash flow, growing at a constant rate, and paid at regular time intervals forever.

ILLUSTRATION **A3.8   Valuing a Stock with Stable Growth in Dividends**

In 1992, Southwestern Bell paid dividends per share of $2.73. Its earnings and dividends had grown at 6% a year between 1988 and 1992 and were expected to grow at the same rate in the long term. The rate of return required by investors on stocks of equivalent risk was 12.23%.

Current Dividends per Share = $2.73

Expected Growth Rate in Earnings and Dividends = 6%

Discount Rate = 12.23%

$$\text{Value of Stock} = \$2.73 *1.06 / (.1223 - .06) = \$46.45$$

As an interesting aside, the stock was actually trading at $70 per share. This price could be justified by using a higher growth rate. The value of the stock is graphed in Figure A3.6 as a function of the expected growth rate.

The growth rate would have to be approximately 8% to justify a price of $70. This growth rate is often referred to as an *implied growth rate.*

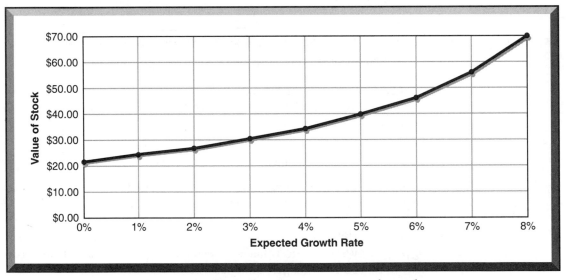

Figure A3.6   SW Bell—value versus expected growth.

Combinations and Uneven Cash Flows

In the real world, a number of different types of cash flows may exist contempareneously, including annuities, simple cash flows, and sometimes perpetuities. Some examples are discussed below.

- A conventional bond pays a fixed coupon every period for the lifetime of the bond and the face value of the bond at maturity. In terms of a timeline:

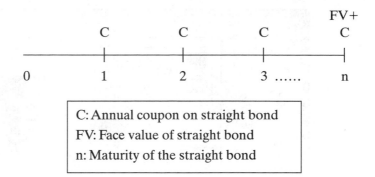

C: Annual coupon on straight bond
FV: Face value of straight bond
n: Maturity of the straight bond

Since coupons are fixed and paid at regular intervals, they represent an annuity, while the face value of the bond is a single cash flow that has to be discounted separately. The value of a straight bond can then be written as follows:

Value of Straight Bond = Coupon (PV of an Annuity for the Life of the Bond)
                         + Face Value (PV of a Single Cash Flow)

ILLUSTRATION A3.9   The Value of a Straight Bond

Say you are trying to value a straight bond with a 15-year maturity and a 10.75% coupon rate. The current interest rate on bonds of this risk level is 8.5%.

PV of Cash Flows on Bond = 107.50* PV(A,8.5%, 15 years) + $1000/1.085^{15}$ = $1186.85

If interest rates rise to 10%:

PV of Cash Flows on Bond = 107.50* PV(A,10%, 15 years) + $1000/1.10^{15}$ = $1,057.05
Percentage change in Price = ($1057.05 − $1186.85)/$1186.85 = − 10.94%

If interest rates fall to 7%:

PV of Cash Flows on Bond = 107.50* PV(A,7%, 15 years) + $1000/1.07^{15}$ = $1,341.55
Percentage Change in Price = ($1341.55 − $1186.85)/$1186.85 = +13.03%

This asymmetric response to interest rate changes is called *convexity*.

ILLUSTRATION A3.10   Contrasting Short-term versus Long-term Bonds

Now say you are valuing four different bonds—1-year, 5-year, 15-year, and 30-year—with the same coupon rate of 10.75%. Figure A3.7 contrasts the price changes on these three bonds as a function of interest rate changes.

Bond Pricing Proposition 1: The longer the maturity of a bond, the more sensitive it is to changes in interest rates.

ILLUSTRATION A3.11   Contrasting Low Coupon and High Coupon Bonds

Suppose you are valuing four different bonds, all with the same maturity - 15 years − but different coupon rates − 0%, 5%, 10.75%, and 12%. Figure A3.8 contrasts the effects of changing interest rates on each of these bonds.

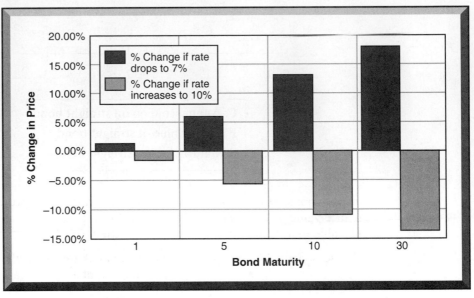

Figure A3.7   Price changes as a function of bond maturities.

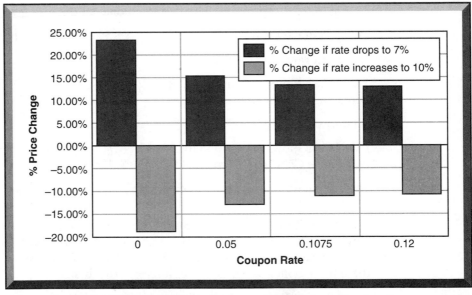

Figure A3.8   Bond price changes as a function of coupon rates.

Bond Pricing Proposition 2: The lower the coupon rate on the bond, the more sensitive it is to changes in interest rates.

• In the case of the stock of a company that expects high growth in the near future and lower and more stable growth forever after that, the expected dividends take the following form:

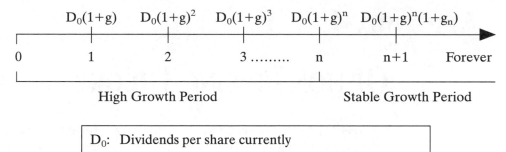

D_0: Dividends per share currently
$g =$ Expected growth rate in high growth period (n years)
$g_n =$ Expected growth rate after high growth period

The dividends over the high-growth period represent a growing annuity, while the dividends after that satisfy the conditions of a growing perpetuity. The value of the stock can thus be written as the sum of the two present values.

$$P_0 = \frac{D_0 * (1 + g) * \left(1 - \dfrac{(1 + g)^n}{(1 + r)^n}\right)}{r - g} + \frac{D_{n+1}}{(r - g_n)(1 + r)^n}$$

Growing Annuity   Growing Perpetuity—Discounted Back

where

$P_0 =$ Present value of expected dividends
$g =$ Extraordinary growth rate for the first n years (n = high-growth period)
$g_n =$ Growth rate forever after year n
$D_0 =$ Current dividends per share
$D_t =$ Dividends per share in year t
$r =$ Required rate of return $\rightarrow$ discount rate

Appendix 4:

Option Pricing Theory

Options are derivative securities; that is, they are securities that derive their value from an underlying asset. Though traded options are of comparatively recent origin, option-like securities have existed for a very long time. In this appendix, we will look at a number of questions relating to the determinants of option value:

- What are the characteristics of call or put options?
- What are the determinants of option value?
- What are the basic option pricing models, and on what assumptions are they built? In particular, what is a replicating portfolio and how can it help in pricing options?

The technology available for valuing options has expanded dramatically in the last three decades, especially since the development of the basic option pricing model by Black and Scholes. Their model, while setting the general framework for valuing options, has been modified to work in a variety of settings. An alternative model for option pricing, the binomial model, provides more insight into the determinants of option value.

What is an Option?

An option provides the holder with the right to buy or sell a specified quantity of an *underlying asset* at a fixed price (called a *strike price* or an *exercise price*) on or before the expiration date of the option. Since it is a right and not an obligation, the holder can choose not to exercise the right and allow the option to expire. There are two types of options—*call options* and *put options*.

Call Options

A call option gives the buyer of the option the right to buy the underlying asset at a fixed price, called the strike or the exercise price, at any time prior to the expiration date of the option: The buyer pays a price for this right. If at expiration, the value of the asset is less than the strike price, the option is not exercised and expires worthless. If, on the other hand, the value of the asset is greater than the strike price, the option is exercised—the buyer of the option buys the stock at the exercise price and the difference between the asset value and the exercise price comprises the gross profit on the investment. The net profit on the investment is the difference between the gross profit and the price paid for the call initially. Table A4.1 summarizes the transactions involved in a call option.

A payoff diagram illustrates the cash payoff on an option at expiration. For a call, the net payoff is negative (and equal to the price paid for the call) if the value of the underlying asset is less than the strike price. If the price of the underlying asset exceeds the strike price, the gross payoff is the difference between the value of the underlying asset and the strike price, and the net payoff is the difference between the gross payoff and the price of the call. This is illustrated in Figure A4.1.

■ **Strike Price:** This is the price at which the holder of a call (put) option can buy (sell) the underlying asset any time before expiration.

■ **Call Option:** A call option gives its holder the right to buy the underlying asset at a fixed price any time before the expiration of the option.

■ **Payoff Diagram:** A payoff diagram shows the cash flows on a call or put option as a function of the price of the underlying asset at expiration.

Put Options

A put option gives the buyer of the option the right to sell the underlying asset at a fixed price, again called the strike or exercise price, at any time prior to the expiration

Table A4.1   A SUMMARY OF TRANSACTIONS IN A CALL OPTION

	Now	At Expiration
Buyer of call	pays the call price and gets the right to exercise.	If asset value (S) > strike price (K), buyer exercises. Gross profit = S − K Net profit = S − K − call price
Seller of call	receives the call price and agrees to deliver the asset at the exercise price if the buyer demands it any time before expiration.	If asset value < strike price, buyer does not exercise. Buyer's loss = call price Seller's gain = call price

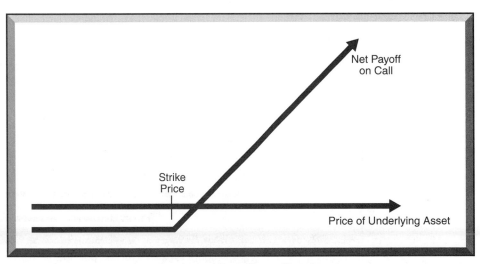

Figure A4.1   Payoff on call option.

date of the option. The buyer pays a price for this right. If the price of the underlying asset is greater than the strike price, the option will not be exercised and will expire worthless. If on the other hand, the price of the underlying asset is less than the strike price, the owner of the put option will exercise the option and sell the stock at the strike price, claiming the difference between the strike price and the market value of the asset as the gross profit. Again, netting out the initial cost paid for the put yields the net profit from the transaction. Table A4.2 summarizes the transactions involved in a put.

Put Option: A put option gives its holder the right to sell the underlying asset at a fixed price any time before the expiration of the option.

A Payoff Diagram

A put has a negative net payoff if the value of the underlying asset exceeds the strike price, and has a gross payoff equal to the difference between the strike price and the value of the underlying asset if the asset value is less than the strike price. This is summarized in Figure A4.2.

Table A4.2   A SUMMARY OF TRANSACTIONS IN A PUT OPTION

	Now	At Maturity
Buyer of put	pays the put price and gets the right to exercise.	If asset value (S) < strike price (K), buyer exercises. Gross profit = K − S Net profit = K − S − put price
Seller of put	receives the put price and agrees to buy the asset at the exercise price if the buyer demands it.	If asset value > strike price, buyer does not exercise. Buyer's loss = put price Seller's gain = put price

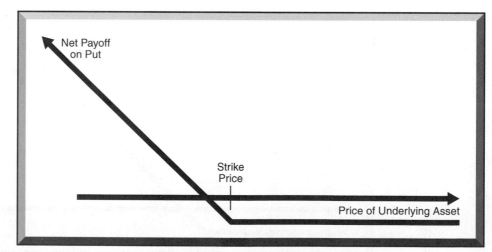

Figure A4.2   Payoff on put option.

DETERMINANTS OF OPTION VALUE

The value of an option is determined by a number of variables relating to the underlying asset and financial markets.

Variables Relating to the Underlying Asset
Current Value of the Underlying Asset
Options are assets that derive value from an underlying asset. Consequently, changes in the value of the underlying asset affect the value of the options on that asset. Since calls provide the right to buy the underlying asset at a fixed price, an increase in the value of the asset will increase the value of the calls. Puts, on the other hand, become less valuable as the value of the asset increases.

Variance in Value of the Underlying Asset
The buyer of an option acquires the right to buy or sell the underlying asset at a fixed price. The higher the variance in the value of the underlying asset, the greater the value of the option. This is true for both calls and puts. While it may seem counterintuitive that an increase in a risk measure (variance) should increase value, options are different from other securities since buyers of options can never lose more than the price they pay for them; in fact, they have the potential to earn significant returns from large price movements.

Dividends Paid on the Underlying Asset
The value of the underlying asset can be expected to decrease if dividend payments are made on the asset during the life of the option. Consequently, the value of a call on the asset is a *decreasing* function of the size of expected dividend payments, and the value of a put is an *increasing* function of expected dividend payments.

Variables Relating to the Option Characteristics
Strike Price of Option
A key characteristic used to describe an option is the strike price. In the case of calls, where the holder acquires the right to buy at a fixed price, the value of the call will decline as the strike price increases. In the case of puts, where the holder has the right to sell at a fixed price, the value will increase as the strike price increases.

Time to Expiration on Option
Both calls and puts become more valuable as the time to expiration increases. This is because the longer time to expiration provides more time for the value of the underlying asset to move, increasing the value of both types of options. Additionally, in the case of a call, where the buyer has to pay a fixed price at expiration, the present value of this fixed price decreases as the life of the option increases, increasing the value of the call. In the case of a put, the present value of the expected proceeds from the sale of the asset at the exercise price at expiration decreases as the time to expiration is extended.

Variables Relating to Financial Markets
Riskless Interest Rate Corresponding to Life of Option

Since the buyer of an option pays the price of the option up front, an opportunity cost is involved. This cost will depend upon the level of interest rates and the time to expiration on the option. The riskless interest rate also enters into the valuation of options when the present value of the exercise price is calculated, since the exercise price does not have to be paid (received) until expiration on calls (puts). Increases in the interest rate will increase the value of calls and reduce the value of puts.

American versus European Options: Variables Relating to Early Exercise

A primary distinction between American and European options is that American options can be exercised at any time prior to its expiration, while European options can be exercised only at expiration. The possibility of early exercise makes American options more valuable than otherwise similar European options; it also makes them more difficult to value. There is one compensating factor that enables the former to be valued using models designed for the latter. In most cases, the time premium associated with the remaining life of an option makes early exercise suboptimal.

While early exercise is not optimal generally, there are at least two exceptions to this rule. One is a case where the underlying asset pays large dividends, thus reducing the value of the asset, and any call options on that asset. In this case, call options may be exercised just before an ex-dividend date, if the time premium on the options is less than the expected decline in asset value as a consequence of the dividend payment. The other exception arises when an investor holds both the underlying asset and *deep in-the-money puts* on that asset at a time when interest rates are high. In this case, the time premium on the put may be less than the potential gain from exercising the put early and earning interest on the exercise price.

In-the-Money Put (Call): An in-the-money put (call) is one where the strike price is higher (lower) than the stock price right now; in other words, there would be a positive cash flow from immediate exercise. A deep in-the-money call or put is one where the difference between the strike price and the stock price is large.

A Summary of the Determinants of Option Value

Table A4.3 summarizes the variables and their predicted effects on call and put prices.

OPTION PRICING MODELS

Option pricing theory has made vast strides since 1972, when Black and Scholes published their path-breaking paper providing a model for valuing dividend-protected European options. Black and Scholes used a "replicating portfolio"—a portfolio

Table A4.3   SUMMARY OF VARIABLES AFFECTING CALL AND PUT PRICES

Factor	Effect on	
	Call Value	Put Value
Increase in underlying asset's value	Increases	Decreases
Increase in strike price	Decreases	Increases
Increase in variance of underlying asset	Increases	Increases
Increase in time to expiration	Increases	Increases
Increase in interest rates	Increases	Decreases
Increase in dividends paid	Decreases	Increases

composed of the underlying asset and the risk-free asset that had the same cash flows as the option being valued—to come up with their final formulation. While their derivation is mathematically complicated, there is a simpler binomial model for valuing options that draws on the same logic.

Replicating Portfolio: A replicating portfolio is a portfolio composed of the underlying asset and a riskless asset that generates the same cash flow as a specified call or put option.

The Binomial Model

The *binomial option pricing model* is based upon a simple formulation for the asset price process, in which the asset, in any time period, can move to one of two possible prices. The general formulation of a stock price process that follows the binomial is shown in Figure A4.3.

In this figure, S is the current stock price; the price moves up to S_u with probability p and down to S_d with probability $1 - p$ in any time period. $[S_u = s*u; S_d = S*d]$

Creating a Replicating Portfolio

The objective in creating a replicating portfolio is to use a combination of risk-free borrowing/lending and the underlying asset to create the same cash flows as the option being valued. The principles of arbitrage apply here, and the value of the option must be equal to the value of the replicating portfolio. In the case of the general formulation above, where stock prices can either move up to S_u or down to S_d in any time period, the replicating portfolio for a call with strike price K will involve borrowing $B and acquiring Δ of the underlying asset, where:

Δ = Number of Units of the Underlying Asset Bought = $(C_u - C_d)/(S_u - S_d)$

where

C_u = Value of the call if the stock price is S_u
C_d = Value of the call if the stock price is S_d

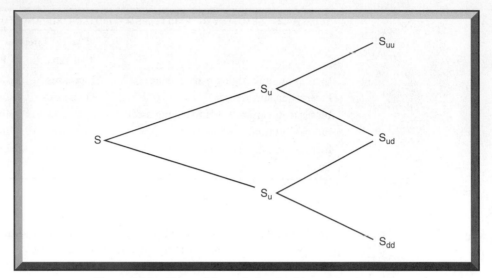

Figure A4.3   General formulation for binomial price path.

In a multiperiod binomial process, the valuation has to proceed iteratively (i.e., starting with the last time period and moving backward in time until the current point in time). The portfolios replicating the option are created at each step and valued, providing the values for the option in that time period. The final output from the binomial option pricing model is a statement of the value of the option in terms of the replicating portfolio, composed of Δ shares (option delta) of the underlying asset and risk-free borrowing/lending.

Value of the Call = Current Value of Underlying Asset * Option Delta −
Borrowing Needed to Replicate the Option

The Determinants of Value
The binomial model provides insight into the determinants of option value. The value of an option is not determined by the *expected* price of the asset but by its *current* price, which, of course, reflects expectations about the future. This is a direct consequence of arbitrage. If the option value deviates from the value of the replicating portfolio, investors can create an arbitrage position (i.e., one that requires no investment, involves no risk, and delivers positive returns). The option value increases as the time to expiration is extended, as the price movements (u and d) increase, and with increases in the interest rate.

The Black-Scholes Model
While the binomial model provides an intuitive feel for the determinants of option value, it requires a large number of inputs in terms of expected future prices at each node. The Black-Scholes model is not an entirely different model; rather, it is one limiting case of the binomial, but it reduces the informational requirements substantially.

The binomial model is a discrete-time model for asset price movements, including a time interval t between price movements. As the time interval is shortened, the limiting distribution, as $t \to 0$, can take one of two forms. If as $t \to 0$, price changes become smaller, the limiting distribution is the normal distribution and the price process is a continuous one. If as $t \to 0$, price changes remain large, the limiting distribution is the Poisson distribution (i.e., a distribution that allows for price jumps). The Black-Scholes model applies when the limiting distribution is the normal distribution,[1] and it explicitly assumes that the price process is continuous and that there are no jumps in asset prices.

The Model

The version of the model presented by Black and Scholes was designed to value European options, which were dividend-protected. Thus, neither the possibility of early exercise nor the payment of dividends affects the value of options in this model.

The value of a call option in the Black-Scholes model can be written as a function of the following variables:

S = Current value of the underlying asset
K = Strike price of the option
t = Life to expiration of the option
r = Riskless interest rate corresponding to the life of the option
σ^2 = Variance in the ln(value) of the underlying asset

The model itself can be written as:

$$\text{Value of call} = S\, N\,(d_1) - K\, e^{-rt}\, N(d_2)$$

where

$$d_1 = \frac{\ln\left(\frac{S}{K}\right) + (r + \frac{\sigma^2}{2})t}{\sigma\sqrt{t}}$$

$$d_2 = d_1 - \sigma\sqrt{t}$$

The process of valuation of options using the Black-Scholes model involves the following steps:

Step 1:   The inputs to the Black-Scholes model are used to estimate d_1 and d_2.

Step 2:   The cumulative normal distribution functions, $N(d_1)$ and $N(d_2)$, corresponding to these standardized normal variables are estimated.

---

[1]Stock prices cannot drop below zero, because of the limited liability of stockholders in publicly listed firms. Hence, stock prices, by themselves, cannot be normally distributed, since a normal distribution requires some probability of infinitely negative values. The distribution of the natural logs of stock prices are assumed to follow a normal distribution in the Black-Scholes model. This is why the variance used in this model is the variance in the log of stock prices.

Step 3: The present value of the exercise price is estimated, using the continuous time version of the present value formulation:
Present Value of Exercise Price $= K e^{-rt}$

Step 4: The value of the call is estimated from the Black-Scholes model.

The Determinants of Value

The determinants of value in the Black-Scholes model are the same as those in the binomial—the current value of the stock price, the variability in stock prices, the time to expiration on the option, the strike price, and the riskless interest rate. The principle of replicating portfolios that is used in binomial valuation also underlies the Black-Scholes model. Table A4.4 provides the replicating portfolios for calls and puts, using the binomial and the Black-Scholes models, where B, B', Δ, and Δ' are estimated from the binomial process.

Model Limitations and Fixes

The version of the Black-Scholes model presented above does not take into account the possibility of early exercise or the payment of dividends, both of which impact the value of options. However, adjustments exist, which while not perfect, provide partial corrections to value.

Dividends

The payment of dividends reduces the stock price. Consequently, call options will become less valuable and put options more valuable as dividend payments increase. There are two possible adjustments for dividends, one for short-term options and the other for long-term options.

Short-term Options

When options have only a short time to expiration (less than one year), the present value of the expected dividends during the life of the option can be estimated and subtracted from the current value of the asset to obtain a

---

Table A4.4 REPLICATING PORTFOLIO FOR CALL AND PUT OPTIONS WITH MODELS

Option Position	Replicating Portfolio	
	With Binomial	**With Black-Scholes**
Buy call option	Borrow $ B	Borrow $K e^{-rt} N(d_2)$
	Buy Δ shares of stock	Buy $N(d_1)$ shares of stock
Sell call option	Lend $B	Lend $K e^{-rt} N(d_2)$
	Sell short Δ shares	Sell short $N(d_1)$ shares
Buy put option	Lend $B'	Lend $K e^{-rt} (1 - N(d_2))$
	Sell short Δ' shares	Sell short $(1 - N(d_1))$ shares
Sell put option	Borrow $B'	Borrow $K e^{-rt} (1 - N(d_2))$
	Buy Δ' shares	Buy $(1 - N((d_1))$ shares

"dividend-adjusted value," which can be used as the input for S in the Black-Scholes model:

$$\text{Adjusted Stock Price} = S' = S - \sum \frac{\text{Div}_t}{(1 + r)^t}$$

$$\text{Value of Call} = S' N(d_1) - K\,e^{-rt}\,N(d_2)$$

where

$$d_1 = \frac{\ln\left(\dfrac{S'}{K}\right) + \left(r + \dfrac{\sigma^2}{2}\right)t}{\sigma\sqrt{t}}$$

$$d_2 = d_1 - \sigma\sqrt{t}$$

IN PRACTICE: A Note on Estimating the Inputs to the Black-Scholes Model

The Black-Scholes model requires inputs that are consistent on time measurement. As presented here, all the inputs have to be annualized. The variance, estimated from ln(asset prices), can be annualized easily because variances are linear in time if the serial correlation is zero. Thus, if monthly (weekly) prices are used to estimate variance, the variance is annualized by multiplying by 12 (52).

Long-term Options

The present-value approach to dealing with dividends becomes tedious and difficult to apply to long-term options. If the dividend yield (y = dividends/current value of the asset) of the underlying asset is expected to remain unchanged during the life of the option, the Black-Scholes model can be modified to take dividends into account:

$$C = S\,e^{-yt}\,N(d_1) - K\,e^{-rt}\,N(d_2)$$

where

$$d_1 = \frac{\ln\left(\dfrac{S}{K}\right) + \left(r - y + \dfrac{\sigma^2}{2}\right)t}{\sigma\sqrt{t}}$$

$$d_2 = d_1 - \sigma\sqrt{t}$$

From an intuitive standpoint, the adjustments have two effects. First, the value of the asset is discounted back to the present at the dividend yield to take into account the expected drop in value from dividend payments. Second, the interest rate is offset by the dividend yield to reflect the lower carrying cost from holding the stock (in the replicating portfolio).

Early Exercise

There are two basic approaches for dealing with the possibility of early exercise. One values the option to each ex-dividend day and chooses the maximum of the estimated call values; the other uses a modified version of the binomial model to consider the possibility of early exercise.

Approach 1: Pseudo-American Valuation

Step 1:   Define when dividends will be paid and how much the dividends will be.

Step 2:   Value the call option to each ex-dividend date using the dividend-adjusted approach described above, whereby the stock price is reduced by the present value of expected dividends.

Step 3:   Choose the maximum of the call values estimated for each ex-dividend day.

Approach 2: Using the Binomial

Step 1:   If the variance in log (stock prices) has been estimated for the Black-Scholes, convert these into inputs for the binomial model:

$$u = \exp\left[(r - \sigma^2/2)(T/m) + \sqrt{(\sigma^2 T/m)}\right]$$

$$d = \exp\left[(r - \sigma^2/2)(T/m) - \sqrt{(\sigma^2 T/m)}\right]$$

where u and d are the up and down movements per unit time for the binomial, T is the life of the option, and m is the number of periods within that lifetime.

Step 2:   Specify the period in which the dividends will be paid and make the assumption that the price will drop by the amount of the dividend in that period.

Step 3:   Value the call at each node of the tree, allowing for the possibility of early exercise just before ex-dividend dates. There will be early exercise if the remaining time premium on the option is less than the expected drop in option value as a consequence of the dividend payment.

Step 4:   Value the call at time 0, using the standard binomial approach.

The Impact of Exercise on the Value of the Underlying Asset

The derivation of the Black-Scholes model is based upon the assumption that exercising an option does not affect the value of the underlying asset. This may be true for listed options on stocks, but it is not true for some types of options. For instance, the exercise of warrants increases the number of shares outstanding and brings fresh cash into the firm, both of which will affect the stock price.[2] The expected negative

---

[2]Warrants are call options issued by firms, either as part of management compensation contracts or to raise equity.

impact (dilution) of exercise will decrease the value of warrants compared to otherwise similar call options.

Valuing Puts
The value of a put is related to the value of a call with the same strike price and the same expiration date through an arbitrage relationship that specifies that:

$$C - P = S - K e^{-rt}$$

where C is the value of the call and P is the value of the put (with the same life and exercise price).

This arbitrage relationship can be derived fairly easily and is called *put-call parity*. To see why put-call parity holds, consider creating the following portfolio:

(a) Sell a call and buy a put with exercise price K.

(b) Buy the stock at current stock price S.

The payoff from this position is riskless and always yields K at expiration t. To see this, assume that the stock price at expiration is S*:

POSITION	PAYOFFS AT T IF S*>K	PAYOFFS AT T IF S*<K
Sell call	−(S*−K)	0
Buy put	0	K−S*
Buy stock	S*	S*
Total	K	K

Since this position always yields K risklessly, its value must be equal to the present value of K at the riskless rate ($K e^{-rt}$).

$$S + P - C = K e^{-rt}$$
$$C - P = S - K e^{-rt}$$

This relationship can be used to value puts. Substituting the Black-Scholes formulation for the value of an equivalent call:

$$\text{Value of Put} = S e^{-yt} (N(d_1) - 1) - K e^{-rt} (N(d_2) - 1)$$

where

$$d_1 = \frac{\ln\left(\frac{S}{K}\right) + (r - y + \frac{\sigma^2}{2})t}{\sigma\sqrt{t}}$$

$$d_2 = d_1 - \sigma \sqrt{t}$$

BIBLIOGRAPHY

Aharony, J. and I. Swary, 1981, "Quarterly Dividends and Earnings Announcements and Stockholders' Returns: An Empirical Analysis," *Journal of Finance,* Vol. 36, 1–12.

Altman, E. I., 1968, "Financial Ratios, Discriminant Analysis and the Prediction of Corporate Bankruptcy," *Journal of Finance,* Vol. 23, 589–609.

Altman, E. I., 1994, "Defaults and Returns on High Yield Bonds," Working Paper, Salomon Center, New York University.

Altman, E. I. and V. Kishore, 1996, "The Default Experience of U.S. Bonds," Working Paper, Salomon Center, New York University.

Amihud, Y., B. Christensen, and H. Mendelson, 1992, "Further Evidence on the Risk-Return Relationship," Working Paper, New York University.

Asquith, P. and D. W. Mullins, Jr., 1983, "The Impact of Initiating Dividend Payments on Shareholder Wealth," *Journal of Business,* Vol. 56, 77–96.

Bailey, W., "Canada's Dual Class Shares: Further Evidence on the Market Value of Cash Dividends," *Journal of Finance,* 1988, Vol. 43(5), 1143–1160.

Baker, H. Kent, Gail E. Farrelly, and Richard B. Edelman, 1985, "A Survey of Management Views on Dividend Policy," *Financial Management,* Vol. 14(3), 78–84.

Barry, Christopher B., Chris J. Muscarella, and Michael R. Vetsuypens, 1991, "Underwriter Warrants, Underwriter Compensation, and the Costs of Going Public," *Journal of Financial Economics,* Vol. 29(1), 113–136.

Barry, Christopher B., Chris J. Muscarella, John W. Peavy, III, and Michael R. Vetsuypens, 1990, "The Role of Venture Capital in the Creation of Public Companies: Evidence from the Going-Public Process," *Journal of Financial Economics,* Vol. 27(2), 447–472.

Baumol, William J., 1952, "The Transactions Demand for Cash: An Inventory Theoretic Approach," *Quarterly Journal of Economics,* Vol. 66(4), 545–556.

Beaver, William H., Paul Kettler, and Myron Scholes, 1970, "The Association Between Market Determined and Accounting Determined Risk Measures," *Accounting Review,* Vol. 45(4), 654–682.

Bhide, A., 1993, "Reversing Corporate Diversification," in *The New Corporate Finance— Where Theory Meets Practice,* ed. D.H. Chew Jr., New York, McGraw Hill.

Black, F. and M. Scholes, 1972, "The Valuation of Option Contracts and a Test of Market Efficiency," *Journal of Finance,* Vol. 27, 399–417.

Black, F. and M. Scholes, 1974, "The Effects of Dividend Yields and Dividend Policy on Common Stock Prices and Returns," *Journal of Financial Economics,* Vol. 1, 1-22.

Block, Stanley B. and Timothy J. Gallagher, 1986, "The Use of Interest Rate Futures and Options by Corporate Financial Managers," *Financial Management,* Vol. 15(3), 73–78.

Block, Stanley B. and Timothy J. Gallagher, 1988, "How Much Do Bank Trust Departments Use Derivatives?" *Journal of Portfolio Management,* Vol. 15(1), 12–15.

Booth, James R., Richard L. Smith, and Richard W. Stolz, 1984, "Use of Interest Rate Futures by Financial Institutions," *Journal of Bank Research,* Vol. 15(1), 15–20.

Bradley, M., A. Desai, and E. H. Kim, 1983, "The Rationale Behind Interfirm Tender Offers," *Journal of Financial Economics,* Vol. 11, 183–206.

Bradley, M., A. Desai, and E. H. Kim, 1988, "Synergistic Gains from Corporate Acquisitions and Their Division Between the Stockholders of Target and Acquiring Firms," *Journal of Financial Economics,* Vol. 21, 3–40.

Bradley, M., Gregg A. Jarrell, and E. Han Kim, 1984, "On the Existence of an Optimal Capital Structure: Theory and Evidence," *Journal of Finance,* Vol. 39(3), 857–878.

Brennan, M. J. and E. S. Schwartz, 1985, "Evaluating Natural Resource Investments," *Journal of Business,* Vol. 58, 135–158.

Brickley, James A., Ronald C. Lease, and Clifford W. Smith, Jr., 1988, "Ownership Structure and Voting on Antitakeover Amendments," *Journal of Financial Economics,* Vol. 20(1/2), 267–292.

Chan, L. K. and J. Lakonsihok, 1992, "Are the Reports of Beta's Death Premature?" Working Paper, University of Illinois.

Charest, Guy, 1978, "Split Information, Stock Returns and Market Efficiency—I," *Journal of Financial Economics,* Vol. 6(2/3), 265–296.

Chen, N., R. Roll, and S. A. Ross, 1986, "Economic Forces and the Stock Market," *Journal of Business,* Vol. 59, 383–404.

Choi, F. D. S. and R. M. Levich, 1990, "The Capital Market Effects of International Accounting Diversity," Dow Jones Irwin, 1990.

Cootner, P. H., 1961, "Common Elements in Futures Markets for Commodities and Bonds," *American Economic Review,* Vol. 51(2), 173–183.

Copeland, Thomas E., 1979, "Liquidity Changes Following Stock Splits," *Journal of Finance,* Vol. 34(1), 115–141.

Copeland, T. E., T. Koller, and J. Murrin, 1990, *Valuation: Measuring and Managing the Value of Companies,* New York, Wiley.

Copeland, T. E., E. F. Lemgruber, and D. Mayers, 1987, "Corporate Spinoffs: Multiple Announcement and Ex-Date Abnormal Performance," in *Modern Finance and Industrial Economics,* Basil Blackwell, New York.

Cornell, Bradford and Alan C. Shapiro, Spring 1987, "Corporate Stakeholders and Corporate Finance," *Financial Management,* 5–14.

Damodaran, A., 1989, "The Weekend Effect in Information Releases: A Study of Earnings and Dividend Announcements," *Review of Financial Studies,* Vol. 2(4), 607–623.

Damodaran, A., 1994, *Investment Valuation,* Wiley, New York.

Dann, L. Y. and H. DeAngelo, 1983, "Standstill Agreements, Privately Negotiated Stock Repurchases, and the Market for Corporate Control," *Journal of Financial Economics,* Vol. 11, 275–300.

Dann, L. Y. and H. DeAngelo, 1988, "Corporate Financial Policy and Corporate Control: A Study of Defensive Adjustments in Asset and Ownership Structure," *Journal of Financial Economics,* Vol. 20, 87–128.

Dann, Y., David Mayers, and Robert J. Raab, Jr., 1977, "Trading Rules, Large Blocks and the Speed of Price Adjustment," *Journal of Financial Economics,* Vol. 4(1), 3–22.

Davis, H., "The 1989 Treasury Survey: New Directions in Financial Risk Management," 1989 Business International Corporation.

DeAngelo, H. and L. DeAngelo, 1985, "Managerial Ownership of Voting Rights: A Study of Public Corporations with Dual Classes of Common Stock," *Journal of Financial Economics,* Vol. 14, 33–69.

DeAngelo, H. and E. M. Rice, 1983, "Antitakeover Charter Amendments and Stockholder Wealth," *Journal of Financial Economics,* Vol. 11, 329–360.

DeAngelo, H., L. DeAngelo, and E. M. Rice, 1984, "Going Private: The Effects of a Change in Corporate Ownership Structure," *Midland Corporate Finance Journal,* 35–43.

DeBondt, W. F. M. and R. Thaler, 1985, "Does the Stock Market Overreact?" *Journal of Finance,* Vol. 40, 793–805.

DeBondt, W. F. M. and R. Thaler, 1987, "Further Evidence on Investor Overreaction and Stock Market Seasonality," *Journal of Finance,* Vol. 42, 557–581.

Denis, David J. and Diane K. Denis, 1993, "Leveraged Recaps in the Curbing of Corporate Overinvestment," *Journal of Applied Corporate Finance,* Vol. 6(1), 60–71.

Dubofsky, P. and P. R. Varadarajan, 1987, "Diversification and Measures of Performance: Additional Empirical Evidence," *Academy of Management Journal,* 597–608.

Elton, Edwin J., Martin J. Gruber, and Joel Rentzler, 1984, "The Ex-Dividend Day Behavior of Stock Prices—A Reexamination of the Clientele Effect: A Comment," *Journal of Finance,* Vol. 39(2), 551–556.

Fama, E. F., 1965, "The Behavior of Stock Market Prices," *Journal of Business,* Vol. 38, 34–105.

Fama, E. F., 1970, "Efficient Capital Markets: A Review of Theory and Empirical Work," *Journal of Finance,* Vol. 25, 383–417.

Fama, E. F. and Harvey Babiak, 1968, "Dividend Policy: An Empirical Analysis," *Journal of the American Statistical Association,* Vol. 63(324), 1132–1161.

Fama, E. F. and K. R. French, 1992, "The Cross-Section of Expected Returns," *Journal of Finance,* Vol. 47, 427–466.

Fama, E. F. and G. William Schwert, 1977, "Asset Returns and Inflation," *Journal of Financial Economics,* Vol. 5(2), 115–146.

Fama, F., Lawrence Fisher, Michael C. Jensen, and Richard Roll, 1969, "The Adjustment of Stock Prices to New Information," *International Economic Review,* Vol. 10(1), 1–21.

Feldstein, Martin, 1980, "Fiscal Policies, Inflation, and Capital Formation," *American Economic Review,* Vol. 70(4), 636–650.

Flannery, Mark J., 1986, "Asymmetric Information and Risky Debt Maturity Choice," *Journal of Finance,* Vol. 41(1), 19–38.

Fruhan, W. E., 1979, *Financial Strategy: Studies in the Creation, Transfer and Destruction of Shareholder Value,* Homewood, Ill., Irwin.

Fruhan, W. E., W. C. Kester, S. P. Mason, T. R. Piper, and R. S. Ruback, 1992, *Case Problems in Finance,* Homewood, Ill., Irwin.

Ghosh, C. and J. Randall Woolridge, 1988, "An Analysis of Shareholder Reaction to Dividend Cuts and Omissions," *Journal of Financial Research,* Vol. 11(4), 281–294.

Ghosh, C. and J. R. Woolridge, 1989, "Stock-Market Reaction to Growth-Induced Dividend Cuts: Are Investors Myopic?" *Managerial Decision Economics,* Vol. 10(1), 25–35.

Gitman, Lawrence J., Edward A. Moses, and I. Thomas White, 1979, "An Assessment of Corporate Cash Management Practices," *Financial Management,* Vol. 8(1), 32–41.

Goswami, Gautam, Thomas Noe, and Michael Rebello, 1995, "Debt Financing Under Asymmetric Information," *Journal of Finance,* Vol. 50(2), 633–659.

Grinblatt, Mark S., Ronald W. Masulis, and Sheridan Titman, 1984, "The Valuation Effects of Stock Splits and Stock Dividends," *Journal of Financial Economics,* Vol. 13(4), 461–490.

Hand, John R. M., Robert W. Holthausen, and Richard W. Leftwich, 1992, "The Effect of Bond Rating Agency Announcements on Bond and Stock Prices," *Journal of Finance,* Vol. 47(2), 733–752.

Haugen, R. A., 1990, *Modern Investment Theory,* Englewood Cliffs, N.J., Prentice Hall.

Healy, P. M., K. G. Palepu, and R. S. Ruback, 1989, "Do Mergers Improve Corporate Performance?" Working Paper, Harvard Business School.

Hite, G. L. and J. E. Owens, 1983, "Security Price Reactions Around Corporate Spin-off Announcements," *Journal of Financial Economics,* Vol. 12, 409–436.

Hong, Hai, Robert S. Kaplan, and Gershon Mandelker, 1978, "Pooling vs. Purchase: The Effects of Accounting for Mergers on Stock Prices," *Accounting Review,* Vol. 53(1), 31–47.

Ibbotson, R. G. and G. P. Brinson, 1993, *Global Investing,* New York: McGraw-Hill.

Ibbotson, R. G. and R. A. Sinquefield, 1996, "Stocks, Bonds, Bills and Inflation," Ibbotson Associates, Chicago.

Ibbotson, R. G., Jody L. Sindelar, and Jay R. Ritter, 1988, "Initial Public Offerings," *Journal of Applied Corporate Finance,* Vol. 1(2), 37–45.

Ibbotson, Roger G., Jody L. Sindelar, and Jay R. Ritter, 1994, "The Market's Problems with the Pricing of Initial Public Offerings," *Journal of Applied Corporate Finance,* Vol. 7(1), 66–74.

Jain, P. C., 1985, "The Effect of Voluntary Sell-off Announcements on Shareholder Wealth," *Journal of Finance,* Vol. 40, 209–224.

Jarrell, G. A. and A. B. Poulsen, 1988, "Dual Class Recapitalizations as Antitakeover Mechanisms: The Recent Evidence," *Journal of Financial Economics,* Vol. 20, 129–152.

Jarrell, G. A., J. A. Brickley, and J. M. Netter, 1988, "The Market for Corporate Control: The Empirical Evidence Since 1980," *Journal of Economic Perspectives,* Vol. 2, 49–68.

Jennergren, L. P., 1975, "Filer Tests of Swedish Share Prices," *International Capital Markets,* North-Holland, New York 55–67.

Jennergren, L. P., and P. E. Korsvold, 1974, "Price Formation in the Norwegian and Swedish Stock Markets—Some Random Walk Tests," *Swedish Journal of Economics,* Vol. 76, 171–185.

Jensen, M. C., 1969, "Risk, the Pricing of Capital Assets, and the Evaluation of Investment Portfolios," *Journal of Business,* Vol. 42, 167–247.

Jensen, M. C., 1986, "Agency Costs of Free Cashflow, Corporate Finance and Takeovers," *American Economic Review,* Vol. 76, 323–329.

Jensen, M. C. and R. S. Ruback, 1983, "The Market for Corporate Control," *Journal of Financial Economics,* Vol. 11, 5–50.

Kale, Jayant R. and Thomas H. Noe, 1990, "Risky Debt Maturity Choice in a Sequential Game Equilibrium," *Journal of Financial Research,* Vol. 8, 155–165.

Kaplan, R. S. and R. Roll, 1972, "Investor Evaluation of Accounting Information: Some Empirical Evidence," *Journal of Business,* 225–257.

Karpoff, J. M. and P. H. Malatesta, 1990, "The Wealth Effects of Second-Generation State Takeover Legislation," *Journal of Financial Economics,* Vol. 25, 291–322.

Keynes, J. M., *The General Theory of Employment, Interest and Money,* New York, Harcourt, Brace and World, 1936.

Krishna G. Palepu and Healy, Paul M., 1989, "How Investors Interpret Changes in Corporate Financial Policy," *Journal of Applied Corporate Finance,* Vol. 2(3), 59–64.

Lang, L. H. P., R. M. Stulz, and R. A. Walkling, 1989, "Managerial Performance, Tobin's Q and the Gains from Successful Tender Offers," *Journal of Financial Economics,* Vol. 24, 137–154.

Lease, R. C., J. J. McConnell, and W. H. Mikkelson, 1983, "The Market Value of Control in Publicly-Traded Corporations," *Journal of Financial Economics,* Vol. 11, 439–471.

Leibowitz, Martin L. and Stanley Kogelman, 1992, "Franchise Value and the Growth Process," *Financial Analyst Journal,* Vol. 48(1), 53–62.

Lewellen, W. G., 1971, "A Pure Financial Rationale for the Conglomerate Merger," *Journal of Finance,* Vol. 26, 521–537.

Lewent, Judy C. and A. John Kearney, 1990, "Identifying, Measuring, and Hedging Currency Risk at Merck," *Journal of Applied Corporate Finance,* Vol. 2(4), 19–28.

Linn, S. and J. J. McConnell, 1983, "An Empirical Investigation of the Impact of Anti-Takeover Amendments on Common Stock Prices," *Journal of Financial Economics,* Vol. 11, 361–399.

Linn, S. C. and Michael S. Rozeff, 1985, "The Effect of Voluntary Spin-Offs on Stock Prices: The Anergy Hypothesis," *Advances in Financial Planning and Forecasting,* Vol. 1(1), 265–292.

Lintner, J., 1956, "Distribution of Incomes of Corporations Among Dividends, Retained Earnings, and Taxes," *American Economic Review,* Vol. 46(2), 97–113.

Litzenberger, R. H. and K. Ramaswamy, 1979, "The Effect of Personal Taxes and Dividends on Capital Asset Prices: Theory and Empirical Evidence," *Journal of Financial Economics,* Vol. 7, 163–196.

Long, John B., Jr., 1978, "The Market Valuation of Cash Dividends: A Case to Consider," *Journal of Financial Economics,* Vol. 6(2/3), 235–264.

Markowitz, Harry M., 1991, "Foundations of Portfolio Theory," *Journal of Finance,* Vol. 46(2), 469–478.

Mathur, Ike and David Loy, 1981, "Foreign Currency Translation: Survey of Corporate Treasurers," *Management Accounting,* Vol. 63(3), 33–42.

Mayers, David and Clifford W. Smith, Jr., 1982, "On the Corporate Demand for Insurance," *Journal of Business,* Vol. 55(2), 281–296.

McConnell, J. J. and C. J. Muscarella, 1985, "Corporate Capital Expenditure Decisions and the Market Value of the Firm," *Journal of Financial Economics,* Vol. 14, 399–422.

Merton, R. C., 1973, "The Theory of Rational Option Pricing," *Bell Journal of Economics,* Vol. 4(1), 141–183.

Michel, A. and I. Shaked, 1984, "Does Business Diversification Affect Performance?" *Financial Management,* Vol. 13, 5–14.

Mikkelson, Wayne H., 1981, "Convertible Calls and Security Returns," *Journal of Financial Economics,* Vol. 9(3), 237–264.

Miles, J. A. and J. D. Rosenfeld, 1983, "The Effect of Voluntary Spin-off Announcements on Shareholder Wealth," *Journal of Finance,* Vol. 38, 1597–1606.

Miller, M., 1977, "Debt and Taxes," *Journal of Finance,* Vol. 32, 261–275.

Miller, M. and F. Modigliani, 1961, "Dividend Policy, Growth and the Valuation of Shares," *Journal of Business,* Vol. 34, 411–433.

Miller, Merton H. and Daniel Orr, 1966, "A Model of the Demand for Money by Firms," *Quarterly Journal of Economics,* Vol. 80(3), 413–435.

Miller, Merton H. and Myron S. Scholes, 1978, "Dividends and Taxes," *Journal of Financial Economics,* Vol. 6(4), 333–364.

Miller, Merton H. and Myron S. Scholes, 1982, "Dividends and Taxes: Some Empirical Evidence," *Journal of Political Economy,* Vol. 90(6), 1118–1141.

Mitchell, M. L. and K. Lehn, 1990, "Do Bad Bidders Make Good Targets?" *Journal of Applied Corporate Finance,* Vol. 3, 60–69.

Modigliani, F. and M. Miller, 1958, "The Cost of Capital, Corporation Finance and the Theory of Investment," *American Economic Review,* Vol. 53, 261–297.

Muscarella, Chris J. and Michael R. Vetsuypens, 1989, "A Simple Test of Baron's Model of IPO Underpricing," *Journal of Financial Economics,* Vol. 24, 125–136.

Myers, Stewart C., 1977, "Determinants of Corporate Borrowing," *Journal of Financial Economics,* Vol. 5(2), 147–175.

Myers, S. C. and N. S. Majluf, 1984, "Corporate Financing and Investment Decisions When Firms Have Information That Investors Do Not Have," *Journal of Financial Economics,* Vol. 13, 187–221.

Palepu, Krishna G., 1986, "Predicting Takeover Targets: A Methodological and Empirical Analysis," *Journal of Accounting and Economics,* Vol. 8(1), 3–35.

Partch, M. Megan, 1987, "The Creation of a Class of Limited Voting Common Stock and Shareholder Wealth," *Journal of Financial Economics,* Vol. 18(2), 313–340.

Penman, Stephen H., 1987, "The Distribution of Earnings News over Time and Seasonalities in Aggregate Stock Returns," *Journal of Financial Economics,* Vol. 18(2), 199–228.

Pinegar, J. Michael and Lisa Wilbricht, 1989, "What Managers Think of Capital Structure Theory: A Survey," *Financial Management,* Vol. 18(4), 82–91.

Porter, M. E., 1980, *Competitive Strategy: Techniques for Analyzing Industries and Competitors,* New York, Free Press.

Praetz, Peter D., 1972, "The Distribution of Share Price Changes," *Journal of Business,* Vol. 45(1), 49–55.

Rajan, Raghuram G. and Luigi Zingales, 1995, "What Do We Know About Capital Structure? Some Evidence from International Data," *Journal of Finance,* Vol. 50(5), 1421–1460.

Rawls, S. Waite, III and Charles W. Smithson, 1989, "The Evolution of Risk Management Products," *Journal of Applied Corporate Finance,* Vol. 1(4), 18–26.

Roll, R., 1977, "A Critique of the Asset Pricing Theory's Tests: Part I: On Past and Potential Testability of Theory," *Journal of Financial Economics,* Vol. 4, 129–176.

Rosenberg, Barr and James Guy, 1976, "Beta and Investment Fundamentals," *Financial Analyst Journal,* Vol. 32(3), 60–72.

Rosenberg, Barr and James Guy, 1976, "Beta and Investment Fundamentals—II," *Financial Analyst Journal,* Vol. 32(4), 62–70.

Rosenberg, Barr and James Guy, 1995, "Prediction of Beta from Investment Fundamentals," *Financial Analyst Journal,* Vol. 51(1), 101–112.

Rosenberg, Barr and V. Marathe, 1979, "Tests of Capital Asset Pricing Hypotheses," *Research in Finance,* Vol. 1, 115–124.

Ross, Marc, 1986, "Capital Budgeting Practices of Twelve Large Manufacturers," *Financial Management,* Vol. 15(4), 15–22.

Ross, Stephen A., 1976, "The Arbitrage Theory of Capital Asset Pricing," *Journal of Economic Theory,* Vol. 13(3), 341–360.

Schipper, K. and A. Smith, 1983, "Effects of Recontracting on Shareholder Wealth: The Case of Voluntary Spin-offs," *Journal of Financial Economics,* Vol. 12, 437–468.

Schipper, K. and A. Smith, 1986, "A Comparison of Equity Carve-outs and Seasoned Equity Offerings: Share Price Effects and Corporate Restructuring," *Journal of Financial Economics,* Vol. 15, 153–186.

Scott, David F., Jr. and John D. Martin, 1975, "Industry Influence on Financial Structure," *Financial Management,* Vol. 4(1), 67–73.

Shapiro, A., 1985, "Corporate Strategy and the Capital Budgeting Decision," *Midland Corporate Finance Journal,* Vol. 4, 22–36.

Shapiro, A., 1989a, *Modern Corporate Finance,* New York, Macmillan.

Shapiro, A., 1989b, *Multinational Financial Management,* London, Allyn & Bacon.

Siegel, D., J. Smith, and J. Paddock, 1993, "Valuing Offshore Oil Properties with Option Pricing Models," in *The New Corporate Finance,* ed. D. H. Chew, Jr., New York, McGraw-Hill.

Silber, W. L., 1991, "Discounts on Restricted Stock: The Impact of Illiquidity on Stock Prices," *Financial Analysts Journal,* Vol. 24, 60–64.

Smith, C. W., 1993, "Raising Capital: Theory and Evidence," in *The New Corporate Finance,* ed. D. H. Chew, Jr., New York, McGraw-Hill.

Stapleton, R. C., 1985, "A Note on Default Risk, Leverage and the MM Theorem," *Journal of Financial Economics,* Vol. 2, 377–381.

Statman, Meir and Tyzoon T. Tyebjee, 1985, "Optimistic Capital Budgeting Forecasts: An Experiment," *Financial Management,* Vol. 14(3), 27–33.

Stewart, B., 1990, "The Quest for Value," Harper Business, New York.

Titman, S., 1984, "The Effect of Capital Structure on a Firm's Liquidation Decision," *Journal of Financial Economics,* Vol. 13, 137–183.

Tull, Donald S., 1967, "The Relationship of Actual and Predicted Sales and Profits in New-Product Introductions," *Journal of Business,* Vol. 40(3), 233–253.

Varadarajan, P.R., and V. Ramanujam, 1987, "Diversification and Performance: A Reexamination Using a New Two-Dimensional Conceptualization of Diversity in Firms," *Academy of Management Journal,* Vol. 30, 369–380.

Vermaelen, Theo, 1981, "Common Stock Repurchases and Market Signalling: An Empirical Study," *Journal of Financial Economics,* Vol. 9(2), 138–183.

Warner, Jerold B., 1977, "Bankruptcy Costs: Some Evidence," *Journal of Finance,* Vol. 32(2), 337–347.

Womack, K., 1996, "Do Brokerage Analysts' Recommendations Have Investment Value?" *Journal of Finance,* Vol. 51.

Woodruff, Catherine S. and A. J. Senchack, Jr., 1988, "Intradaily Price-Volume Adjustments of NYSE Stocks to Unexpected Earnings," *Journal of Finance,* Vol. 43(2), 467–491.

Woolridge, R., 1993, "Competitive Decline and Corporate Restructuring," in *The New Corporate Finance,* ed. D. H. Chew, Jr., New York, McGraw-Hill.

INDEX